FoxTrot
en masse

Other Fox Trot Books by Bill Amend

Fox Trot
Pass the Loot
Black Bart Says Draw
Eight Yards, Down and Out
Enormously Fox Trot

Anthology

Fox Trot: The Works

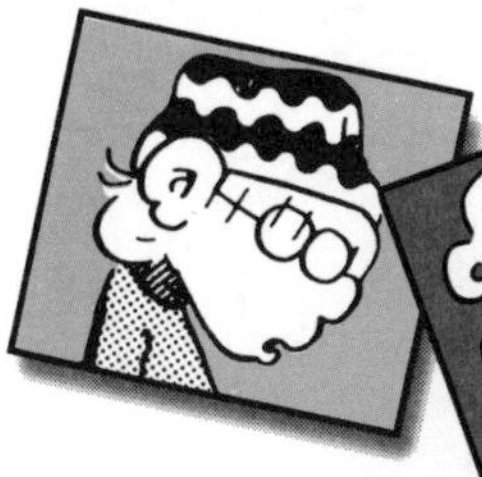
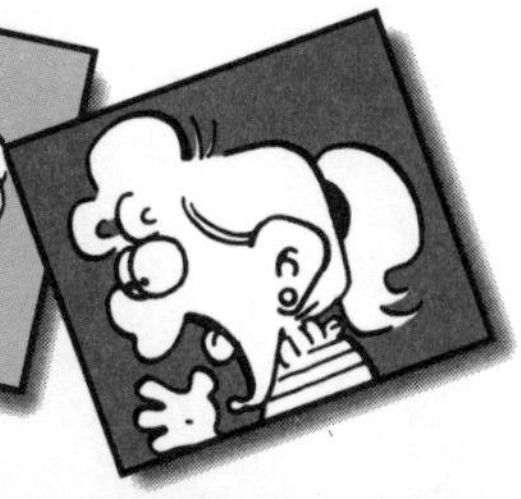
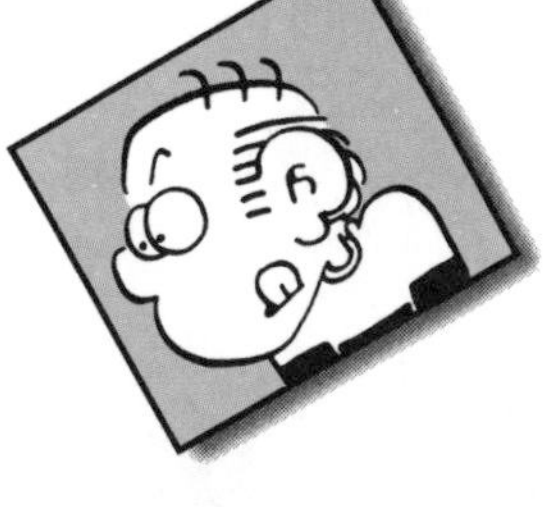
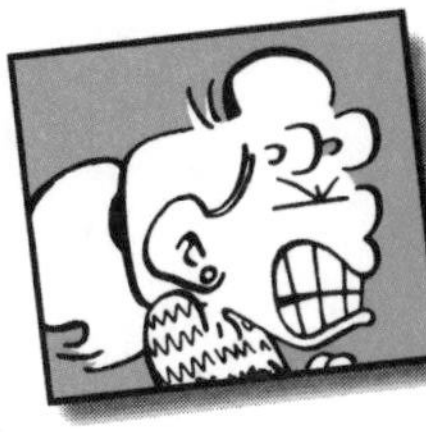
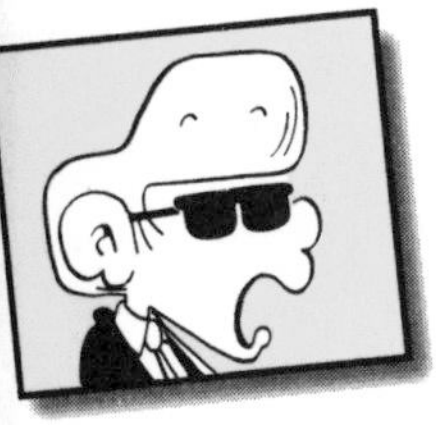
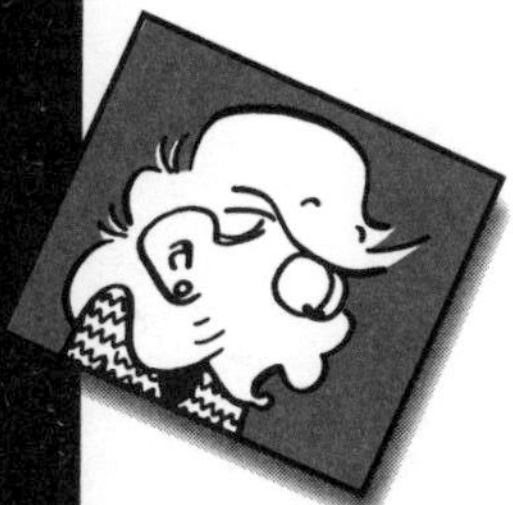

FoxTrot en masse

by Bill Amend

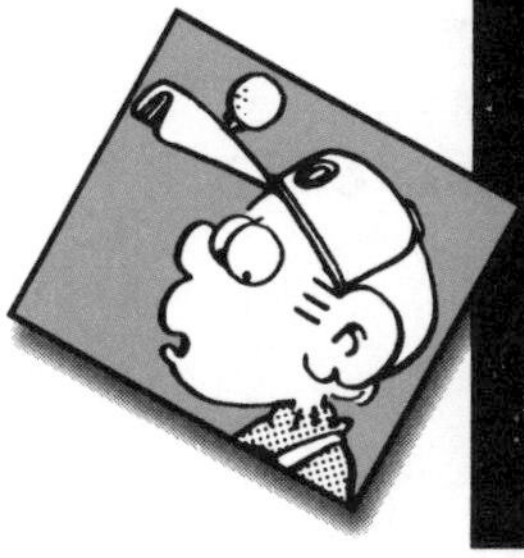
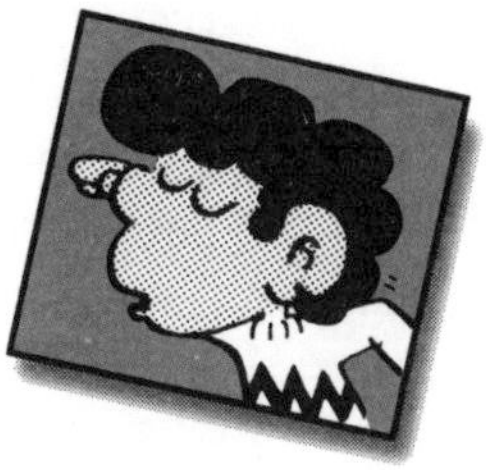
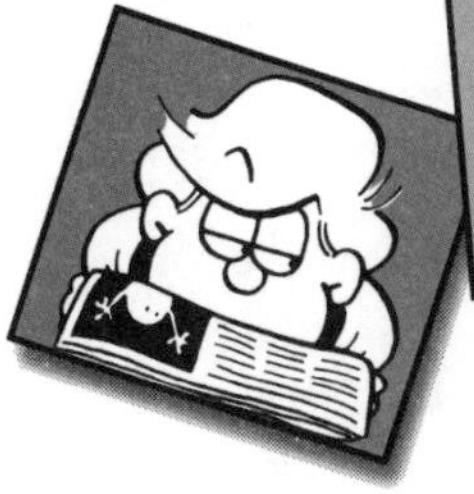
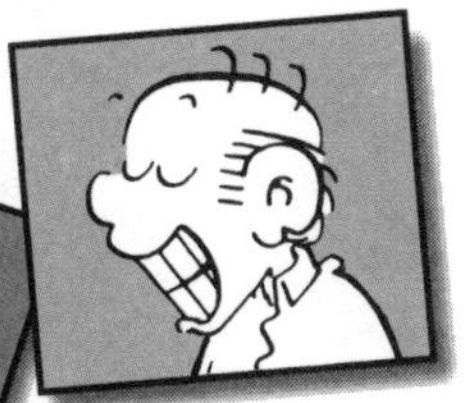
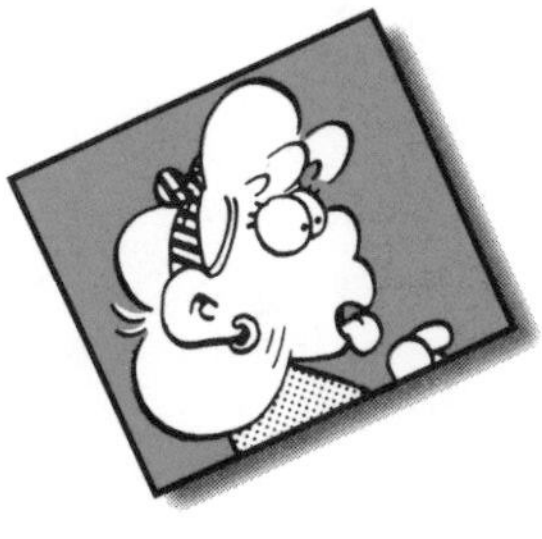
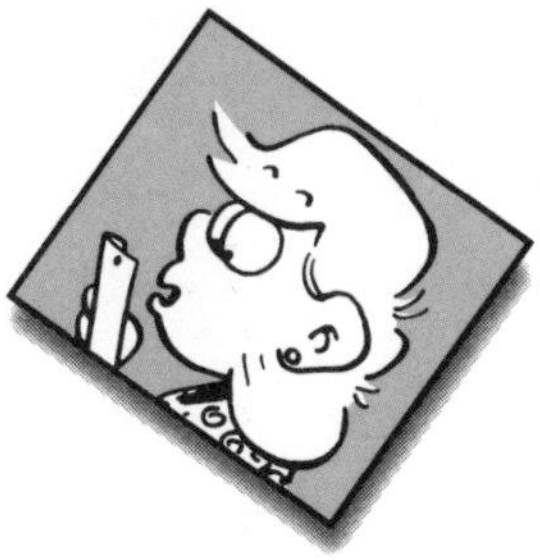
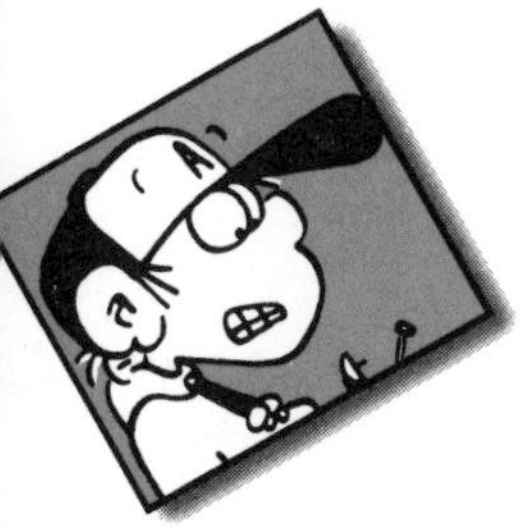
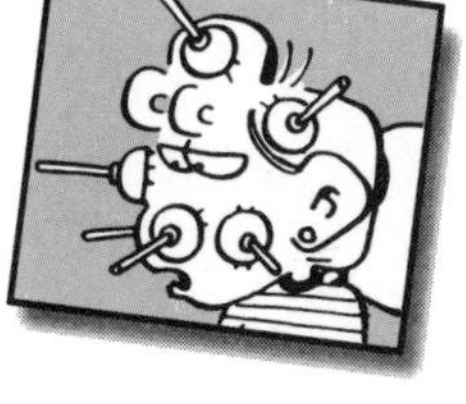
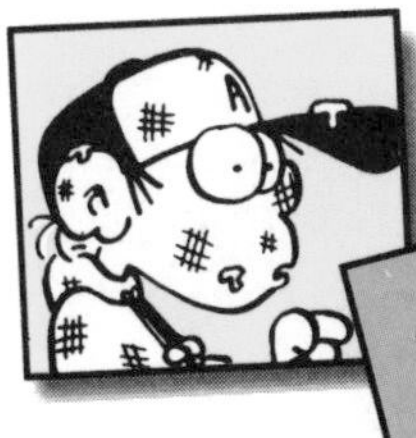
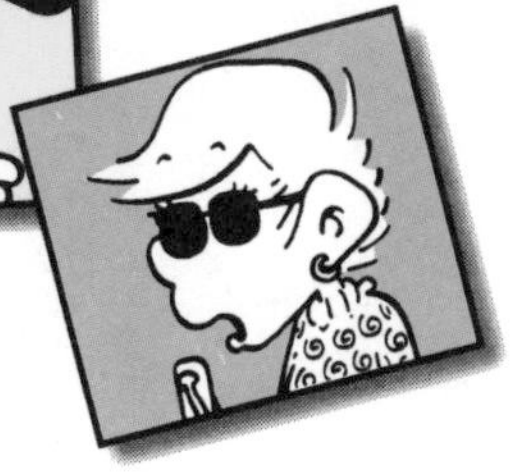

Andrews and McMeel
A Universal Press Syndicate Company
Kansas City

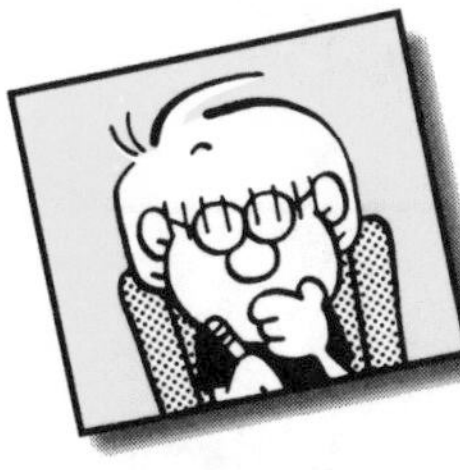
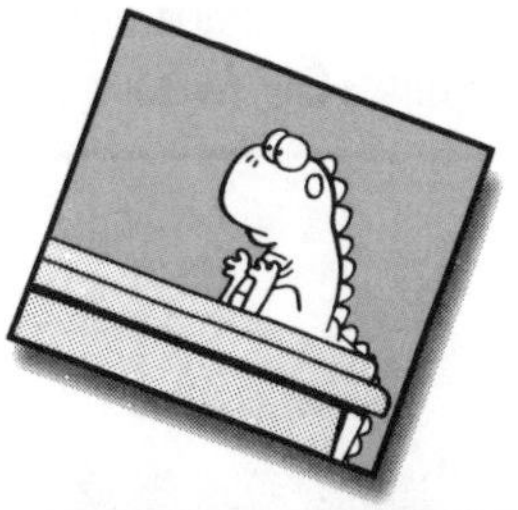
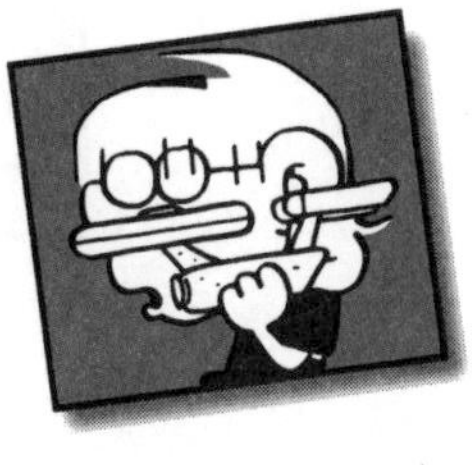

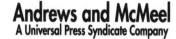

FOX TROT is distributed internationally by Universal Press Syndicate.

Fox Trot en masse copyright © 1992 by Universal Press Syndicate. All rights reserved. Printed in the United States of America. No part of this book may be used or reproduced in any manner whatsoever without written permission except in the case of reprints in the context of reviews. For information write Andrews and McMeel, a Universal Press Syndicate Company, 4900 Main Street, Kansas City, Missouri 64112.

ISBN: 0-8362-1897-3

Library of Congress Catalog Card Number: 92-72246

First Printing, September 1992
Second Printing, October 1994

——— ATTENTION: SCHOOLS AND BUSINESSES ———

Andrews and McMeel books are available at quantity discounts with bulk purchase for educational, business, or sales promotional use. For information, write to: Special Sales Department, Andrews and McMeel, 4900 Main Street, Kansas City, Missouri 64112.

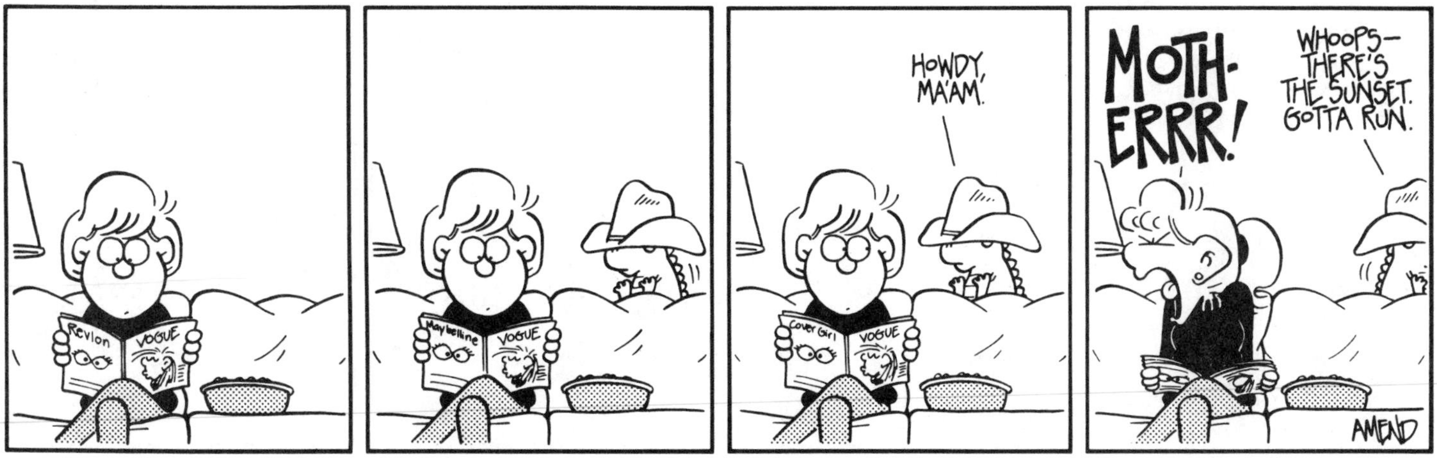
Revlon
VOGUE
Maybelline
VOGUE
HOWDY, MA'AM.
Cover Girl
VOGUE
MOTH-ERRR!
WHOOPS— THERE'S THE SUNSET. GOTTA RUN.
AMEND

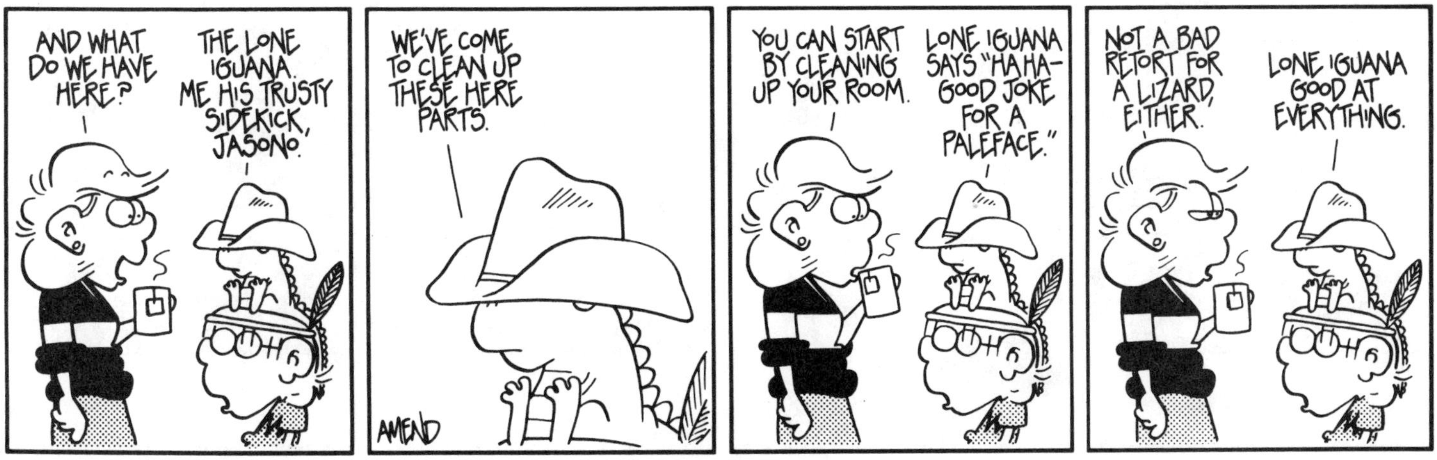
AND WHAT DO WE HAVE HERE?
THE LONE IGUANA. ME HIS TRUSTY SIDEKICK, JASONO.
WE'VE COME TO CLEAN UP THESE HERE PARTS.
AMEND
YOU CAN START BY CLEANING UP YOUR ROOM.
LONE IGUANA SAYS "HA HA- GOOD JOKE FOR A PALEFACE."
NOT A BAD RETORT FOR A LIZARD, EITHER.
LONE IGUANA GOOD AT EVERYTHING.

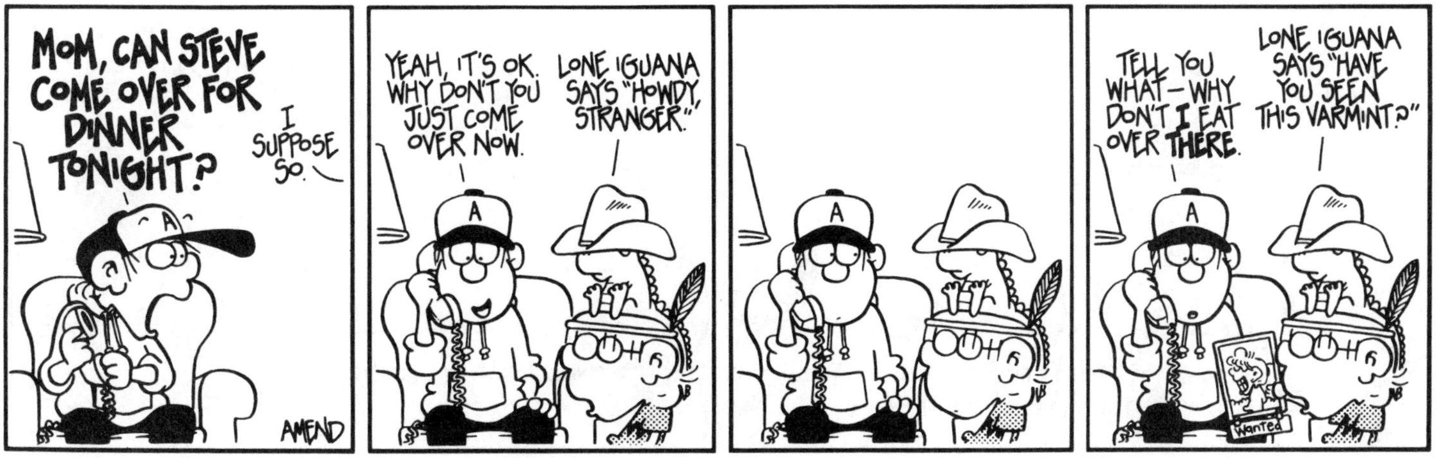
MOM, CAN STEVE COME OVER FOR DINNER TONIGHT?
I SUPPOSE SO.
AMEND
YEAH, IT'S OK. WHY DON'T YOU JUST COME OVER NOW.
LONE IGUANA SAYS "HOWDY, STRANGER."
TELL YOU WHAT— WHY DON'T I EAT OVER THERE.
LONE IGUANA SAYS "HAVE YOU SEEN THIS VARMINT?"
Wanted

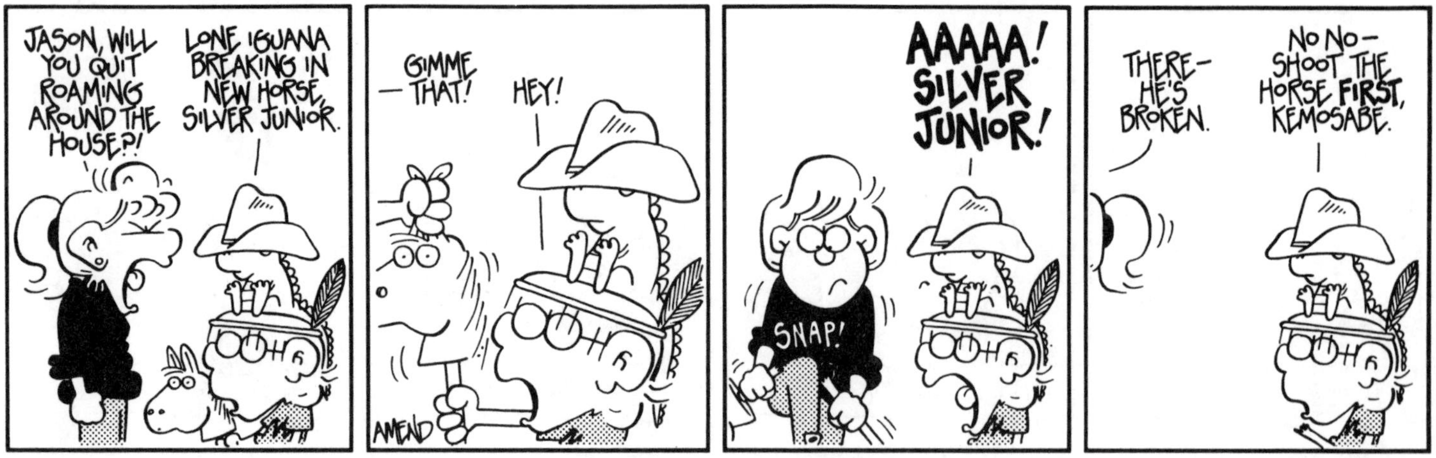
JASON, WILL YOU QUIT ROAMING AROUND THE HOUSE?!
LONE IGUANA BREAKING IN NEW HORSE, SILVER JUNIOR.
GIMME THAT!
HEY!
AMEND
SNAP!
AAAAA! SILVER JUNIOR!
THERE— HE'S BROKEN.
NO NO— SHOOT THE HORSE FIRST, KEMOSABE.

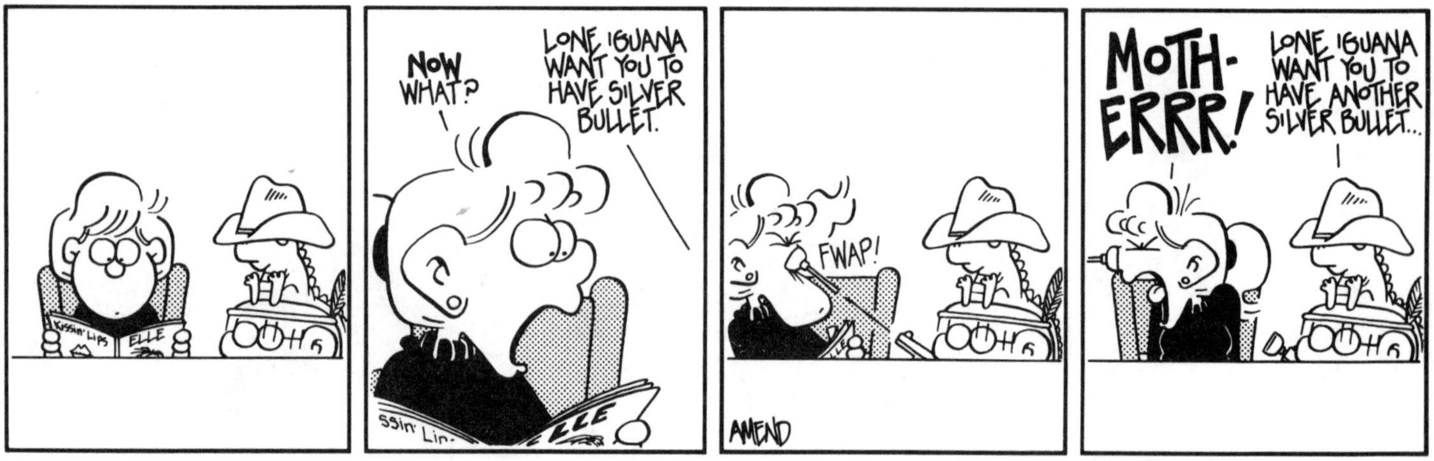
KISSIN' LIPS
ELLE
NOW WHAT?
LONE IGUANA WANT YOU TO HAVE SILVER BULLET.
FWAP!
AMEND
MOTH-ERRR!
LONE IGUANA WANT YOU TO HAVE ANOTHER SILVER BULLET...

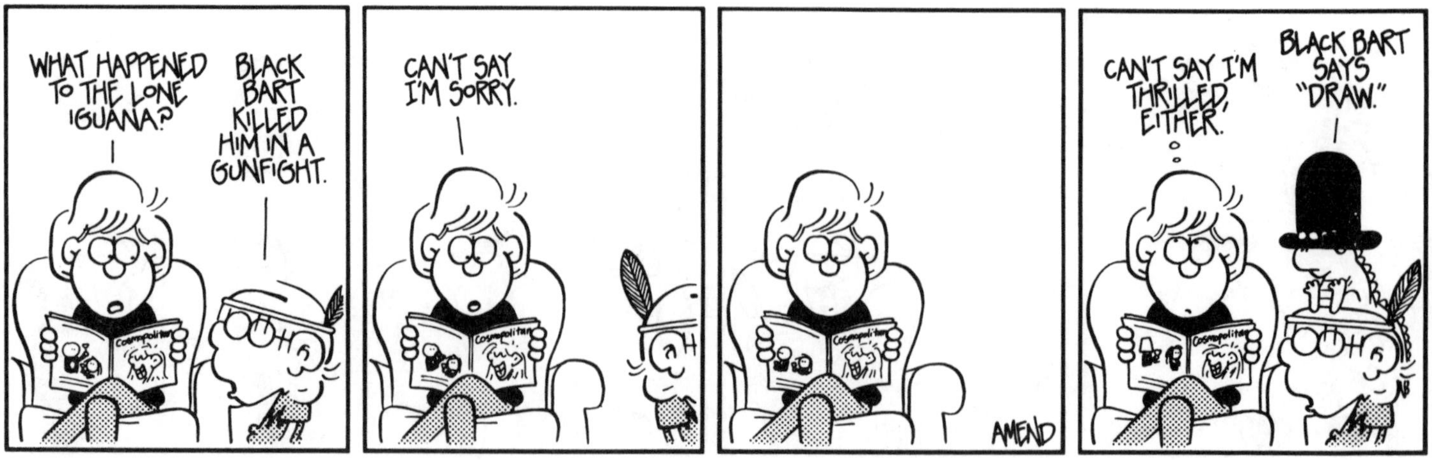
WHAT HAPPENED TO THE LONE IGUANA?
BLACK BART KILLED HIM IN A GUNFIGHT.
CAN'T SAY I'M SORRY.
AMEND
CAN'T SAY I'M THRILLED, EITHER.
BLACK BART SAYS "DRAW."

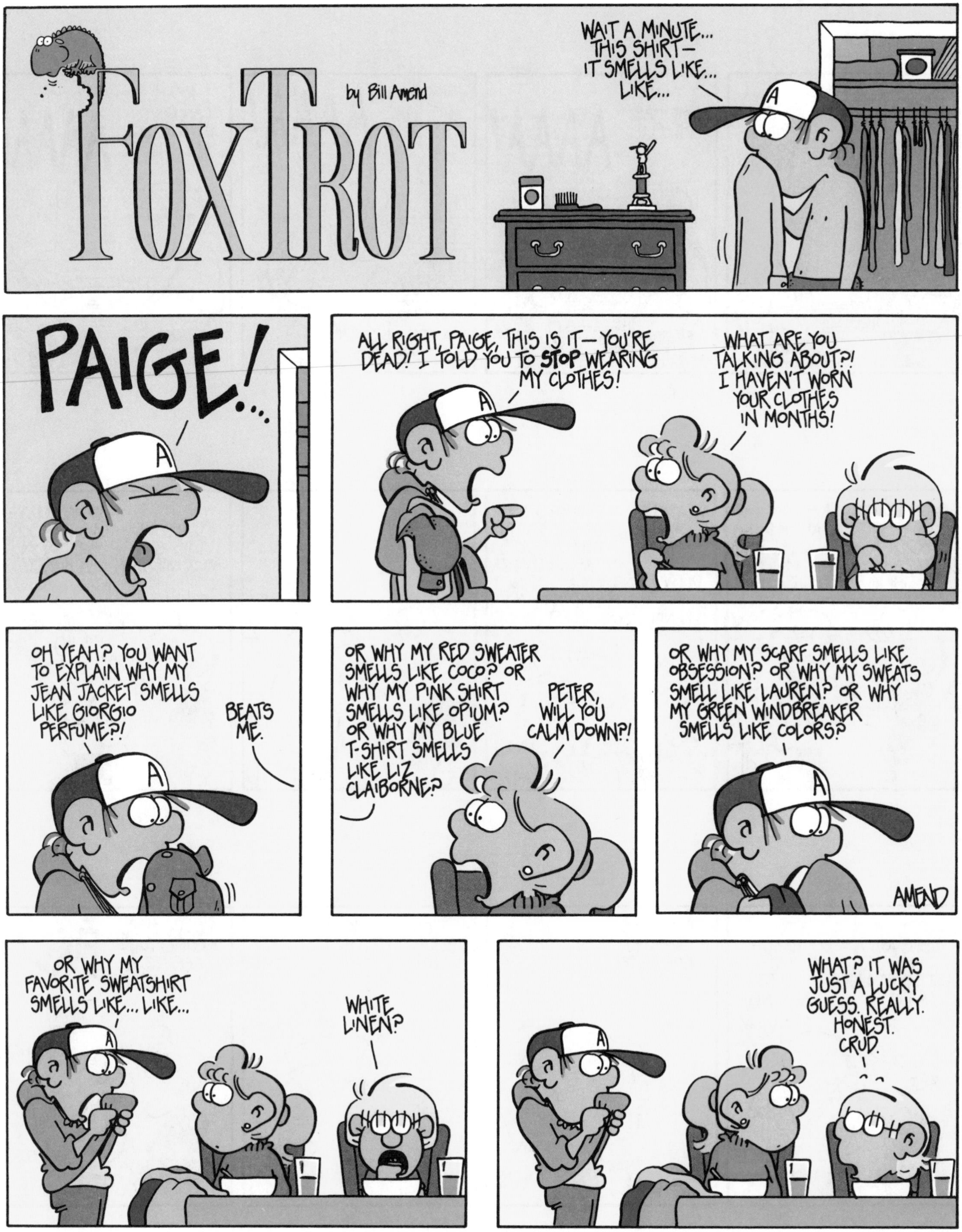
FoxTrot
by Bill Amend
WAIT A MINUTE... THIS SHIRT— IT SMELLS LIKE... LIKE...
PAIGE!...
ALL RIGHT, PAIGE, THIS IS IT—YOU'RE DEAD! I TOLD YOU TO STOP WEARING MY CLOTHES!
WHAT ARE YOU TALKING ABOUT?! I HAVEN'T WORN YOUR CLOTHES IN MONTHS!
OH YEAH? YOU WANT TO EXPLAIN WHY MY JEAN JACKET SMELLS LIKE GIORGIO PERFUME?!
BEATS ME.
OR WHY MY RED SWEATER SMELLS LIKE COCO? OR WHY MY PINK SHIRT SMELLS LIKE OPIUM? OR WHY MY BLUE T-SHIRT SMELLS LIKE LIZ CLAIBORNE?
PETER, WILL YOU CALM DOWN?!
OR WHY MY SCARF SMELLS LIKE OBSESSION? OR WHY MY SWEATS SMELL LIKE LAUREN? OR WHY MY GREEN WINDBREAKER SMELLS LIKE COLORS?
AMEND
OR WHY MY FAVORITE SWEATSHIRT SMELLS LIKE... LIKE...
WHITE LINEN?
WHAT? IT WAS JUST A LUCKY GUESS. REALLY. HONEST. CRUD.

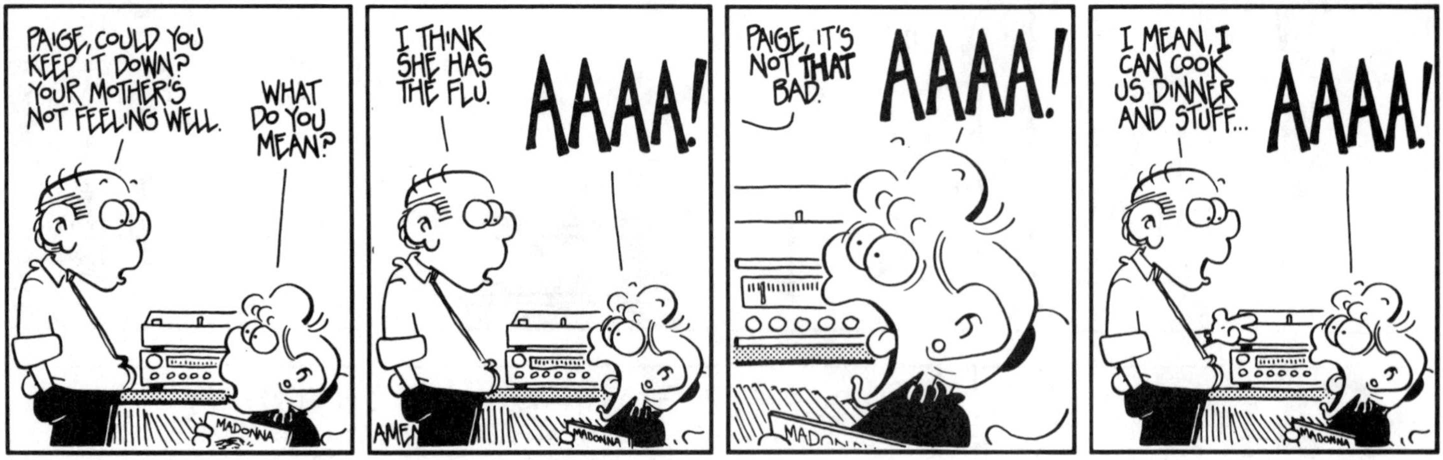
PAIGE, COULD YOU KEEP IT DOWN? YOUR MOTHER'S NOT FEELING WELL.
WHAT DO YOU MEAN?
MADONNA
I THINK SHE HAS THE FLU.
AAAA!
AMEND
MADONNA
PAIGE, IT'S NOT **THAT** BAD.
AAAA!
MADONNA
I MEAN, I CAN COOK US DINNER AND STUFF...
AAAA!
MADONNA

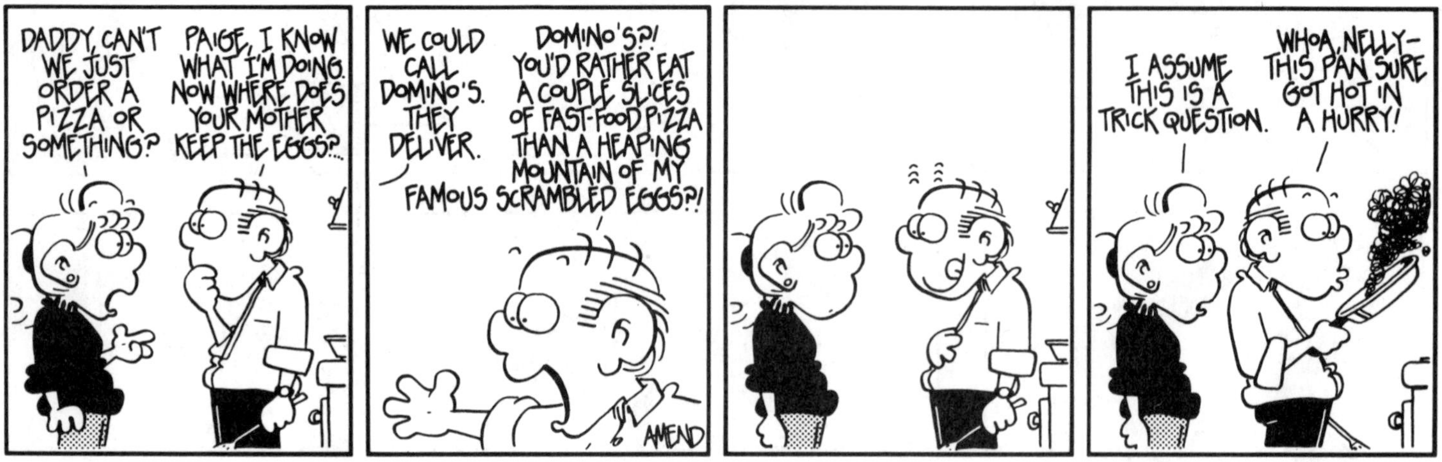
DADDY, CAN'T WE JUST ORDER A PIZZA OR SOMETHING?
PAIGE, I KNOW WHAT I'M DOING. NOW WHERE DOES YOUR MOTHER KEEP THE EGGS?...
WE COULD CALL DOMINO'S. THEY DELIVER.
DOMINO'S?! YOU'D RATHER EAT A COUPLE SLICES OF FAST-FOOD PIZZA THAN A HEAPING MOUNTAIN OF MY FAMOUS SCRAMBLED EGGS?!
AMEND
I ASSUME THIS IS A TRICK QUESTION.
WHOA, NELLY- THIS PAN SURE GOT HOT IN A HURRY!

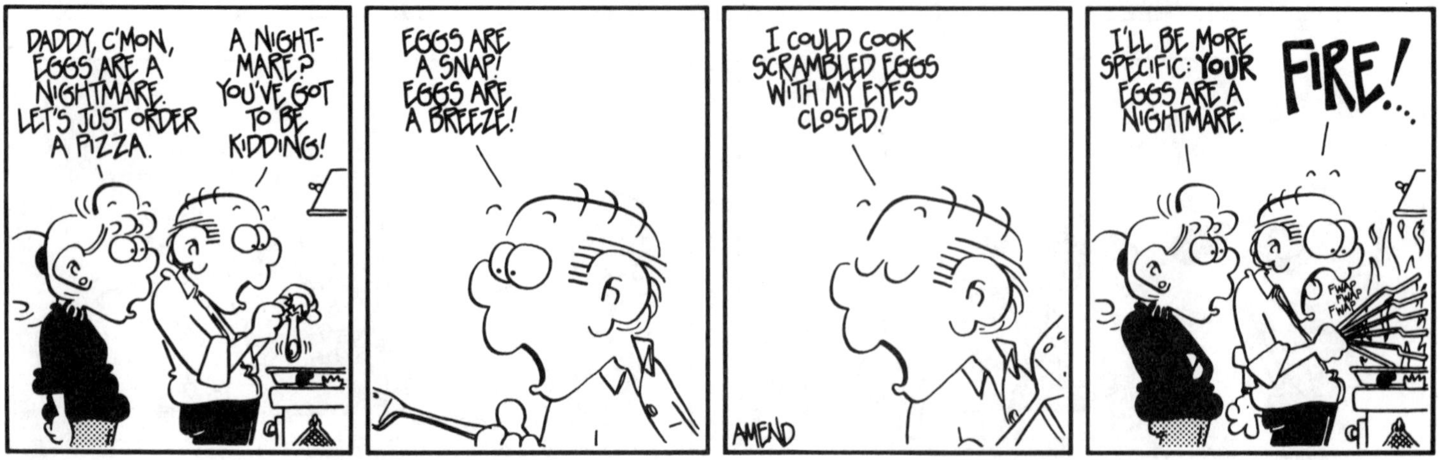
DADDY, C'MON, EGGS ARE A NIGHTMARE. LET'S JUST ORDER A PIZZA.
A NIGHT-MARE? YOU'VE GOT TO BE KIDDING!
EGGS ARE A SNAP! EGGS ARE A BREEZE!
I COULD COOK SCRAMBLED EGGS WITH MY EYES CLOSED!
AMEND
I'LL BE MORE SPECIFIC: **YOUR** EGGS ARE A NIGHTMARE.
FIRE!...
FWAP FWAP FWAP

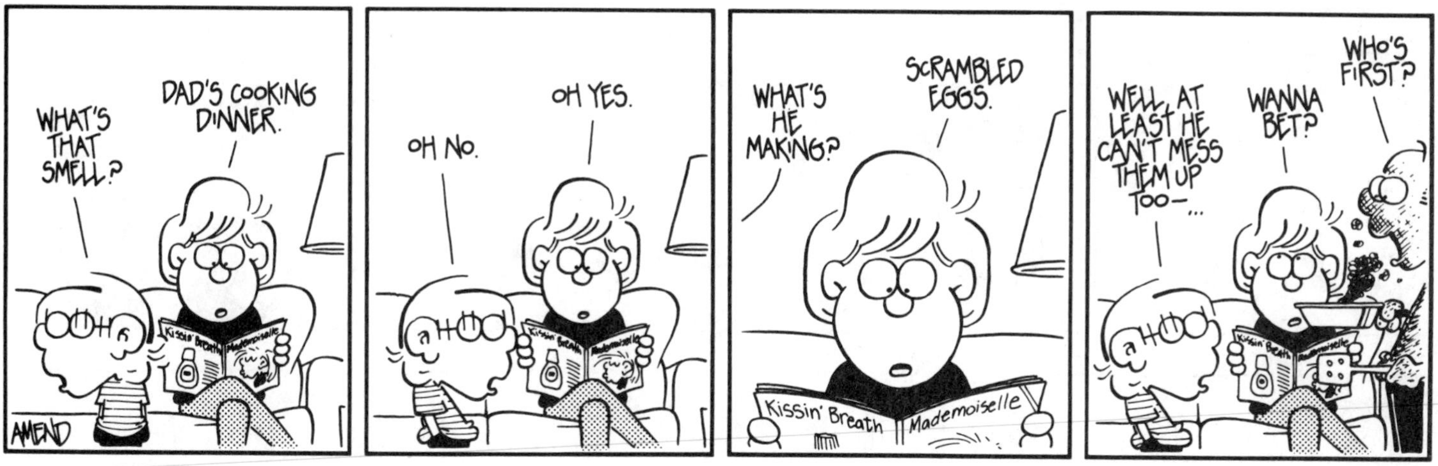
AMEND
WHAT'S THAT SMELL?
DAD'S COOKING DINNER.
OH NO.
OH YES.
Kissin' Breath
Mademoiselle
WHAT'S HE MAKING?
SCRAMBLED EGGS.
WELL, AT LEAST HE CAN'T MESS THEM UP TOO–...
WANNA BET?
WHO'S FIRST?

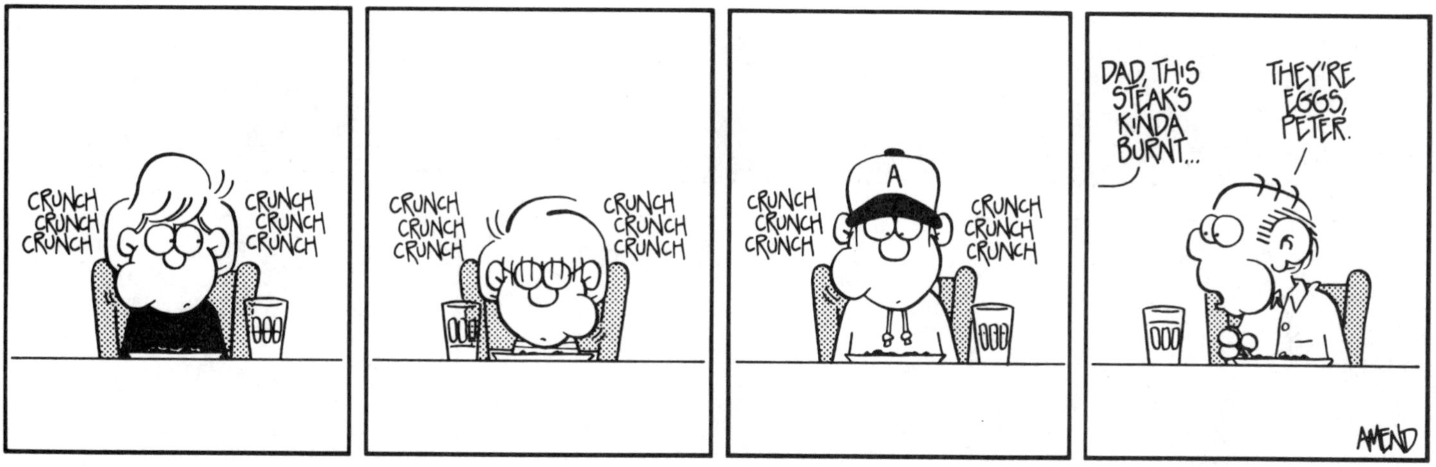
CRUNCH CRUNCH CRUNCH
CRUNCH CRUNCH CRUNCH
CRUNCH CRUNCH CRUNCH
CRUNCH CRUNCH CRUNCH
CRUNCH CRUNCH CRUNCH
CRUNCH CRUNCH CRUNCH
DAD, THIS STEAK'S KINDA BURNT...
THEY'RE EGGS, PETER.
AMEND

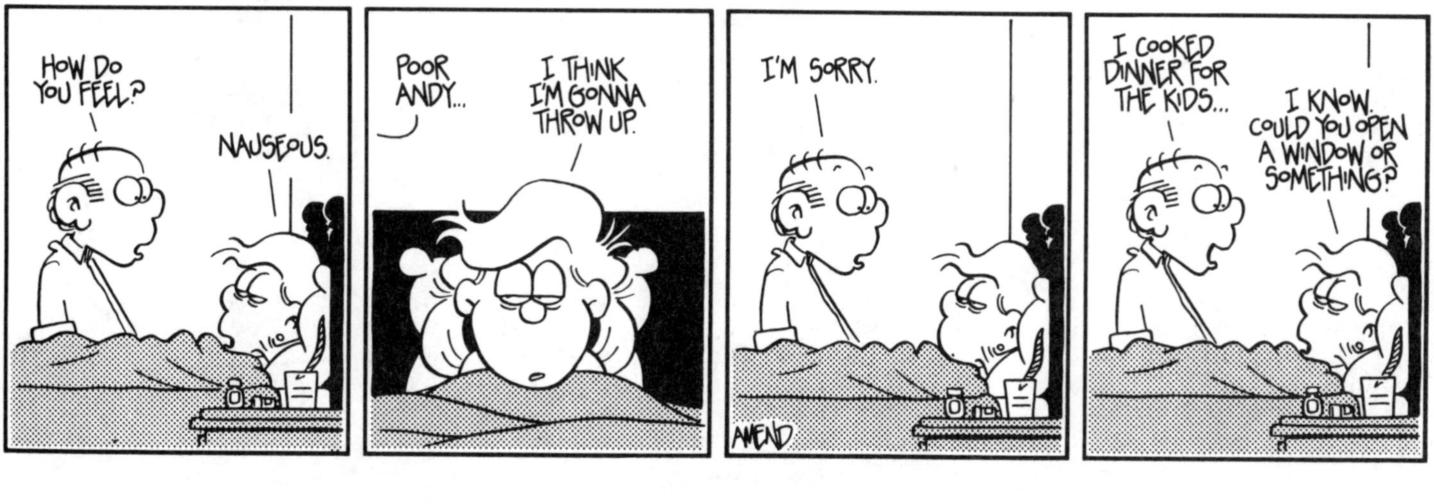
HOW DO YOU FEEL?
NAUSEOUS.
POOR ANDY...
I THINK I'M GONNA THROW UP.
I'M SORRY.
AMEND
I COOKED DINNER FOR THE KIDS...
I KNOW. COULD YOU OPEN A WINDOW OR SOMETHING?

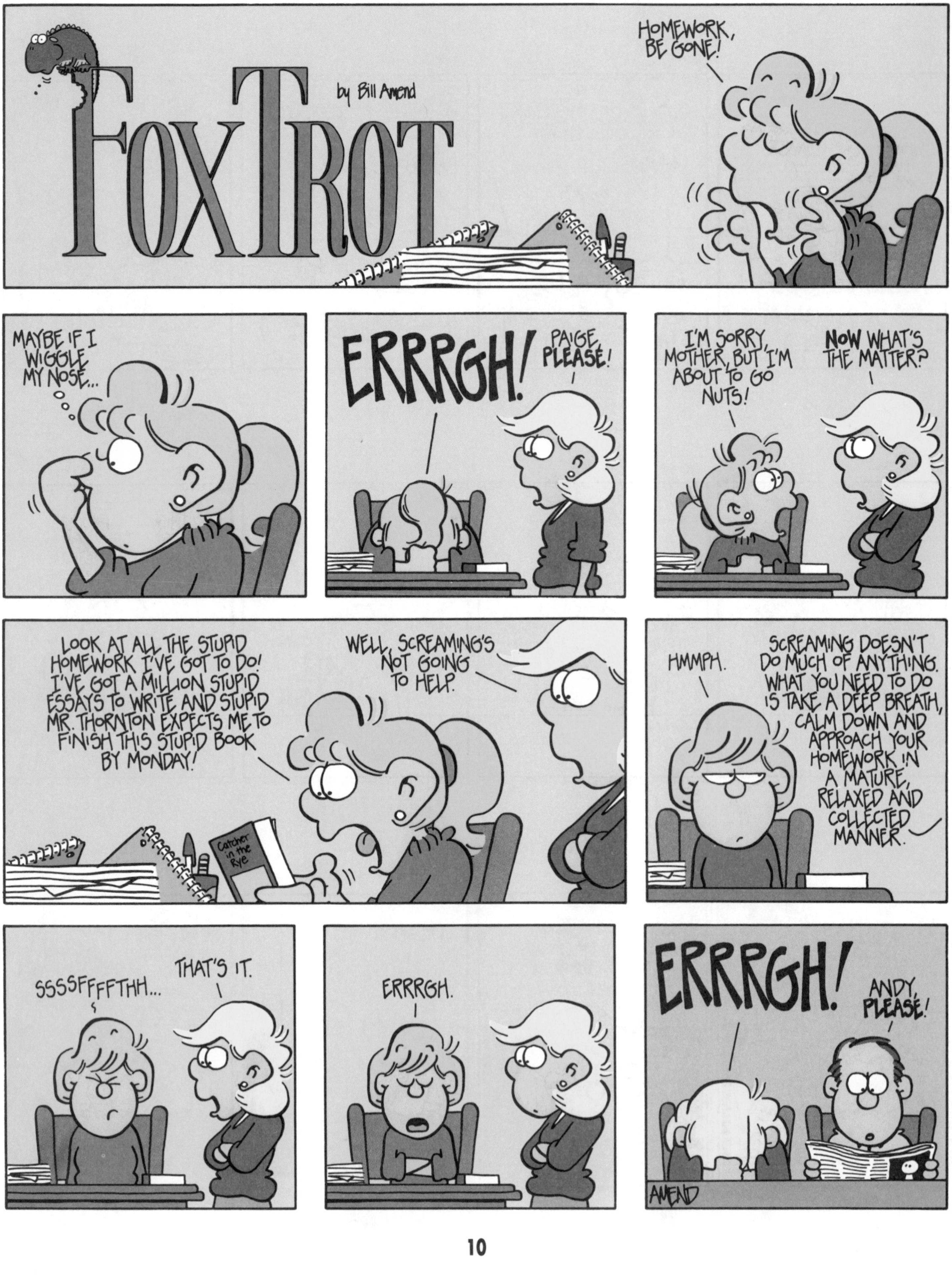

FoxTrot
by Bill Amend
HOMEWORK, BE GONE!
MAYBE IF I WIGGLE MY NOSE...
ERRRGH!
PAIGE, PLEASE!
I'M SORRY, MOTHER, BUT I'M ABOUT TO GO NUTS!
NOW WHAT'S THE MATTER?
LOOK AT ALL THE STUPID HOMEWORK I'VE GOT TO DO! I'VE GOT A MILLION STUPID ESSAYS TO WRITE AND STUPID MR. THORNTON EXPECTS ME TO FINISH THIS STUPID BOOK BY MONDAY!
Catcher in the Rye
WELL, SCREAMING'S NOT GOING TO HELP.
HMMPH.
SCREAMING DOESN'T DO MUCH OF ANYTHING. WHAT YOU NEED TO DO IS TAKE A DEEP BREATH, CALM DOWN AND APPROACH YOUR HOMEWORK IN A MATURE, RELAXED AND COLLECTED MANNER.
SSSSFFFFTHH...
THAT'S IT.
ERRRGH.
ERRRGH!
ANDY, PLEASE!
AMEND

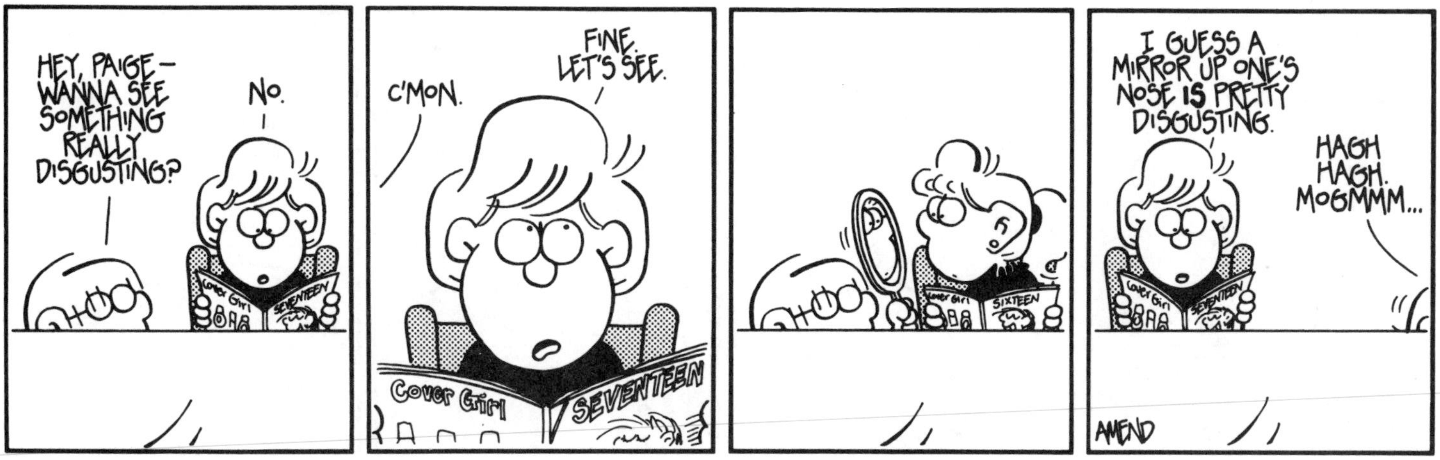
HEY, PAIGE— WANNA SEE SOMETHING REALLY DISGUSTING?
NO.
C'MON.
FINE. LET'S SEE.
I GUESS A MIRROR UP ONE'S NOSE **IS** PRETTY DISGUSTING.
HAGH HAGH. MOGMMM...
AMEND

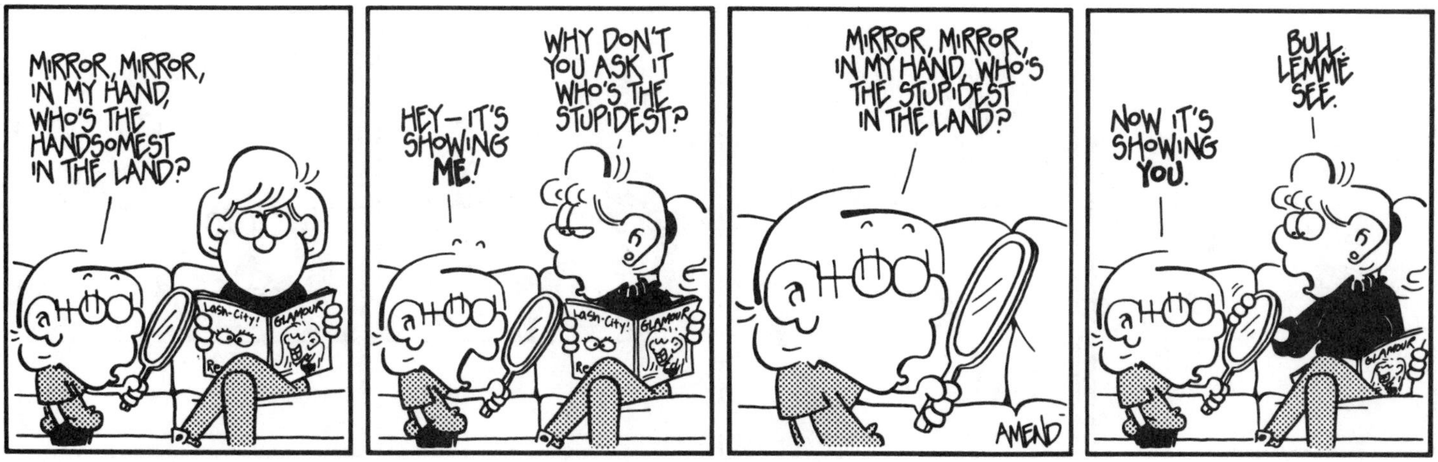
MIRROR, MIRROR, IN MY HAND, WHO'S THE HANDSOMEST IN THE LAND?
HEY— IT'S SHOWING **ME**!
WHY DON'T YOU ASK IT WHO'S THE STUPIDEST?
MIRROR, MIRROR, IN MY HAND, WHO'S THE STUPIDEST IN THE LAND?
AMEND
NOW IT'S SHOWING **YOU**.
BULL. LEMME SEE.

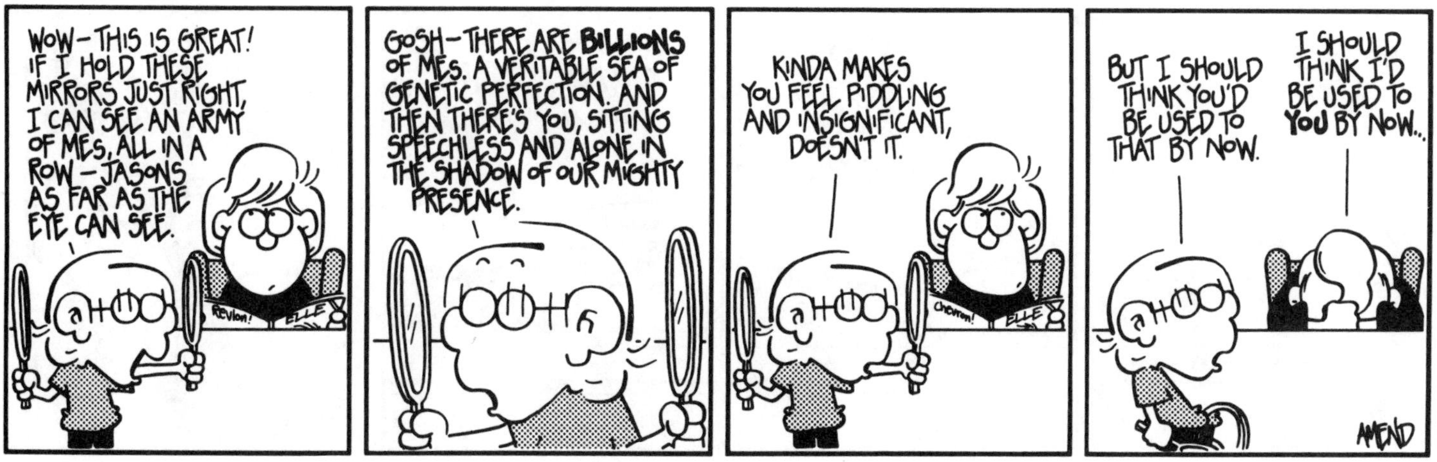
WOW— THIS IS GREAT! IF I HOLD THESE MIRRORS JUST RIGHT, I CAN SEE AN ARMY OF MES, ALL IN A ROW— JASONS AS FAR AS THE EYE CAN SEE.
GOSH— THERE ARE **BILLIONS** OF MES. A VERITABLE SEA OF GENETIC PERFECTION. AND THEN THERE'S YOU, SITTING SPEECHLESS AND ALONE IN THE SHADOW OF OUR MIGHTY PRESENCE.
KINDA MAKES YOU FEEL PIDDLING AND INSIGNIFICANT, DOESN'T IT.
BUT I SHOULD THINK YOU'D BE USED TO THAT BY NOW.
I SHOULD THINK I'D BE USED TO **YOU** BY NOW...
AMEND

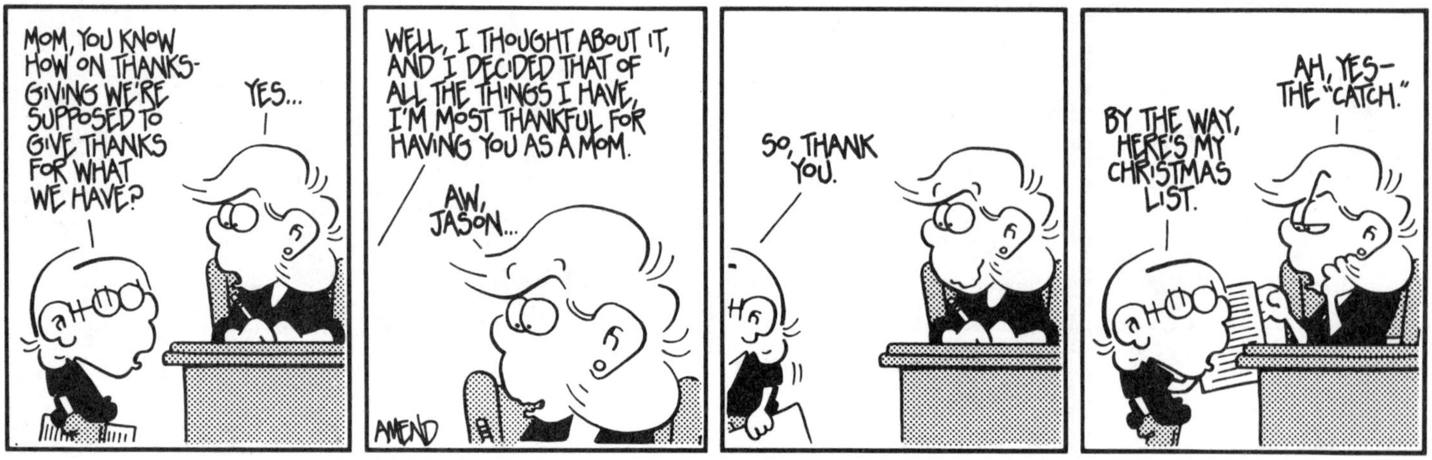
MOM, YOU KNOW HOW ON THANKSGIVING WE'RE SUPPOSED TO GIVE THANKS FOR WHAT WE HAVE?
YES...
WELL, I THOUGHT ABOUT IT, AND I DECIDED THAT OF ALL THE THINGS I HAVE, I'M MOST THANKFUL FOR HAVING YOU AS A MOM.
AW, JASON...
AMEND
SO, THANK YOU.
BY THE WAY, HERE'S MY CHRISTMAS LIST.
AH, YES— THE "CATCH."

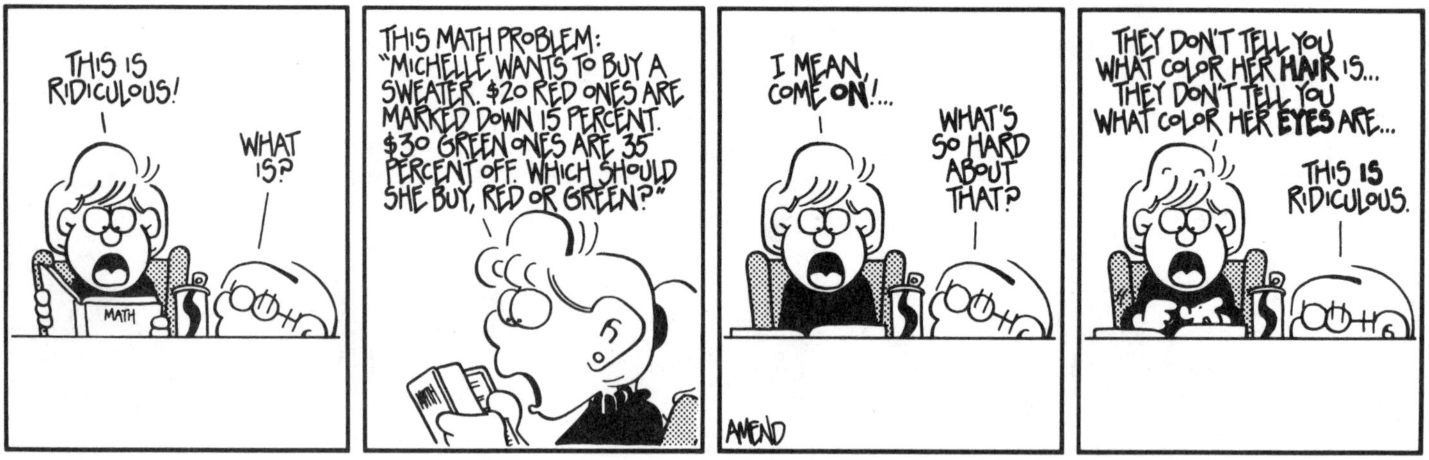
THIS IS RIDICULOUS!
WHAT IS?
MATH
THIS MATH PROBLEM: "MICHELLE WANTS TO BUY A SWEATER. $20 RED ONES ARE MARKED DOWN 15 PERCENT. $30 GREEN ONES ARE 35 PERCENT OFF. WHICH SHOULD SHE BUY, RED OR GREEN?"
MATH
I MEAN, COME **ON**!...
WHAT'S SO HARD ABOUT THAT?
AMEND
THEY DON'T TELL YOU WHAT COLOR HER **HAIR** IS... THEY DON'T TELL YOU WHAT COLOR HER **EYES** ARE...
THIS **IS** RIDICULOUS.

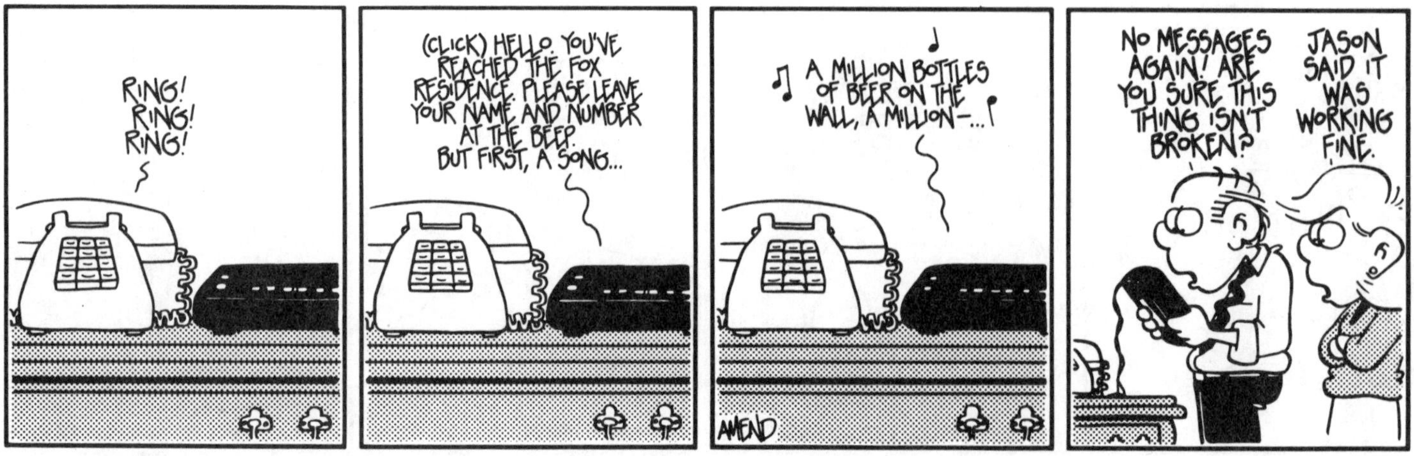
RING! RING! RING!
(CLICK) HELLO. YOU'VE REACHED THE FOX RESIDENCE. PLEASE LEAVE YOUR NAME AND NUMBER AT THE BEEP. BUT FIRST, A SONG...
♫ A MILLION BOTTLES OF BEER ON THE WALL, A MILLION—...
AMEND
NO MESSAGES AGAIN! ARE YOU SURE THIS THING ISN'T BROKEN?
JASON SAID IT WAS WORKING FINE.

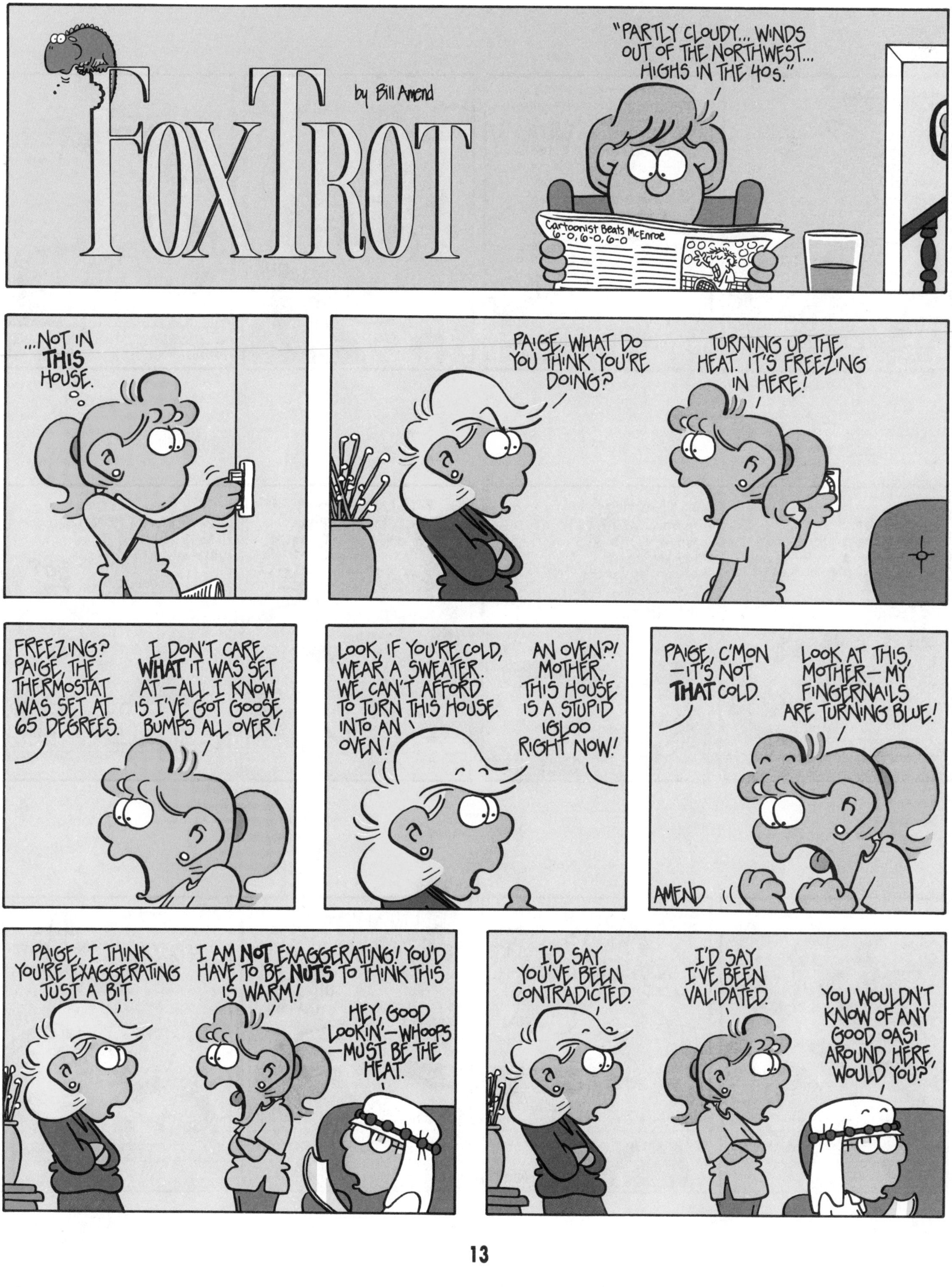
FoxTrot
by Bill Amend
"PARTLY CLOUDY... WINDS OUT OF THE NORTHWEST... HIGHS IN THE 40s."
Cartoonist Beats McEnroe 6-0, 6-0, 6-0
...NOT IN THIS HOUSE.
PAIGE, WHAT DO YOU THINK YOU'RE DOING?
TURNING UP THE HEAT. IT'S FREEZING IN HERE!
FREEZING? PAIGE, THE THERMOSTAT WAS SET AT 65 DEGREES.
I DON'T CARE WHAT IT WAS SET AT—ALL I KNOW IS I'VE GOT GOOSE BUMPS ALL OVER!
LOOK, IF YOU'RE COLD, WEAR A SWEATER. WE CAN'T AFFORD TO TURN THIS HOUSE INTO AN OVEN!
AN OVEN?! MOTHER, THIS HOUSE IS A STUPID IGLOO RIGHT NOW!
PAIGE, C'MON—IT'S NOT THAT COLD.
LOOK AT THIS, MOTHER—MY FINGERNAILS ARE TURNING BLUE!
AMEND
PAIGE, I THINK YOU'RE EXAGGERATING JUST A BIT.
I AM NOT EXAGGERATING! YOU'D HAVE TO BE NUTS TO THINK THIS IS WARM!
HEY, GOOD LOOKIN'—WHOOPS—MUST BE THE HEAT.
I'D SAY YOU'VE BEEN CONTRADICTED.
I'D SAY I'VE BEEN VALIDATED.
YOU WOULDN'T KNOW OF ANY GOOD OASI AROUND HERE, WOULD YOU?

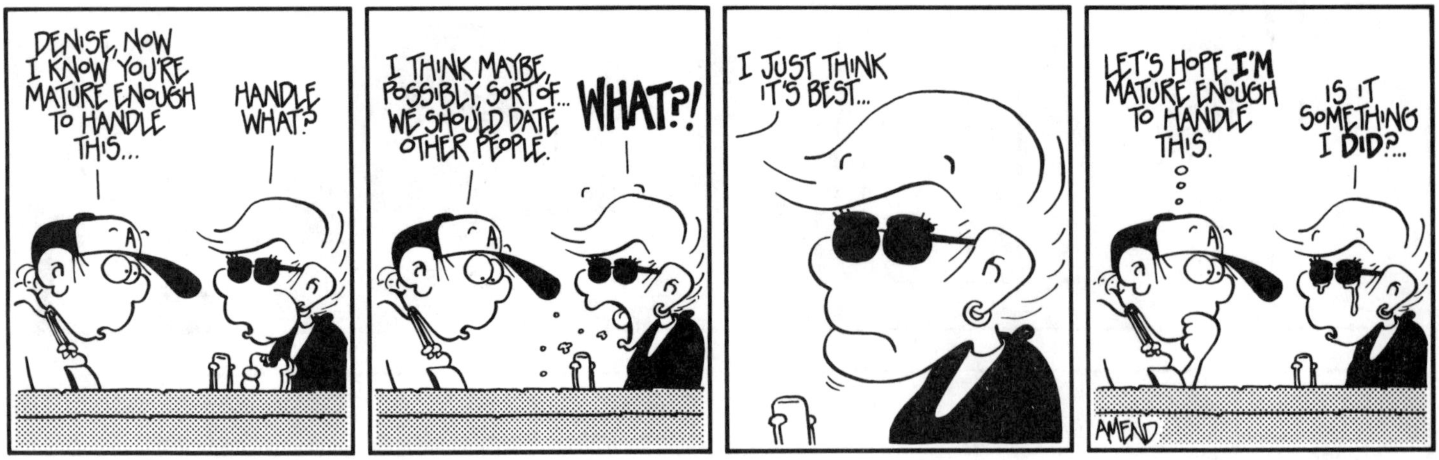
DENISE, NOW I KNOW YOU'RE MATURE ENOUGH TO HANDLE THIS...
HANDLE WHAT?
I THINK MAYBE, POSSIBLY, SORT OF... WE SHOULD DATE OTHER PEOPLE.
WHAT?!
I JUST THINK IT'S BEST...
LET'S HOPE I'M MATURE ENOUGH TO HANDLE THIS.
IS IT SOMETHING I DID?...
AMEND

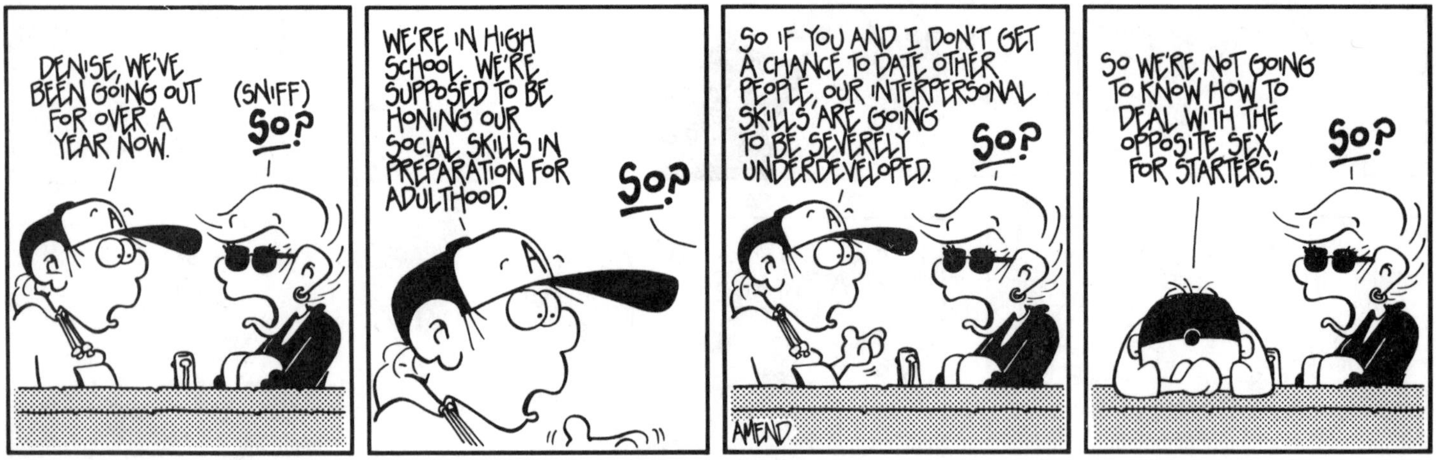
DENISE, WE'VE BEEN GOING OUT FOR OVER A YEAR NOW.
(SNIFF) SO?
WE'RE IN HIGH SCHOOL. WE'RE SUPPOSED TO BE HONING OUR SOCIAL SKILLS IN PREPARATION FOR ADULTHOOD.
SO?
SO IF YOU AND I DON'T GET A CHANCE TO DATE OTHER PEOPLE, OUR INTERPERSONAL SKILLS ARE GOING TO BE SEVERELY UNDERDEVELOPED.
SO?
AMEND
SO WE'RE NOT GOING TO KNOW HOW TO DEAL WITH THE OPPOSITE SEX, FOR STARTERS.
SO?

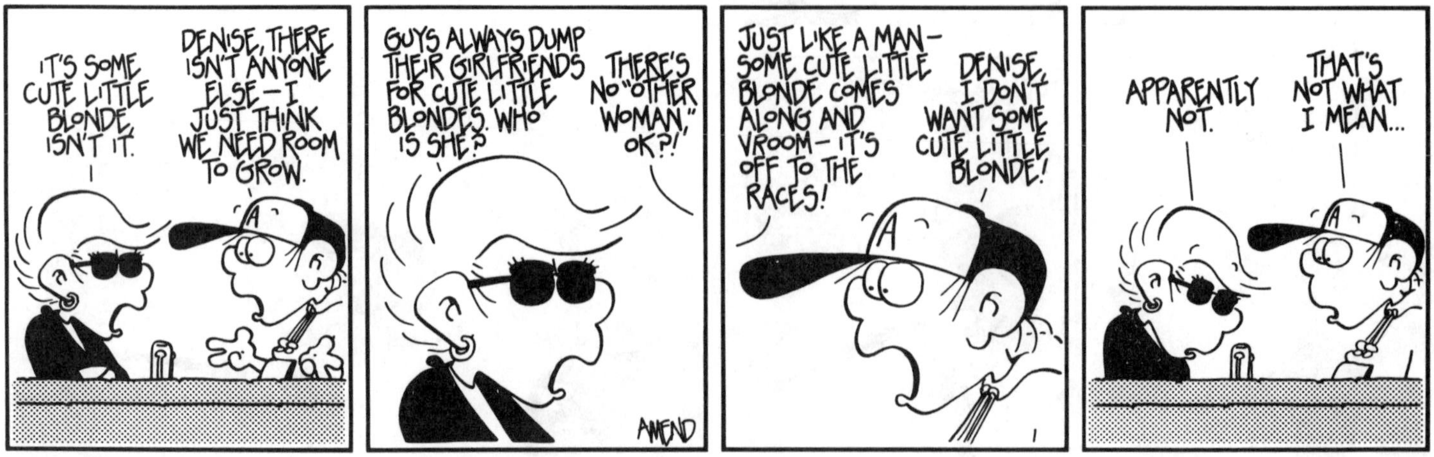
IT'S SOME CUTE LITTLE BLONDE, ISN'T IT.
DENISE, THERE ISN'T ANYONE ELSE — I JUST THINK WE NEED ROOM TO GROW.
GUYS ALWAYS DUMP THEIR GIRLFRIENDS FOR CUTE LITTLE BLONDES. WHO IS SHE?
THERE'S NO "OTHER WOMAN," OK?!
AMEND
JUST LIKE A MAN — SOME CUTE LITTLE BLONDE COMES ALONG AND VROOM — IT'S OFF TO THE RACES!
DENISE, I DON'T WANT SOME CUTE LITTLE BLONDE!
APPARENTLY NOT.
THAT'S NOT WHAT I MEAN...

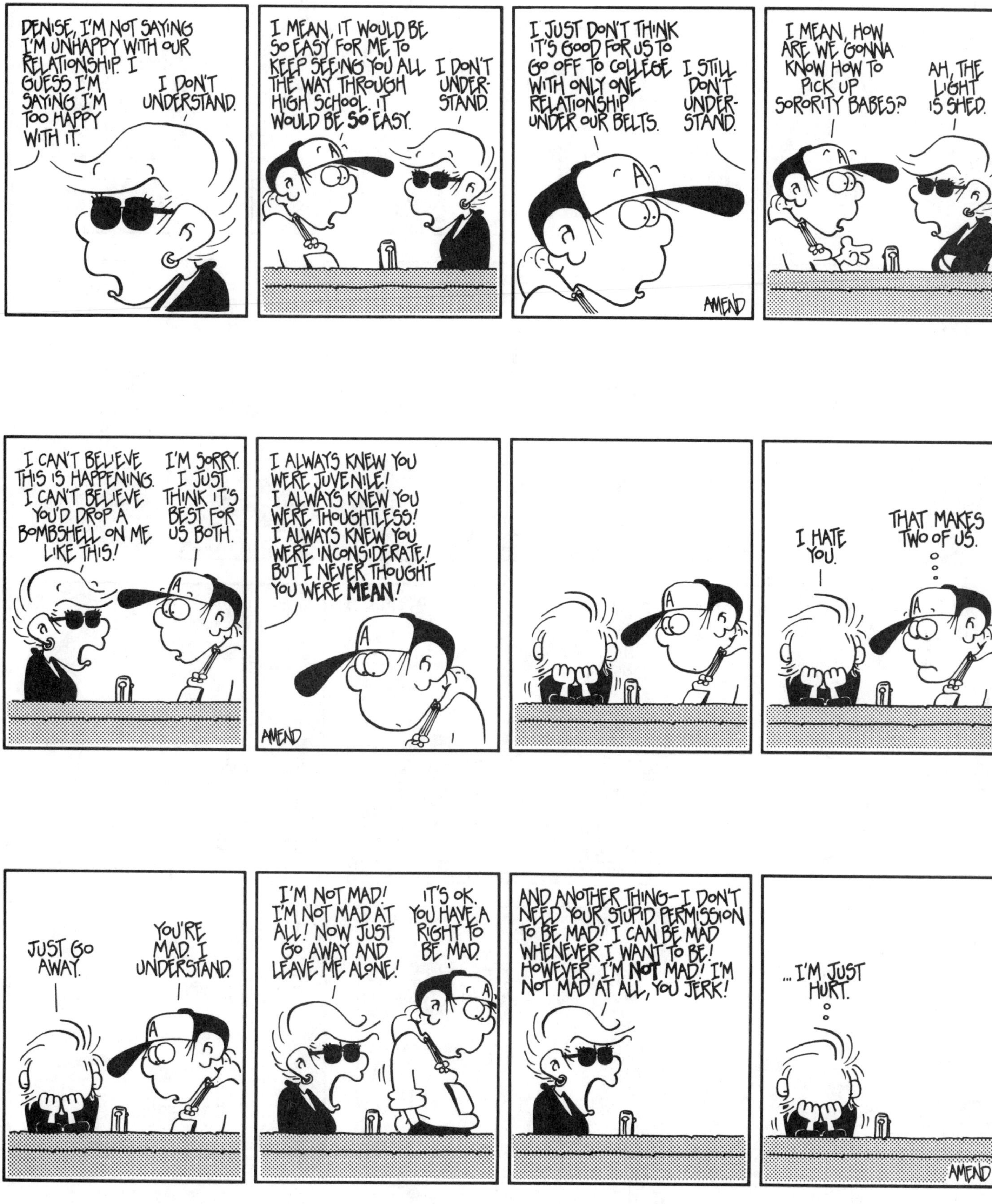
DENISE, I'M NOT SAYING I'M UNHAPPY WITH OUR RELATIONSHIP. I GUESS I'M SAYING I'M TOO HAPPY WITH IT.
I DON'T UNDERSTAND.
I MEAN, IT WOULD BE SO EASY FOR ME TO KEEP SEEING YOU ALL THE WAY THROUGH HIGH SCHOOL. IT WOULD BE SO EASY.
I DON'T UNDERSTAND.
I JUST DON'T THINK IT'S GOOD FOR US TO GO OFF TO COLLEGE WITH ONLY ONE RELATIONSHIP UNDER OUR BELTS.
I STILL DON'T UNDERSTAND.
AMEND
I MEAN, HOW ARE WE GONNA KNOW HOW TO PICK UP SORORITY BABES?
AH, THE LIGHT IS SHED.
I CAN'T BELIEVE THIS IS HAPPENING. I CAN'T BELIEVE YOU'D DROP A BOMBSHELL ON ME LIKE THIS!
I'M SORRY. I JUST THINK IT'S BEST FOR US BOTH.
I ALWAYS KNEW YOU WERE JUVENILE! I ALWAYS KNEW YOU WERE THOUGHTLESS! I ALWAYS KNEW YOU WERE INCONSIDERATE! BUT I NEVER THOUGHT YOU WERE MEAN!
AMEND
I HATE YOU.
THAT MAKES TWO OF US.
JUST GO AWAY.
YOU'RE MAD. I UNDERSTAND.
I'M NOT MAD! I'M NOT MAD AT ALL! NOW JUST GO AWAY AND LEAVE ME ALONE!
IT'S OK. YOU HAVE A RIGHT TO BE MAD.
AND ANOTHER THING—I DON'T NEED YOUR STUPID PERMISSION TO BE MAD! I CAN BE MAD WHENEVER I WANT TO BE! HOWEVER, I'M NOT MAD! I'M NOT MAD AT ALL, YOU JERK!
...I'M JUST HURT.
AMEND

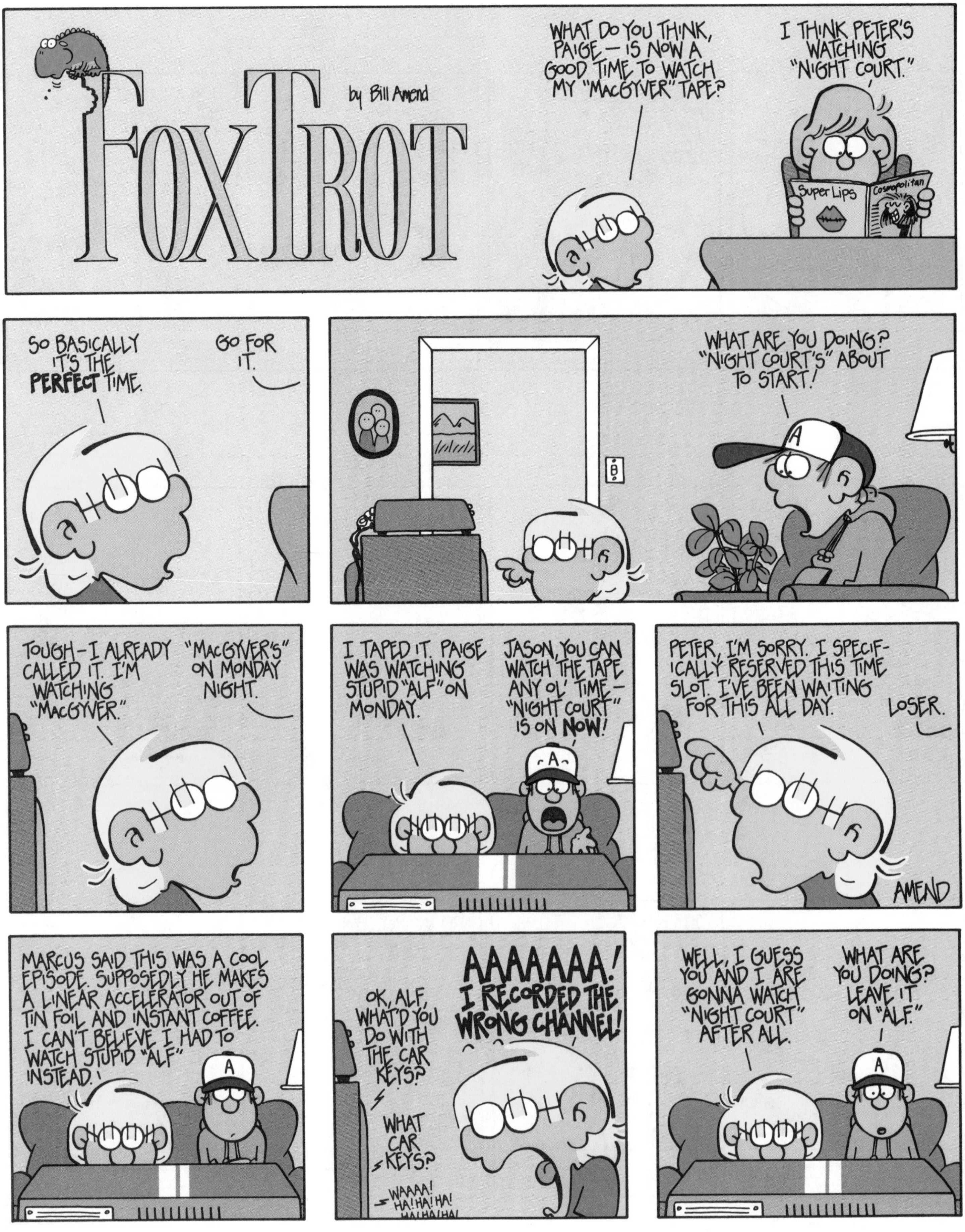
FoxTrot
by Bill Amend
WHAT DO YOU THINK, PAIGE — IS NOW A GOOD TIME TO WATCH MY "MACGYVER" TAPE?
I THINK PETER'S WATCHING "NIGHT COURT."
Super Lips
Cosmopolitan
SO BASICALLY IT'S THE PERFECT TIME.
GO FOR IT.
WHAT ARE YOU DOING? "NIGHT COURT'S" ABOUT TO START!
TOUGH — I ALREADY CALLED IT. I'M WATCHING "MACGYVER."
"MACGYVER'S" ON MONDAY NIGHT.
I TAPED IT. PAIGE WAS WATCHING STUPID "ALF" ON MONDAY.
JASON, YOU CAN WATCH THE TAPE ANY OL' TIME — "NIGHT COURT" IS ON NOW!
PETER, I'M SORRY. I SPECIFICALLY RESERVED THIS TIME SLOT. I'VE BEEN WAITING FOR THIS ALL DAY.
LOSER.
AMEND
MARCUS SAID THIS WAS A COOL EPISODE. SUPPOSEDLY HE MAKES A LINEAR ACCELERATOR OUT OF TIN FOIL AND INSTANT COFFEE. I CAN'T BELIEVE I HAD TO WATCH STUPID "ALF" INSTEAD.
OK, ALF, WHAT'D YOU DO WITH THE CAR KEYS?
WHAT CAR KEYS?
WAAAA! HA! HA! HA!
AAAAAAA! I RECORDED THE WRONG CHANNEL!
WELL, I GUESS YOU AND I ARE GONNA WATCH "NIGHT COURT" AFTER ALL.
WHAT ARE YOU DOING? LEAVE IT ON "ALF."

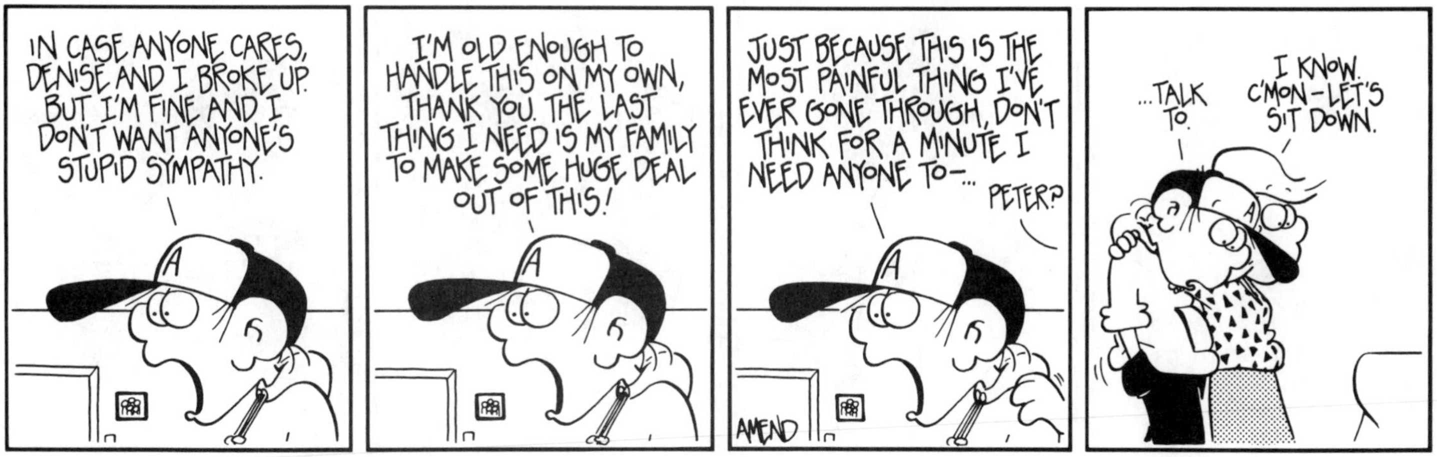
IN CASE ANYONE CARES, DENISE AND I BROKE UP. BUT I'M FINE AND I DON'T WANT ANYONE'S STUPID SYMPATHY.
I'M OLD ENOUGH TO HANDLE THIS ON MY OWN, THANK YOU. THE LAST THING I NEED IS MY FAMILY TO MAKE SOME HUGE DEAL OUT OF THIS!
JUST BECAUSE THIS IS THE MOST PAINFUL THING I'VE EVER GONE THROUGH, DON'T THINK FOR A MINUTE I NEED ANYONE TO–...
PETER?
...TALK TO.
I KNOW. C'MON–LET'S SIT DOWN.
AMEND

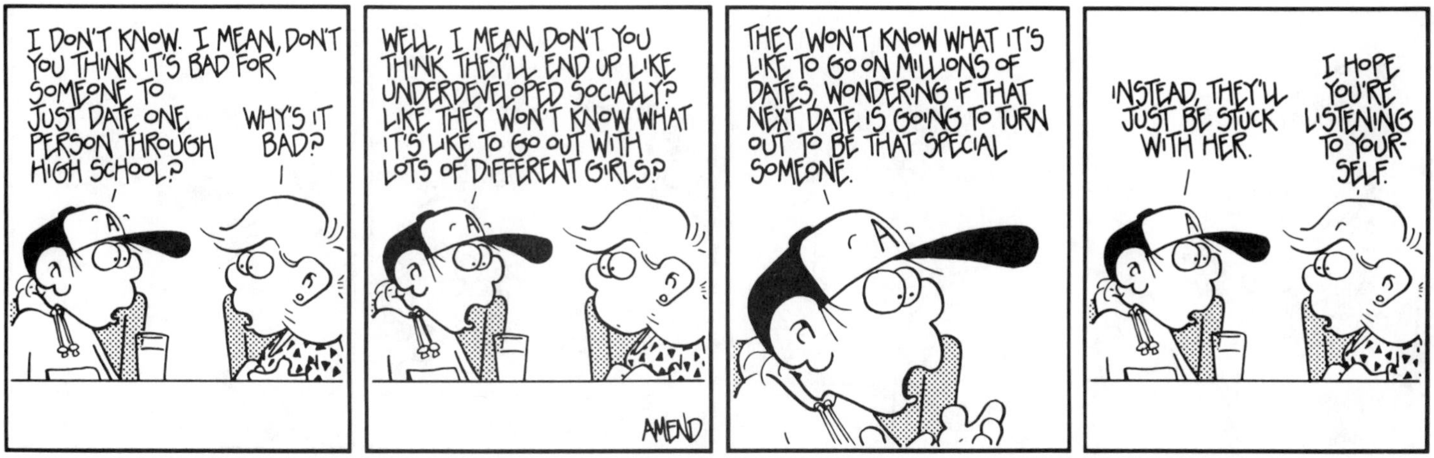
I DON'T KNOW. I MEAN, DON'T YOU THINK IT'S BAD FOR SOMEONE TO JUST DATE ONE PERSON THROUGH HIGH SCHOOL?
WHY'S IT BAD?
WELL, I MEAN, DON'T YOU THINK THEY'LL END UP LIKE UNDERDEVELOPED SOCIALLY? LIKE THEY WON'T KNOW WHAT IT'S LIKE TO GO OUT WITH LOTS OF DIFFERENT GIRLS?
AMEND
THEY WON'T KNOW WHAT IT'S LIKE TO GO ON MILLIONS OF DATES, WONDERING IF THAT NEXT DATE IS GOING TO TURN OUT TO BE THAT SPECIAL SOMEONE.
INSTEAD, THEY'LL JUST BE STUCK WITH HER.
I HOPE YOU'RE LISTENING TO YOURSELF.

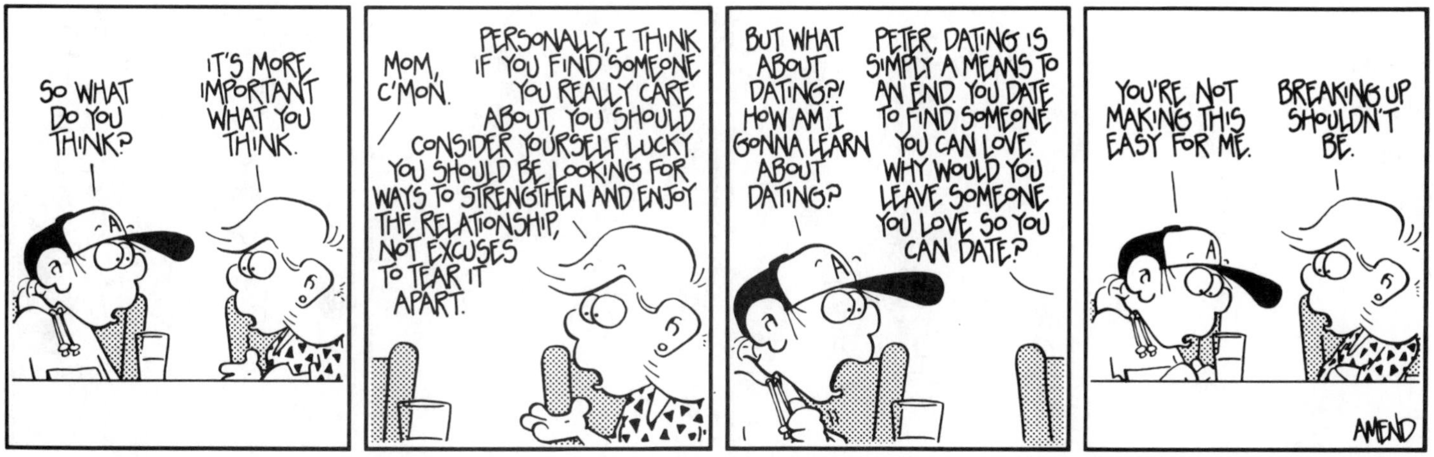
SO WHAT DO YOU THINK?
IT'S MORE IMPORTANT WHAT YOU THINK.
PERSONALLY, I THINK IF YOU FIND SOMEONE YOU REALLY CARE ABOUT, YOU SHOULD CONSIDER YOURSELF LUCKY. YOU SHOULD BE LOOKING FOR WAYS TO STRENGTHEN AND ENJOY THE RELATIONSHIP, NOT EXCUSES TO TEAR IT APART.
MOM, C'MON.
BUT WHAT ABOUT DATING?! HOW AM I GONNA LEARN ABOUT DATING?
PETER, DATING IS SIMPLY A MEANS TO AN END. YOU DATE TO FIND SOMEONE YOU CAN LOVE. WHY WOULD YOU LEAVE SOMEONE YOU LOVE SO YOU CAN DATE?
YOU'RE NOT MAKING THIS EASY FOR ME.
BREAKING UP SHOULDN'T BE.
AMEND

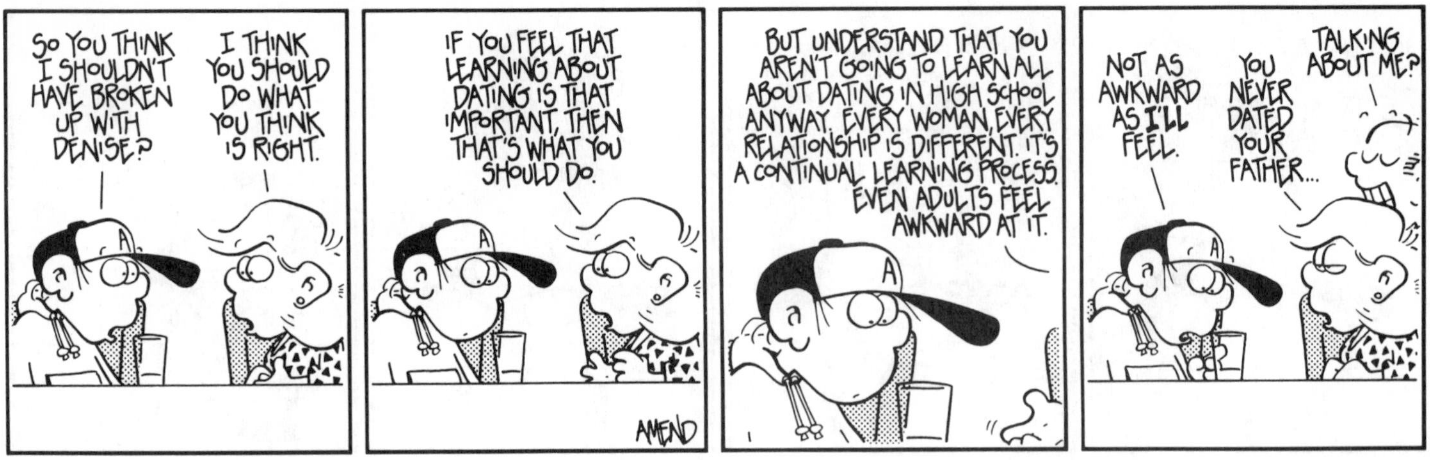
SO YOU THINK I SHOULDN'T HAVE BROKEN UP WITH DENISE?
I THINK YOU SHOULD DO WHAT YOU THINK IS RIGHT.
IF YOU FEEL THAT LEARNING ABOUT DATING IS THAT IMPORTANT, THEN THAT'S WHAT YOU SHOULD DO.
AMEND
BUT UNDERSTAND THAT YOU AREN'T GOING TO LEARN ALL ABOUT DATING IN HIGH SCHOOL ANYWAY. EVERY WOMAN, EVERY RELATIONSHIP IS DIFFERENT. IT'S A CONTINUAL LEARNING PROCESS. EVEN ADULTS FEEL AWKWARD AT IT.
NOT AS AWKWARD AS **I'LL** FEEL.
YOU NEVER DATED YOUR FATHER...
TALKING ABOUT ME?

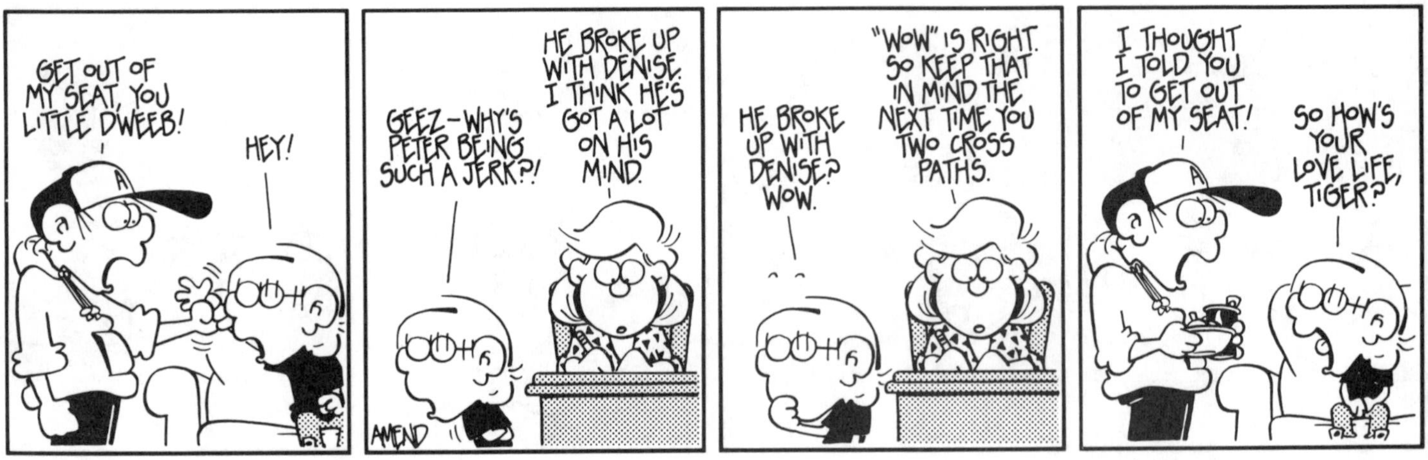
GET OUT OF MY SEAT, YOU LITTLE DWEEB!
HEY!
GEEZ–WHY'S PETER BEING SUCH A JERK?!
HE BROKE UP WITH DENISE. I THINK HE'S GOT A LOT ON HIS MIND.
AMEND
HE BROKE UP WITH DENISE? WOW.
"WOW" IS RIGHT. SO KEEP THAT IN MIND THE NEXT TIME YOU TWO CROSS PATHS.
I THOUGHT I TOLD YOU TO GET OUT OF MY SEAT!
SO HOW'S YOUR LOVE LIFE, TIGER?

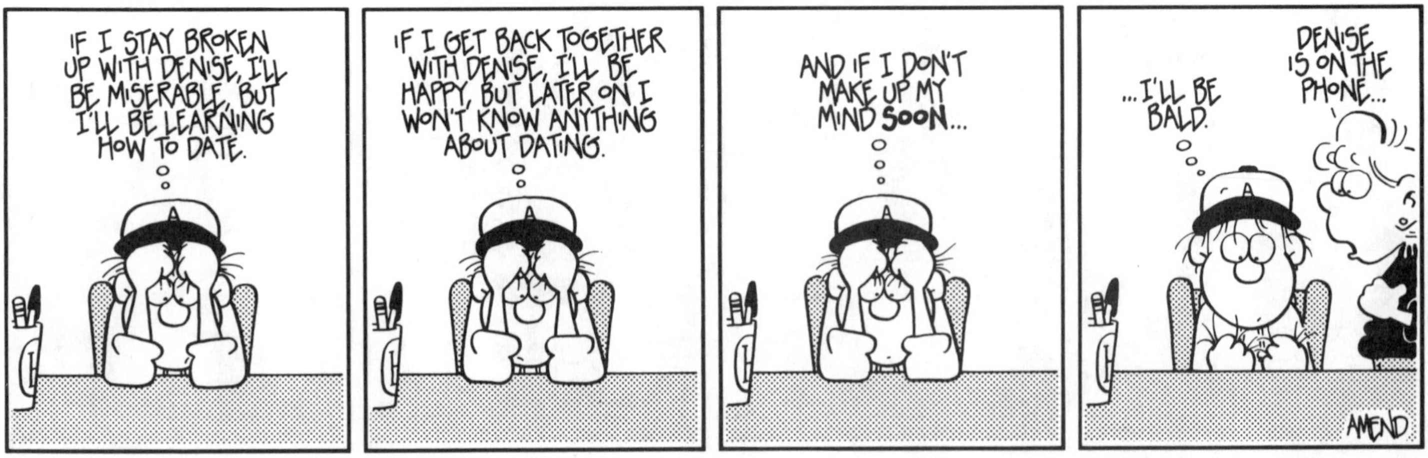
IF I STAY BROKEN UP WITH DENISE, I'LL BE MISERABLE, BUT I'LL BE LEARNING HOW TO DATE.
IF I GET BACK TOGETHER WITH DENISE, I'LL BE HAPPY, BUT LATER ON I WON'T KNOW ANYTHING ABOUT DATING.
AND IF I DON'T MAKE UP MY MIND **SOON**...
...I'LL BE BALD.
DENISE IS ON THE PHONE...
AMEND

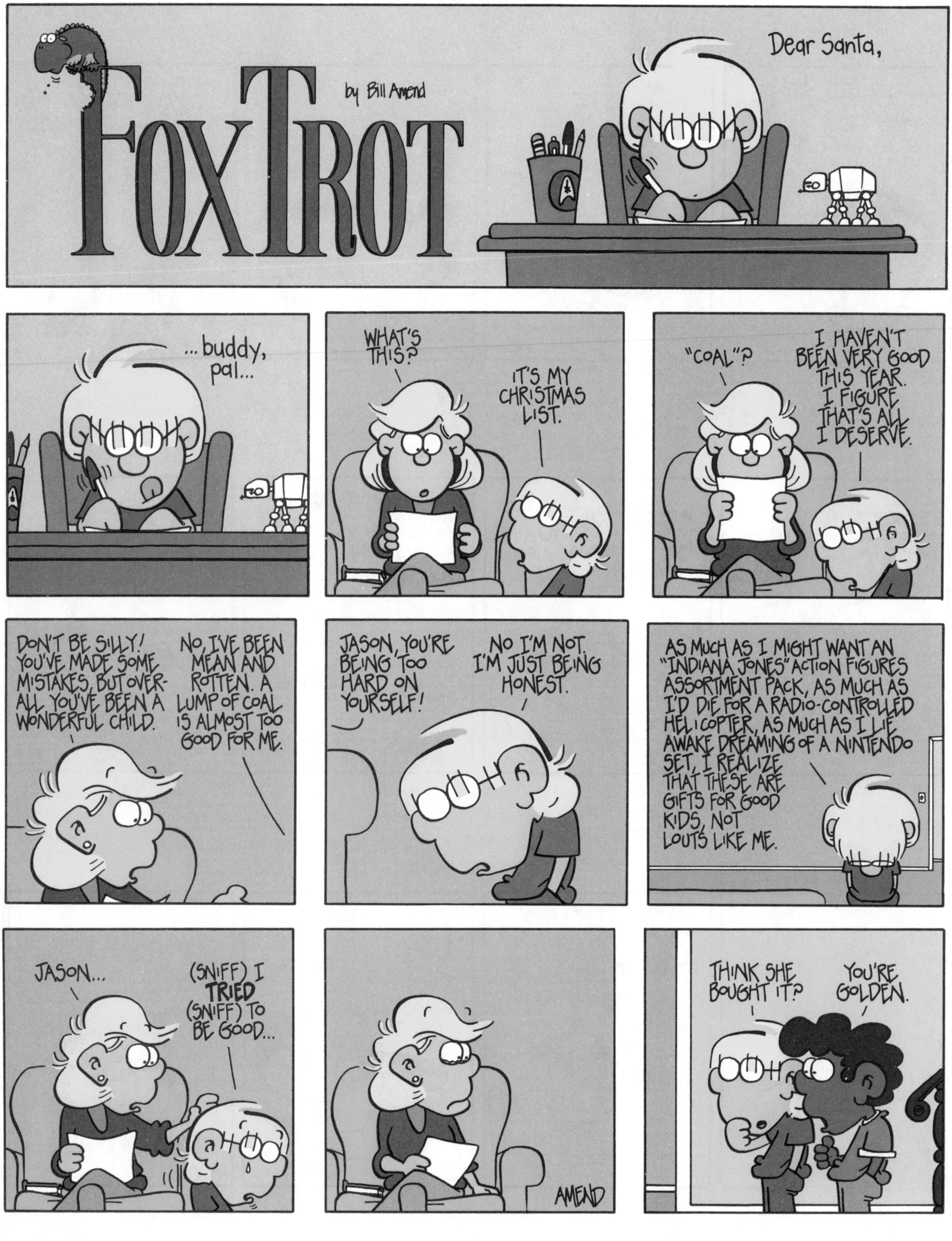
FoxTrot
by Bill Amend
Dear Santa,
...buddy, pal...
WHAT'S THIS?
IT'S MY CHRISTMAS LIST.
"COAL"?
I HAVEN'T BEEN VERY GOOD THIS YEAR. I FIGURE THAT'S ALL I DESERVE.
DON'T BE SILLY! YOU'VE MADE SOME MISTAKES, BUT OVERALL YOU'VE BEEN A WONDERFUL CHILD.
NO, I'VE BEEN MEAN AND ROTTEN. A LUMP OF COAL IS ALMOST TOO GOOD FOR ME.
JASON, YOU'RE BEING TOO HARD ON YOURSELF!
NO I'M NOT. I'M JUST BEING HONEST.
AS MUCH AS I MIGHT WANT AN "INDIANA JONES" ACTION FIGURES ASSORTMENT PACK, AS MUCH AS I'D DIE FOR A RADIO-CONTROLLED HELICOPTER, AS MUCH AS I LIE AWAKE DREAMING OF A NINTENDO SET, I REALIZE THAT THESE ARE GIFTS FOR GOOD KIDS, NOT LOUTS LIKE ME.
JASON...
(SNIFF) I **TRIED** (SNIFF) TO BE GOOD...
AMEND
THINK SHE BOUGHT IT?
YOU'RE GOLDEN.

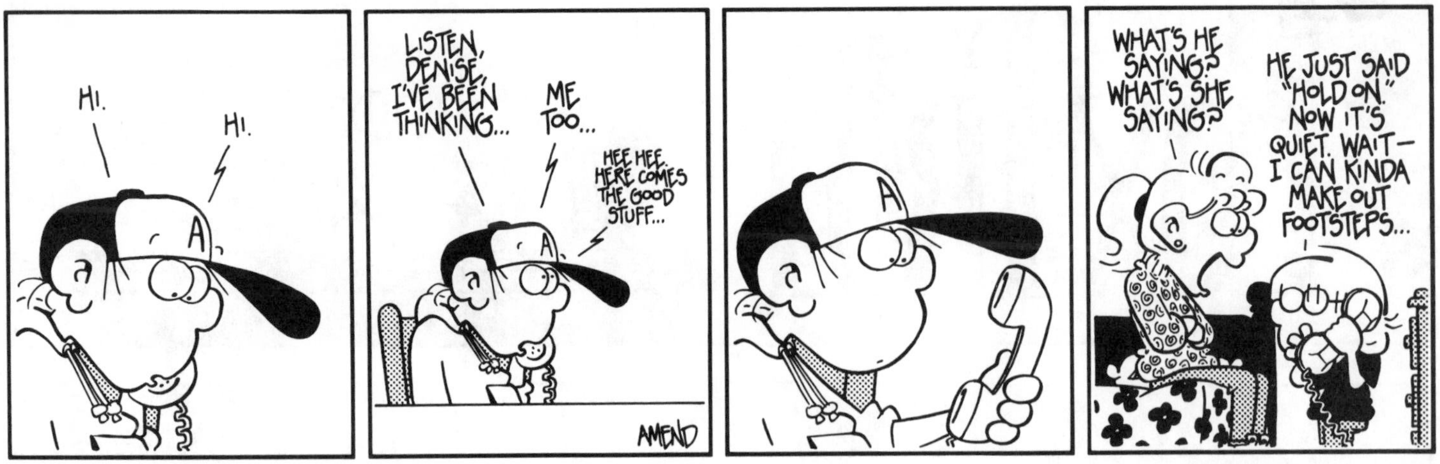
HI.
HI.
LISTEN, DENISE, I'VE BEEN THINKING...
ME TOO...
HEE HEE. HERE COMES THE GOOD STUFF...
AMEND
WHAT'S HE SAYING? WHAT'S SHE SAYING?
HE JUST SAID "HOLD ON." NOW IT'S QUIET. WAIT— I CAN KINDA MAKE OUT FOOTSTEPS...

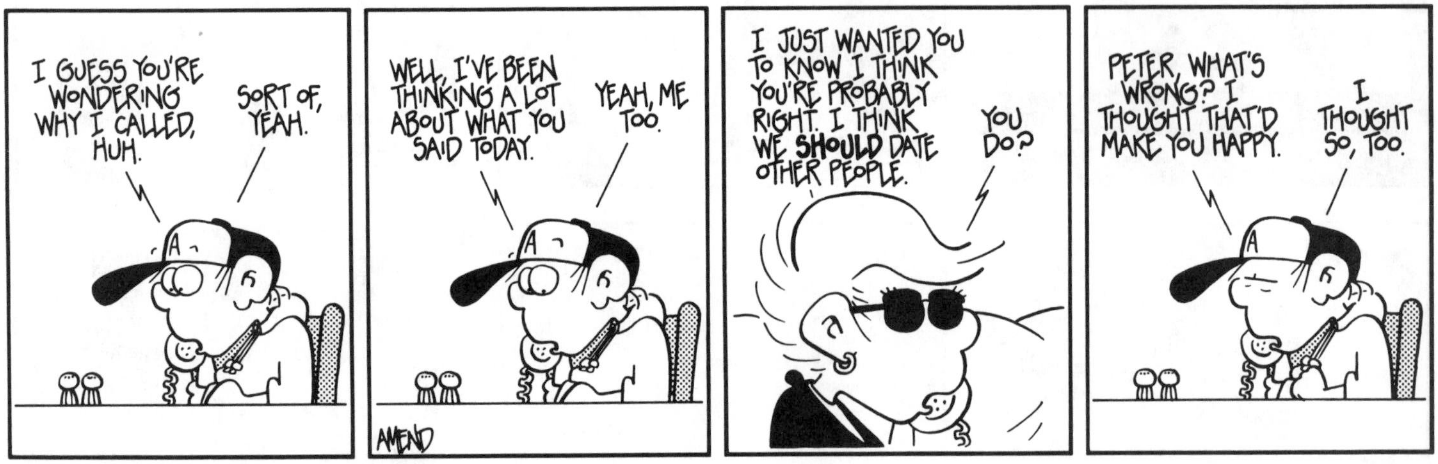
I GUESS YOU'RE WONDERING WHY I CALLED, HUH.
SORT OF, YEAH.
WELL, I'VE BEEN THINKING A LOT ABOUT WHAT YOU SAID TODAY.
YEAH, ME TOO.
AMEND
I JUST WANTED YOU TO KNOW I THINK YOU'RE PROBABLY RIGHT. I THINK WE SHOULD DATE OTHER PEOPLE.
YOU DO?
PETER, WHAT'S WRONG? I THOUGHT THAT'D MAKE YOU HAPPY.
I THOUGHT SO, TOO.

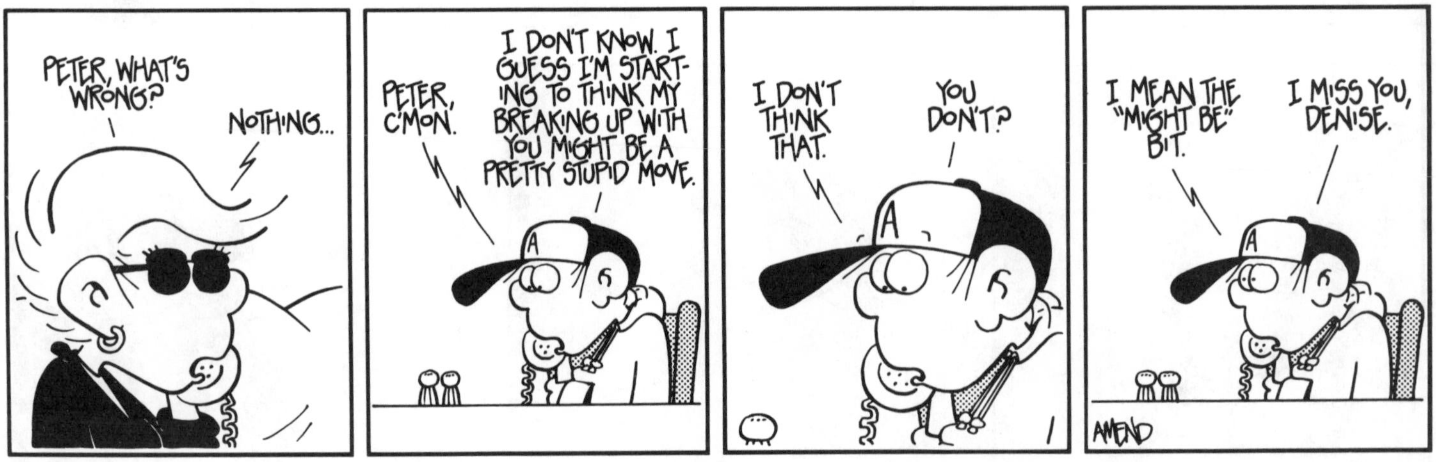
PETER, WHAT'S WRONG?
NOTHING...
PETER, C'MON.
I DON'T KNOW. I GUESS I'M STARTING TO THINK MY BREAKING UP WITH YOU MIGHT BE A PRETTY STUPID MOVE.
I DON'T THINK THAT.
YOU DON'T?
I MEAN THE "MIGHT BE" BIT.
I MISS YOU, DENISE.
AMEND

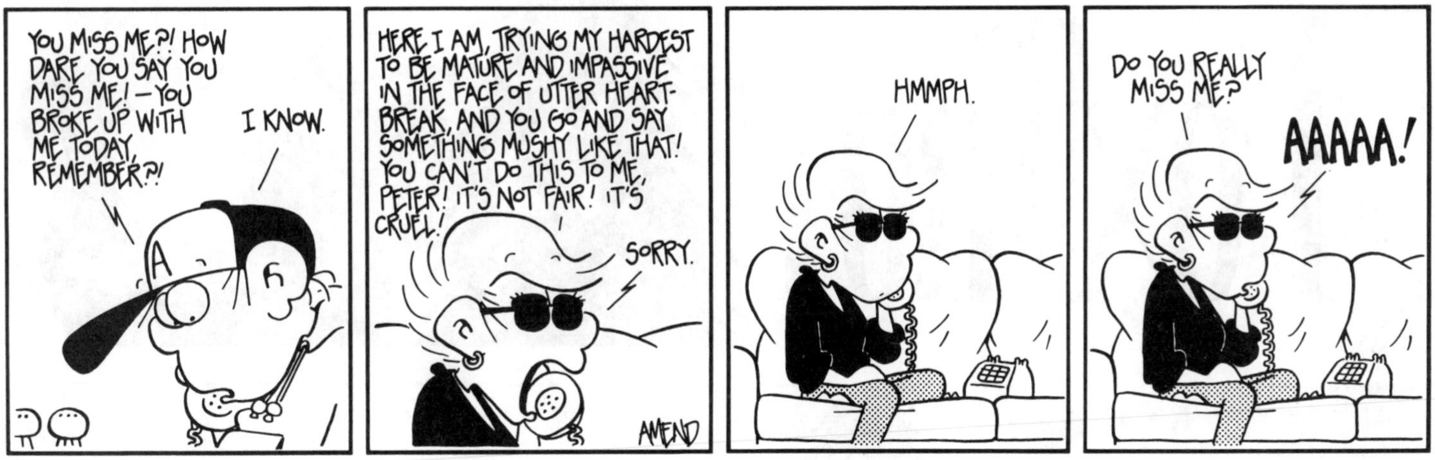
YOU MISS ME?! HOW DARE YOU SAY YOU MISS ME! —YOU BROKE UP WITH ME TODAY, REMEMBER?!
I KNOW.
HERE I AM, TRYING MY HARDEST TO BE MATURE AND IMPASSIVE IN THE FACE OF UTTER HEART-BREAK, AND YOU GO AND SAY SOMETHING MUSHY LIKE THAT! YOU CAN'T DO THIS TO ME, PETER! IT'S NOT FAIR! IT'S CRUEL!
SORRY.
AMEND
HMMPH.
DO YOU REALLY MISS ME?
AAAAA!

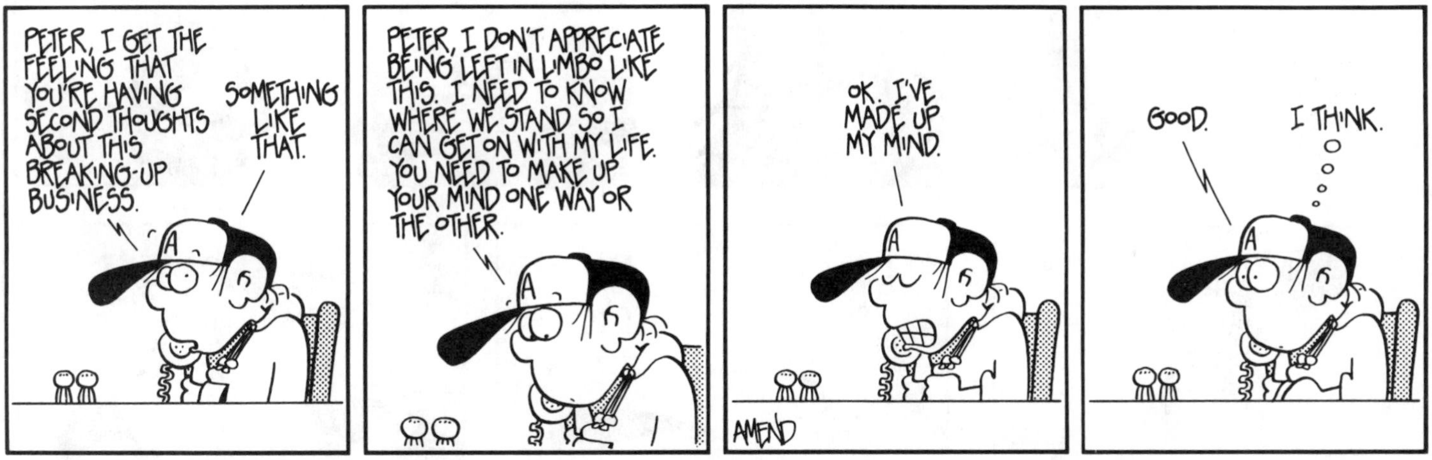
PETER, I GET THE FEELING THAT YOU'RE HAVING SECOND THOUGHTS ABOUT THIS BREAKING-UP BUSINESS.
SOMETHING LIKE THAT.
PETER, I DON'T APPRECIATE BEING LEFT IN LIMBO LIKE THIS. I NEED TO KNOW WHERE WE STAND SO I CAN GET ON WITH MY LIFE. YOU NEED TO MAKE UP YOUR MIND ONE WAY OR THE OTHER.
OK. I'VE MADE UP MY MIND.
AMEND
GOOD.
I THINK.

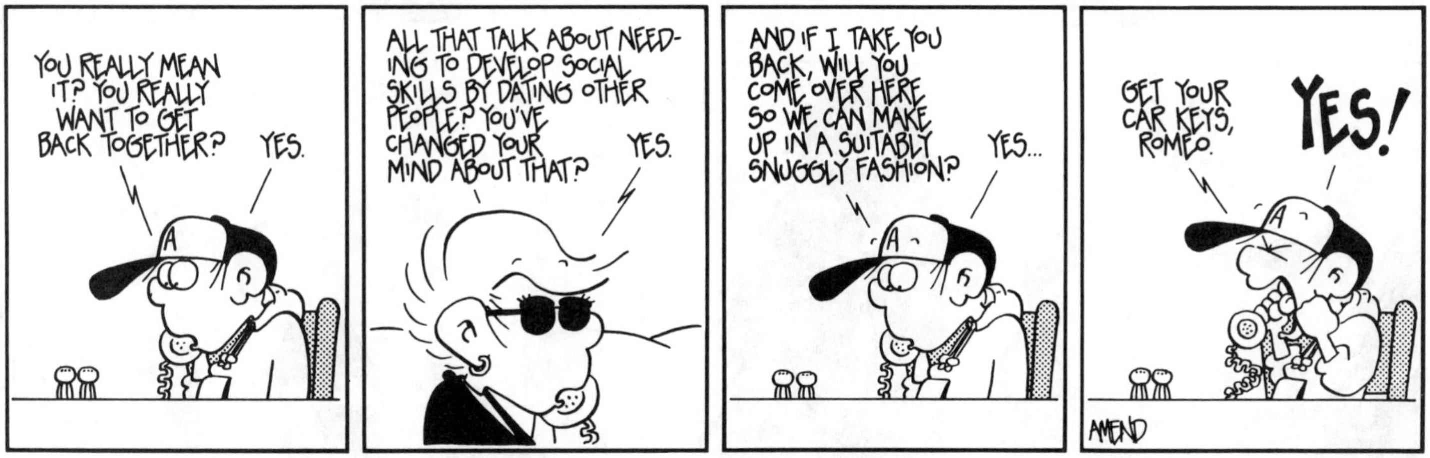
YOU REALLY MEAN IT? YOU REALLY WANT TO GET BACK TOGETHER?
YES.
ALL THAT TALK ABOUT NEED-ING TO DEVELOP SOCIAL SKILLS BY DATING OTHER PEOPLE? YOU'VE CHANGED YOUR MIND ABOUT THAT?
YES.
AND IF I TAKE YOU BACK, WILL YOU COME OVER HERE SO WE CAN MAKE UP IN A SUITABLY SNUGGLY FASHION?
YES...
GET YOUR CAR KEYS, ROMEO.
YES!
AMEND

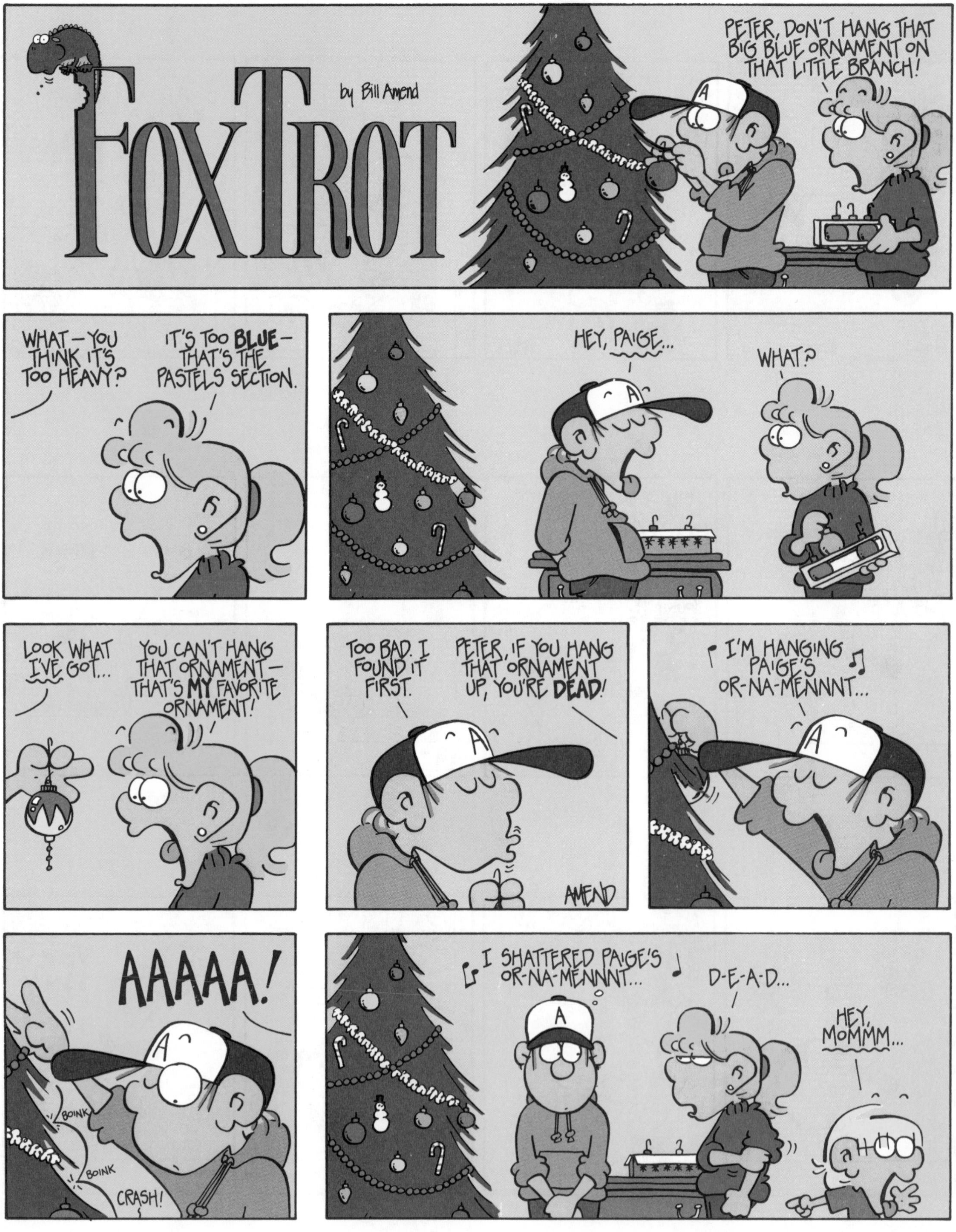
FoxTrot
by Bill Amend
PETER, DON'T HANG THAT BIG BLUE ORNAMENT ON THAT LITTLE BRANCH!
WHAT—YOU THINK IT'S TOO HEAVY?
IT'S TOO **BLUE**—THAT'S THE PASTELS SECTION.
HEY, PAIGE...
WHAT?
LOOK WHAT I'VE GOT...
YOU CAN'T HANG THAT ORNAMENT—THAT'S **MY** FAVORITE ORNAMENT!
TOO BAD. I FOUND IT FIRST.
PETER, IF YOU HANG THAT ORNAMENT UP, YOU'RE **DEAD**!
AMEND
I'M HANGING PAIGE'S OR-NA-MENNNT...
AAAAA!
BOINK
BOINK
CRASH!
I SHATTERED PAIGE'S OR-NA-MENNNT...
D-E-A-D...
HEY, MOMMM...

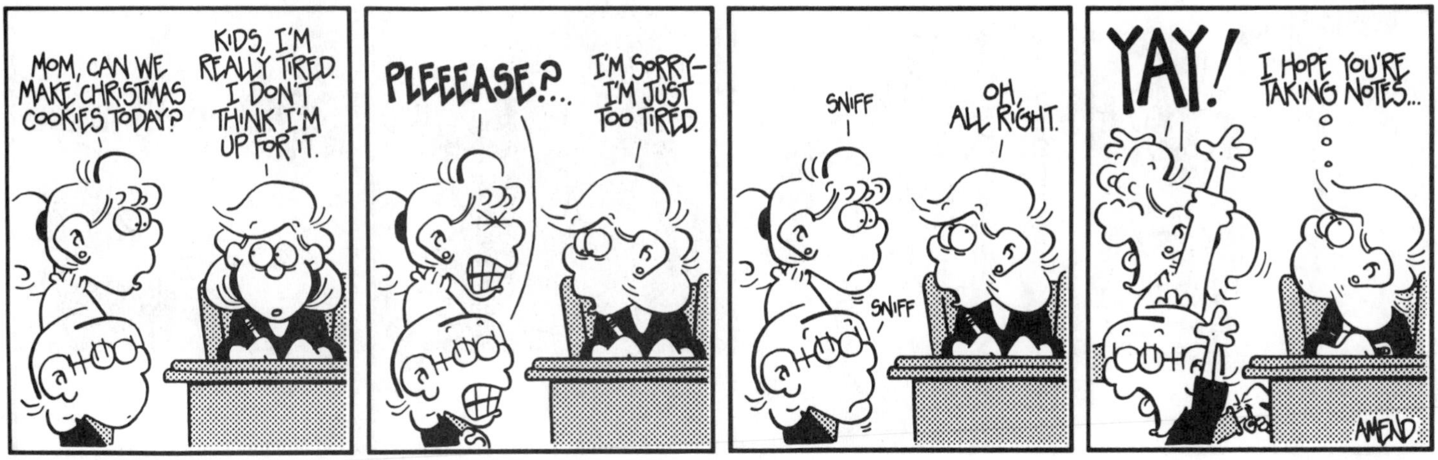
MOM, CAN WE MAKE CHRISTMAS COOKIES TODAY?
KIDS, I'M REALLY TIRED. I DON'T THINK I'M UP FOR IT.
PLEEEASE?...
I'M SORRY— I'M JUST TOO TIRED.
SNIFF
SNIFF
OH, ALL RIGHT.
YAY!
I HOPE YOU'RE TAKING NOTES...
AMEND

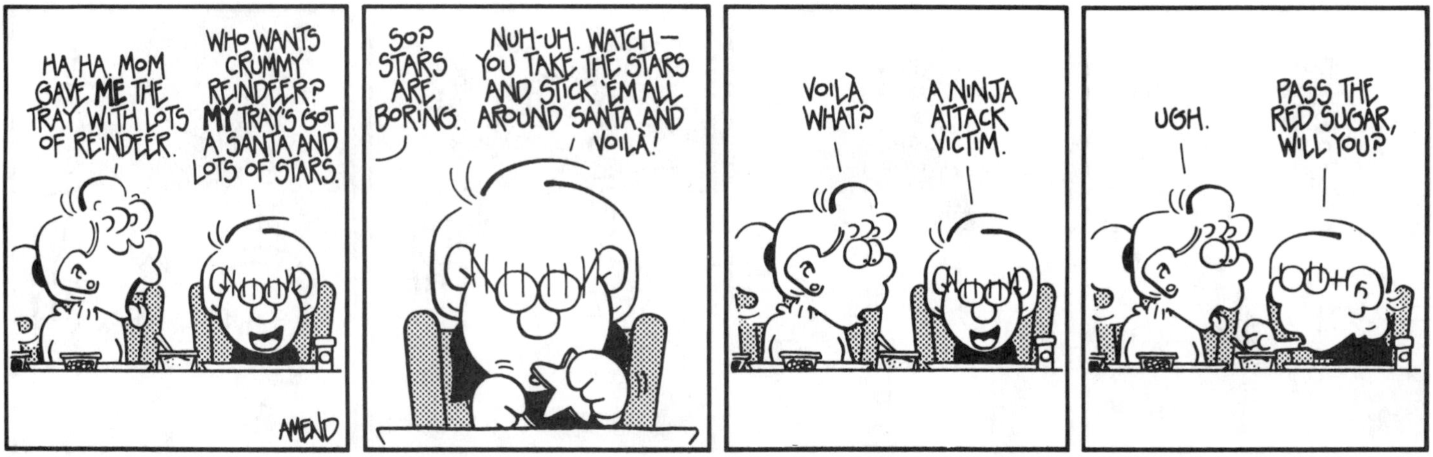
HA HA. MOM GAVE **ME** THE TRAY WITH LOTS OF REINDEER.
WHO WANTS CRUMMY REINDEER? **MY** TRAY'S GOT A SANTA AND LOTS OF STARS.
AMEND
SO? STARS ARE BORING.
NUH-UH. WATCH— YOU TAKE THE STARS AND STICK 'EM ALL AROUND SANTA AND VOILÀ!
VOILÀ WHAT?
A NINJA ATTACK VICTIM.
UGH.
PASS THE RED SUGAR, WILL YOU?

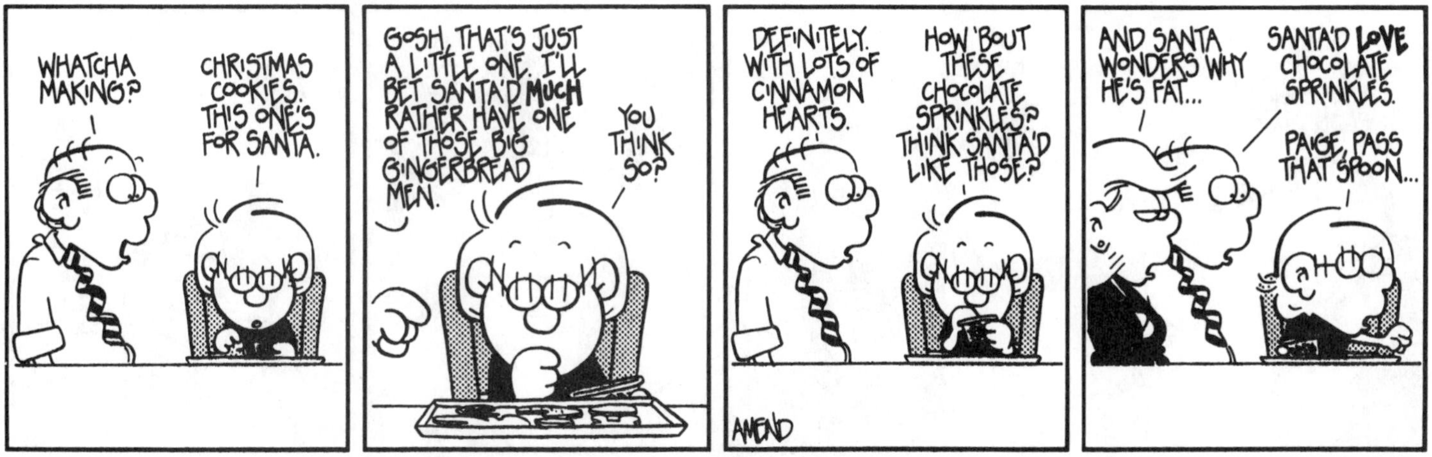
WHATCHA MAKING?
CHRISTMAS COOKIES. THIS ONE'S FOR SANTA.
GOSH, THAT'S JUST A LITTLE ONE. I'LL BET SANTA'D **MUCH** RATHER HAVE ONE OF THOSE BIG GINGERBREAD MEN.
YOU THINK SO?
DEFINITELY. WITH LOTS OF CINNAMON HEARTS.
HOW 'BOUT THESE CHOCOLATE SPRINKLES? THINK SANTA'D LIKE THOSE?
AMEND
AND SANTA WONDERS WHY HE'S FAT...
SANTA'D **LOVE** CHOCOLATE SPRINKLES.
PAIGE, PASS THAT SPOON...

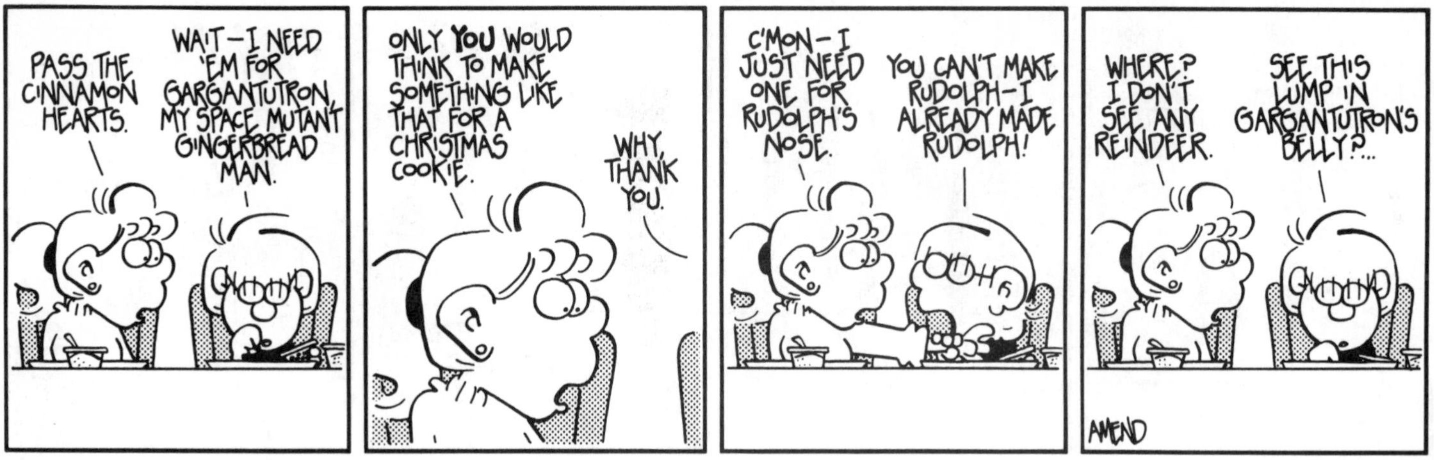
PASS THE CINNAMON HEARTS.
WAIT—I NEED 'EM FOR GARGANTUTRON, MY SPACE MUTANT GINGERBREAD MAN.
ONLY **YOU** WOULD THINK TO MAKE SOMETHING LIKE THAT FOR A CHRISTMAS COOKIE.
WHY, THANK YOU.
C'MON—I JUST NEED ONE FOR RUDOLPH'S NOSE.
YOU CAN'T MAKE RUDOLPH—I ALREADY MADE RUDOLPH!
WHERE? I DON'T SEE ANY REINDEER.
SEE THIS LUMP IN GARGANTUTRON'S BELLY?...
AMEND

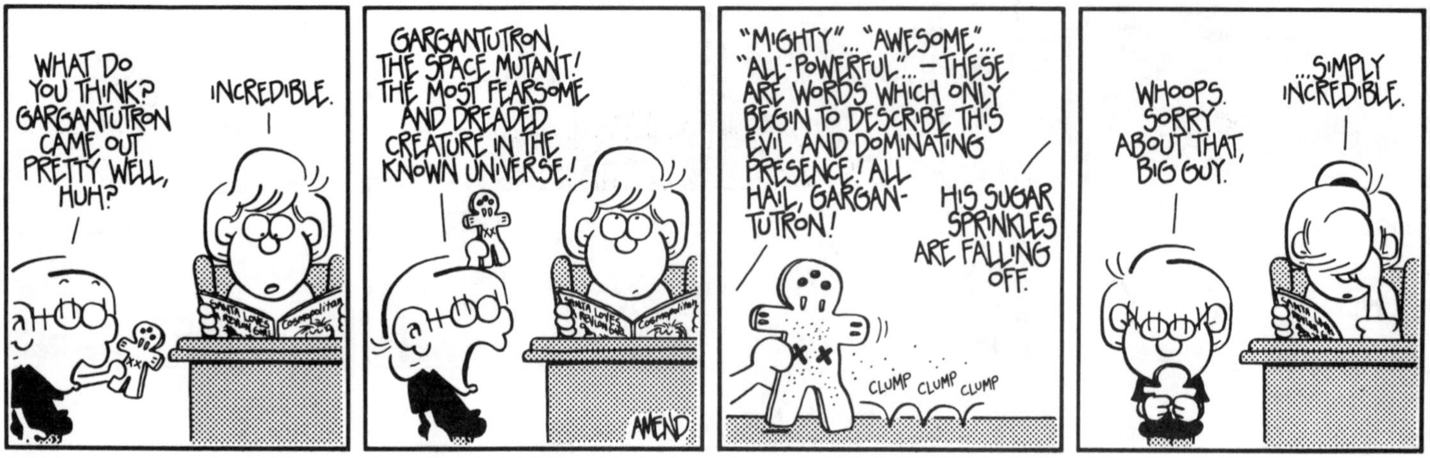
WHAT DO YOU THINK? GARGANTUTRON CAME OUT PRETTY WELL, HUH?
INCREDIBLE.
GARGANTUTRON, THE SPACE MUTANT! THE MOST FEARSOME AND DREADED CREATURE IN THE KNOWN UNIVERSE!
AMEND
"MIGHTY"... "AWESOME"... "ALL-POWERFUL"...—THESE ARE WORDS WHICH ONLY BEGIN TO DESCRIBE THIS EVIL AND DOMINATING PRESENCE! ALL HAIL, GARGANTUTRON!
HIS SUGAR SPRINKLES ARE FALLING OFF.
CLUMP CLUMP CLUMP
WHOOPS. SORRY ABOUT THAT, BIG GUY.
...SIMPLY INCREDIBLE.

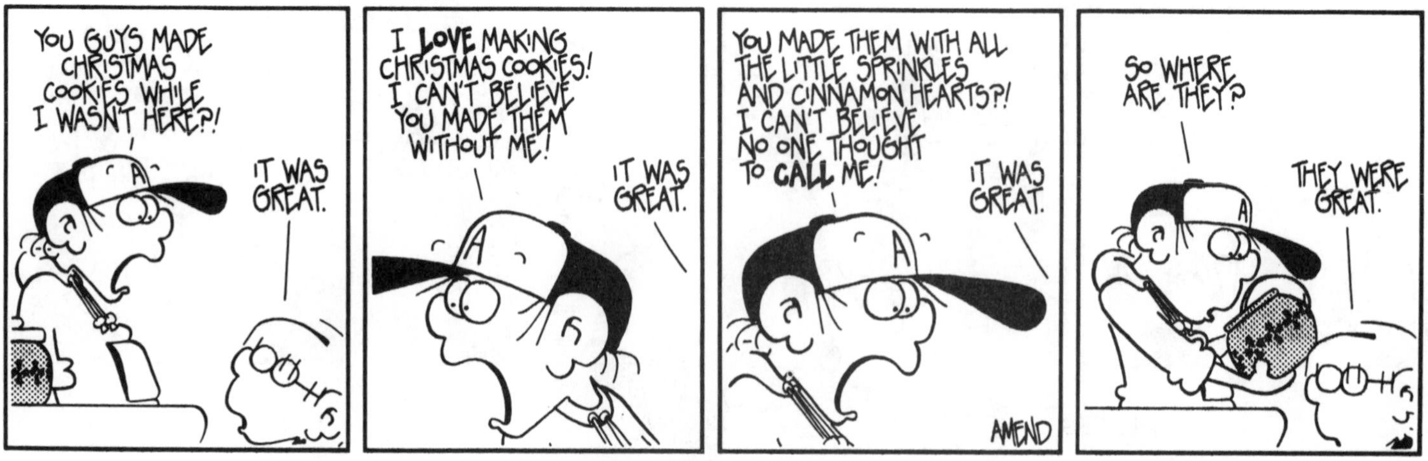
YOU GUYS MADE CHRISTMAS COOKIES WHILE I WASN'T HERE?!
IT WAS GREAT.
I **LOVE** MAKING CHRISTMAS COOKIES! I CAN'T BELIEVE YOU MADE THEM WITHOUT ME!
IT WAS GREAT.
YOU MADE THEM WITH ALL THE LITTLE SPRINKLES AND CINNAMON HEARTS?! I CAN'T BELIEVE NO ONE THOUGHT TO **CALL** ME!
IT WAS GREAT.
AMEND
SO WHERE ARE THEY?
THEY WERE GREAT.

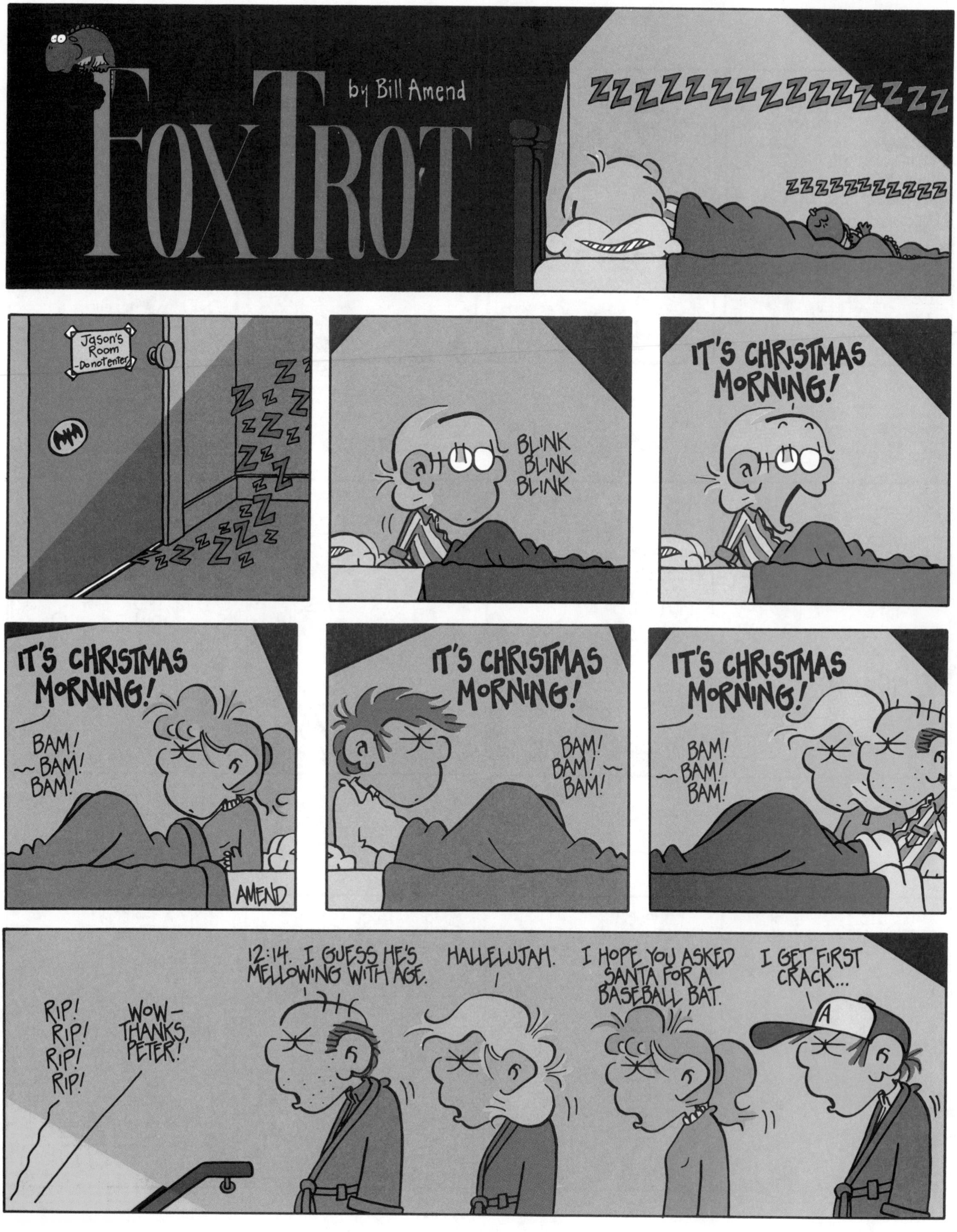
FoxTrot
by Bill Amend
ZZZZZZZZZZZZZZZZ
ZZZZZZZZZZZ
Jason's Room -Do not enter
BLINK BLINK BLINK
IT'S CHRISTMAS MORNING!
IT'S CHRISTMAS MORNING!
BAM! BAM! BAM!
AMEND
IT'S CHRISTMAS MORNING!
BAM! BAM! BAM!
IT'S CHRISTMAS MORNING!
BAM! BAM! BAM!
RIP! RIP! RIP! RIP!
WOW— THANKS, PETER!
12:14. I GUESS HE'S MELLOWING WITH AGE.
HALLELUJAH.
I HOPE YOU ASKED SANTA FOR A BASEBALL BAT.
I GET FIRST CRACK...

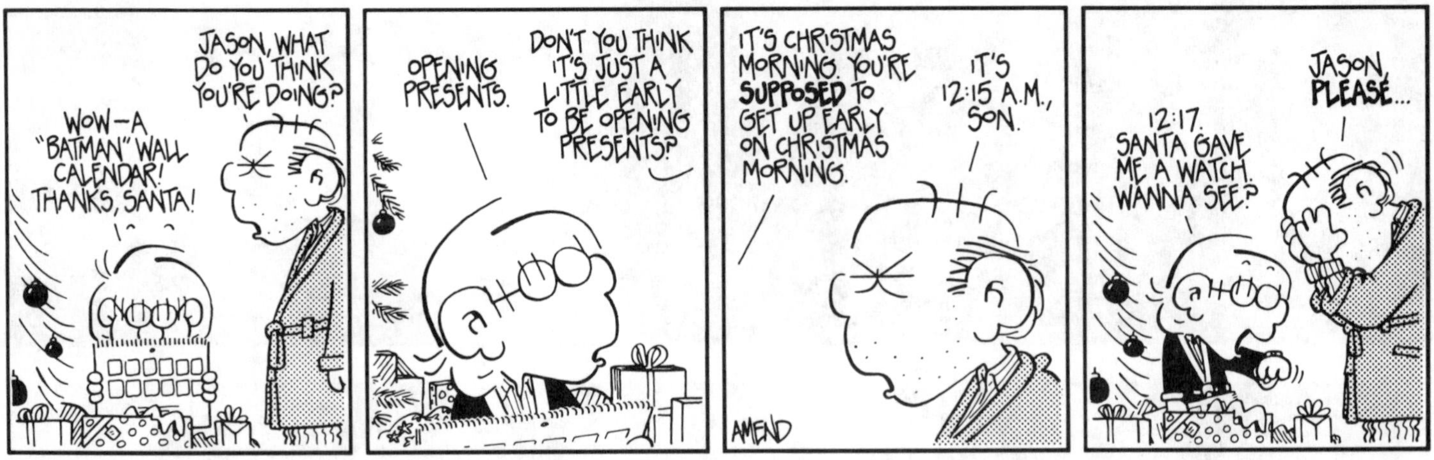
JASON, WHAT DO YOU THINK YOU'RE DOING?
WOW—A "BATMAN" WALL CALENDAR! THANKS, SANTA!
OPENING PRESENTS.
DON'T YOU THINK IT'S JUST A LITTLE EARLY TO BE OPENING PRESENTS?
IT'S CHRISTMAS MORNING. YOU'RE **SUPPOSED** TO GET UP EARLY ON CHRISTMAS MORNING.
IT'S 12:15 A.M., SON.
AMEND
12:17. SANTA GAVE ME A WATCH. WANNA SEE?
JASON, **PLEASE**...

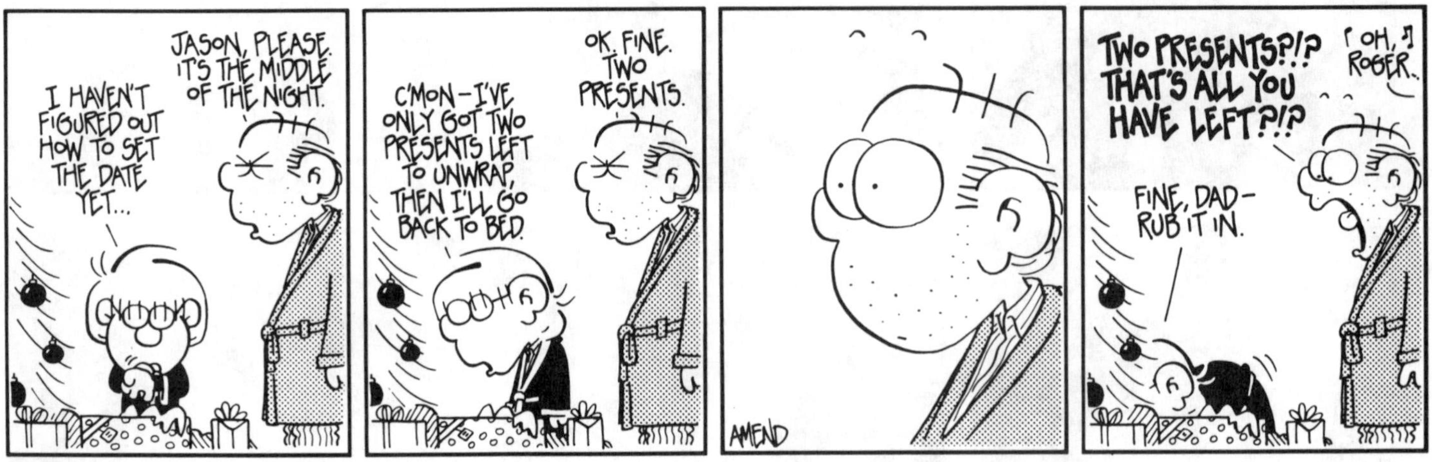
JASON, PLEASE. IT'S THE MIDDLE OF THE NIGHT.
I HAVEN'T FIGURED OUT HOW TO SET THE DATE YET...
C'MON—I'VE ONLY GOT TWO PRESENTS LEFT TO UNWRAP, THEN I'LL GO BACK TO BED.
OK, FINE. TWO PRESENTS.
AMEND
TWO PRESENTS?!? THAT'S ALL YOU HAVE LEFT?!?
OH, ROGER...
FINE, DAD—RUB IT IN.

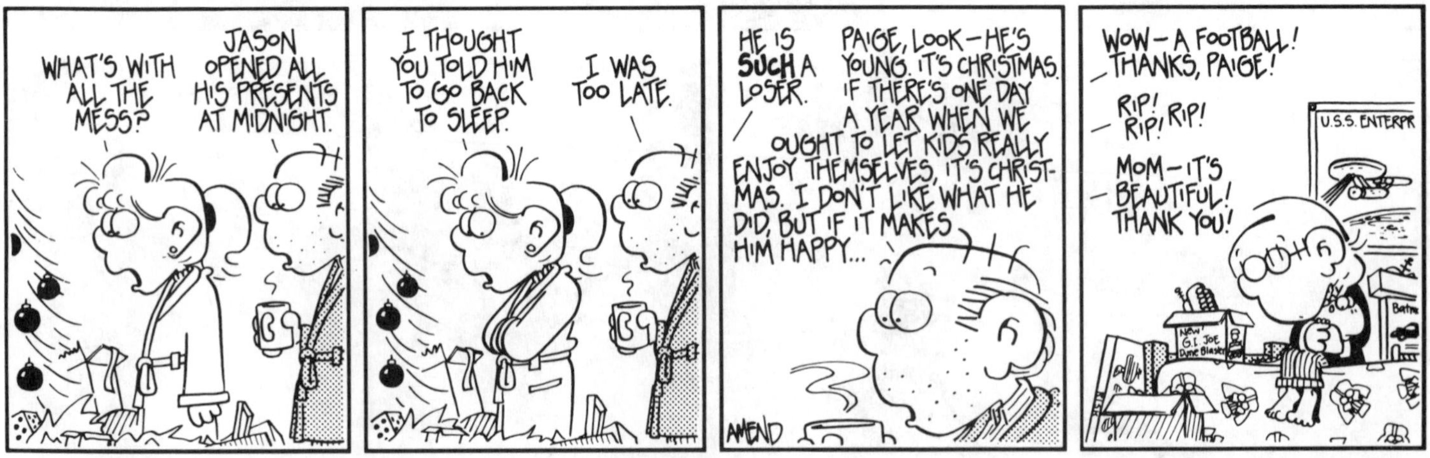
WHAT'S WITH ALL THE MESS?
JASON OPENED ALL HIS PRESENTS AT MIDNIGHT.
I THOUGHT YOU TOLD HIM TO GO BACK TO SLEEP.
I WAS TOO LATE.
HE IS **SUCH** A LOSER.
PAIGE, LOOK—HE'S YOUNG. IT'S CHRISTMAS. IF THERE'S ONE DAY A YEAR WHEN WE OUGHT TO LET KIDS REALLY ENJOY THEMSELVES, IT'S CHRISTMAS. I DON'T LIKE WHAT HE DID, BUT IF IT MAKES HIM HAPPY...
AMEND
WOW—A FOOTBALL! THANKS, PAIGE!
RIP! RIP! RIP!
MOM—IT'S BEAUTIFUL! THANK YOU!
U.S.S. ENTERPR

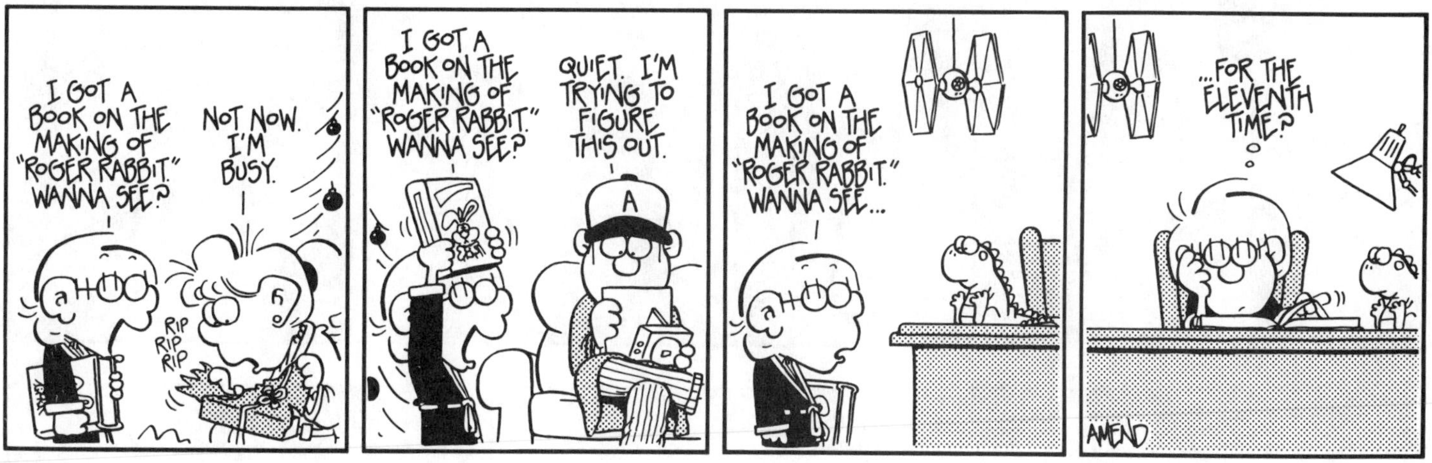
I GOT A BOOK ON THE MAKING OF "ROGER RABBIT." WANNA SEE?
NOT NOW. I'M BUSY.
RIP RIP RIP
I GOT A BOOK ON THE MAKING OF "ROGER RABBIT." WANNA SEE?
QUIET. I'M TRYING TO FIGURE THIS OUT.
I GOT A BOOK ON THE MAKING OF "ROGER RABBIT." WANNA SEE...
...FOR THE ELEVENTH TIME?
AMEND

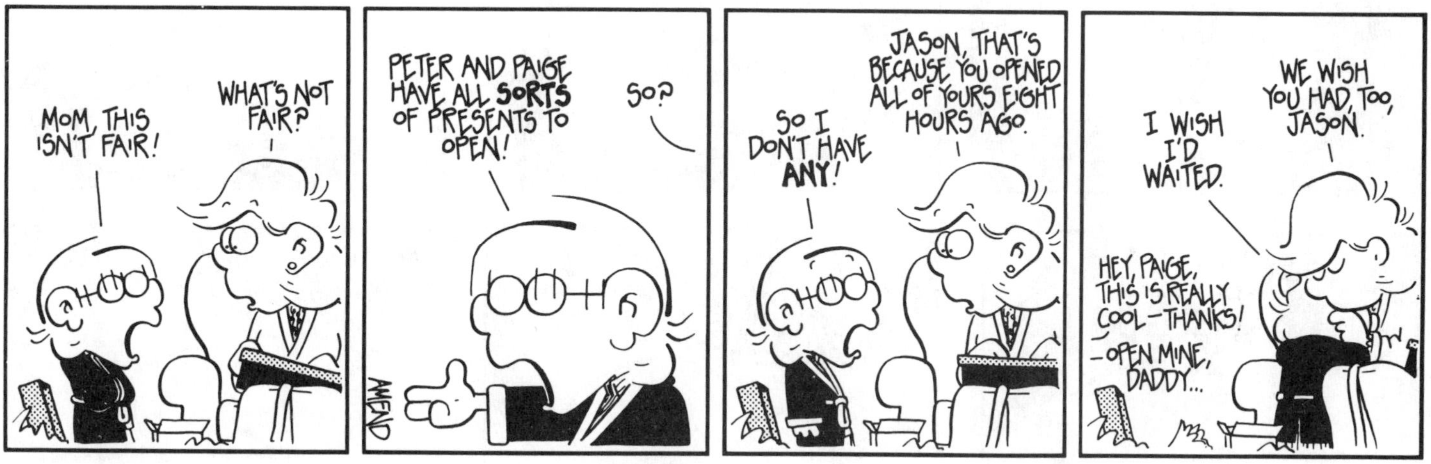
MOM, THIS ISN'T FAIR!
WHAT'S NOT FAIR?
PETER AND PAIGE HAVE ALL SORTS OF PRESENTS TO OPEN!
SO?
AMEND
SO I DON'T HAVE ANY!
JASON, THAT'S BECAUSE YOU OPENED ALL OF YOURS EIGHT HOURS AGO.
I WISH I'D WAITED.
WE WISH YOU HAD, TOO, JASON.
HEY, PAIGE, THIS IS REALLY COOL—THANKS!
—OPEN MINE, DADDY...

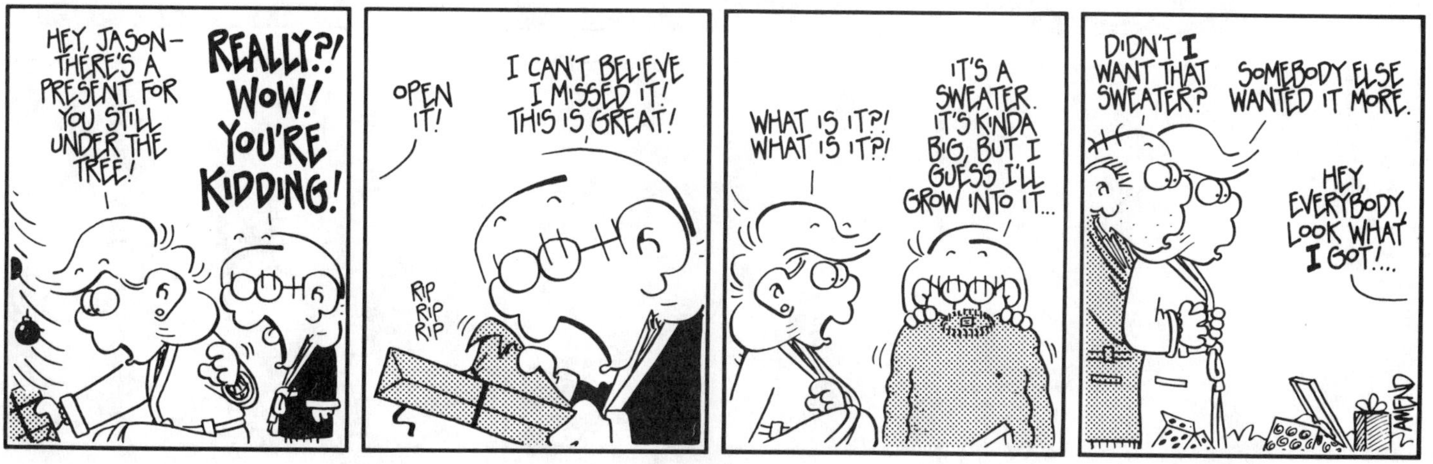
HEY, JASON—THERE'S A PRESENT FOR YOU STILL UNDER THE TREE!
REALLY?! WOW! YOU'RE KIDDING!
OPEN IT!
I CAN'T BELIEVE I MISSED IT! THIS IS GREAT!
RIP RIP RIP
WHAT IS IT?! WHAT IS IT?!
IT'S A SWEATER. IT'S KINDA BIG, BUT I GUESS I'LL GROW INTO IT...
DIDN'T I WANT THAT SWEATER?
SOMEBODY ELSE WANTED IT MORE.
HEY, EVERYBODY, LOOK WHAT I GOT!...
AMEND

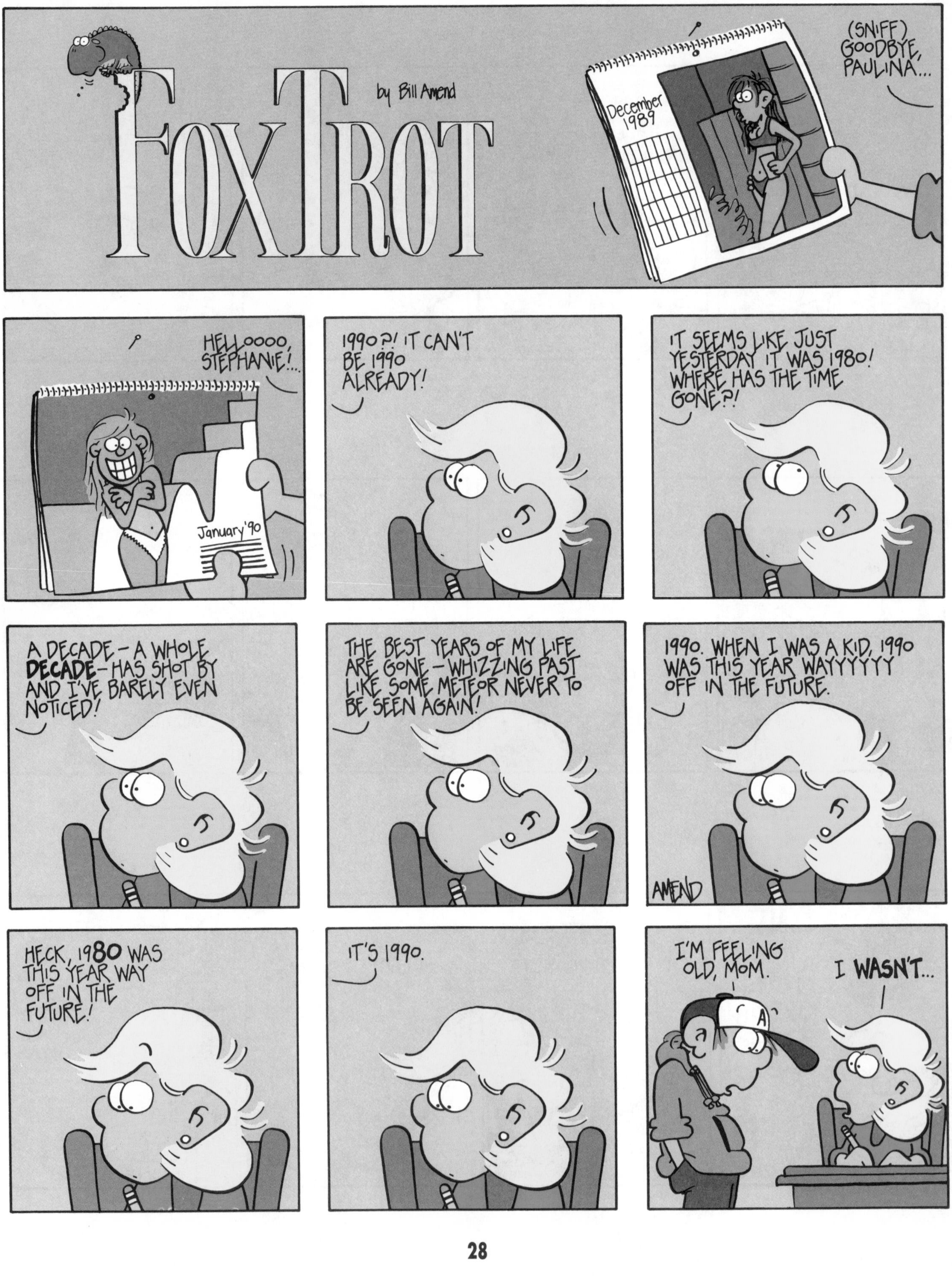
FoxTrot
by Bill Amend
December 1989
(SNIFF) GOODBYE, PAULINA...
HELLOOOO, STEPHANIE!...
January '90
1990?! IT CAN'T BE 1990 ALREADY!
IT SEEMS LIKE JUST YESTERDAY IT WAS 1980! WHERE HAS THE TIME GONE?!
A DECADE—A WHOLE DECADE—HAS SHOT BY AND I'VE BARELY EVEN NOTICED!
THE BEST YEARS OF MY LIFE ARE GONE—WHIZZING PAST LIKE SOME METEOR NEVER TO BE SEEN AGAIN!
1990. WHEN I WAS A KID, 1990 WAS THIS YEAR WAYYYYYY OFF IN THE FUTURE.
AMEND
HECK, 1980 WAS THIS YEAR WAY OFF IN THE FUTURE!
IT'S 1990.
I'M FEELING OLD, MOM.
I WASN'T...

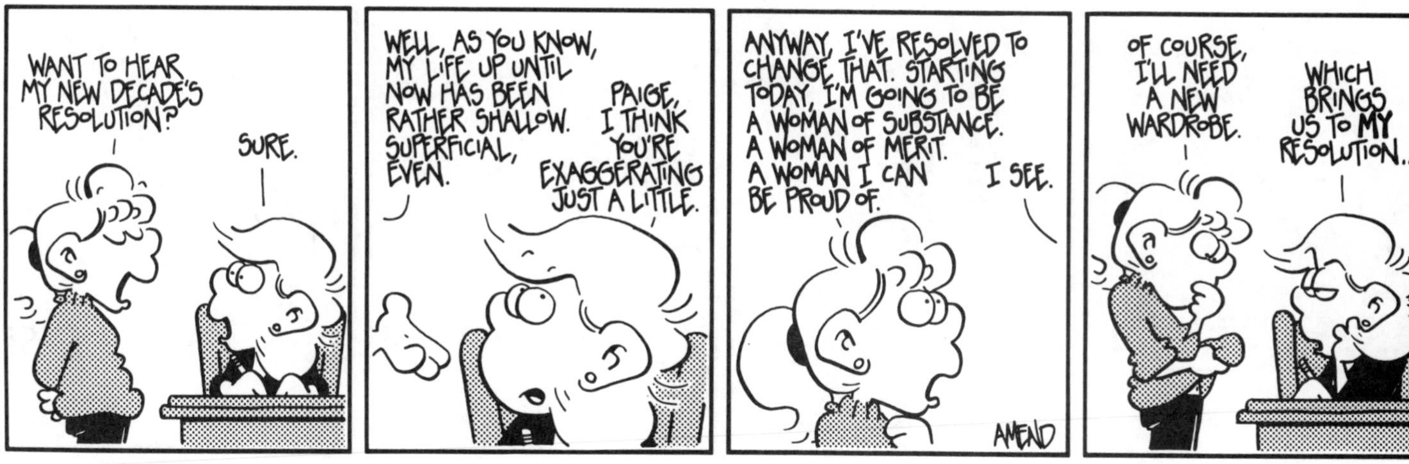
WANT TO HEAR MY NEW DECADE'S RESOLUTION?
SURE.
WELL, AS YOU KNOW, MY LIFE UP UNTIL NOW HAS BEEN RATHER SHALLOW. SUPERFICIAL, EVEN.
PAIGE, I THINK YOU'RE EXAGGERATING JUST A LITTLE.
ANYWAY, I'VE RESOLVED TO CHANGE THAT. STARTING TODAY, I'M GOING TO BE A WOMAN OF SUBSTANCE. A WOMAN OF MERIT. A WOMAN I CAN BE PROUD OF.
I SEE.
AMEND
OF COURSE, I'LL NEED A NEW WARDROBE.
WHICH BRINGS US TO MY RESOLUTION...

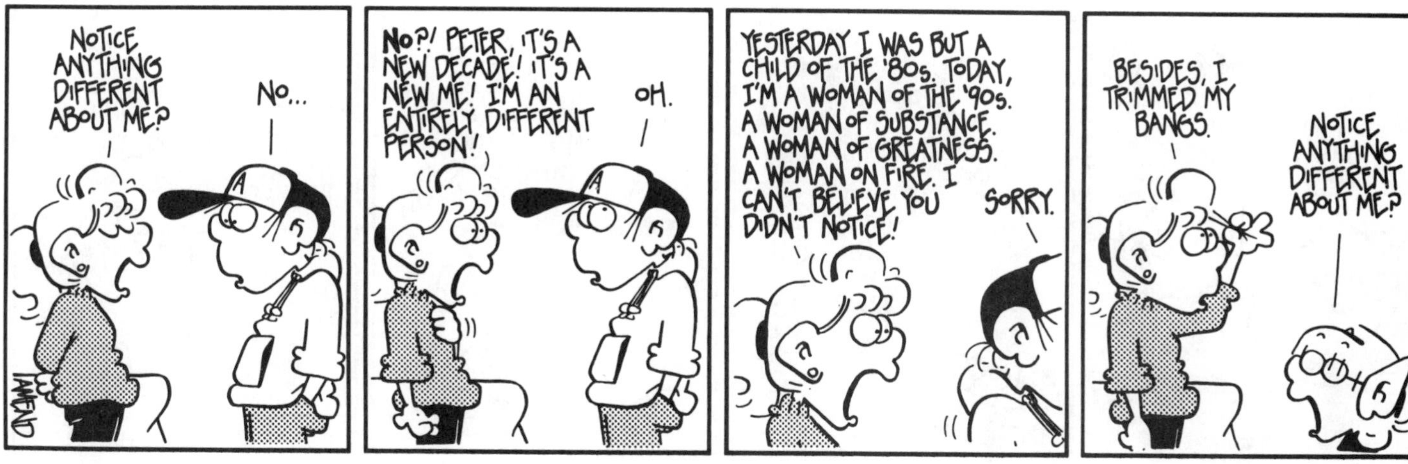
NOTICE ANYTHING DIFFERENT ABOUT ME?
NO...
AMEND
NO?! PETER, IT'S A NEW DECADE! IT'S A NEW ME! I'M AN ENTIRELY DIFFERENT PERSON!
OH.
YESTERDAY I WAS BUT A CHILD OF THE '80s. TODAY, I'M A WOMAN OF THE '90s. A WOMAN OF SUBSTANCE. A WOMAN OF GREATNESS. A WOMAN ON FIRE. I CAN'T BELIEVE YOU DIDN'T NOTICE!
SORRY.
BESIDES, I TRIMMED MY BANGS.
NOTICE ANYTHING DIFFERENT ABOUT ME?

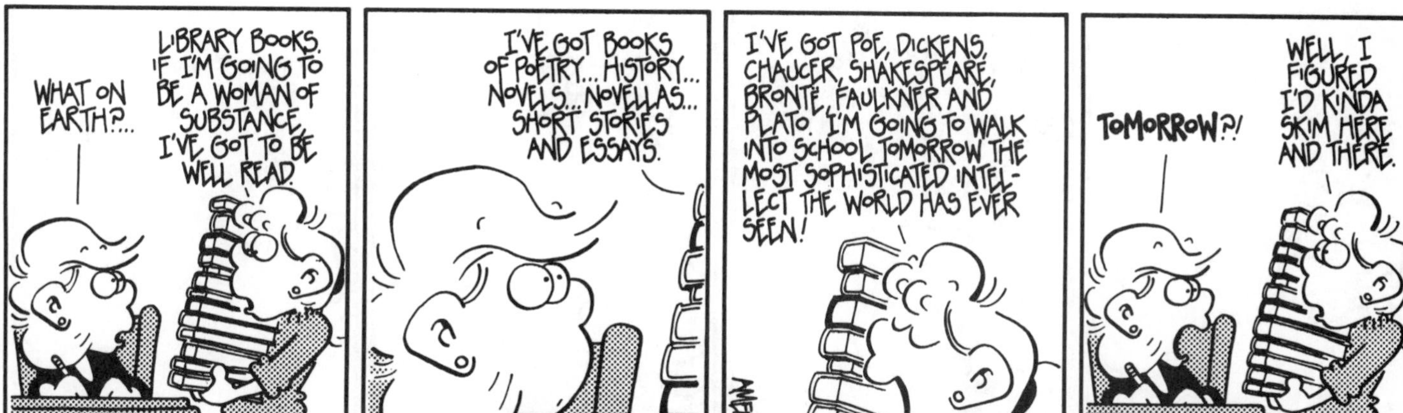
WHAT ON EARTH?...
LIBRARY BOOKS. IF I'M GOING TO BE A WOMAN OF SUBSTANCE, I'VE GOT TO BE WELL READ.
I'VE GOT BOOKS OF POETRY... HISTORY... NOVELS... NOVELLAS... SHORT STORIES AND ESSAYS.
I'VE GOT POE, DICKENS, CHAUCER, SHAKESPEARE, BRONTË, FAULKNER AND PLATO. I'M GOING TO WALK INTO SCHOOL TOMORROW THE MOST SOPHISTICATED INTELLECT THE WORLD HAS EVER SEEN!
AMEND
TOMORROW?!
WELL, I FIGURED I'D KINDA SKIM HERE AND THERE.

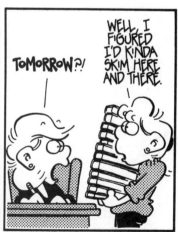

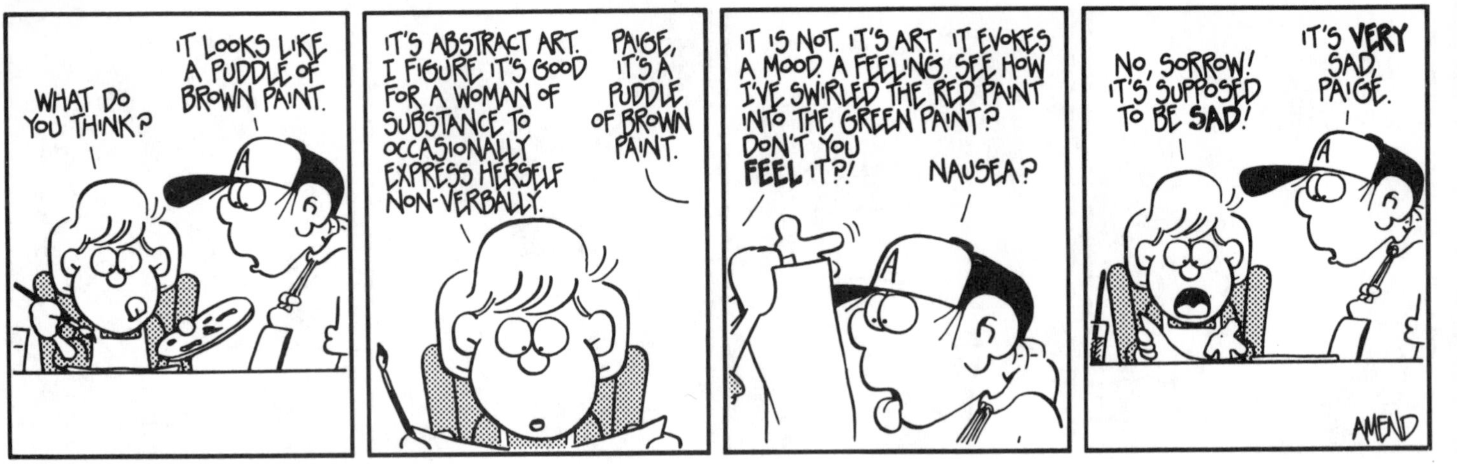
WHAT DO YOU THINK?
IT LOOKS LIKE A PUDDLE OF BROWN PAINT.
IT'S ABSTRACT ART. I FIGURE IT'S GOOD FOR A WOMAN OF SUBSTANCE TO OCCASIONALLY EXPRESS HERSELF NON-VERBALLY.
PAIGE, IT'S A PUDDLE OF BROWN PAINT.
IT IS NOT. IT'S ART. IT EVOKES A MOOD. A FEELING. SEE HOW I'VE SWIRLED THE RED PAINT INTO THE GREEN PAINT? DON'T YOU FEEL IT?!
NAUSEA?
NO, SORROW! IT'S SUPPOSED TO BE SAD!
IT'S VERY SAD, PAIGE.
AMEND

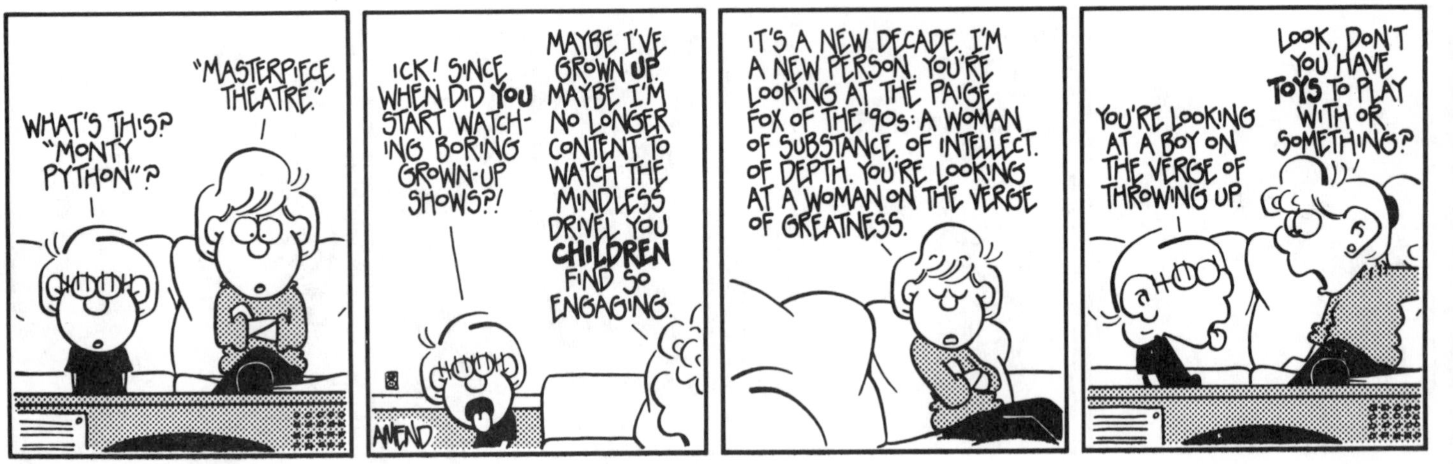
WHAT'S THIS? "MONTY PYTHON"?
"MASTERPIECE THEATRE."
ICK! SINCE WHEN DID YOU START WATCHING BORING GROWN-UP SHOWS?!
MAYBE I'VE GROWN UP. MAYBE I'M NO LONGER CONTENT TO WATCH THE MINDLESS DRIVEL YOU CHILDREN FIND SO ENGAGING.
AMEND
IT'S A NEW DECADE. I'M A NEW PERSON. YOU'RE LOOKING AT THE PAIGE FOX OF THE '90s: A WOMAN OF SUBSTANCE, OF INTELLECT, OF DEPTH. YOU'RE LOOKING AT A WOMAN ON THE VERGE OF GREATNESS.
YOU'RE LOOKING AT A BOY ON THE VERGE OF THROWING UP.
LOOK, DON'T YOU HAVE TOYS TO PLAY WITH OR SOMETHING?

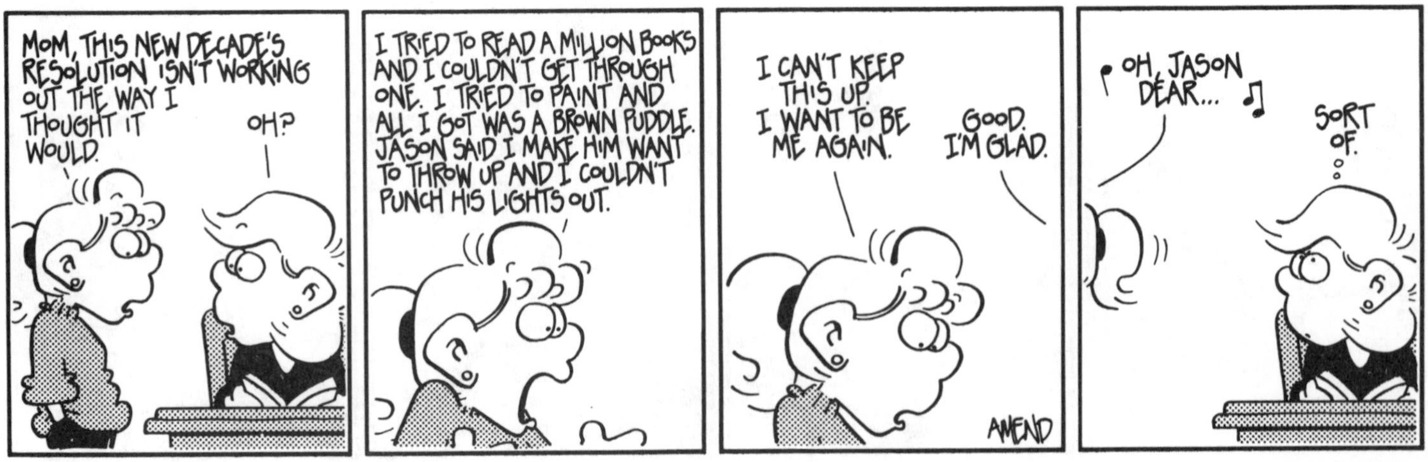
MOM, THIS NEW DECADE'S RESOLUTION ISN'T WORKING OUT THE WAY I THOUGHT IT WOULD.
OH?
I TRIED TO READ A MILLION BOOKS AND I COULDN'T GET THROUGH ONE. I TRIED TO PAINT AND ALL I GOT WAS A BROWN PUDDLE. JASON SAID I MAKE HIM WANT TO THROW UP AND I COULDN'T PUNCH HIS LIGHTS OUT.
I CAN'T KEEP THIS UP. I WANT TO BE ME AGAIN.
GOOD. I'M GLAD.
AMEND
OH, JASON DEAR...
SORT OF.

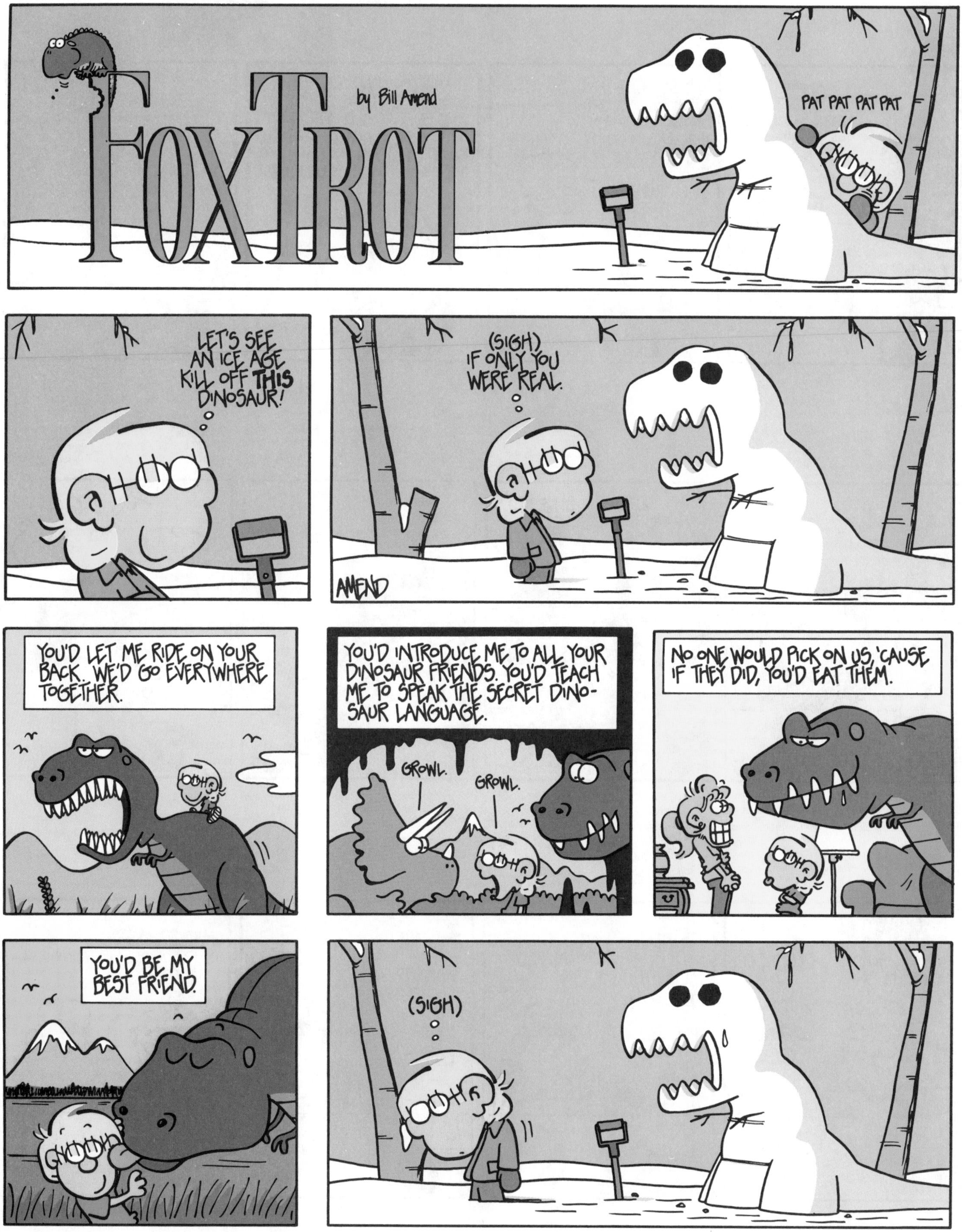
FOXTROT
by Bill Amend
PAT PAT PAT PAT
LET'S SEE AN ICE AGE KILL OFF THIS DINOSAUR!
(SIGH) IF ONLY YOU WERE REAL.
AMEND
YOU'D LET ME RIDE ON YOUR BACK. WE'D GO EVERYWHERE TOGETHER.
YOU'D INTRODUCE ME TO ALL YOUR DINOSAUR FRIENDS. YOU'D TEACH ME TO SPEAK THE SECRET DINOSAUR LANGUAGE.
GROWL.
GROWL.
NO ONE WOULD PICK ON US, 'CAUSE IF THEY DID, YOU'D EAT THEM.
YOU'D BE MY BEST FRIEND.
(SIGH)

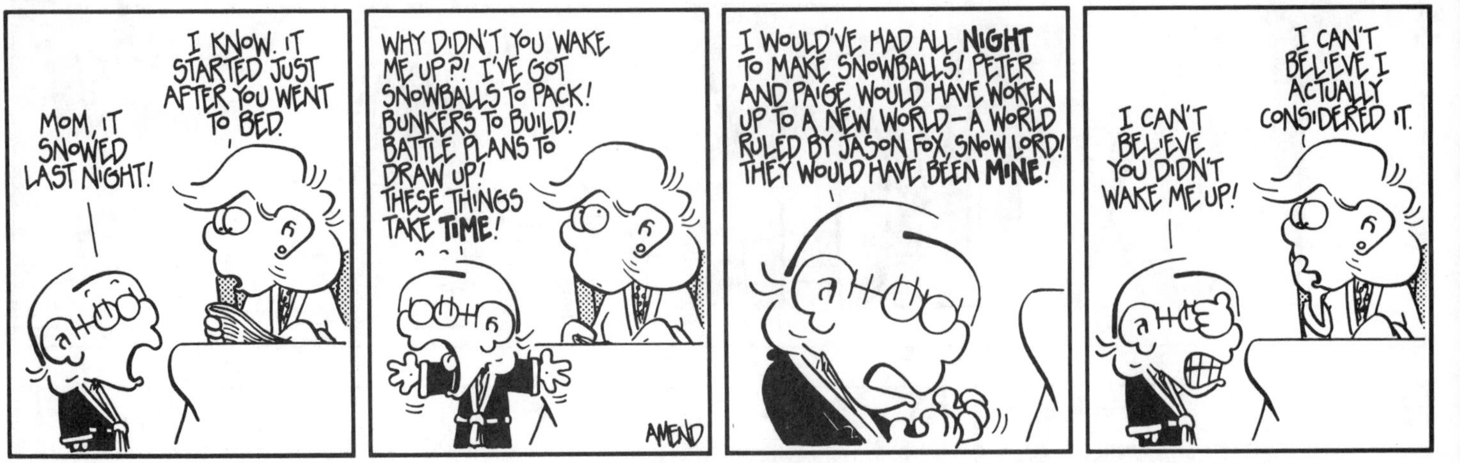
MOM, IT SNOWED LAST NIGHT!
I KNOW. IT STARTED JUST AFTER YOU WENT TO BED.
WHY DIDN'T YOU WAKE ME UP?! I'VE GOT SNOWBALLS TO PACK! BUNKERS TO BUILD! BATTLE PLANS TO DRAW UP! THESE THINGS TAKE TIME!
AMEND
I WOULD'VE HAD ALL NIGHT TO MAKE SNOWBALLS! PETER AND PAIGE WOULD HAVE WOKEN UP TO A NEW WORLD—A WORLD RULED BY JASON FOX, SNOW LORD! THEY WOULD HAVE BEEN MINE!
I CAN'T BELIEVE YOU DIDN'T WAKE ME UP!
I CAN'T BELIEVE I ACTUALLY CONSIDERED IT.

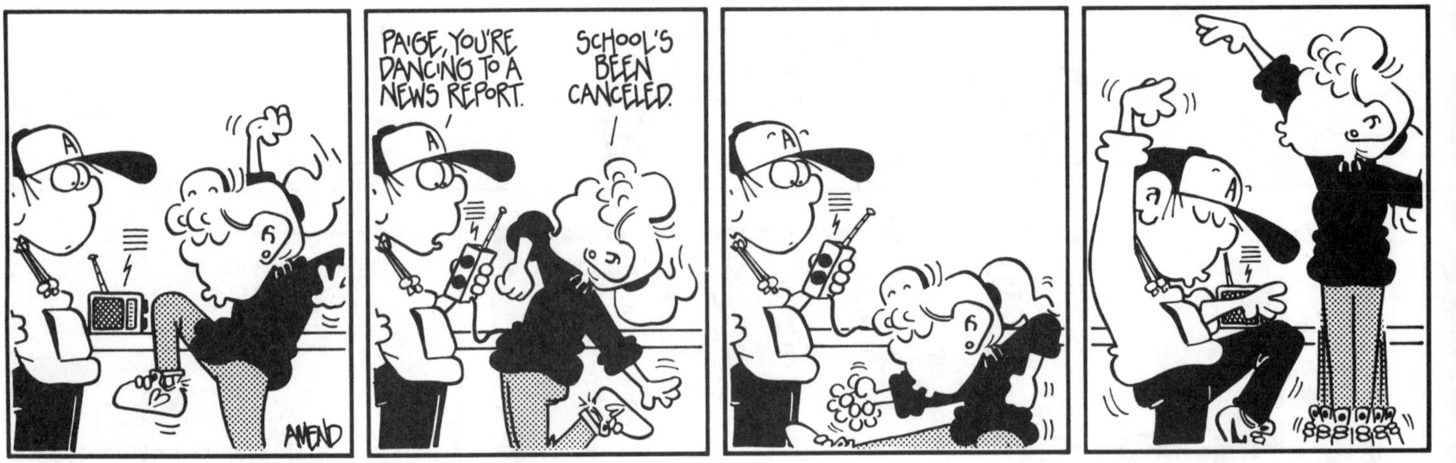
AMEND
PAIGE, YOU'RE DANCING TO A NEWS REPORT.
SCHOOL'S BEEN CANCELED.

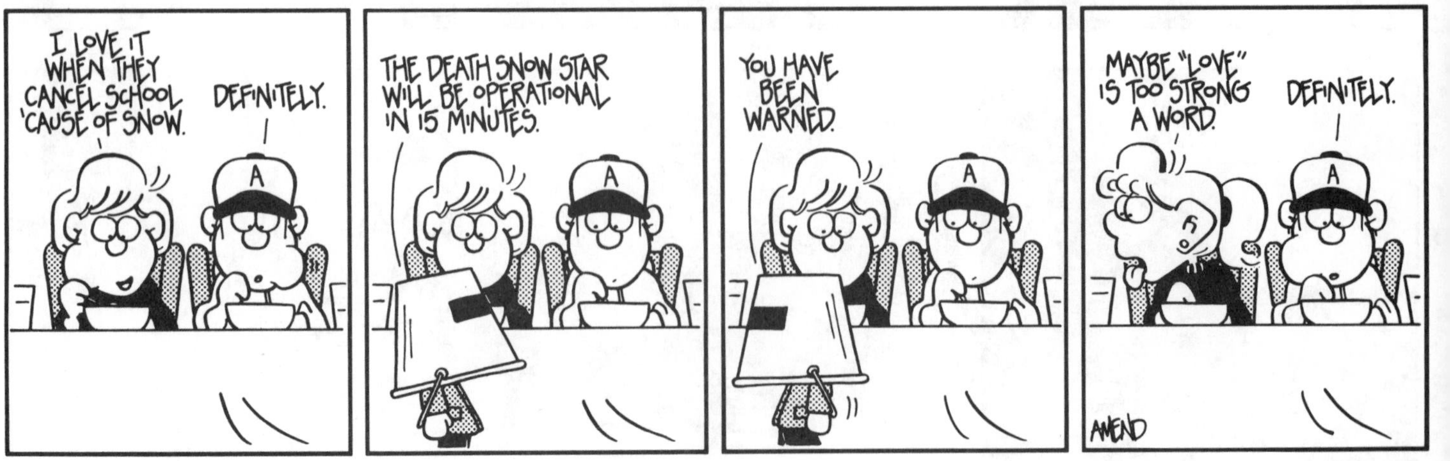
I LOVE IT WHEN THEY CANCEL SCHOOL 'CAUSE OF SNOW.
DEFINITELY.
THE DEATH SNOW STAR WILL BE OPERATIONAL IN 15 MINUTES.
YOU HAVE BEEN WARNED.
MAYBE "LOVE" IS TOO STRONG A WORD.
DEFINITELY.
AMEND

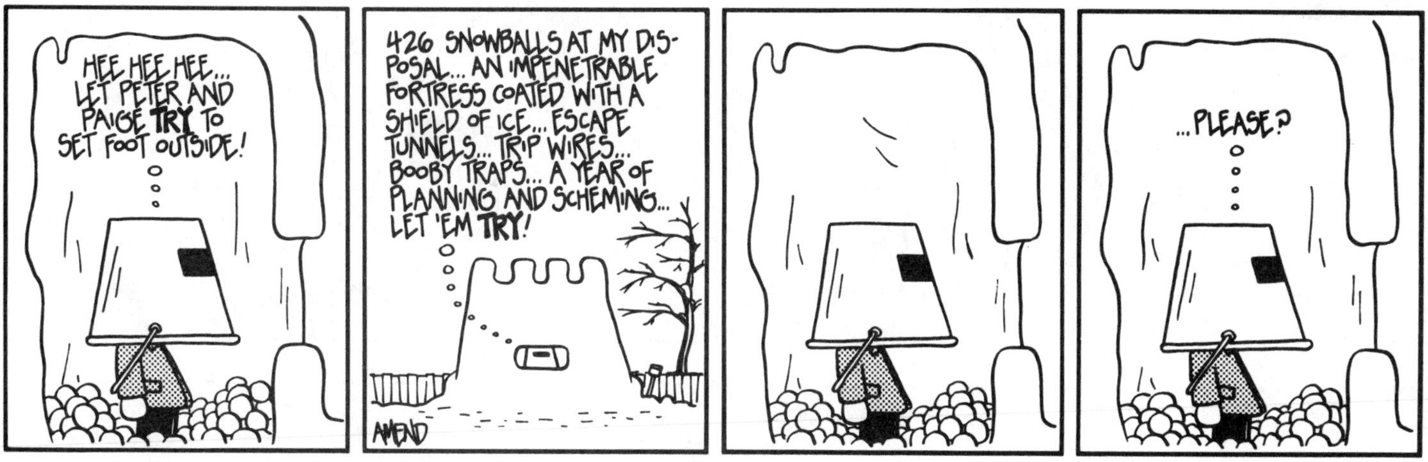
HEE HEE HEE... LET PETER AND PAIGE TRY TO SET FOOT OUTSIDE!
426 SNOWBALLS AT MY DISPOSAL... AN IMPENETRABLE FORTRESS COATED WITH A SHIELD OF ICE... ESCAPE TUNNELS... TRIP WIRES... BOOBY TRAPS... A YEAR OF PLANNING AND SCHEMING... LET 'EM TRY!
AMEND
...PLEASE?

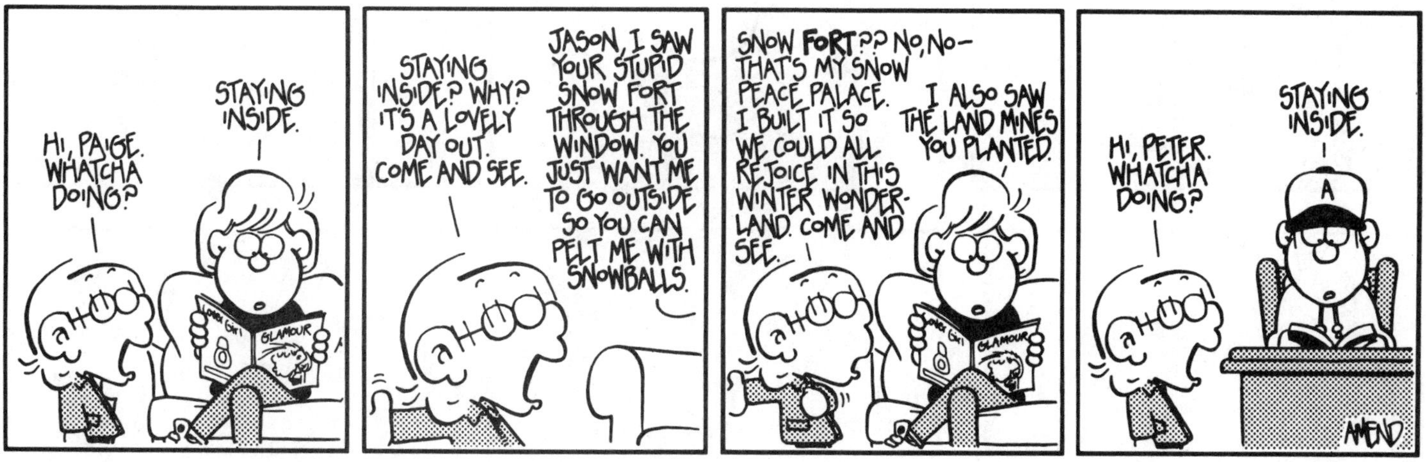
HI, PAIGE. WHATCHA DOING?
STAYING INSIDE.
STAYING INSIDE? WHY? IT'S A LOVELY DAY OUT. COME AND SEE.
JASON, I SAW YOUR STUPID SNOW FORT THROUGH THE WINDOW. YOU JUST WANT ME TO GO OUTSIDE SO YOU CAN PELT ME WITH SNOWBALLS.
SNOW FORT?? NO, NO– THAT'S MY SNOW PEACE PALACE. I BUILT IT SO WE COULD ALL REJOICE IN THIS WINTER WONDERLAND. COME AND SEE.
I ALSO SAW THE LAND MINES YOU PLANTED.
HI, PETER. WHATCHA DOING?
STAYING INSIDE.
AMEND

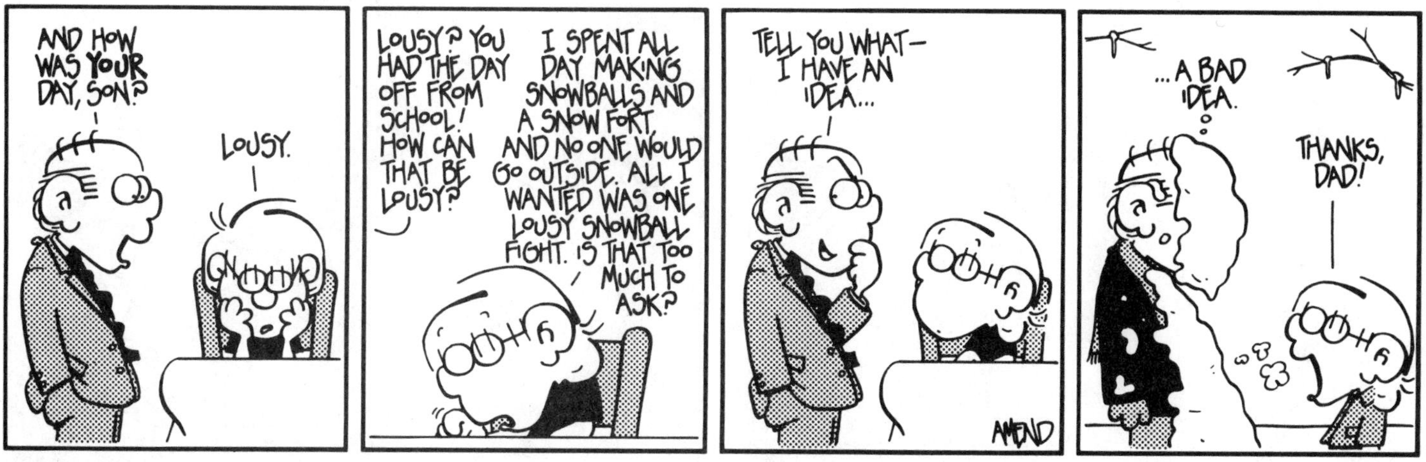
AND HOW WAS YOUR DAY, SON?
LOUSY.
LOUSY? YOU HAD THE DAY OFF FROM SCHOOL! HOW CAN THAT BE LOUSY?
I SPENT ALL DAY MAKING SNOWBALLS AND A SNOW FORT, AND NO ONE WOULD GO OUTSIDE. ALL I WANTED WAS ONE LOUSY SNOWBALL FIGHT. IS THAT TOO MUCH TO ASK?
TELL YOU WHAT– I HAVE AN IDEA...
AMEND
...A BAD IDEA.
THANKS, DAD!

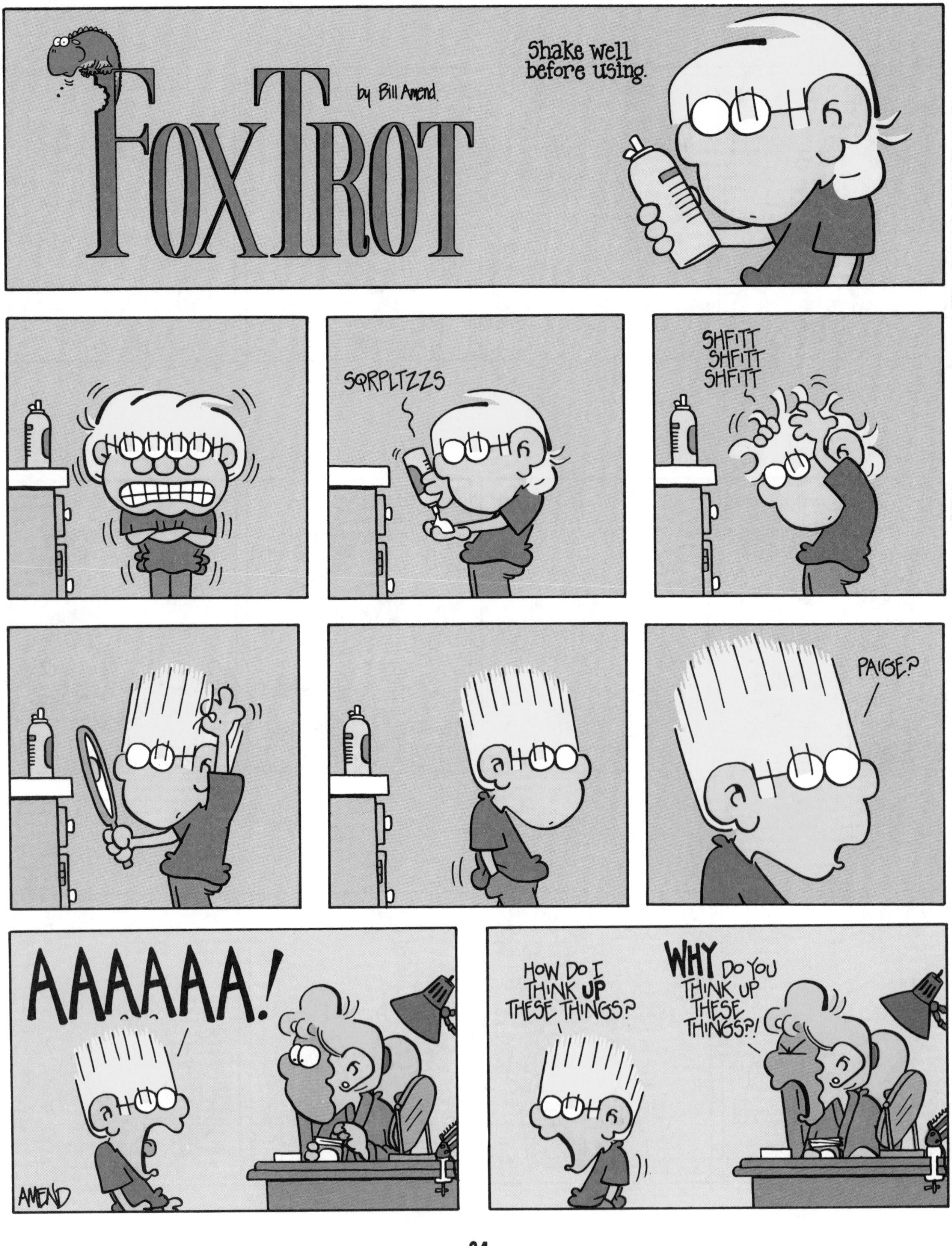
FoxTrot
by Bill Amend.
Shake well before using.
SQRPLTZZZS
SHFITT SHFITT SHFITT
PAIGE?
AAAAAA!
AMEND
HOW DO I THINK UP THESE THINGS?
WHY DO YOU THINK UP THESE THINGS?!

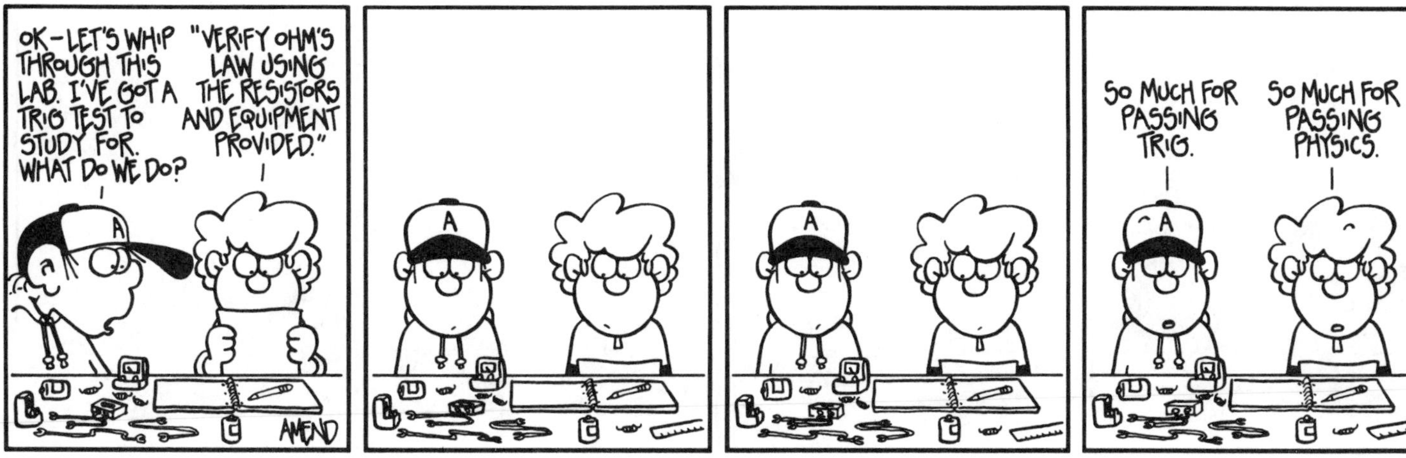
OK–LET'S WHIP THROUGH THIS LAB. I'VE GOT A TRIG TEST TO STUDY FOR. WHAT DO WE DO?
"VERIFY OHM'S LAW USING THE RESISTORS AND EQUIPMENT PROVIDED."
SO MUCH FOR PASSING TRIG.
SO MUCH FOR PASSING PHYSICS.
AMEND

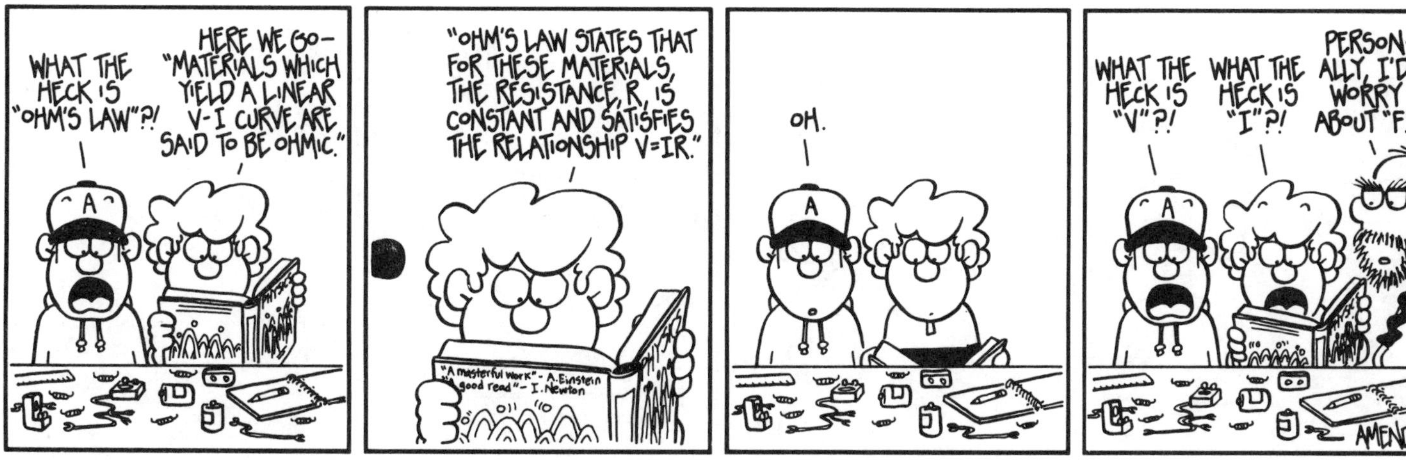
WHAT THE HECK IS "OHM'S LAW"?!
HERE WE GO– "MATERIALS WHICH YIELD A LINEAR V-I CURVE ARE SAID TO BE OHMIC."
"OHM'S LAW STATES THAT FOR THESE MATERIALS, THE RESISTANCE, R, IS CONSTANT AND SATISFIES THE RELATIONSHIP V=IR."
"A masterful work" - A. Einstein
"A good read" - I. Newton
OH.
WHAT THE HECK IS "V"?!
WHAT THE HECK IS "I"?!
PERSON-ALLY, I'D WORRY ABOUT "F."
AMEND

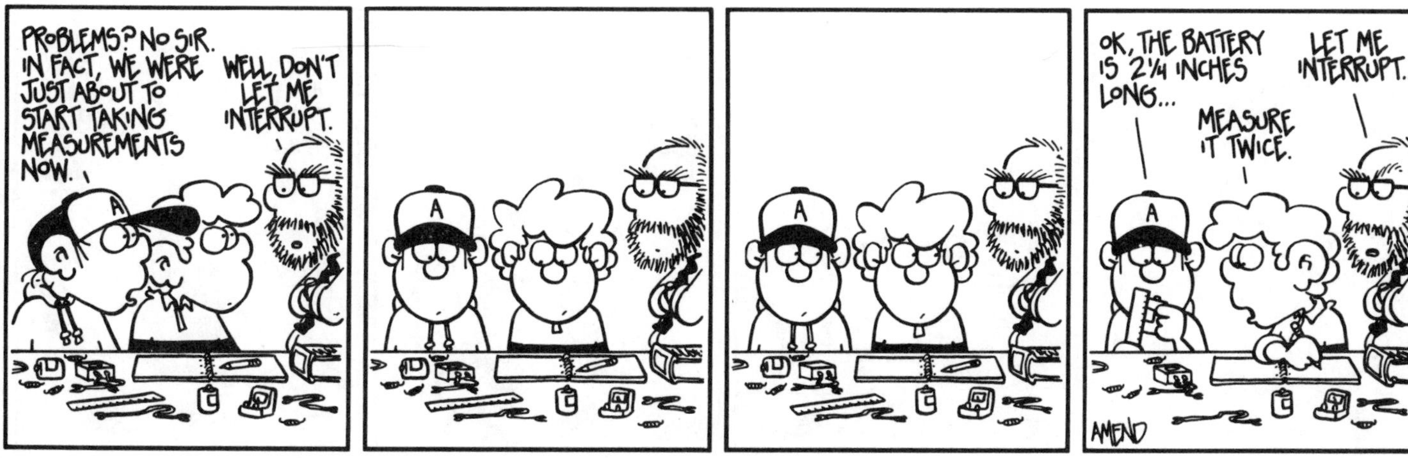
PROBLEMS? NO SIR. IN FACT, WE WERE JUST ABOUT TO START TAKING MEASUREMENTS NOW.
WELL, DON'T LET ME INTERRUPT.
OK, THE BATTERY IS 2¼ INCHES LONG...
MEASURE IT TWICE.
LET ME INTERRUPT...
AMEND

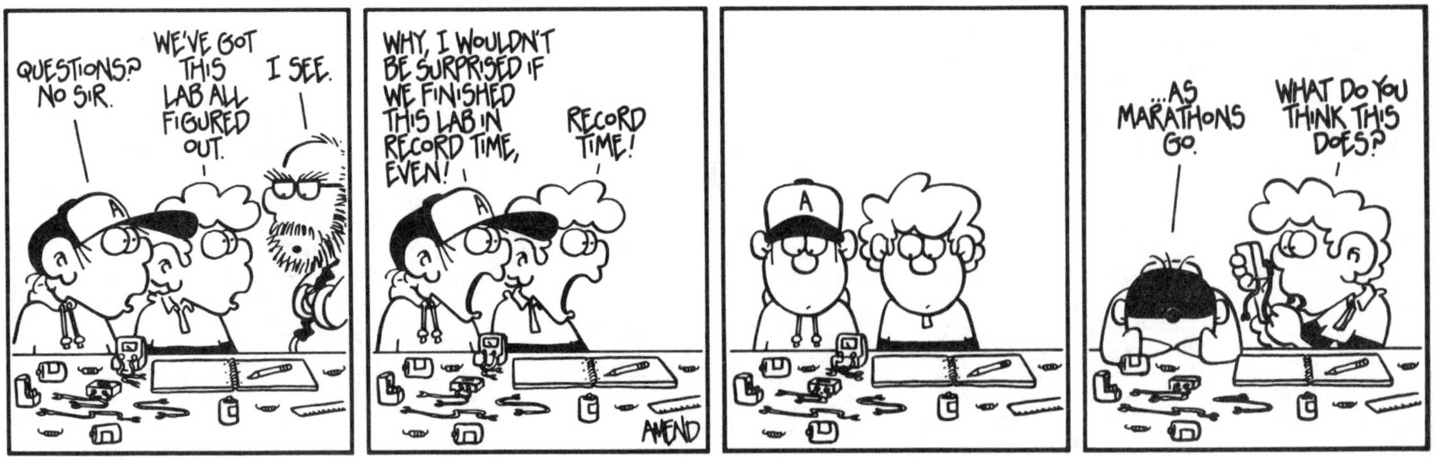
QUESTIONS? NO SIR.
WE'VE GOT THIS LAB ALL FIGURED OUT.
I SEE.
WHY, I WOULDN'T BE SURPRISED IF WE FINISHED THIS LAB IN RECORD TIME, EVEN!
RECORD TIME!
AMEND
...AS MARATHONS GO.
WHAT DO YOU THINK THIS DOES?

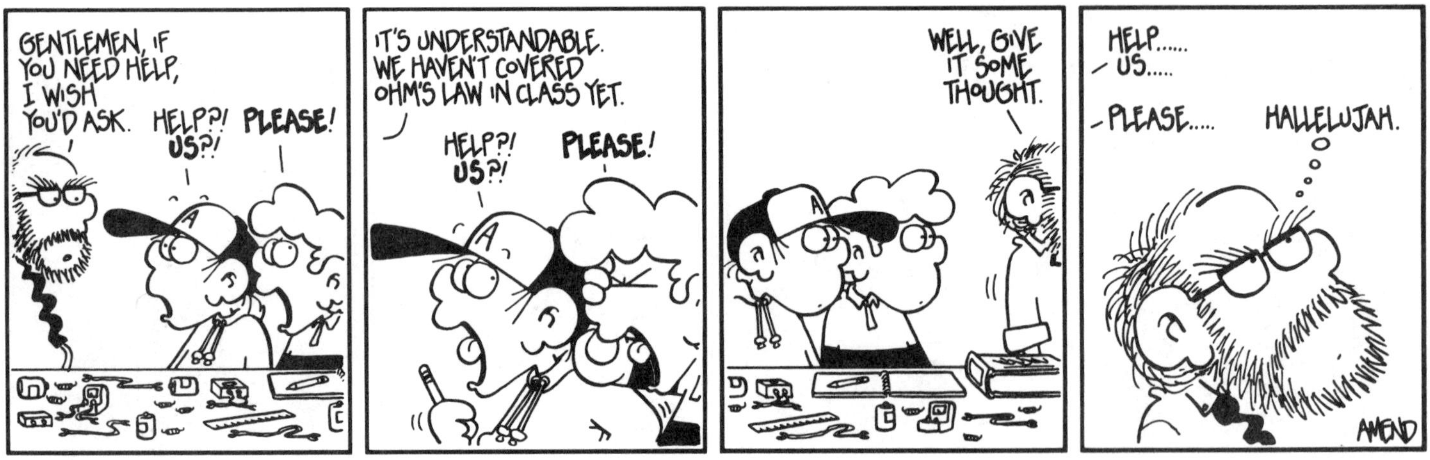
GENTLEMEN, IF YOU NEED HELP, I WISH YOU'D ASK.
HELP?! US?!
PLEASE!
IT'S UNDERSTANDABLE. WE HAVEN'T COVERED OHM'S LAW IN CLASS YET.
HELP?! US?!
PLEASE!
WELL, GIVE IT SOME THOUGHT.
HELP...... US.....
PLEASE.....
HALLELUJAH.
AMEND

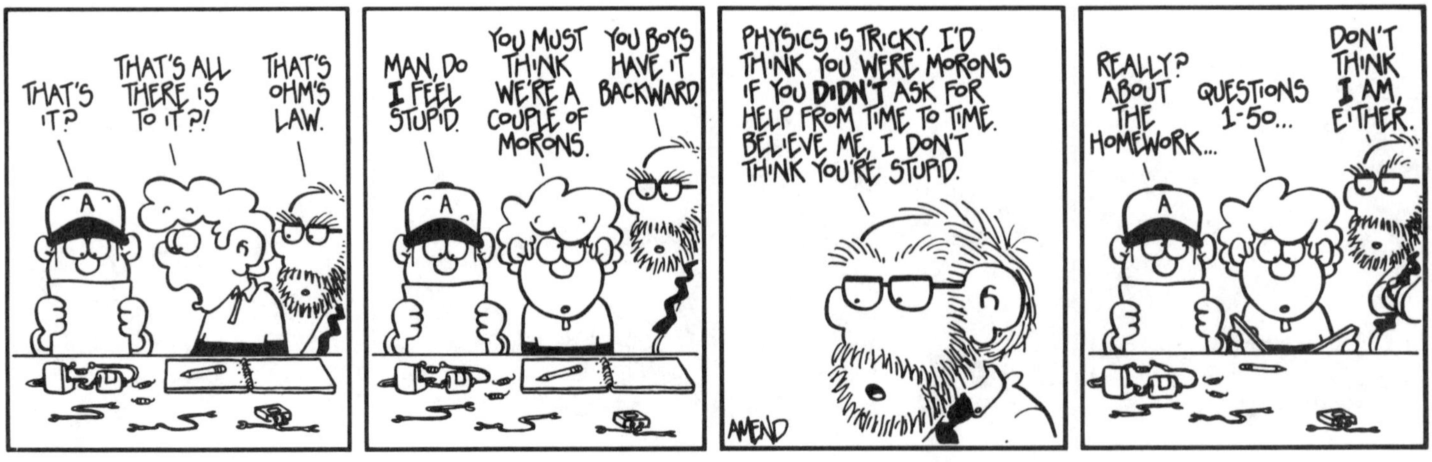
THAT'S IT?
THAT'S ALL THERE IS TO IT?!
THAT'S OHM'S LAW.
MAN, DO I FEEL STUPID.
YOU MUST THINK WE'RE A COUPLE OF MORONS.
YOU BOYS HAVE IT BACKWARD.
PHYSICS IS TRICKY. I'D THINK YOU WERE MORONS IF YOU DIDN'T ASK FOR HELP FROM TIME TO TIME. BELIEVE ME, I DON'T THINK YOU'RE STUPID.
AMEND
REALLY? ABOUT THE HOMEWORK...
QUESTIONS 1-50...
DON'T THINK I AM, EITHER.

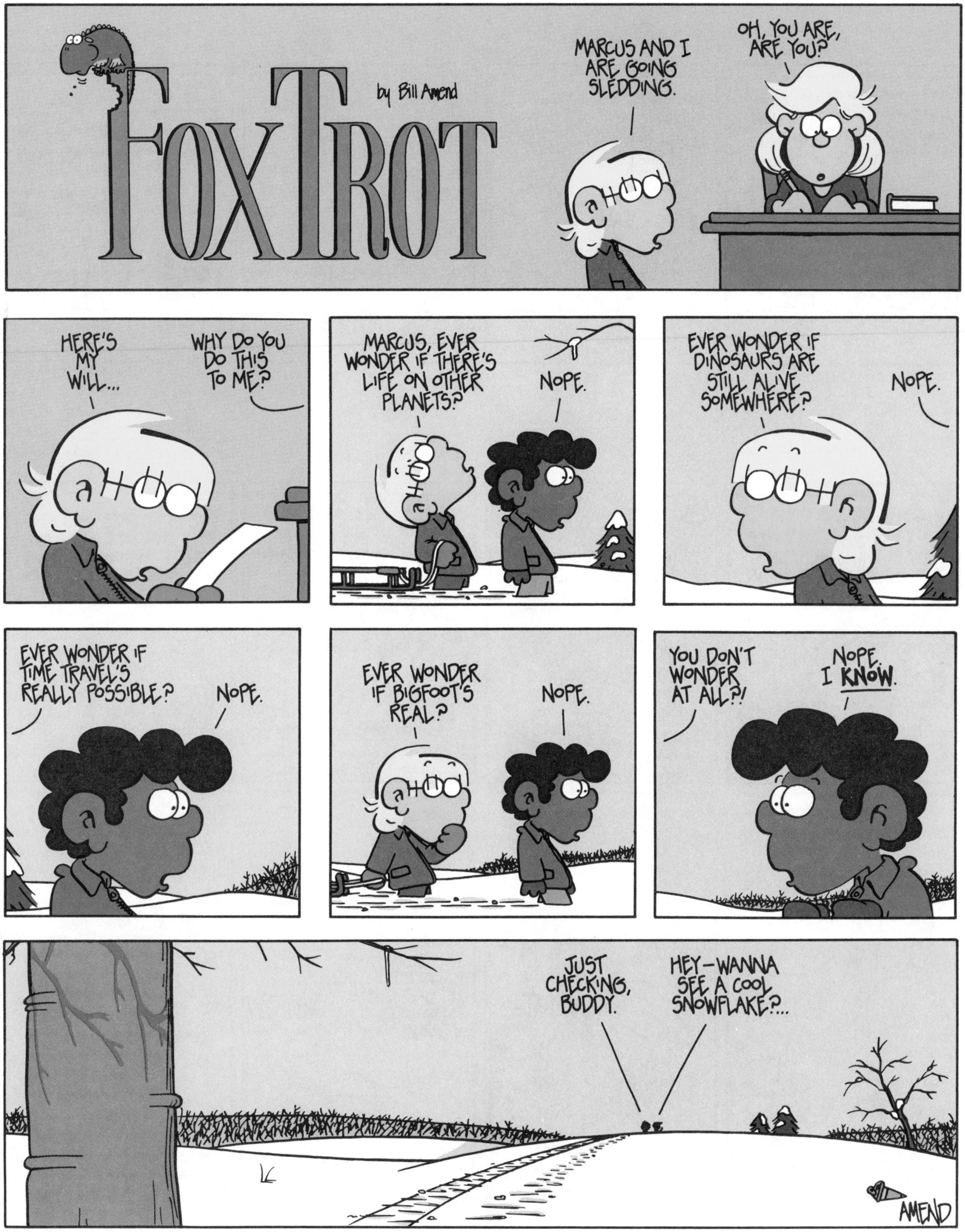
FoxTrot
by Bill Amend
MARCUS AND I ARE GOING SLEDDING.
OH, YOU ARE, ARE YOU?
HERE'S MY WILL...
WHY DO YOU DO THIS TO ME?
MARCUS, EVER WONDER IF THERE'S LIFE ON OTHER PLANETS?
NOPE.
EVER WONDER IF DINOSAURS ARE STILL ALIVE SOMEWHERE?
NOPE.
EVER WONDER IF TIME TRAVEL'S REALLY POSSIBLE?
NOPE.
EVER WONDER IF BIGFOOT'S REAL?
NOPE.
YOU DON'T WONDER AT ALL?!
NOPE. I KNOW.
JUST CHECKING, BUDDY.
HEY—WANNA SEE A COOL SNOWFLAKE?...
AMEND

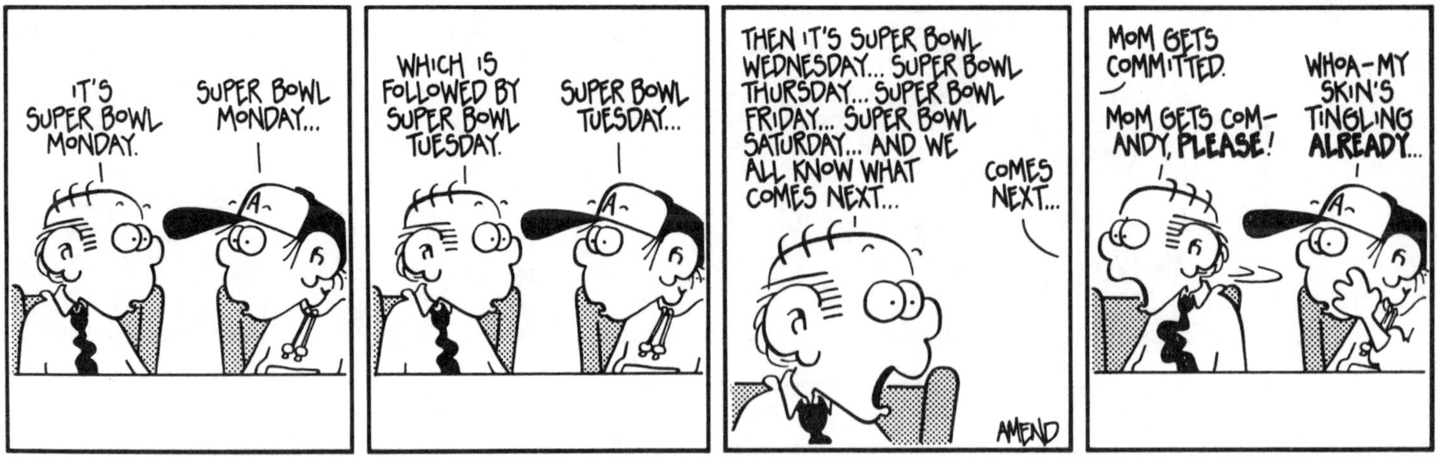
IT'S SUPER BOWL MONDAY.
SUPER BOWL MONDAY...
WHICH IS FOLLOWED BY SUPER BOWL TUESDAY.
SUPER BOWL TUESDAY...
THEN IT'S SUPER BOWL WEDNESDAY... SUPER BOWL THURSDAY... SUPER BOWL FRIDAY... SUPER BOWL SATURDAY... AND WE ALL KNOW WHAT COMES NEXT...
COMES NEXT...
AMEND
MOM GETS COMMITTED.
MOM GETS COM- ANDY, PLEASE!
WHOA-MY SKIN'S TINGLING ALREADY...

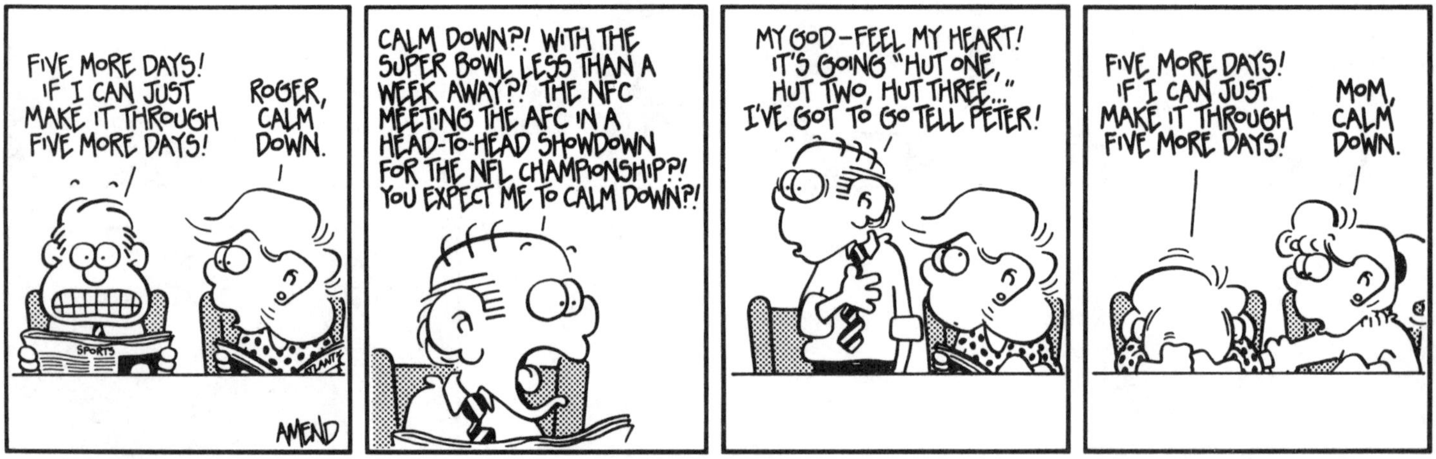
FIVE MORE DAYS! IF I CAN JUST MAKE IT THROUGH FIVE MORE DAYS!
ROGER, CALM DOWN.
SPORTS
AMEND
CALM DOWN?! WITH THE SUPER BOWL LESS THAN A WEEK AWAY?! THE NFC MEETING THE AFC IN A HEAD-TO-HEAD SHOWDOWN FOR THE NFL CHAMPIONSHIP?! YOU EXPECT ME TO CALM DOWN?!
MY GOD-FEEL MY HEART! IT'S GOING "HUT ONE, HUT TWO, HUT THREE..." I'VE GOT TO GO TELL PETER!
FIVE MORE DAYS! IF I CAN JUST MAKE IT THROUGH FIVE MORE DAYS!
MOM, CALM DOWN.

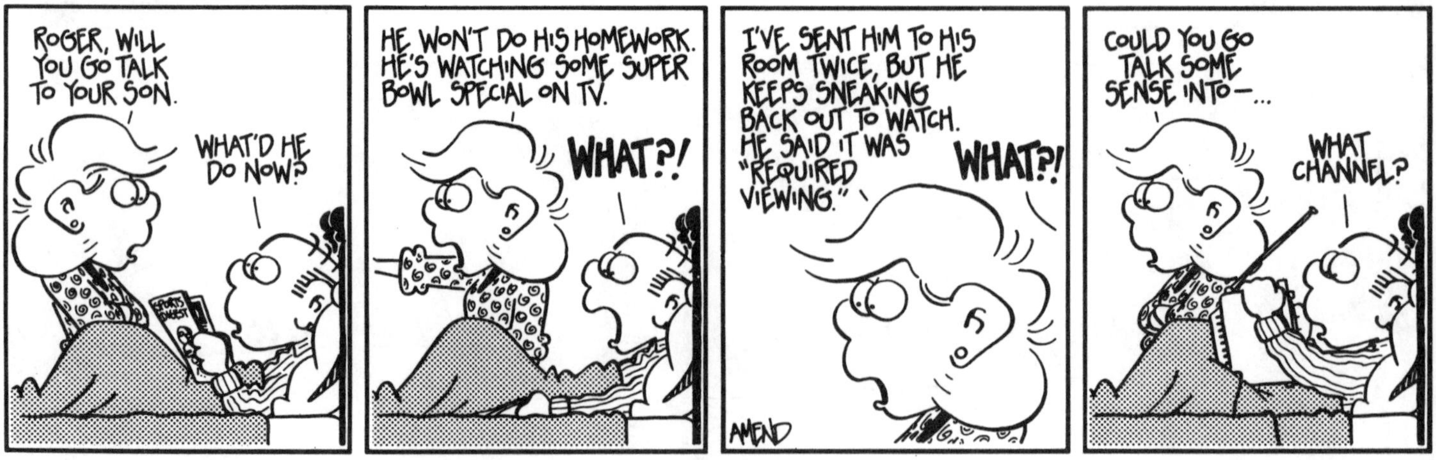
ROGER, WILL YOU GO TALK TO YOUR SON.
WHAT'D HE DO NOW?
SPORTS DIGEST
HE WON'T DO HIS HOMEWORK. HE'S WATCHING SOME SUPER BOWL SPECIAL ON TV.
WHAT?!
I'VE SENT HIM TO HIS ROOM TWICE, BUT HE KEEPS SNEAKING BACK OUT TO WATCH. HE SAID IT WAS "REQUIRED VIEWING."
WHAT?!
AMEND
COULD YOU GO TALK SOME SENSE INTO-...
WHAT CHANNEL?

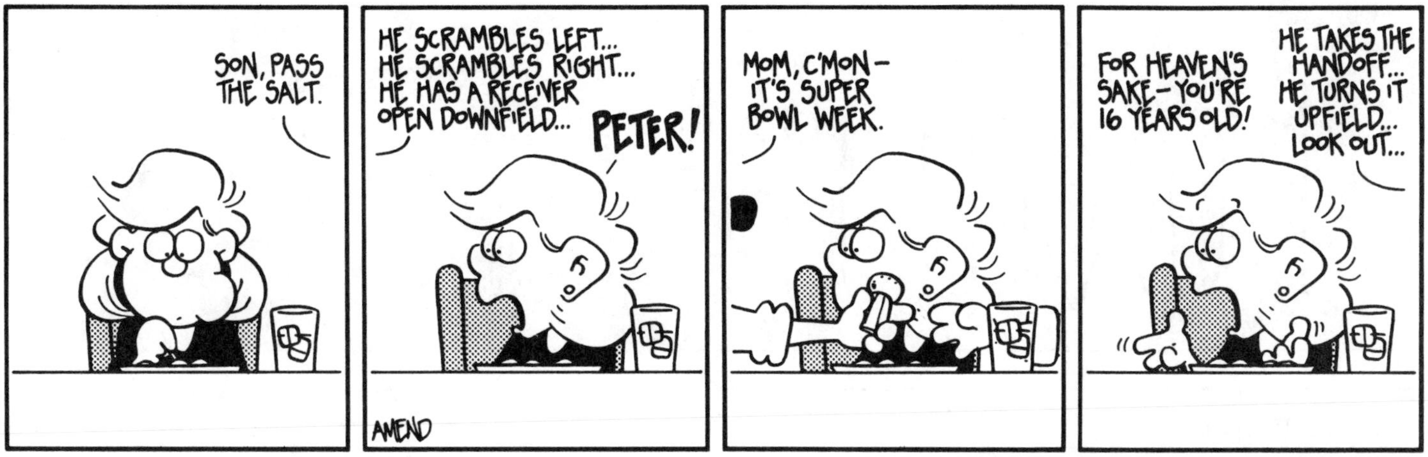
SON, PASS THE SALT.
HE SCRAMBLES LEFT... HE SCRAMBLES RIGHT... HE HAS A RECEIVER OPEN DOWNFIELD...
PETER!
AMEND
MOM, C'MON – IT'S SUPER BOWL WEEK.
FOR HEAVEN'S SAKE – YOU'RE 16 YEARS OLD!
HE TAKES THE HANDOFF... HE TURNS IT UPFIELD... LOOK OUT...

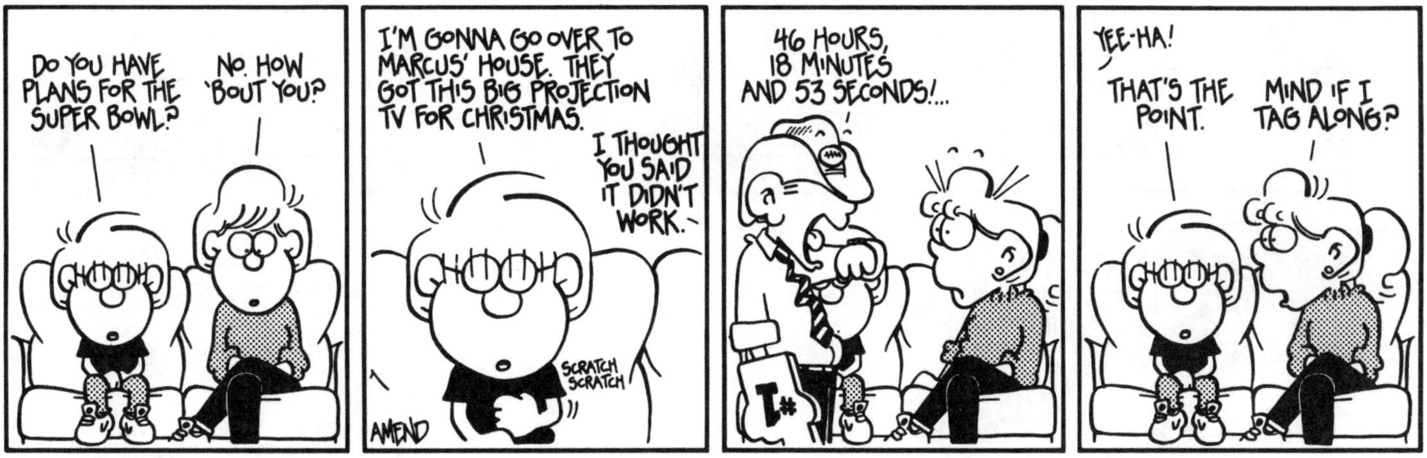
DO YOU HAVE PLANS FOR THE SUPER BOWL?
NO. HOW 'BOUT YOU?
I'M GONNA GO OVER TO MARCUS' HOUSE. THEY GOT THIS BIG PROJECTION TV FOR CHRISTMAS.
I THOUGHT YOU SAID IT DIDN'T WORK.
SCRATCH SCRATCH
AMEND
46 HOURS, 18 MINUTES AND 53 SECONDS!...
YEE-HA!
THAT'S THE POINT.
MIND IF I TAG ALONG?

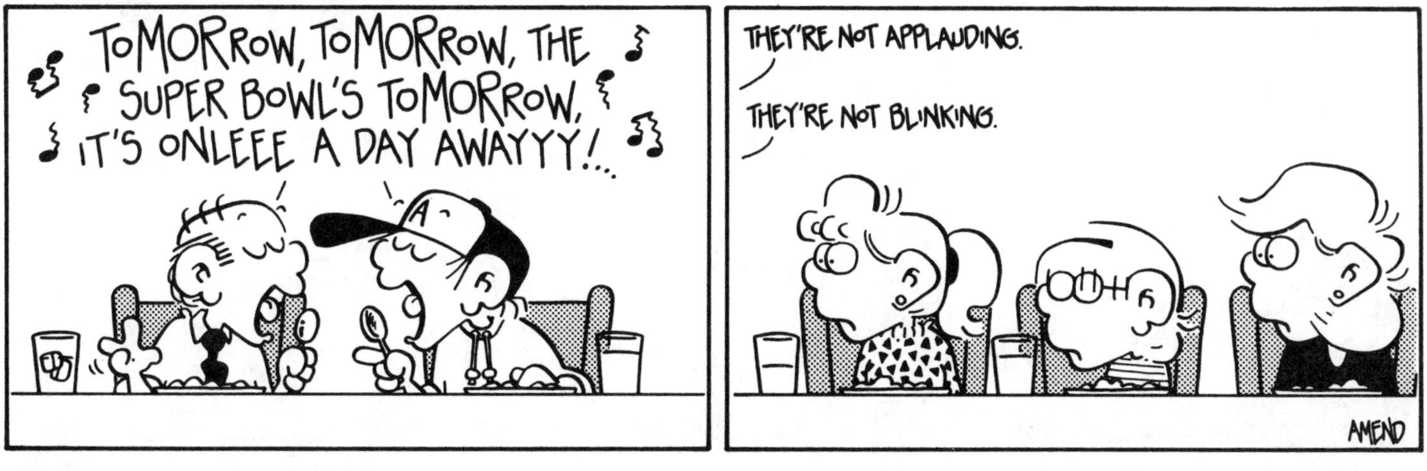
TOMORROW, TOMORROW, THE SUPER BOWL'S TOMORROW, IT'S ONLEEE A DAY AWAYYY!...
THEY'RE NOT APPLAUDING.
THEY'RE NOT BLINKING.
AMEND

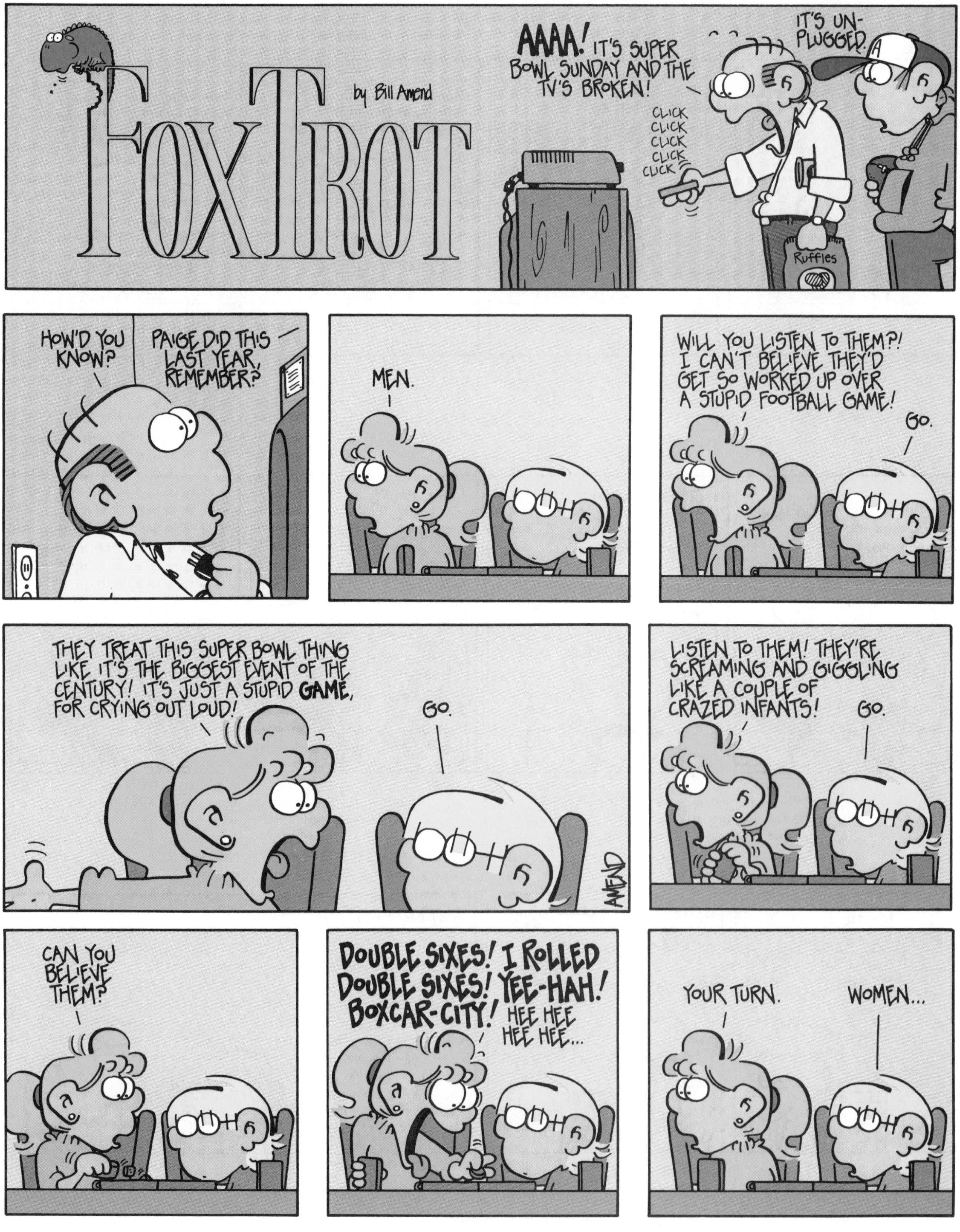
FoxTrot
by Bill Amend
AAAA! IT'S SUPER BOWL SUNDAY AND THE TV'S BROKEN!
CLICK CLICK CLICK CLICK CLICK
IT'S UN-PLUGGED.
Ruffles
HOW'D YOU KNOW?
PAIGE DID THIS LAST YEAR, REMEMBER?
MEN.
WILL YOU LISTEN TO THEM?! I CAN'T BELIEVE THEY'D GET SO WORKED UP OVER A STUPID FOOTBALL GAME!
GO.
THEY TREAT THIS SUPER BOWL THING LIKE IT'S THE BIGGEST EVENT OF THE CENTURY! IT'S JUST A STUPID GAME, FOR CRYING OUT LOUD!
GO.
AMEND
LISTEN TO THEM! THEY'RE SCREAMING AND GIGGLING LIKE A COUPLE OF CRAZED INFANTS!
GO.
CAN YOU BELIEVE THEM?
DOUBLE SIXES! I ROLLED DOUBLE SIXES! YEE-HAH! BOXCAR-CITY!
HEE HEE HEE HEE...
YOUR TURN.
WOMEN...

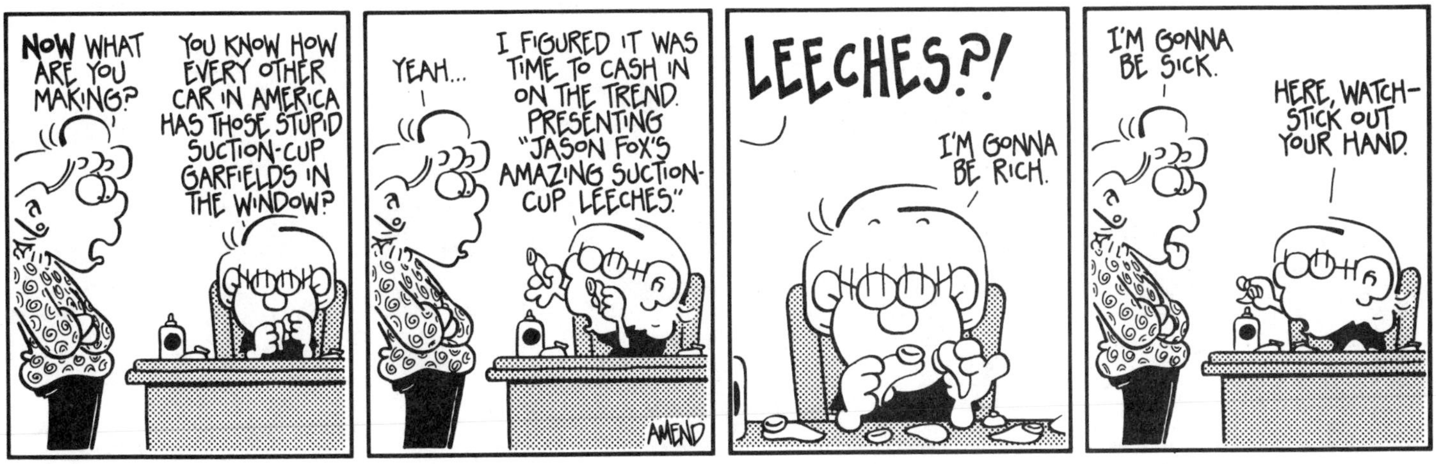
NOW WHAT ARE YOU MAKING?
YOU KNOW HOW EVERY OTHER CAR IN AMERICA HAS THOSE STUPID SUCTION-CUP GARFIELDS IN THE WINDOW?
YEAH...
I FIGURED IT WAS TIME TO CASH IN ON THE TREND. PRESENTING "JASON FOX'S AMAZING SUCTION-CUP LEECHES."
AMEND
LEECHES?!
I'M GONNA BE RICH.
I'M GONNA BE SICK.
HERE, WATCH- STICK OUT YOUR HAND.

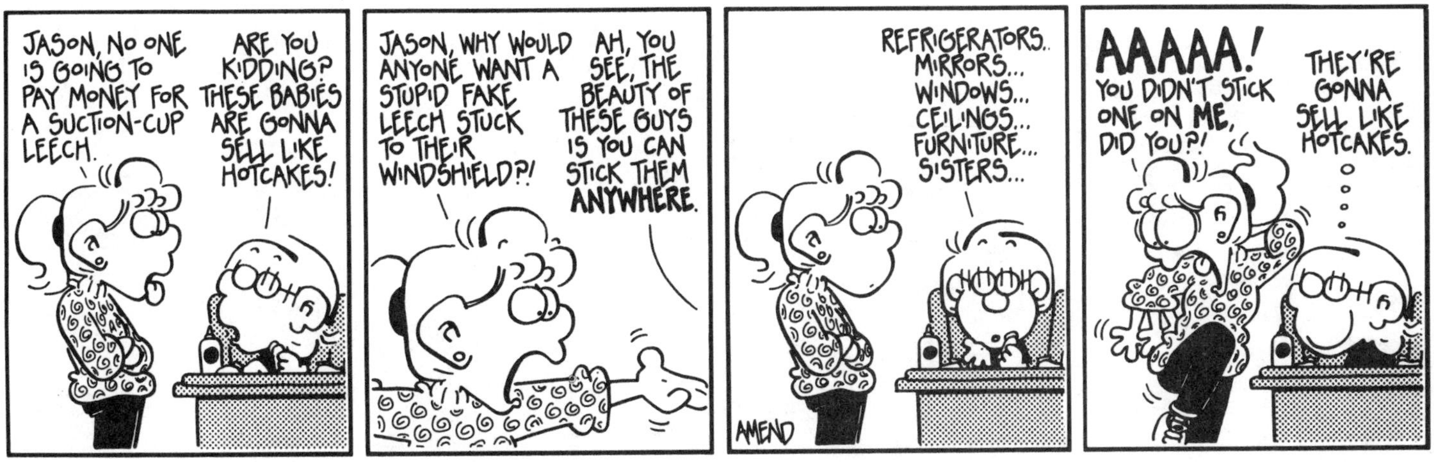
JASON, NO ONE IS GOING TO PAY MONEY FOR A SUCTION-CUP LEECH.
ARE YOU KIDDING? THESE BABIES ARE GONNA SELL LIKE HOTCAKES!
JASON, WHY WOULD ANYONE WANT A STUPID FAKE LEECH STUCK TO THEIR WINDSHIELD?!
AH, YOU SEE, THE BEAUTY OF THESE GUYS IS YOU CAN STICK THEM ANYWHERE.
REFRIGERATORS... MIRRORS... WINDOWS... CEILINGS... FURNITURE... SISTERS...
AMEND
AAAAA! YOU DIDN'T STICK ONE ON ME, DID YOU?!
THEY'RE GONNA SELL LIKE HOTCAKES.

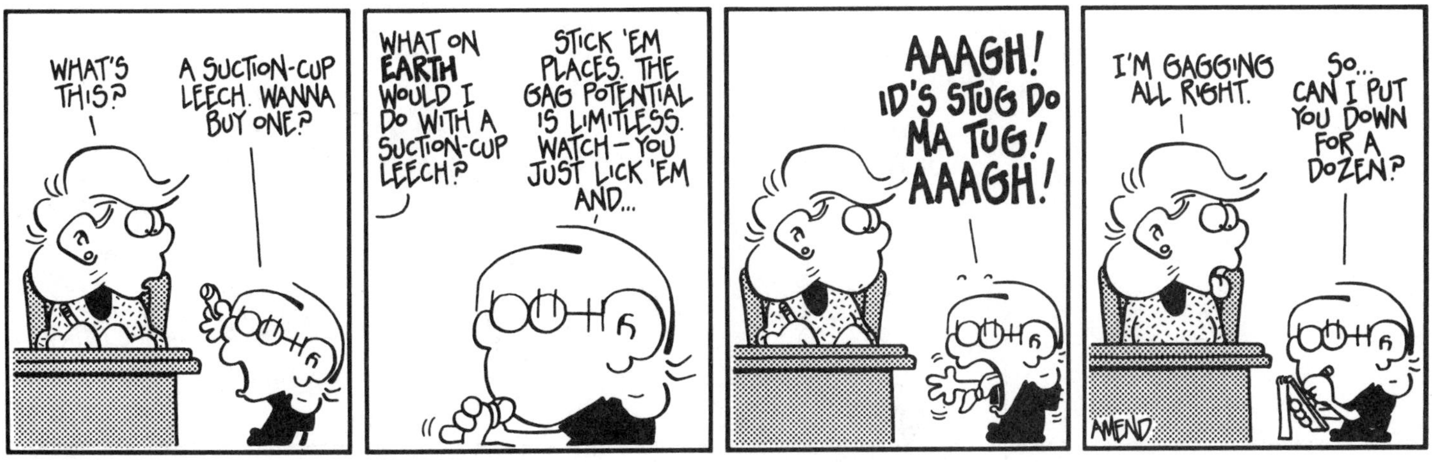
WHAT'S THIS?
A SUCTION-CUP LEECH. WANNA BUY ONE?
WHAT ON EARTH WOULD I DO WITH A SUCTION-CUP LEECH?
STICK 'EM PLACES. THE GAG POTENTIAL IS LIMITLESS. WATCH- YOU JUST LICK 'EM AND...
AAAGH! ID'S STUG DO MA TUG! AAAGH!
I'M GAGGING ALL RIGHT.
SO... CAN I PUT YOU DOWN FOR A DOZEN?
AMEND

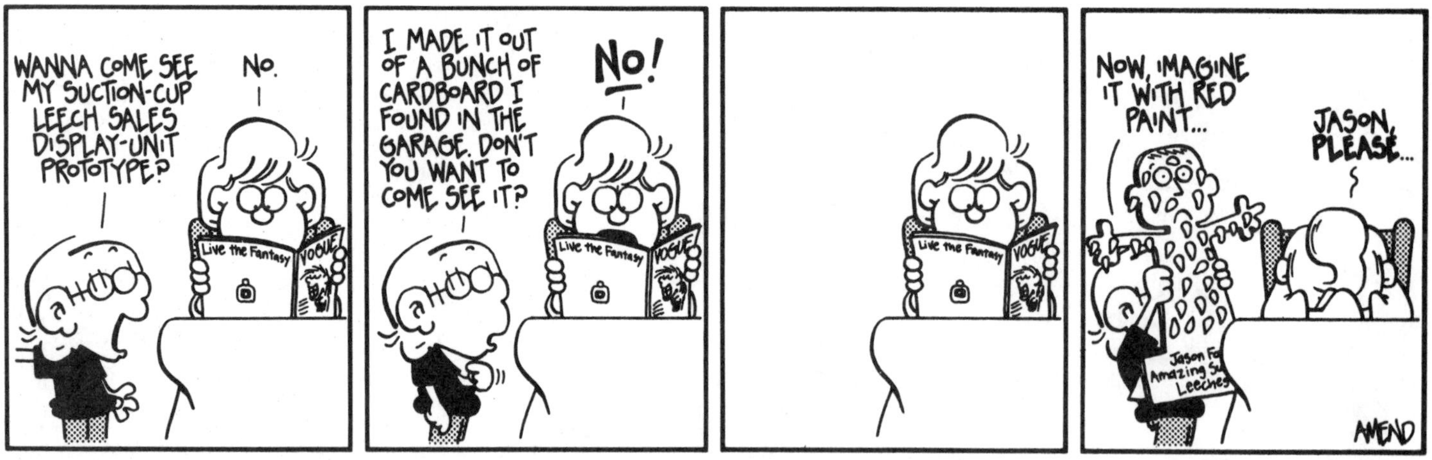
WANNA COME SEE MY SUCTION-CUP LEECH SALES DISPLAY-UNIT PROTOTYPE?
NO.
Live the Fantasy
VOGUE
I MADE IT OUT OF A BUNCH OF CARDBOARD I FOUND IN THE GARAGE. DON'T YOU WANT TO COME SEE IT?
NO!
NOW, IMAGINE IT WITH RED PAINT...
JASON, PLEASE...
Jason Fox's Amazing Suction-Cup Leeches
AMEND

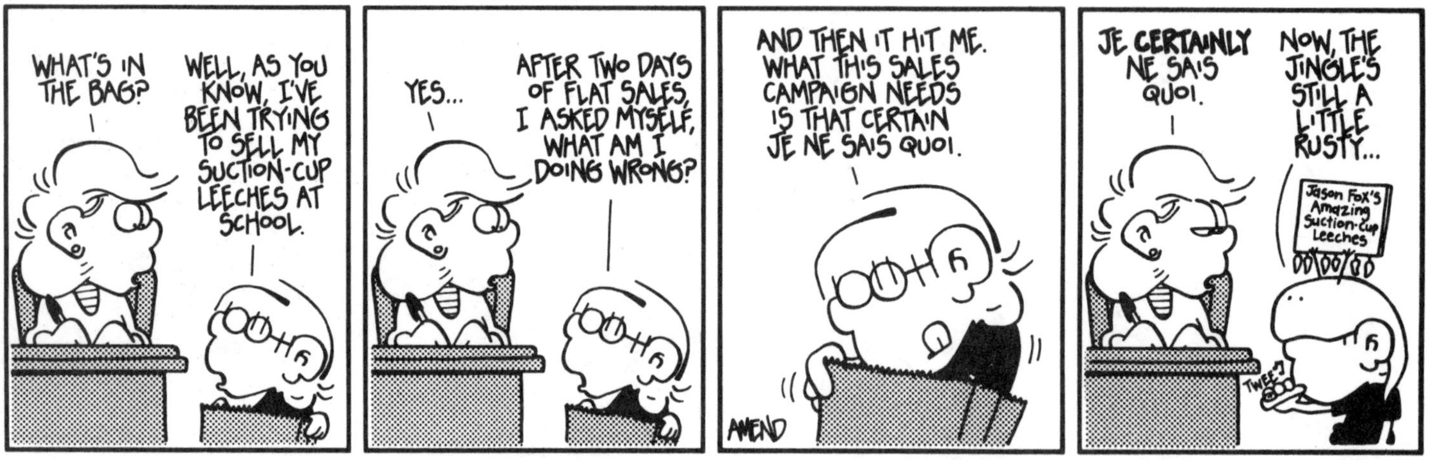
WHAT'S IN THE BAG?
WELL, AS YOU KNOW, I'VE BEEN TRYING TO SELL MY SUCTION-CUP LEECHES AT SCHOOL.
YES...
AFTER TWO DAYS OF FLAT SALES, I ASKED MYSELF, WHAT AM I DOING WRONG?
AND THEN IT HIT ME. WHAT THIS SALES CAMPAIGN NEEDS IS THAT CERTAIN JE NE SAIS QUOI.
AMEND
JE CERTAINLY NE SAIS QUOI.
NOW, THE JINGLE'S STILL A LITTLE RUSTY...
Jason Fox's Amazing Suction-Cup Leeches

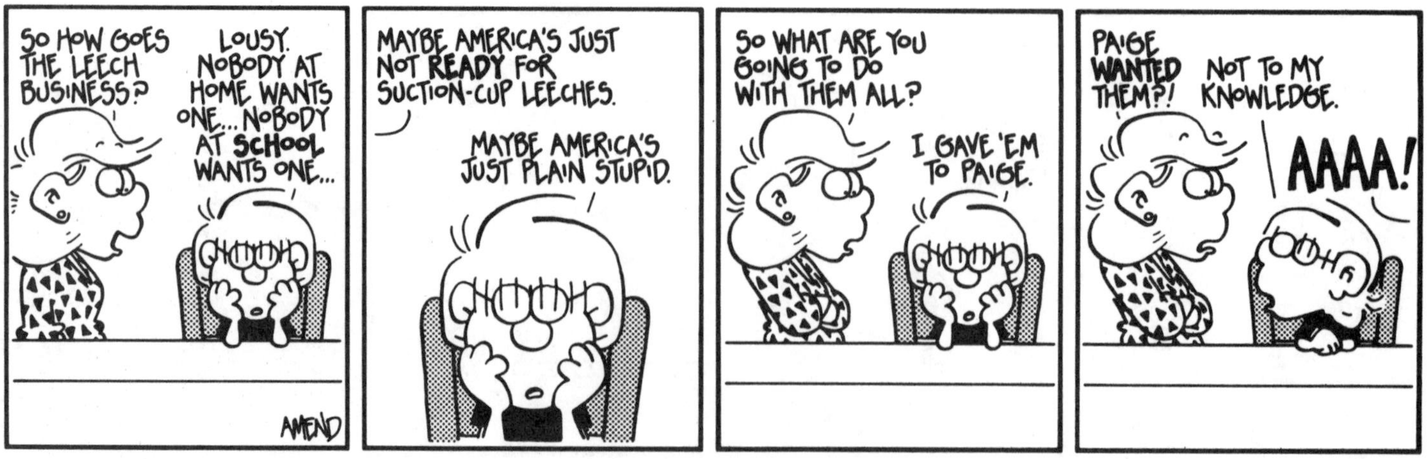
SO HOW GOES THE LEECH BUSINESS?
LOUSY. NOBODY AT HOME WANTS ONE... NOBODY AT SCHOOL WANTS ONE...
AMEND
MAYBE AMERICA'S JUST NOT READY FOR SUCTION-CUP LEECHES.
MAYBE AMERICA'S JUST PLAIN STUPID.
SO WHAT ARE YOU GOING TO DO WITH THEM ALL?
I GAVE 'EM TO PAIGE.
PAIGE WANTED THEM?!
NOT TO MY KNOWLEDGE.
AAAA!

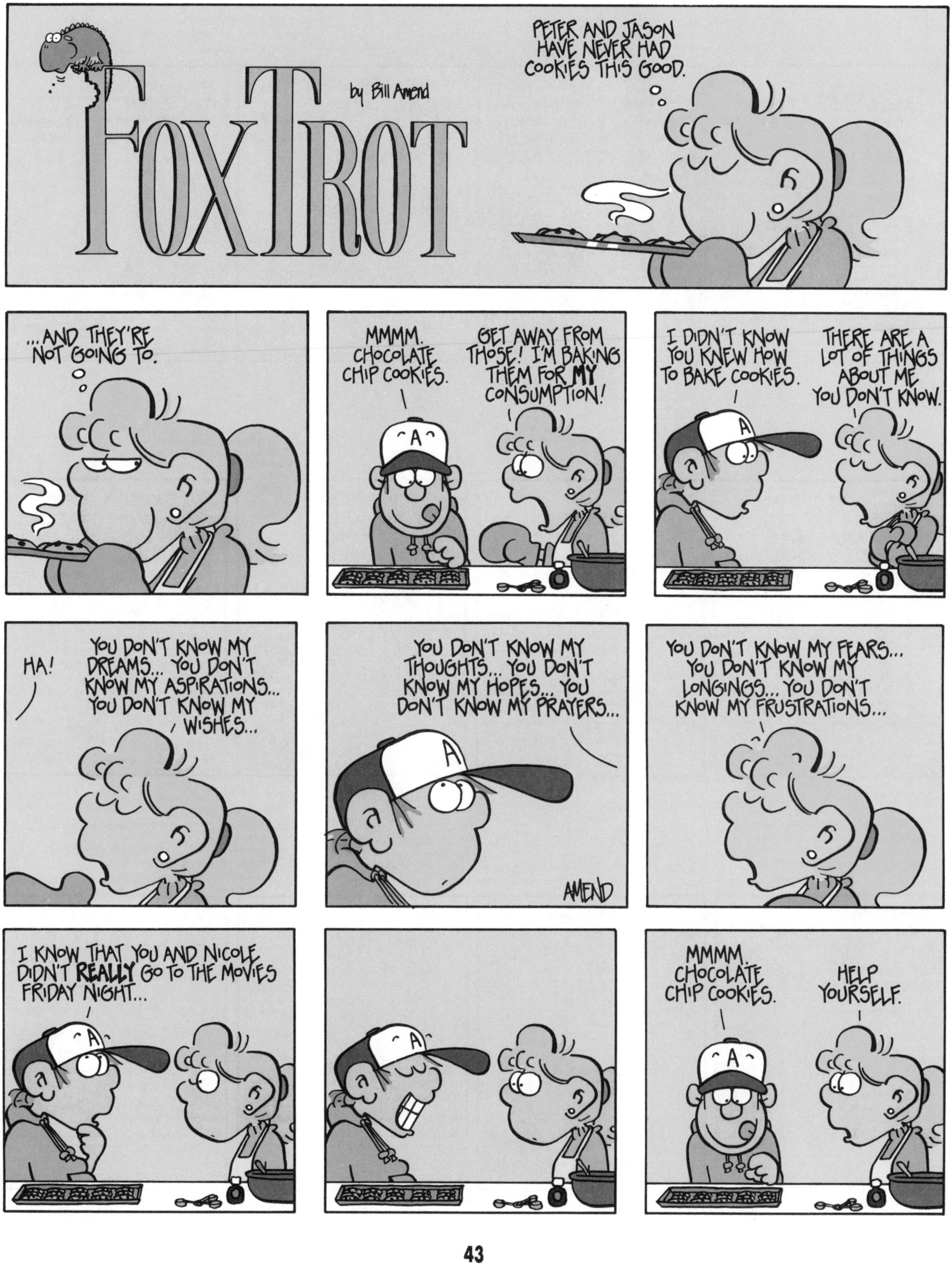
FoxTrot
by Bill Amend
PETER AND JASON HAVE NEVER HAD COOKIES THIS GOOD.
...AND THEY'RE NOT GOING TO.
MMMM. CHOCOLATE CHIP COOKIES.
GET AWAY FROM THOSE! I'M BAKING THEM FOR MY CONSUMPTION!
I DIDN'T KNOW YOU KNEW HOW TO BAKE COOKIES.
THERE ARE A LOT OF THINGS ABOUT ME YOU DON'T KNOW.
HA!
YOU DON'T KNOW MY DREAMS... YOU DON'T KNOW MY ASPIRATIONS... YOU DON'T KNOW MY WISHES...
YOU DON'T KNOW MY THOUGHTS... YOU DON'T KNOW MY HOPES... YOU DON'T KNOW MY PRAYERS...
AMEND
YOU DON'T KNOW MY FEARS... YOU DON'T KNOW MY LONGINGS... YOU DON'T KNOW MY FRUSTRATIONS...
I KNOW THAT YOU AND NICOLE DIDN'T REALLY GO TO THE MOVIES FRIDAY NIGHT...
MMMM. CHOCOLATE CHIP COOKIES.
HELP YOURSELF.

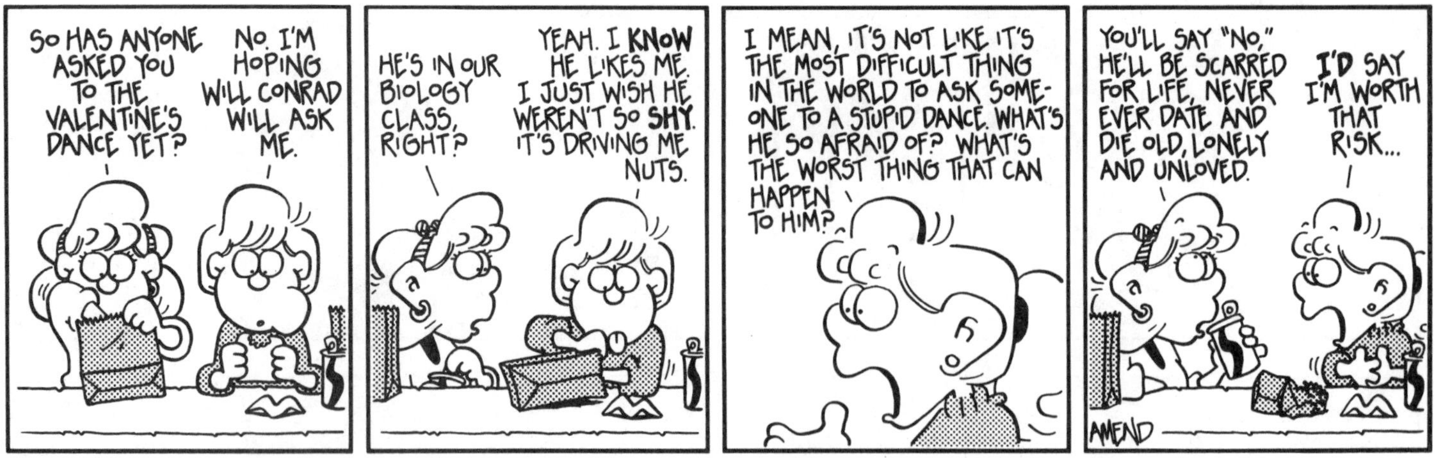
SO HAS ANYONE ASKED YOU TO THE VALENTINE'S DANCE YET?
NO. I'M HOPING WILL CONRAD WILL ASK ME.
HE'S IN OUR BIOLOGY CLASS, RIGHT?
YEAH. I **KNOW** HE LIKES ME. I JUST WISH HE WEREN'T SO **SHY**. IT'S DRIVING ME NUTS.
I MEAN, IT'S NOT LIKE IT'S THE MOST DIFFICULT THING IN THE WORLD TO ASK SOMEONE TO A STUPID DANCE. WHAT'S HE SO AFRAID OF? WHAT'S THE WORST THING THAT CAN HAPPEN TO HIM?
YOU'LL SAY "NO," HE'LL BE SCARRED FOR LIFE, NEVER EVER DATE AND DIE OLD, LONELY AND UNLOVED.
I'D SAY I'M WORTH THAT RISK...
AMEND

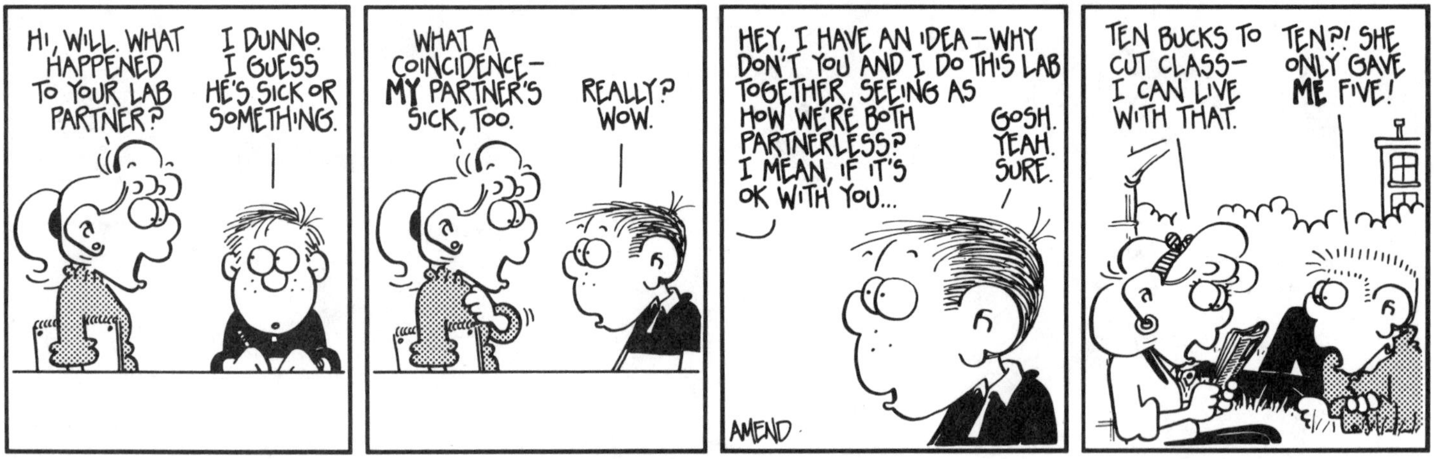
HI, WILL. WHAT HAPPENED TO YOUR LAB PARTNER?
I DUNNO. I GUESS HE'S SICK OR SOMETHING.
WHAT A COINCIDENCE— **MY** PARTNER'S SICK, TOO.
REALLY? WOW.
HEY, I HAVE AN IDEA—WHY DON'T YOU AND I DO THIS LAB TOGETHER, SEEING AS HOW WE'RE BOTH PARTNERLESS? I MEAN, IF IT'S OK WITH YOU...
GOSH. YEAH. SURE.
AMEND
TEN BUCKS TO CUT CLASS— I CAN LIVE WITH THAT.
TEN?! SHE ONLY GAVE **ME** FIVE!

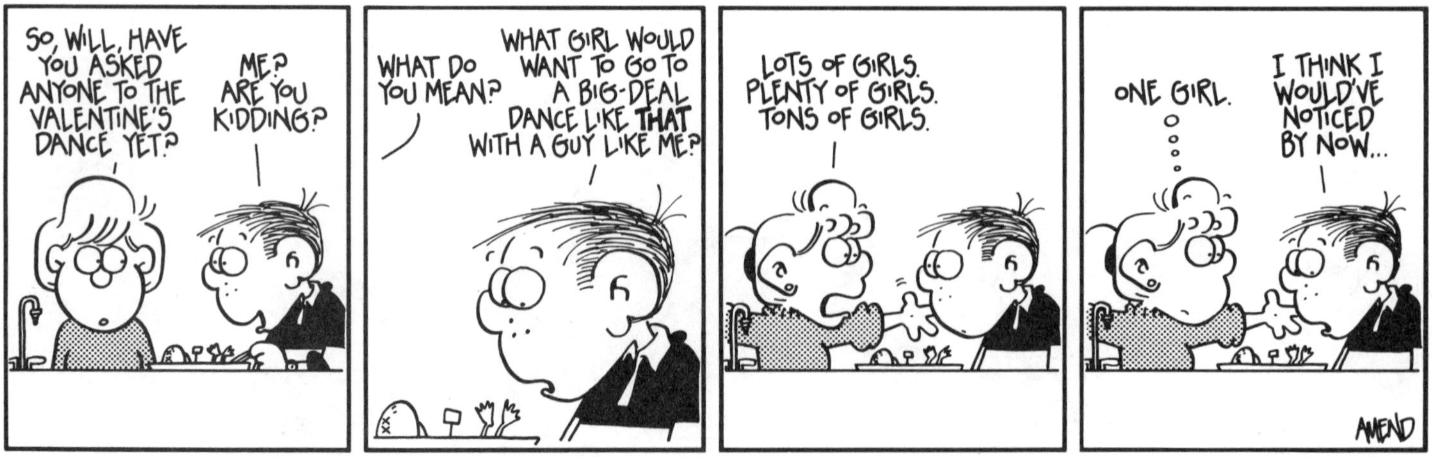
SO, WILL, HAVE YOU ASKED ANYONE TO THE VALENTINE'S DANCE YET?
ME? ARE YOU KIDDING?
WHAT DO YOU MEAN?
WHAT GIRL WOULD WANT TO GO TO A BIG-DEAL DANCE LIKE **THAT** WITH A GUY LIKE ME?
LOTS OF GIRLS. PLENTY OF GIRLS. TONS OF GIRLS.
ONE GIRL.
I THINK I WOULD'VE NOTICED BY NOW...
AMEND

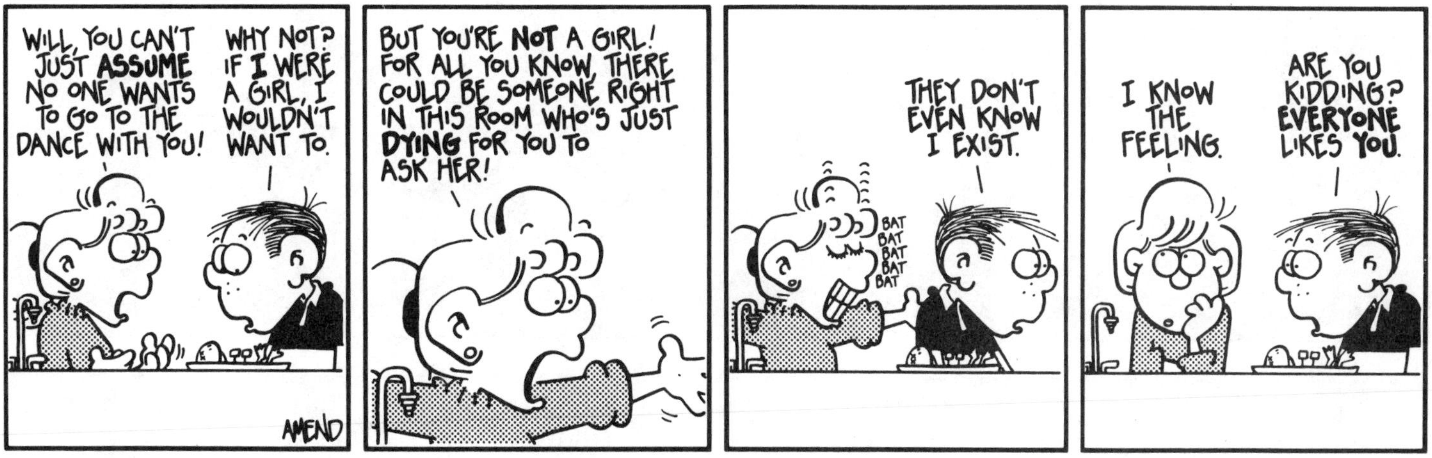
WILL, YOU CAN'T JUST **ASSUME** NO ONE WANTS TO GO TO THE DANCE WITH YOU!
WHY NOT? IF **I** WERE A GIRL, I WOULDN'T WANT TO.
BUT YOU'RE **NOT** A GIRL! FOR ALL YOU KNOW, THERE COULD BE SOMEONE RIGHT IN THIS ROOM WHO'S JUST **DYING** FOR YOU TO ASK HER!
BAT BAT BAT BAT BAT
THEY DON'T EVEN KNOW I EXIST.
I KNOW THE FEELING.
ARE YOU KIDDING? **EVERYONE** LIKES **YOU**.
AMEND

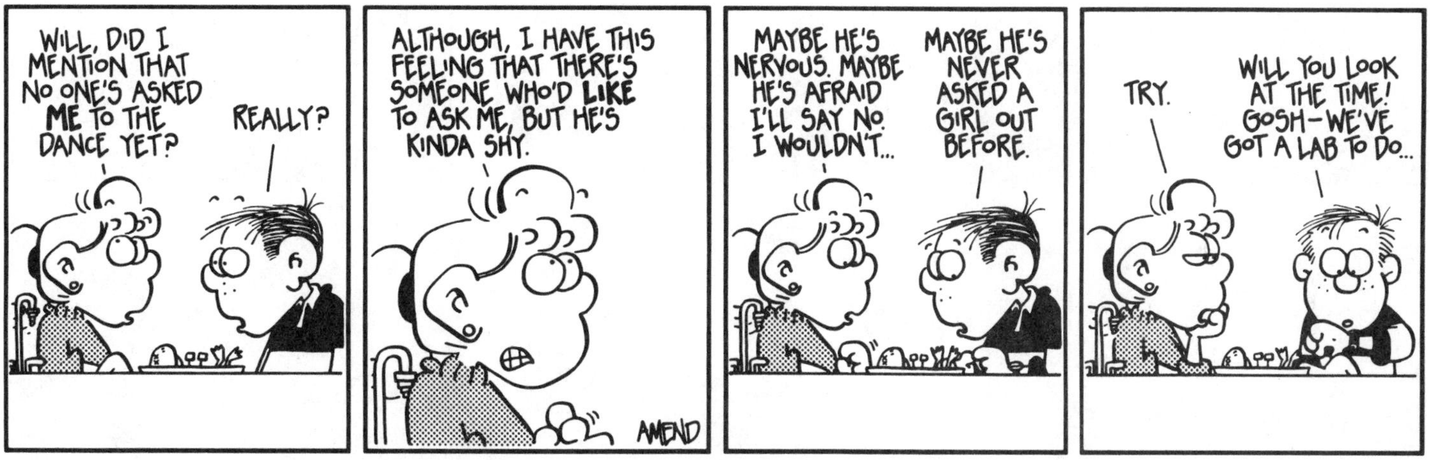
WILL, DID I MENTION THAT NO ONE'S ASKED **ME** TO THE DANCE YET?
REALLY?
ALTHOUGH, I HAVE THIS FEELING THAT THERE'S SOMEONE WHO'D **LIKE** TO ASK ME, BUT HE'S KINDA SHY.
AMEND
MAYBE HE'S NERVOUS. MAYBE HE'S AFRAID I'LL SAY NO. I WOULDN'T...
MAYBE HE'S NEVER ASKED A GIRL OUT BEFORE.
TRY.
WILL YOU LOOK AT THE TIME! GOSH—WE'VE GOT A LAB TO DO...

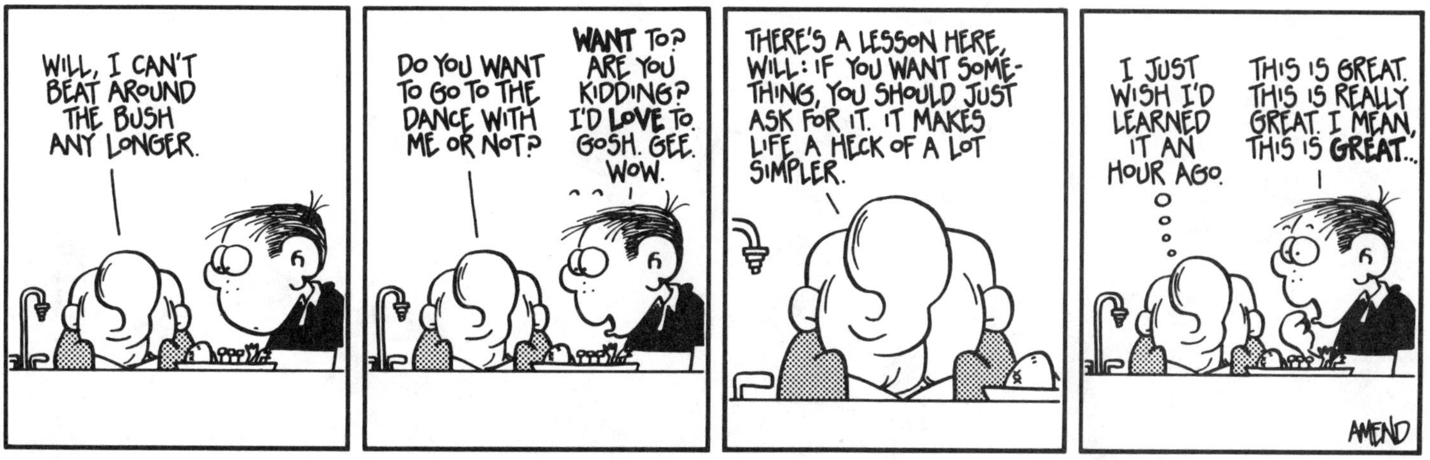
WILL, I CAN'T BEAT AROUND THE BUSH ANY LONGER.
DO YOU WANT TO GO TO THE DANCE WITH ME OR NOT?
WANT TO? ARE YOU KIDDING? I'D **LOVE** TO. GOSH. GEE. WOW.
THERE'S A LESSON HERE, WILL: IF YOU WANT SOMETHING, YOU SHOULD JUST ASK FOR IT. IT MAKES LIFE A HECK OF A LOT SIMPLER.
I JUST WISH I'D LEARNED IT AN HOUR AGO.
THIS IS GREAT. THIS IS REALLY GREAT. I MEAN, THIS IS **GREAT**...
AMEND

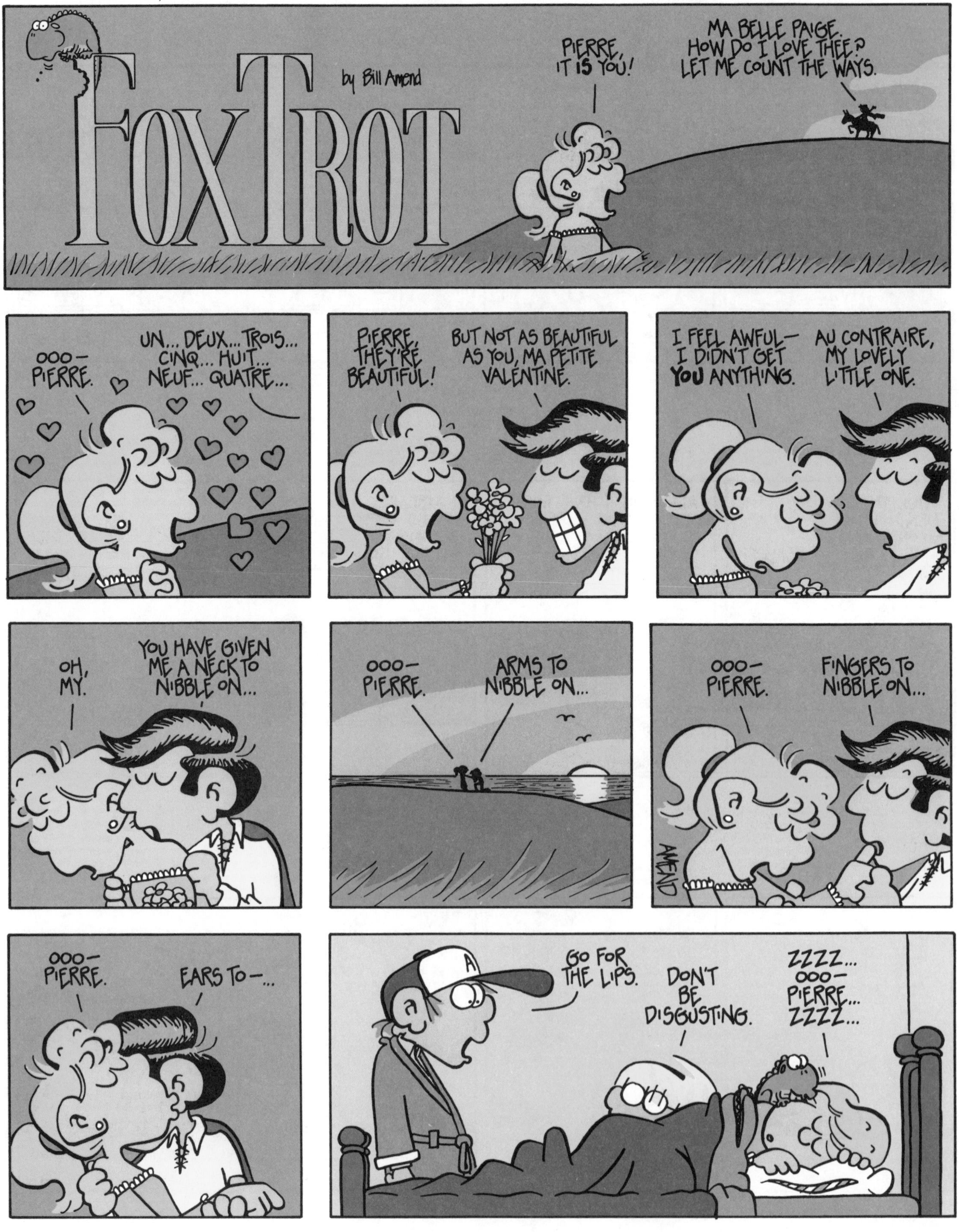
FoxTrot
by Bill Amend
PIERRE, IT **IS** YOU!
MA BELLE PAIGE. HOW DO I LOVE THEE? LET ME COUNT THE WAYS.
OOO— PIERRE.
UN... DEUX... TROIS... CINQ... HUIT... NEUF... QUATRE...
PIERRE, THEY'RE BEAUTIFUL!
BUT NOT AS BEAUTIFUL AS YOU, MA PETITE VALENTINE.
I FEEL AWFUL— I DIDN'T GET **YOU** ANYTHING.
AU CONTRAIRE, MY LOVELY LITTLE ONE.
OH, MY.
YOU HAVE GIVEN ME A NECK TO NIBBLE ON...
OOO— PIERRE.
ARMS TO NIBBLE ON...
OOO— PIERRE.
FINGERS TO NIBBLE ON...
AMEND
OOO— PIERRE.
EARS TO—...
GO FOR THE LIPS.
DON'T BE DISGUSTING.
ZZZZ... OOO— PIERRE... ZZZZ...

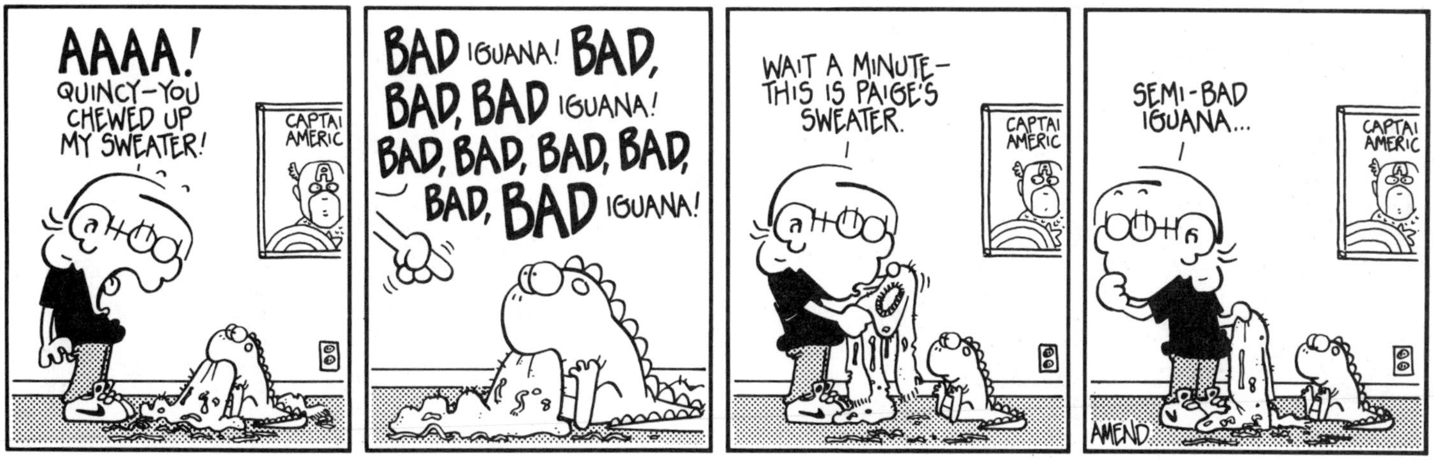
AAAA! QUINCY—YOU CHEWED UP MY SWEATER!
CAPTAI AMERIC
BAD IGUANA! BAD, BAD, BAD IGUANA! BAD, BAD, BAD, BAD, BAD, BAD IGUANA!
WAIT A MINUTE— THIS IS PAIGE'S SWEATER.
SEMI-BAD IGUANA...
AMEND

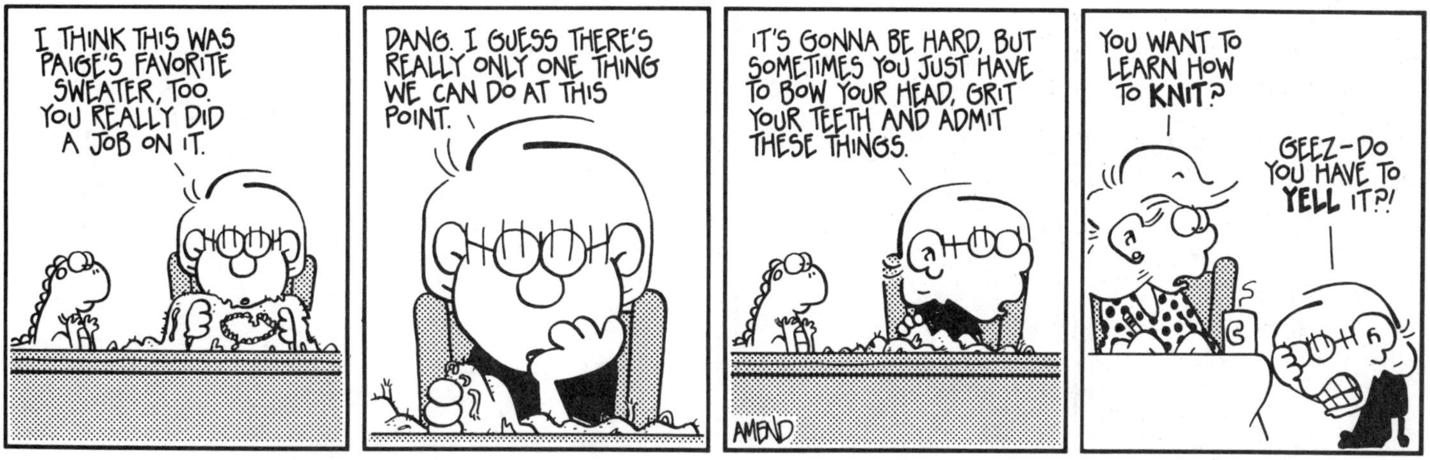
I THINK THIS WAS PAIGE'S FAVORITE SWEATER, TOO. YOU REALLY DID A JOB ON IT.
DANG. I GUESS THERE'S REALLY ONLY ONE THING WE CAN DO AT THIS POINT.
IT'S GONNA BE HARD, BUT SOMETIMES YOU JUST HAVE TO BOW YOUR HEAD, GRIT YOUR TEETH AND ADMIT THESE THINGS.
AMEND
YOU WANT TO LEARN HOW TO **KNIT**?
GEEZ—DO YOU HAVE TO **YELL** IT?!

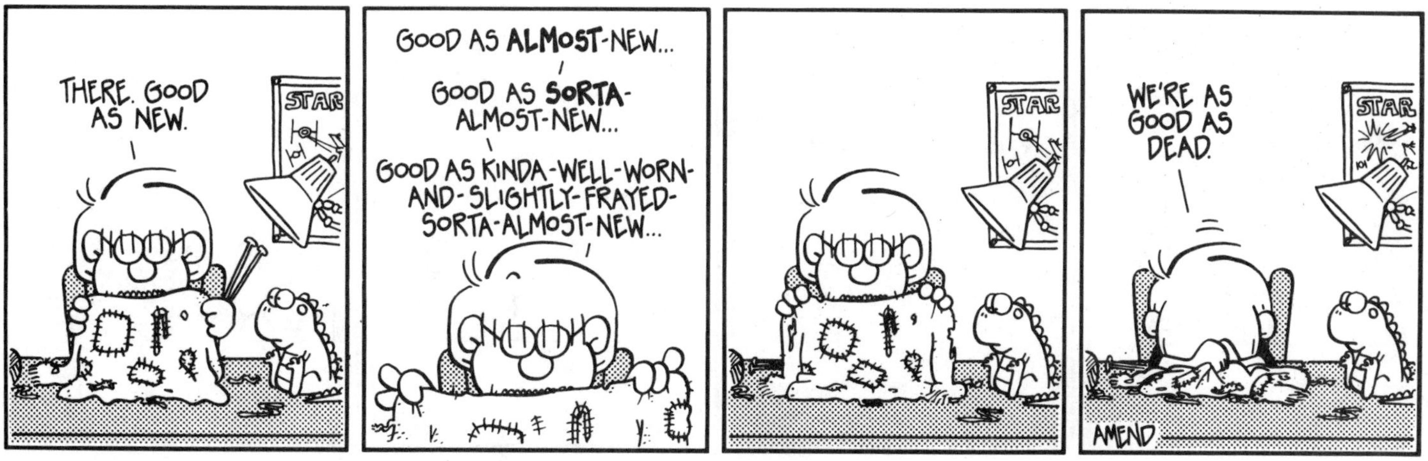
THERE. GOOD AS NEW.
STAR
GOOD AS **ALMOST**-NEW...
GOOD AS **SORTA**-ALMOST-NEW...
GOOD AS KINDA-WELL-WORN-AND-SLIGHTLY-FRAYED-SORTA-ALMOST-NEW...
WE'RE AS GOOD AS DEAD.
AMEND

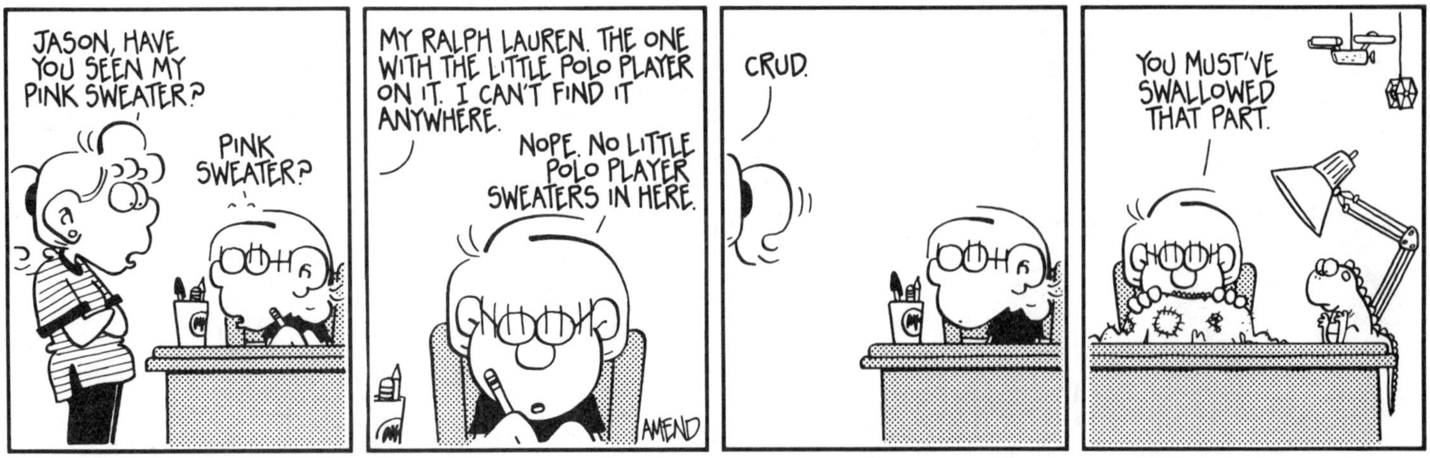
JASON, HAVE YOU SEEN MY PINK SWEATER?
PINK SWEATER?
MY RALPH LAUREN. THE ONE WITH THE LITTLE POLO PLAYER ON IT. I CAN'T FIND IT ANYWHERE.
NOPE. NO LITTLE POLO PLAYER SWEATERS IN HERE.
AMEND
CRUD.
YOU MUST'VE SWALLOWED THAT PART.

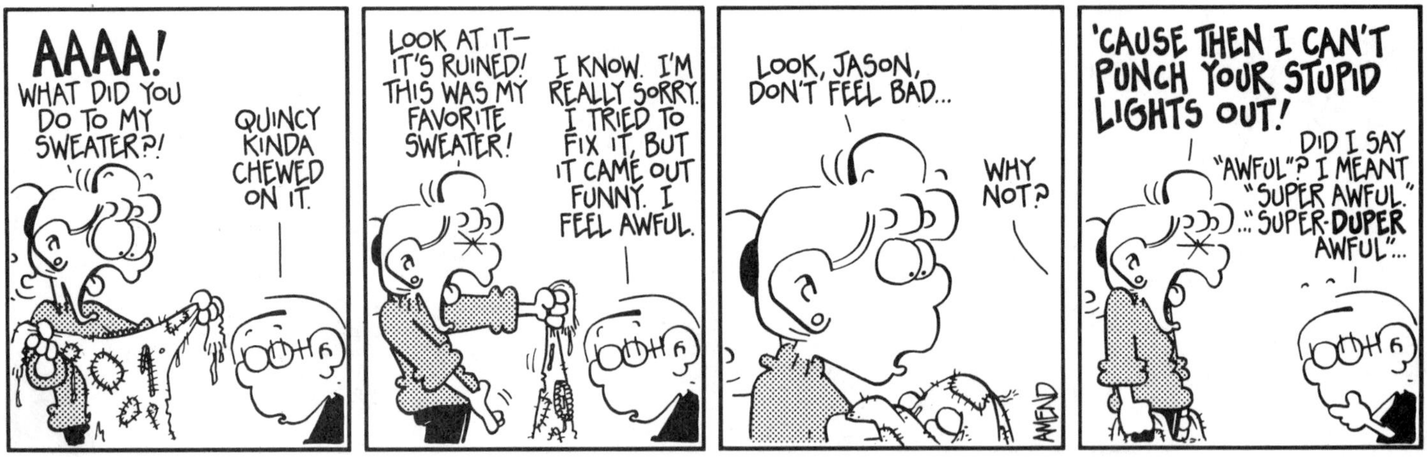
AAAA!
WHAT DID YOU DO TO MY SWEATER?!
QUINCY KINDA CHEWED ON IT.
LOOK AT IT— IT'S RUINED! THIS WAS MY FAVORITE SWEATER!
I KNOW. I'M REALLY SORRY. I TRIED TO FIX IT, BUT IT CAME OUT FUNNY. I FEEL AWFUL.
LOOK, JASON, DON'T FEEL BAD...
WHY NOT?
AMEND
'CAUSE THEN I CAN'T PUNCH YOUR STUPID LIGHTS OUT!
DID I SAY "AWFUL"? I MEANT "SUPER AWFUL."... "SUPER-DUPER AWFUL"...

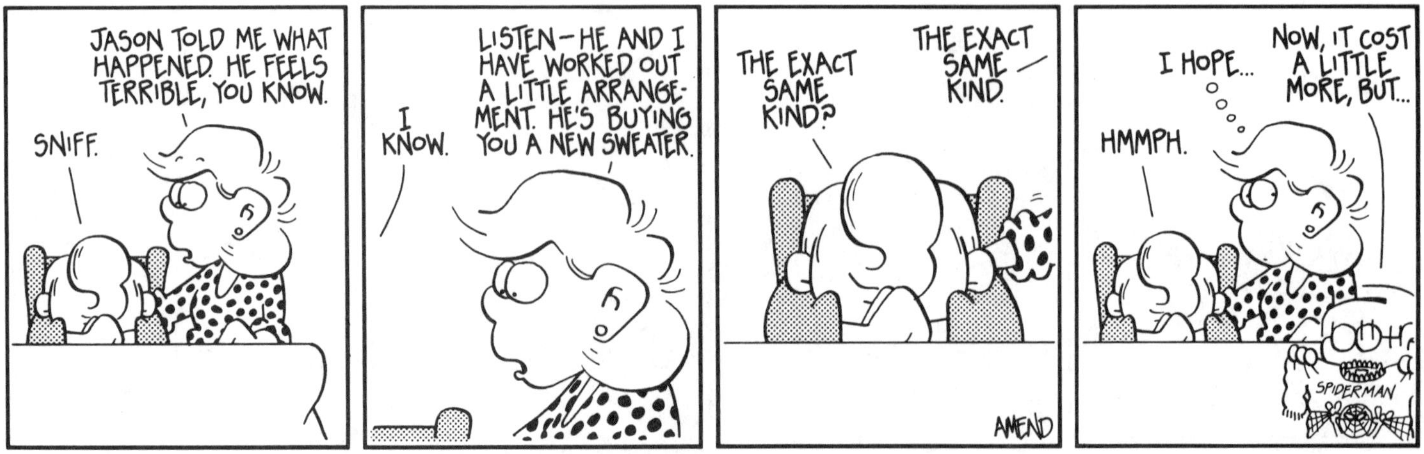
JASON TOLD ME WHAT HAPPENED. HE FEELS TERRIBLE, YOU KNOW.
SNIFF.
I KNOW.
LISTEN—HE AND I HAVE WORKED OUT A LITTLE ARRANGEMENT. HE'S BUYING YOU A NEW SWEATER.
THE EXACT SAME KIND?
THE EXACT SAME KIND.
AMEND
I HOPE...
NOW, IT COST A LITTLE MORE, BUT...
HMMPH.
SPIDERMAN

by Bill Amend

FoxTrot

LET'S SEE... DO I WANT HEAT-SEEKING MISSILES OR A NUCLEAR-POWERED X-RAY LASER?

DESIGNING A HOUSE CAN BE SO CONFUSING.

WHAT **ARE** YOU DOING?

DRAWING UP BLUE-PRINTS FOR THE MANSION I'M GOING TO BUILD SOMEDAY. I'M CALLING IT JASON MANOR.

OF COURSE.

I FIGURE I'LL SAVE TIME BY PLANNING IT OUT NOW.

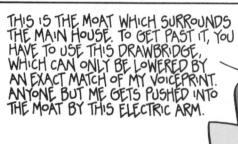

THIS IS THE MOAT WHICH SURROUNDS THE MAIN HOUSE. TO GET PAST IT, YOU HAVE TO USE THIS DRAWBRIDGE, WHICH CAN ONLY BE LOWERED BY AN EXACT MATCH OF MY VOICEPRINT. ANYONE BUT ME GETS PUSHED INTO THE MOAT BY THIS ELECTRIC ARM.

AMEND

THIS IS THE FRONT HALL. ANYONE BUT ME FALLS THROUGH A TRAPDOOR AND SLIDES DOWN A CHUTE INTO THE MOAT. THIS IS THE STAIRCASE. FOR ANYONE BUT ME, IT TURNS INTO A RAMP AND SENDS THEM TUMBLING OUT THE FRONT DOOR AND INTO THE MOAT.

THIS IS THE TV ROOM. ALL THE CHAIRS ARE TUNED TO MY EXACT WEIGHT. ANYONE BUT ME IS EJECTED THROUGH THE SKYLIGHT, OVER THE HOUSE, AND INTO THE MOAT. THIS IS THE KITCHEN—...

JASON, THIS IS RIDICULOUS! WHAT IF, FOR INSTANCE, I COME OVER TO VISIT?

WHOOPS—I HADN'T THOUGHT OF THAT...

TONING DOWN THE BOOBY TRAPS?

PUTTING SHARKS IN THE MOAT.

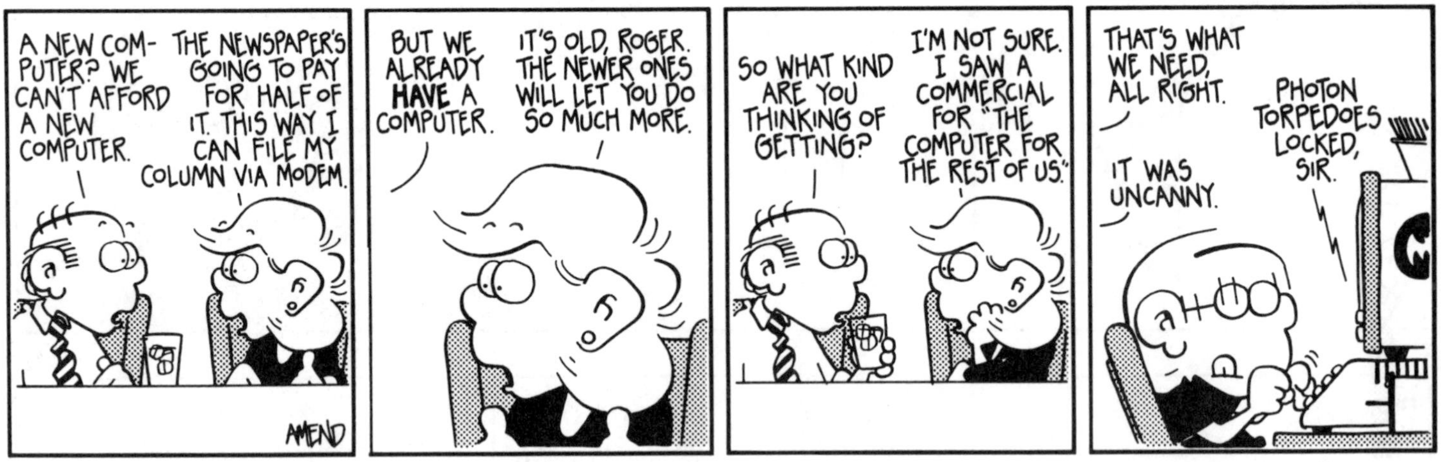
A NEW COMPUTER? WE CAN'T AFFORD A NEW COMPUTER.
THE NEWSPAPER'S GOING TO PAY FOR HALF OF IT. THIS WAY I CAN FILE MY COLUMN VIA MODEM.
AMEND
BUT WE ALREADY **HAVE** A COMPUTER.
IT'S OLD, ROGER. THE NEWER ONES WILL LET YOU DO SO MUCH MORE.
SO WHAT KIND ARE YOU THINKING OF GETTING?
I'M NOT SURE. I SAW A COMMERCIAL FOR "THE COMPUTER FOR THE REST OF US."
THAT'S WHAT WE NEED, ALL RIGHT.
IT WAS UNCANNY.
PHOTON TORPEDOES LOCKED, SIR.

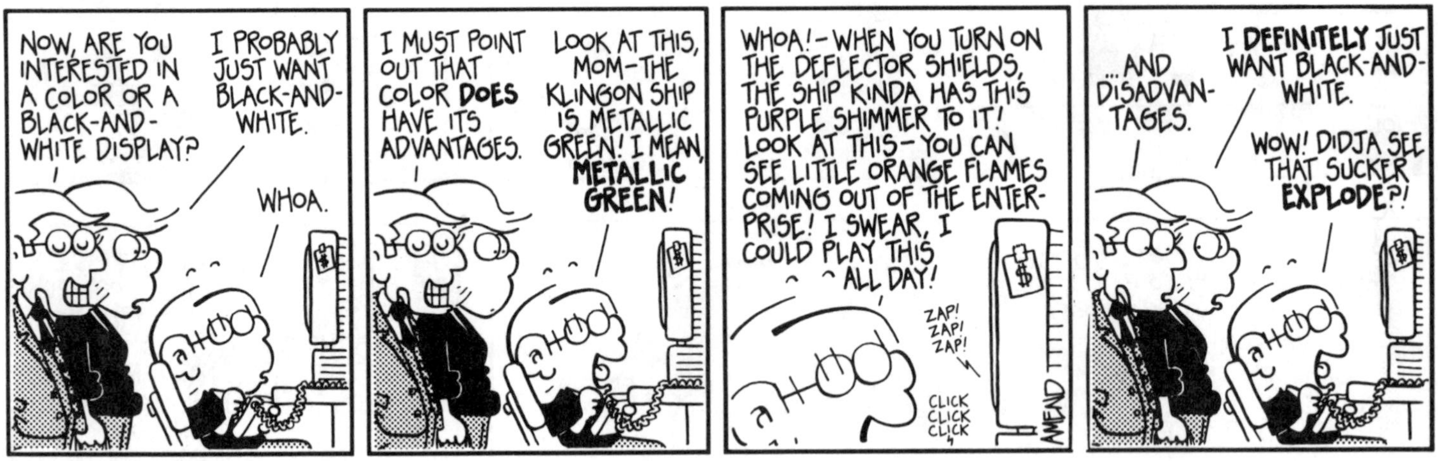
NOW, ARE YOU INTERESTED IN A COLOR OR A BLACK-AND-WHITE DISPLAY?
I PROBABLY JUST WANT BLACK-AND-WHITE.
WHOA.
I MUST POINT OUT THAT COLOR **DOES** HAVE ITS ADVANTAGES.
LOOK AT THIS, MOM—THE KLINGON SHIP IS METALLIC GREEN! I MEAN, **METALLIC GREEN**!
WHOA!—WHEN YOU TURN ON THE DEFLECTOR SHIELDS, THE SHIP KINDA HAS THIS PURPLE SHIMMER TO IT! LOOK AT THIS—YOU CAN SEE LITTLE ORANGE FLAMES COMING OUT OF THE ENTERPRISE! I SWEAR, I COULD PLAY THIS ALL DAY!
ZAP! ZAP! ZAP!
CLICK CLICK CLICK
AMEND
...AND DISADVANTAGES.
I **DEFINITELY** JUST WANT BLACK-AND-WHITE.
WOW! DIDJA SEE THAT SUCKER **EXPLODE**?!

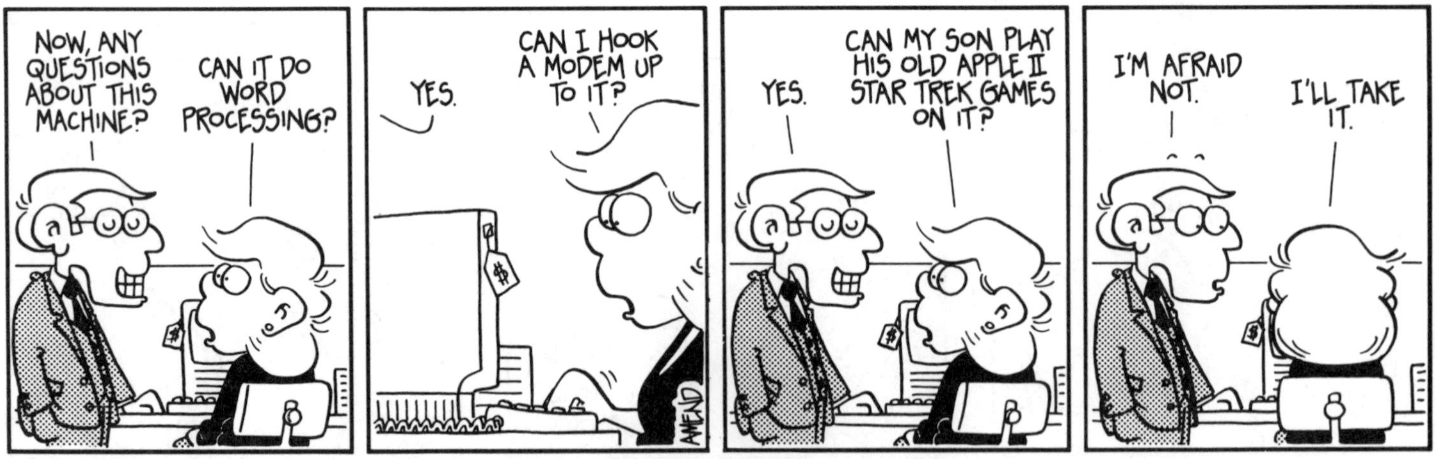
NOW, ANY QUESTIONS ABOUT THIS MACHINE?
CAN IT DO WORD PROCESSING?
YES.
CAN I HOOK A MODEM UP TO IT?
AMEND
YES.
CAN MY SON PLAY HIS OLD APPLE II STAR TREK GAMES ON IT?
I'M AFRAID NOT.
I'LL TAKE IT.

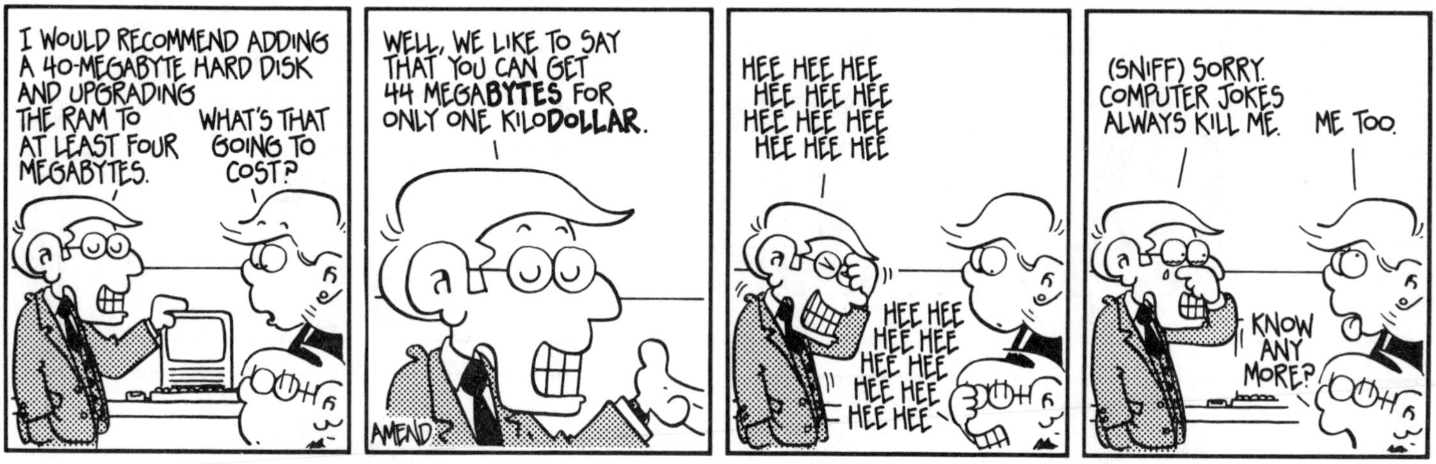
I WOULD RECOMMEND ADDING A 40-MEGABYTE HARD DISK AND UPGRADING THE RAM TO AT LEAST FOUR MEGABYTES.
WHAT'S THAT GOING TO COST?
WELL, WE LIKE TO SAY THAT YOU CAN GET 44 MEGABYTES FOR ONLY ONE KILODOLLAR.
AMEND
HEE HEE HEE HEE HEE HEE HEE HEE HEE HEE HEE HEE
HEE HEE HEE HEE HEE HEE HEE HEE HEE HEE
(SNIFF) SORRY. COMPUTER JOKES ALWAYS KILL ME.
ME TOO.
KNOW ANY MORE?

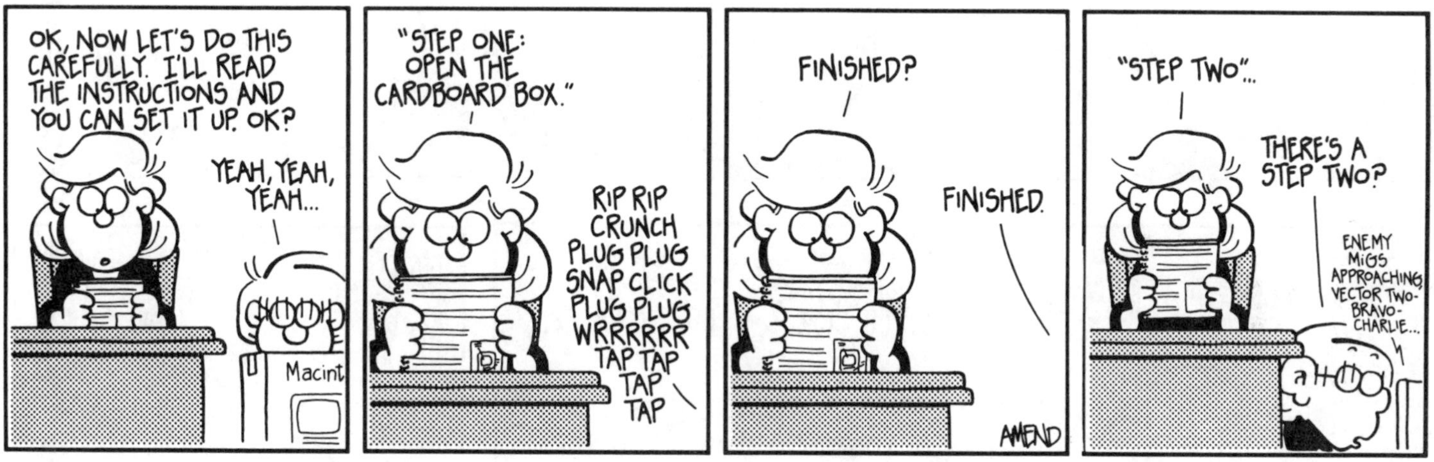
OK, NOW LET'S DO THIS CAREFULLY. I'LL READ THE INSTRUCTIONS AND YOU CAN SET IT UP. OK?
YEAH, YEAH, YEAH...
Macint
"STEP ONE: OPEN THE CARDBOARD BOX."
RIP RIP CRUNCH PLUG PLUG SNAP CLICK PLUG PLUG WRRRRRR TAP TAP TAP TAP
FINISHED?
FINISHED.
AMEND
"STEP TWO"...
THERE'S A STEP TWO?
ENEMY MIGS APPROACHING. VECTOR TWO-BRAVO-CHARLIE...

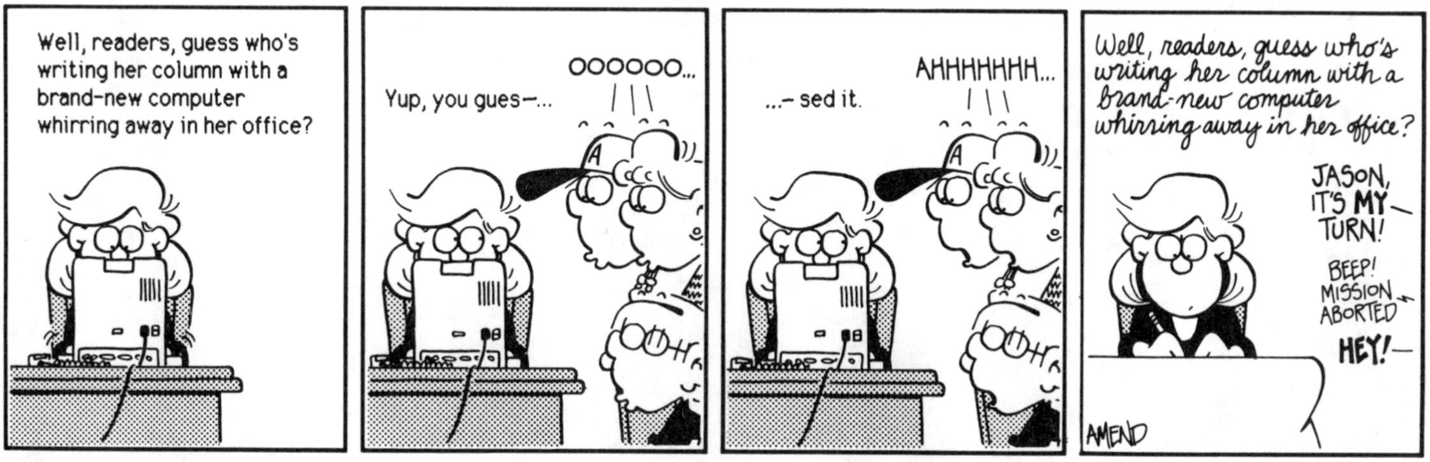
Well, readers, guess who's writing her column with a brand-new computer whirring away in her office?
Yup, you gues—...
OOOOOO...
...–sed it.
AHHHHHHH...
Well, readers, guess who's writing her column with a brand-new computer whirring away in her office?
JASON, IT'S MY TURN!
BEEP! MISSION ABORTED
HEY!
AMEND

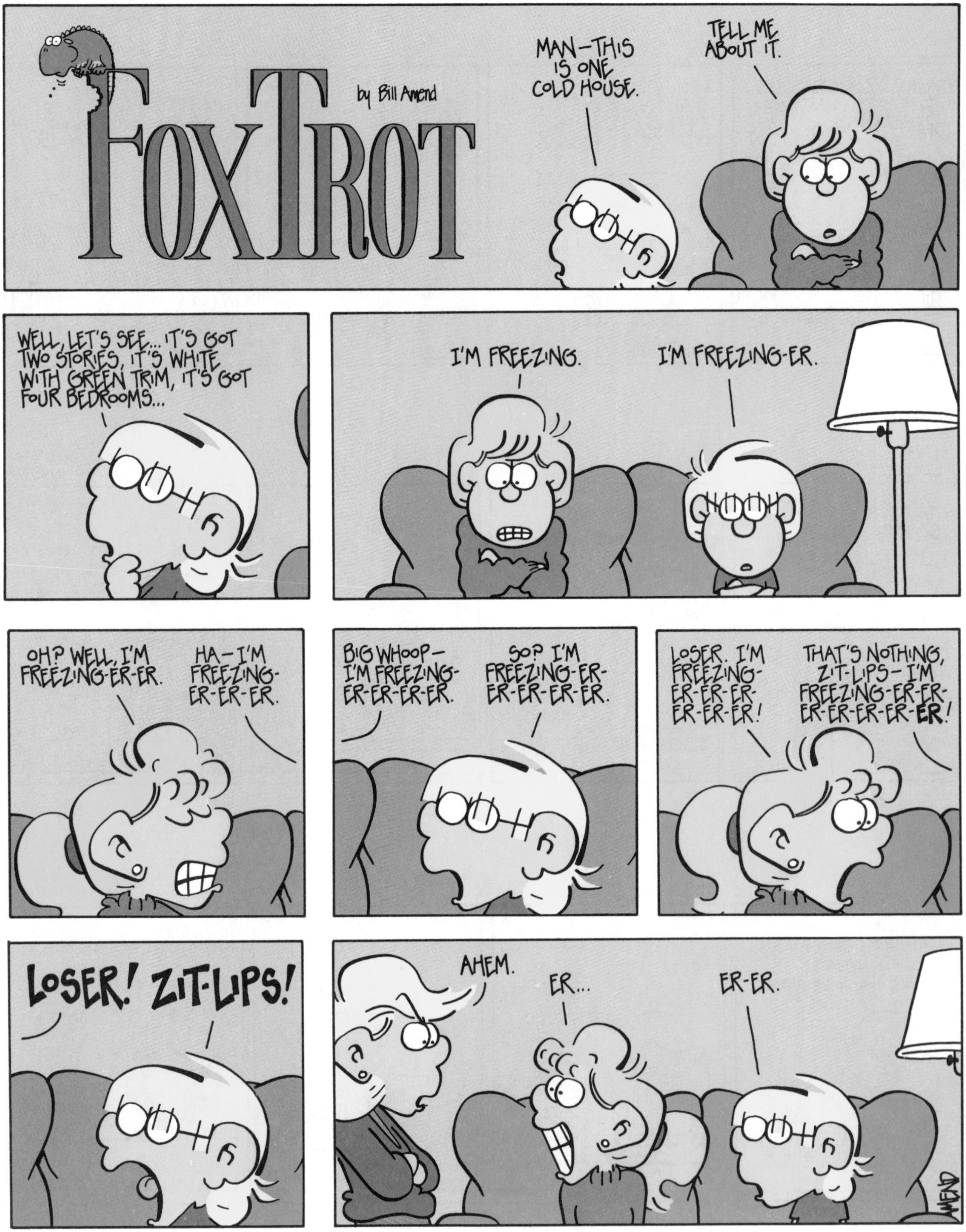
FoxTrot
by Bill Amend
MAN—THIS IS ONE COLD HOUSE.
TELL ME ABOUT IT.
WELL, LET'S SEE... IT'S GOT TWO STORIES, IT'S WHITE WITH GREEN TRIM, IT'S GOT FOUR BEDROOMS...
I'M FREEZING.
I'M FREEZING-ER.
OH? WELL, I'M FREEZING-ER-ER.
HA—I'M FREEZING-ER-ER-ER.
BIG WHOOP—I'M FREEZING-ER-ER-ER-ER.
SO? I'M FREEZING-ER-ER-ER-ER-ER.
LOSER. I'M FREEZING-ER-ER-ER-ER-ER-ER!
THAT'S NOTHING, ZIT-LIPS—I'M FREEZING-ER-ER-ER-ER-ER-ER-**ER**!
LOSER! ZIT-LIPS!
AHEM.
ER...
ER-ER.
AMEND

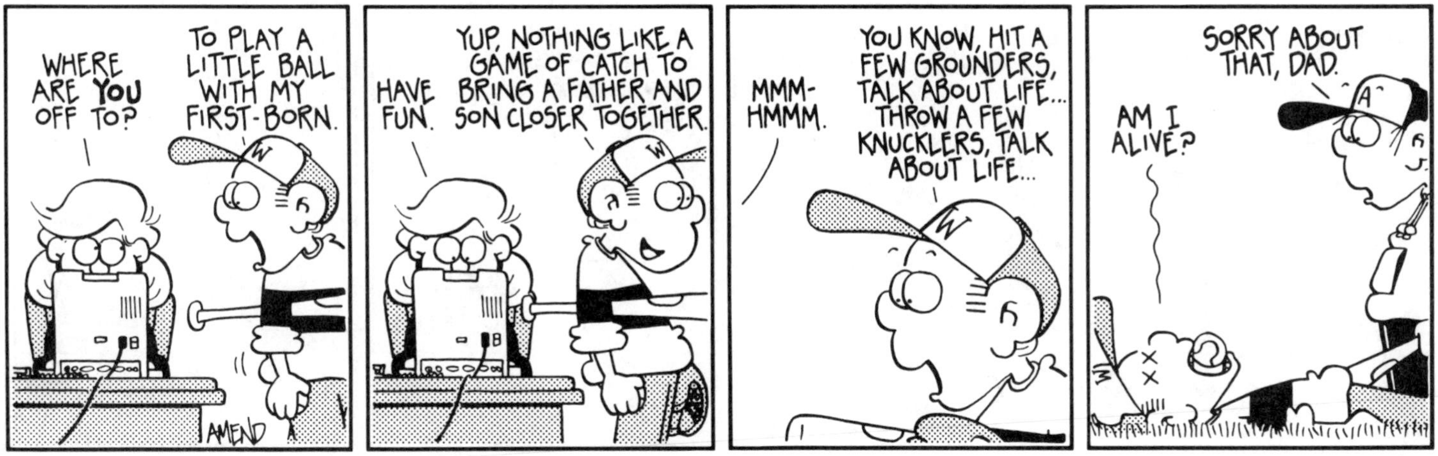
WHERE ARE **YOU** OFF TO?
TO PLAY A LITTLE BALL WITH MY FIRST-BORN.
HAVE FUN.
YUP, NOTHING LIKE A GAME OF CATCH TO BRING A FATHER AND SON CLOSER TOGETHER.
MMM-HMMM.
YOU KNOW, HIT A FEW GROUNDERS, TALK ABOUT LIFE... THROW A FEW KNUCKLERS, TALK ABOUT LIFE...
SORRY ABOUT THAT, DAD.
AM I ALIVE?
AMEND

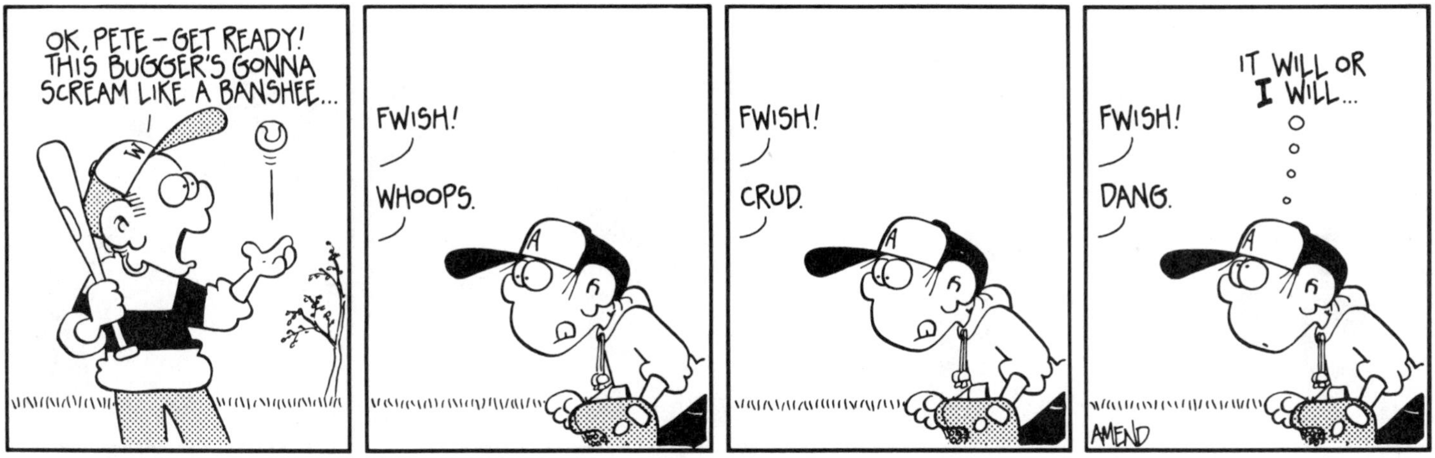
OK, PETE – GET READY! THIS BUGGER'S GONNA SCREAM LIKE A BANSHEE...
FWISH!
WHOOPS.
FWISH!
CRUD.
FWISH!
DANG.
IT WILL OR **I** WILL...
AMEND

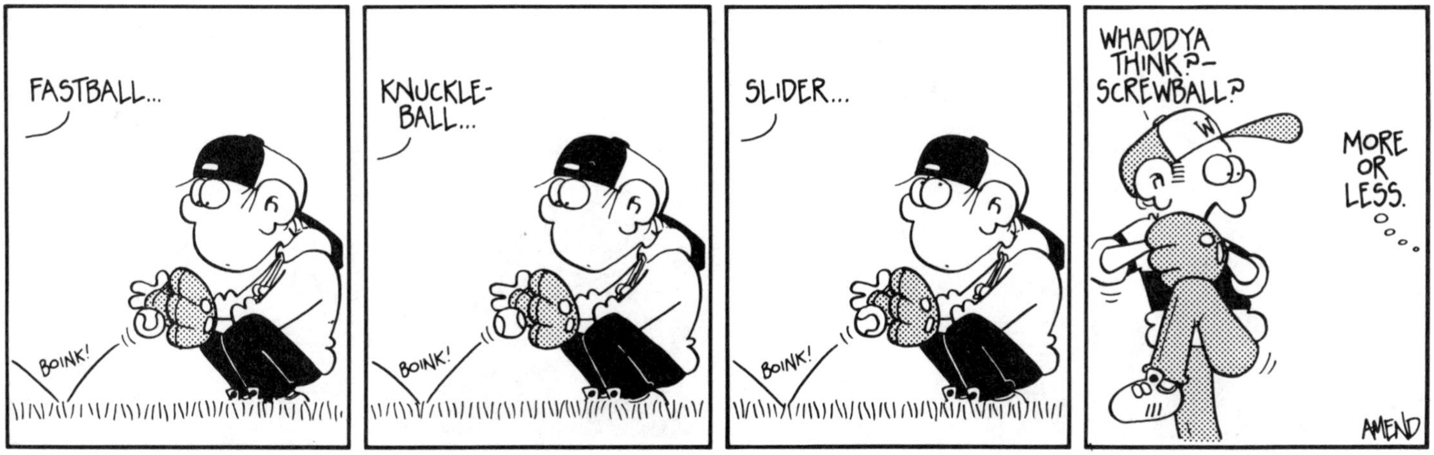
FASTBALL...
BOINK!
KNUCKLE-BALL...
BOINK!
SLIDER...
BOINK!
WHADDYA THINK?– SCREWBALL?
MORE OR LESS.
AMEND

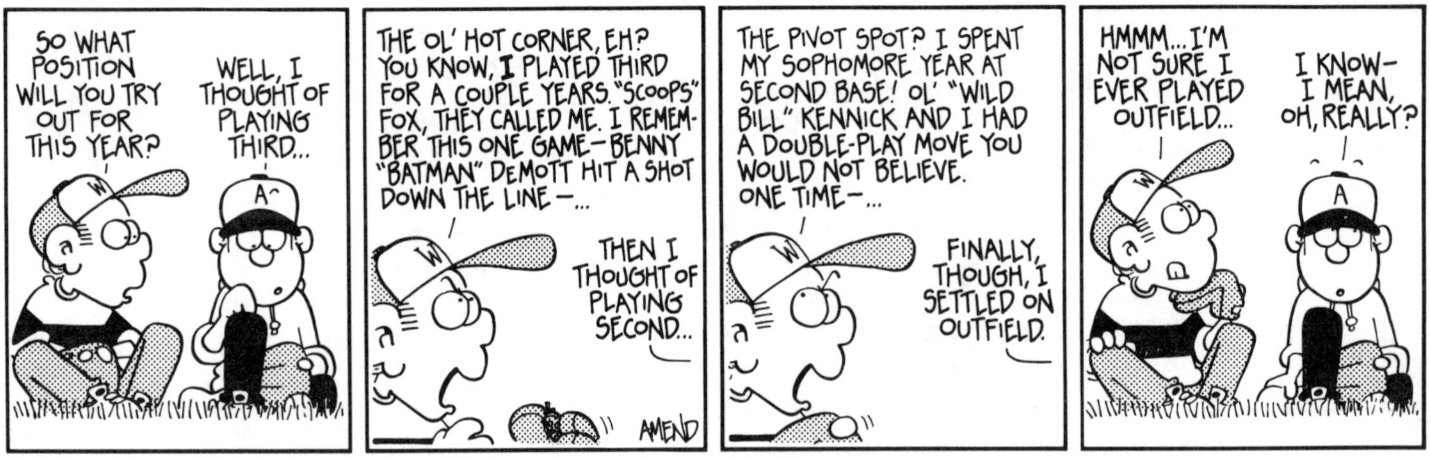
SO WHAT POSITION WILL YOU TRY OUT FOR THIS YEAR?
WELL, I THOUGHT OF PLAYING THIRD...
THE OL' HOT CORNER, EH? YOU KNOW, I PLAYED THIRD FOR A COUPLE YEARS. "SCOOPS" FOX, THEY CALLED ME. I REMEMBER THIS ONE GAME—BENNY "BATMAN" DEMOTT HIT A SHOT DOWN THE LINE—...
THEN I THOUGHT OF PLAYING SECOND...
AMEND
THE PIVOT SPOT? I SPENT MY SOPHOMORE YEAR AT SECOND BASE! OL' "WILD BILL" KENNICK AND I HAD A DOUBLE-PLAY MOVE YOU WOULD NOT BELIEVE. ONE TIME—...
FINALLY, THOUGH, I SETTLED ON OUTFIELD.
HMMM... I'M NOT SURE I EVER PLAYED OUTFIELD...
I KNOW—I MEAN, OH, REALLY?

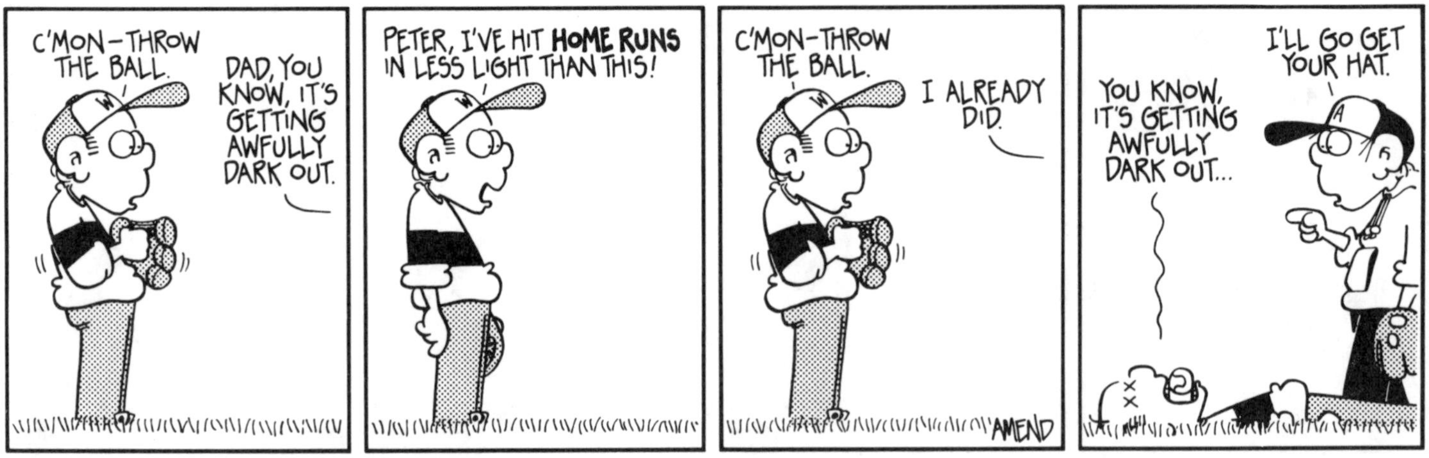
C'MON—THROW THE BALL.
DAD, YOU KNOW, IT'S GETTING AWFULLY DARK OUT.
PETER, I'VE HIT **HOME RUNS** IN LESS LIGHT THAN THIS!
C'MON—THROW THE BALL.
I ALREADY DID.
AMEND
YOU KNOW, IT'S GETTING AWFULLY DARK OUT...
I'LL GO GET YOUR HAT.

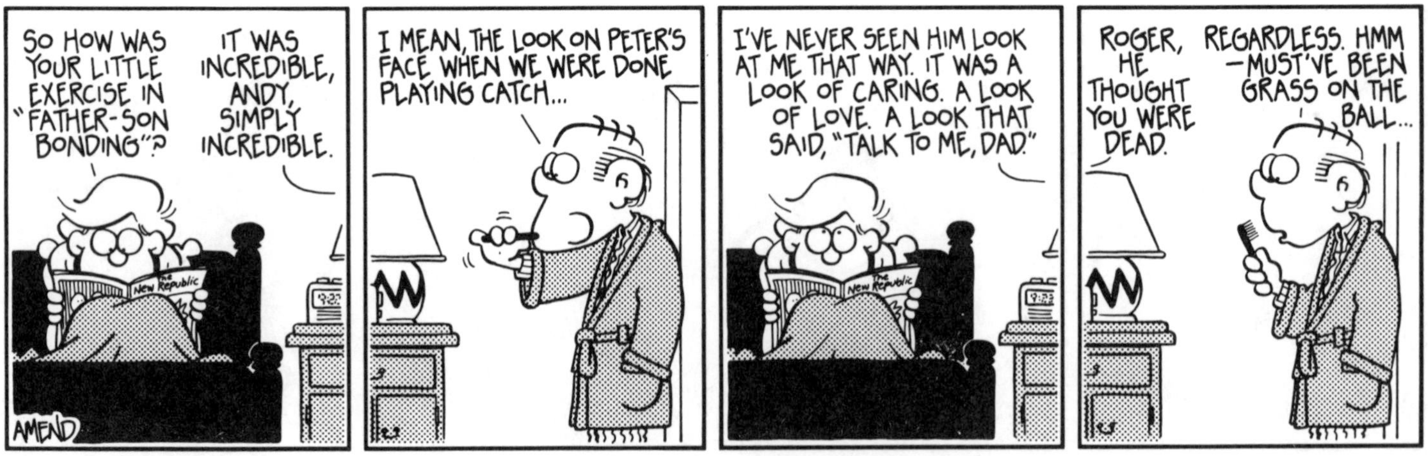
SO HOW WAS YOUR LITTLE EXERCISE IN "FATHER-SON BONDING"?
IT WAS INCREDIBLE, ANDY, SIMPLY INCREDIBLE.
AMEND
I MEAN, THE LOOK ON PETER'S FACE WHEN WE WERE DONE PLAYING CATCH...
I'VE NEVER SEEN HIM LOOK AT ME THAT WAY. IT WAS A LOOK OF CARING. A LOOK OF LOVE. A LOOK THAT SAID, "TALK TO ME, DAD."
ROGER, HE THOUGHT YOU WERE DEAD.
REGARDLESS. HMM—MUST'VE BEEN GRASS ON THE BALL...

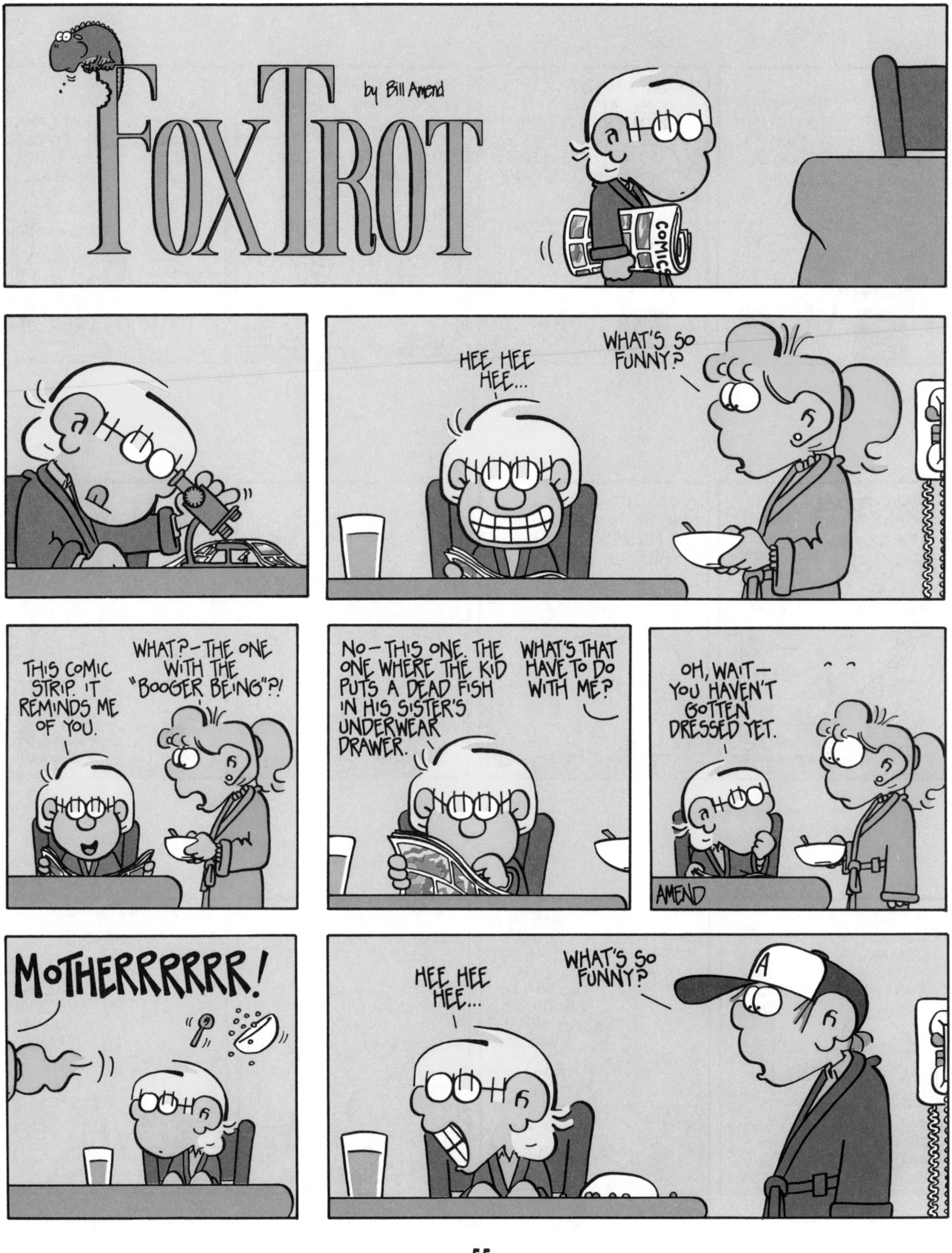
FoxTrot
by Bill Amend
COMICS
HEE HEE HEE...
WHAT'S SO FUNNY?
THIS COMIC STRIP. IT REMINDS ME OF YOU.
WHAT?– THE ONE WITH THE "BOOGER BEING"?!
NO– THIS ONE. THE ONE WHERE THE KID PUTS A DEAD FISH IN HIS SISTER'S UNDERWEAR DRAWER.
WHAT'S THAT HAVE TO DO WITH ME?
OH, WAIT– YOU HAVEN'T GOTTEN DRESSED YET.
AMEND
MOTHERRRRRR!
HEE HEE HEE...
WHAT'S SO FUNNY?

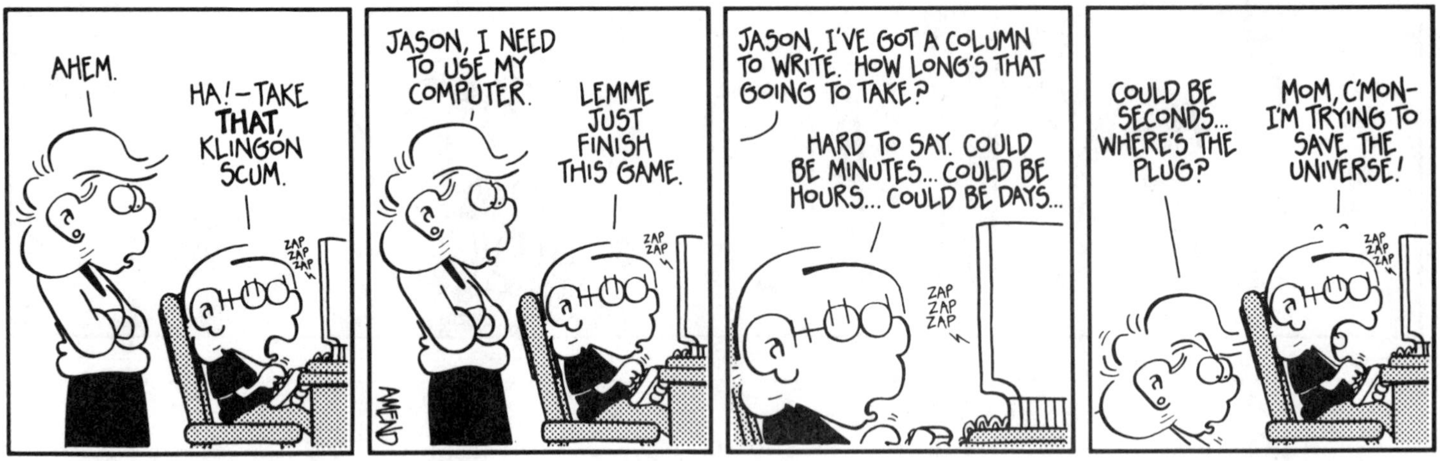
AHEM.
HA! –TAKE **THAT**, KLINGON SCUM.
ZAP ZAP ZAP
JASON, I NEED TO USE MY COMPUTER.
LEMME JUST FINISH THIS GAME.
ZAP ZAP
AMEND
JASON, I'VE GOT A COLUMN TO WRITE. HOW LONG'S THAT GOING TO TAKE?
HARD TO SAY. COULD BE MINUTES... COULD BE HOURS... COULD BE DAYS...
ZAP ZAP ZAP
MOM, C'MON– I'M TRYING TO SAVE THE UNIVERSE!
COULD BE SECONDS... WHERE'S THE PLUG?
ZAP ZAP ZAP

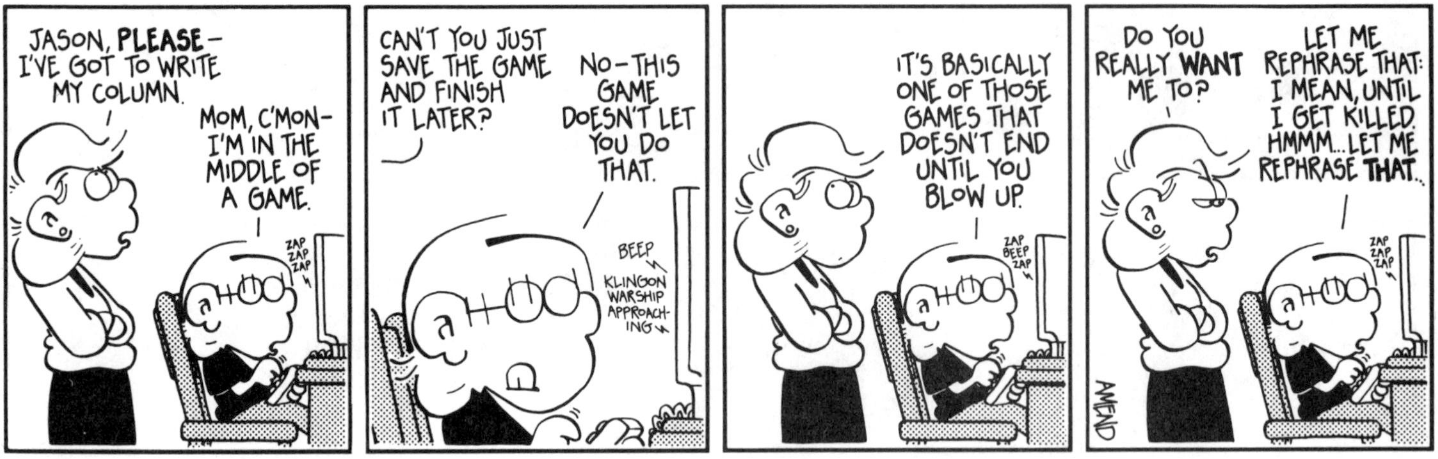
JASON, **PLEASE**– I'VE GOT TO WRITE MY COLUMN.
MOM, C'MON– I'M IN THE MIDDLE OF A GAME.
ZAP ZAP ZAP
CAN'T YOU JUST SAVE THE GAME AND FINISH IT LATER?
NO–THIS GAME DOESN'T LET YOU DO THAT.
BEEP
KLINGON WARSHIP APPROACHING
IT'S BASICALLY ONE OF THOSE GAMES THAT DOESN'T END UNTIL YOU BLOW UP.
ZAP BEEP ZAP
DO YOU REALLY **WANT** ME TO?
LET ME REPHRASE THAT: I MEAN, UNTIL I GET KILLED. HMMM... LET ME REPHRASE **THAT**...
ZAP ZAP ZAP
AMEND

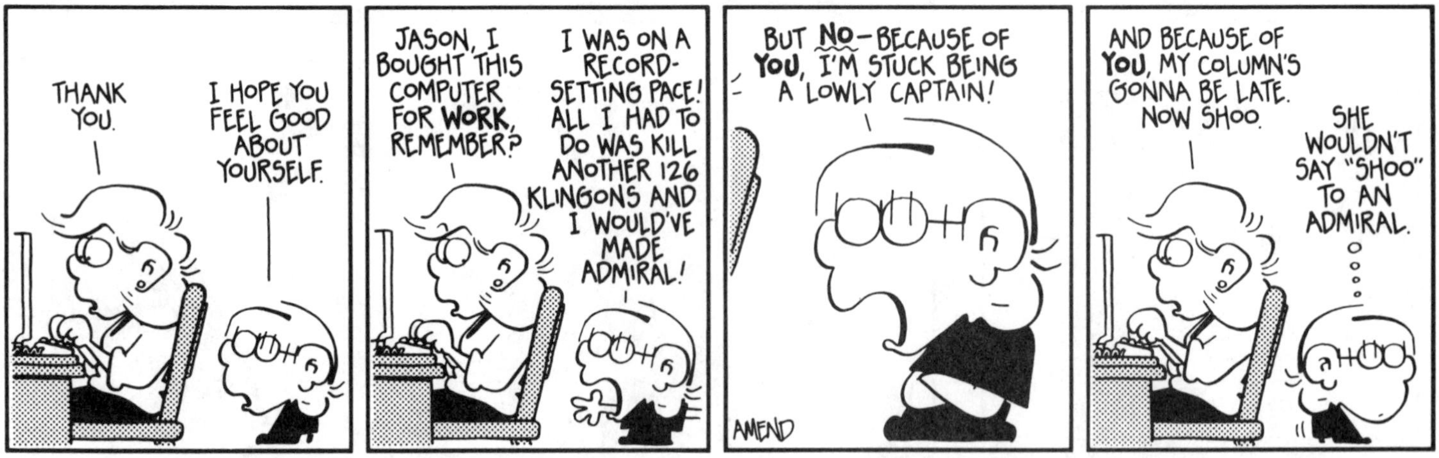
THANK YOU.
I HOPE YOU FEEL GOOD ABOUT YOURSELF.
JASON, I BOUGHT THIS COMPUTER FOR **WORK**, REMEMBER?
I WAS ON A RECORD-SETTING PACE! ALL I HAD TO DO WAS KILL ANOTHER 126 KLINGONS AND I WOULD'VE MADE ADMIRAL!
BUT NO– BECAUSE OF **YOU**, I'M STUCK BEING A LOWLY CAPTAIN!
AMEND
AND BECAUSE OF **YOU**, MY COLUMN'S GONNA BE LATE. NOW SHOO.
SHE WOULDN'T SAY "SHOO" TO AN ADMIRAL.

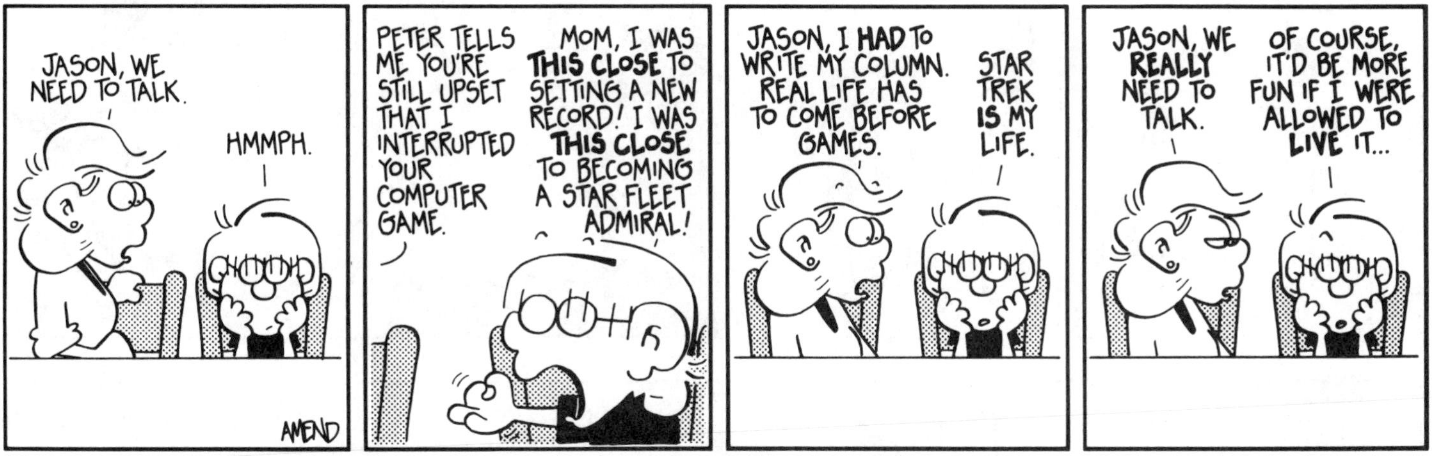
JASON, WE NEED TO TALK.
HMMPH.
PETER TELLS ME YOU'RE STILL UPSET THAT I INTERRUPTED YOUR COMPUTER GAME.
MOM, I WAS THIS CLOSE TO SETTING A NEW RECORD! I WAS THIS CLOSE TO BECOMING A STAR FLEET ADMIRAL!
JASON, I HAD TO WRITE MY COLUMN. REAL LIFE HAS TO COME BEFORE GAMES.
STAR TREK IS MY LIFE.
JASON, WE REALLY NEED TO TALK.
OF COURSE, IT'D BE MORE FUN IF I WERE ALLOWED TO LIVE IT...
AMEND

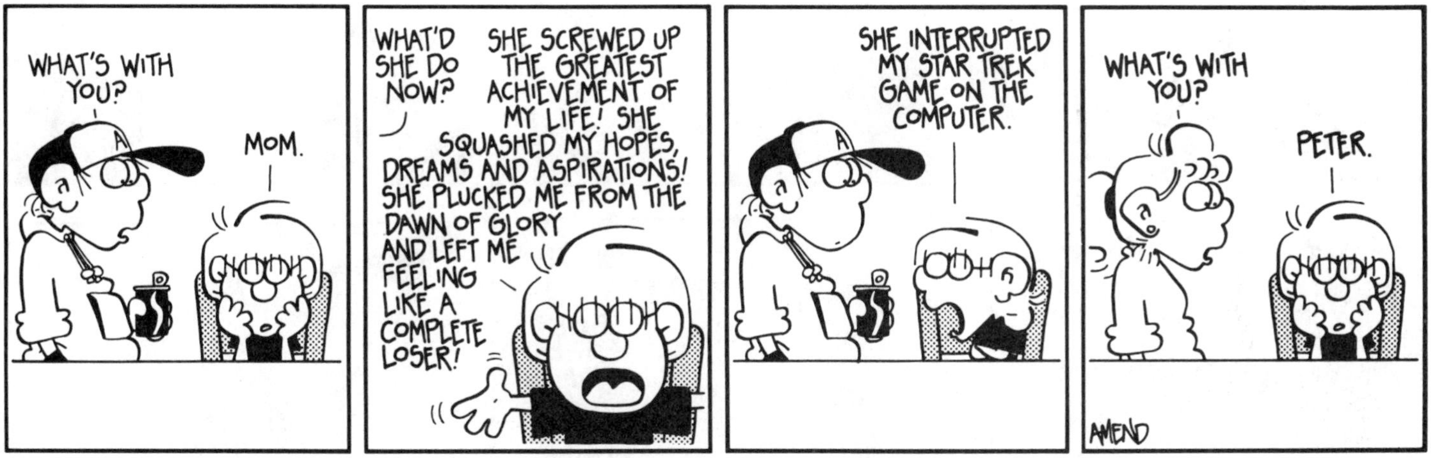
WHAT'S WITH YOU?
MOM.
WHAT'D SHE DO NOW?
SHE SCREWED UP THE GREATEST ACHIEVEMENT OF MY LIFE! SHE SQUASHED MY HOPES, DREAMS AND ASPIRATIONS! SHE PLUCKED ME FROM THE DAWN OF GLORY AND LEFT ME FEELING LIKE A COMPLETE LOSER!
SHE INTERRUPTED MY STAR TREK GAME ON THE COMPUTER.
WHAT'S WITH YOU?
PETER.
AMEND

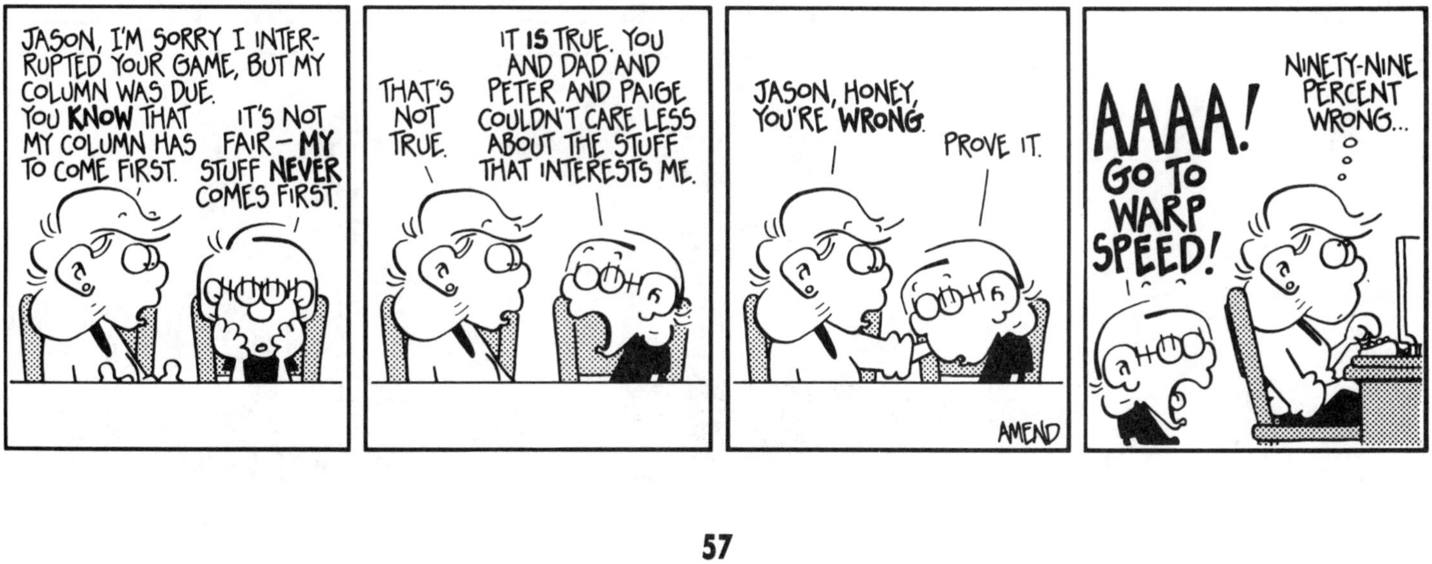
JASON, I'M SORRY I INTERRUPTED YOUR GAME, BUT MY COLUMN WAS DUE. YOU KNOW THAT MY COLUMN HAS TO COME FIRST.
IT'S NOT FAIR—MY STUFF NEVER COMES FIRST.
THAT'S NOT TRUE.
IT IS TRUE. YOU AND DAD AND PETER AND PAIGE COULDN'T CARE LESS ABOUT THE STUFF THAT INTERESTS ME.
JASON, HONEY, YOU'RE WRONG.
PROVE IT.
AMEND
AAAA! GO TO WARP SPEED!
NINETY-NINE PERCENT WRONG...

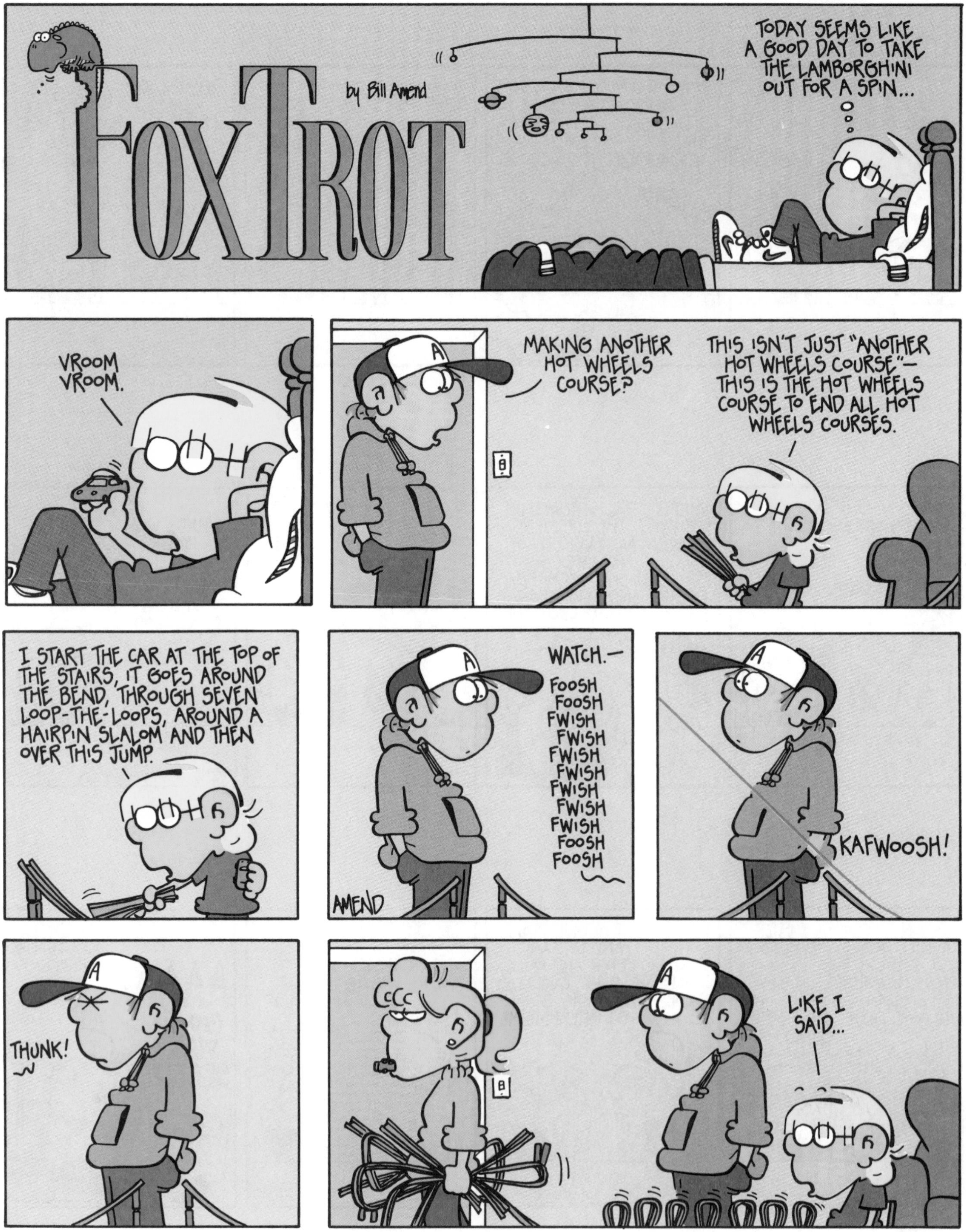
FoxTrot
by Bill Amend
TODAY SEEMS LIKE A GOOD DAY TO TAKE THE LAMBORGHINI OUT FOR A SPIN...
VROOM VROOM.
MAKING ANOTHER HOT WHEELS COURSE?
THIS ISN'T JUST "ANOTHER HOT WHEELS COURSE"— THIS IS THE HOT WHEELS COURSE TO END ALL HOT WHEELS COURSES.
I START THE CAR AT THE TOP OF THE STAIRS, IT GOES AROUND THE BEND, THROUGH SEVEN LOOP-THE-LOOPS, AROUND A HAIRPIN SLALOM AND THEN OVER THIS JUMP.
WATCH.—
FOOSH FOOSH FWISH FWISH FWISH FWISH FWISH FWISH FWISH FOOSH FOOSH
AMEND
KAFWOOSH!
THUNK!
LIKE I SAID...

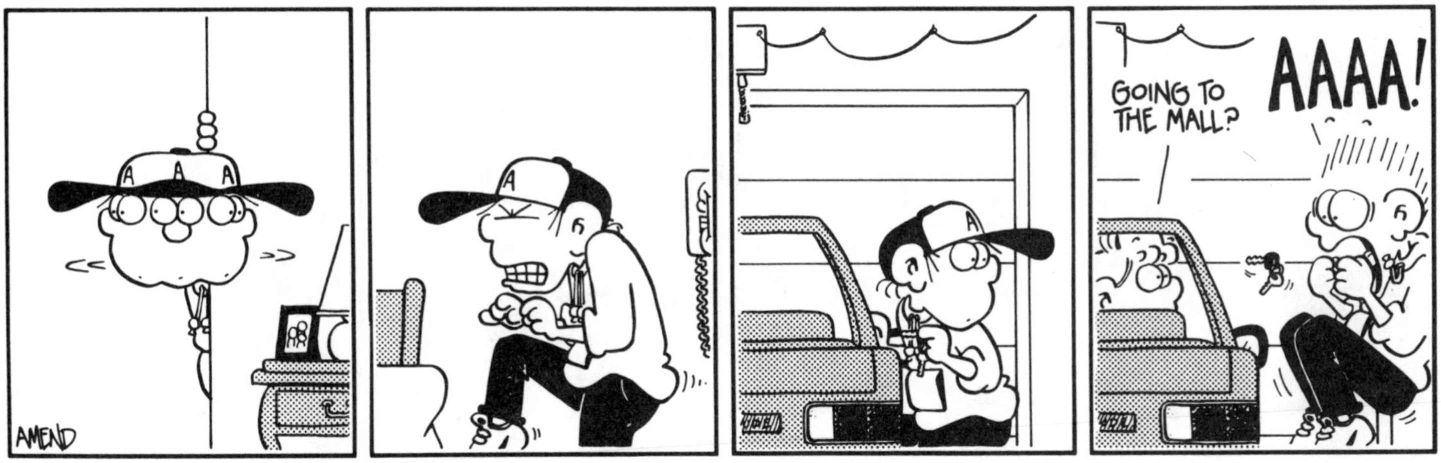
AMEND
GOING TO THE MALL?
AAAA!

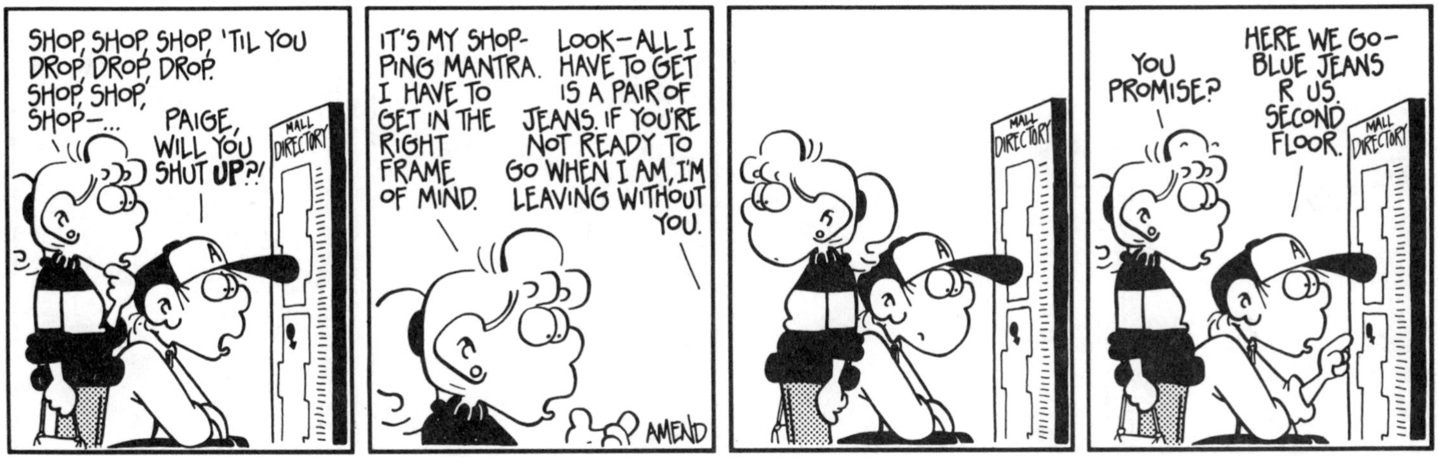
SHOP, SHOP, SHOP, 'TIL YOU DROP, DROP, DROP. SHOP, SHOP, SHOP—...
PAIGE, WILL YOU SHUT **UP**?!
MALL DIRECTORY
IT'S MY SHOPPING MANTRA. I HAVE TO GET IN THE RIGHT FRAME OF MIND.
LOOK—ALL I HAVE TO GET IS A PAIR OF JEANS. IF YOU'RE NOT READY TO GO WHEN I AM, I'M LEAVING WITHOUT YOU.
AMEND
MALL DIRECTORY
YOU PROMISE?
HERE WE GO—BLUE JEANS R US. SECOND FLOOR.
MALL DIRECTORY

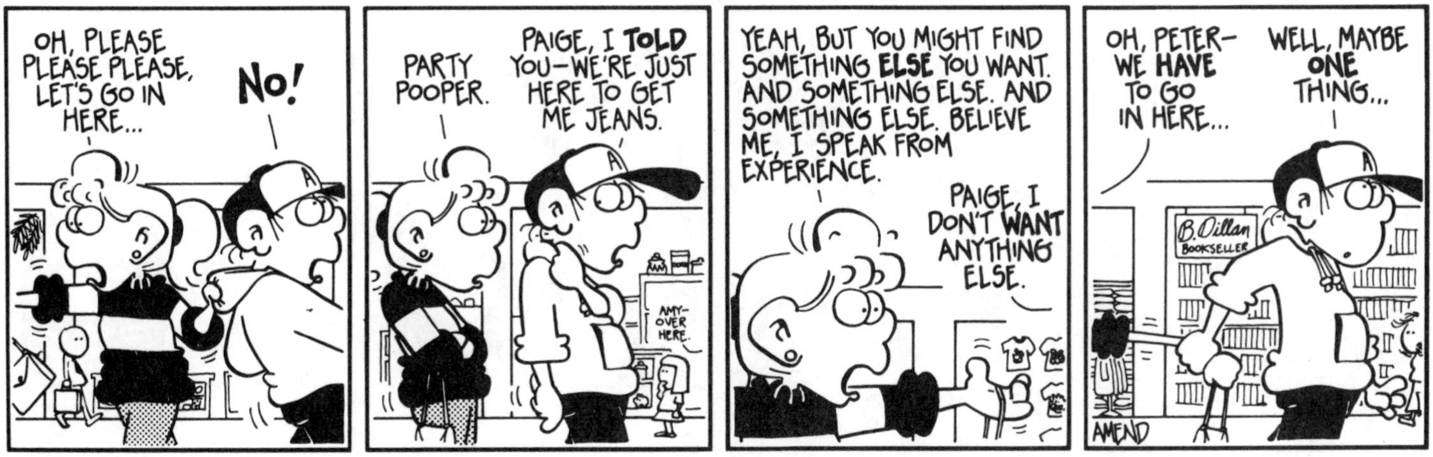
OH, PLEASE PLEASE PLEASE, LET'S GO IN HERE...
No!
PARTY POOPER.
PAIGE, I **TOLD** YOU—WE'RE JUST HERE TO GET ME JEANS.
AMY—OVER HERE.
YEAH, BUT YOU MIGHT FIND SOMETHING **ELSE** YOU WANT. AND SOMETHING ELSE. AND SOMETHING ELSE. BELIEVE ME, I SPEAK FROM EXPERIENCE.
PAIGE, I DON'T **WANT** ANYTHING ELSE.
OH, PETER—WE **HAVE** TO GO IN HERE...
WELL, MAYBE **ONE** THING...
B. Dillan BOOKSELLER
AMEND

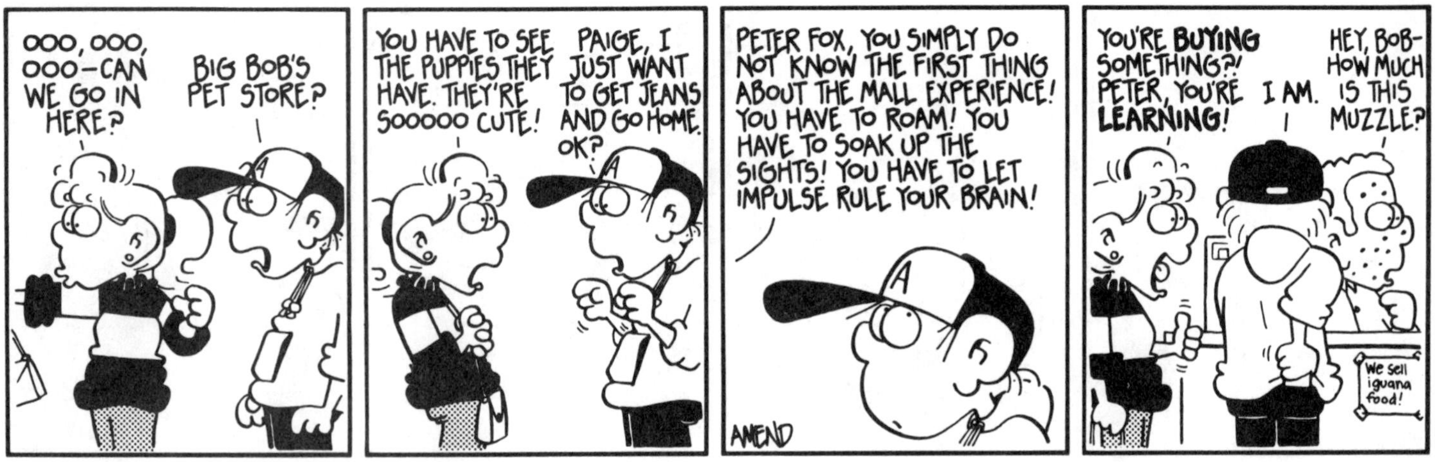
OOO, OOO, OOO—CAN WE GO IN HERE?
BIG BOB'S PET STORE?
YOU HAVE TO SEE THE PUPPIES THEY HAVE. THEY'RE SOOOOO CUTE!
PAIGE, I JUST WANT TO GET JEANS AND GO HOME. OK?
PETER FOX, YOU SIMPLY DO NOT KNOW THE FIRST THING ABOUT THE MALL EXPERIENCE! YOU HAVE TO ROAM! YOU HAVE TO SOAK UP THE SIGHTS! YOU HAVE TO LET IMPULSE RULE YOUR BRAIN!
AMEND
YOU'RE **BUYING** SOMETHING?! PETER, YOU'RE **LEARNING**!
I AM.
HEY, BOB—HOW MUCH IS THIS MUZZLE?
We sell iguana food!

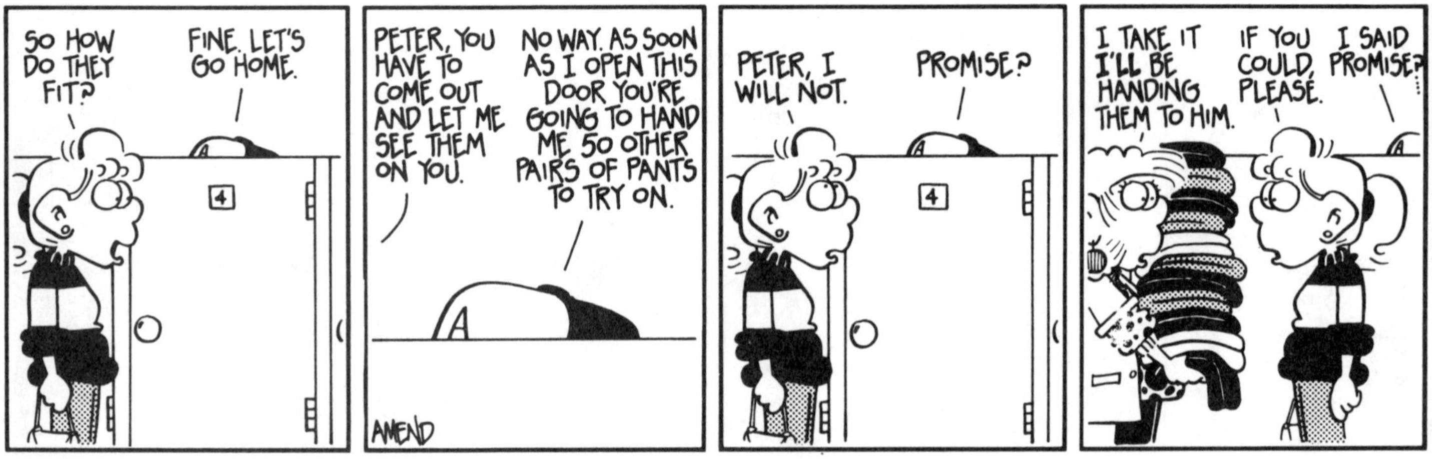
SO HOW DO THEY FIT?
FINE. LET'S GO HOME.
4
PETER, YOU HAVE TO COME OUT AND LET ME SEE THEM ON YOU.
NO WAY. AS SOON AS I OPEN THIS DOOR YOU'RE GOING TO HAND ME 50 OTHER PAIRS OF PANTS TO TRY ON.
AMEND
PETER, I WILL NOT.
PROMISE?
4
I TAKE IT **I'LL** BE HANDING THEM TO HIM.
IF YOU COULD, PLEASE.
I SAID PROMISE?

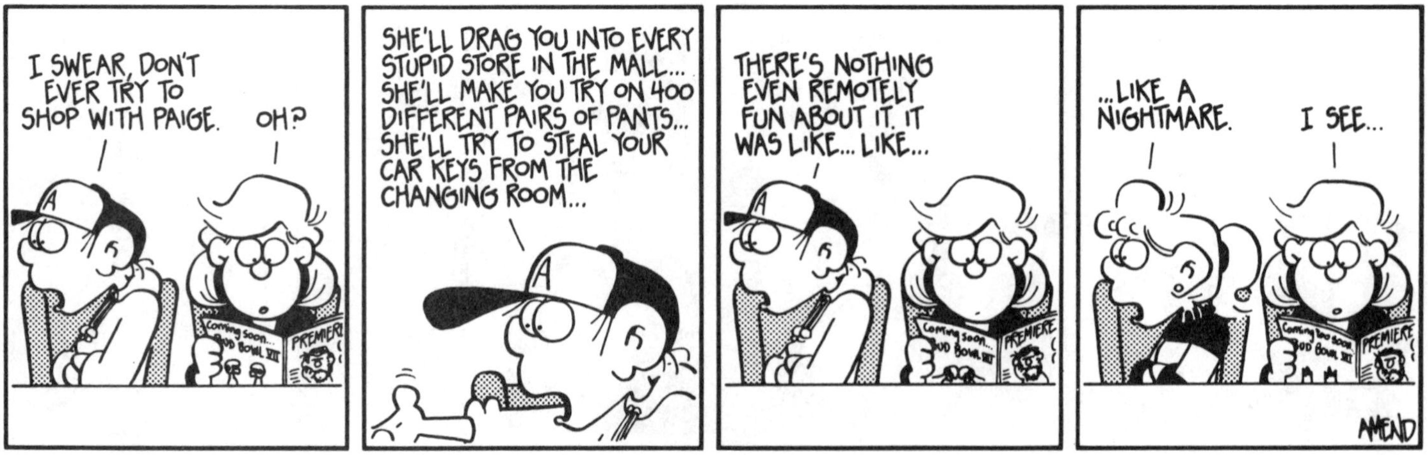
I SWEAR, DON'T EVER TRY TO SHOP WITH PAIGE.
OH?
SHE'LL DRAG YOU INTO EVERY STUPID STORE IN THE MALL... SHE'LL MAKE YOU TRY ON 400 DIFFERENT PAIRS OF PANTS... SHE'LL TRY TO STEAL YOUR CAR KEYS FROM THE CHANGING ROOM...
THERE'S NOTHING EVEN REMOTELY FUN ABOUT IT. IT WAS LIKE... LIKE...
...LIKE A NIGHTMARE.
I SEE...
AMEND

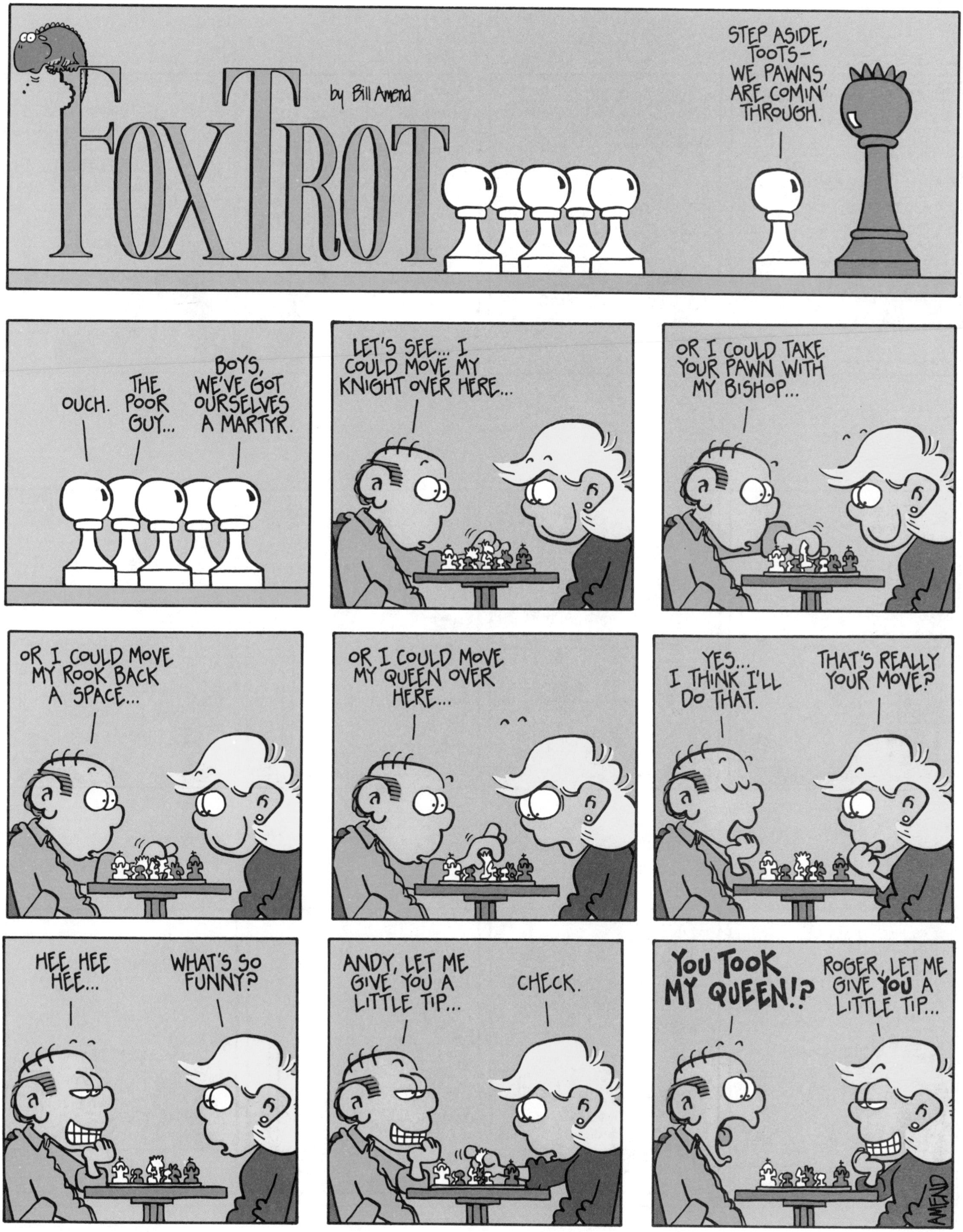
FoxTrot
by Bill Amend
STEP ASIDE, TOOTS– WE PAWNS ARE COMIN' THROUGH.
OUCH.
THE POOR GUY...
BOYS, WE'VE GOT OURSELVES A MARTYR.
LET'S SEE... I COULD MOVE MY KNIGHT OVER HERE...
OR I COULD TAKE YOUR PAWN WITH MY BISHOP...
OR I COULD MOVE MY ROOK BACK A SPACE...
OR I COULD MOVE MY QUEEN OVER HERE...
YES... I THINK I'LL DO THAT.
THAT'S REALLY YOUR MOVE?
HEE HEE HEE...
WHAT'S SO FUNNY?
ANDY, LET ME GIVE YOU A LITTLE TIP...
CHECK.
YOU TOOK MY QUEEN!?
ROGER, LET ME GIVE YOU A LITTLE TIP...
AMEND

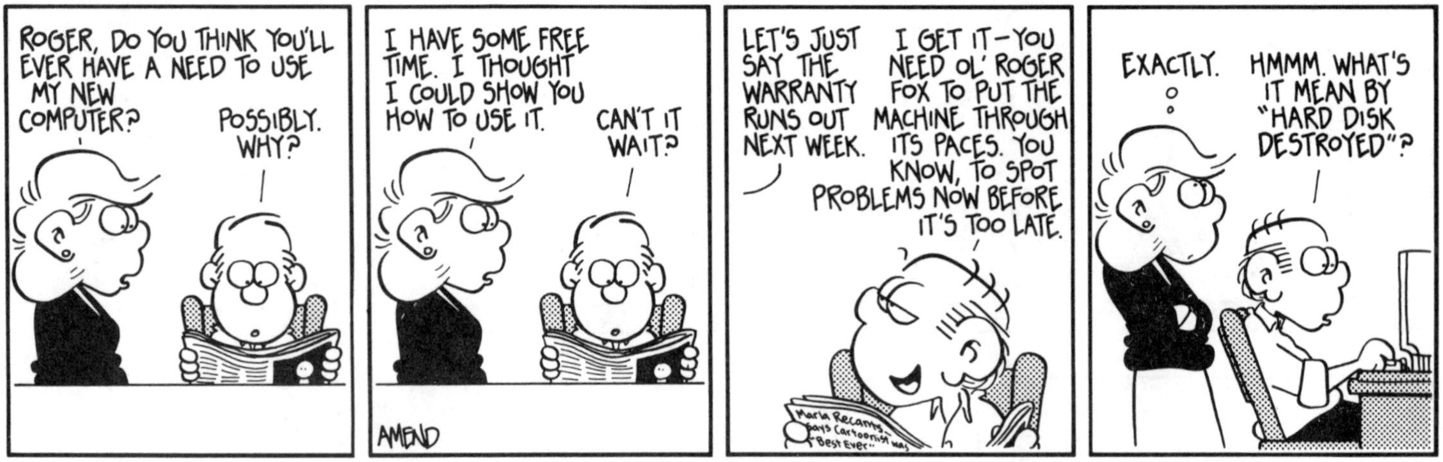
ROGER, DO YOU THINK YOU'LL EVER HAVE A NEED TO USE MY NEW COMPUTER?
POSSIBLY. WHY?
I HAVE SOME FREE TIME. I THOUGHT I COULD SHOW YOU HOW TO USE IT.
CAN'T IT WAIT?
AMEND
LET'S JUST SAY THE WARRANTY RUNS OUT NEXT WEEK.
I GET IT—YOU NEED OL' ROGER FOX TO PUT THE MACHINE THROUGH ITS PACES. YOU KNOW, TO SPOT PROBLEMS NOW BEFORE IT'S TOO LATE.
EXACTLY.
HMMM. WHAT'S IT MEAN BY "HARD DISK DESTROYED"?

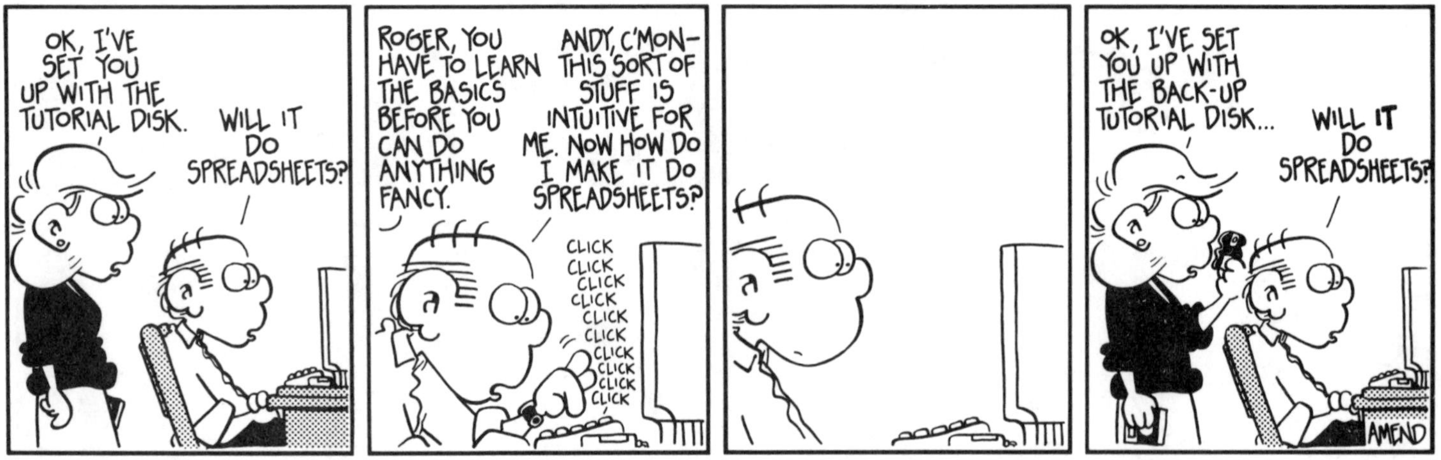
OK, I'VE SET YOU UP WITH THE TUTORIAL DISK.
WILL IT DO SPREADSHEETS?
ROGER, YOU HAVE TO LEARN THE BASICS BEFORE YOU CAN DO ANYTHING FANCY.
ANDY, C'MON—THIS SORT OF STUFF IS INTUITIVE FOR ME. NOW HOW DO I MAKE IT DO SPREADSHEETS?
CLICK CLICK CLICK CLICK CLICK CLICK CLICK CLICK CLICK CLICK
OK, I'VE SET YOU UP WITH THE BACK-UP TUTORIAL DISK...
WILL **IT** DO SPREADSHEETS?
AMEND

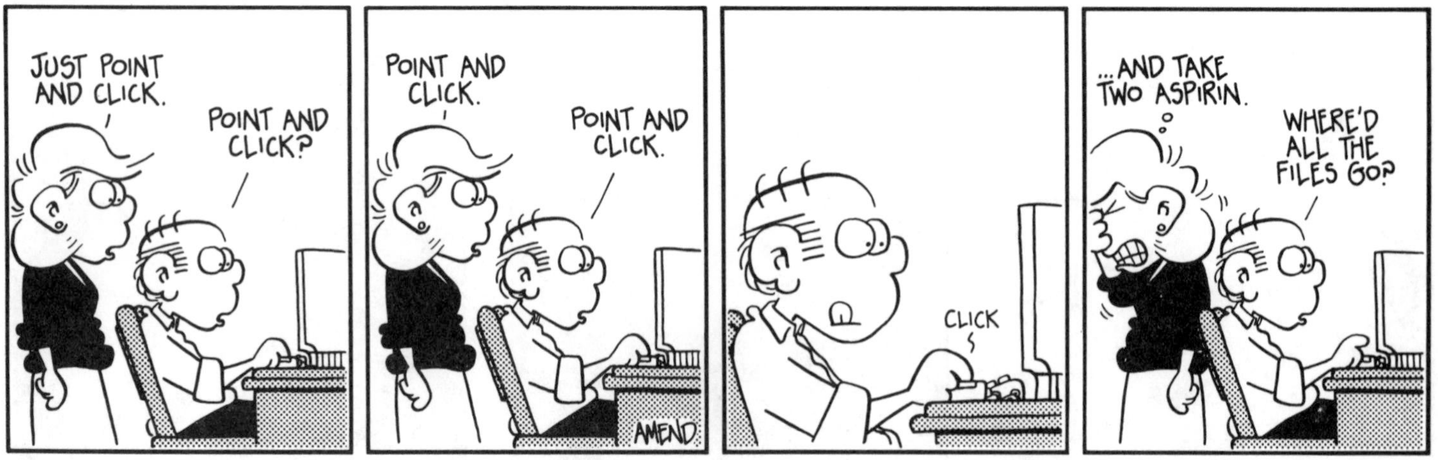
JUST POINT AND CLICK.
POINT AND CLICK?
POINT AND CLICK.
POINT AND CLICK.
AMEND
CLICK
...AND TAKE TWO ASPIRIN.
WHERE'D ALL THE FILES GO?

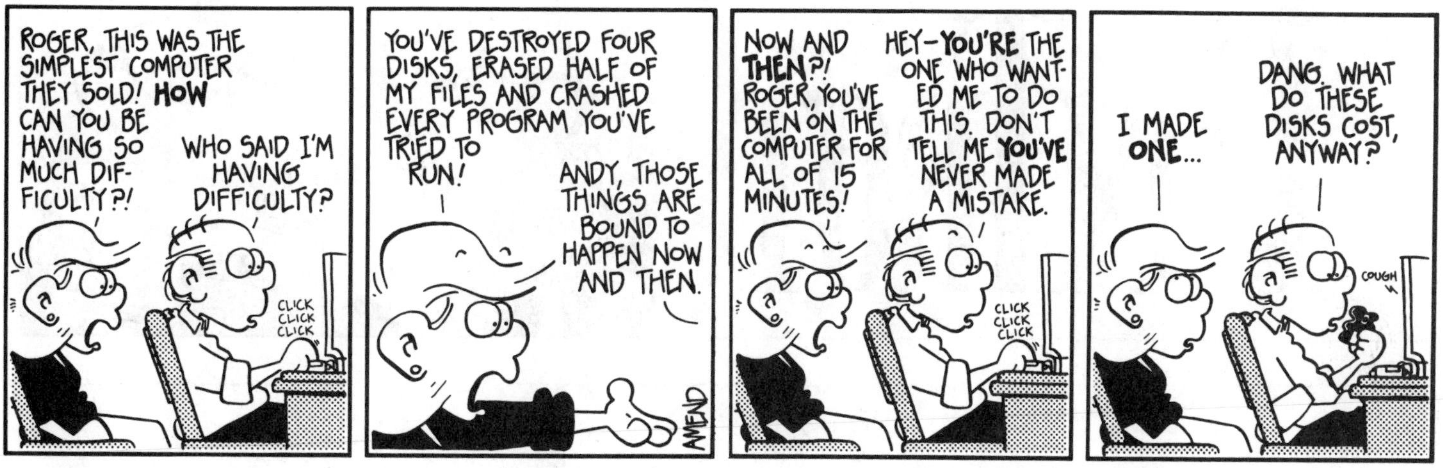
ROGER, THIS WAS THE SIMPLEST COMPUTER THEY SOLD! **HOW** CAN YOU BE HAVING SO MUCH DIFFICULTY?!
WHO SAID I'M HAVING DIFFICULTY?
CLICK CLICK CLICK
YOU'VE DESTROYED FOUR DISKS, ERASED HALF OF MY FILES AND CRASHED EVERY PROGRAM YOU'VE TRIED TO RUN!
ANDY, THOSE THINGS ARE BOUND TO HAPPEN NOW AND THEN.
AMEND
NOW AND **THEN**?! ROGER, YOU'VE BEEN ON THE COMPUTER FOR ALL OF 15 MINUTES!
HEY—**YOU'RE** THE ONE WHO WANTED ME TO DO THIS. DON'T TELL ME **YOU'VE** NEVER MADE A MISTAKE.
CLICK CLICK CLICK
I MADE **ONE**...
DANG. WHAT DO THESE DISKS COST, ANYWAY?
COUGH

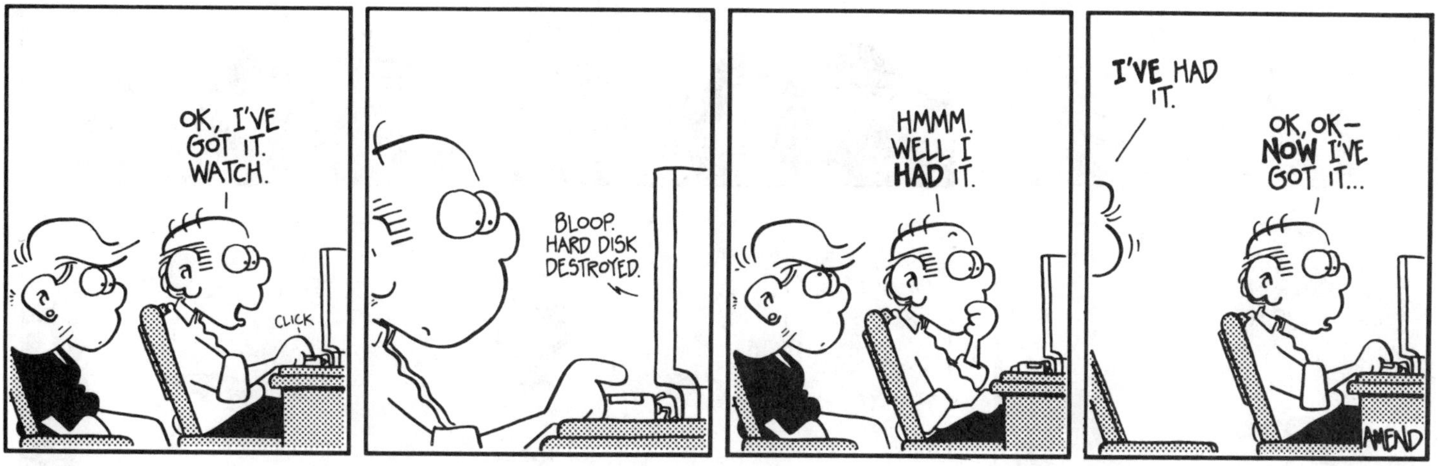
OK, I'VE GOT IT. WATCH.
CLICK
BLOOP. HARD DISK DESTROYED.
HMMM. WELL I **HAD** IT.
I'VE HAD IT.
OK, OK— **NOW** I'VE GOT IT...
AMEND

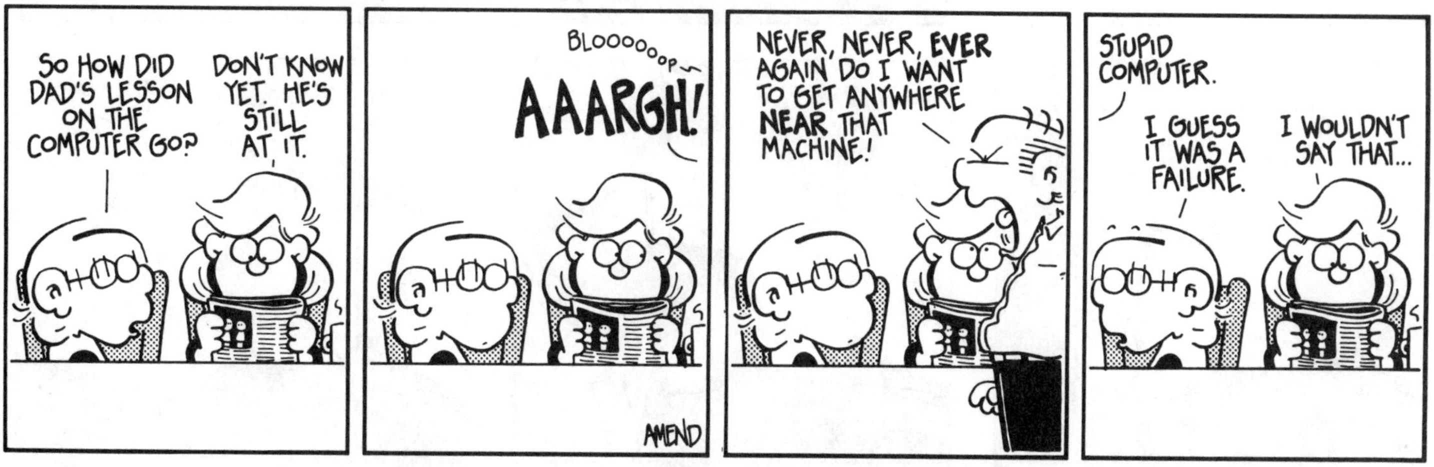
SO HOW DID DAD'S LESSON ON THE COMPUTER GO?
DON'T KNOW YET. HE'S STILL AT IT.
BLOOOOOOOP
AAARGH!
AMEND
NEVER, NEVER, **EVER** AGAIN DO I WANT TO GET ANYWHERE **NEAR** THAT MACHINE!
STUPID COMPUTER.
I GUESS IT WAS A FAILURE.
I WOULDN'T SAY THAT...

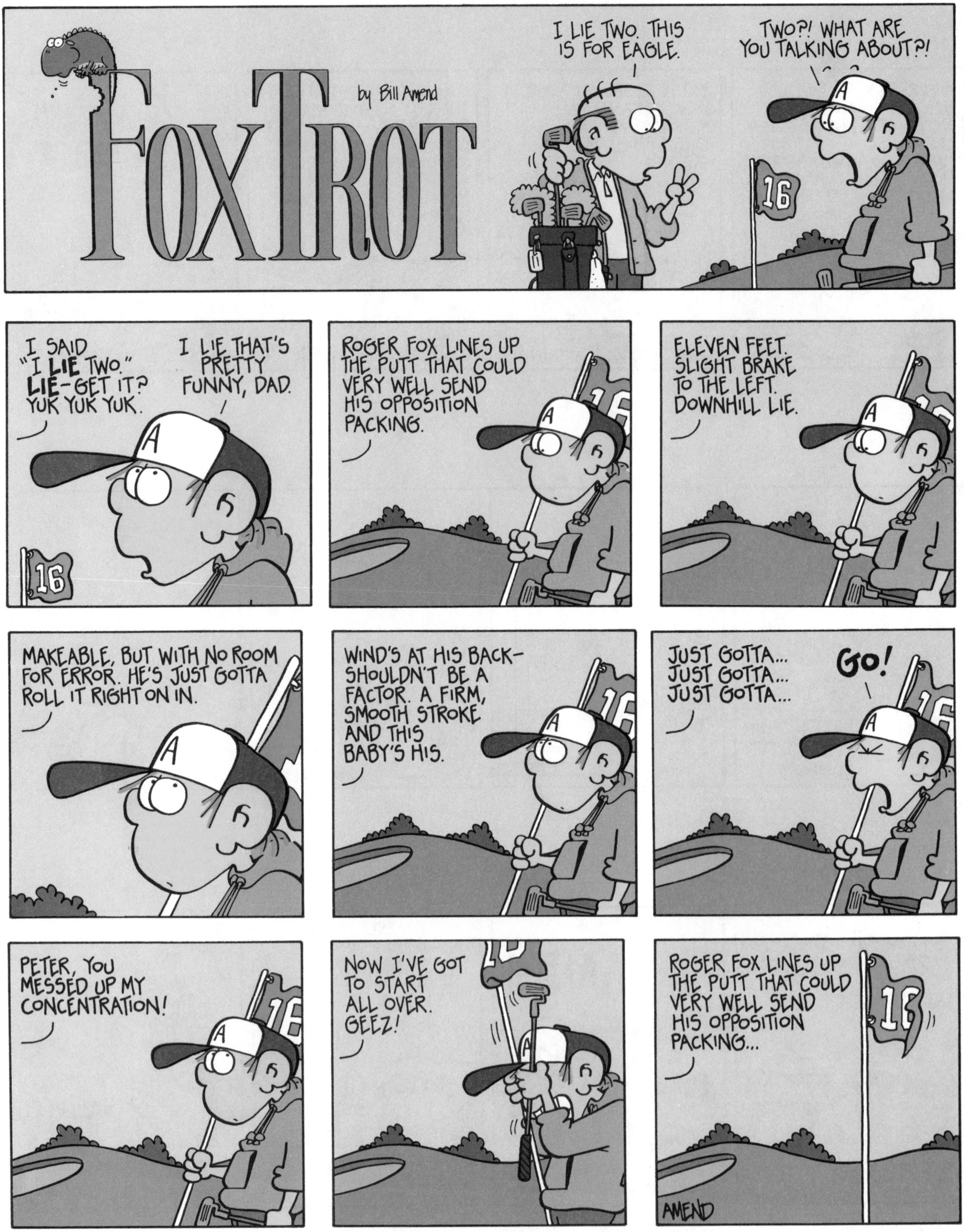
FoxTrot
by Bill Amend
I LIE TWO. THIS IS FOR EAGLE.
TWO?! WHAT ARE YOU TALKING ABOUT?!
I SAID "I LIE TWO." LIE-GET IT? YUK YUK YUK.
I LIE THAT'S PRETTY FUNNY, DAD.
ROGER FOX LINES UP THE PUTT THAT COULD VERY WELL SEND HIS OPPOSITION PACKING.
ELEVEN FEET. SLIGHT BRAKE TO THE LEFT. DOWNHILL LIE.
MAKEABLE, BUT WITH NO ROOM FOR ERROR. HE'S JUST GOTTA ROLL IT RIGHT ON IN.
WIND'S AT HIS BACK-SHOULDN'T BE A FACTOR. A FIRM, SMOOTH STROKE AND THIS BABY'S HIS.
JUST GOTTA... JUST GOTTA... JUST GOTTA...
GO!
PETER, YOU MESSED UP MY CONCENTRATION!
NOW I'VE GOT TO START ALL OVER. GEEZ!
ROGER FOX LINES UP THE PUTT THAT COULD VERY WELL SEND HIS OPPOSITION PACKING...
AMEND

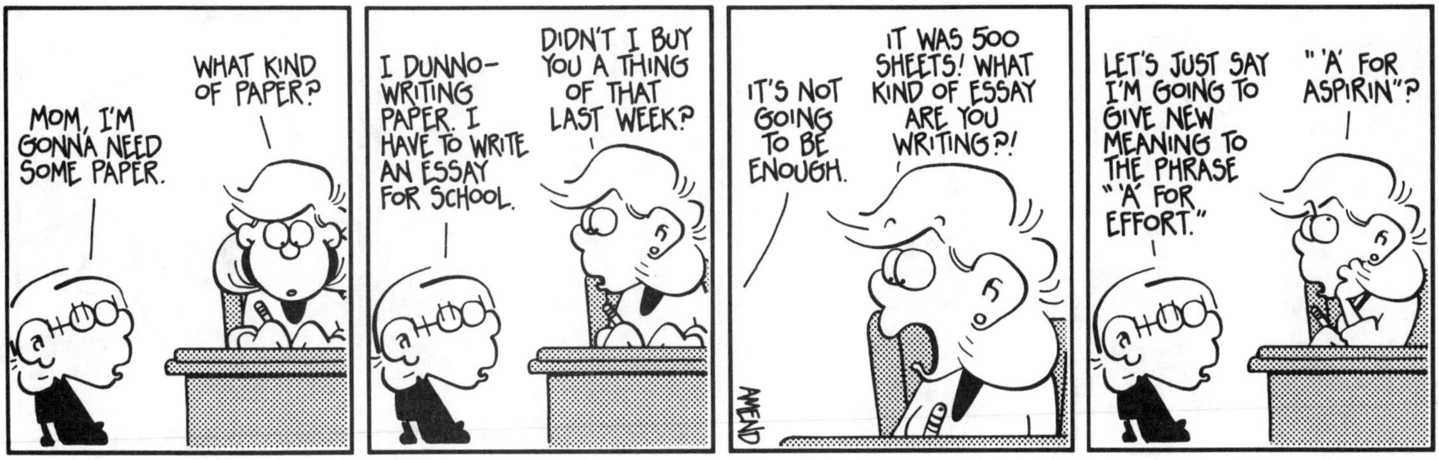
MOM, I'M GONNA NEED SOME PAPER.
WHAT KIND OF PAPER?
I DUNNO– WRITING PAPER. I HAVE TO WRITE AN ESSAY FOR SCHOOL.
DIDN'T I BUY YOU A THING OF THAT LAST WEEK?
IT'S NOT GOING TO BE ENOUGH.
IT WAS 500 SHEETS! WHAT KIND OF ESSAY ARE YOU WRITING?!
AMEND
LET'S JUST SAY I'M GOING TO GIVE NEW MEANING TO THE PHRASE "'A' FOR EFFORT."
"'A' FOR ASPIRIN"?

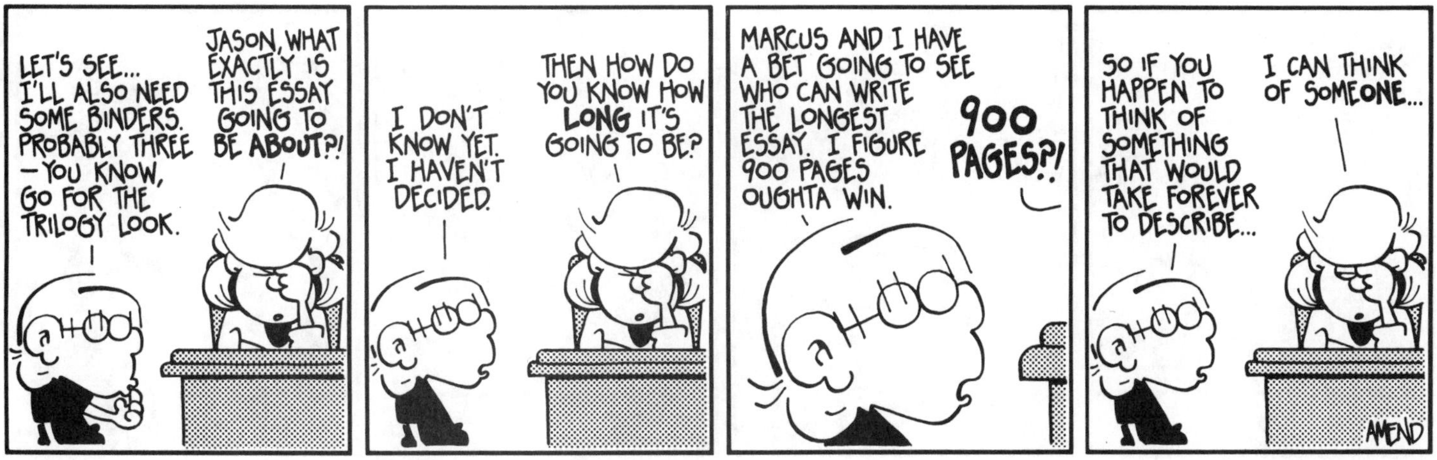
LET'S SEE... I'LL ALSO NEED SOME BINDERS. PROBABLY THREE –YOU KNOW, GO FOR THE TRILOGY LOOK.
JASON, WHAT EXACTLY IS THIS ESSAY GOING TO BE ABOUT?!
I DON'T KNOW YET. I HAVEN'T DECIDED.
THEN HOW DO YOU KNOW HOW LONG IT'S GOING TO BE?
MARCUS AND I HAVE A BET GOING TO SEE WHO CAN WRITE THE LONGEST ESSAY. I FIGURE 900 PAGES OUGHTA WIN.
900 PAGES?!
SO IF YOU HAPPEN TO THINK OF SOMETHING THAT WOULD TAKE FOREVER TO DESCRIBE...
I CAN THINK OF SOMEONE...
AMEND

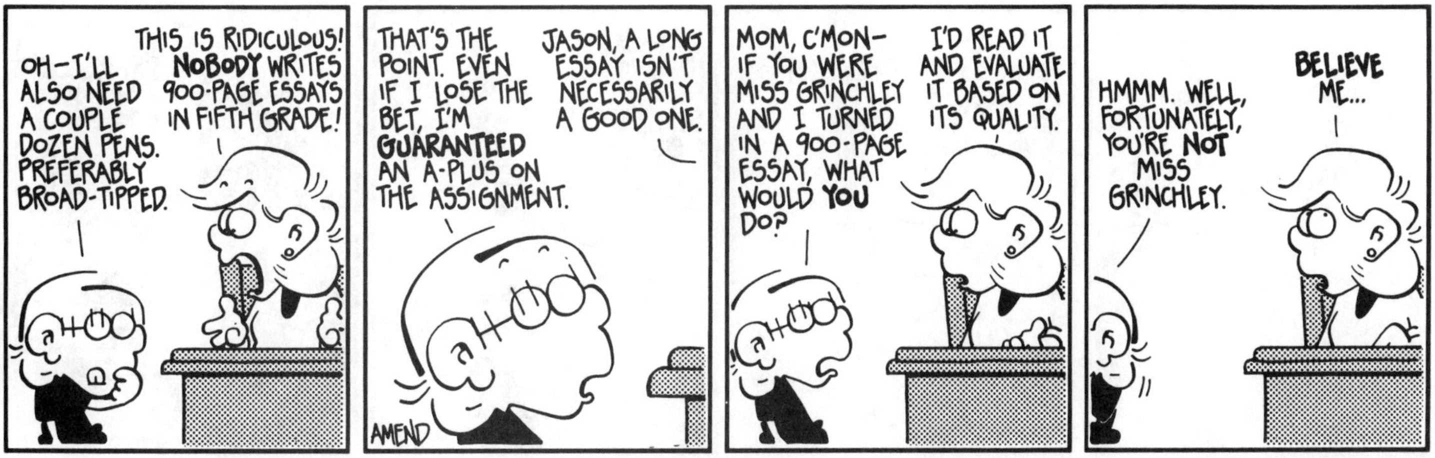
OH–I'LL ALSO NEED A COUPLE DOZEN PENS. PREFERABLY BROAD-TIPPED.
THIS IS RIDICULOUS! NOBODY WRITES 900-PAGE ESSAYS IN FIFTH GRADE!
THAT'S THE POINT. EVEN IF I LOSE THE BET, I'M GUARANTEED AN A-PLUS ON THE ASSIGNMENT.
JASON, A LONG ESSAY ISN'T NECESSARILY A GOOD ONE.
AMEND
MOM, C'MON– IF YOU WERE MISS GRINCHLEY AND I TURNED IN A 900-PAGE ESSAY, WHAT WOULD YOU DO?
I'D READ IT AND EVALUATE IT BASED ON ITS QUALITY.
HMMM. WELL, FORTUNATELY, YOU'RE NOT MISS GRINCHLEY.
BELIEVE ME...

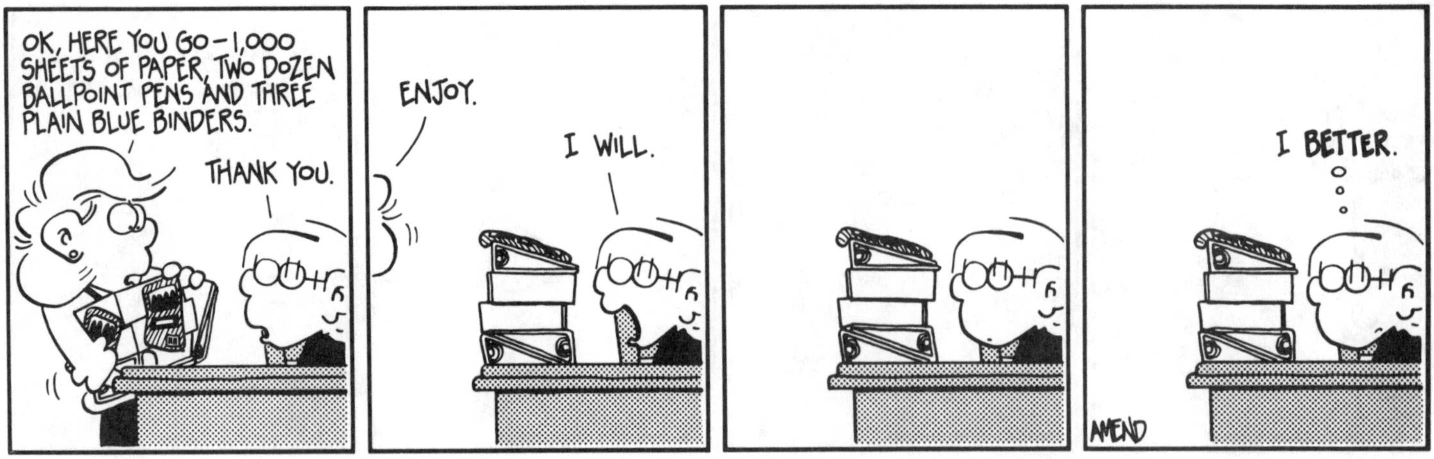
OK, HERE YOU GO — 1,000 SHEETS OF PAPER, TWO DOZEN BALLPOINT PENS AND THREE PLAIN BLUE BINDERS.
THANK YOU.
ENJOY.
I WILL.
I BETTER.
AMEND

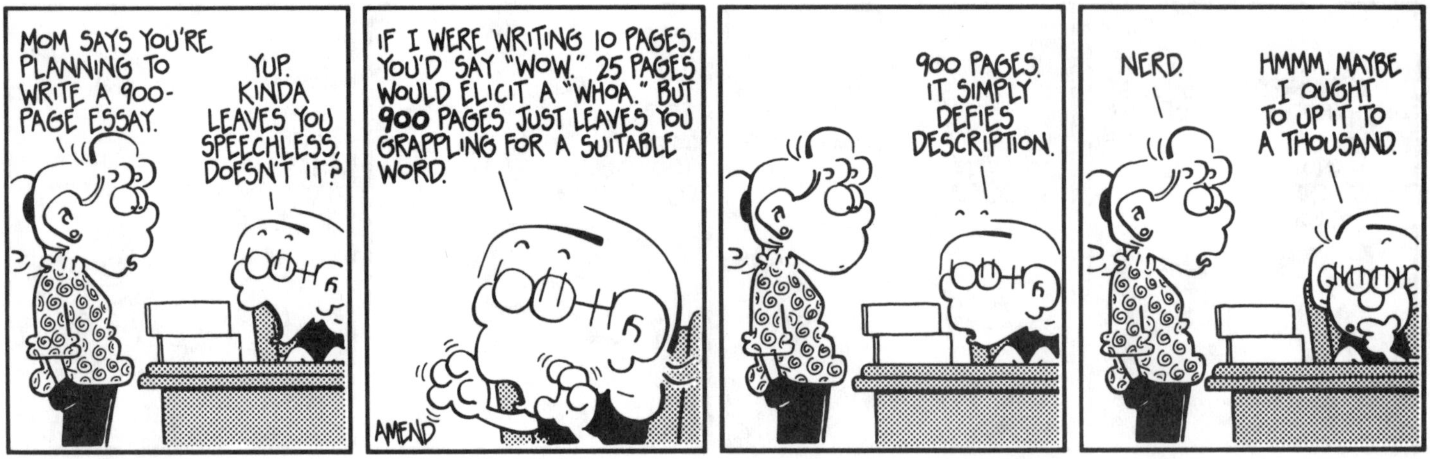
MOM SAYS YOU'RE PLANNING TO WRITE A 900-PAGE ESSAY.
YUP. KINDA LEAVES YOU SPEECHLESS, DOESN'T IT?
IF I WERE WRITING 10 PAGES, YOU'D SAY "WOW." 25 PAGES WOULD ELICIT A "WHOA." BUT 900 PAGES JUST LEAVES YOU GRAPPLING FOR A SUITABLE WORD.
AMEND
900 PAGES. IT SIMPLY DEFIES DESCRIPTION.
NERD.
HMMM. MAYBE I OUGHT TO UP IT TO A THOUSAND.

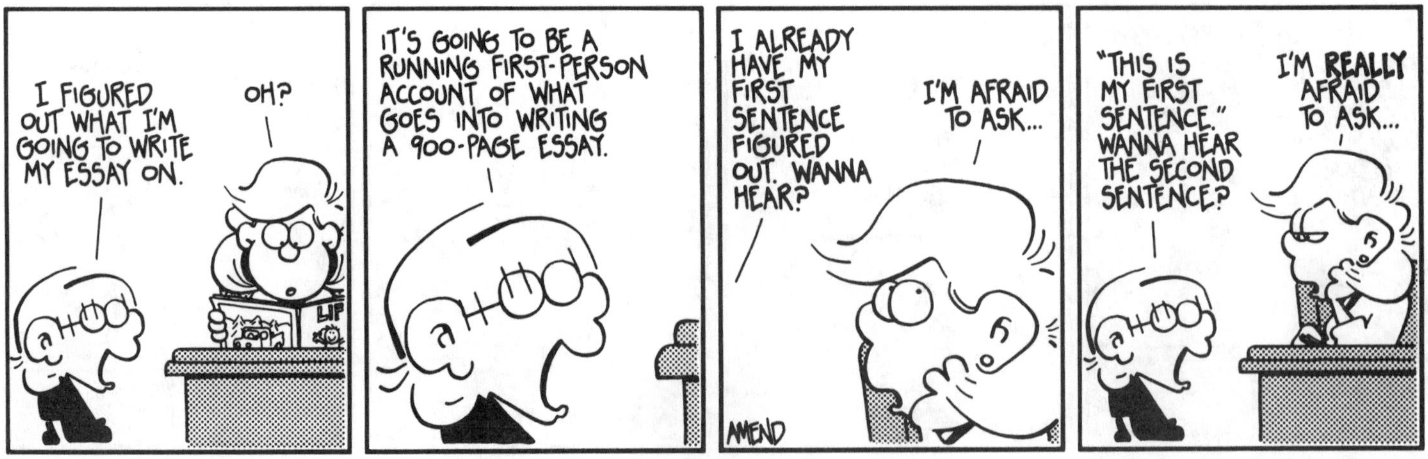
I FIGURED OUT WHAT I'M GOING TO WRITE MY ESSAY ON.
OH?
IT'S GOING TO BE A RUNNING FIRST-PERSON ACCOUNT OF WHAT GOES INTO WRITING A 900-PAGE ESSAY.
I ALREADY HAVE MY FIRST SENTENCE FIGURED OUT. WANNA HEAR?
I'M AFRAID TO ASK...
AMEND
"THIS IS MY FIRST SENTENCE." WANNA HEAR THE SECOND SENTENCE?
I'M REALLY AFRAID TO ASK...

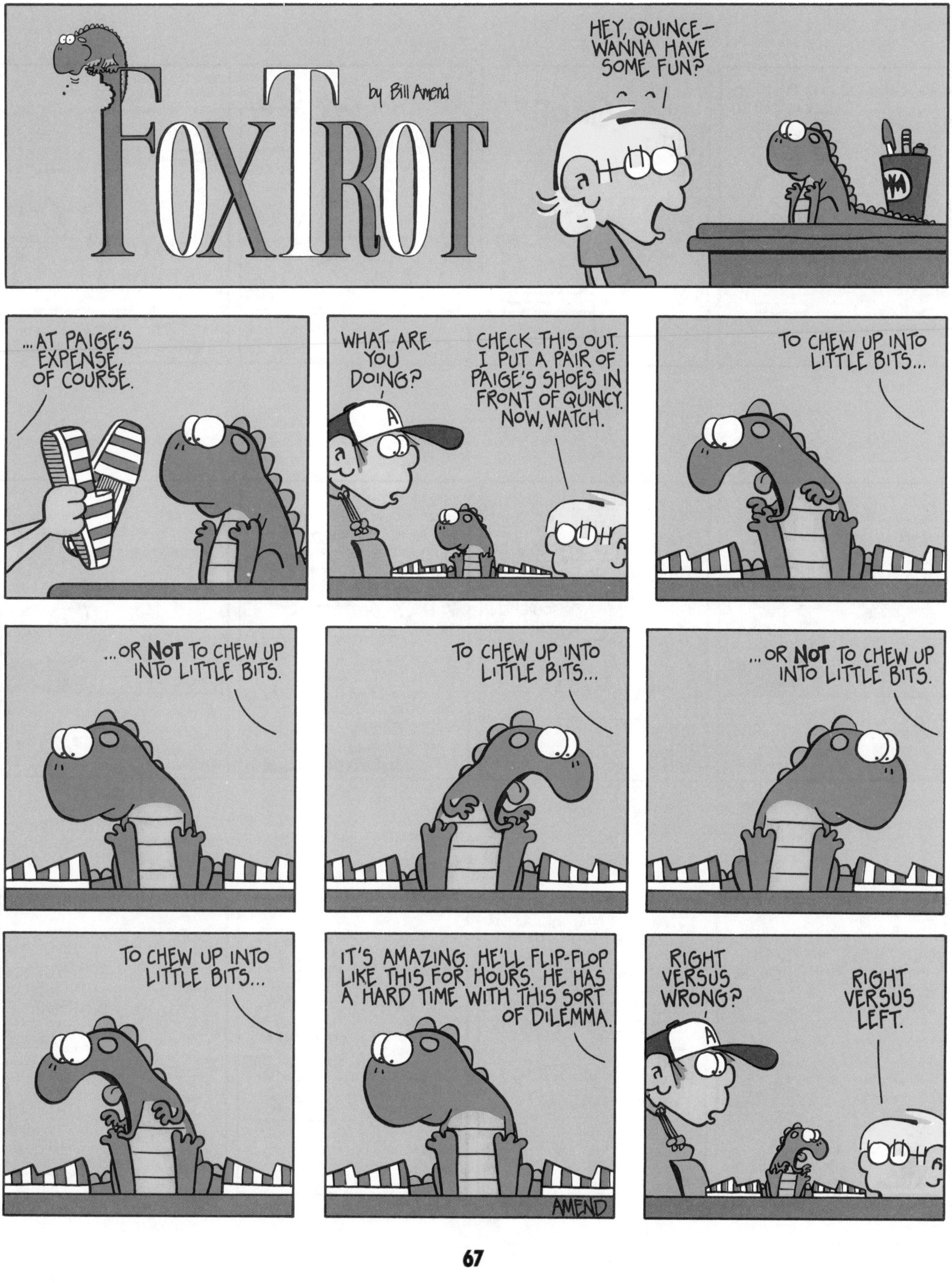
FoxTrot
by Bill Amend
HEY, QUINCE— WANNA HAVE SOME FUN?
...AT PAIGE'S EXPENSE, OF COURSE.
WHAT ARE YOU DOING?
CHECK THIS OUT. I PUT A PAIR OF PAIGE'S SHOES IN FRONT OF QUINCY. NOW, WATCH.
TO CHEW UP INTO LITTLE BITS...
...OR **NOT** TO CHEW UP INTO LITTLE BITS.
TO CHEW UP INTO LITTLE BITS...
...OR **NOT** TO CHEW UP INTO LITTLE BITS.
TO CHEW UP INTO LITTLE BITS...
IT'S AMAZING. HE'LL FLIP-FLOP LIKE THIS FOR HOURS. HE HAS A HARD TIME WITH THIS SORT OF DILEMMA.
AMEND
RIGHT VERSUS WRONG?
RIGHT VERSUS LEFT.

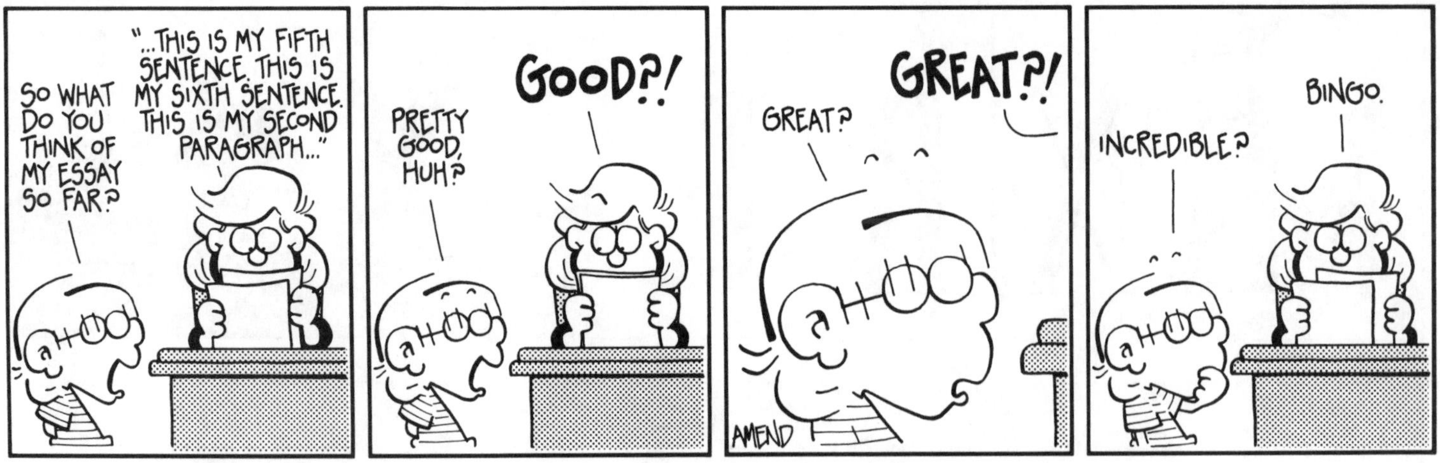
SO WHAT DO YOU THINK OF MY ESSAY SO FAR?
"...THIS IS MY FIFTH SENTENCE. THIS IS MY SIXTH SENTENCE. THIS IS MY SECOND PARAGRAPH..."
PRETTY GOOD, HUH?
GOOD?!
GREAT?
GREAT?!
AMEND
INCREDIBLE?
BINGO.

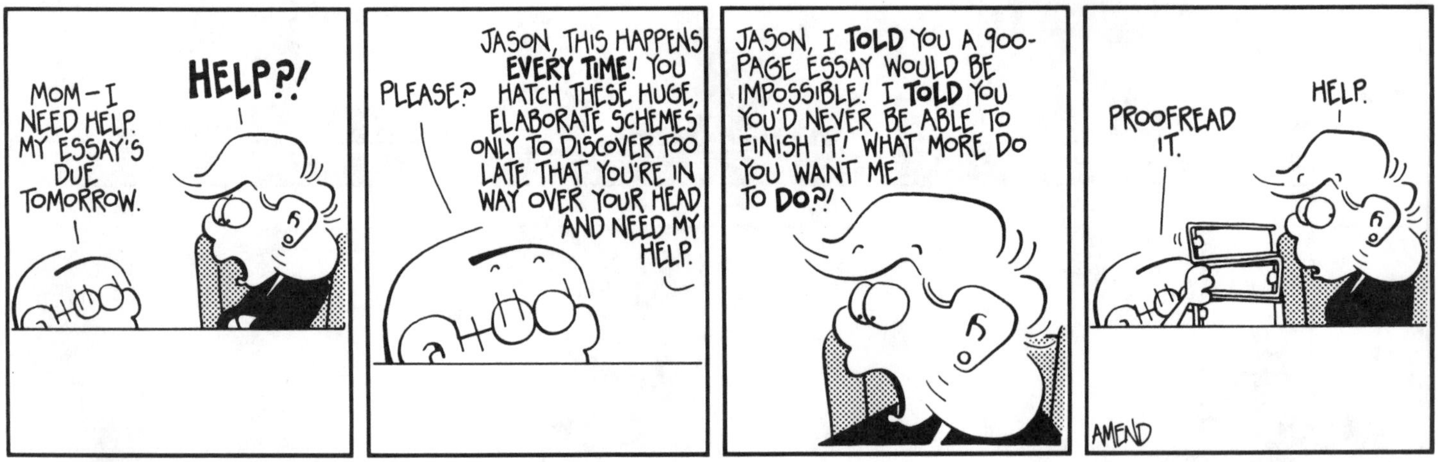
MOM–I NEED HELP. MY ESSAY'S DUE TOMORROW.
HELP?!
PLEASE?
JASON, THIS HAPPENS **EVERY TIME**! YOU HATCH THESE HUGE, ELABORATE SCHEMES ONLY TO DISCOVER TOO LATE THAT YOU'RE IN WAY OVER YOUR HEAD AND NEED MY HELP.
JASON, I **TOLD** YOU A 900-PAGE ESSAY WOULD BE IMPOSSIBLE! I **TOLD** YOU YOU'D NEVER BE ABLE TO FINISH IT! WHAT MORE DO YOU WANT ME TO **DO**?!
PROOFREAD IT.
HELP.
AMEND

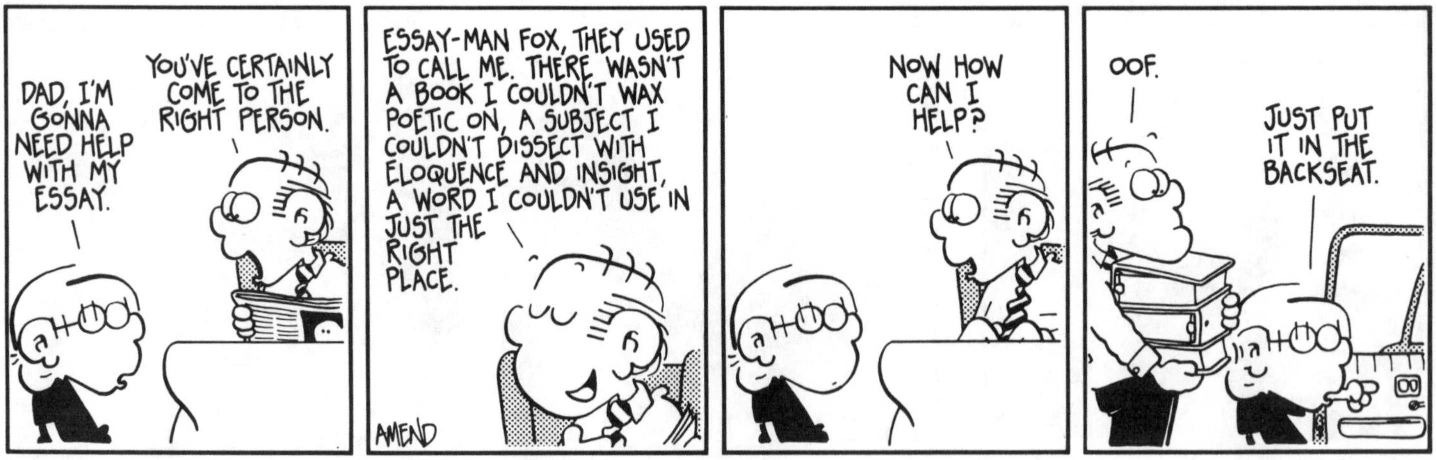
DAD, I'M GONNA NEED HELP WITH MY ESSAY.
YOU'VE CERTAINLY COME TO THE RIGHT PERSON.
ESSAY-MAN FOX, THEY USED TO CALL ME. THERE WASN'T A BOOK I COULDN'T WAX POETIC ON, A SUBJECT I COULDN'T DISSECT WITH ELOQUENCE AND INSIGHT, A WORD I COULDN'T USE IN JUST THE RIGHT PLACE.
AMEND
NOW HOW CAN I HELP?
OOF.
JUST PUT IT IN THE BACKSEAT.

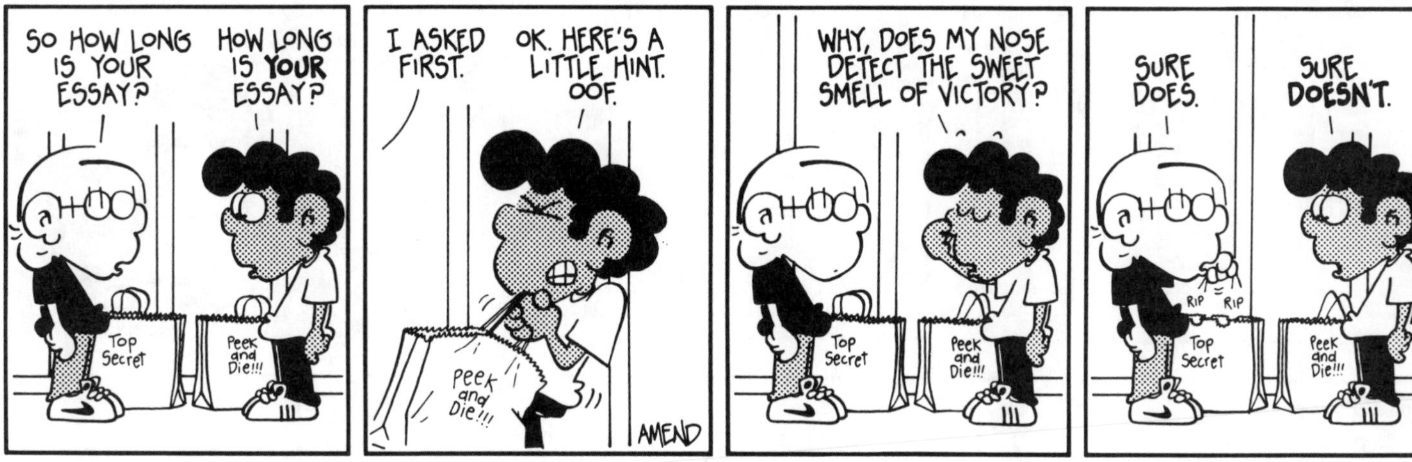
SO HOW LONG IS YOUR ESSAY?
HOW LONG IS **YOUR** ESSAY?
Top Secret
Peek and Die!!!
I ASKED FIRST.
OK. HERE'S A LITTLE HINT. OOF.
Peek and Die!!!
AMEND
WHY, DOES MY NOSE DETECT THE SWEET SMELL OF VICTORY?
Top Secret
Peek and Die!!!
SURE DOES.
SURE **DOESN'T**.
RIP
RIP
Top Secret
Peek and Die!!!

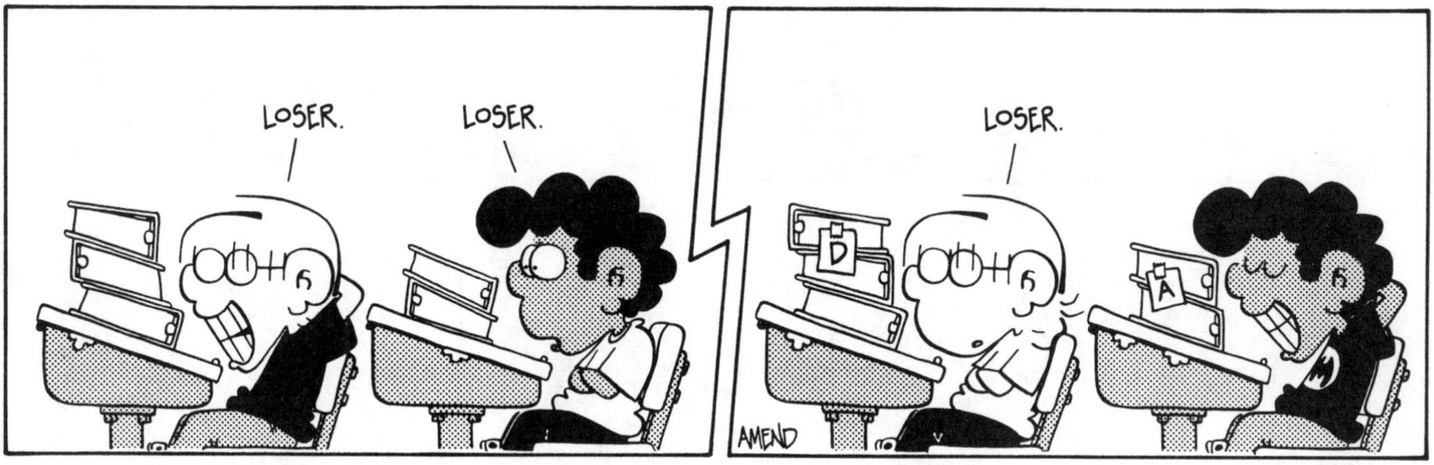
LOSER.
LOSER.
LOSER.
D
A
AMEND

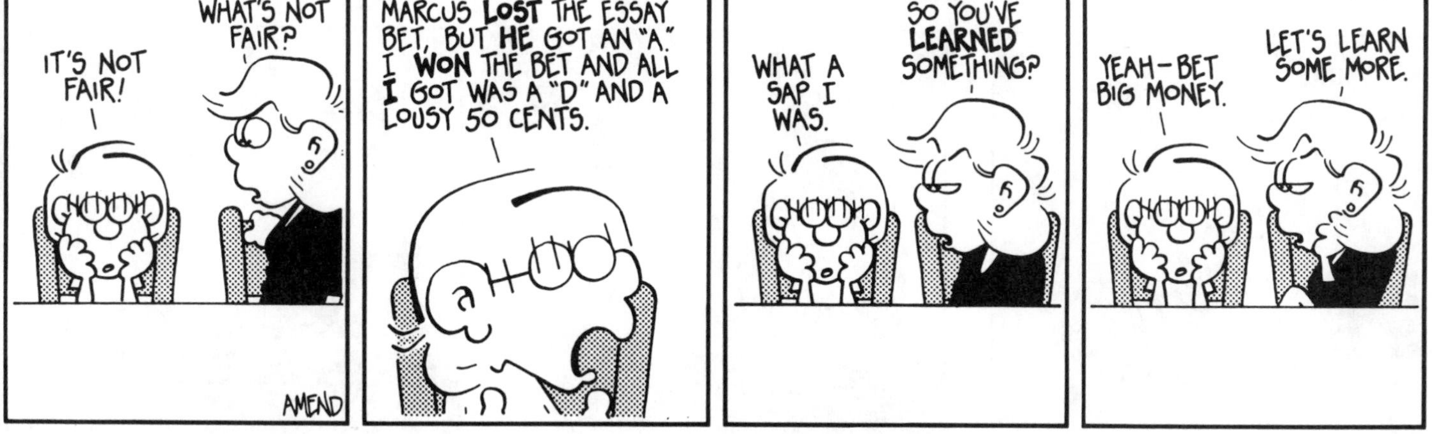
IT'S NOT FAIR!
WHAT'S NOT FAIR?
AMEND
MARCUS **LOST** THE ESSAY BET, BUT **HE** GOT AN "A." I **WON** THE BET AND ALL **I** GOT WAS A "D" AND A LOUSY 50 CENTS.
WHAT A SAP I WAS.
SO YOU'VE **LEARNED** SOMETHING?
YEAH-BET BIG MONEY.
LET'S LEARN SOME MORE.

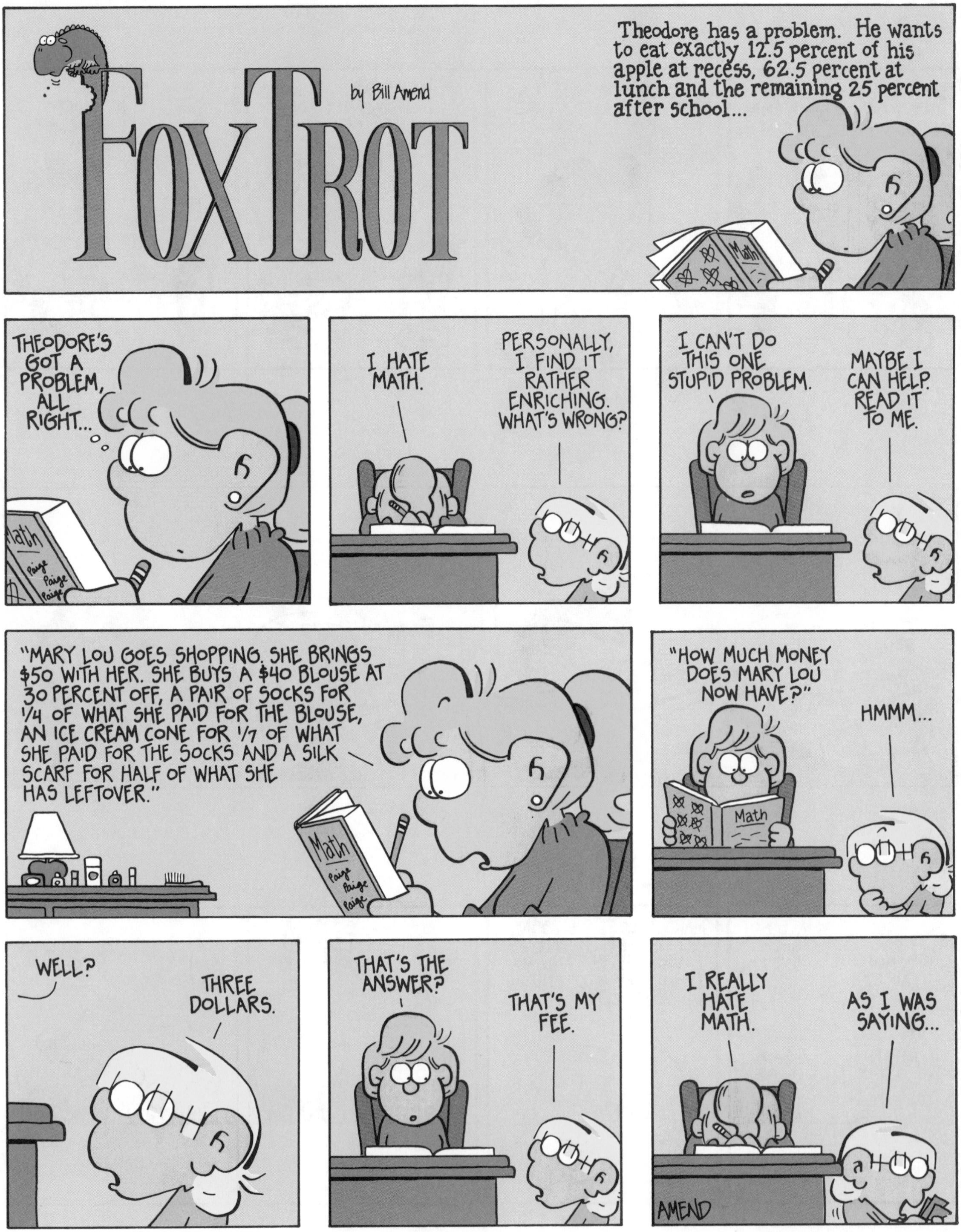
FoxTrot
by Bill Amend
Theodore has a problem. He wants to eat exactly 12.5 percent of his apple at recess, 62.5 percent at lunch and the remaining 25 percent after school...
Math
THEODORE'S GOT A PROBLEM, ALL RIGHT...
Math
Paige Paige Paige
I HATE MATH.
PERSONALLY, I FIND IT RATHER ENRICHING. WHAT'S WRONG?
I CAN'T DO THIS ONE STUPID PROBLEM.
MAYBE I CAN HELP. READ IT TO ME.
"MARY LOU GOES SHOPPING. SHE BRINGS $50 WITH HER. SHE BUYS A $40 BLOUSE AT 30 PERCENT OFF, A PAIR OF SOCKS FOR 1/4 OF WHAT SHE PAID FOR THE BLOUSE, AN ICE CREAM CONE FOR 1/7 OF WHAT SHE PAID FOR THE SOCKS AND A SILK SCARF FOR HALF OF WHAT SHE HAS LEFTOVER."
Math
Paige Paige Paige
"HOW MUCH MONEY DOES MARY LOU NOW HAVE?"
Math
HMMM...
WELL?
THREE DOLLARS.
THAT'S THE ANSWER?
THAT'S MY FEE.
I REALLY HATE MATH.
AS I WAS SAYING...
AMEND

I REALLY WISH THE KIDS DIDN'T HAVE THE WHOLE WEEK OFF FROM SCHOOL.

WE'LL LIVE.

I REALLY WISH THEY'D AT LEAST FIND ANOTHER HOUSE TO TEAR APART.

WE'LL GET THROUGH THIS.

I REALLY WISH THEY COULD GO FIVE MINUTES WITHOUT FIGHTING.

WE'LL SURVIVE.

SPORTS
CARTOONIST TO TAKE MOUND OPENING DAY
"Damn Right I'm Scared" says Flustered Will Clark

I REALLY WISH YOU'D STOP SAYING "WE."

WHOA— I'M LATE FOR WORK.

AMEND

WHATCHA WATCHING?

"MATLOCK." IT'S A GOOD ONE. THERE ARE LIKE 25 SUSPECTS.

HAVEN'T YOU SEEN THIS ONE ALREADY?

NO.

AMEND

SURE YOU HAVE. IT'S THE ONE WHERE THE GIRL KILLS HER BROTHER.

I WALKED RIGHT INTO **THAT** ONE...

SUCH AN OBVIOUS MOTIVE. I'M DISAPPOINTED.

IT'S AMAZING HOW MUCH SPRING VACATION CHANGES WHEN YOU GET OLDER.

FOR NOW, IT MEANS JUST SITTING AROUND PLAYING VIDEO GAMES AND WATCHING "BULLWINKLE" RE-RUNS ALL DAY.

BUT IN ANOTHER 10 YEARS, IT'LL MEAN CHUGGING BEERS ON THE BEACH WHILE ENDLESS PARADES OF WOMEN COMPETE IN WET T-SHIRT CONTESTS.

AMEND

BETTER ENJOY IT WHILE WE CAN.

PASS THE HO-HOS.

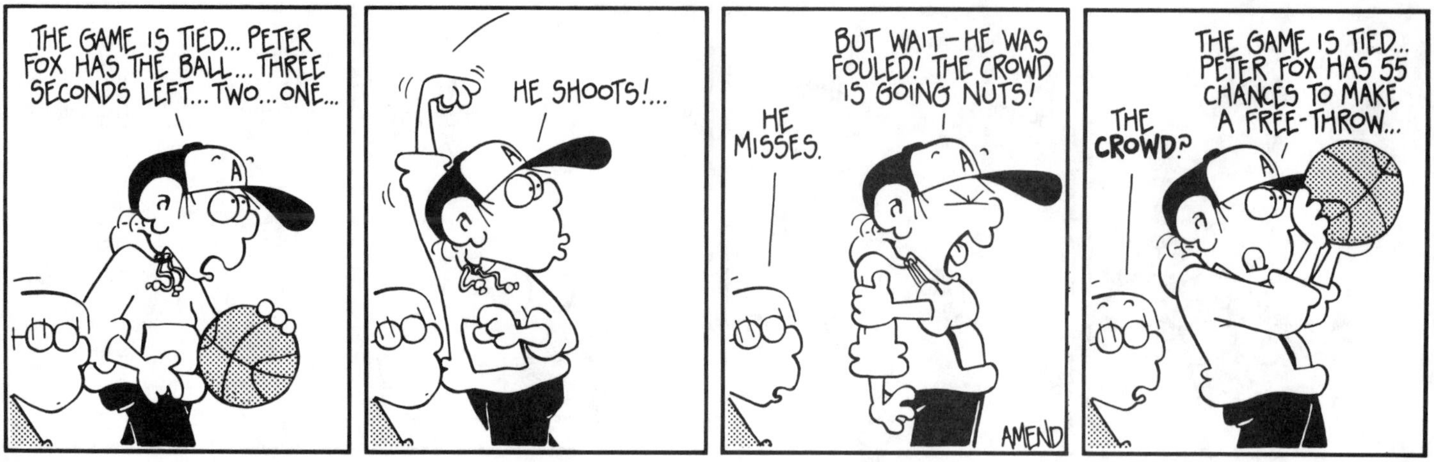
THE GAME IS TIED... PETER FOX HAS THE BALL... THREE SECONDS LEFT...TWO...ONE...
HE SHOOTS!...
HE MISSES.
BUT WAIT—HE WAS FOULED! THE CROWD IS GOING NUTS!
THE CROWD?
THE GAME IS TIED... PETER FOX HAS 55 CHANCES TO MAKE A FREE-THROW...
AMEND

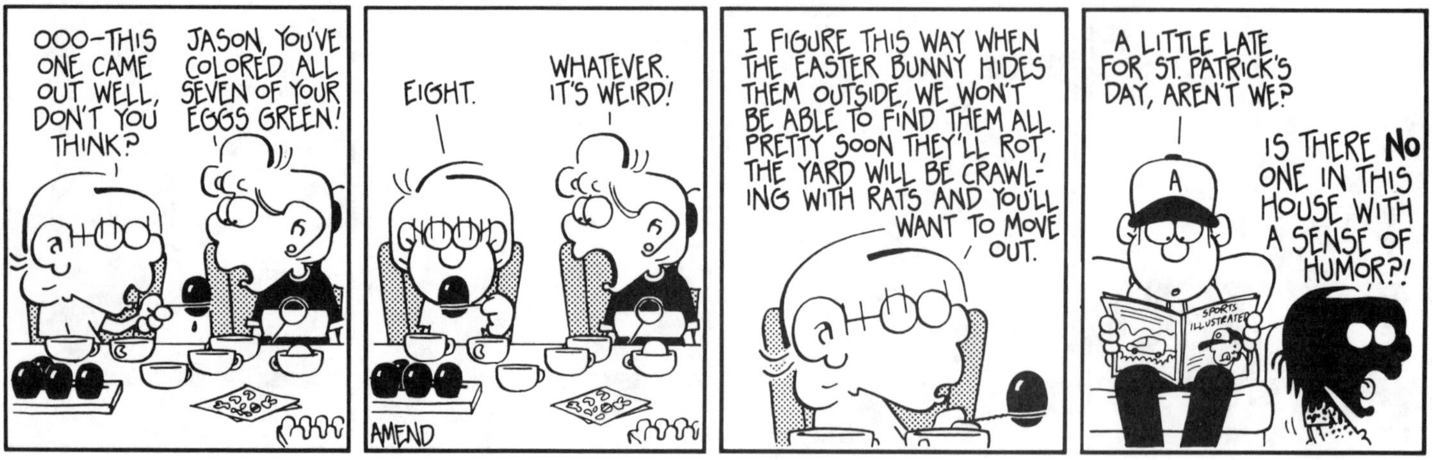
OOO—THIS ONE CAME OUT WELL, DON'T YOU THINK?
JASON, YOU'VE COLORED ALL SEVEN OF YOUR EGGS GREEN!
EIGHT.
WHATEVER. IT'S WEIRD!
AMEND
I FIGURE THIS WAY WHEN THE EASTER BUNNY HIDES THEM OUTSIDE, WE WON'T BE ABLE TO FIND THEM ALL. PRETTY SOON THEY'LL ROT, THE YARD WILL BE CRAWLING WITH RATS AND YOU'LL WANT TO MOVE OUT.
A LITTLE LATE FOR ST. PATRICK'S DAY, AREN'T WE?
IS THERE NO ONE IN THIS HOUSE WITH A SENSE OF HUMOR?!
SPORTS ILLUSTRATED

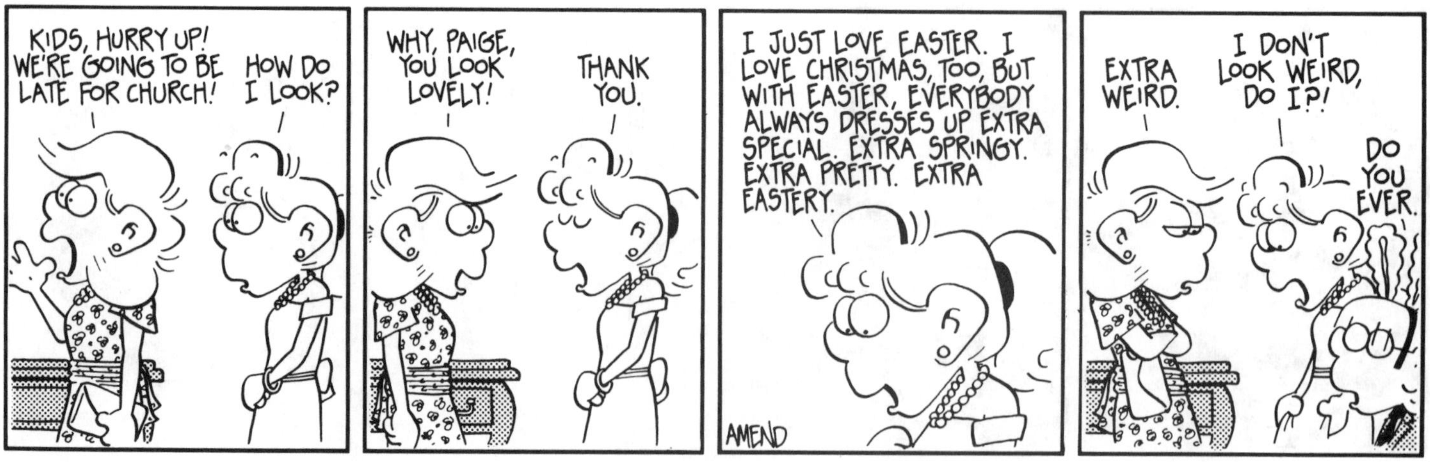
KIDS, HURRY UP! WE'RE GOING TO BE LATE FOR CHURCH!
HOW DO I LOOK?
WHY, PAIGE, YOU LOOK LOVELY!
THANK YOU.
I JUST LOVE EASTER. I LOVE CHRISTMAS, TOO, BUT WITH EASTER, EVERYBODY ALWAYS DRESSES UP EXTRA SPECIAL. EXTRA SPRINGY. EXTRA PRETTY. EXTRA EASTERY.
AMEND
EXTRA WEIRD.
I DON'T LOOK WEIRD, DO I?!
DO YOU EVER.

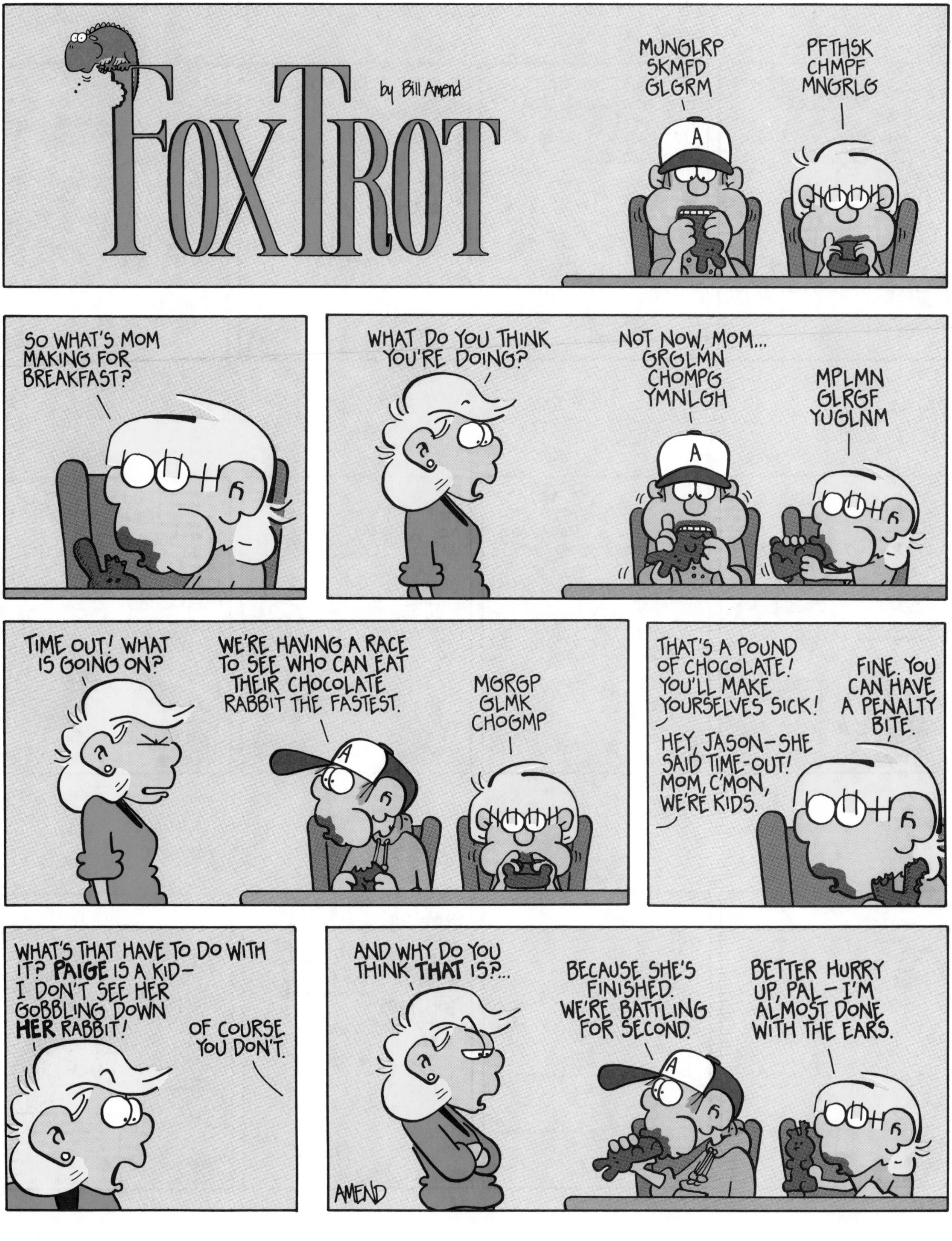
FoxTrot
by Bill Amend
MUNGLRP SKMFD GLGRM
PFTHSK CHMPF MNGRLG
SO WHAT'S MOM MAKING FOR BREAKFAST?
WHAT DO YOU THINK YOU'RE DOING?
NOT NOW, MOM... GRGLMN CHOMPG YMNLGH
MPLMN GLRGF YUGLNM
TIME OUT! WHAT IS GOING ON?
WE'RE HAVING A RACE TO SEE WHO CAN EAT THEIR CHOCOLATE RABBIT THE FASTEST.
MGRGP GLMK CHOGMP
THAT'S A POUND OF CHOCOLATE! YOU'LL MAKE YOURSELVES SICK!
FINE. YOU CAN HAVE A PENALTY BITE.
HEY, JASON–SHE SAID TIME-OUT! MOM, C'MON, WE'RE KIDS.
WHAT'S THAT HAVE TO DO WITH IT? PAIGE IS A KID– I DON'T SEE HER GOBBLING DOWN HER RABBIT!
OF COURSE YOU DON'T.
AND WHY DO YOU THINK THAT IS?...
BECAUSE SHE'S FINISHED. WE'RE BATTLING FOR SECOND.
BETTER HURRY UP, PAL–I'M ALMOST DONE WITH THE EARS.
AMEND

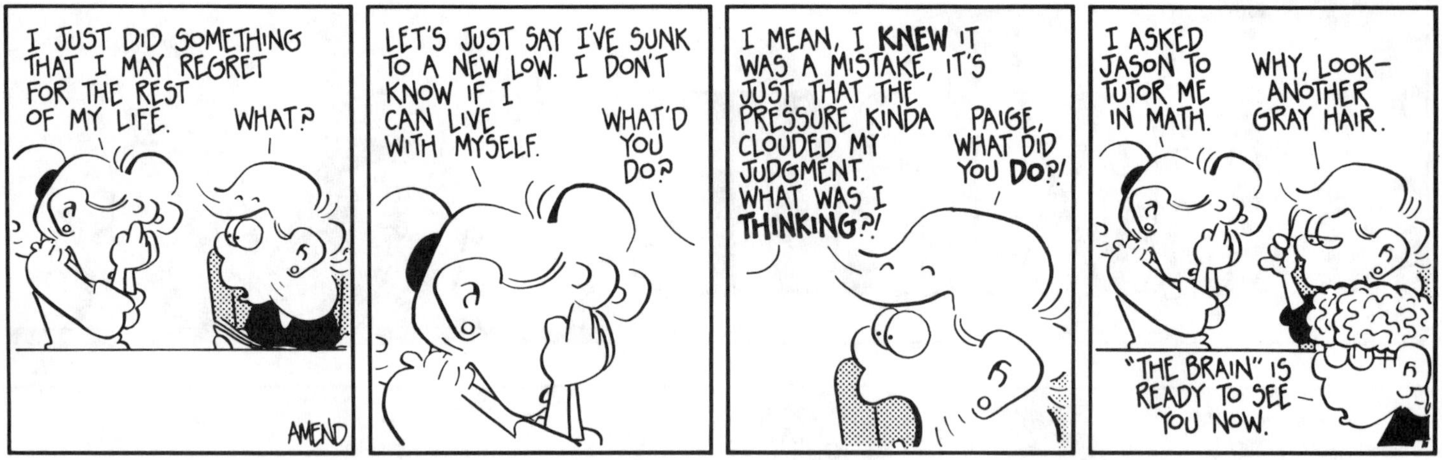
I JUST DID SOMETHING THAT I MAY REGRET FOR THE REST OF MY LIFE.
WHAT?
LET'S JUST SAY I'VE SUNK TO A NEW LOW. I DON'T KNOW IF I CAN LIVE WITH MYSELF.
WHAT'D YOU DO?
I MEAN, I **KNEW** IT WAS A MISTAKE, IT'S JUST THAT THE PRESSURE KINDA CLOUDED MY JUDGMENT. WHAT WAS I **THINKING**?!
PAIGE, WHAT DID YOU **DO**?!
I ASKED JASON TO TUTOR ME IN MATH.
WHY, LOOK– ANOTHER GRAY HAIR.
"THE BRAIN" IS READY TO SEE YOU NOW.
AMEND

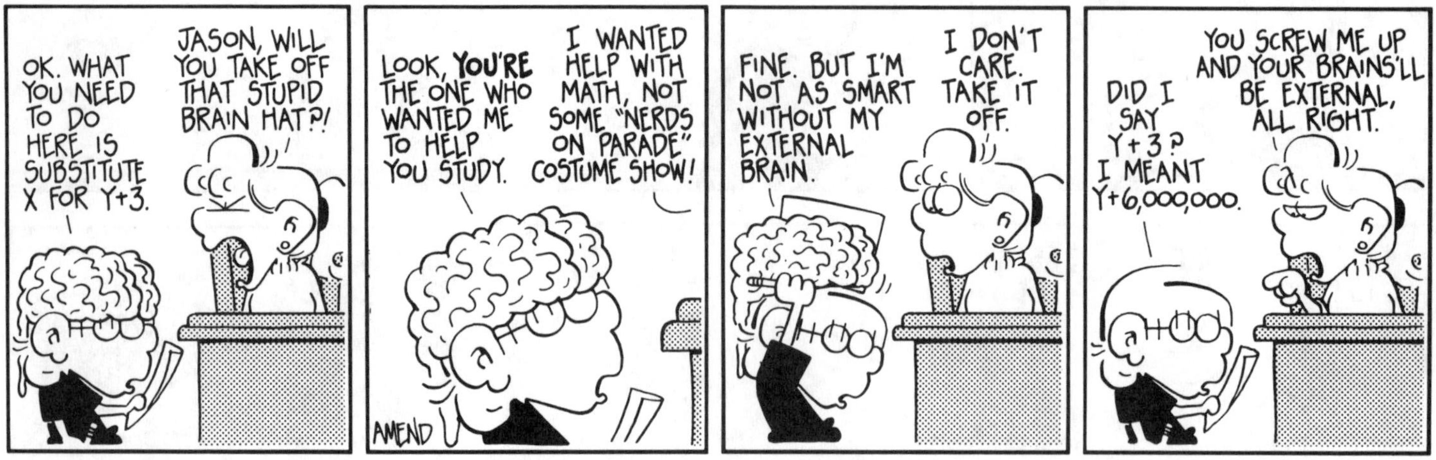
OK. WHAT YOU NEED TO DO HERE IS SUBSTITUTE X FOR Y+3.
JASON, WILL YOU TAKE OFF THAT STUPID BRAIN HAT?!
LOOK, **YOU'RE** THE ONE WHO WANTED ME TO HELP YOU STUDY.
I WANTED HELP WITH MATH, NOT SOME "NERDS ON PARADE" COSTUME SHOW!
AMEND
FINE. BUT I'M NOT AS SMART WITHOUT MY EXTERNAL BRAIN.
I DON'T CARE. TAKE IT OFF.
DID I SAY Y+3? I MEANT Y+6,000,000.
YOU SCREW ME UP AND YOUR BRAINS'LL BE EXTERNAL, ALL RIGHT.

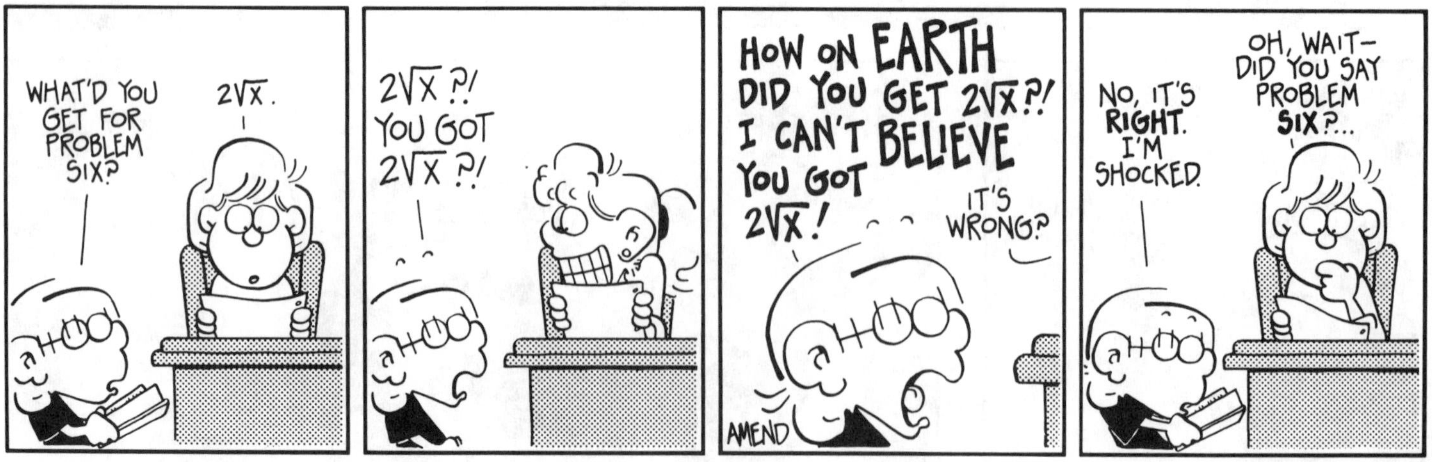
WHAT'D YOU GET FOR PROBLEM SIX?
2√X.
2√X ?! YOU GOT 2√X ?!
HOW ON EARTH DID YOU GET 2√X ?! I CAN'T BELIEVE YOU GOT 2√X!
IT'S WRONG?
AMEND
NO, IT'S **RIGHT**. I'M SHOCKED.
OH, WAIT– DID YOU SAY PROBLEM **SIX**?...

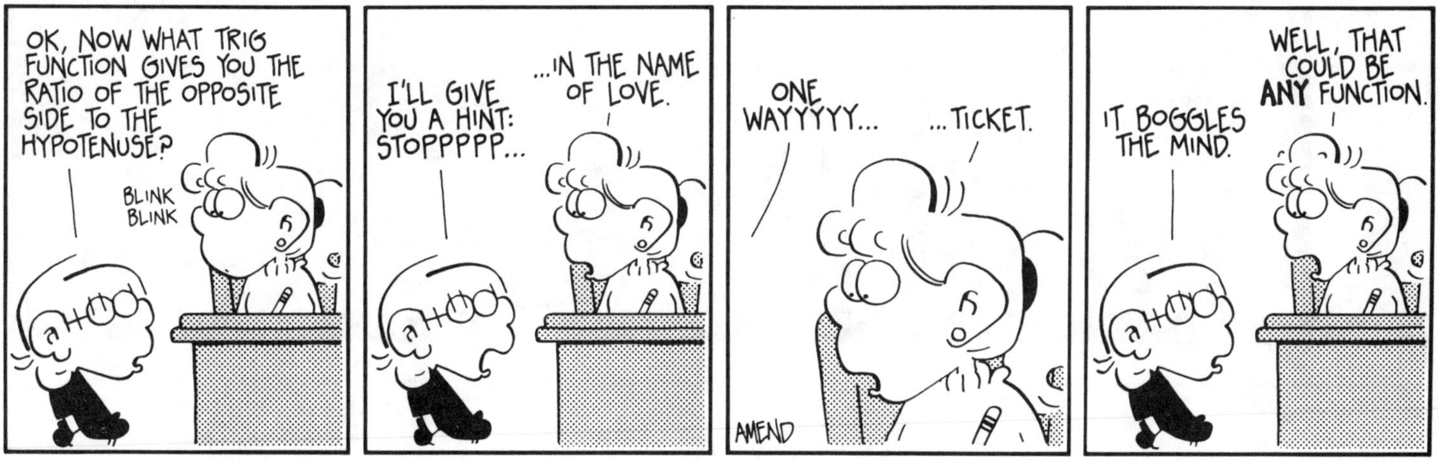
OK, NOW WHAT TRIG FUNCTION GIVES YOU THE RATIO OF THE OPPOSITE SIDE TO THE HYPOTENUSE?
BLINK BLINK
I'LL GIVE YOU A HINT: STOPPPPP...
...IN THE NAME OF LOVE.
ONE WAYYYYY...
...TICKET.
AMEND
IT BOGGLES THE MIND.
WELL, THAT COULD BE ANY FUNCTION.

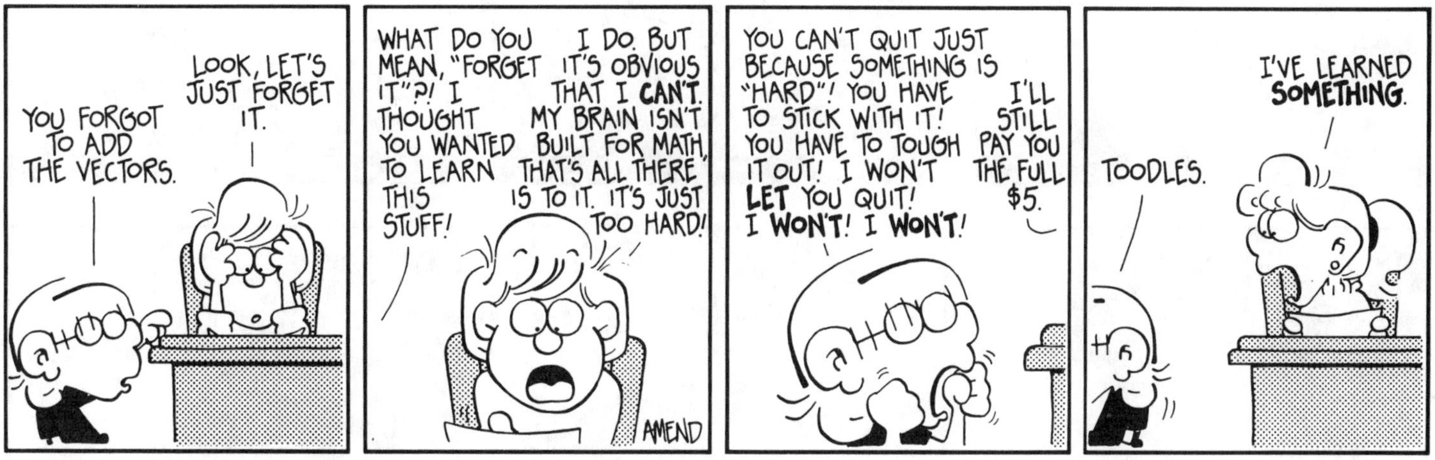
YOU FORGOT TO ADD THE VECTORS.
LOOK, LET'S JUST FORGET IT.
WHAT DO YOU MEAN, "FORGET IT"?! I THOUGHT YOU WANTED TO LEARN THIS STUFF!
I DO. BUT IT'S OBVIOUS THAT I CAN'T. MY BRAIN ISN'T BUILT FOR MATH, THAT'S ALL THERE IS TO IT. IT'S JUST TOO HARD!
AMEND
YOU CAN'T QUIT JUST BECAUSE SOMETHING IS "HARD"! YOU HAVE TO STICK WITH IT! YOU HAVE TO TOUGH IT OUT! I WON'T LET YOU QUIT! I WON'T! I WON'T!
I'LL STILL PAY YOU THE FULL $5.
TOODLES.
I'VE LEARNED SOMETHING.

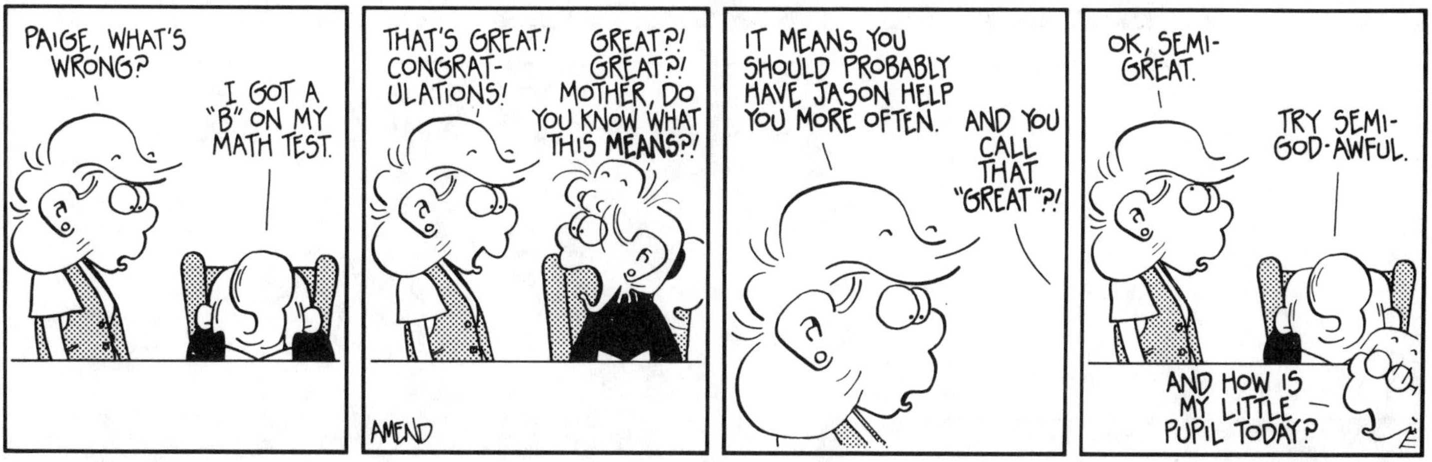
PAIGE, WHAT'S WRONG?
I GOT A "B" ON MY MATH TEST.
THAT'S GREAT! CONGRAT-ULATIONS!
GREAT?! GREAT?! MOTHER, DO YOU KNOW WHAT THIS MEANS?!
AMEND
IT MEANS YOU SHOULD PROBABLY HAVE JASON HELP YOU MORE OFTEN.
AND YOU CALL THAT "GREAT"?!
OK, SEMI-GREAT.
TRY SEMI-GOD-AWFUL.
AND HOW IS MY LITTLE PUPIL TODAY?

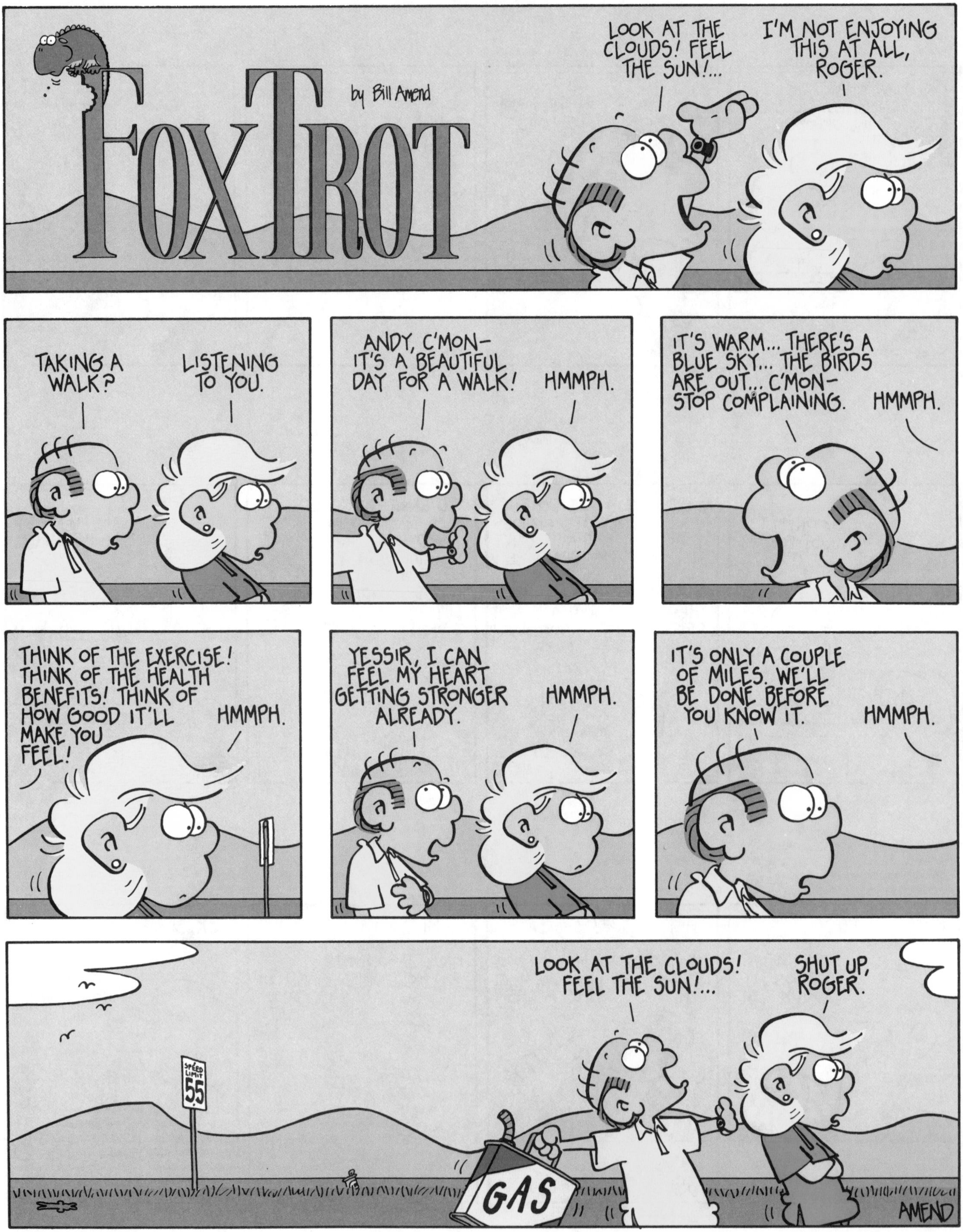
FoxTrot
by Bill Amend
LOOK AT THE CLOUDS! FEEL THE SUN!...
I'M NOT ENJOYING THIS AT ALL, ROGER.
TAKING A WALK?
LISTENING TO YOU.
ANDY, C'MON— IT'S A BEAUTIFUL DAY FOR A WALK!
HMMPH.
IT'S WARM... THERE'S A BLUE SKY... THE BIRDS ARE OUT... C'MON— STOP COMPLAINING.
HMMPH.
THINK OF THE EXERCISE! THINK OF THE HEALTH BENEFITS! THINK OF HOW GOOD IT'LL MAKE YOU FEEL!
HMMPH.
YESSIR, I CAN FEEL MY HEART GETTING STRONGER ALREADY.
HMMPH.
IT'S ONLY A COUPLE OF MILES. WE'LL BE DONE BEFORE YOU KNOW IT.
HMMPH.
SPEED LIMIT 55
LOOK AT THE CLOUDS! FEEL THE SUN!...
SHUT UP, ROGER.
GAS
AMEND

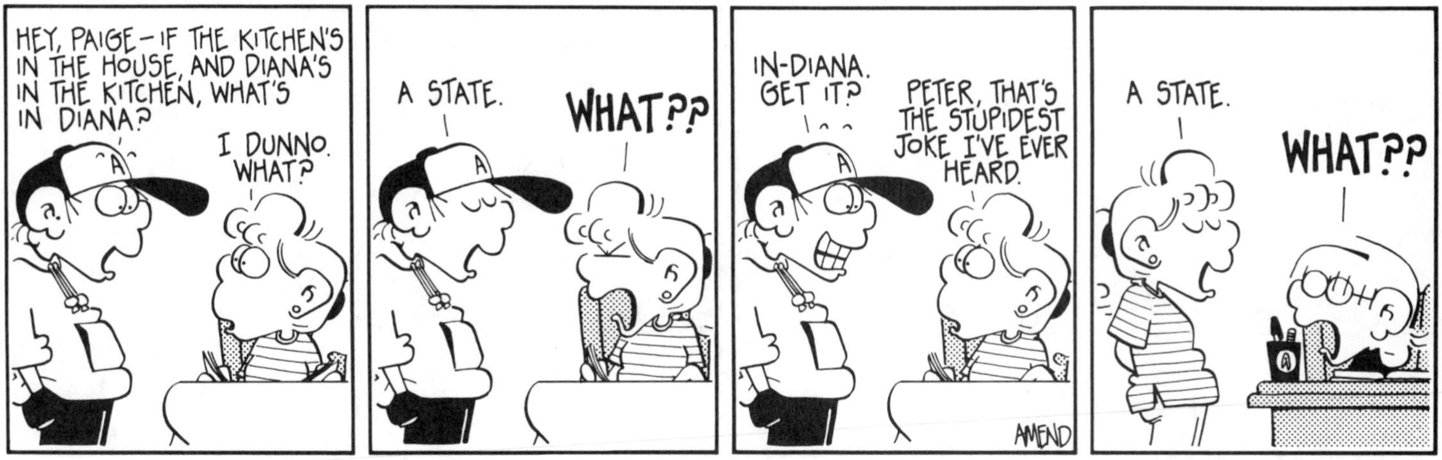
HEY, PAIGE– IF THE KITCHEN'S IN THE HOUSE, AND DIANA'S IN THE KITCHEN, WHAT'S IN DIANA?
I DUNNO. WHAT?
A STATE.
WHAT??
IN-DIANA. GET IT?
PETER, THAT'S THE STUPIDEST JOKE I'VE EVER HEARD.
AMEND
A STATE.
WHAT??

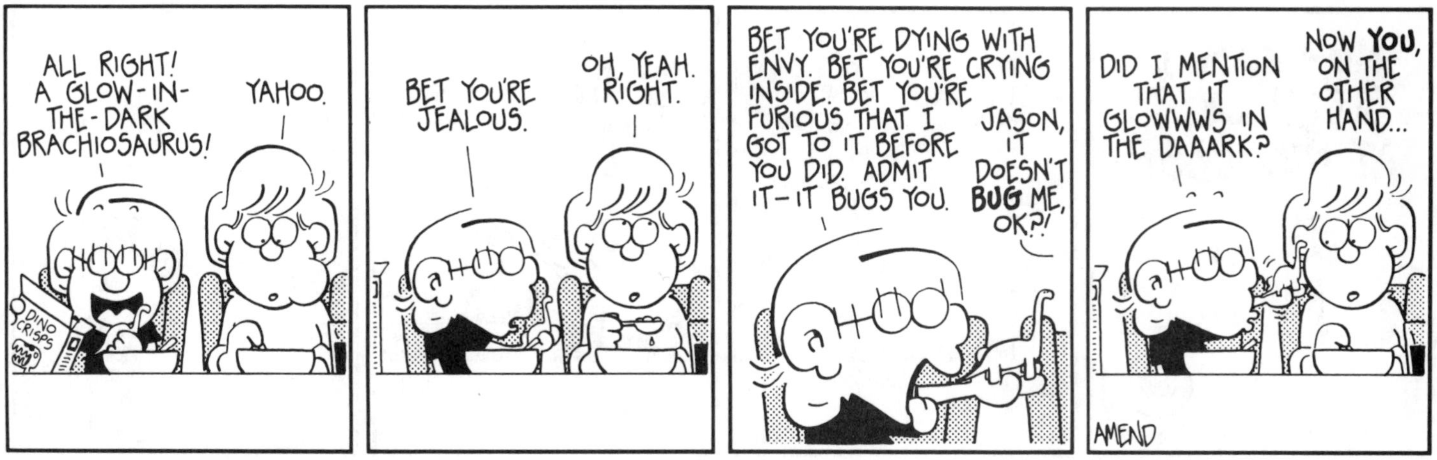
ALL RIGHT! A GLOW-IN-THE-DARK BRACHIOSAURUS!
YAHOO.
DINO CRISPS
BET YOU'RE JEALOUS.
OH, YEAH. RIGHT.
BET YOU'RE DYING WITH ENVY. BET YOU'RE CRYING INSIDE. BET YOU'RE FURIOUS THAT I GOT TO IT BEFORE YOU DID. ADMIT IT– IT BUGS YOU.
JASON, IT DOESN'T **BUG** ME, OK?!
DID I MENTION THAT IT GLOWWWS IN THE DAAARK?
NOW **YOU**, ON THE OTHER HAND...
AMEND

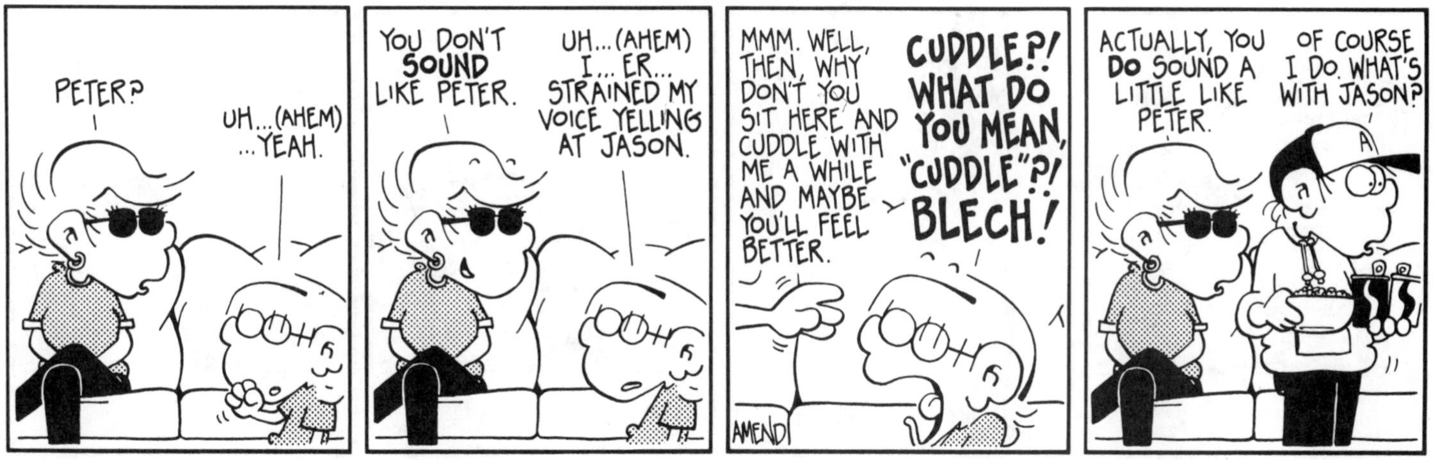
PETER?
UH...(AHEM) ...YEAH.
YOU DON'T **SOUND** LIKE PETER.
UH...(AHEM) I... ER... STRAINED MY VOICE YELLING AT JASON.
MMM. WELL, THEN, WHY DON'T YOU SIT HERE AND CUDDLE WITH ME A WHILE AND MAYBE YOU'LL FEEL BETTER.
CUDDLE?! WHAT DO YOU MEAN, "CUDDLE"?! BLECH!
AMEND
ACTUALLY, YOU **DO** SOUND A LITTLE LIKE PETER.
OF COURSE I DO. **WHAT'S** WITH JASON?

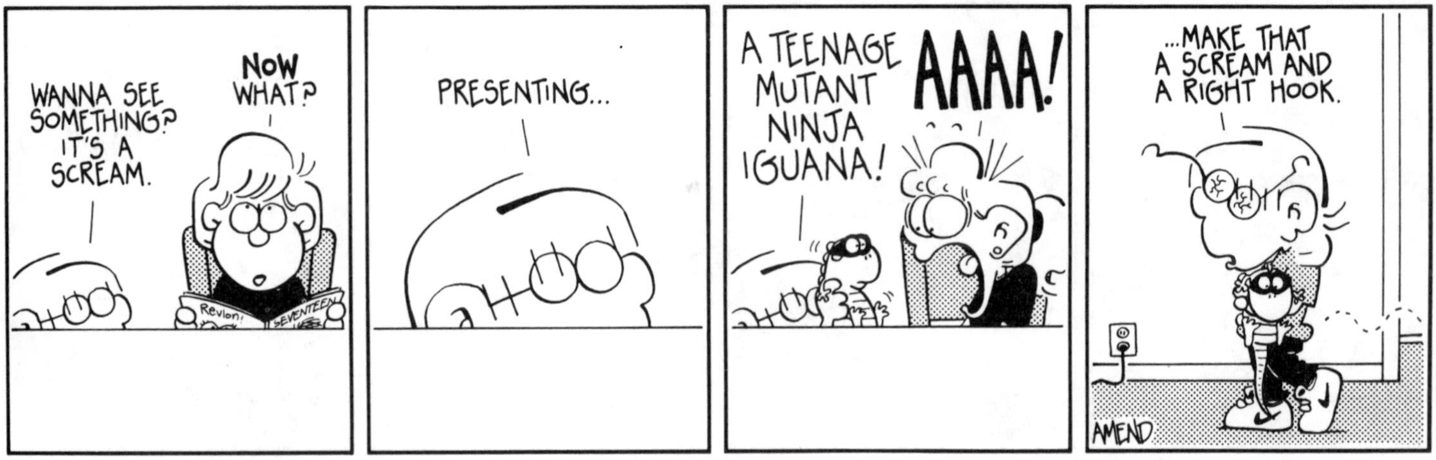
WANNA SEE SOMETHING? IT'S A SCREAM.
NOW WHAT?
Revlon!
SEVENTEEN
PRESENTING...
A TEENAGE MUTANT NINJA IGUANA!
AAAA!
...MAKE THAT A SCREAM AND A RIGHT HOOK.
AMEND

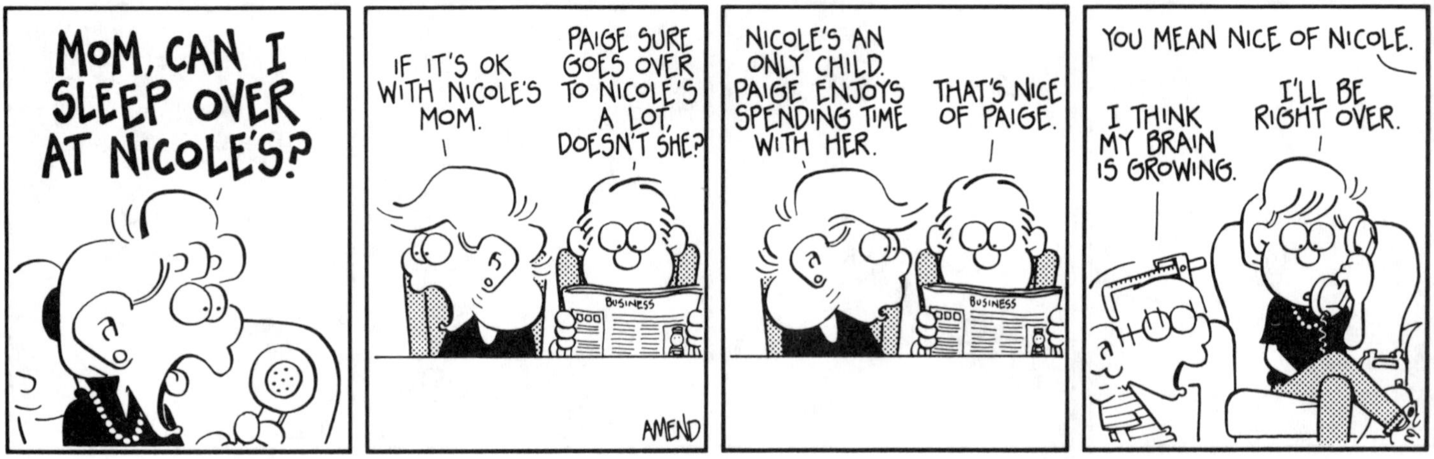
MOM, CAN I SLEEP OVER AT NICOLE'S?
IF IT'S OK WITH NICOLE'S MOM.
PAIGE SURE GOES OVER TO NICOLE'S A LOT, DOESN'T SHE?
BUSINESS
AMEND
NICOLE'S AN ONLY CHILD. PAIGE ENJOYS SPENDING TIME WITH HER.
THAT'S NICE OF PAIGE.
BUSINESS
YOU MEAN NICE OF NICOLE.
I THINK MY BRAIN IS GROWING.
I'LL BE RIGHT OVER.

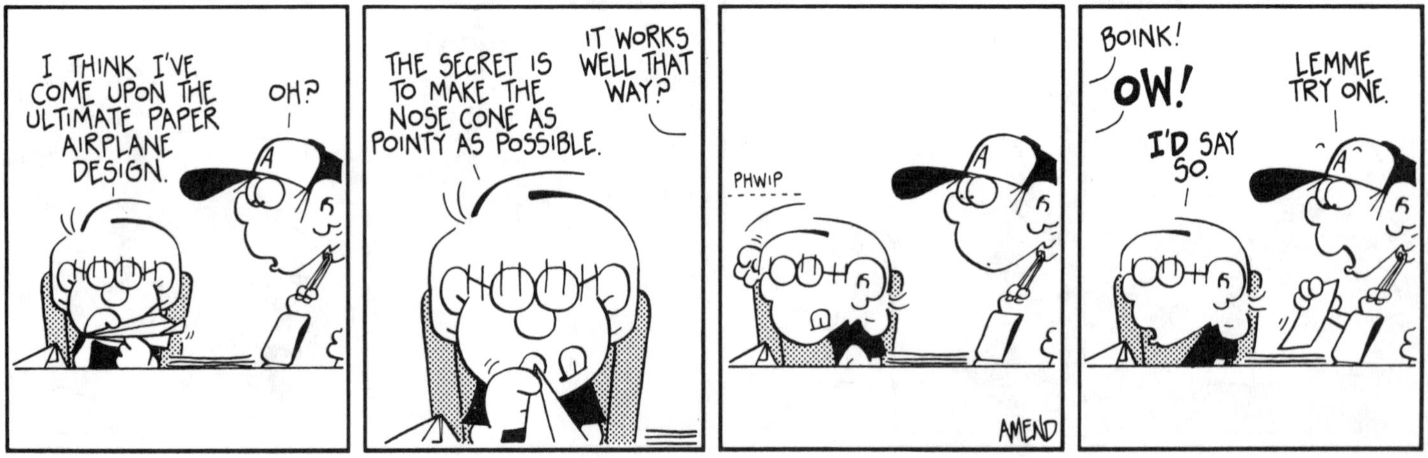
I THINK I'VE COME UPON THE ULTIMATE PAPER AIRPLANE DESIGN.
OH?
THE SECRET IS TO MAKE THE NOSE CONE AS POINTY AS POSSIBLE.
IT WORKS WELL THAT WAY?
PHWIP
AMEND
BOINK!
OW!
I'D SAY SO.
LEMME TRY ONE.

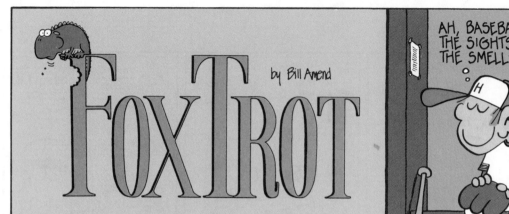

by Bill Amend

FoxTrot

AH, BASEBALL! THE SIGHTS... THE SMELLS...

FOX—WHAT ARE YOU DOING?! GET YOUR @#☆!! OUT ON THE FIELD!

THE SOUNDS...

PETER FOX, CENTERFIELDER EXTRAORDINAIRE, SETS HIMSELF FOR THE FINAL OUT OF THE GAME.

HIS TEAM, UP BY A RUN, IS ONLY THREE STRIKES AWAY FROM AN UPSET VICTORY.

THE BASES ARE LOADED. THEIR BEST HITTER IS AT THE PLATE.

AMEND

THE AIR IS FRAUGHT WITH TENSION. THIS IS IT, FOLKS. CRUNCH TIME.

ALL EYES FOCUS ON THE BATTER. NEVER MIND THE GREEN GRASS, THE BROWN DIRT, THE BLUE, CLOUDLESS SKY...

MAKE THAT SEMI-CLOUDLESS.

WHAP!

THE CROWD RISES AS ONE...

79

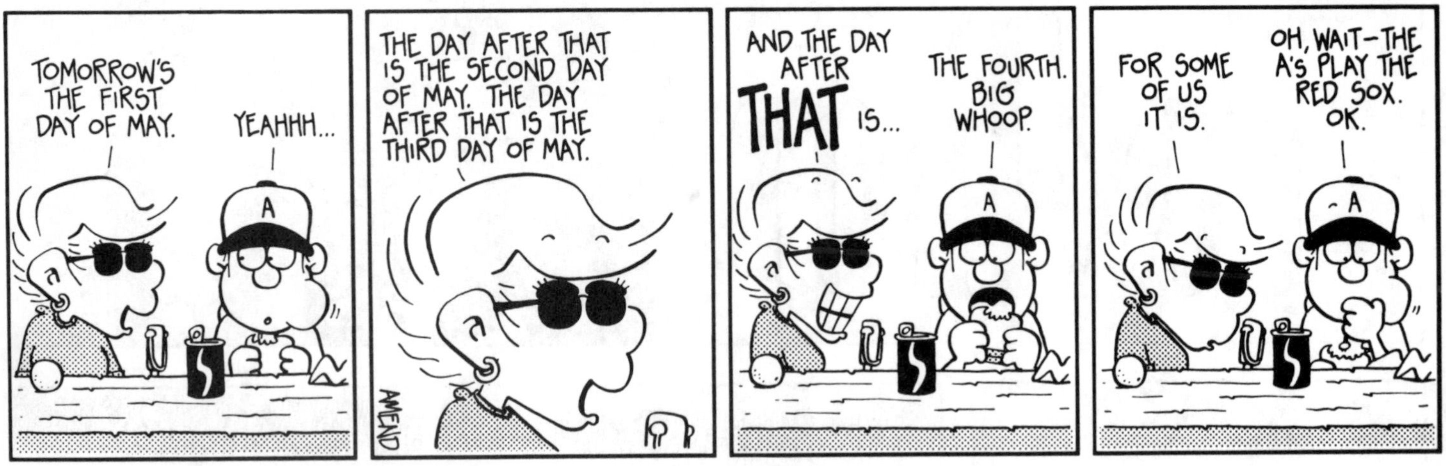
TOMORROW'S THE FIRST DAY OF MAY.
YEAHHH...
THE DAY AFTER THAT IS THE SECOND DAY OF MAY. THE DAY AFTER THAT IS THE THIRD DAY OF MAY.
AMEND
AND THE DAY AFTER THAT IS...
THE FOURTH. BIG WHOOP.
FOR SOME OF US IT IS.
OH, WAIT—THE A'S PLAY THE RED SOX. OK.

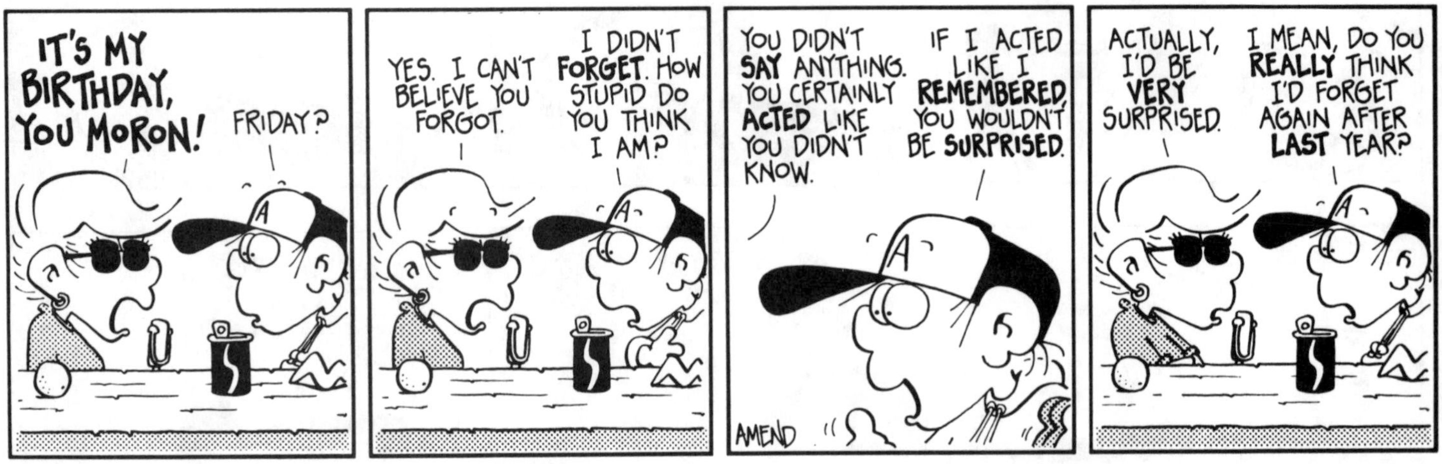
IT'S MY BIRTHDAY, YOU MORON!
FRIDAY?
YES. I CAN'T BELIEVE YOU FORGOT.
I DIDN'T FORGET. HOW STUPID DO YOU THINK I AM?
YOU DIDN'T SAY ANYTHING. YOU CERTAINLY ACTED LIKE YOU DIDN'T KNOW.
IF I ACTED LIKE I REMEMBERED, YOU WOULDN'T BE SURPRISED.
AMEND
ACTUALLY, I'D BE VERY SURPRISED.
I MEAN, DO YOU REALLY THINK I'D FORGET AGAIN AFTER LAST YEAR?

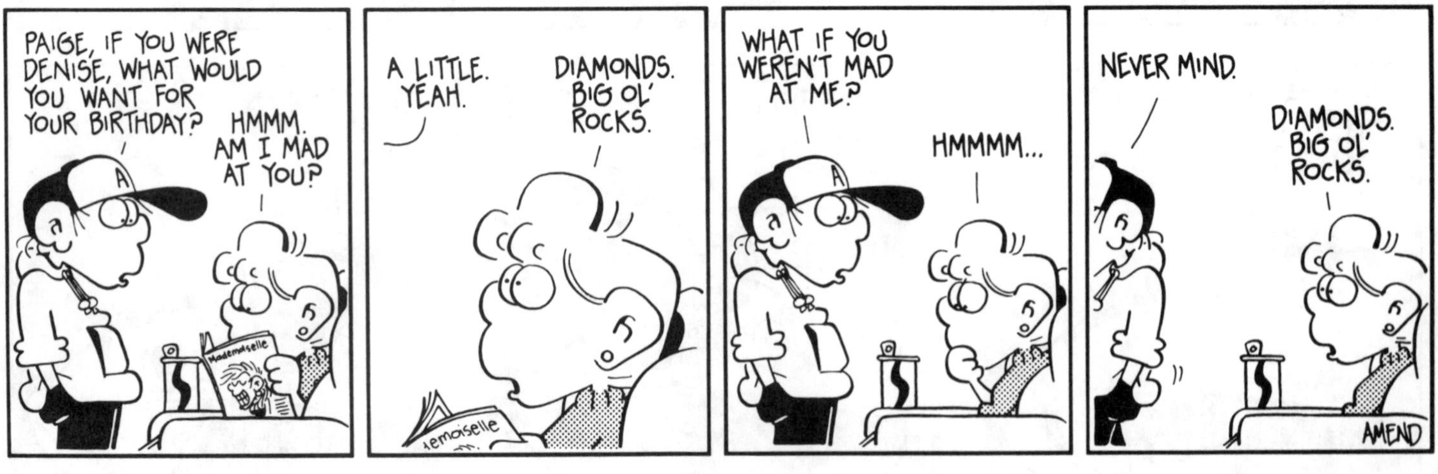
PAIGE, IF YOU WERE DENISE, WHAT WOULD YOU WANT FOR YOUR BIRTHDAY?
HMMM. AM I MAD AT YOU?
Mademoiselle
A LITTLE. YEAH.
DIAMONDS. BIG OL' ROCKS.
WHAT IF YOU WEREN'T MAD AT ME?
HMMMM...
NEVER MIND.
DIAMONDS. BIG OL' ROCKS.
AMEND

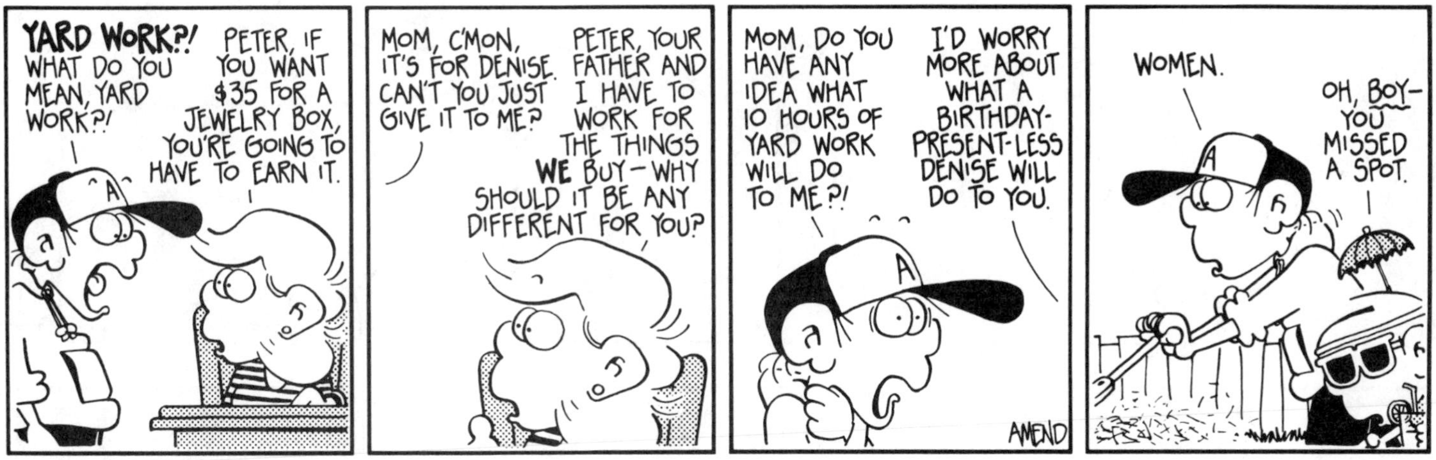
YARD WORK?! WHAT DO YOU MEAN, YARD WORK?!
PETER, IF YOU WANT $35 FOR A JEWELRY BOX, YOU'RE GOING TO HAVE TO EARN IT.
MOM, C'MON, IT'S FOR DENISE. CAN'T YOU JUST GIVE IT TO ME?
PETER, YOUR FATHER AND I HAVE TO WORK FOR THE THINGS WE BUY—WHY SHOULD IT BE ANY DIFFERENT FOR YOU?
MOM, DO YOU HAVE ANY IDEA WHAT 10 HOURS OF YARD WORK WILL DO TO ME?!
I'D WORRY MORE ABOUT WHAT A BIRTHDAY-PRESENT-LESS DENISE WILL DO TO YOU.
AMEND
WOMEN.
OH, BOY—YOU MISSED A SPOT.

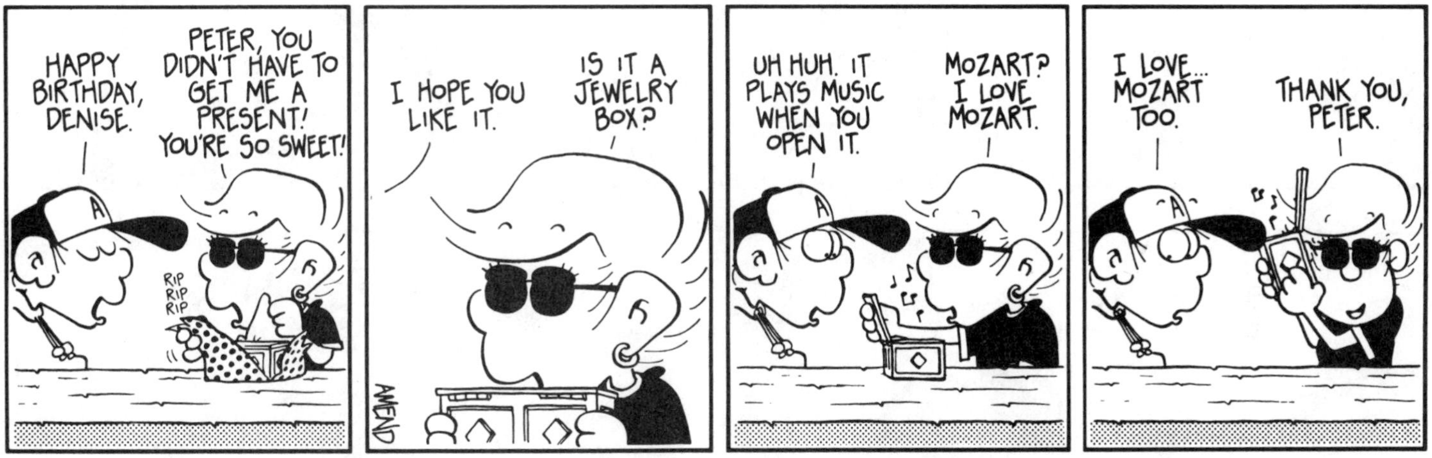
HAPPY BIRTHDAY, DENISE.
PETER, YOU DIDN'T HAVE TO GET ME A PRESENT! YOU'RE SO SWEET!
RIP RIP RIP
AMEND
I HOPE YOU LIKE IT.
IS IT A JEWELRY BOX?
UH HUH. IT PLAYS MUSIC WHEN YOU OPEN IT.
MOZART? I LOVE MOZART.
I LOVE... MOZART TOO.
THANK YOU, PETER.

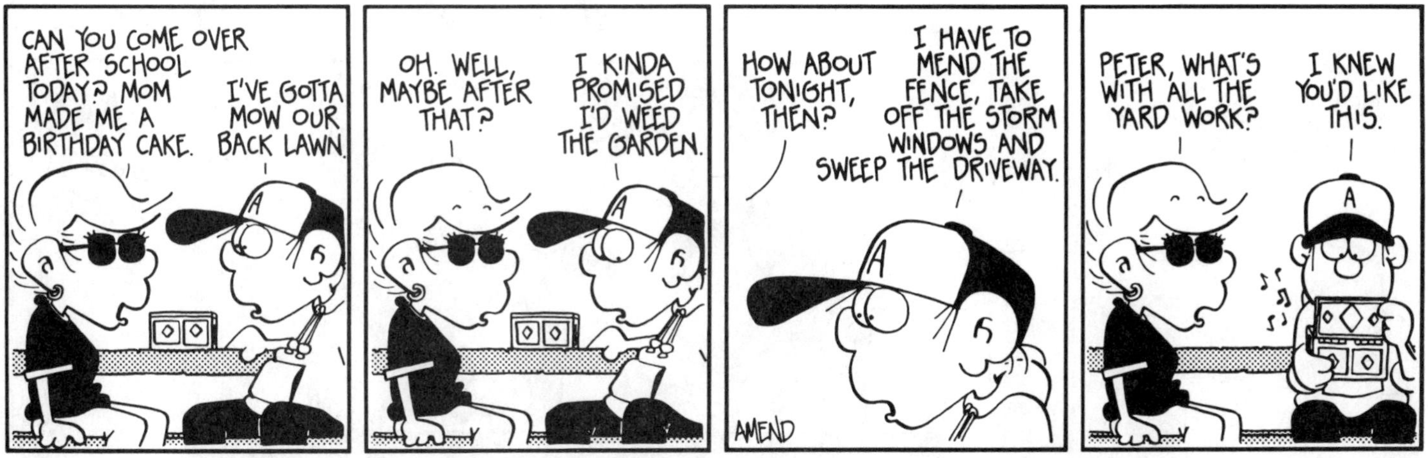
CAN YOU COME OVER AFTER SCHOOL TODAY? MOM MADE ME A BIRTHDAY CAKE.
I'VE GOTTA MOW OUR BACK LAWN.
OH. WELL, MAYBE AFTER THAT?
I KINDA PROMISED I'D WEED THE GARDEN.
HOW ABOUT TONIGHT, THEN?
I HAVE TO MEND THE FENCE, TAKE OFF THE STORM WINDOWS AND SWEEP THE DRIVEWAY.
AMEND
PETER, WHAT'S WITH ALL THE YARD WORK?
I KNEW YOU'D LIKE THIS.

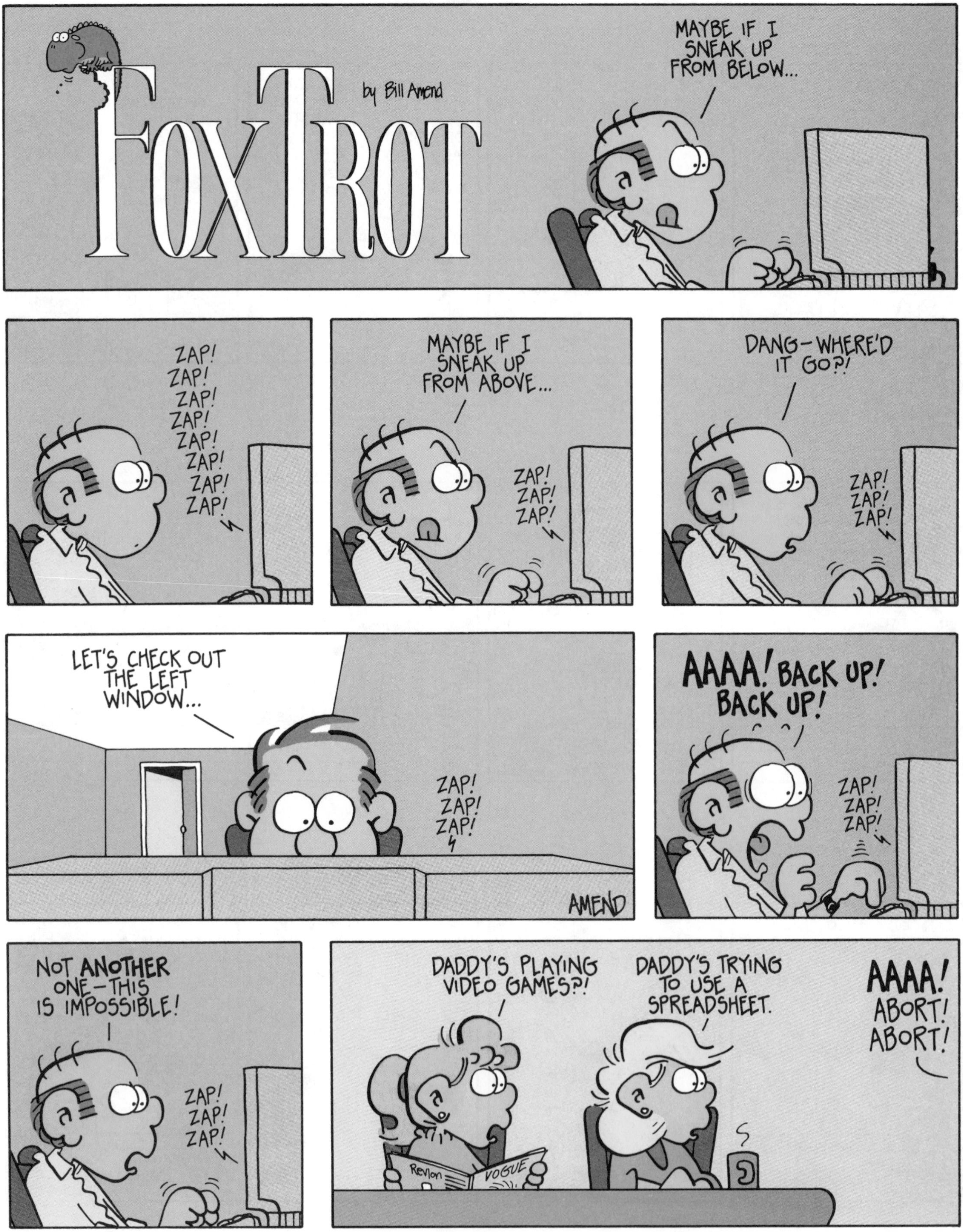
FoxTrot
by Bill Amend
MAYBE IF I SNEAK UP FROM BELOW...
ZAP! ZAP! ZAP! ZAP! ZAP! ZAP! ZAP! ZAP!
MAYBE IF I SNEAK UP FROM ABOVE...
ZAP! ZAP! ZAP!
DANG—WHERE'D IT GO?!
ZAP! ZAP! ZAP!
LET'S CHECK OUT THE LEFT WINDOW...
ZAP! ZAP! ZAP!
AMEND
AAAA! BACK UP! BACK UP!
ZAP! ZAP! ZAP!
NOT ANOTHER ONE—THIS IS IMPOSSIBLE!
ZAP! ZAP! ZAP!
DADDY'S PLAYING VIDEO GAMES?!
DADDY'S TRYING TO USE A SPREADSHEET.
AAAA! ABORT! ABORT!
Revlon
VOGUE

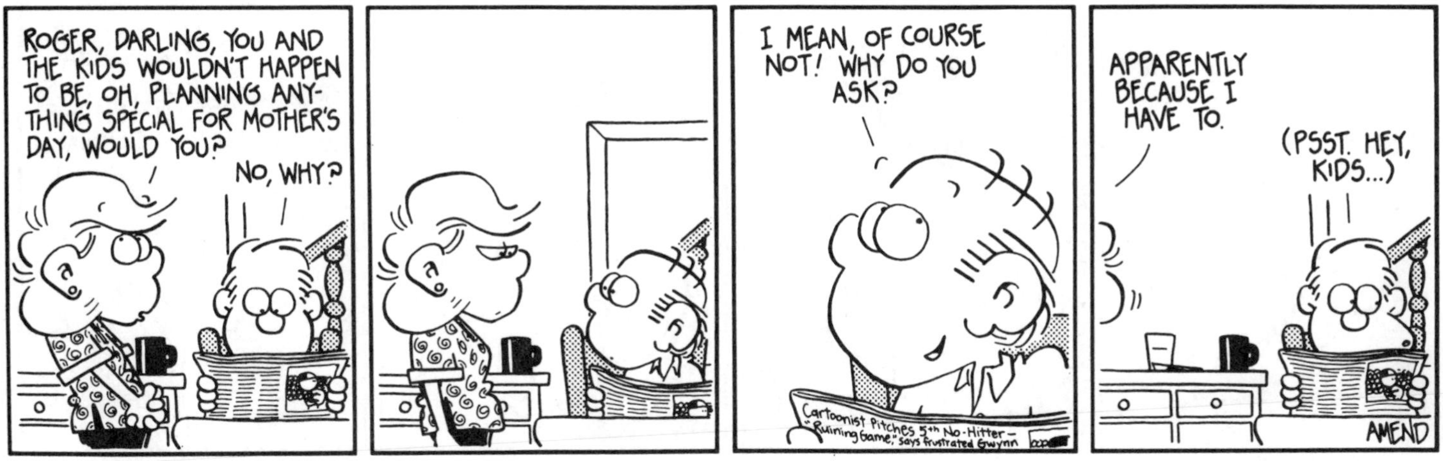
ROGER, DARLING, YOU AND THE KIDS WOULDN'T HAPPEN TO BE, OH, PLANNING ANYTHING SPECIAL FOR MOTHER'S DAY, WOULD YOU?
NO, WHY?
I MEAN, OF COURSE NOT! WHY DO YOU ASK?
Cartoonist Pitches 5th No-Hitter — "Ruining Game," Says Frustrated Gwynn
APPARENTLY BECAUSE I HAVE TO.
(PSST. HEY, KIDS...)
AMEND

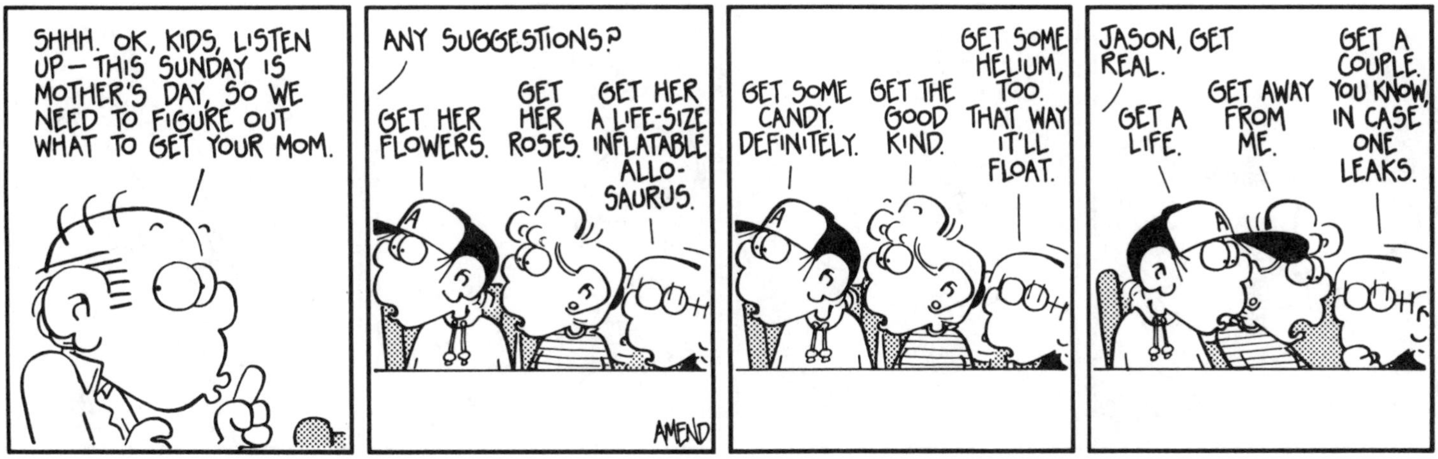
SHHH. OK, KIDS, LISTEN UP — THIS SUNDAY IS MOTHER'S DAY, SO WE NEED TO FIGURE OUT WHAT TO GET YOUR MOM.
ANY SUGGESTIONS?
GET HER FLOWERS.
GET HER ROSES.
GET HER A LIFE-SIZE INFLATABLE ALLOSAURUS.
AMEND
GET SOME CANDY. DEFINITELY.
GET THE GOOD KIND.
GET SOME HELIUM, TOO. THAT WAY IT'LL FLOAT.
JASON, GET REAL.
GET A LIFE.
GET AWAY FROM ME.
GET A COUPLE. YOU KNOW, IN CASE ONE LEAKS.

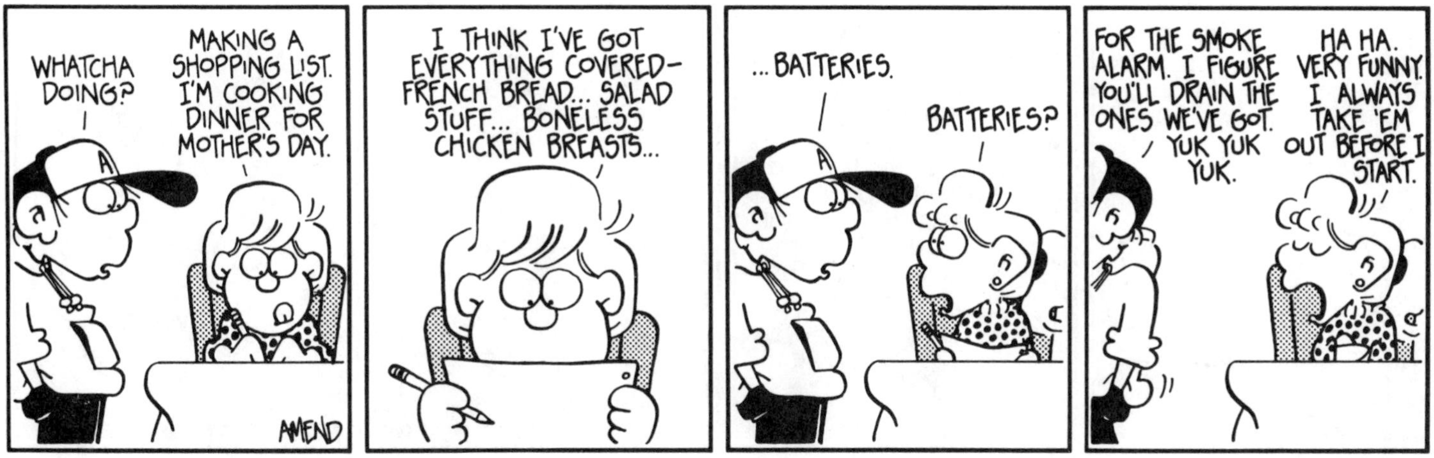
WHATCHA DOING?
MAKING A SHOPPING LIST. I'M COOKING DINNER FOR MOTHER'S DAY.
AMEND
I THINK I'VE GOT EVERYTHING COVERED — FRENCH BREAD... SALAD STUFF... BONELESS CHICKEN BREASTS...
...BATTERIES.
BATTERIES?
FOR THE SMOKE ALARM. I FIGURE YOU'LL DRAIN THE ONES WE'VE GOT. YUK YUK YUK.
HA HA. VERY FUNNY. I ALWAYS TAKE 'EM OUT BEFORE I START.

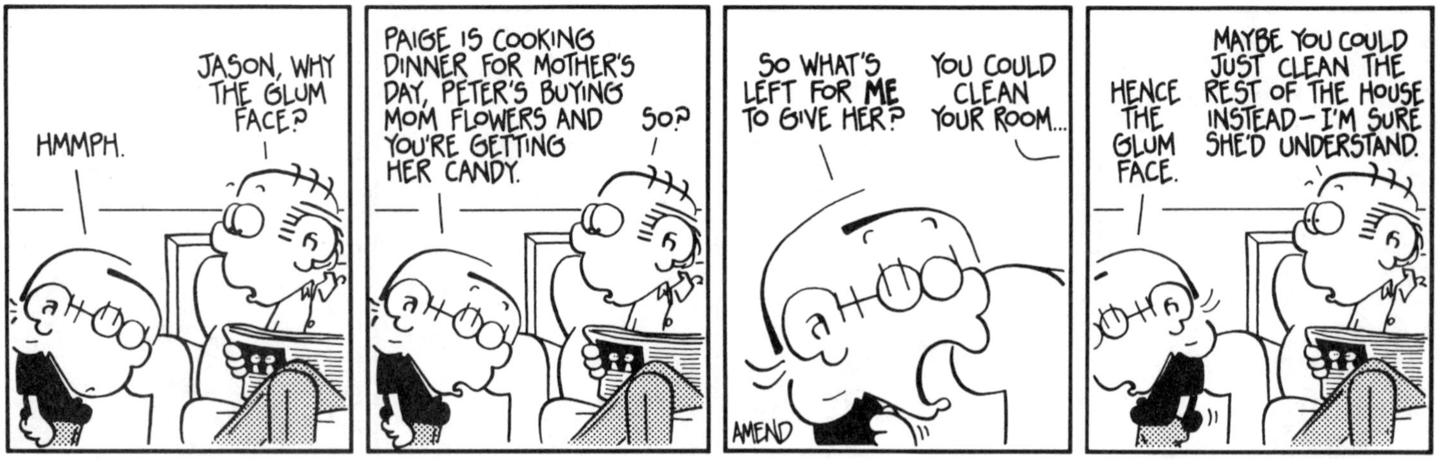
HMMPH.
JASON, WHY THE GLUM FACE?
PAIGE IS COOKING DINNER FOR MOTHER'S DAY, PETER'S BUYING MOM FLOWERS AND YOU'RE GETTING HER CANDY.
SO?
SO WHAT'S LEFT FOR **ME** TO GIVE HER?
YOU COULD CLEAN YOUR ROOM...
AMEND
HENCE THE GLUM FACE.
MAYBE YOU COULD JUST CLEAN THE REST OF THE HOUSE INSTEAD—I'M SURE SHE'D UNDERSTAND.

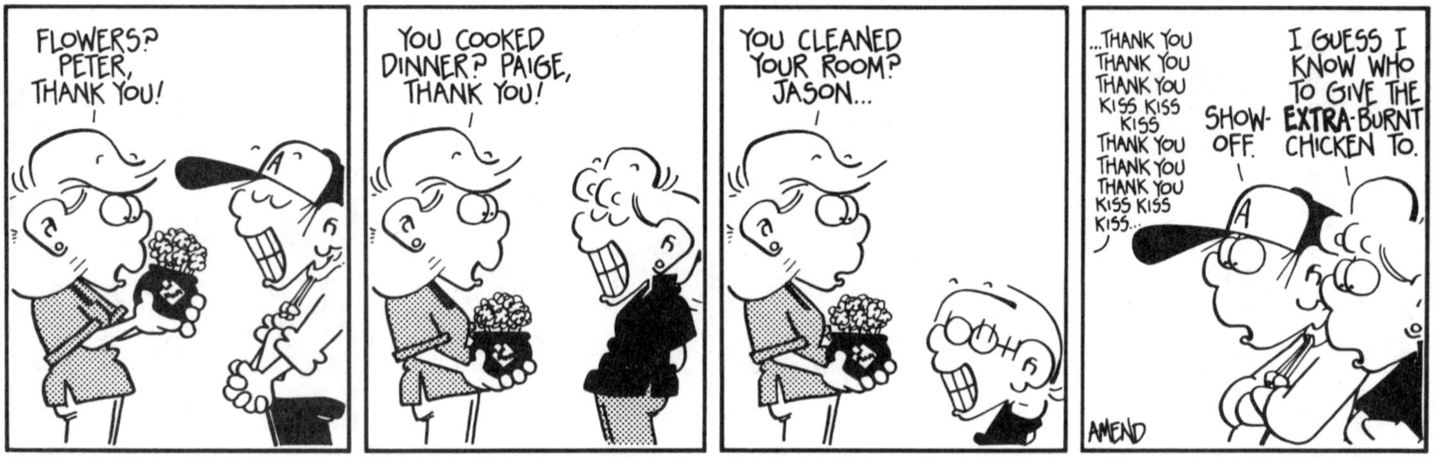
FLOWERS? PETER, THANK YOU!
YOU COOKED DINNER? PAIGE, THANK YOU!
YOU CLEANED YOUR ROOM? JASON...
...THANK YOU THANK YOU THANK YOU KISS KISS KISS THANK YOU THANK YOU THANK YOU KISS KISS KISS...
SHOW-OFF.
I GUESS I KNOW WHO TO GIVE THE **EXTRA**-BURNT CHICKEN TO.
AMEND

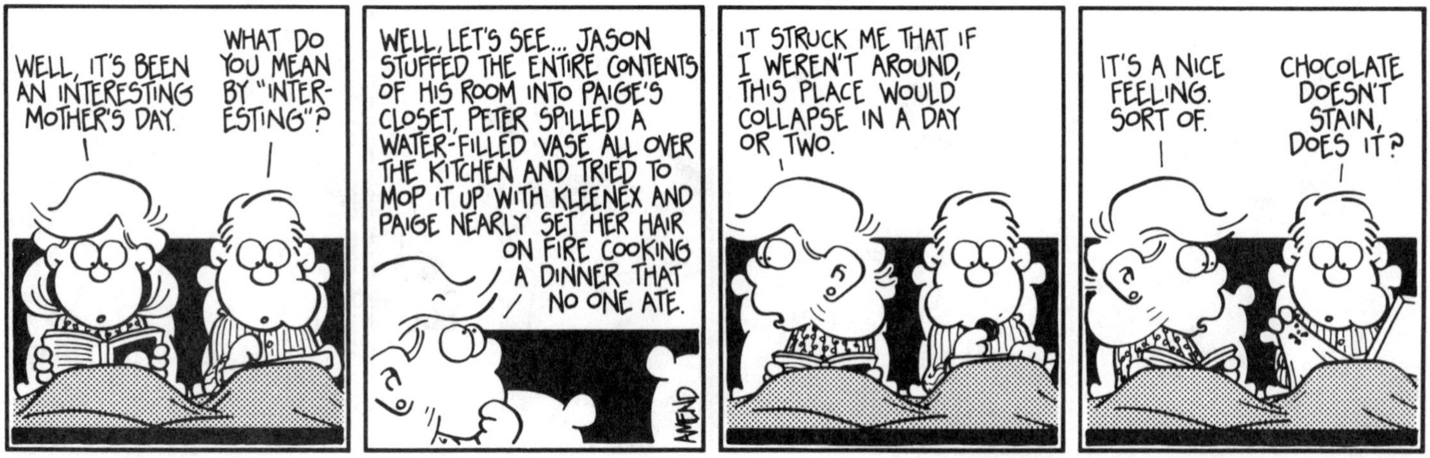
WELL, IT'S BEEN AN INTERESTING MOTHER'S DAY.
WHAT DO YOU MEAN BY "INTER-ESTING"?
WELL, LET'S SEE... JASON STUFFED THE ENTIRE CONTENTS OF HIS ROOM INTO PAIGE'S CLOSET, PETER SPILLED A WATER-FILLED VASE ALL OVER THE KITCHEN AND TRIED TO MOP IT UP WITH KLEENEX AND PAIGE NEARLY SET HER HAIR ON FIRE COOKING A DINNER THAT NO ONE ATE.
AMEND
IT STRUCK ME THAT IF I WEREN'T AROUND, THIS PLACE WOULD COLLAPSE IN A DAY OR TWO.
IT'S A NICE FEELING. SORT OF.
CHOCOLATE DOESN'T STAIN, DOES IT?

by Bill Amend

FoxTrot

WAAA HA HA HA HA HA HA HA HA HA HA HA HA HA HA HA HA HA HA HA HA HA HA

HEE HEE HEE HEE HEE HEE

GIGGLE GIGGLE GIGGLE (SNIFF)

DANG, I'M FUNNY.

WHAT ARE YOU DOING?

DRAWING A COMIC STRIP.

WHAT FOR?

DOES EVERYTHING HAVE TO HAVE A REASON? CAN'T SOMEONE CREATE SOMETHING SIMPLY FOR THE SHEER JOY OF IT?

EXCUSE ME, MR. PHILOSOPHER.

HAVEN'T YOU EVER HEARD OF SELF-EXPRESSION? HAVEN'T YOU EVER HEARD OF ART FOR ART'S SAKE?

AMEND

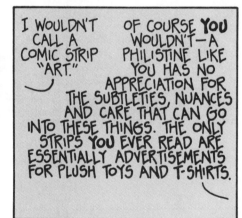

I WOULDN'T CALL A COMIC STRIP "ART."

OF COURSE YOU WOULDN'T—A PHILISTINE LIKE YOU HAS NO APPRECIATION FOR THE SUBTLETIES, NUANCES AND CARE THAT CAN GO INTO THESE THINGS. THE ONLY STRIPS YOU EVER READ ARE ESSENTIALLY ADVERTISEMENTS FOR PLUSH TOYS AND T-SHIRTS.

I, ON THE OTHER HAND, RECOGNIZE THE LIMITLESS POTENTIAL OF THE ART FORM AND SIT HERE NOW SAVORING NOT THE ANTICIPATION OF A HUGE LICENSING DEAL, BUT RATHER THE BEAUTIFUL AND CHALLENGING ACT OF CREATION.

AND IT IS BEAUTIFUL.

"BARF AND ARF"?!

EVEN THE TITLE IS POETRY.

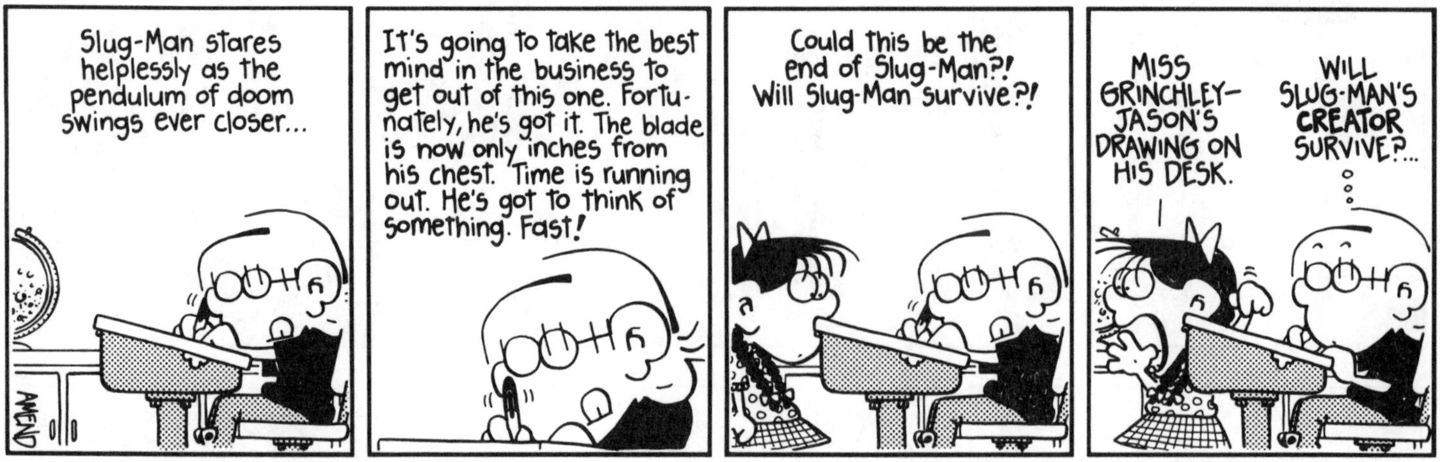
Slug-Man stares helplessly as the pendulum of doom swings ever closer...
AMEND
It's going to take the best mind in the business to get out of this one. Fortunately, he's got it. The blade is now only inches from his chest. Time is running out. He's got to think of something. Fast!
Could this be the end of Slug-Man?! Will Slug-Man survive?!
MISS GRINCHLEY— JASON'S DRAWING ON HIS DESK.
WILL SLUG-MAN'S **CREATOR** SURVIVE?...

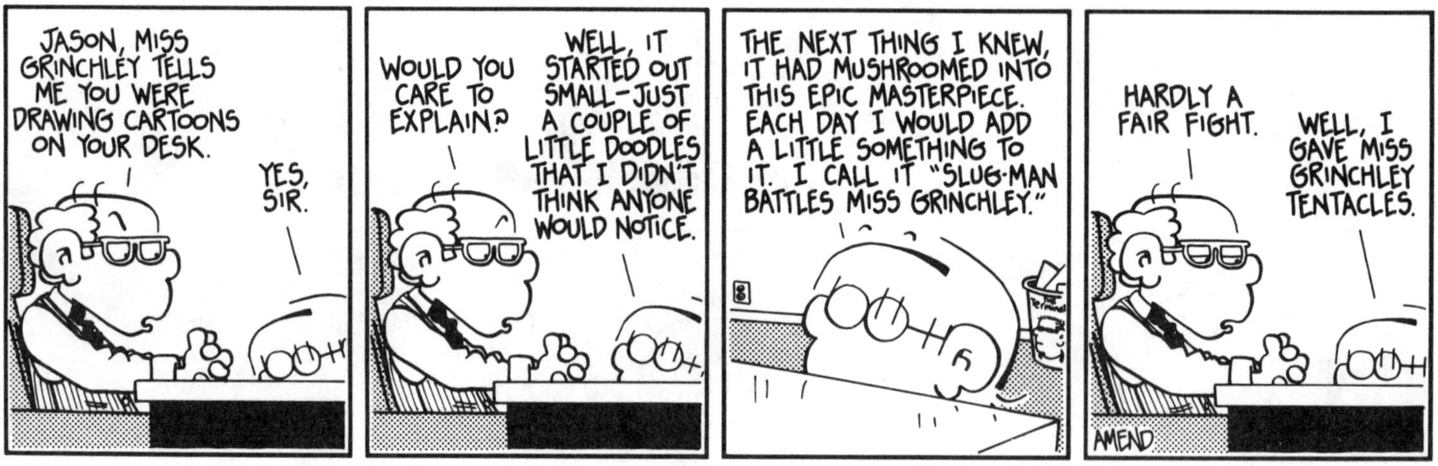
JASON, MISS GRINCHLEY TELLS ME YOU WERE DRAWING CARTOONS ON YOUR DESK.
YES, SIR.
WOULD YOU CARE TO EXPLAIN?
WELL, IT STARTED OUT SMALL—JUST A COUPLE OF LITTLE DOODLES THAT I DIDN'T THINK ANYONE WOULD NOTICE.
THE NEXT THING I KNEW, IT HAD MUSHROOMED INTO THIS EPIC MASTERPIECE. EACH DAY I WOULD ADD A LITTLE SOMETHING TO IT. I CALL IT "SLUG-MAN BATTLES MISS GRINCHLEY."
HARDLY A FAIR FIGHT.
WELL, I GAVE MISS GRINCHLEY TENTACLES.
AMEND

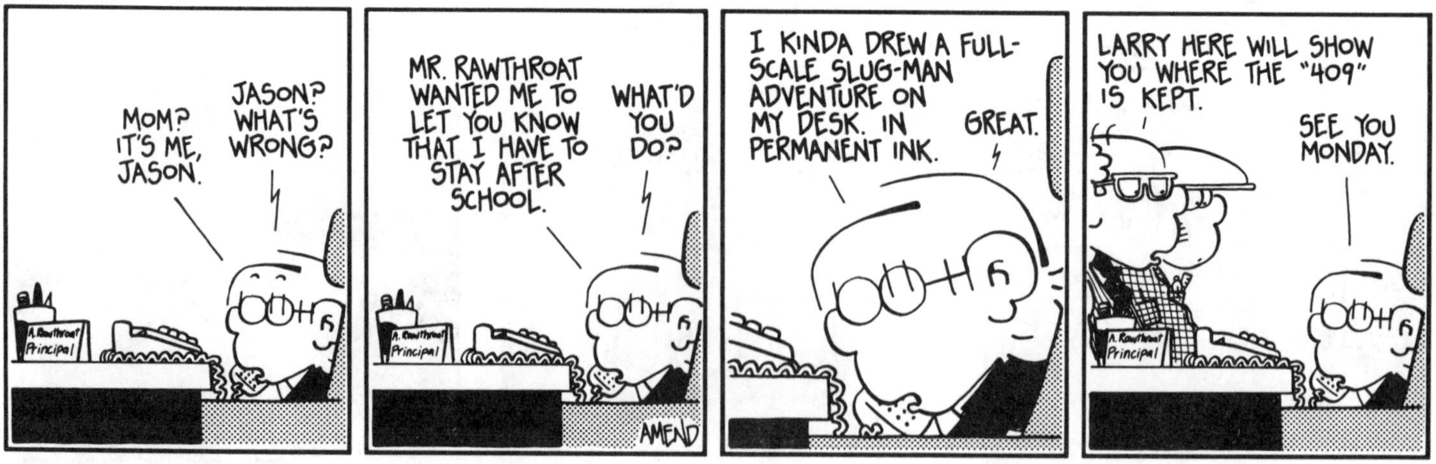
MOM? IT'S ME, JASON.
JASON? WHAT'S WRONG?
A. Rawthroat Principal
MR. RAWTHROAT WANTED ME TO LET YOU KNOW THAT I HAVE TO STAY AFTER SCHOOL.
WHAT'D YOU DO?
AMEND
I KINDA DREW A FULL-SCALE SLUG-MAN ADVENTURE ON MY DESK. IN PERMANENT INK.
GREAT.
LARRY HERE WILL SHOW YOU WHERE THE "409" IS KEPT.
SEE YOU MONDAY.

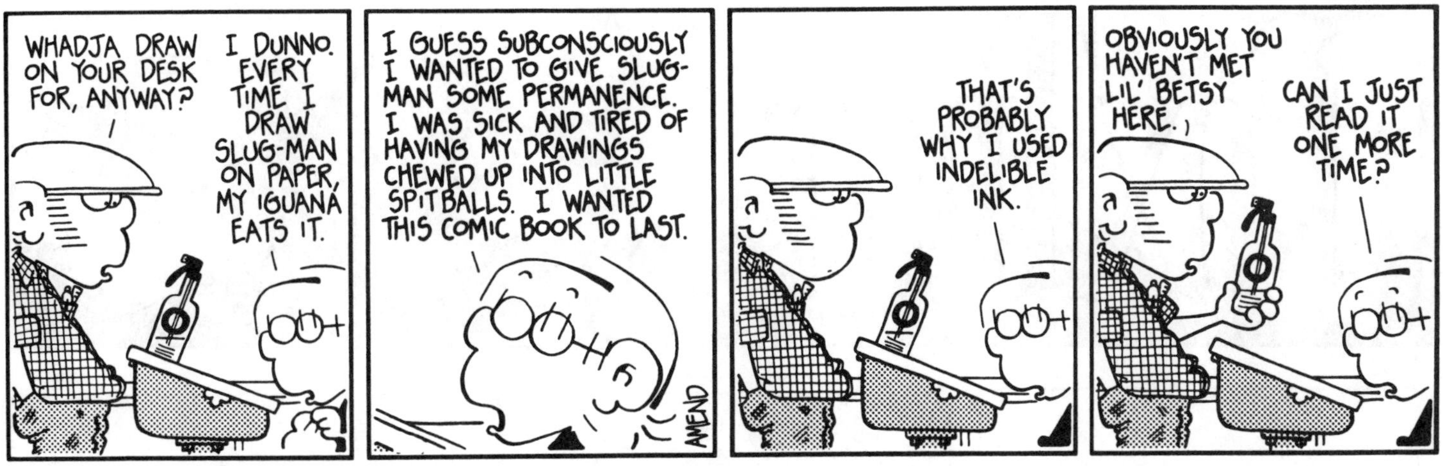
WHADJA DRAW ON YOUR DESK FOR, ANYWAY?
I DUNNO. EVERY TIME I DRAW SLUG-MAN ON PAPER, MY IGUANA EATS IT.
I GUESS SUBCONSCIOUSLY I WANTED TO GIVE SLUG-MAN SOME PERMANENCE. I WAS SICK AND TIRED OF HAVING MY DRAWINGS CHEWED UP INTO LITTLE SPITBALLS. I WANTED THIS COMIC BOOK TO LAST.
AMEND
THAT'S PROBABLY WHY I USED INDELIBLE INK.
OBVIOUSLY YOU HAVEN'T MET LIL' BETSY HERE.
CAN I JUST READ IT ONE MORE TIME?

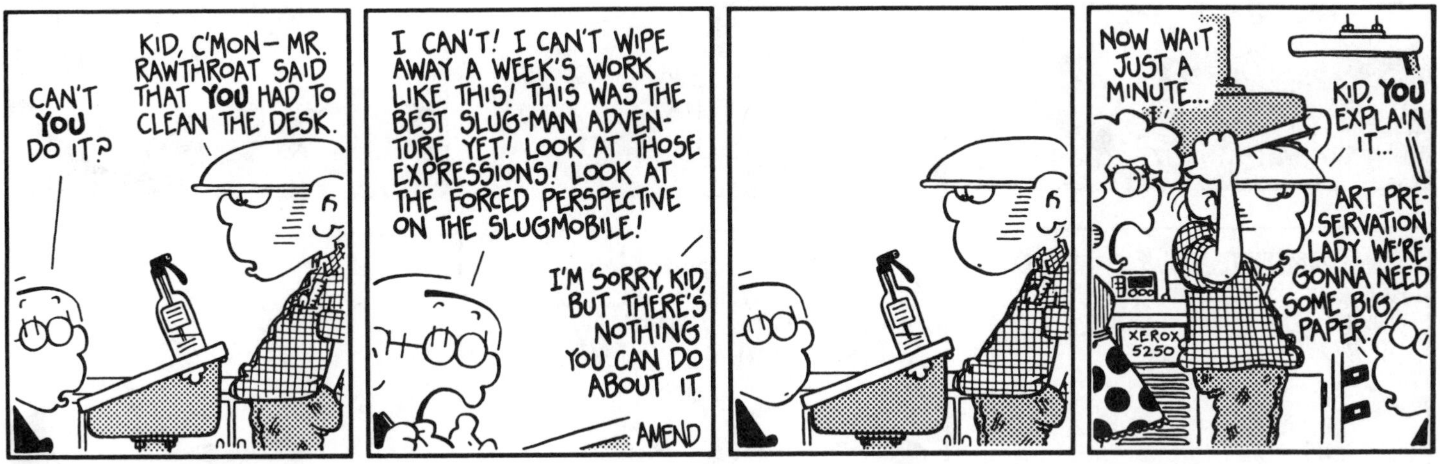
CAN'T **YOU** DO IT?
KID, C'MON— MR. RAWTHROAT SAID THAT **YOU** HAD TO CLEAN THE DESK.
I CAN'T! I CAN'T WIPE AWAY A WEEK'S WORK LIKE THIS! THIS WAS THE BEST SLUG-MAN ADVENTURE YET! LOOK AT THOSE EXPRESSIONS! LOOK AT THE FORCED PERSPECTIVE ON THE SLUGMOBILE!
I'M SORRY, KID, BUT THERE'S NOTHING YOU CAN DO ABOUT IT.
AMEND
NOW WAIT JUST A MINUTE...
KID, **YOU** EXPLAIN IT...
ART PRESERVATION LADY. WE'RE GONNA NEED SOME BIG PAPER.
XEROX 5250

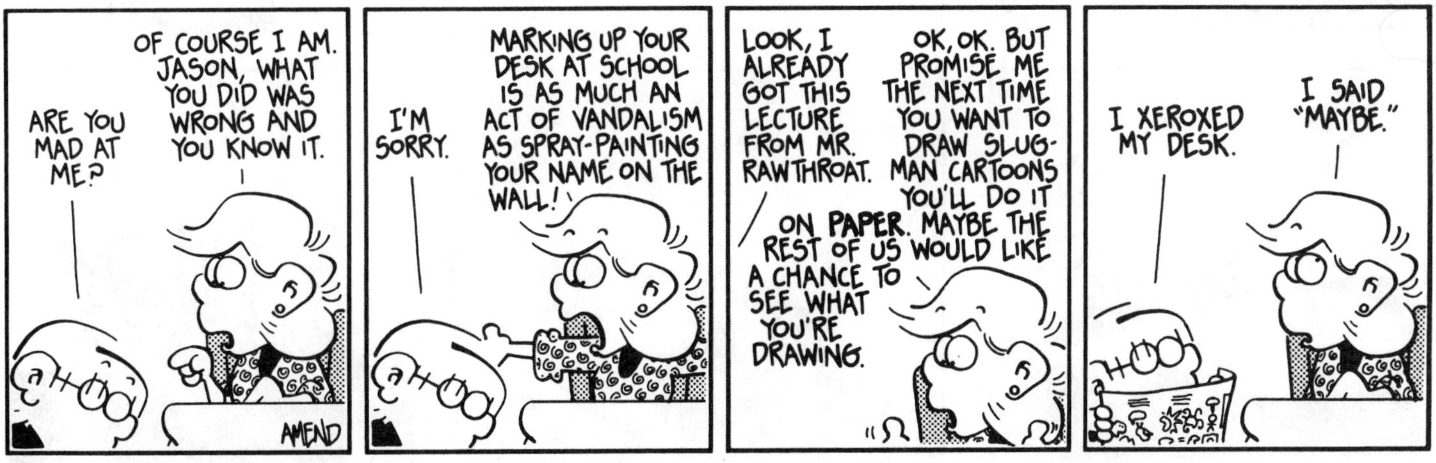
ARE YOU MAD AT ME?
OF COURSE I AM. JASON, WHAT YOU DID WAS WRONG AND YOU KNOW IT.
AMEND
I'M SORRY.
MARKING UP YOUR DESK AT SCHOOL IS AS MUCH AN ACT OF VANDALISM AS SPRAY-PAINTING YOUR NAME ON THE WALL!
LOOK, I ALREADY GOT THIS LECTURE FROM MR. RAWTHROAT.
OK, OK. BUT PROMISE ME THE NEXT TIME YOU WANT TO DRAW SLUG-MAN CARTOONS YOU'LL DO IT ON **PAPER**. MAYBE THE REST OF US WOULD LIKE A CHANCE TO SEE WHAT YOU'RE DRAWING.
I XEROXED MY DESK.
I SAID "MAYBE."

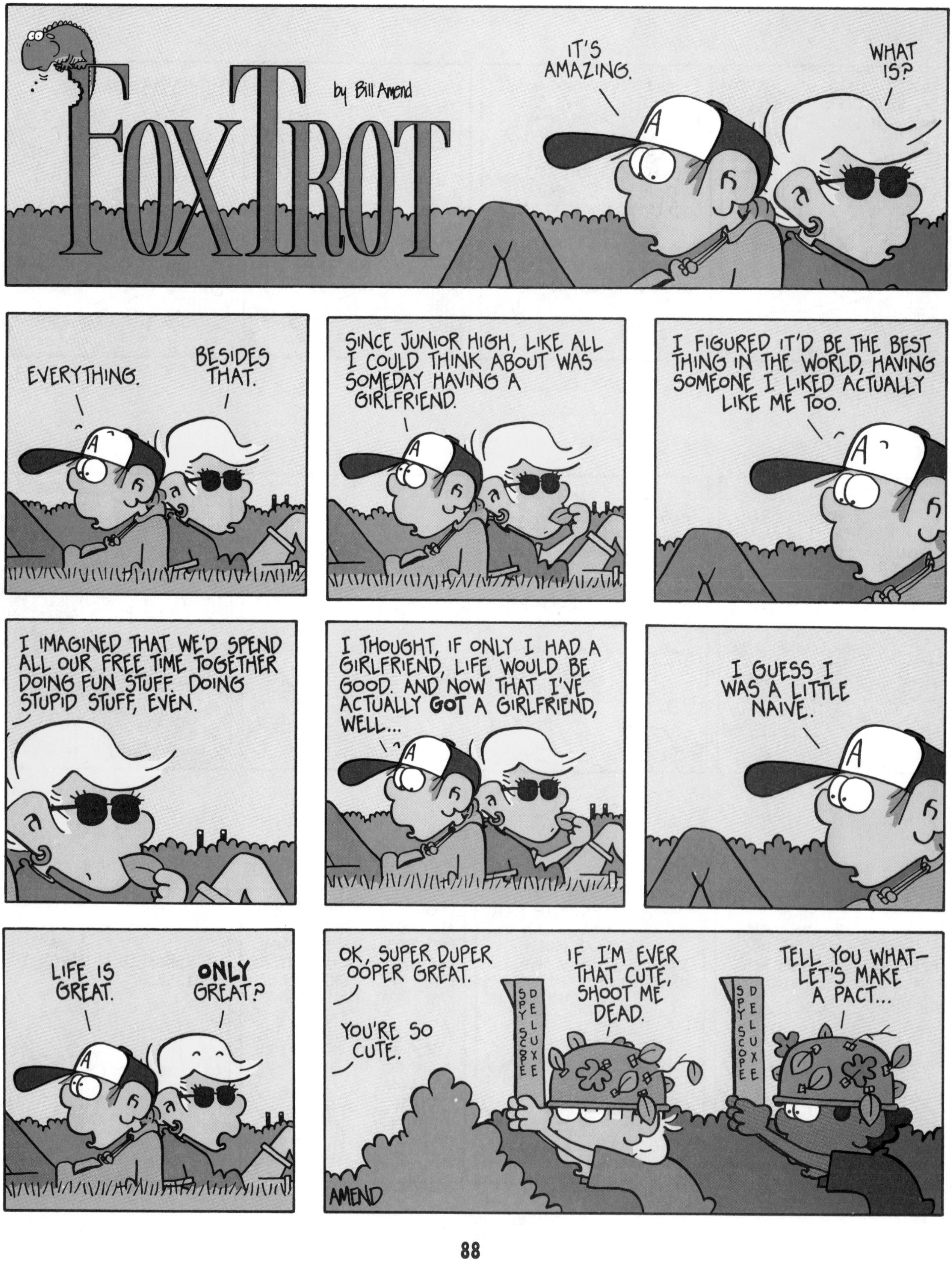
FoxTrot
by Bill Amend
IT'S AMAZING.
WHAT IS?
EVERYTHING.
BESIDES THAT.
SINCE JUNIOR HIGH, LIKE ALL I COULD THINK ABOUT WAS SOMEDAY HAVING A GIRLFRIEND.
I FIGURED IT'D BE THE BEST THING IN THE WORLD, HAVING SOMEONE I LIKED ACTUALLY LIKE ME TOO.
I IMAGINED THAT WE'D SPEND ALL OUR FREE TIME TOGETHER DOING FUN STUFF. DOING STUPID STUFF, EVEN.
I THOUGHT, IF ONLY I HAD A GIRLFRIEND, LIFE WOULD BE GOOD. AND NOW THAT I'VE ACTUALLY **GOT** A GIRLFRIEND, WELL...
I GUESS I WAS A LITTLE NAIVE.
LIFE IS GREAT.
ONLY GREAT?
OK, SUPER DUPER OOPER GREAT.
YOU'RE SO CUTE.
SPY SCOPE DELUXE
IF I'M EVER THAT CUTE, SHOOT ME DEAD.
SPY SCOPE DELUXE
TELL YOU WHAT—LET'S MAKE A PACT...
AMEND

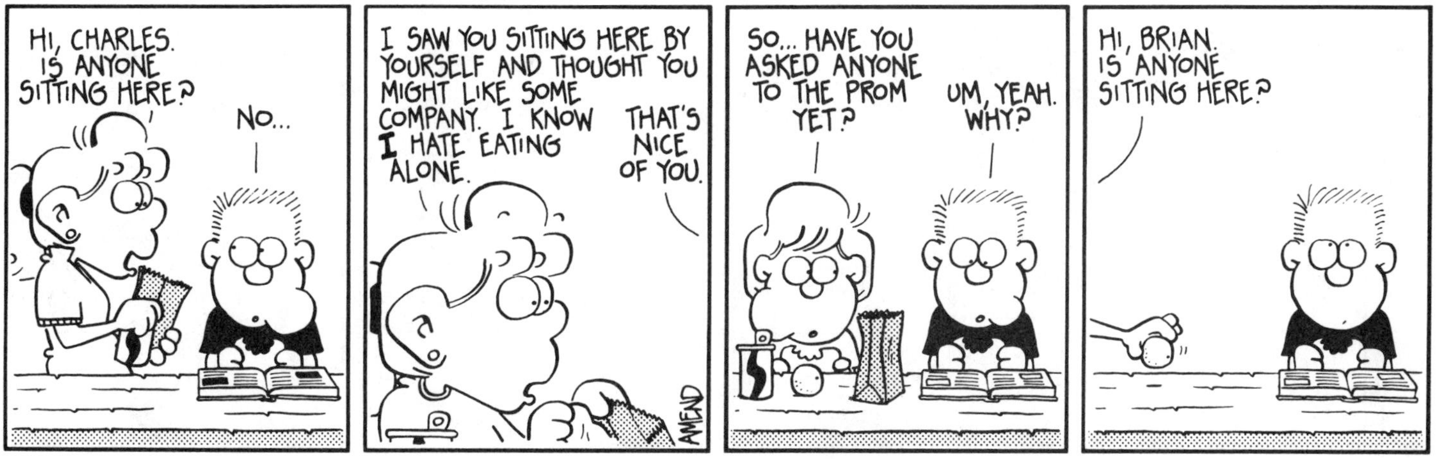
HI, CHARLES. IS ANYONE SITTING HERE?
NO...
I SAW YOU SITTING HERE BY YOURSELF AND THOUGHT YOU MIGHT LIKE SOME COMPANY. I KNOW I HATE EATING ALONE.
THAT'S NICE OF YOU.
AMEND
SO... HAVE YOU ASKED ANYONE TO THE PROM YET?
UM, YEAH. WHY?
HI, BRIAN. IS ANYONE SITTING HERE?

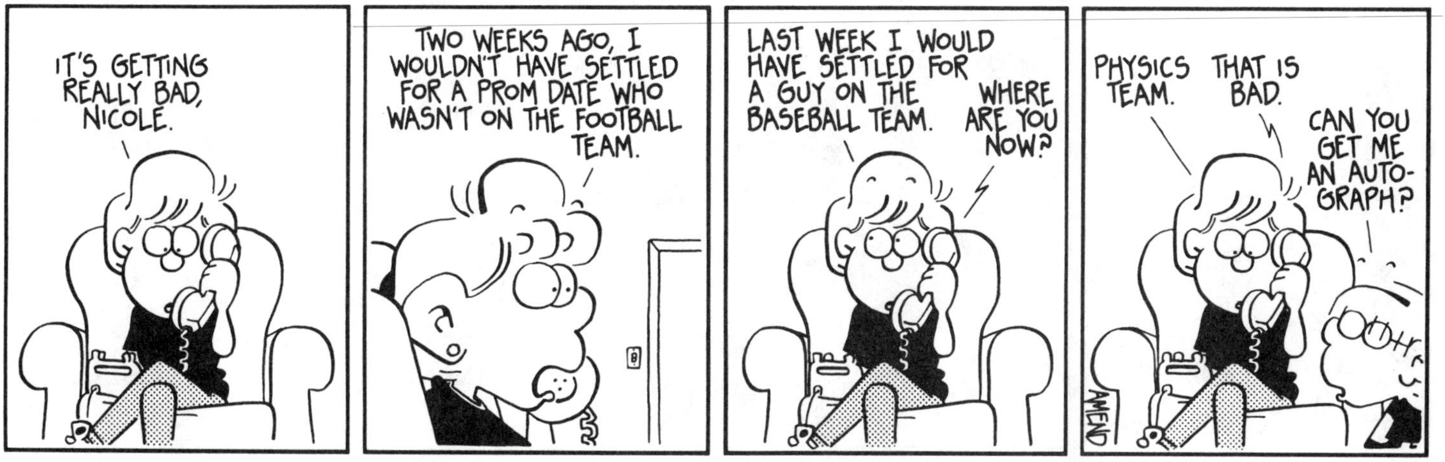
IT'S GETTING REALLY BAD, NICOLE.
TWO WEEKS AGO, I WOULDN'T HAVE SETTLED FOR A PROM DATE WHO WASN'T ON THE FOOTBALL TEAM.
LAST WEEK I WOULD HAVE SETTLED FOR A GUY ON THE BASEBALL TEAM.
WHERE ARE YOU NOW?
PHYSICS TEAM.
THAT IS BAD.
CAN YOU GET ME AN AUTOGRAPH?
AMEND

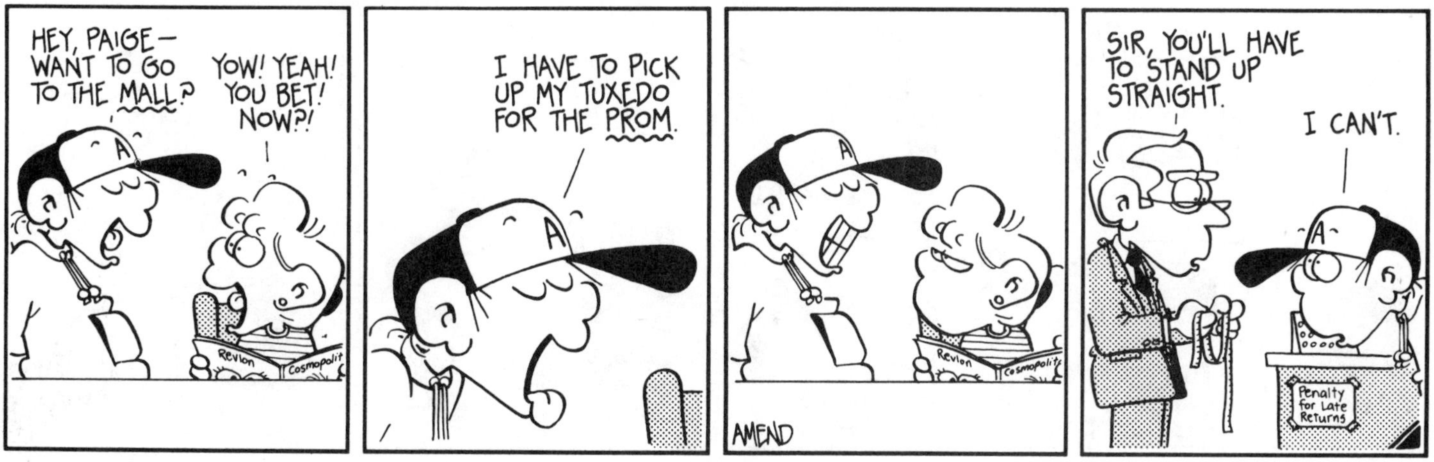
HEY, PAIGE— WANT TO GO TO THE MALL?
YOW! YEAH! YOU BET! NOW?!
Revlon
Cosmopolit
I HAVE TO PICK UP MY TUXEDO FOR THE PROM.
Revlon
Cosmopolit
AMEND
SIR, YOU'LL HAVE TO STAND UP STRAIGHT.
I CAN'T.
Penalty for Late Returns

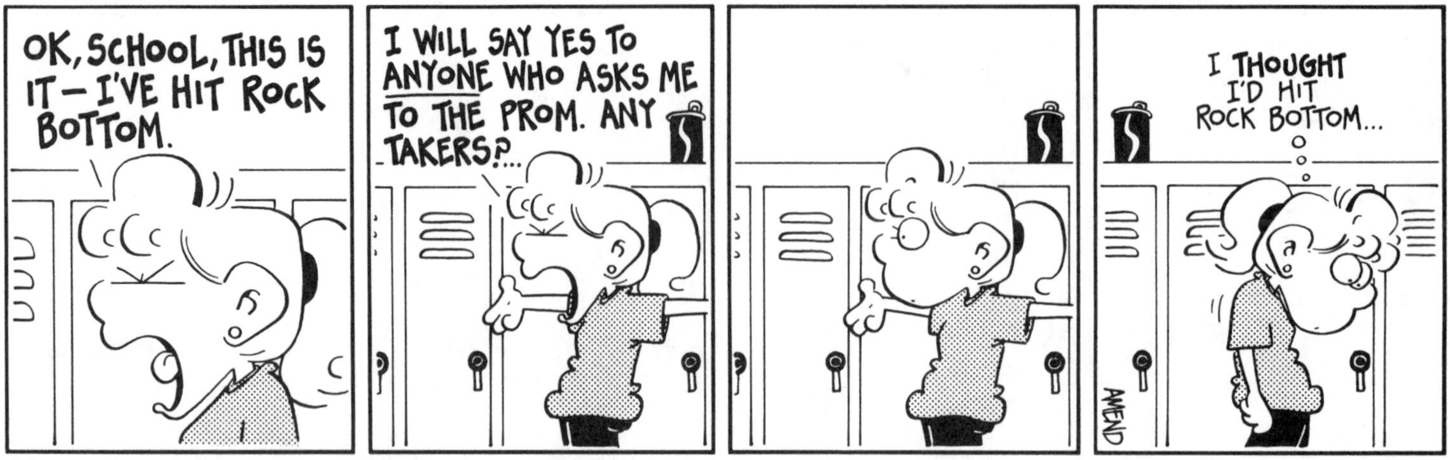
OK, SCHOOL, THIS IS IT—I'VE HIT ROCK BOTTOM.
I WILL SAY YES TO ANYONE WHO ASKS ME TO THE PROM. ANY TAKERS?...
I THOUGHT I'D HIT ROCK BOTTOM...
AMEND

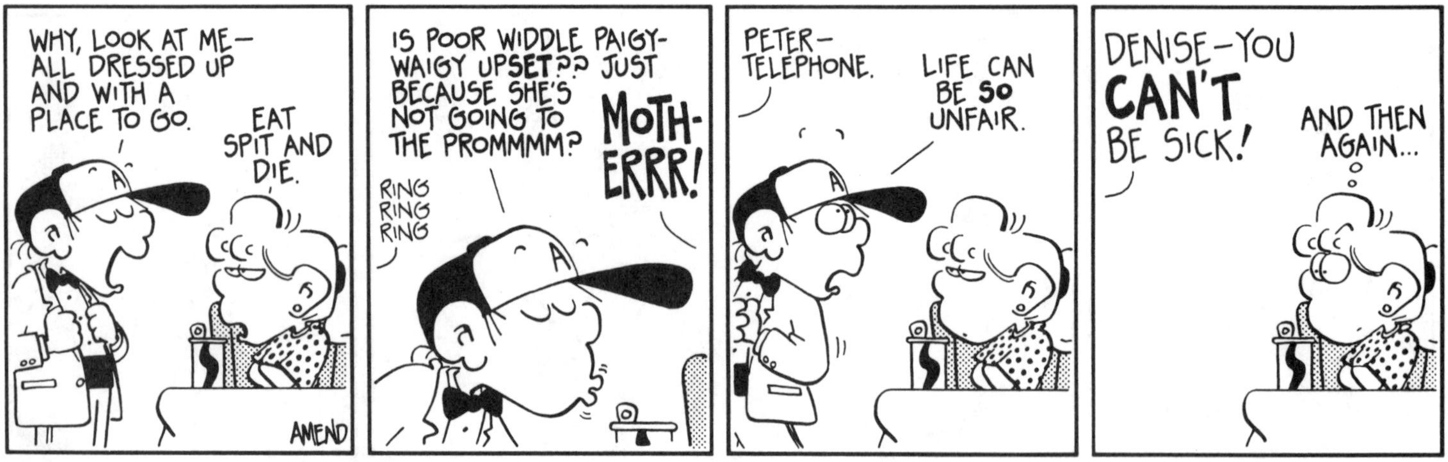
WHY, LOOK AT ME—ALL DRESSED UP AND WITH A PLACE TO GO.
EAT SPIT AND DIE.
AMEND
IS POOR WIDDLE PAIGY-WAIGY UPSET?? JUST BECAUSE SHE'S NOT GOING TO THE PROMMMM?
MOTH-ERRR!
RING RING RING
PETER—TELEPHONE.
LIFE CAN BE SO UNFAIR.
DENISE—YOU CAN'T BE SICK!
AND THEN AGAIN...

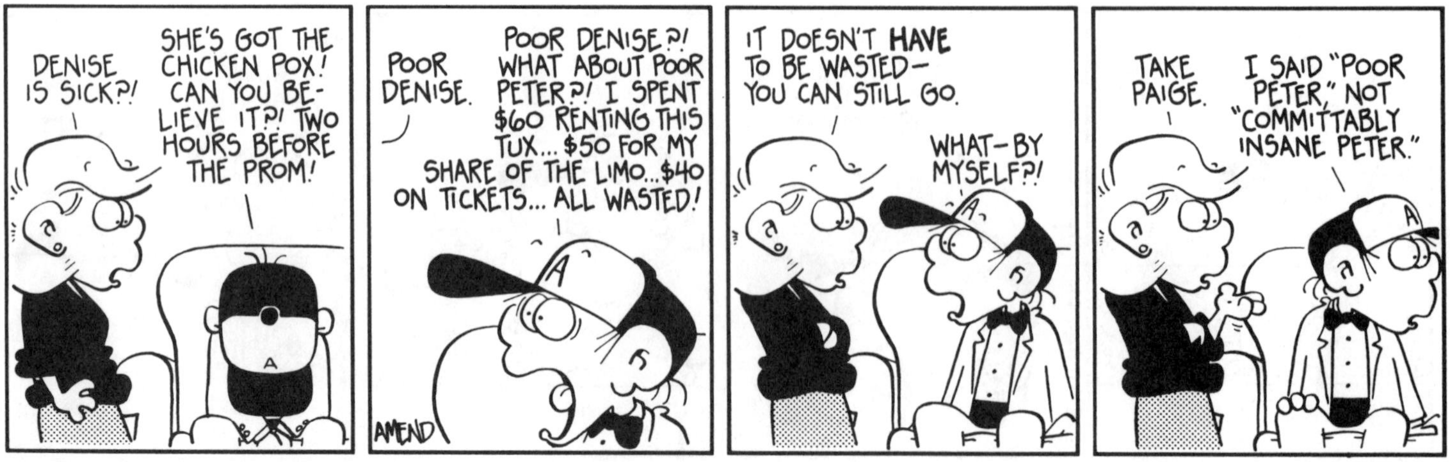
DENISE IS SICK?!
SHE'S GOT THE CHICKEN POX! CAN YOU BELIEVE IT?! TWO HOURS BEFORE THE PROM!
POOR DENISE.
POOR DENISE?! WHAT ABOUT POOR PETER?! I SPENT $60 RENTING THIS TUX... $50 FOR MY SHARE OF THE LIMO... $40 ON TICKETS... ALL WASTED!
AMEND
IT DOESN'T HAVE TO BE WASTED—YOU CAN STILL GO.
WHAT—BY MYSELF?!
TAKE PAIGE.
I SAID "POOR PETER," NOT "COMMITTABLY INSANE PETER."

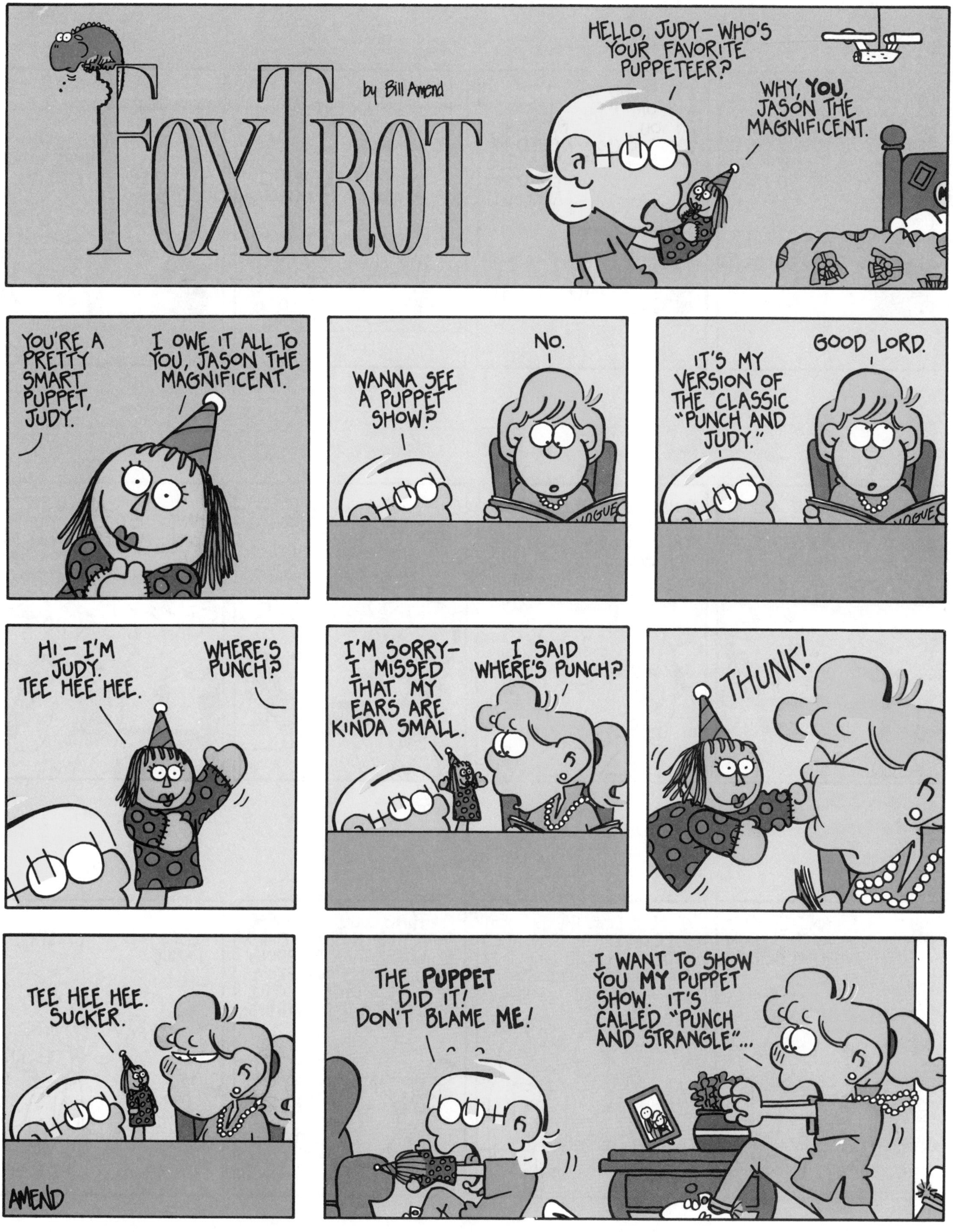
FOXTROT
by Bill Amend
HELLO, JUDY–WHO'S YOUR FAVORITE PUPPETEER?
WHY, YOU, JASON THE MAGNIFICENT.
YOU'RE A PRETTY SMART PUPPET, JUDY.
I OWE IT ALL TO YOU, JASON THE MAGNIFICENT.
WANNA SEE A PUPPET SHOW?
NO.
IT'S MY VERSION OF THE CLASSIC "PUNCH AND JUDY."
GOOD LORD.
HI–I'M JUDY. TEE HEE HEE.
WHERE'S PUNCH?
I'M SORRY–I MISSED THAT. MY EARS ARE KINDA SMALL.
I SAID WHERE'S PUNCH?
THUNK!
TEE HEE HEE. SUCKER.
AMEND
THE PUPPET DID IT! DON'T BLAME ME!
I WANT TO SHOW YOU MY PUPPET SHOW. IT'S CALLED "PUNCH AND STRANGLE"...

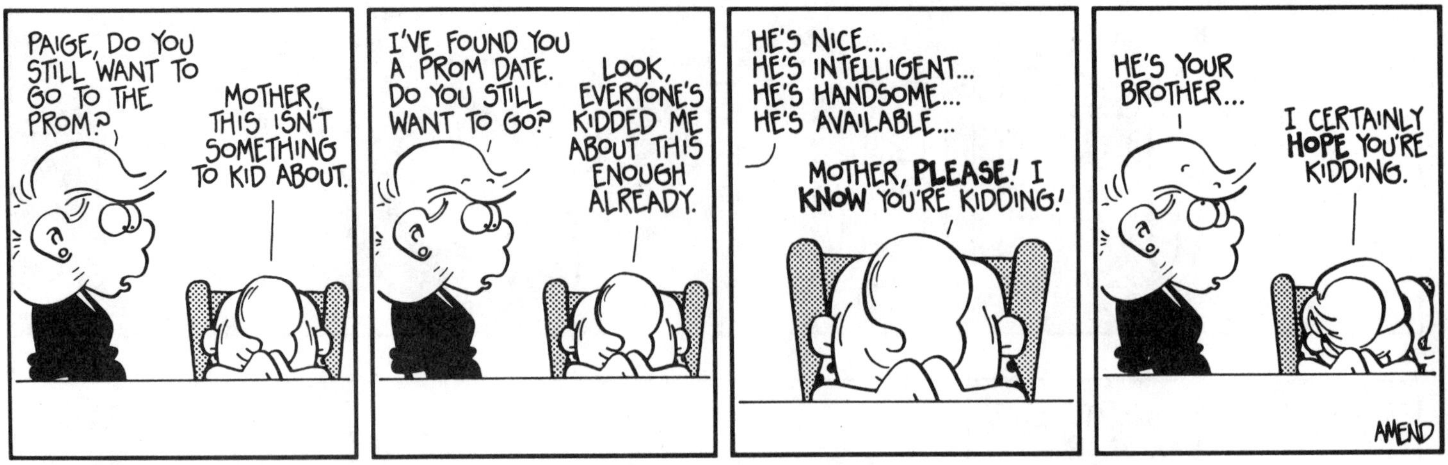
PAIGE, DO YOU STILL WANT TO GO TO THE PROM?
MOTHER, THIS ISN'T SOMETHING TO KID ABOUT.
I'VE FOUND YOU A PROM DATE. DO YOU STILL WANT TO GO?
LOOK, EVERYONE'S KIDDED ME ABOUT THIS ENOUGH ALREADY.
HE'S NICE... HE'S INTELLIGENT... HE'S HANDSOME... HE'S AVAILABLE...
MOTHER, PLEASE! I KNOW YOU'RE KIDDING!
HE'S YOUR BROTHER...
I CERTAINLY HOPE YOU'RE KIDDING.
AMEND

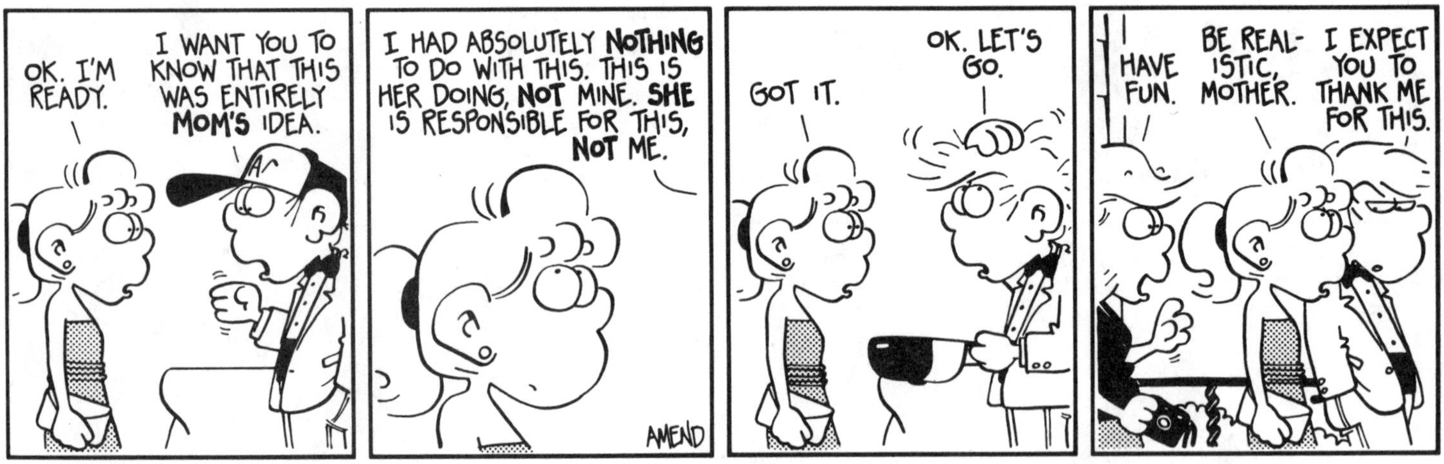
OK. I'M READY.
I WANT YOU TO KNOW THAT THIS WAS ENTIRELY MOM'S IDEA.
I HAD ABSOLUTELY NOTHING TO DO WITH THIS. THIS IS HER DOING, NOT MINE. SHE IS RESPONSIBLE FOR THIS, NOT ME.
AMEND
GOT IT.
OK. LET'S GO.
HAVE FUN.
BE REAL-ISTIC, MOTHER.
I EXPECT YOU TO THANK ME FOR THIS.

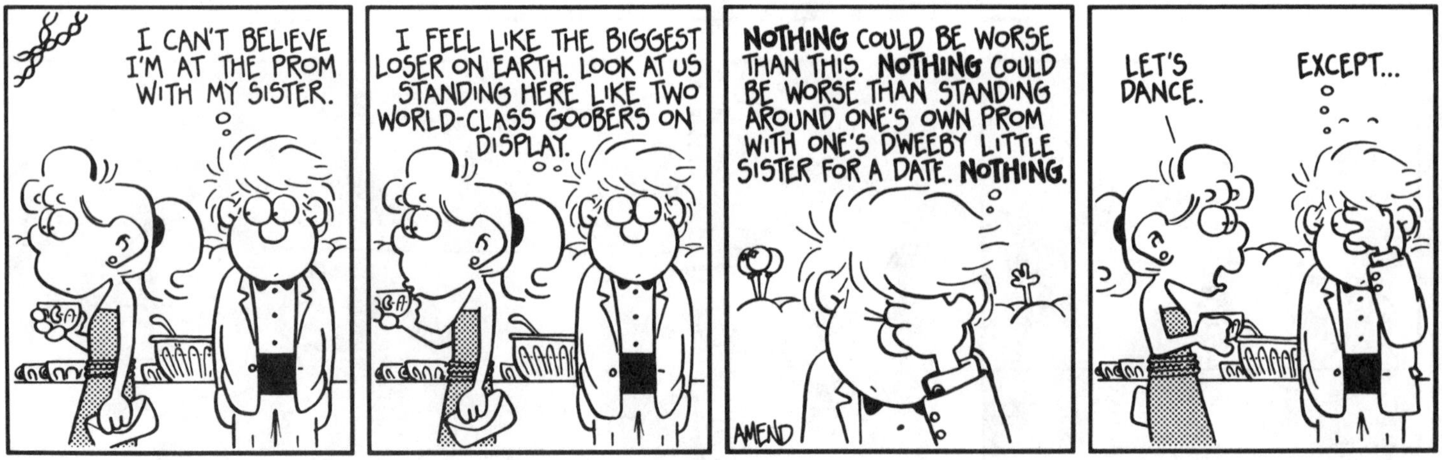
I CAN'T BELIEVE I'M AT THE PROM WITH MY SISTER.
I FEEL LIKE THE BIGGEST LOSER ON EARTH. LOOK AT US STANDING HERE LIKE TWO WORLD-CLASS GOOBERS ON DISPLAY.
NOTHING COULD BE WORSE THAN THIS. NOTHING COULD BE WORSE THAN STANDING AROUND ONE'S OWN PROM WITH ONE'S DWEEBY LITTLE SISTER FOR A DATE. NOTHING.
AMEND
LET'S DANCE.
EXCEPT...

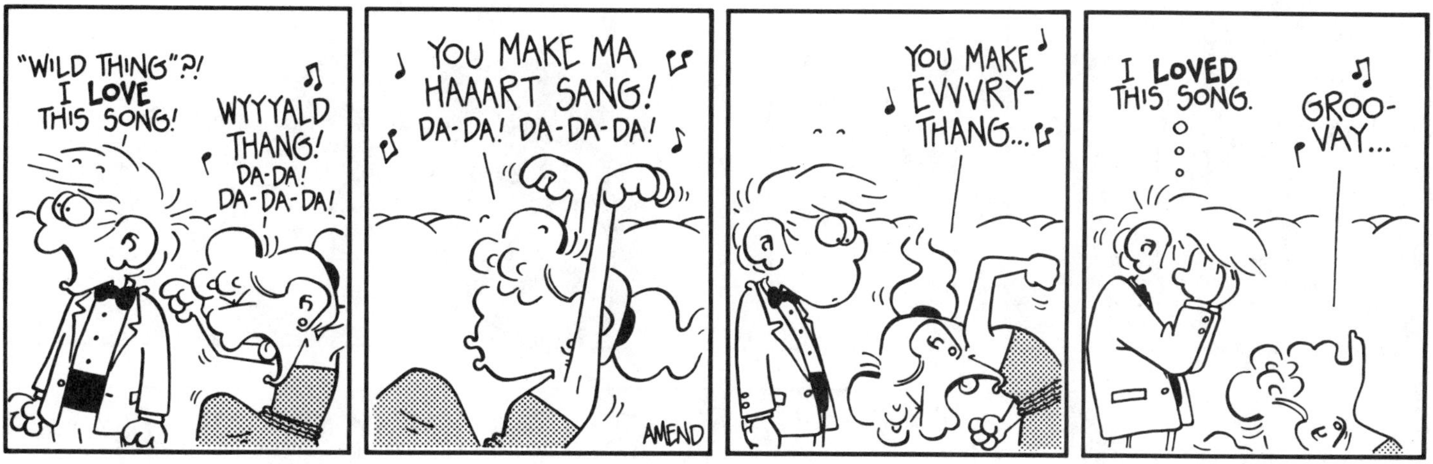
"WILD THING"?! I **LOVE** THIS SONG!
WYYYALD THANG! DA-DA! DA-DA-DA!
YOU MAKE MA HAAART SANG! DA-DA! DA-DA-DA!
YOU MAKE EVVVRY-THANG...
I **LOVED** THIS SONG.
GROO-VAY...
AMEND

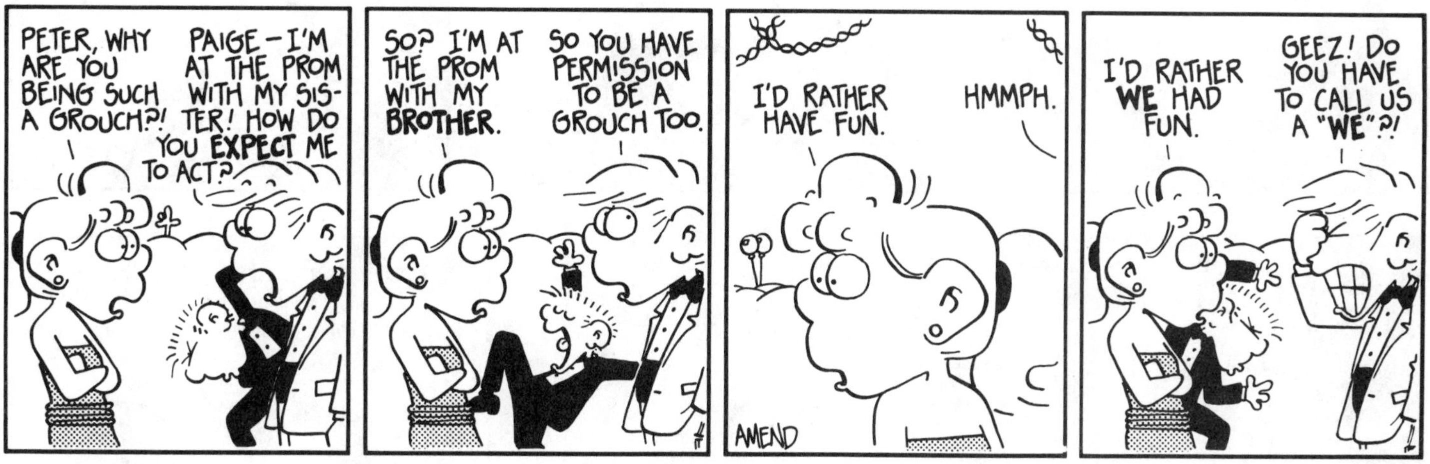
PETER, WHY ARE YOU BEING SUCH A GROUCH?!
PAIGE—I'M AT THE PROM WITH MY SISTER! HOW DO YOU **EXPECT** ME TO ACT?
SO? I'M AT THE PROM WITH MY **BROTHER**.
SO YOU HAVE PERMISSION TO BE A GROUCH TOO.
I'D RATHER HAVE FUN.
HMMPH.
AMEND
I'D RATHER **WE** HAD FUN.
GEEZ! DO YOU HAVE TO CALL US A "**WE**"?!

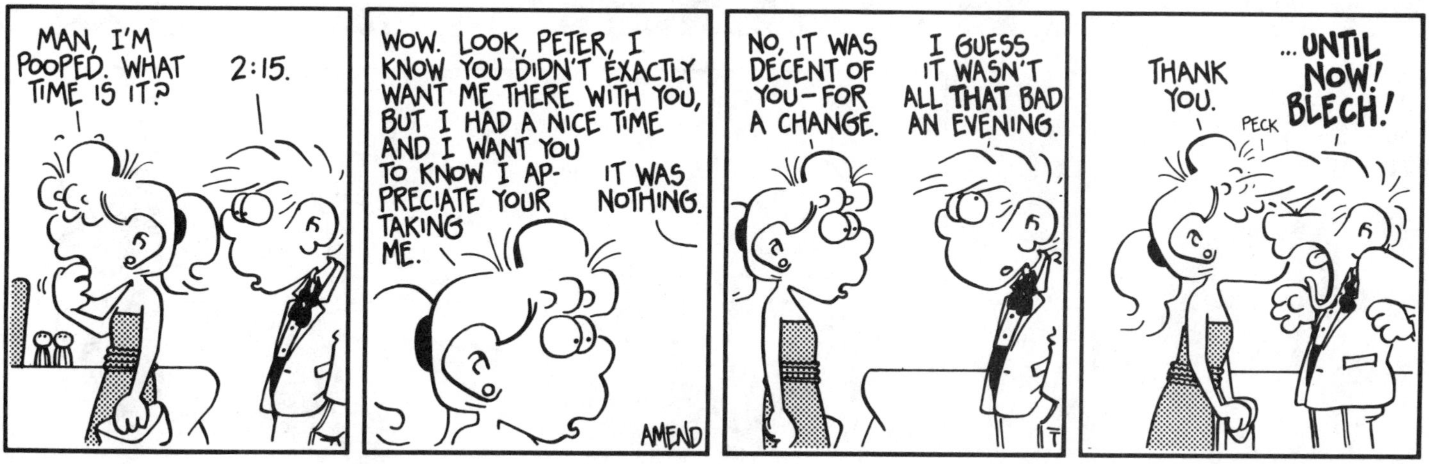
MAN, I'M POOPED. WHAT TIME IS IT?
2:15.
WOW. LOOK, PETER, I KNOW YOU DIDN'T EXACTLY WANT ME THERE WITH YOU, BUT I HAD A NICE TIME AND I WANT YOU TO KNOW I APPRECIATE YOUR TAKING ME.
IT WAS NOTHING.
AMEND
NO, IT WAS DECENT OF YOU—FOR A CHANGE.
I GUESS IT WASN'T ALL **THAT** BAD AN EVENING.
THANK YOU.
PECK
...**UNTIL NOW! BLECH!**

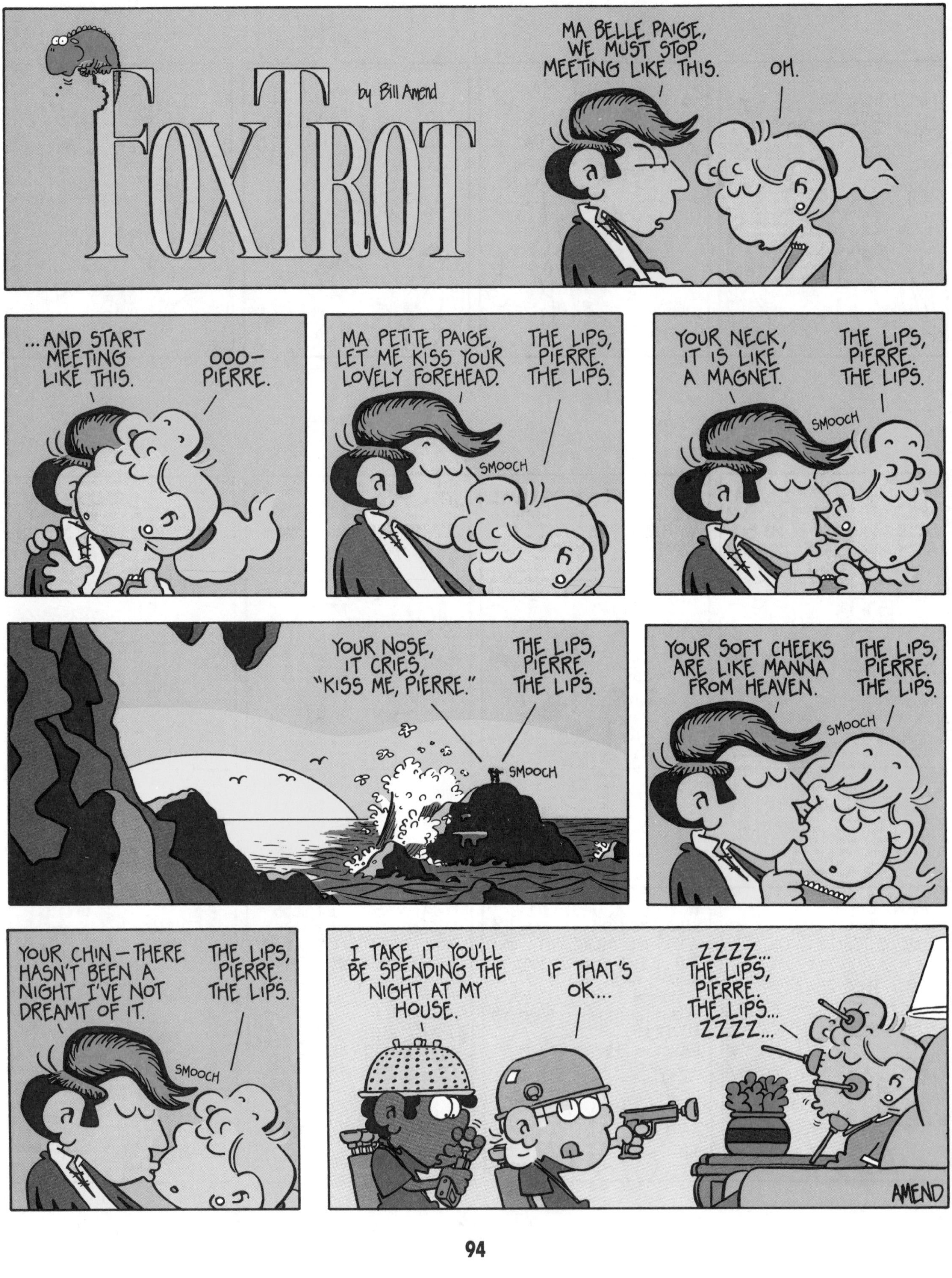
FoxTrot
by Bill Amend
MA BELLE PAIGE, WE MUST STOP MEETING LIKE THIS.
OH.
...AND START MEETING LIKE THIS.
OOO— PIERRE.
MA PETITE PAIGE, LET ME KISS YOUR LOVELY FOREHEAD.
THE LIPS, PIERRE. THE LIPS.
SMOOCH
YOUR NECK, IT IS LIKE A MAGNET.
THE LIPS, PIERRE. THE LIPS.
SMOOCH
YOUR NOSE, IT CRIES, "KISS ME, PIERRE."
THE LIPS, PIERRE. THE LIPS.
SMOOCH
YOUR SOFT CHEEKS ARE LIKE MANNA FROM HEAVEN.
THE LIPS, PIERRE. THE LIPS.
SMOOCH
YOUR CHIN—THERE HASN'T BEEN A NIGHT I'VE NOT DREAMT OF IT.
THE LIPS, PIERRE. THE LIPS.
SMOOCH
I TAKE IT YOU'LL BE SPENDING THE NIGHT AT MY HOUSE.
IF THAT'S OK...
ZZZZ... THE LIPS, PIERRE. THE LIPS... ZZZZ...
AMEND

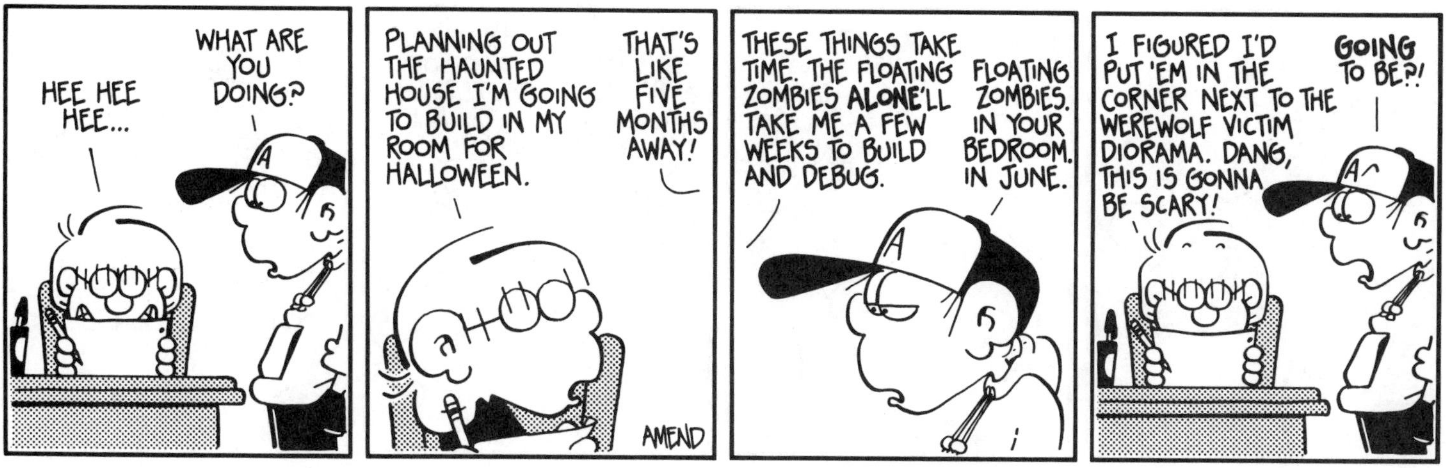
HEE HEE HEE...
WHAT ARE YOU DOING?
PLANNING OUT THE HAUNTED HOUSE I'M GOING TO BUILD IN MY ROOM FOR HALLOWEEN.
THAT'S LIKE FIVE MONTHS AWAY!
AMEND
THESE THINGS TAKE TIME. THE FLOATING ZOMBIES **ALONE**'LL TAKE ME A FEW WEEKS TO BUILD AND DEBUG.
FLOATING ZOMBIES. IN YOUR BEDROOM. IN JUNE.
I FIGURED I'D PUT 'EM IN THE CORNER NEXT TO THE WEREWOLF VICTIM DIORAMA. DANG, THIS IS GONNA BE SCARY!
GOING TO BE?!

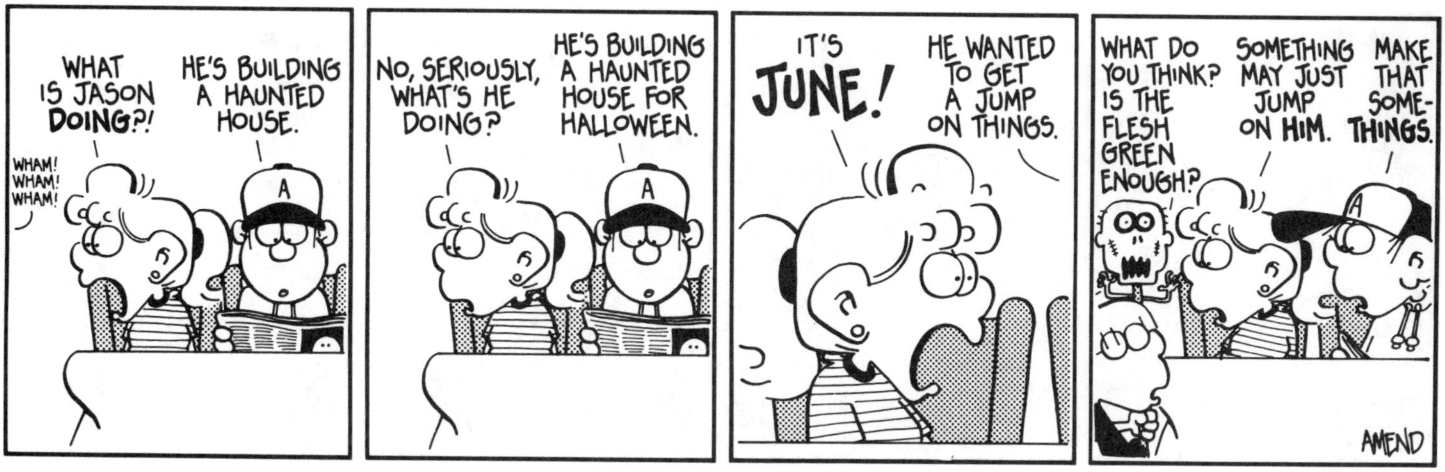
WHAM! WHAM! WHAM!
WHAT IS JASON **DOING**?!
HE'S BUILDING A HAUNTED HOUSE.
NO, SERIOUSLY, WHAT'S HE DOING?
HE'S BUILDING A HAUNTED HOUSE FOR HALLOWEEN.
IT'S **JUNE**!
HE WANTED TO GET A JUMP ON THINGS.
WHAT DO YOU THINK? IS THE FLESH GREEN ENOUGH?
SOMETHING MAY JUST JUMP ON **HIM**.
MAKE THAT SOME-**THINGS**.
AMEND

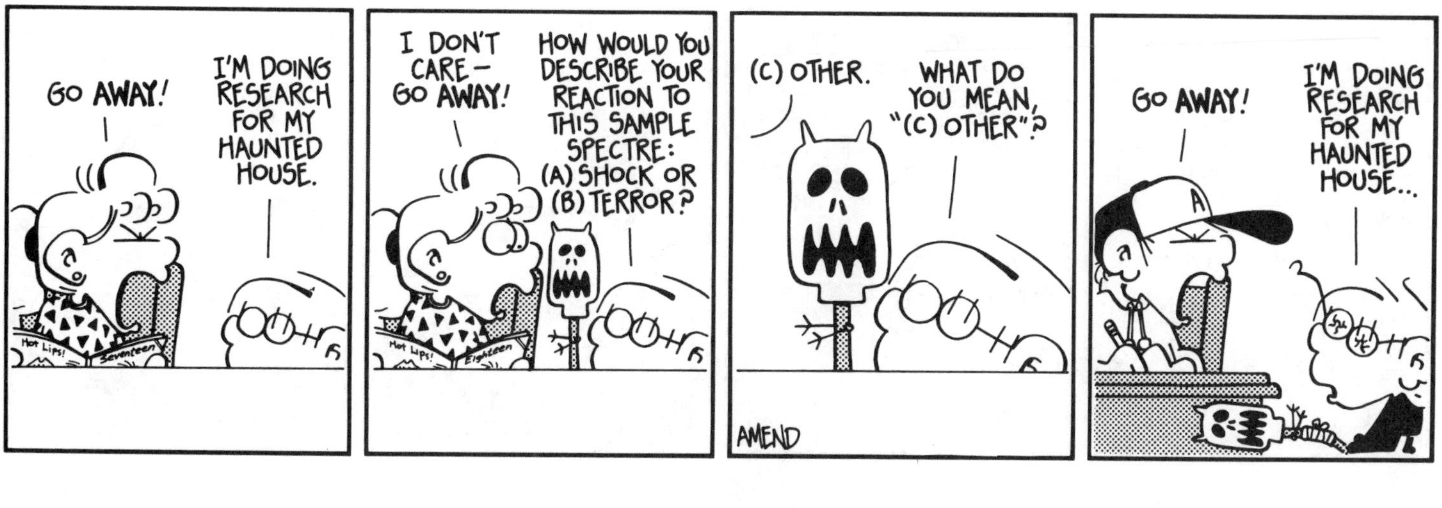
GO **AWAY**!
I'M DOING RESEARCH FOR MY HAUNTED HOUSE.
I DON'T CARE— GO **AWAY**!
HOW WOULD YOU DESCRIBE YOUR REACTION TO THIS SAMPLE SPECTRE: (A) SHOCK OR (B) TERROR?
(C) OTHER.
WHAT DO YOU MEAN, "(C) OTHER"?
AMEND
GO **AWAY**!
I'M DOING RESEARCH FOR MY HAUNTED HOUSE...

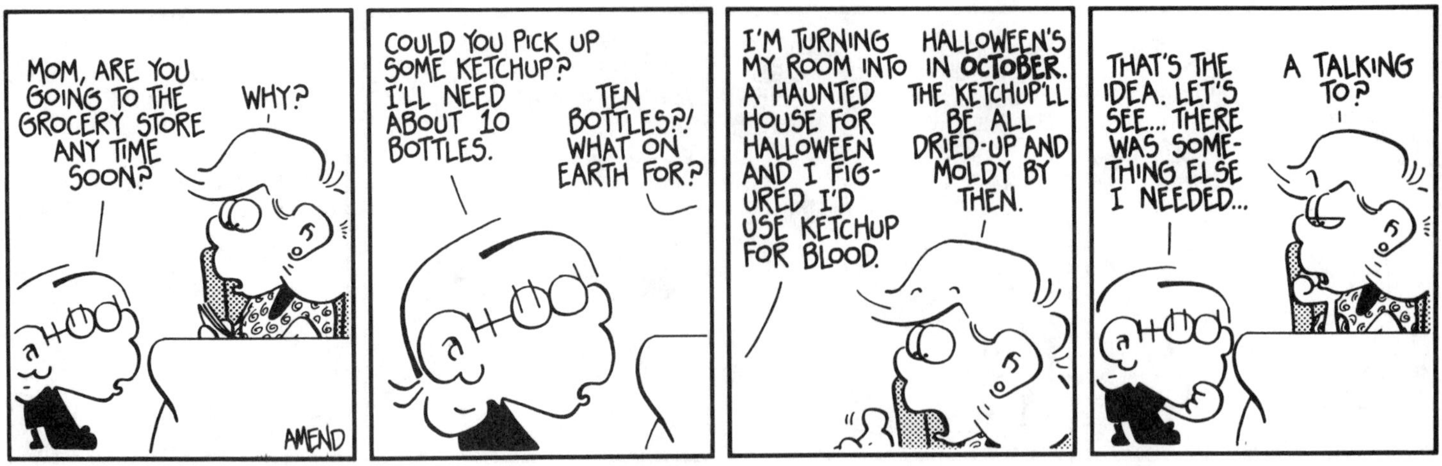

MOM, ARE YOU GOING TO THE GROCERY STORE ANY TIME SOON?
WHY?
AMEND
COULD YOU PICK UP SOME KETCHUP? I'LL NEED ABOUT 10 BOTTLES.
TEN BOTTLES?! WHAT ON EARTH FOR?
I'M TURNING MY ROOM INTO A HAUNTED HOUSE FOR HALLOWEEN AND I FIGURED I'D USE KETCHUP FOR BLOOD.
HALLOWEEN'S IN **OCTOBER**. THE KETCHUP'LL BE ALL DRIED-UP AND MOLDY BY THEN.
THAT'S THE IDEA. LET'S SEE... THERE WAS SOMETHING ELSE I NEEDED...
A TALKING TO?

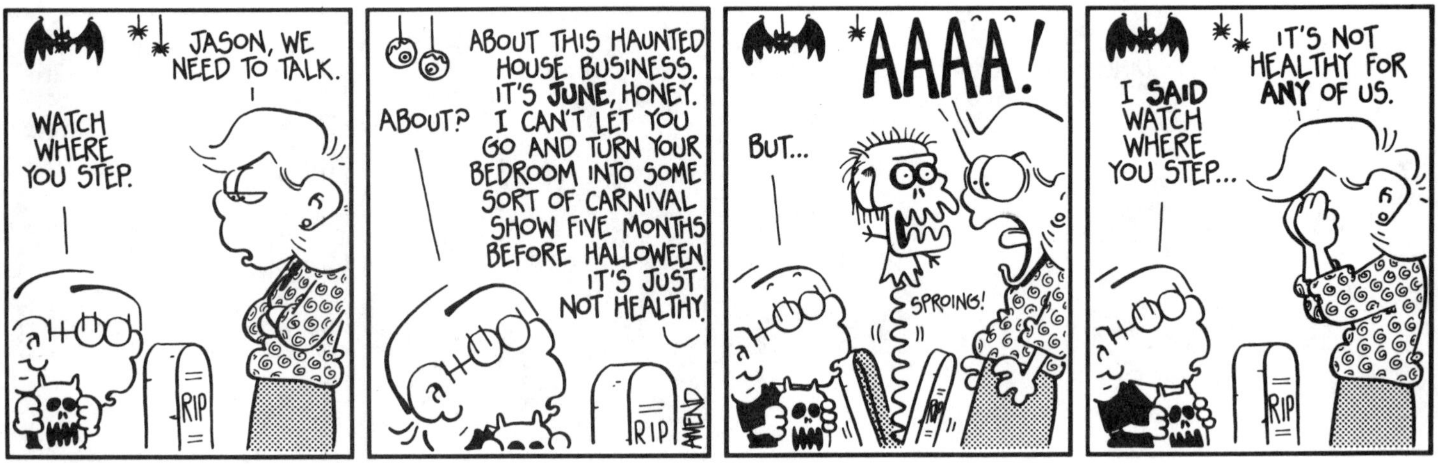

JASON, WE NEED TO TALK.
WATCH WHERE YOU STEP.
RIP
ABOUT?
ABOUT THIS HAUNTED HOUSE BUSINESS. IT'S **JUNE**, HONEY. I CAN'T LET YOU GO AND TURN YOUR BEDROOM INTO SOME SORT OF CARNIVAL SHOW FIVE MONTHS BEFORE HALLOWEEN. IT'S JUST NOT HEALTHY.
RIP
AMEND
BUT...
AAAA!
SPROING!
I **SAID** WATCH WHERE YOU STEP...
IT'S NOT HEALTHY FOR **ANY** OF US.
RIP

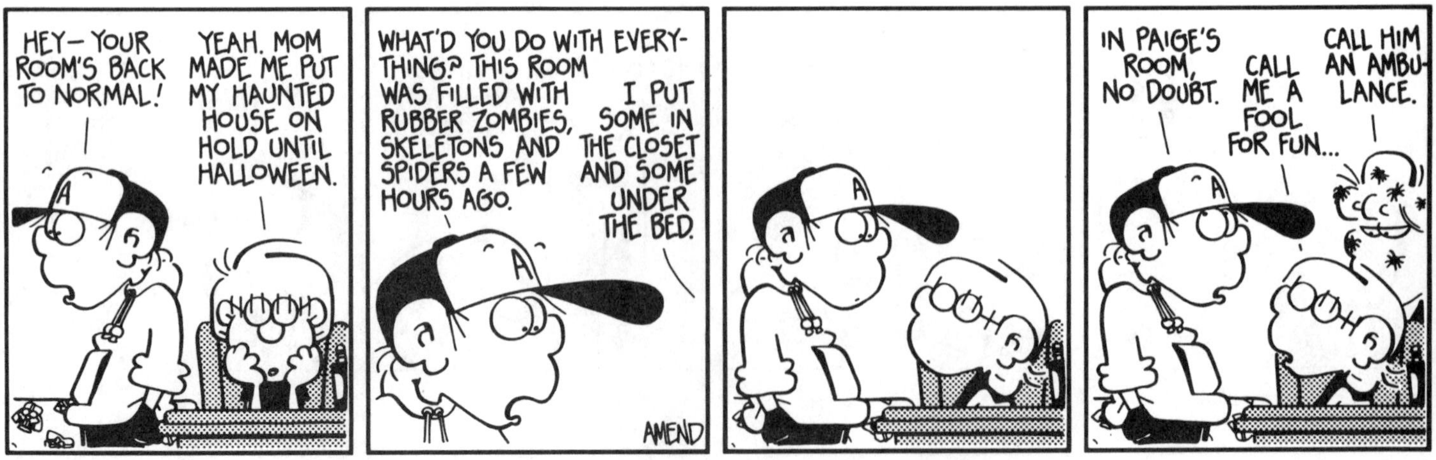

HEY— YOUR ROOM'S BACK TO NORMAL!
YEAH. MOM MADE ME PUT MY HAUNTED HOUSE ON HOLD UNTIL HALLOWEEN.
WHAT'D YOU DO WITH EVERYTHING? THIS ROOM WAS FILLED WITH RUBBER ZOMBIES, SKELETONS AND SPIDERS A FEW HOURS AGO.
I PUT SOME IN THE CLOSET AND SOME UNDER THE BED.
AMEND
IN PAIGE'S ROOM, NO DOUBT.
CALL ME A FOOL FOR FUN...
CALL HIM AN AMBULANCE.

by Bill Amend

FLY, LITTLE ROCK.

FLY LIKE YOU'VE NEVER FLOWN BEFORE.

SOMEHOW I DOUBT THAT'LL BE A PROBLEM.

PETER FOX WINDS AND...

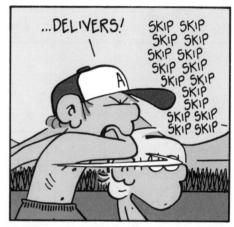

...DELIVERS!

SKIP SKIP
SKIP SKIP
SKIP SKIP
SKIP SKIP
SKIP SKIP
SKIP
SKIP
SKIP SKIP
SKIP SKIP

SIXTEEN SKIPS— A NEW RECORD!

JASON FOX WINDS AND...

...DELIVERS!

SKIP SKIP
SKIP SKIP
BONK!
OW!

...DELIVERS!

ANOTHER SHORT-LIVED RECORD.

"RECORD"?!

SKIP SKIP SKIP SKIP

AMEND

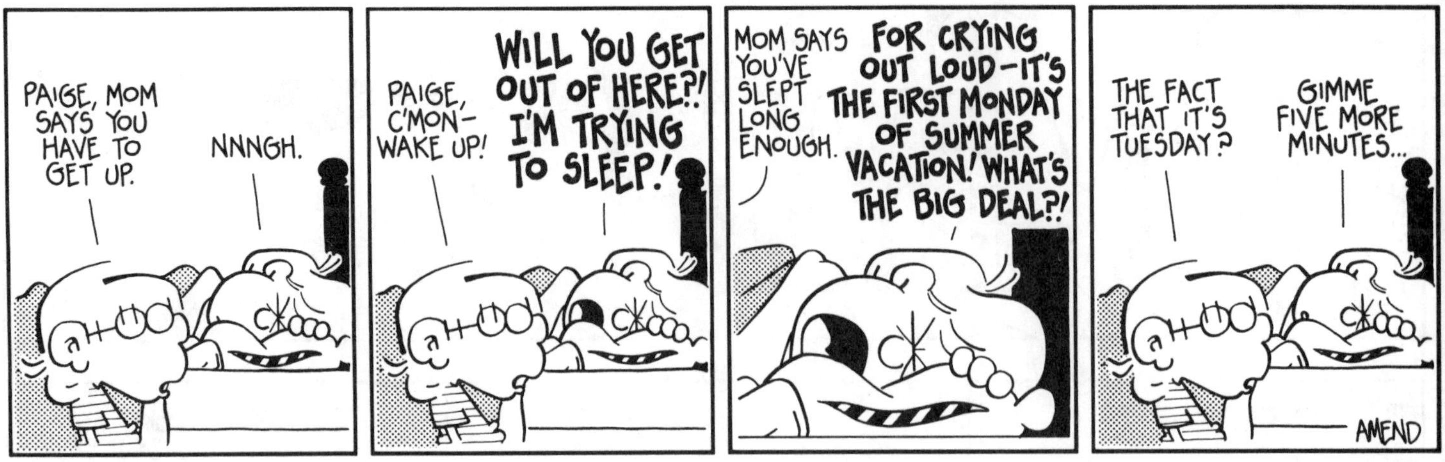
PAIGE, MOM SAYS YOU HAVE TO GET UP.
NNNGH.
PAIGE, C'MON– WAKE UP!
WILL YOU GET OUT OF HERE?! I'M TRYING TO SLEEP!
MOM SAYS YOU'VE SLEPT LONG ENOUGH.
FOR CRYING OUT LOUD–IT'S THE FIRST MONDAY OF SUMMER VACATION! WHAT'S THE BIG DEAL?!
THE FACT THAT IT'S TUESDAY?
GIMME FIVE MORE MINUTES...
AMEND

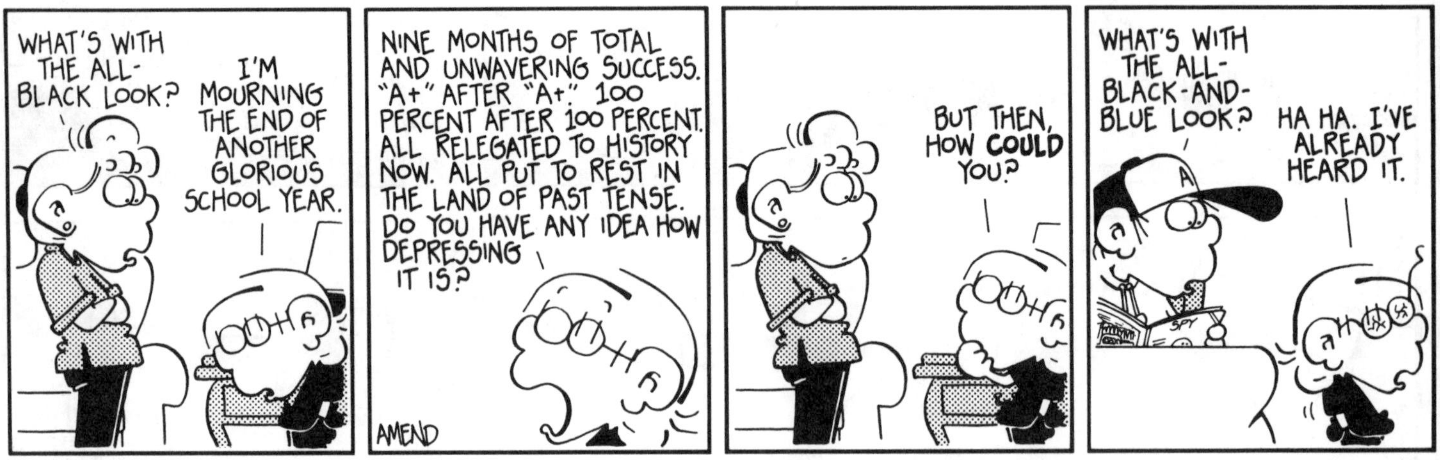
WHAT'S WITH THE ALL-BLACK LOOK?
I'M MOURNING THE END OF ANOTHER GLORIOUS SCHOOL YEAR.
NINE MONTHS OF TOTAL AND UNWAVERING SUCCESS. "A+" AFTER "A+." 100 PERCENT AFTER 100 PERCENT. ALL RELEGATED TO HISTORY NOW. ALL PUT TO REST IN THE LAND OF PAST TENSE. DO YOU HAVE ANY IDEA HOW DEPRESSING IT IS?
AMEND
BUT THEN, HOW COULD YOU?
WHAT'S WITH THE ALL-BLACK-AND-BLUE LOOK?
HA HA. I'VE ALREADY HEARD IT.
SPY

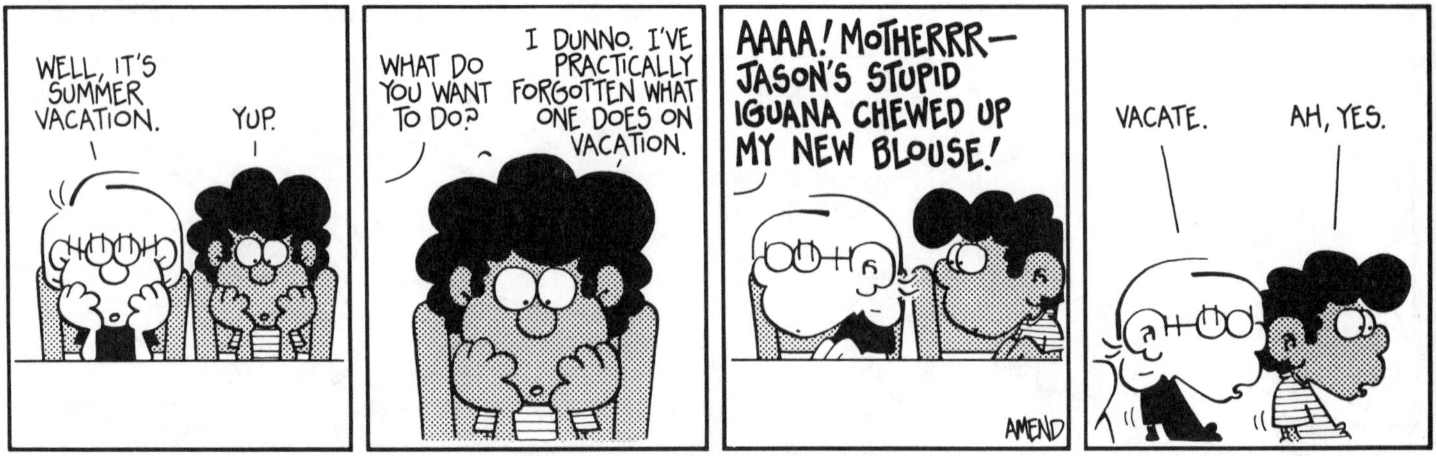
WELL, IT'S SUMMER VACATION.
YUP.
WHAT DO YOU WANT TO DO?
I DUNNO. I'VE PRACTICALLY FORGOTTEN WHAT ONE DOES ON VACATION.
AAAA! MOTHERRR– JASON'S STUPID IGUANA CHEWED UP MY NEW BLOUSE!
AMEND
VACATE.
AH, YES.

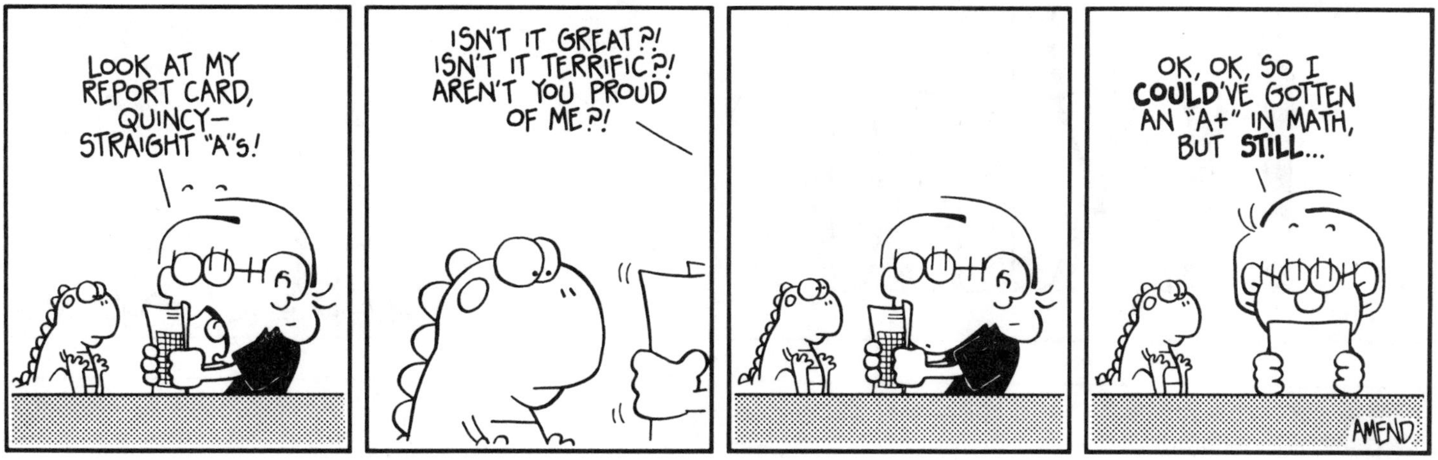
LOOK AT MY REPORT CARD, QUINCY— STRAIGHT "A"s!
ISN'T IT GREAT?! ISN'T IT TERRIFIC?! AREN'T YOU PROUD OF ME?!
OK, OK, SO I **COULD**'VE GOTTEN AN "A+" IN MATH, BUT **STILL**...
AMEND

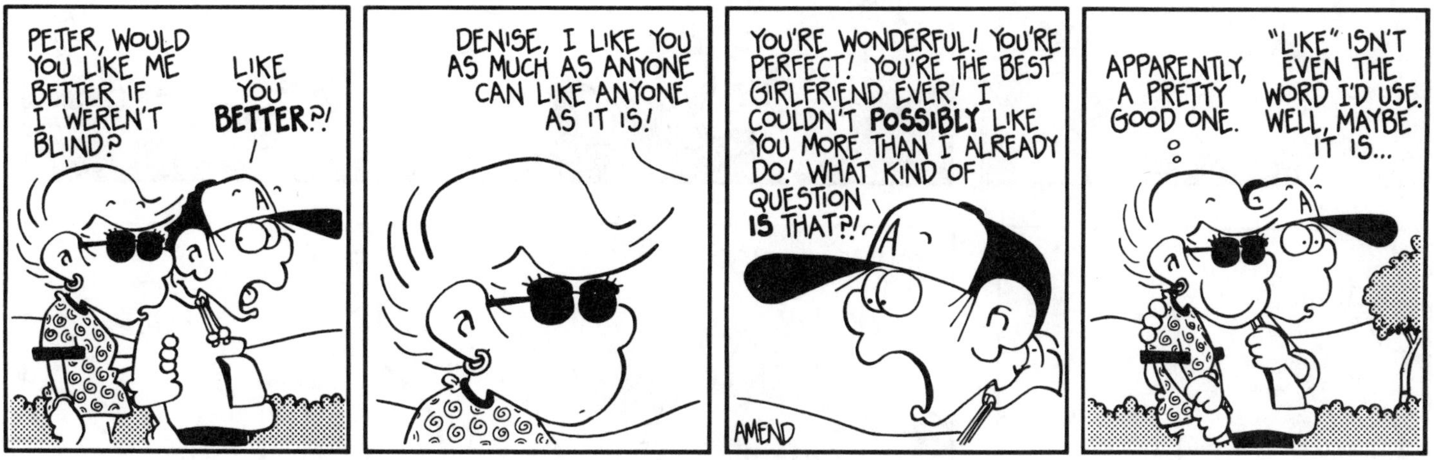
PETER, WOULD YOU LIKE ME BETTER IF I WEREN'T BLIND?
LIKE YOU **BETTER**?!
DENISE, I LIKE YOU AS MUCH AS ANYONE CAN LIKE ANYONE AS IT IS!
YOU'RE WONDERFUL! YOU'RE PERFECT! YOU'RE THE BEST GIRLFRIEND EVER! I COULDN'T **POSSIBLY** LIKE YOU MORE THAN I ALREADY DO! WHAT KIND OF QUESTION **IS** THAT?!
AMEND
APPARENTLY, A PRETTY GOOD ONE.
"LIKE" ISN'T EVEN THE WORD I'D USE. WELL, MAYBE IT IS...

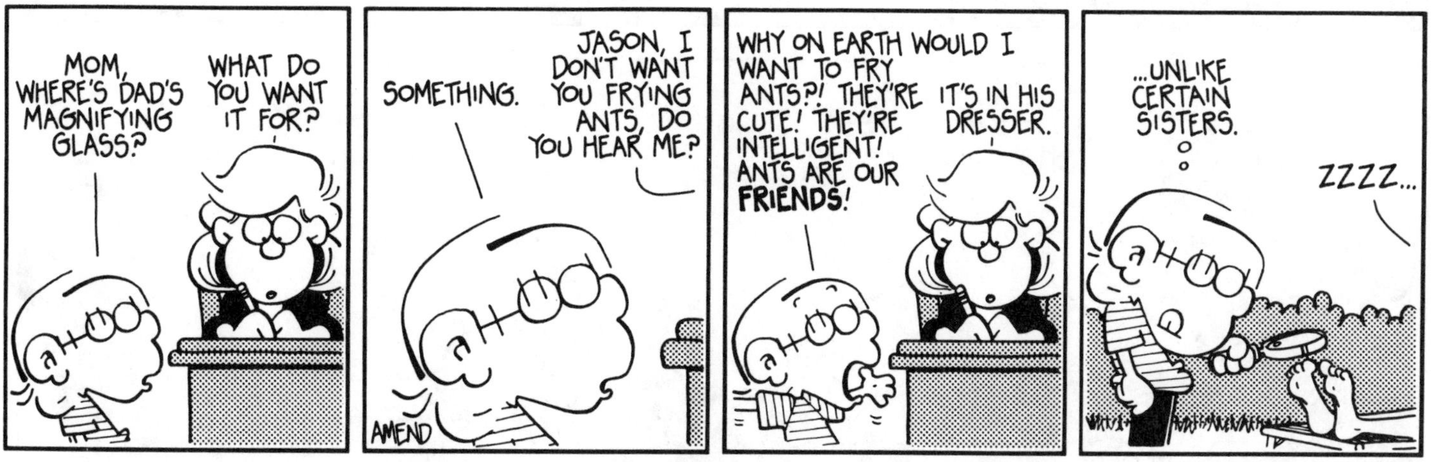
MOM, WHERE'S DAD'S MAGNIFYING GLASS?
WHAT DO YOU WANT IT FOR?
SOMETHING.
JASON, I DON'T WANT YOU FRYING ANTS, DO YOU HEAR ME?
AMEND
WHY ON EARTH WOULD I WANT TO FRY ANTS?! THEY'RE CUTE! THEY'RE INTELLIGENT! ANTS ARE OUR **FRIENDS**!
IT'S IN HIS DRESSER.
...UNLIKE CERTAIN SISTERS.
ZZZZ...

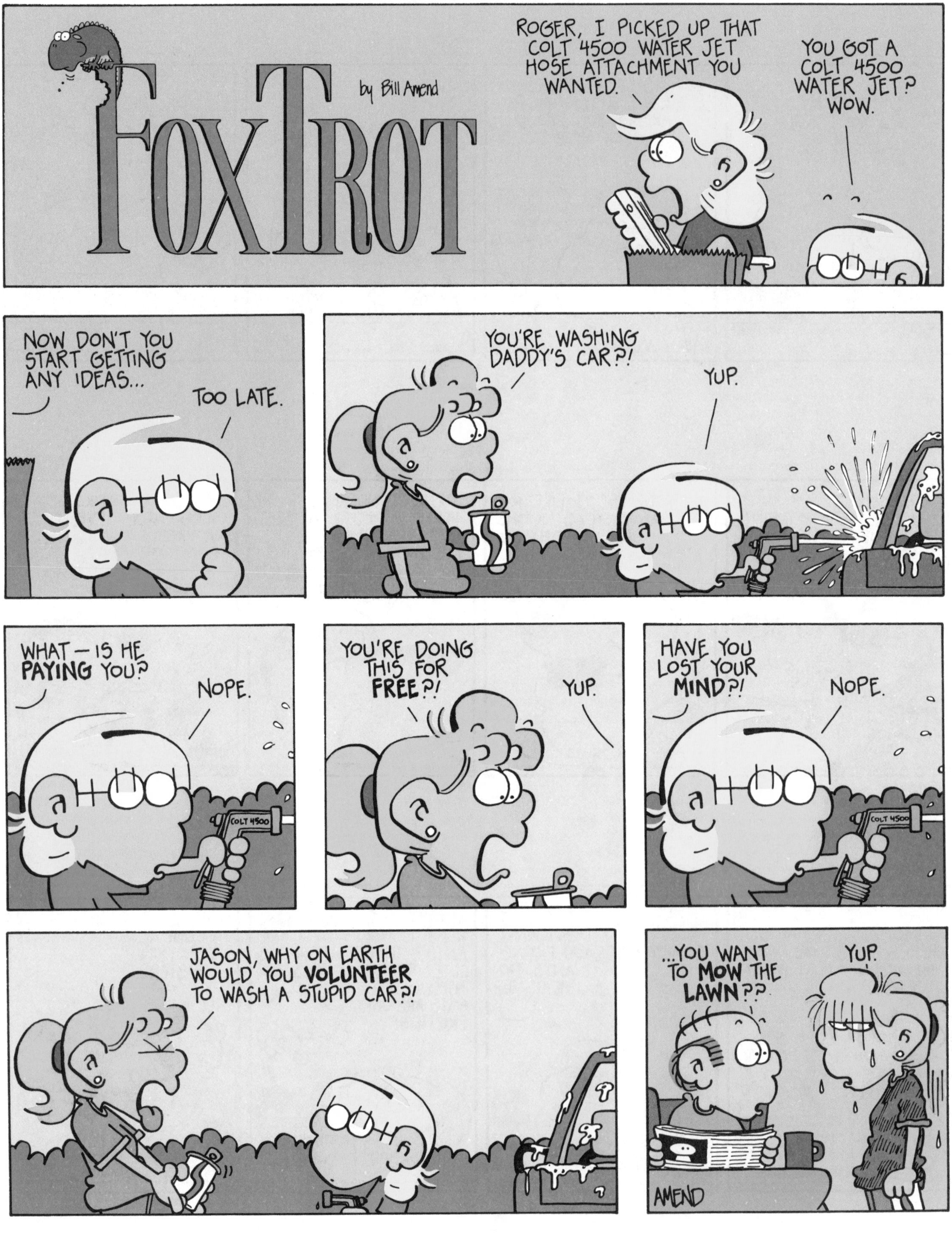
FOXTROT
by Bill Amend
ROGER, I PICKED UP THAT COLT 4500 WATER JET HOSE ATTACHMENT YOU WANTED.
YOU GOT A COLT 4500 WATER JET? WOW.
NOW DON'T YOU START GETTING ANY IDEAS...
TOO LATE.
YOU'RE WASHING DADDY'S CAR?!
YUP.
WHAT — IS HE **PAYING** YOU?
NOPE.
COLT 4500
YOU'RE DOING THIS FOR **FREE**?!
YUP.
HAVE YOU LOST YOUR **MIND**?!
NOPE.
COLT 4500
JASON, WHY ON EARTH WOULD YOU **VOLUNTEER** TO WASH A STUPID CAR?!
...YOU WANT TO **MOW** THE **LAWN**??
YUP.
AMEND

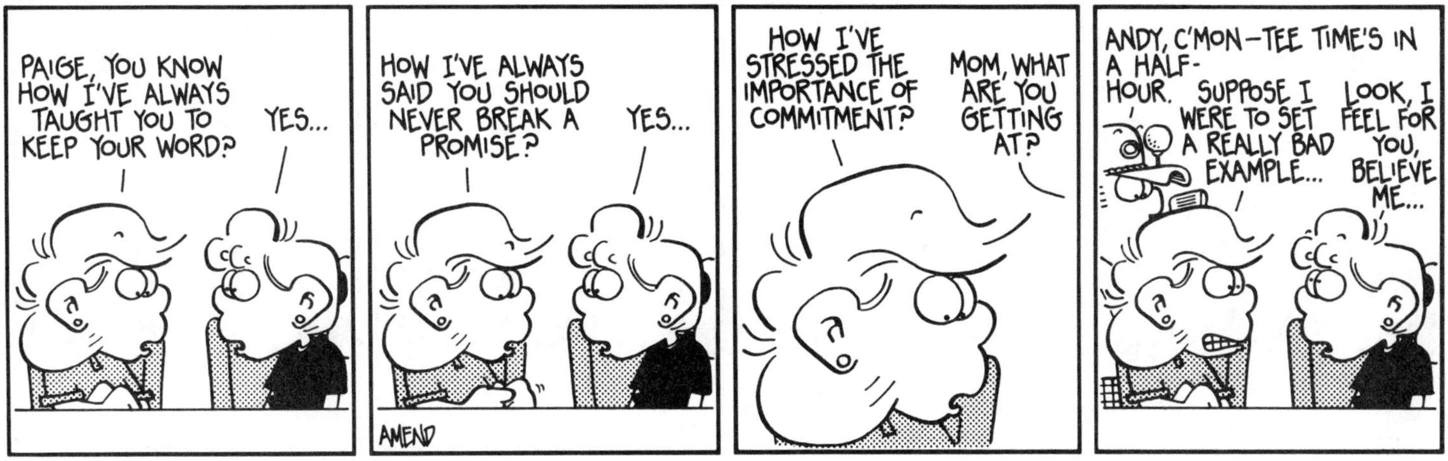
PAIGE, YOU KNOW HOW I'VE ALWAYS TAUGHT YOU TO KEEP YOUR WORD?
YES...
HOW I'VE ALWAYS SAID YOU SHOULD NEVER BREAK A PROMISE?
YES...
AMEND
HOW I'VE STRESSED THE IMPORTANCE OF COMMITMENT?
MOM, WHAT ARE YOU GETTING AT?
ANDY, C'MON—TEE TIME'S IN A HALF-HOUR.
SUPPOSE I WERE TO SET A REALLY BAD EXAMPLE...
LOOK, I FEEL FOR YOU, BELIEVE ME...

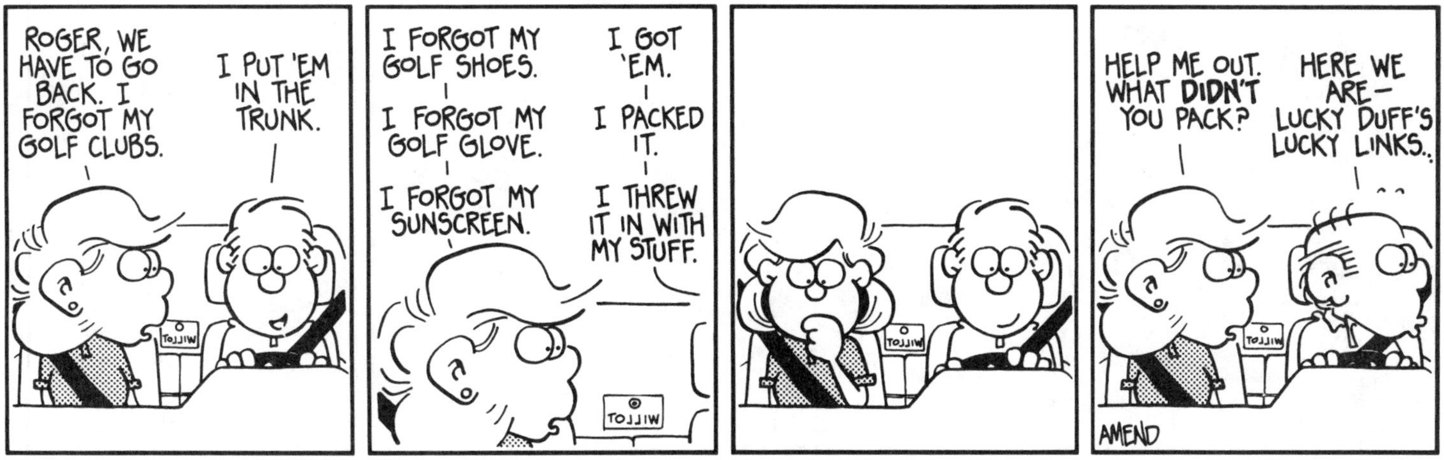
ROGER, WE HAVE TO GO BACK. I FORGOT MY GOLF CLUBS.
I PUT 'EM IN THE TRUNK.
WILLOT
I FORGOT MY GOLF SHOES.
I GOT 'EM.
I FORGOT MY GOLF GLOVE.
I PACKED IT.
I FORGOT MY SUNSCREEN.
I THREW IT IN WITH MY STUFF.
HELP ME OUT. WHAT **DIDN'T** YOU PACK?
HERE WE ARE—LUCKY DUFF'S LUCKY LINKS...
AMEND

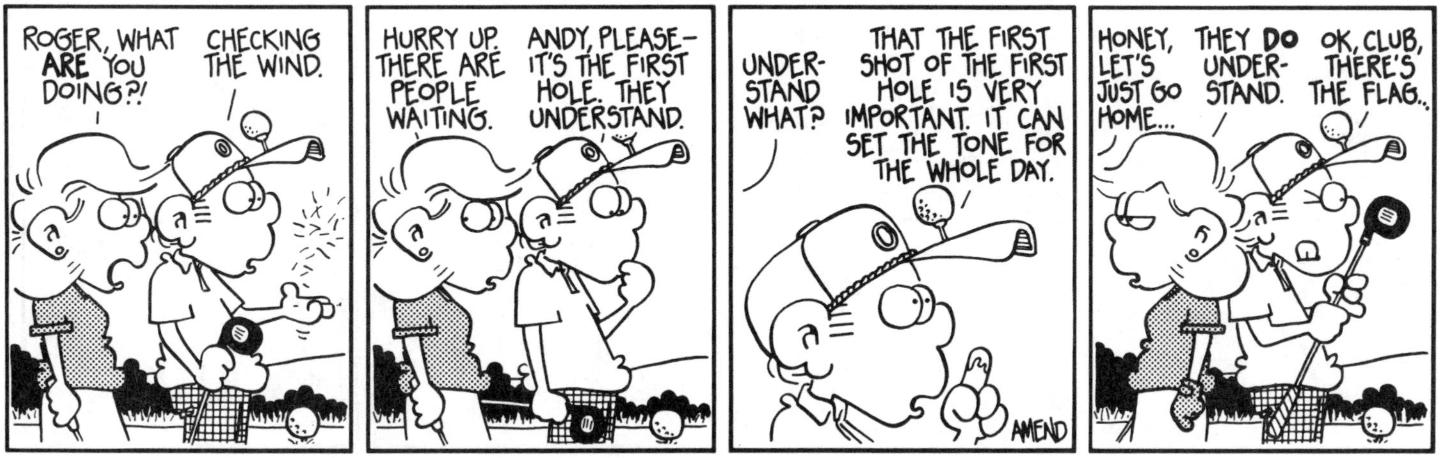
ROGER, WHAT **ARE** YOU DOING?!
CHECKING THE WIND.
HURRY UP. THERE ARE PEOPLE WAITING.
ANDY, PLEASE—IT'S THE FIRST HOLE. THEY UNDERSTAND.
UNDERSTAND WHAT?
THAT THE FIRST SHOT OF THE FIRST HOLE IS VERY IMPORTANT. IT CAN SET THE TONE FOR THE WHOLE DAY.
AMEND
HONEY, LET'S JUST GO HOME...
THEY **DO** UNDERSTAND.
OK, CLUB, THERE'S THE FLAG...

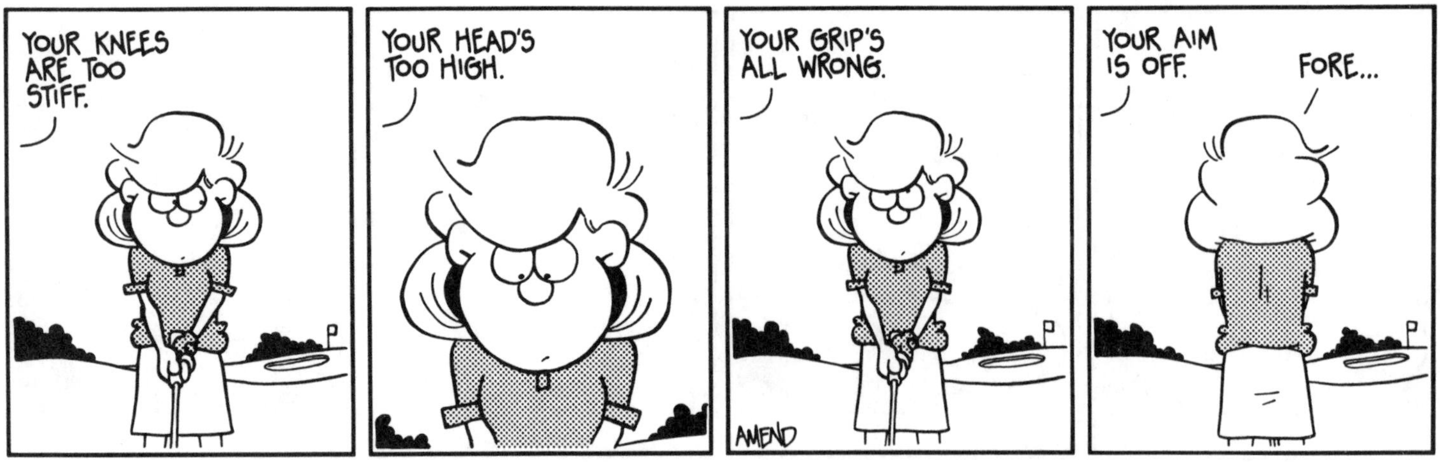
YOUR KNEES ARE TOO STIFF.
YOUR HEAD'S TOO HIGH.
YOUR GRIP'S ALL WRONG.
AMEND
YOUR AIM IS OFF.
FORE...

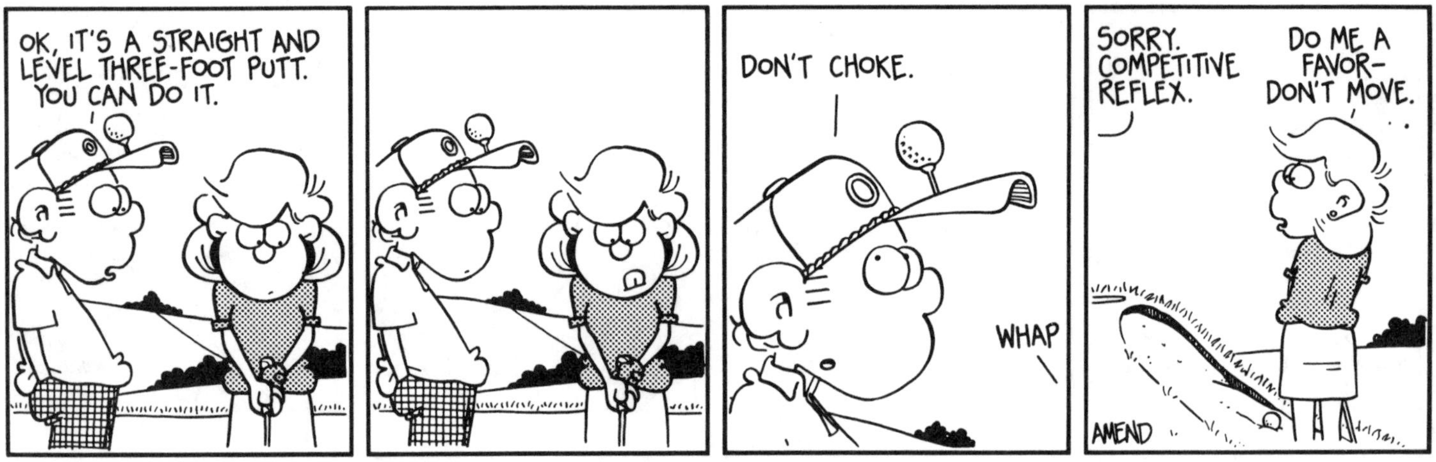
OK, IT'S A STRAIGHT AND LEVEL THREE-FOOT PUTT. YOU CAN DO IT.
DON'T CHOKE.
WHAP
SORRY. COMPETITIVE REFLEX.
DO ME A FAVOR–DON'T MOVE.
AMEND

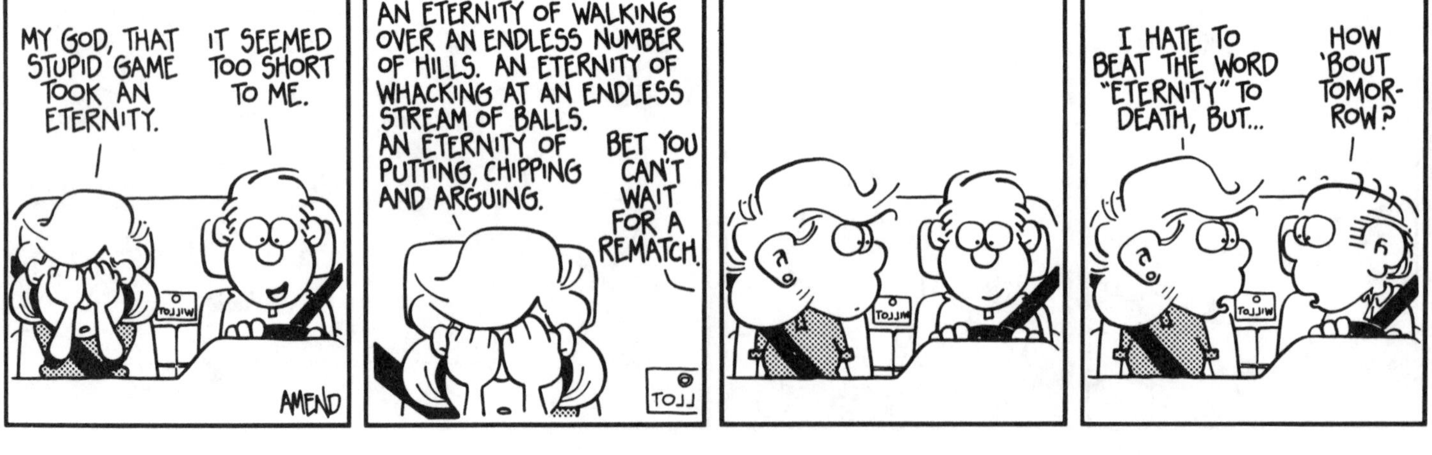
MY GOD, THAT STUPID GAME TOOK AN ETERNITY.
IT SEEMED TOO SHORT TO ME.
AMEND
AN ETERNITY OF WALKING OVER AN ENDLESS NUMBER OF HILLS. AN ETERNITY OF WHACKING AT AN ENDLESS STREAM OF BALLS. AN ETERNITY OF PUTTING, CHIPPING AND ARGUING.
BET YOU CAN'T WAIT FOR A REMATCH.
I HATE TO BEAT THE WORD "ETERNITY" TO DEATH, BUT...
HOW 'BOUT TOMORROW?

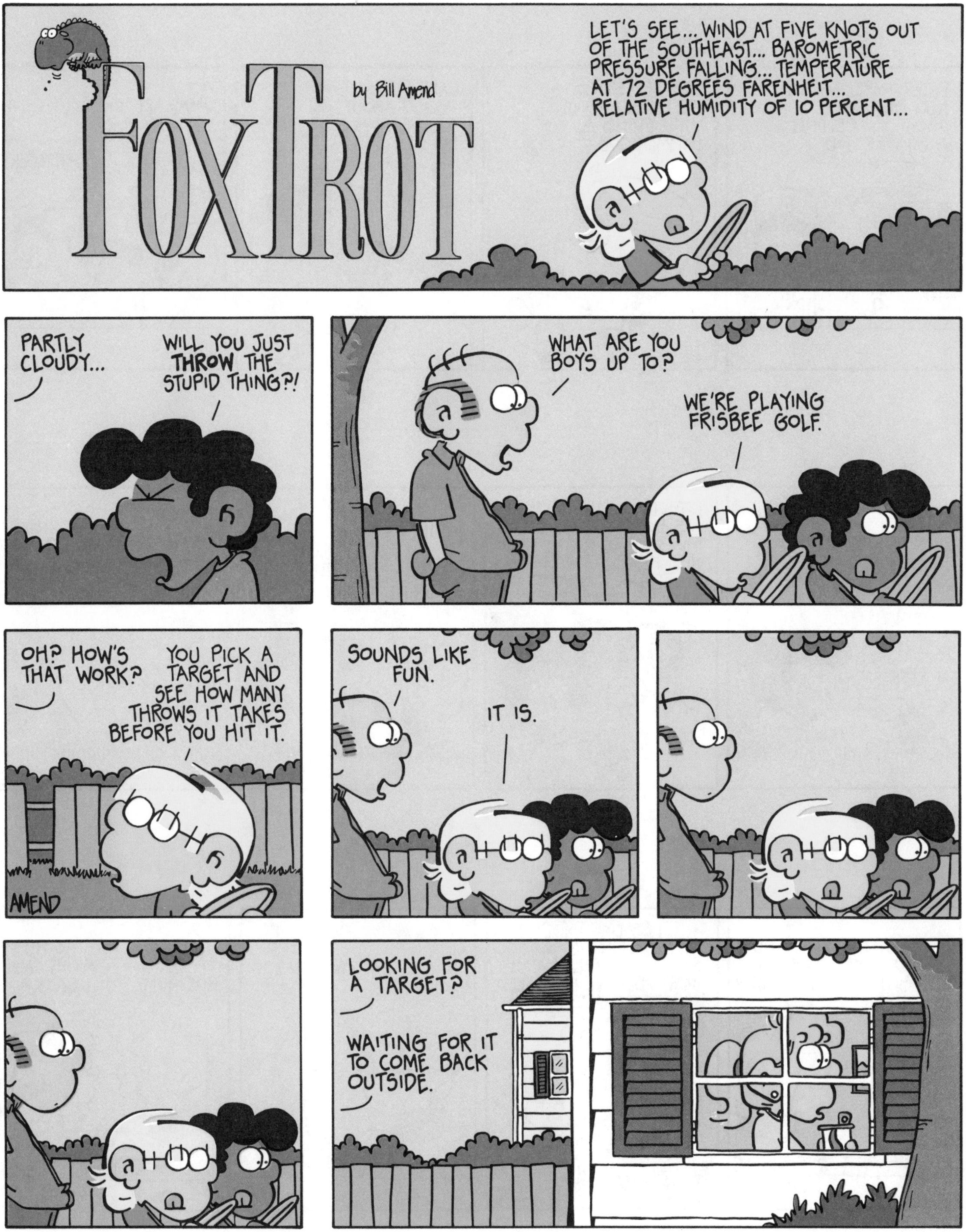
FoxTrot
by Bill Amend
LET'S SEE... WIND AT FIVE KNOTS OUT OF THE SOUTHEAST... BAROMETRIC PRESSURE FALLING... TEMPERATURE AT 72 DEGREES FARENHEIT... RELATIVE HUMIDITY OF 10 PERCENT...
PARTLY CLOUDY...
WILL YOU JUST **THROW** THE STUPID THING?!
WHAT ARE YOU BOYS UP TO?
WE'RE PLAYING FRISBEE GOLF.
OH? HOW'S THAT WORK?
YOU PICK A TARGET AND SEE HOW MANY THROWS IT TAKES BEFORE YOU HIT IT.
AMEND
SOUNDS LIKE FUN.
IT IS.
LOOKING FOR A TARGET?
WAITING FOR IT TO COME BACK OUTSIDE.

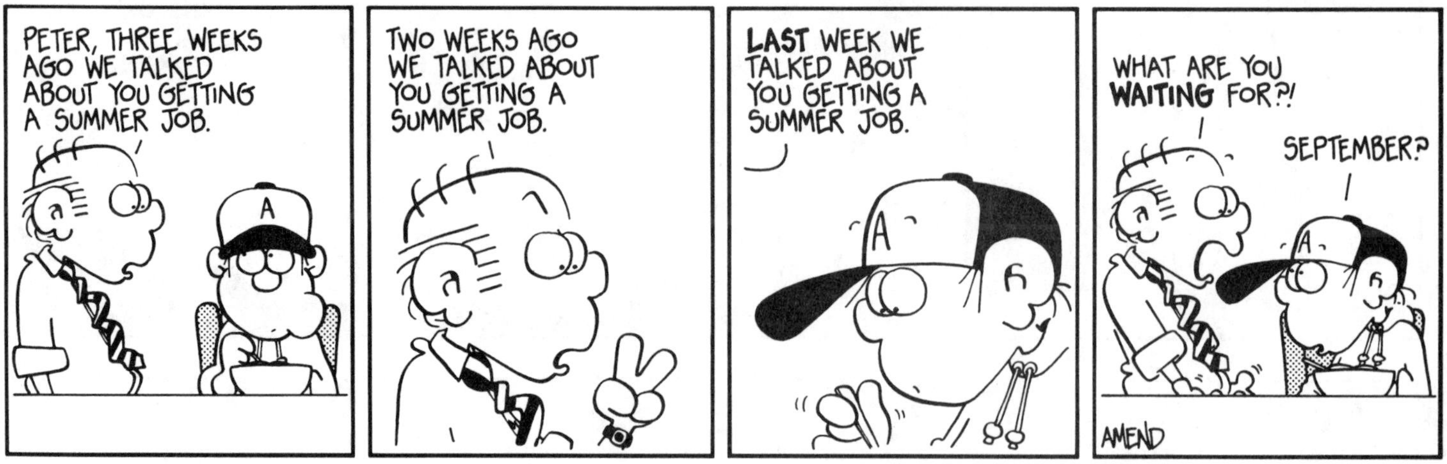
PETER, THREE WEEKS AGO WE TALKED ABOUT YOU GETTING A SUMMER JOB.
TWO WEEKS AGO WE TALKED ABOUT YOU GETTING A SUMMER JOB.
LAST WEEK WE TALKED ABOUT YOU GETTING A SUMMER JOB.
WHAT ARE YOU WAITING FOR?!
SEPTEMBER?
AMEND

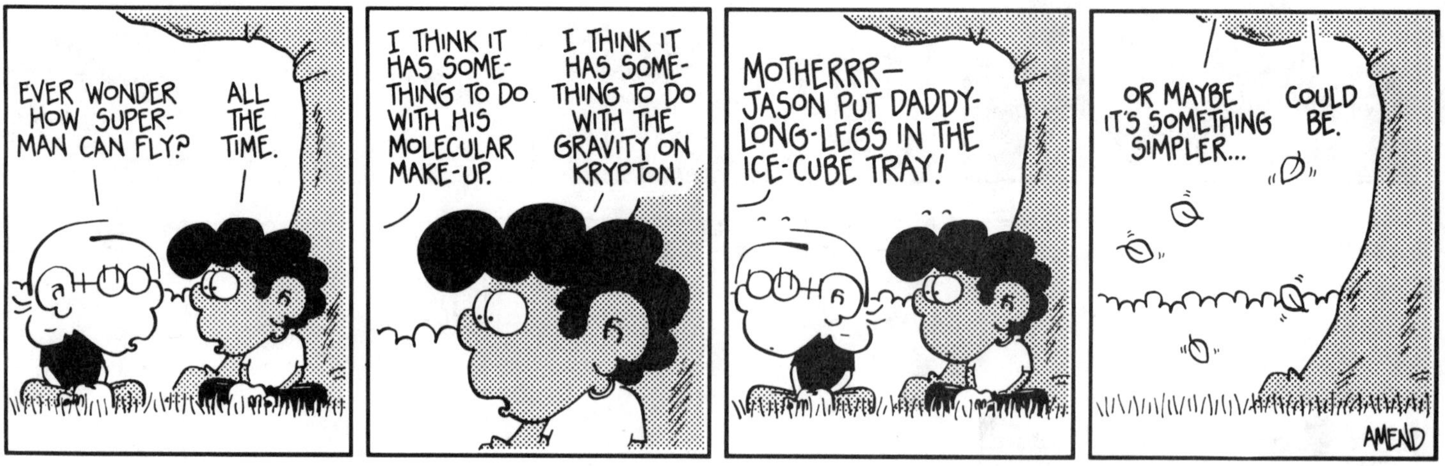
EVER WONDER HOW SUPERMAN CAN FLY?
ALL THE TIME.
I THINK IT HAS SOMETHING TO DO WITH HIS MOLECULAR MAKE-UP.
I THINK IT HAS SOMETHING TO DO WITH THE GRAVITY ON KRYPTON.
MOTHERRR— JASON PUT DADDY-LONG-LEGS IN THE ICE-CUBE TRAY!
OR MAYBE IT'S SOMETHING SIMPLER...
COULD BE.
AMEND

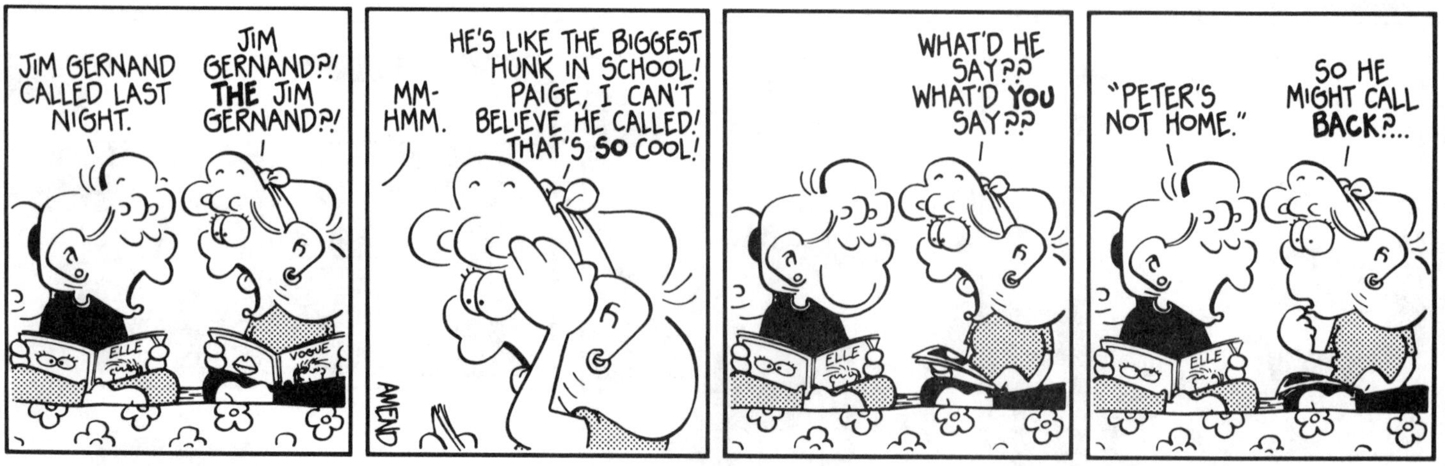
JIM GERNAND CALLED LAST NIGHT.
JIM GERNAND?! THE JIM GERNAND?!
ELLE
VOGUE
MM-HMM.
HE'S LIKE THE BIGGEST HUNK IN SCHOOL! PAIGE, I CAN'T BELIEVE HE CALLED! THAT'S SO COOL!
AMEND
WHAT'D HE SAY?? WHAT'D YOU SAY??
ELLE
"PETER'S NOT HOME."
SO HE MIGHT CALL BACK?...
ELLE

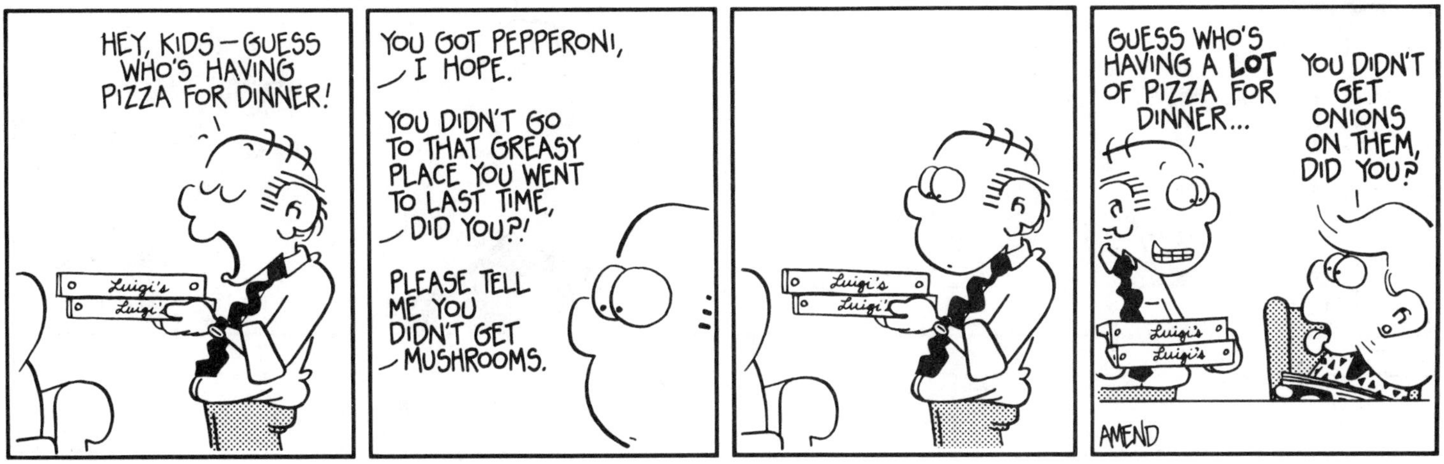
HEY, KIDS — GUESS WHO'S HAVING PIZZA FOR DINNER!
Luigi's
Luigi's
YOU GOT PEPPERONI, I HOPE.
YOU DIDN'T GO TO THAT GREASY PLACE YOU WENT TO LAST TIME, DID YOU?!
PLEASE TELL ME YOU DIDN'T GET MUSHROOMS.
Luigi's
Luigi's
GUESS WHO'S HAVING A **LOT** OF PIZZA FOR DINNER...
YOU DIDN'T GET ONIONS ON THEM, DID YOU?
Luigi's
Luigi's
AMEND

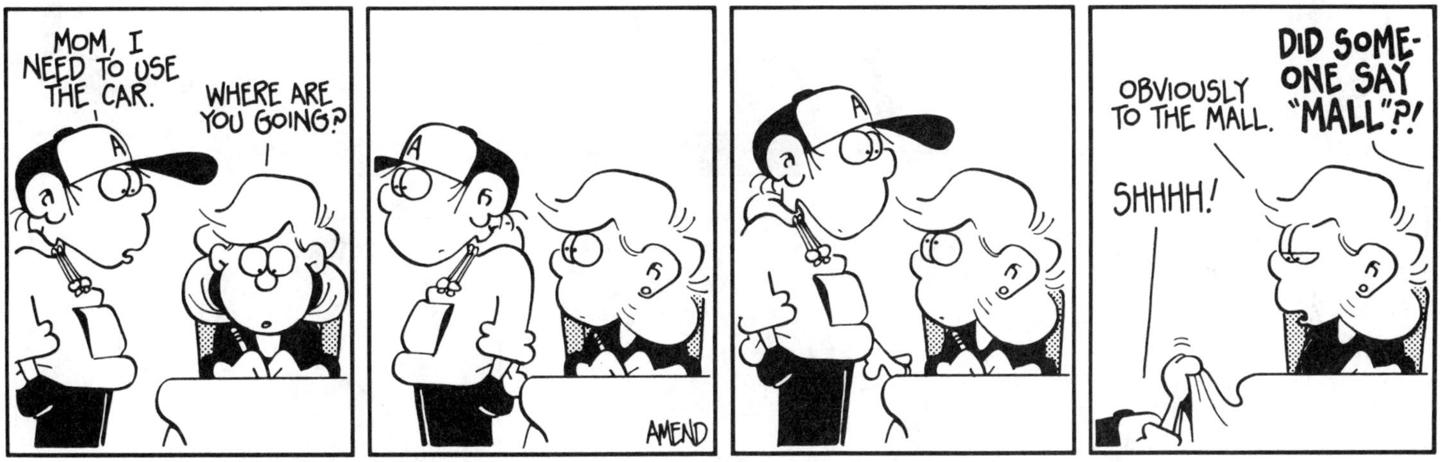
MOM, I NEED TO USE THE CAR.
WHERE ARE YOU GOING?
AMEND
OBVIOUSLY TO THE MALL.
DID SOME-ONE SAY "MALL"?!
SHHHH!

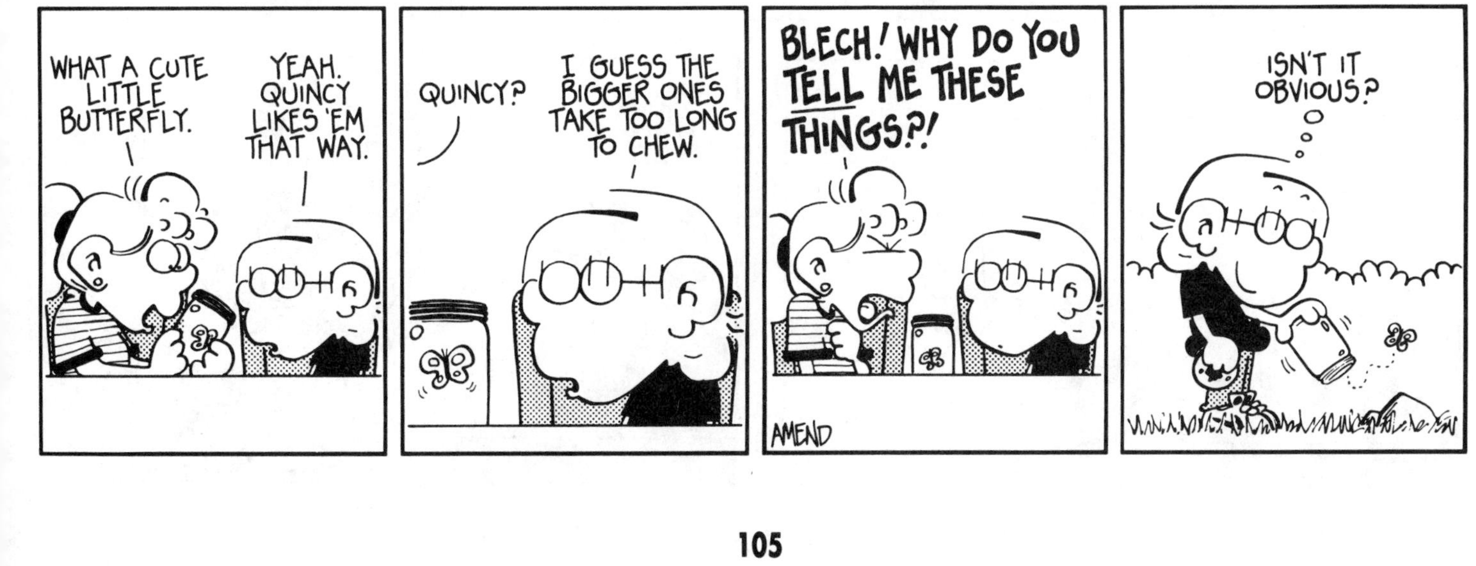
WHAT A CUTE LITTLE BUTTERFLY.
YEAH. QUINCY LIKES 'EM THAT WAY.
QUINCY?
I GUESS THE BIGGER ONES TAKE TOO LONG TO CHEW.
BLECH! WHY DO YOU TELL ME THESE THINGS?!
AMEND
ISN'T IT OBVIOUS?

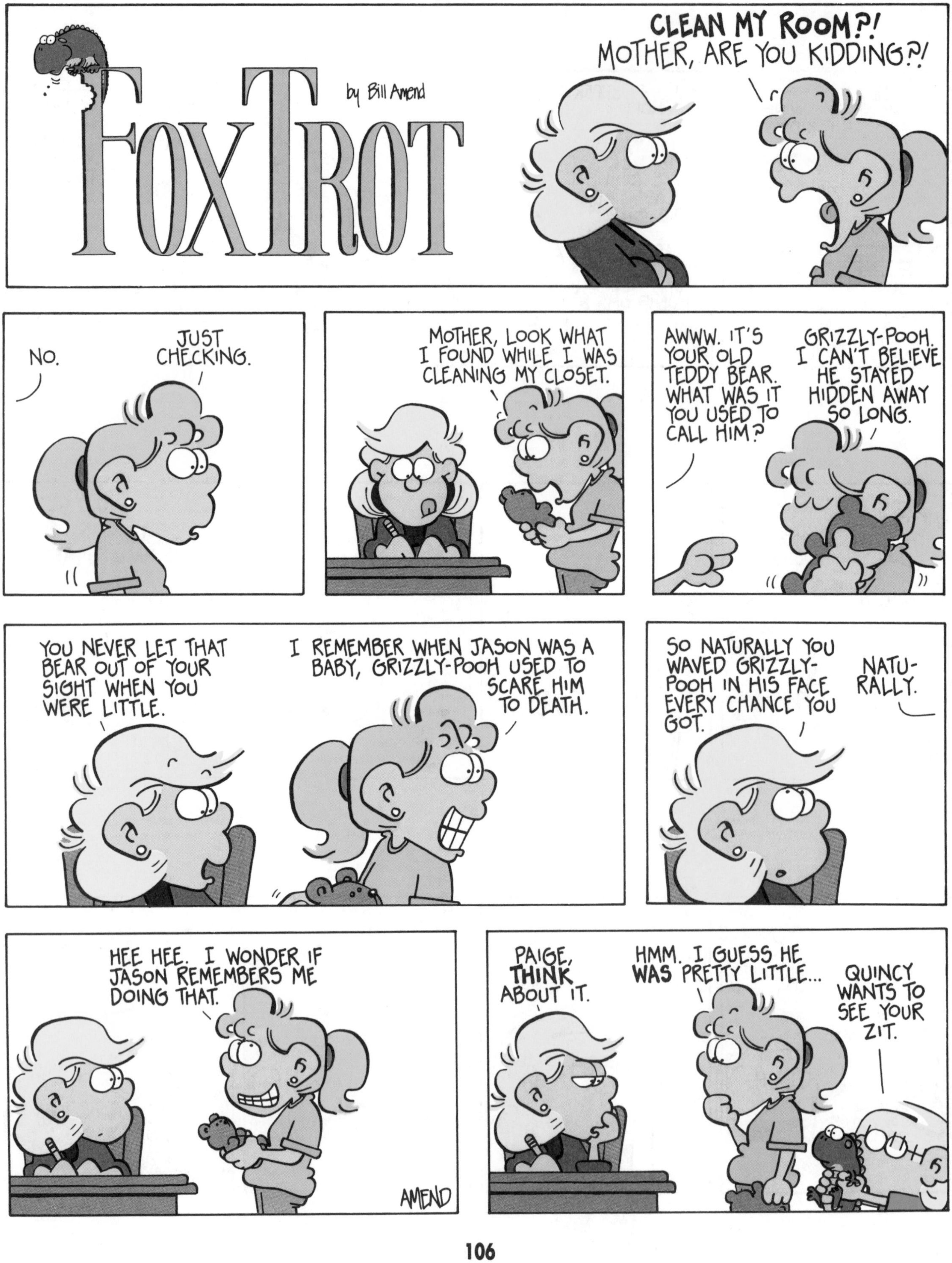
FoxTrot
by Bill Amend
CLEAN MY ROOM?! MOTHER, ARE YOU KIDDING?!
NO.
JUST CHECKING.
MOTHER, LOOK WHAT I FOUND WHILE I WAS CLEANING MY CLOSET.
AWWW. IT'S YOUR OLD TEDDY BEAR. WHAT WAS IT YOU USED TO CALL HIM?
GRIZZLY-POOH. I CAN'T BELIEVE HE STAYED HIDDEN AWAY SO LONG.
YOU NEVER LET THAT BEAR OUT OF YOUR SIGHT WHEN YOU WERE LITTLE.
I REMEMBER WHEN JASON WAS A BABY, GRIZZLY-POOH USED TO SCARE HIM TO DEATH.
SO NATURALLY YOU WAVED GRIZZLY-POOH IN HIS FACE EVERY CHANCE YOU GOT.
NATU-RALLY.
HEE HEE. I WONDER IF JASON REMEMBERS ME DOING THAT.
AMEND
PAIGE, **THINK** ABOUT IT.
HMM. I GUESS HE **WAS** PRETTY LITTLE...
QUINCY WANTS TO SEE YOUR ZIT.

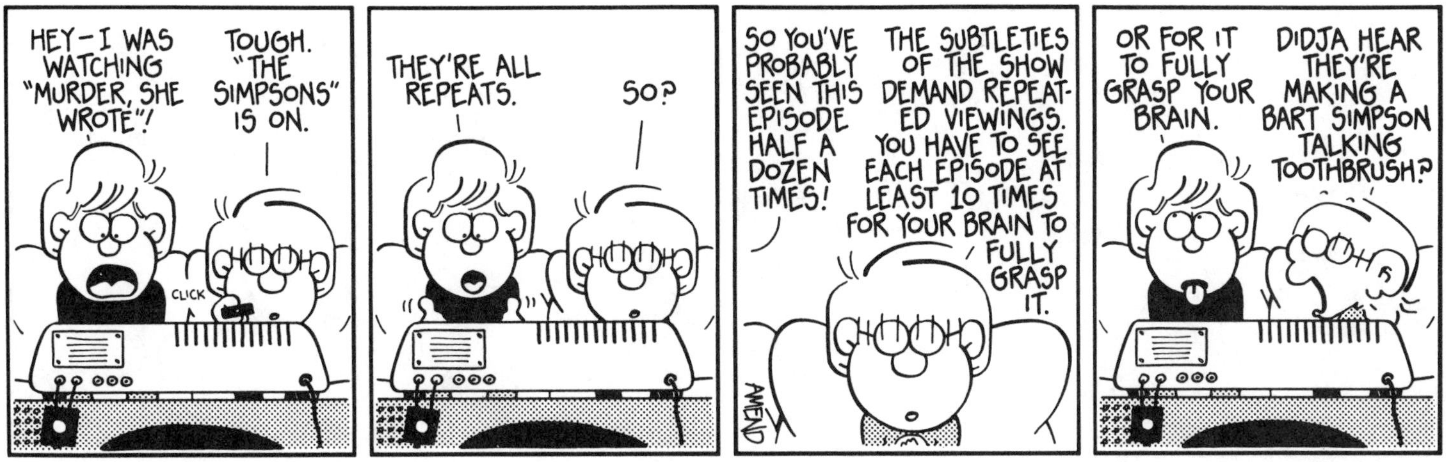
HEY—I WAS WATCHING "MURDER, SHE WROTE"!
TOUGH. "THE SIMPSONS" IS ON.
CLICK
THEY'RE ALL REPEATS.
SO?
SO YOU'VE PROBABLY SEEN THIS EPISODE HALF A DOZEN TIMES!
THE SUBTLETIES OF THE SHOW DEMAND REPEATED VIEWINGS. YOU HAVE TO SEE EACH EPISODE AT LEAST 10 TIMES FOR YOUR BRAIN TO FULLY GRASP IT.
AMEND
OR FOR IT TO FULLY GRASP YOUR BRAIN.
DIDJA HEAR THEY'RE MAKING A BART SIMPSON TALKING TOOTHBRUSH?

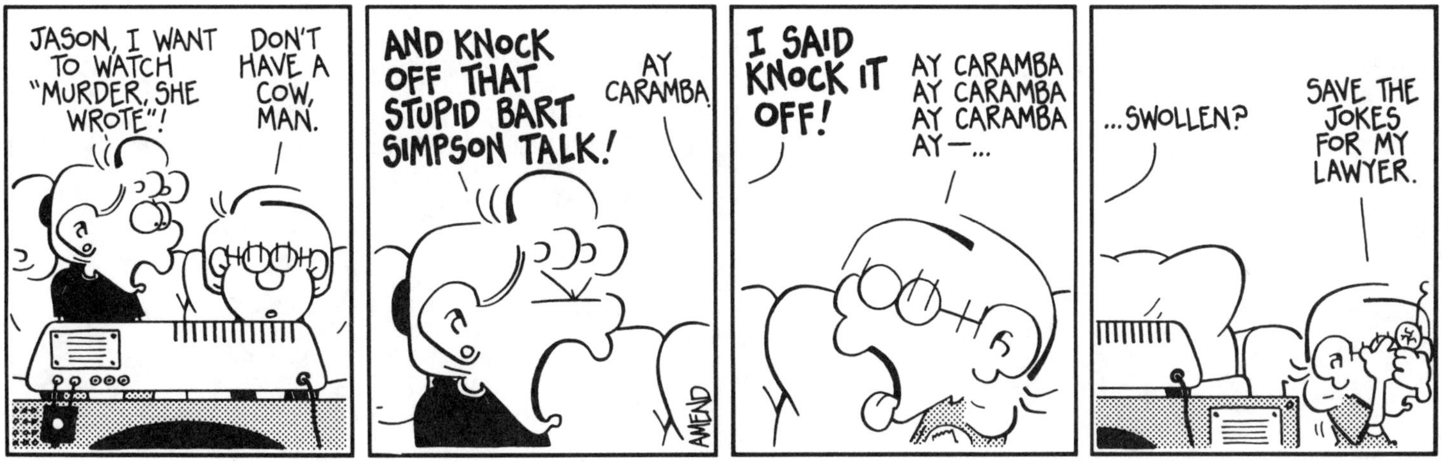
JASON, I WANT TO WATCH "MURDER, SHE WROTE"!
DON'T HAVE A COW, MAN.
AND KNOCK OFF THAT STUPID BART SIMPSON TALK!
AY CARAMBA.
AMEND
I SAID KNOCK IT OFF!
AY CARAMBA AY CARAMBA AY CARAMBA AY—...
...SWOLLEN?
SAVE THE JOKES FOR MY LAWYER.

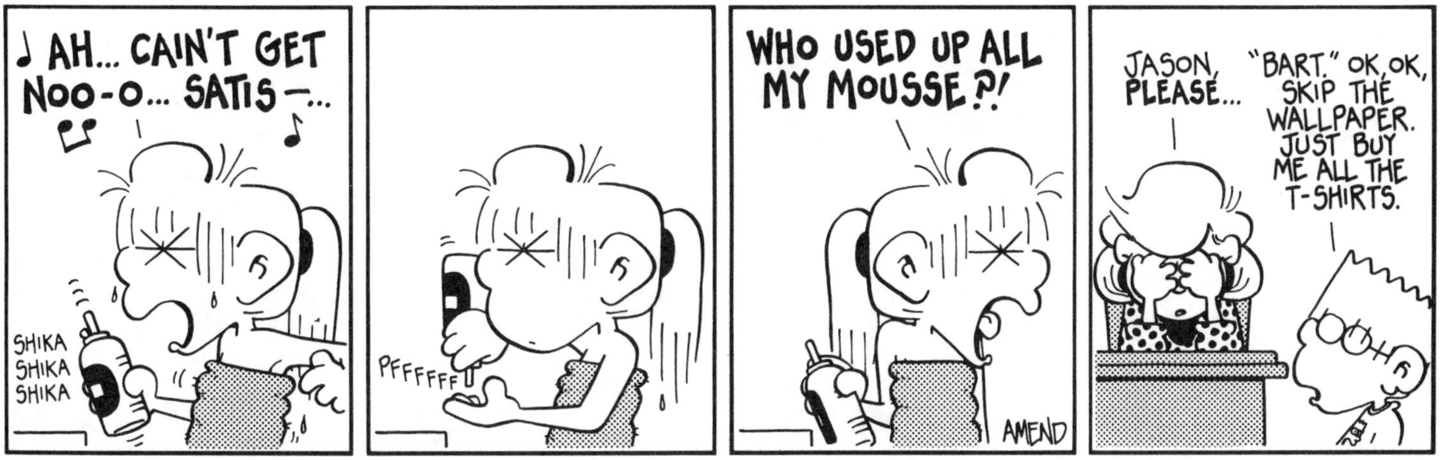
♩ AH... CAIN'T GET NOO-O... SATIS—...
SHIKA SHIKA SHIKA
PFFFFFFF
WHO USED UP ALL MY MOUSSE?!
AMEND
JASON, PLEASE...
"BART." OK, OK, SKIP THE WALLPAPER. JUST BUY ME ALL THE T-SHIRTS.

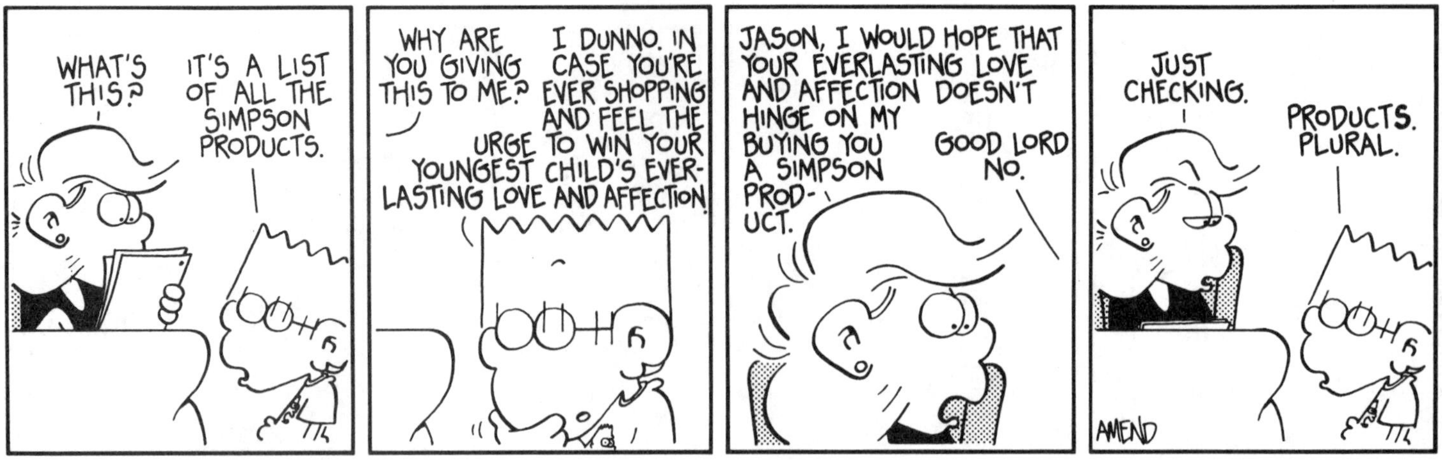
WHAT'S THIS?
IT'S A LIST OF ALL THE SIMPSON PRODUCTS.
WHY ARE YOU GIVING THIS TO ME?
I DUNNO. IN CASE YOU'RE EVER SHOPPING AND FEEL THE URGE TO WIN YOUR YOUNGEST CHILD'S EVERLASTING LOVE AND AFFECTION.
JASON, I WOULD HOPE THAT YOUR EVERLASTING LOVE AND AFFECTION DOESN'T HINGE ON MY BUYING YOU A SIMPSON PRODUCT.
GOOD LORD NO.
JUST CHECKING.
PRODUCTS. PLURAL.
AMEND

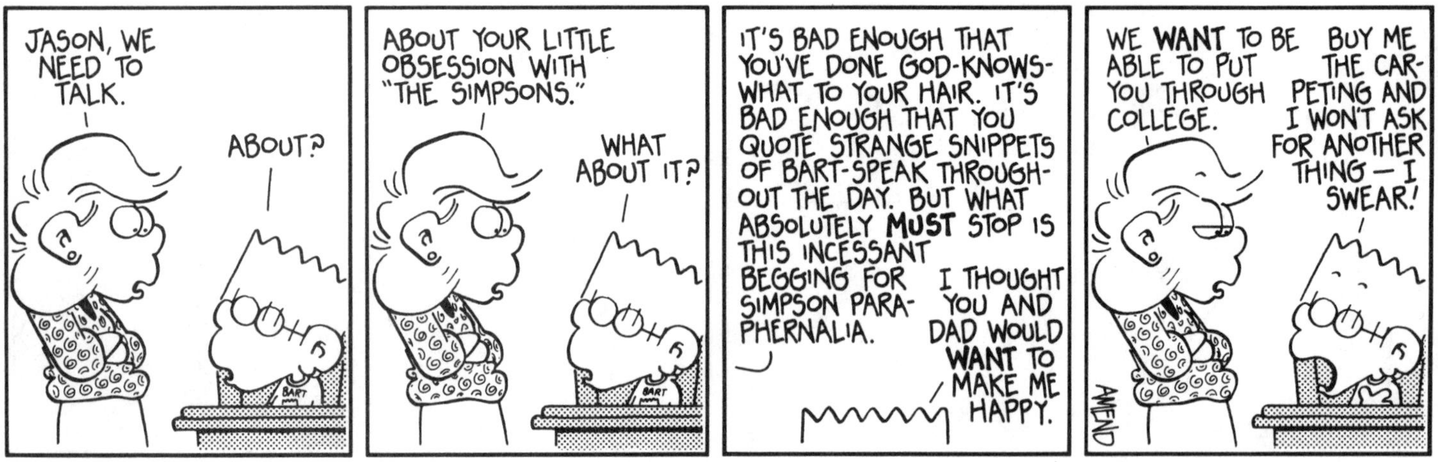
JASON, WE NEED TO TALK.
ABOUT?
BART
ABOUT YOUR LITTLE OBSESSION WITH "THE SIMPSONS."
WHAT ABOUT IT?
BART
IT'S BAD ENOUGH THAT YOU'VE DONE GOD-KNOWS-WHAT TO YOUR HAIR. IT'S BAD ENOUGH THAT YOU QUOTE STRANGE SNIPPETS OF BART-SPEAK THROUGHOUT THE DAY. BUT WHAT ABSOLUTELY MUST STOP IS THIS INCESSANT BEGGING FOR SIMPSON PARAPHERNALIA.
I THOUGHT YOU AND DAD WOULD WANT TO MAKE ME HAPPY.
WE WANT TO BE ABLE TO PUT YOU THROUGH COLLEGE.
BUY ME THE CARPETING AND I WON'T ASK FOR ANOTHER THING — I SWEAR!
AMEND

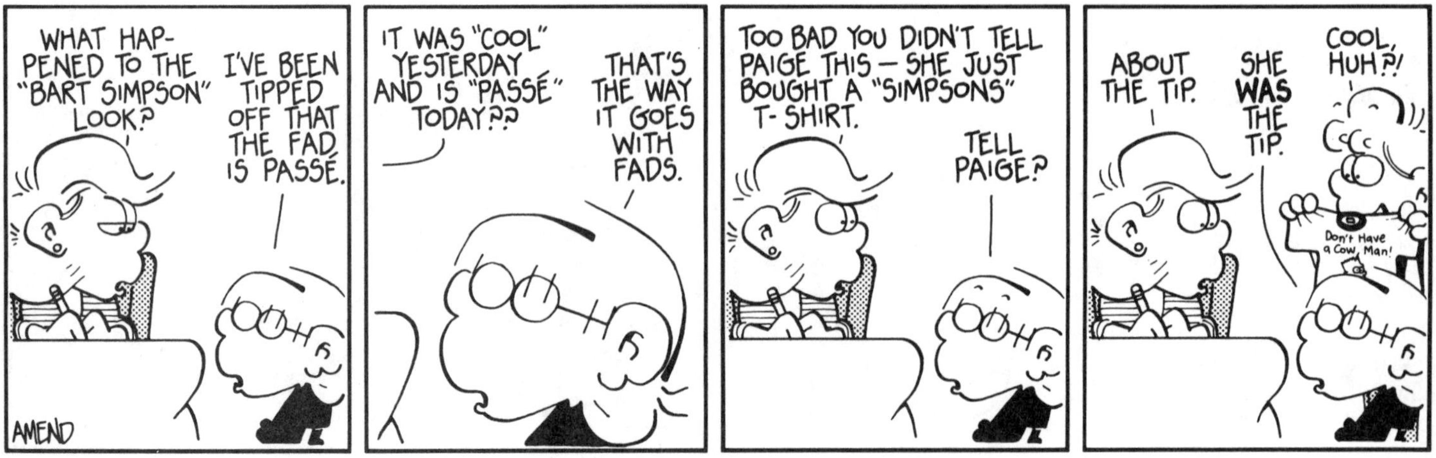
WHAT HAPPENED TO THE "BART SIMPSON" LOOK?
I'VE BEEN TIPPED OFF THAT THE FAD IS PASSÉ.
AMEND
IT WAS "COOL" YESTERDAY AND IS "PASSÉ" TODAY??
THAT'S THE WAY IT GOES WITH FADS.
TOO BAD YOU DIDN'T TELL PAIGE THIS — SHE JUST BOUGHT A "SIMPSONS" T-SHIRT.
TELL PAIGE?
ABOUT THE TIP.
SHE WAS THE TIP.
COOL, HUH?!
Don't Have a Cow, Man!

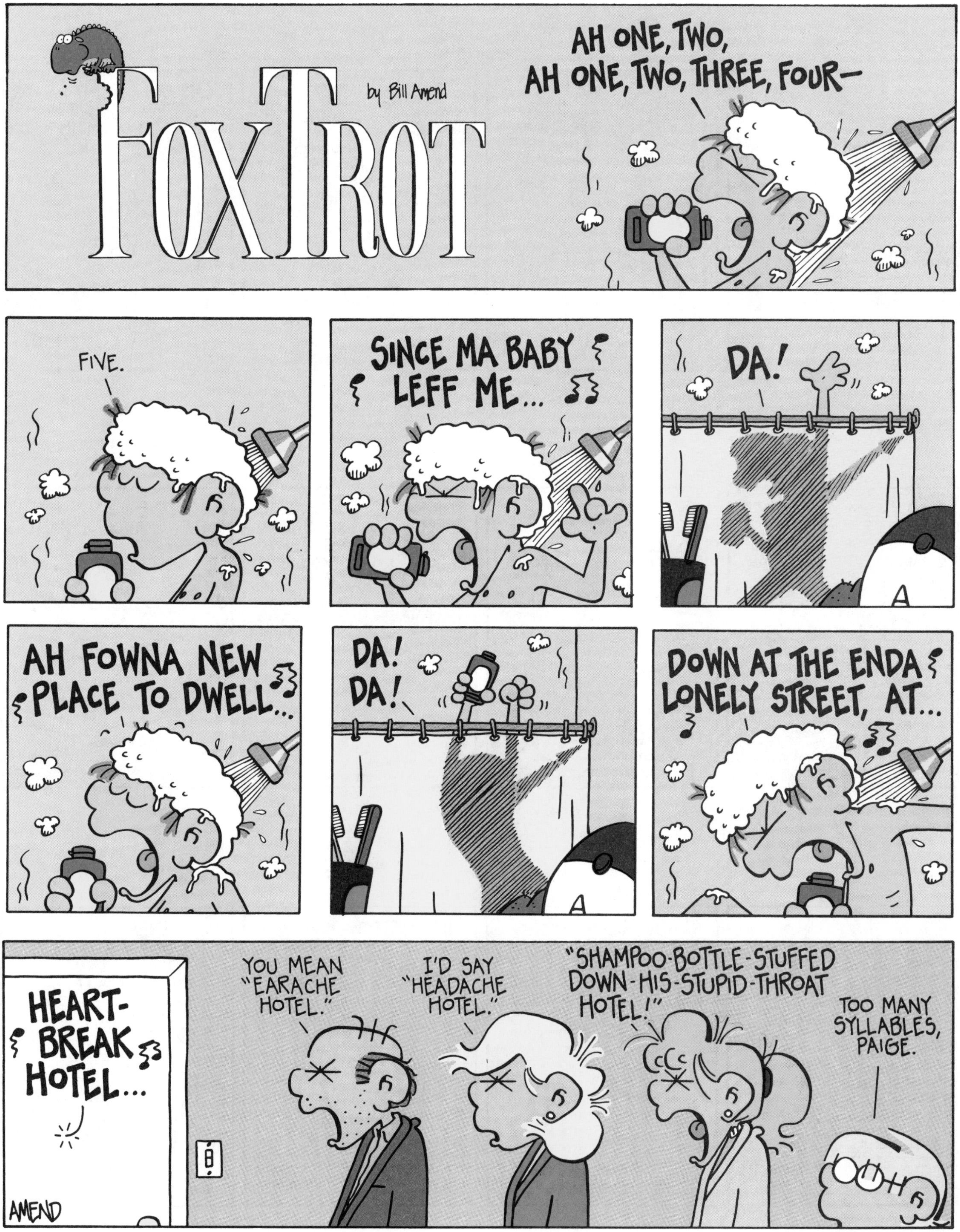
FoxTrot
by Bill Amend
AH ONE, TWO, AH ONE, TWO, THREE, FOUR—
FIVE.
SINCE MA BABY LEFF ME...
DA!
AH FOWNA NEW PLACE TO DWELL...
DA! DA!
DOWN AT THE ENDA LONELY STREET, AT...
HEART-BREAK HOTEL...
YOU MEAN "EARACHE HOTEL."
I'D SAY "HEADACHE HOTEL."
"SHAMPOO-BOTTLE-STUFFED DOWN-HIS-STUPID-THROAT HOTEL!"
TOO MANY SYLLABLES, PAIGE.
AMEND

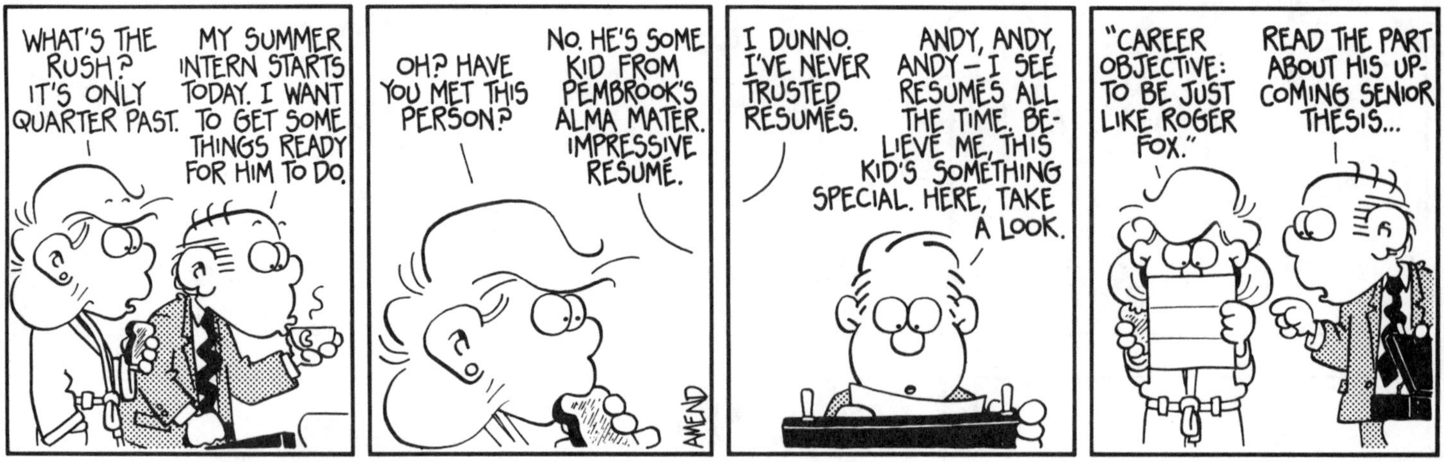
WHAT'S THE RUSH? IT'S ONLY QUARTER PAST.
MY SUMMER INTERN STARTS TODAY. I WANT TO GET SOME THINGS READY FOR HIM TO DO.
OH? HAVE YOU MET THIS PERSON?
NO. HE'S SOME KID FROM PEMBROOK'S ALMA MATER. IMPRESSIVE RESUMÉ.
AMEND
I DUNNO. I'VE NEVER TRUSTED RESUMÉS.
ANDY, ANDY, ANDY – I SEE RESUMÉS ALL THE TIME. BELIEVE ME, THIS KID'S SOMETHING SPECIAL. HERE, TAKE A LOOK.
"CAREER OBJECTIVE: TO BE JUST LIKE ROGER FOX."
READ THE PART ABOUT HIS UPCOMING SENIOR THESIS...

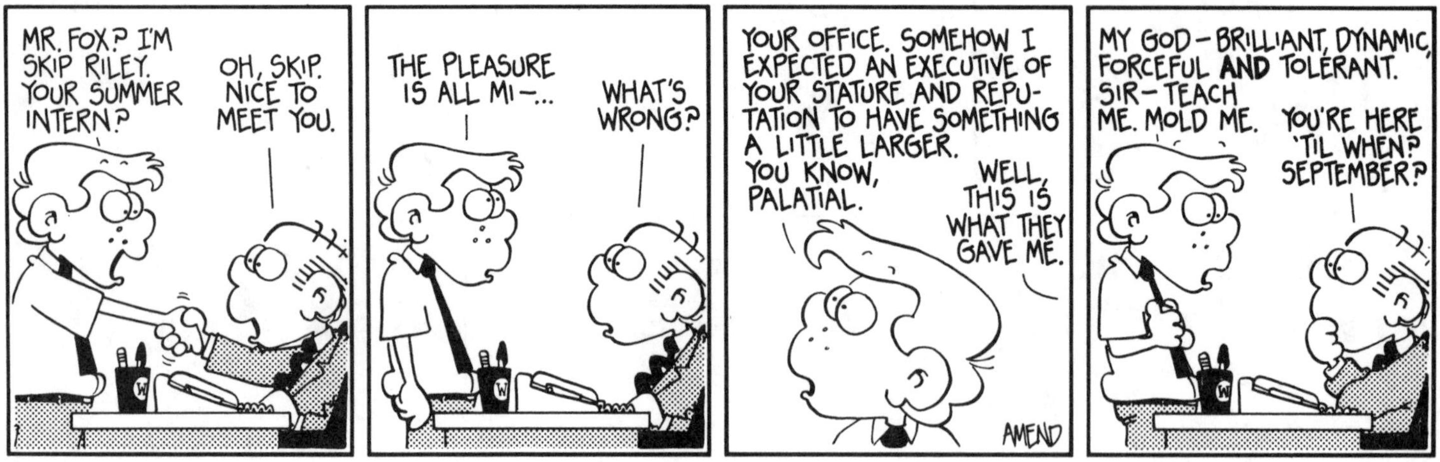
MR. FOX? I'M SKIP RILEY. YOUR SUMMER INTERN?
OH, SKIP. NICE TO MEET YOU.
THE PLEASURE IS ALL MI–...
WHAT'S WRONG?
YOUR OFFICE. SOMEHOW I EXPECTED AN EXECUTIVE OF YOUR STATURE AND REPUTATION TO HAVE SOMETHING A LITTLE LARGER. YOU KNOW, PALATIAL.
WELL, THIS IS WHAT THEY GAVE ME.
AMEND
MY GOD – BRILLIANT, DYNAMIC, FORCEFUL **AND** TOLERANT. SIR – TEACH ME. MOLD ME.
YOU'RE HERE 'TIL WHEN? SEPTEMBER?

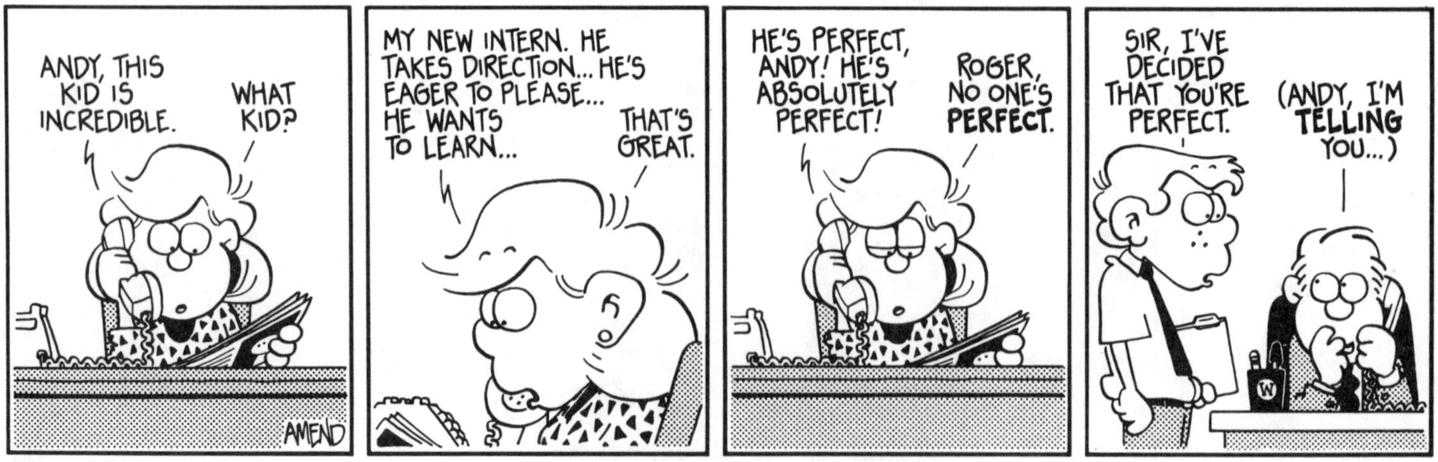
ANDY, THIS KID IS INCREDIBLE.
WHAT KID?
AMEND
MY NEW INTERN. HE TAKES DIRECTION... HE'S EAGER TO PLEASE... HE WANTS TO LEARN...
THAT'S GREAT.
HE'S PERFECT, ANDY! HE'S ABSOLUTELY PERFECT!
ROGER, NO ONE'S **PERFECT**.
SIR, I'VE DECIDED THAT YOU'RE PERFECT.
(ANDY, I'M **TELLING** YOU...)

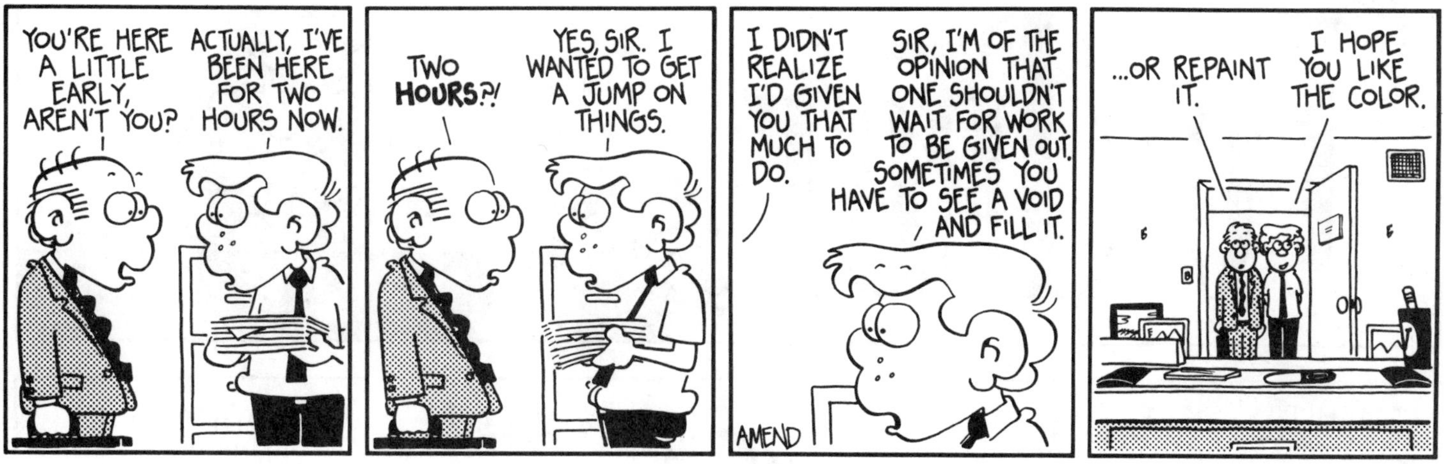
YOU'RE HERE A LITTLE EARLY, AREN'T YOU?
ACTUALLY, I'VE BEEN HERE FOR TWO HOURS NOW.
TWO **HOURS**?!
YES, SIR. I WANTED TO GET A JUMP ON THINGS.
I DIDN'T REALIZE I'D GIVEN YOU THAT MUCH TO DO.
SIR, I'M OF THE OPINION THAT ONE SHOULDN'T WAIT FOR WORK TO BE GIVEN OUT. SOMETIMES YOU HAVE TO SEE A VOID AND FILL IT.
AMEND
...OR REPAINT IT.
I HOPE YOU LIKE THE COLOR.

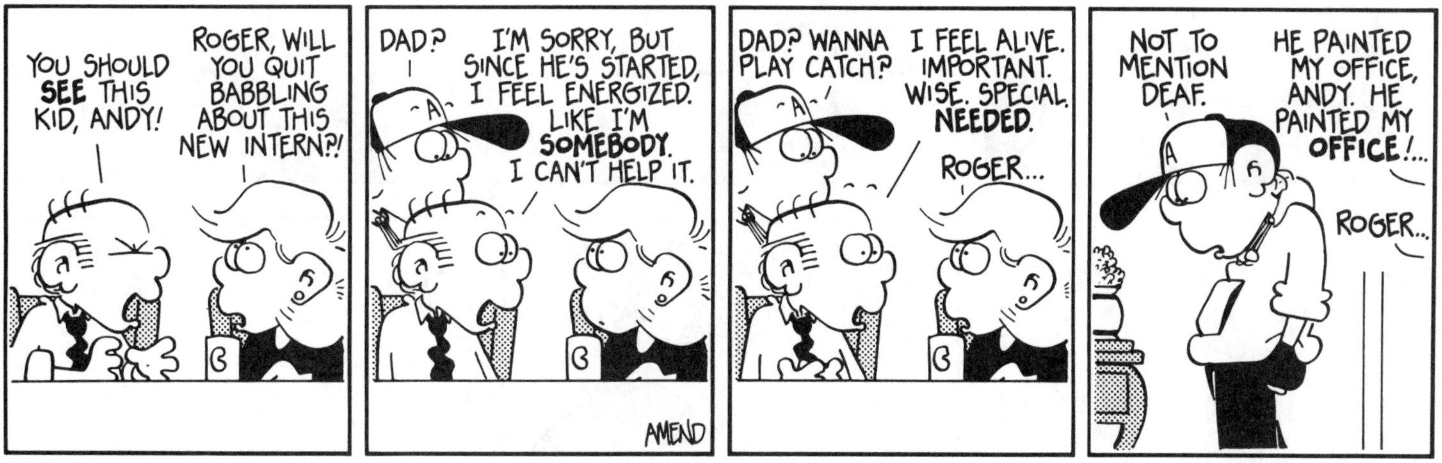
YOU SHOULD **SEE** THIS KID, ANDY!
ROGER, WILL YOU QUIT BABBLING ABOUT THIS NEW INTERN?!
DAD?
I'M SORRY, BUT SINCE HE'S STARTED, I FEEL ENERGIZED. LIKE I'M **SOMEBODY**. I CAN'T HELP IT.
AMEND
DAD? WANNA PLAY CATCH?
I FEEL ALIVE. IMPORTANT. WISE. SPECIAL. **NEEDED**.
ROGER...
NOT TO MENTION DEAF.
HE PAINTED MY OFFICE, ANDY. HE PAINTED MY **OFFICE**!...
ROGER...

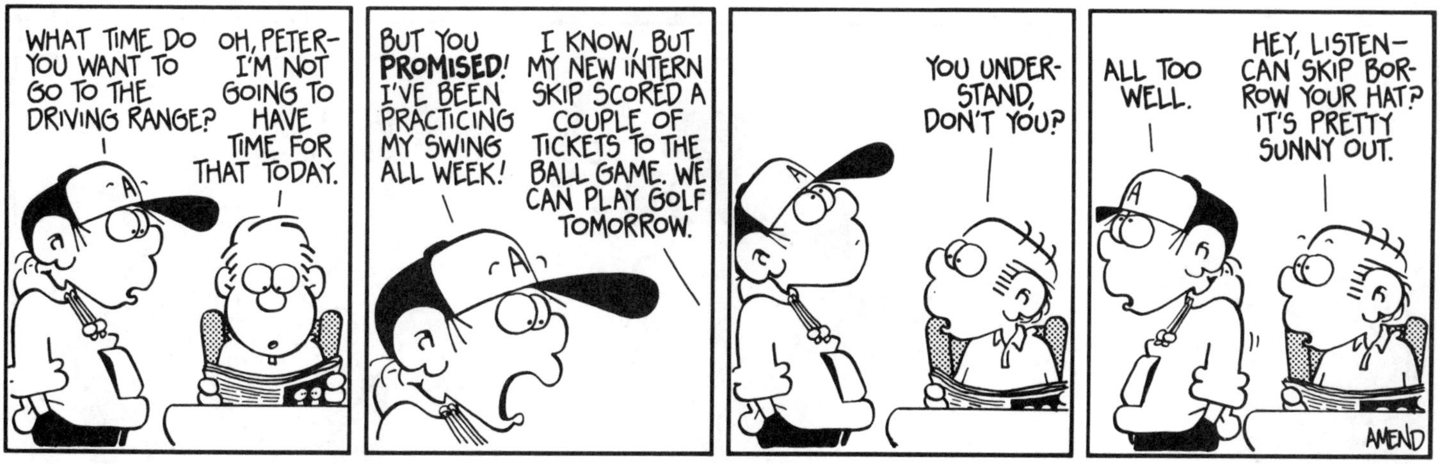
WHAT TIME DO YOU WANT TO GO TO THE DRIVING RANGE?
OH, PETER—I'M NOT GOING TO HAVE TIME FOR THAT TODAY.
BUT YOU **PROMISED**! I'VE BEEN PRACTICING MY SWING ALL WEEK!
I KNOW, BUT MY NEW INTERN SKIP SCORED A COUPLE OF TICKETS TO THE BALL GAME. WE CAN PLAY GOLF TOMORROW.
YOU UNDER-STAND, DON'T YOU?
ALL TOO WELL.
HEY, LISTEN—CAN SKIP BOR-ROW YOUR HAT? IT'S PRETTY SUNNY OUT.
AMEND

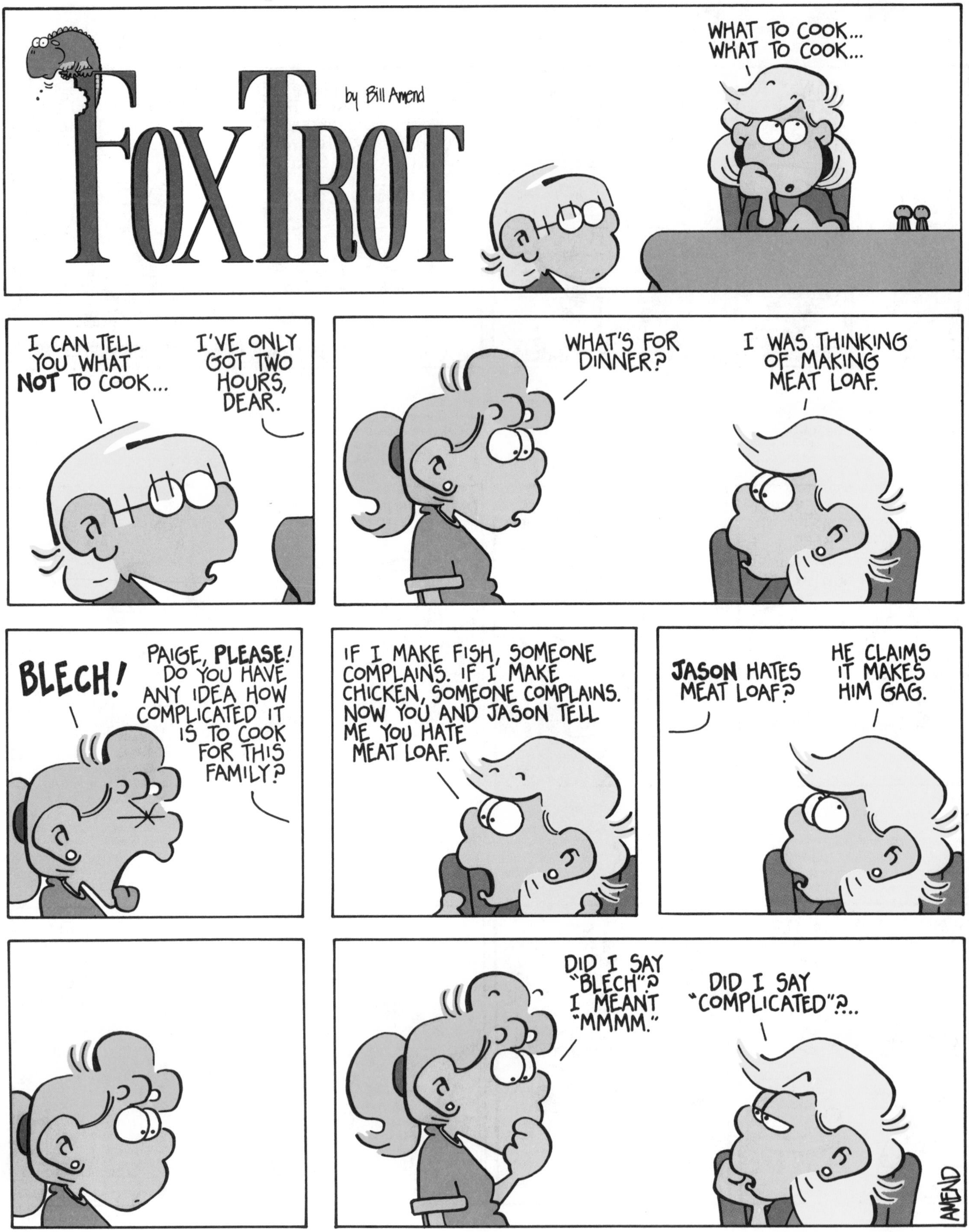
FoxTrot
by Bill Amend
WHAT TO COOK... WHAT TO COOK...
I CAN TELL YOU WHAT **NOT** TO COOK...
I'VE ONLY GOT TWO HOURS, DEAR.
WHAT'S FOR DINNER?
I WAS THINKING OF MAKING MEAT LOAF.
BLECH!
PAIGE, **PLEASE**! DO YOU HAVE ANY IDEA HOW COMPLICATED IT IS TO COOK FOR THIS FAMILY?
IF I MAKE FISH, SOMEONE COMPLAINS. IF I MAKE CHICKEN, SOMEONE COMPLAINS. NOW YOU AND JASON TELL ME YOU HATE MEAT LOAF.
JASON HATES MEAT LOAF?
HE CLAIMS IT MAKES HIM GAG.
DID I SAY "BLECH"? I MEANT "MMMM."
DID I SAY "COMPLICATED"?...
AMEND

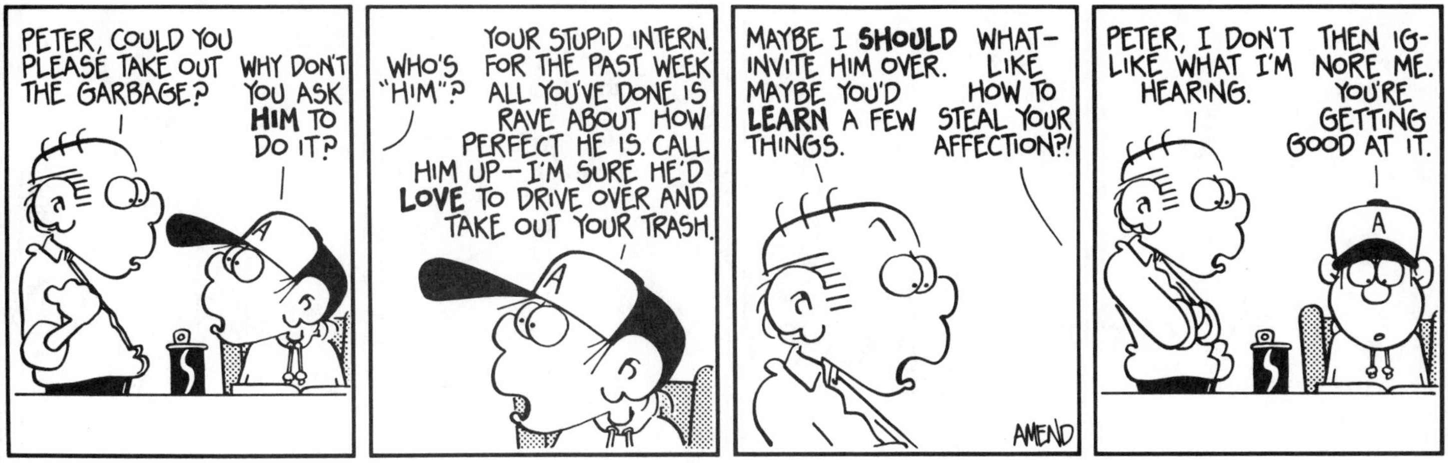
PETER, COULD YOU PLEASE TAKE OUT THE GARBAGE?
WHY DON'T YOU ASK HIM TO DO IT?
WHO'S "HIM"?
YOUR STUPID INTERN. FOR THE PAST WEEK ALL YOU'VE DONE IS RAVE ABOUT HOW PERFECT HE IS. CALL HIM UP—I'M SURE HE'D LOVE TO DRIVE OVER AND TAKE OUT YOUR TRASH.
MAYBE I SHOULD INVITE HIM OVER. MAYBE YOU'D LEARN A FEW THINGS.
WHAT—LIKE HOW TO STEAL YOUR AFFECTION?!
AMEND
PETER, I DON'T LIKE WHAT I'M HEARING.
THEN IGNORE ME. YOU'RE GETTING GOOD AT IT.

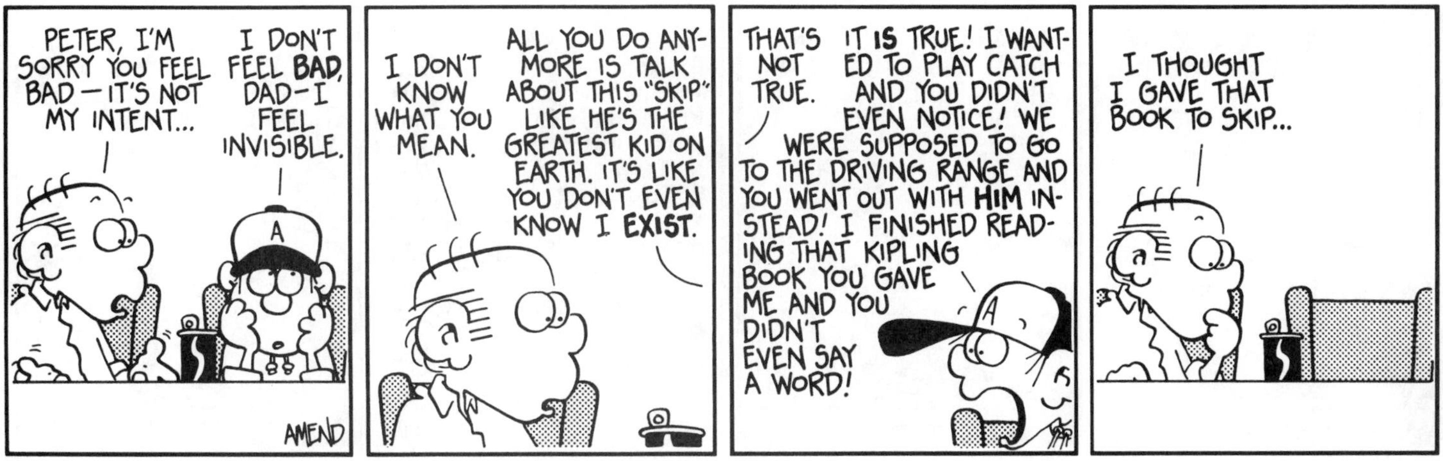
PETER, I'M SORRY YOU FEEL BAD—IT'S NOT MY INTENT...
I DON'T FEEL BAD, DAD—I FEEL INVISIBLE.
AMEND
I DON'T KNOW WHAT YOU MEAN.
ALL YOU DO ANYMORE IS TALK ABOUT THIS "SKIP" LIKE HE'S THE GREATEST KID ON EARTH. IT'S LIKE YOU DON'T EVEN KNOW I EXIST.
THAT'S NOT TRUE.
IT IS TRUE! I WANTED TO PLAY CATCH AND YOU DIDN'T EVEN NOTICE! WE WERE SUPPOSED TO GO TO THE DRIVING RANGE AND YOU WENT OUT WITH HIM INSTEAD! I FINISHED READING THAT KIPLING BOOK YOU GAVE ME AND YOU DIDN'T EVEN SAY A WORD!
I THOUGHT I GAVE THAT BOOK TO SKIP...

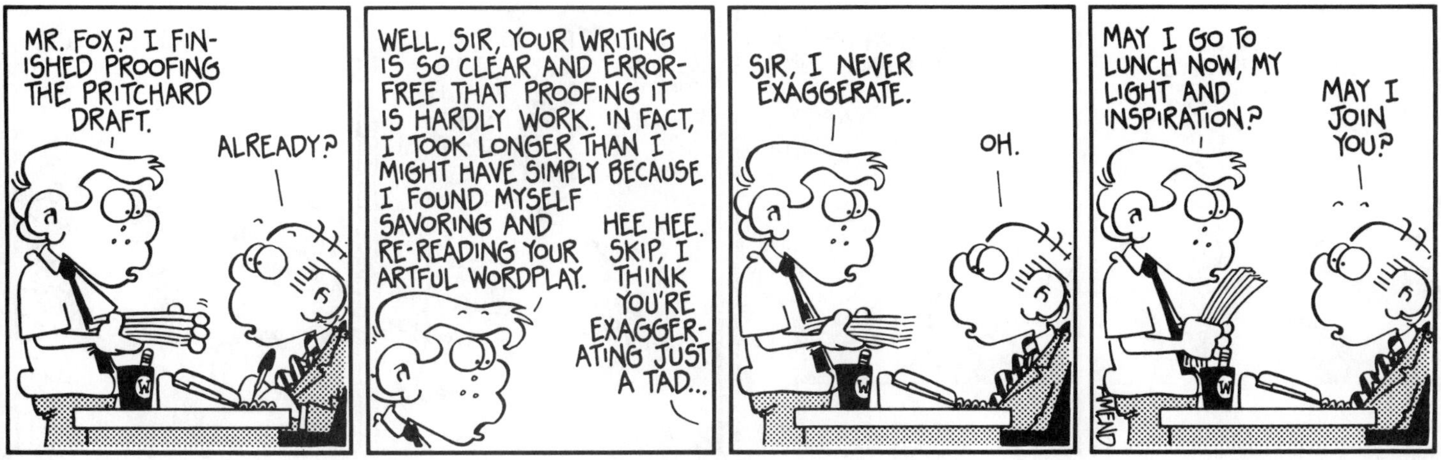
MR. FOX? I FINISHED PROOFING THE PRITCHARD DRAFT.
ALREADY?
WELL, SIR, YOUR WRITING IS SO CLEAR AND ERROR-FREE THAT PROOFING IT IS HARDLY WORK. IN FACT, I TOOK LONGER THAN I MIGHT HAVE SIMPLY BECAUSE I FOUND MYSELF SAVORING AND RE-READING YOUR ARTFUL WORDPLAY.
HEE HEE. SKIP, I THINK YOU'RE EXAGGERATING JUST A TAD...
SIR, I NEVER EXAGGERATE.
OH.
MAY I GO TO LUNCH NOW, MY LIGHT AND INSPIRATION?
MAY I JOIN YOU?
AMEND

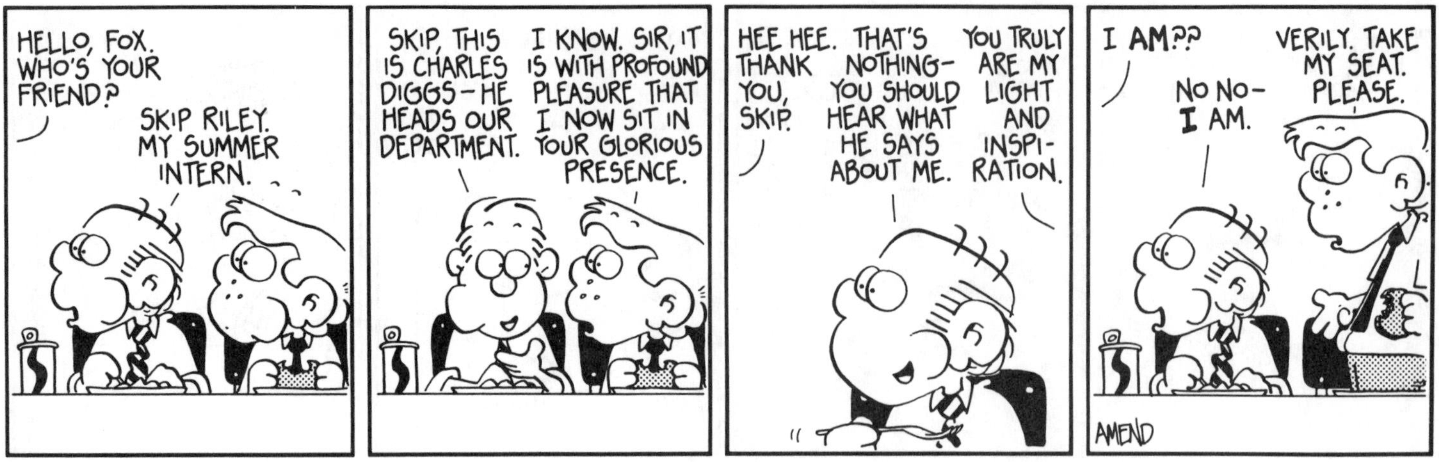
HELLO, FOX. WHO'S YOUR FRIEND?
SKIP RILEY. MY SUMMER INTERN.
SKIP, THIS IS CHARLES DIGGS—HE HEADS OUR DEPARTMENT.
I KNOW. SIR, IT IS WITH PROFOUND PLEASURE THAT I NOW SIT IN YOUR GLORIOUS PRESENCE.
HEE HEE. THANK YOU, SKIP.
THAT'S NOTHING— YOU SHOULD HEAR WHAT HE SAYS ABOUT ME.
YOU TRULY ARE MY LIGHT AND INSPIRATION.
I AM??
NO NO— I AM.
VERILY. TAKE MY SEAT. PLEASE.

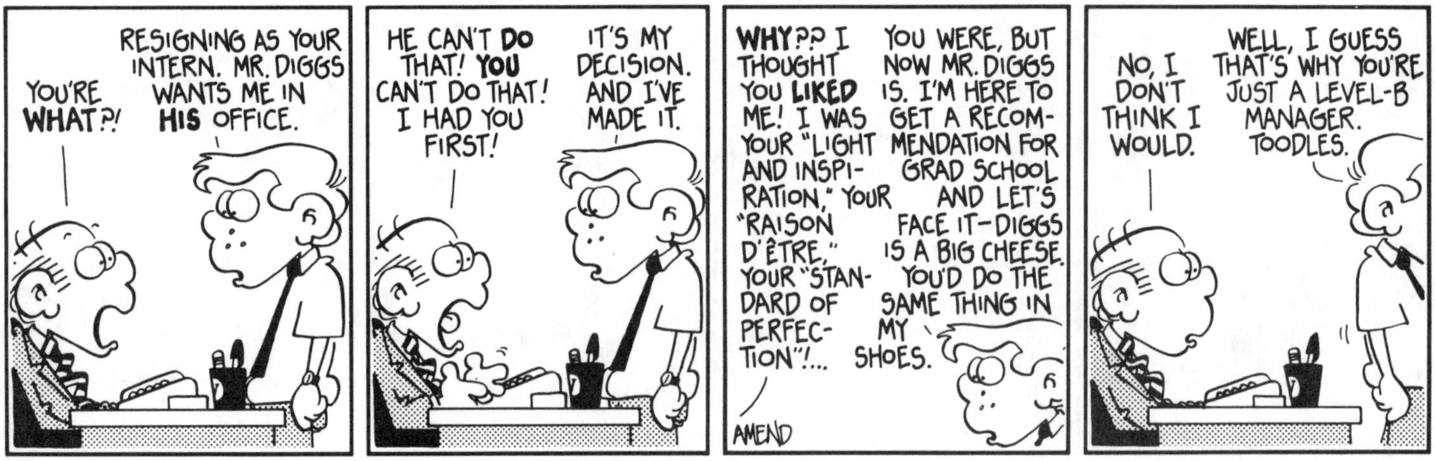
YOU'RE WHAT?!
RESIGNING AS YOUR INTERN. MR. DIGGS WANTS ME IN HIS OFFICE.
HE CAN'T DO THAT! YOU CAN'T DO THAT! I HAD YOU FIRST!
IT'S MY DECISION. AND I'VE MADE IT.
WHY?? I THOUGHT YOU LIKED ME! I WAS YOUR "LIGHT AND INSPIRATION," YOUR "RAISON D'ÊTRE," YOUR "STANDARD OF PERFECTION"!...
YOU WERE, BUT NOW MR. DIGGS IS. I'M HERE TO GET A RECOMMENDATION FOR GRAD SCHOOL AND LET'S FACE IT—DIGGS IS A BIG CHEESE. YOU'D DO THE SAME THING IN MY SHOES.
NO, I DON'T THINK I WOULD.
WELL, I GUESS THAT'S WHY YOU'RE JUST A LEVEL-B MANAGER. TOODLES.

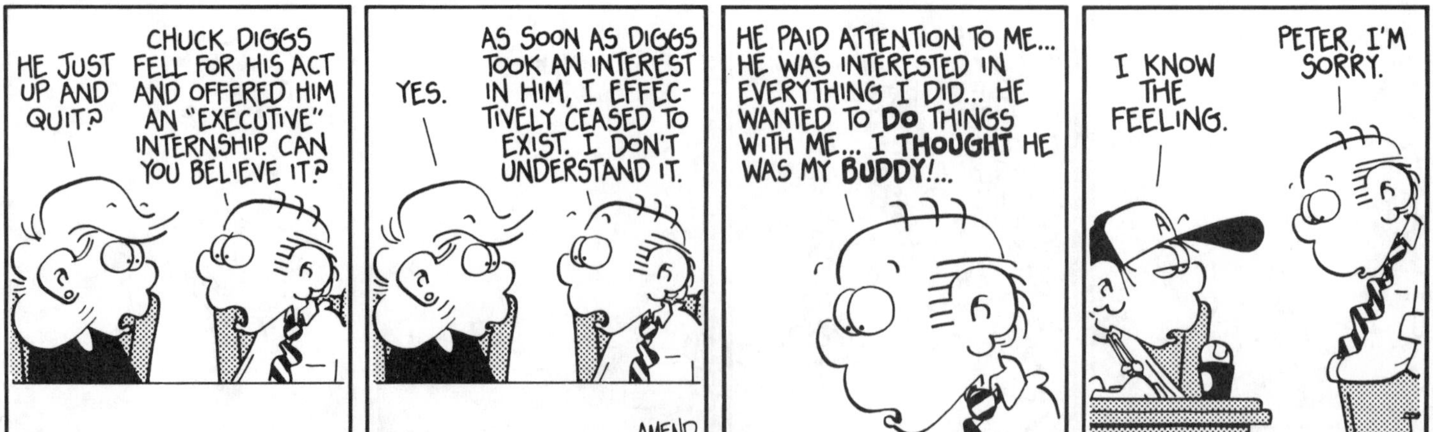
HE JUST UP AND QUIT?
CHUCK DIGGS FELL FOR HIS ACT AND OFFERED HIM AN "EXECUTIVE" INTERNSHIP. CAN YOU BELIEVE IT?
YES.
AS SOON AS DIGGS TOOK AN INTEREST IN HIM, I EFFECTIVELY CEASED TO EXIST. I DON'T UNDERSTAND IT.
HE PAID ATTENTION TO ME... HE WAS INTERESTED IN EVERYTHING I DID... HE WANTED TO DO THINGS WITH ME... I THOUGHT HE WAS MY BUDDY!...
I KNOW THE FEELING.
PETER, I'M SORRY.

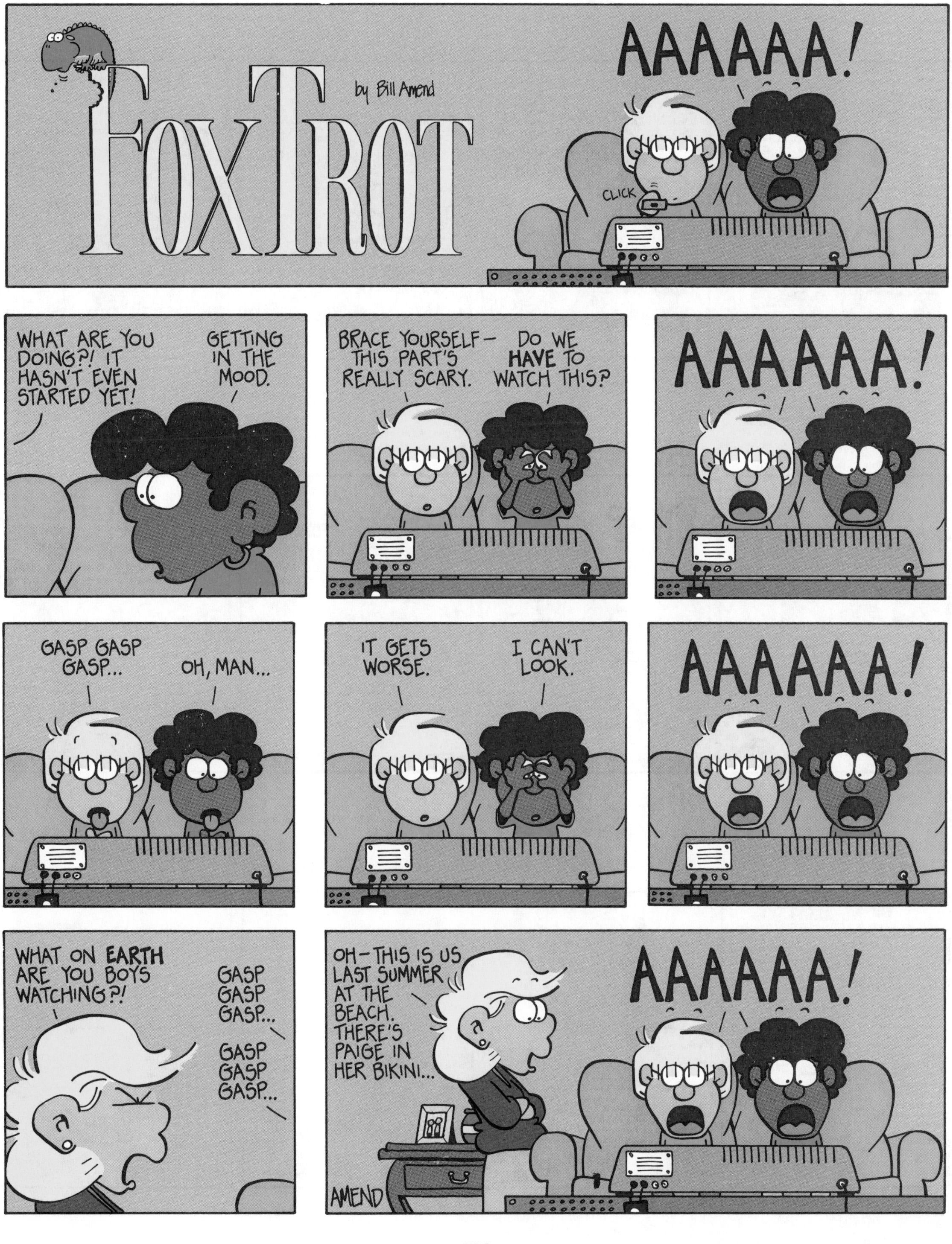
FoxTrot
by Bill Amend
AAAAAA!
CLICK
WHAT ARE YOU DOING?! IT HASN'T EVEN STARTED YET!
GETTING IN THE MOOD.
BRACE YOURSELF— THIS PART'S REALLY SCARY.
DO WE **HAVE** TO WATCH THIS?
AAAAAA!
GASP GASP GASP...
OH, MAN...
IT GETS WORSE.
I CAN'T LOOK.
AAAAAA!
WHAT ON **EARTH** ARE YOU BOYS WATCHING?!
GASP GASP GASP...
GASP GASP GASP...
OH— THIS IS US LAST SUMMER AT THE BEACH. THERE'S PAIGE IN HER BIKINI...
AAAAAA!
AMEND

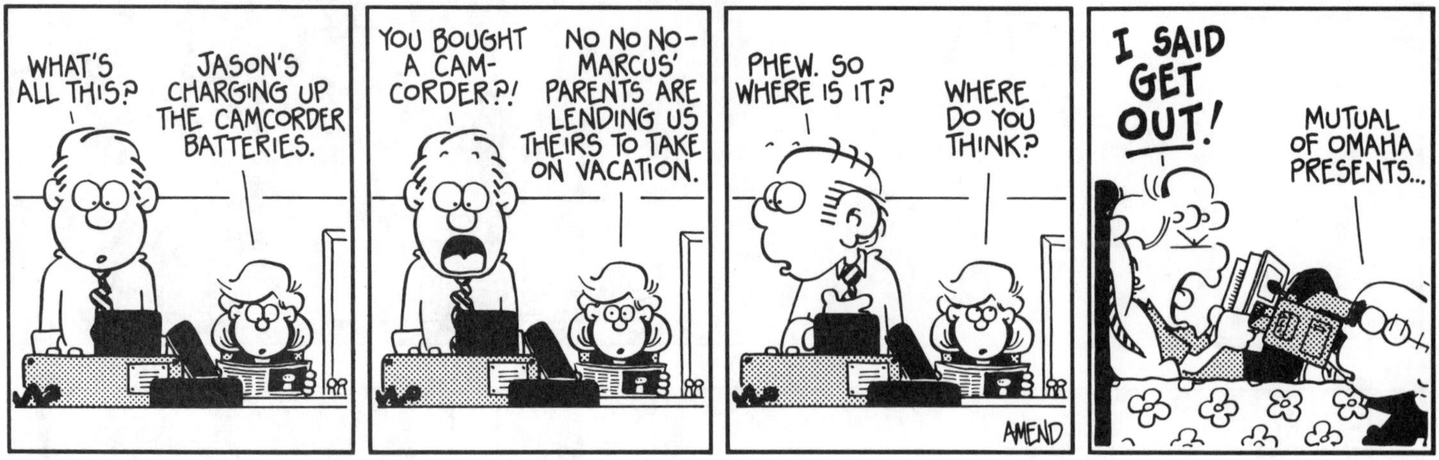
WHAT'S ALL THIS?
JASON'S CHARGING UP THE CAMCORDER BATTERIES.
YOU BOUGHT A CAM-CORDER?!
NO NO NO- MARCUS' PARENTS ARE LENDING US THEIRS TO TAKE ON VACATION.
PHEW. SO WHERE IS IT?
WHERE DO YOU THINK?
AMEND
I SAID GET OUT!
MUTUAL OF OMAHA PRESENTS...

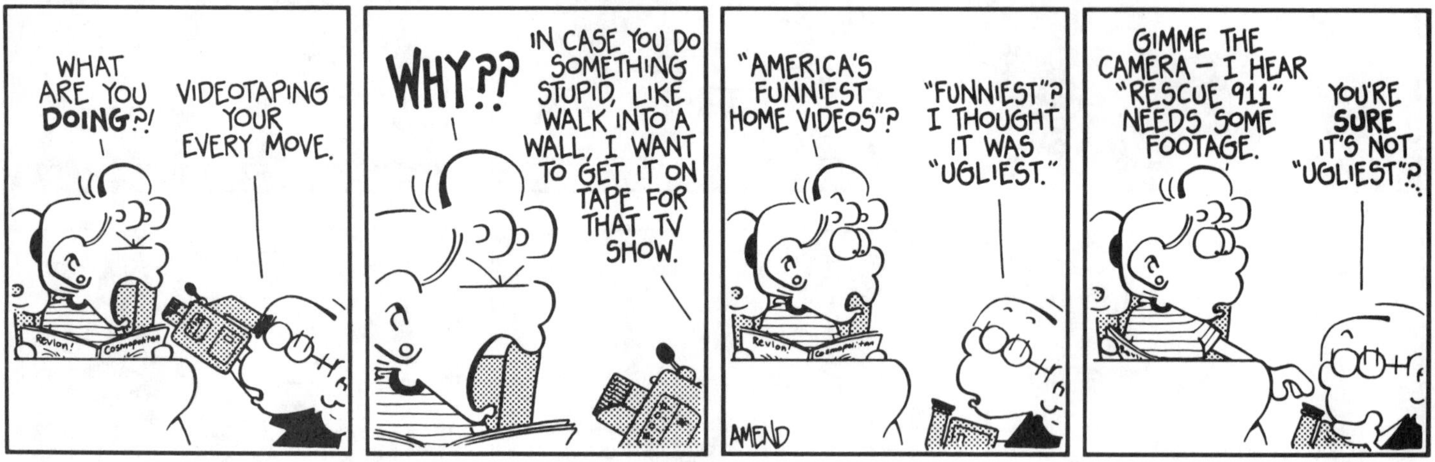
WHAT ARE YOU **DOING**?!
VIDEOTAPING YOUR EVERY MOVE.
Revlon!
Cosmopolitan
WHY??
IN CASE YOU DO SOMETHING STUPID, LIKE WALK INTO A WALL, I WANT TO GET IT ON TAPE FOR THAT TV SHOW.
"AMERICA'S FUNNIEST HOME VIDEOS"?
"FUNNIEST"? I THOUGHT IT WAS "UGLIEST."
AMEND
GIMME THE CAMERA - I HEAR "RESCUE 911" NEEDS SOME FOOTAGE.
YOU'RE **SURE** IT'S NOT "UGLIEST"?

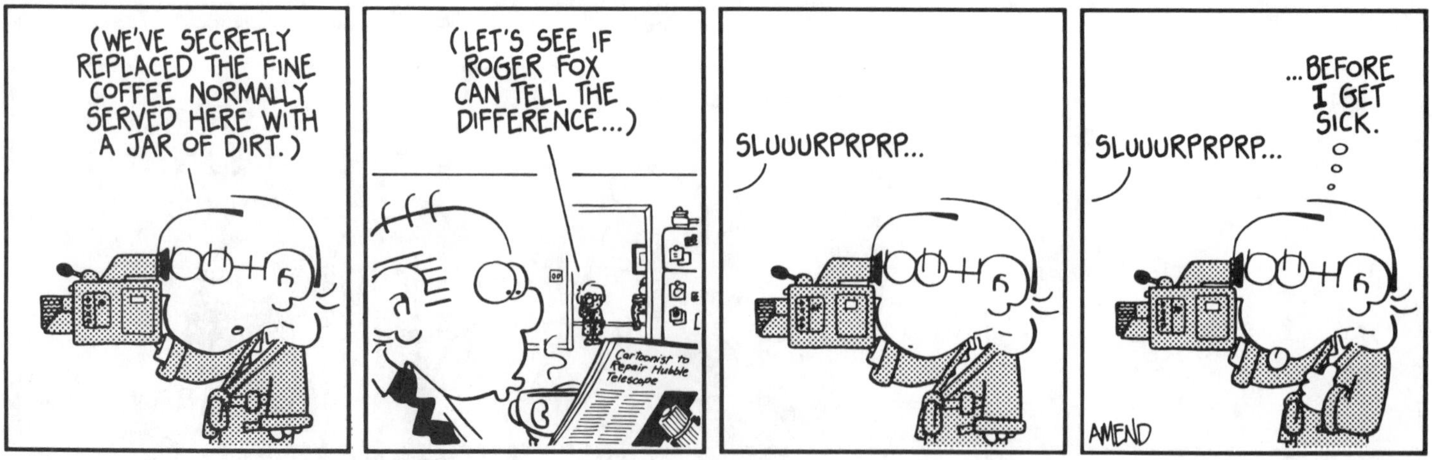
(WE'VE SECRETLY REPLACED THE FINE COFFEE NORMALLY SERVED HERE WITH A JAR OF DIRT.)
(LET'S SEE IF ROGER FOX CAN TELL THE DIFFERENCE...)
Cartoonist to Repair Hubble Telescope
SLUUURPRPRP...
SLUUURPRPRP...
...BEFORE **I** GET SICK.
AMEND

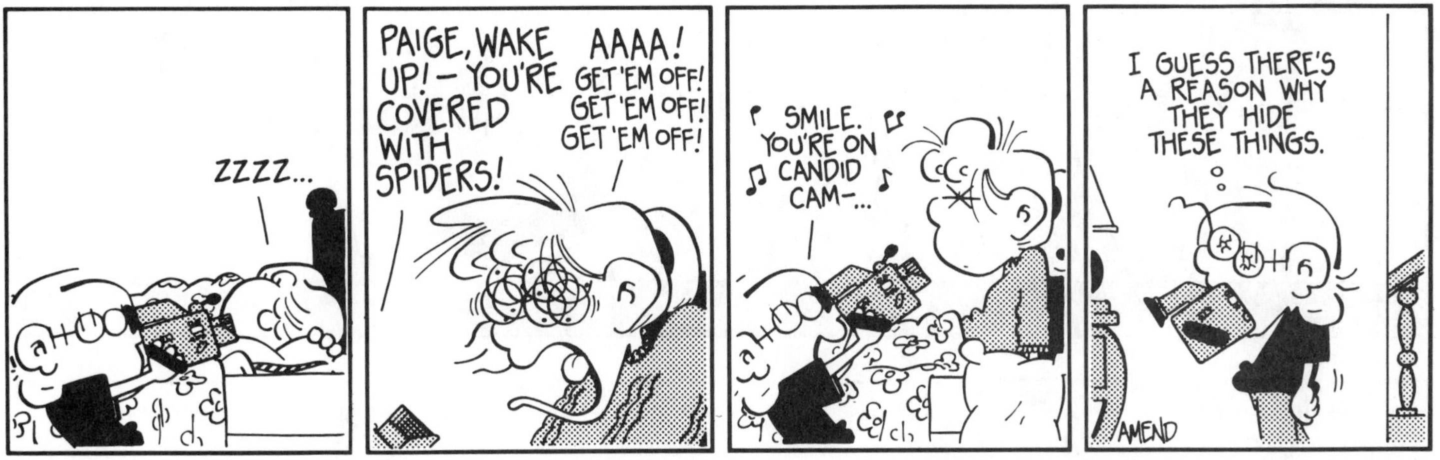
ZZZZ...
PAIGE, WAKE UP! – YOU'RE COVERED WITH SPIDERS!
AAAA! GET 'EM OFF! GET 'EM OFF! GET 'EM OFF!
SMILE. YOU'RE ON CANDID CAM–...
I GUESS THERE'S A REASON WHY THEY HIDE THESE THINGS.
AMEND

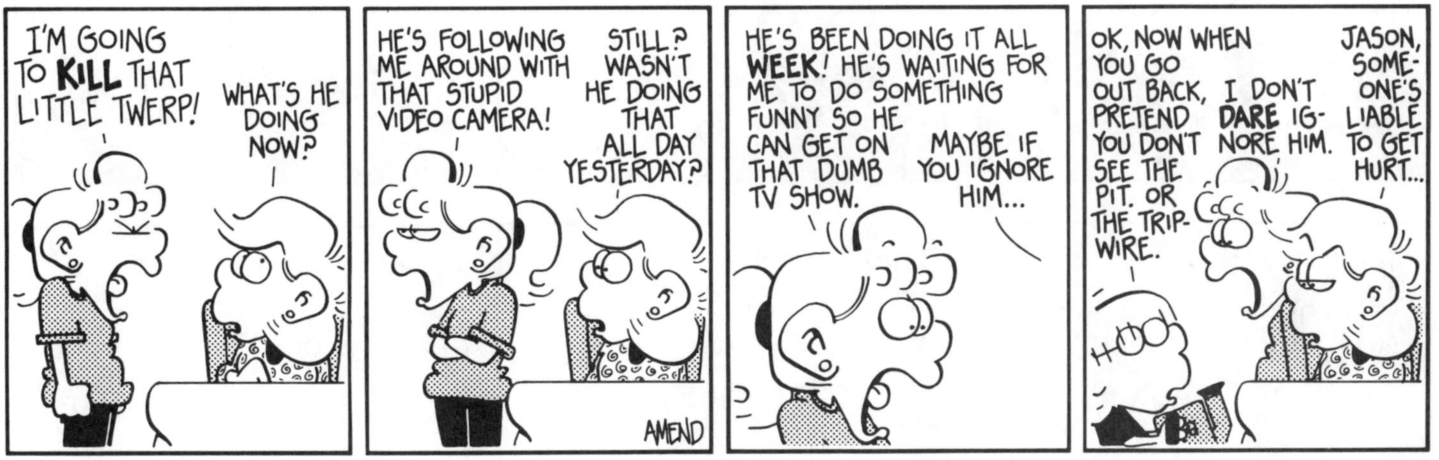
I'M GOING TO **KILL** THAT LITTLE TWERP!
WHAT'S HE DOING NOW?
HE'S FOLLOWING ME AROUND WITH THAT STUPID VIDEO CAMERA!
STILL? WASN'T HE DOING THAT ALL DAY YESTERDAY?
AMEND
HE'S BEEN DOING IT ALL **WEEK**! HE'S WAITING FOR ME TO DO SOMETHING FUNNY SO HE CAN GET ON THAT DUMB TV SHOW.
MAYBE IF YOU IGNORE HIM...
OK, NOW WHEN YOU GO OUT BACK, PRETEND YOU DON'T SEE THE PIT. OR THE TRIP-WIRE.
I DON'T **DARE** IGNORE HIM.
JASON, SOME-ONE'S LIABLE TO GET HURT...

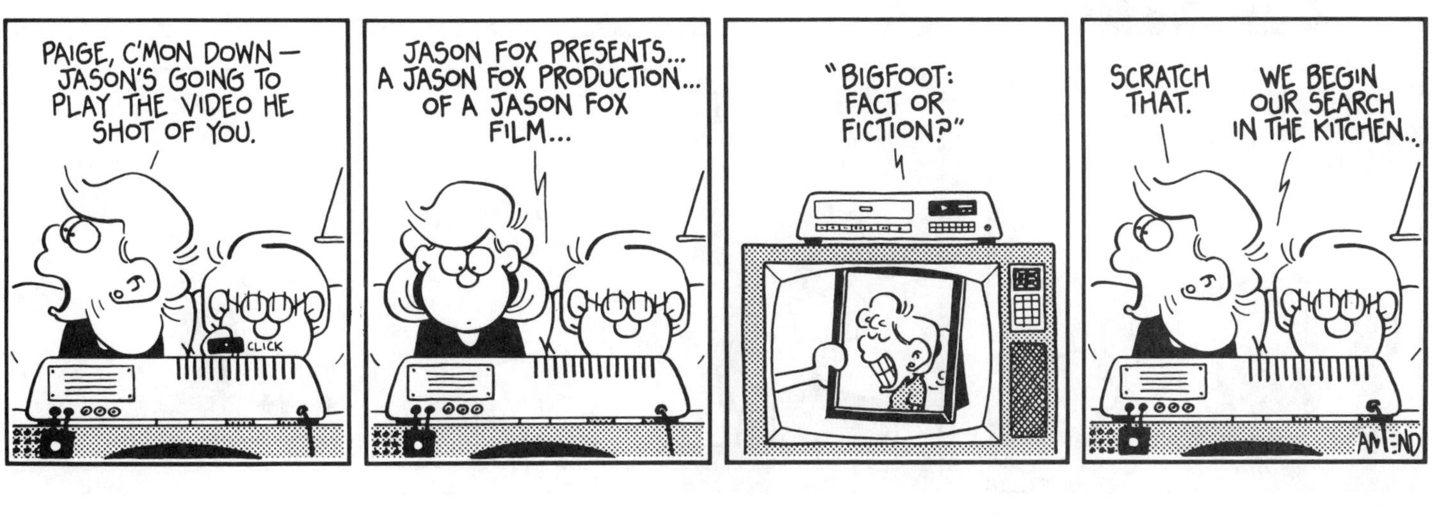
PAIGE, C'MON DOWN – JASON'S GOING TO PLAY THE VIDEO HE SHOT OF YOU.
CLICK
JASON FOX PRESENTS... A JASON FOX PRODUCTION... OF A JASON FOX FILM...
"BIGFOOT: FACT OR FICTION?"
SCRATCH THAT.
WE BEGIN OUR SEARCH IN THE KITCHEN...
AMEND

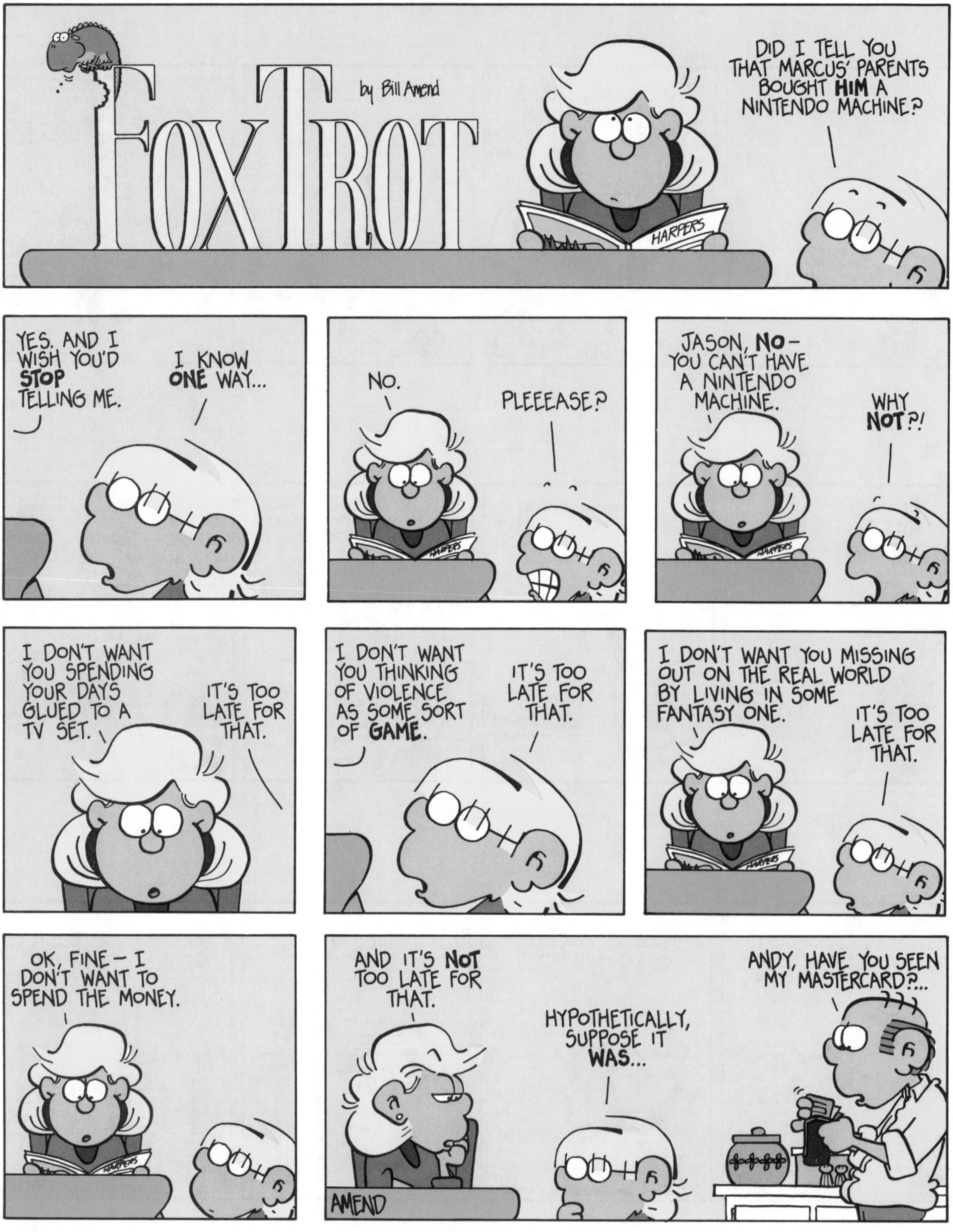
FoxTrot
by Bill Amend
DID I TELL YOU THAT MARCUS' PARENTS BOUGHT **HIM** A NINTENDO MACHINE?
HARPERS
YES. AND I WISH YOU'D **STOP** TELLING ME.
I KNOW **ONE** WAY...
NO.
PLEEEASE?
JASON, **NO**– YOU CAN'T HAVE A NINTENDO MACHINE.
WHY **NOT**?!
I DON'T WANT YOU SPENDING YOUR DAYS GLUED TO A TV SET.
IT'S TOO LATE FOR THAT.
I DON'T WANT YOU THINKING OF VIOLENCE AS SOME SORT OF **GAME**.
IT'S TOO LATE FOR THAT.
I DON'T WANT YOU MISSING OUT ON THE REAL WORLD BY LIVING IN SOME FANTASY ONE.
IT'S TOO LATE FOR THAT.
OK, FINE– I DON'T WANT TO SPEND THE MONEY.
AND IT'S **NOT** TOO LATE FOR THAT.
HYPOTHETICALLY, SUPPOSE IT **WAS**...
ANDY, HAVE YOU SEEN MY MASTERCARD?...
AMEND

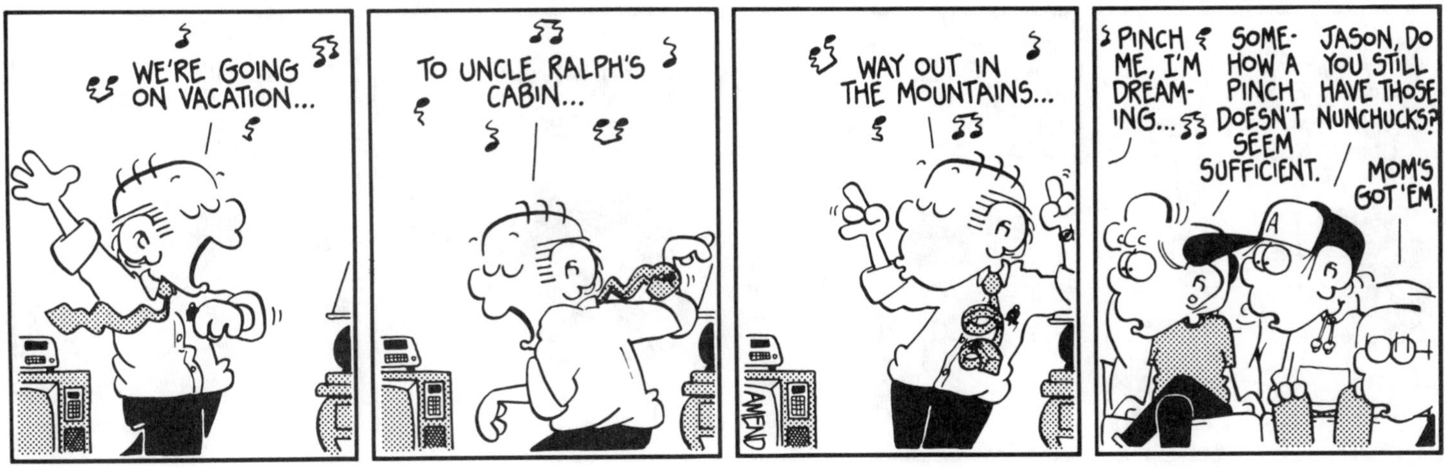
WE'RE GOING ON VACATION...
TO UNCLE RALPH'S CABIN...
WAY OUT IN THE MOUNTAINS...
AMEND
PINCH ME, I'M DREAMING...
SOMEHOW A PINCH DOESN'T SEEM SUFFICIENT.
JASON, DO YOU STILL HAVE THOSE NUNCHUCKS?
MOM'S GOT 'EM.

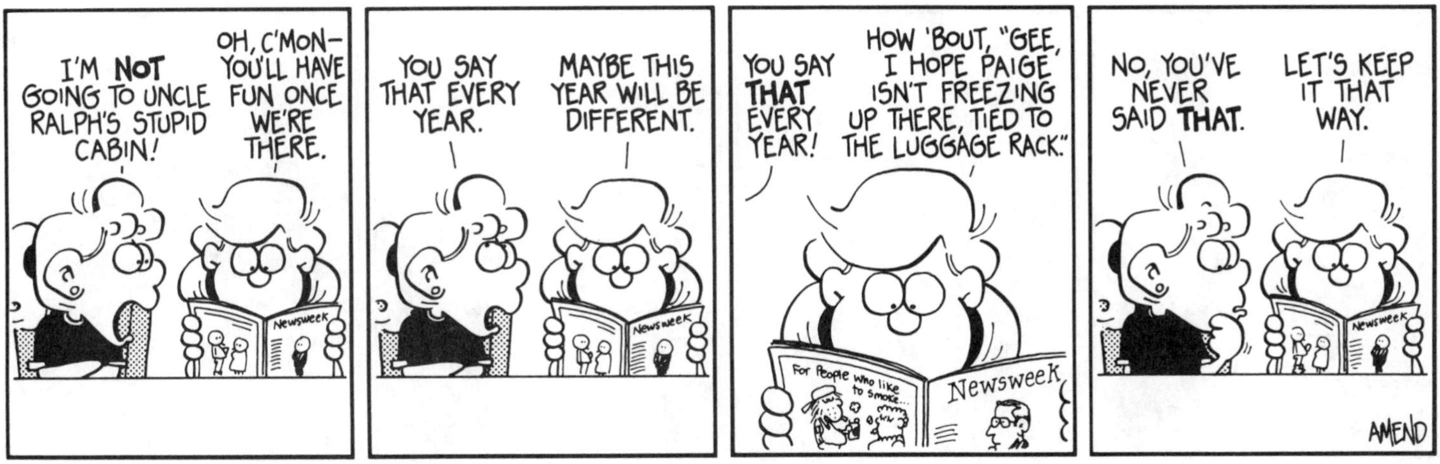
I'M **NOT** GOING TO UNCLE RALPH'S STUPID CABIN!
OH, C'MON— YOU'LL HAVE FUN ONCE WE'RE THERE.
YOU SAY THAT EVERY YEAR.
MAYBE THIS YEAR WILL BE DIFFERENT.
YOU SAY **THAT** EVERY YEAR!
HOW 'BOUT, "GEE, I HOPE PAIGE ISN'T FREEZING UP THERE, TIED TO THE LUGGAGE RACK."
Newsweek
For People who like to Smoke...
NO, YOU'VE NEVER SAID **THAT**.
LET'S KEEP IT THAT WAY.
AMEND

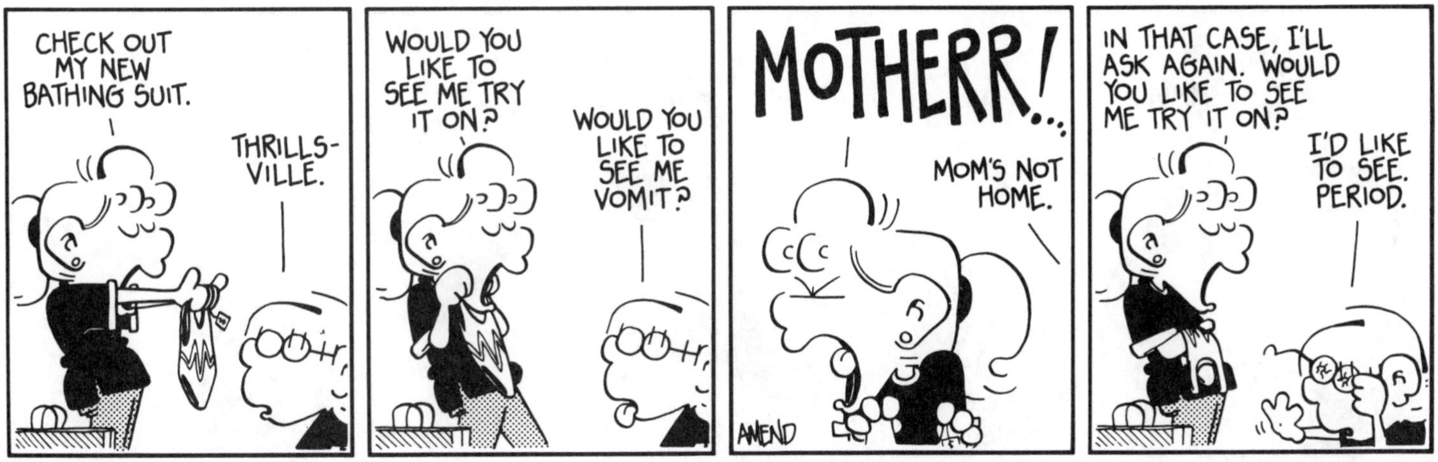
CHECK OUT MY NEW BATHING SUIT.
THRILLSVILLE.
WOULD YOU LIKE TO SEE ME TRY IT ON?
WOULD YOU LIKE TO SEE ME VOMIT?
MOTHERR!...
MOM'S NOT HOME.
AMEND
IN THAT CASE, I'LL ASK AGAIN. WOULD YOU LIKE TO SEE ME TRY IT ON?
I'D LIKE TO SEE. PERIOD.

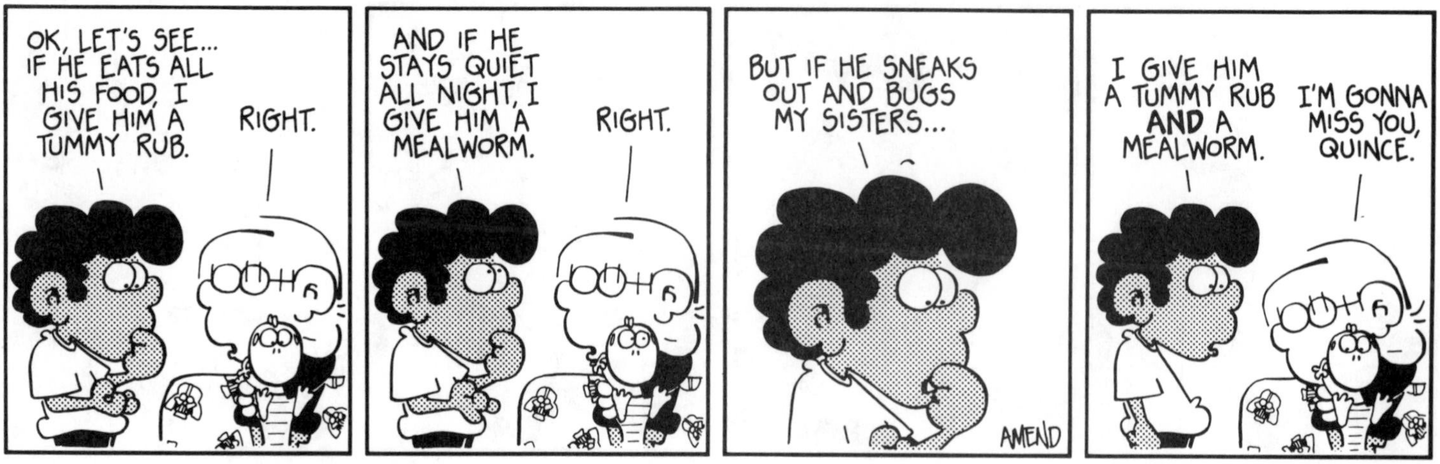
OK, LET'S SEE... IF HE EATS ALL HIS FOOD, I GIVE HIM A TUMMY RUB.
RIGHT.
AND IF HE STAYS QUIET ALL NIGHT, I GIVE HIM A MEALWORM.
RIGHT.
BUT IF HE SNEAKS OUT AND BUGS MY SISTERS...
AMEND
I GIVE HIM A TUMMY RUB **AND** A MEALWORM.
I'M GONNA MISS YOU, QUINCE.

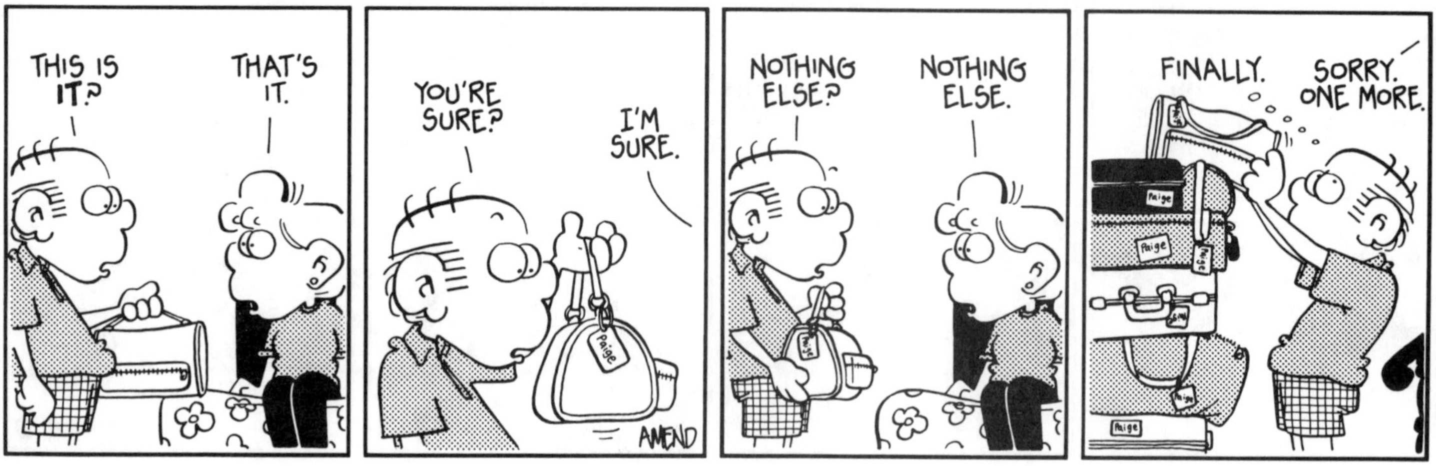
THIS IS **IT**?
THAT'S IT.
YOU'RE SURE?
I'M SURE.
Paige
AMEND
NOTHING ELSE?
NOTHING ELSE.
FINALLY.
SORRY. ONE MORE.

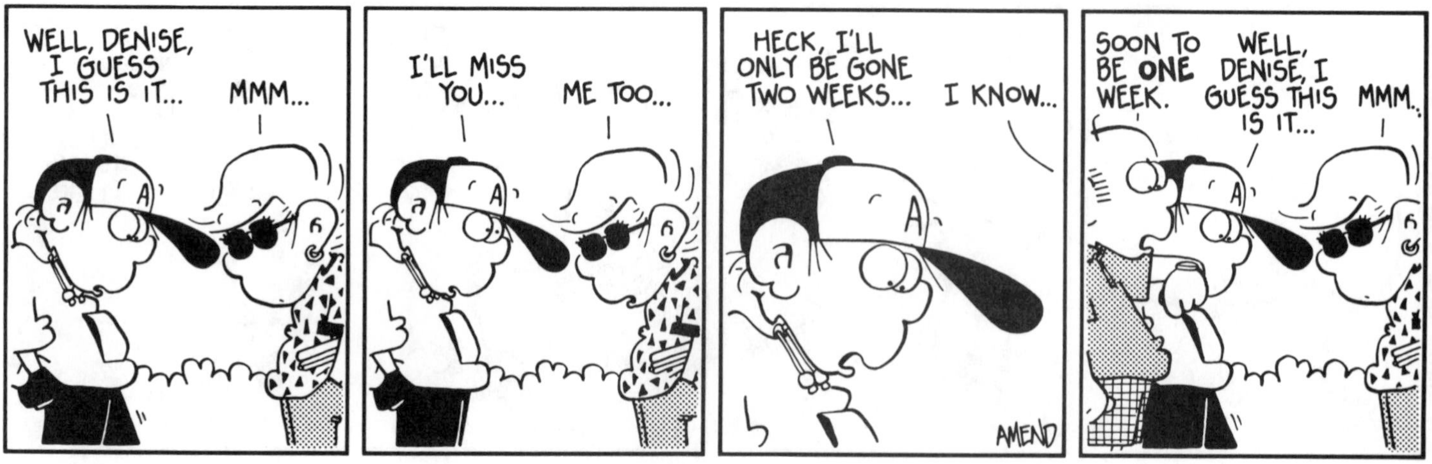
WELL, DENISE, I GUESS THIS IS IT...
MMM...
I'LL MISS YOU...
ME TOO...
HECK, I'LL ONLY BE GONE TWO WEEKS...
I KNOW...
AMEND
SOON TO BE **ONE** WEEK.
WELL, DENISE, I GUESS THIS IS IT...
MMM...

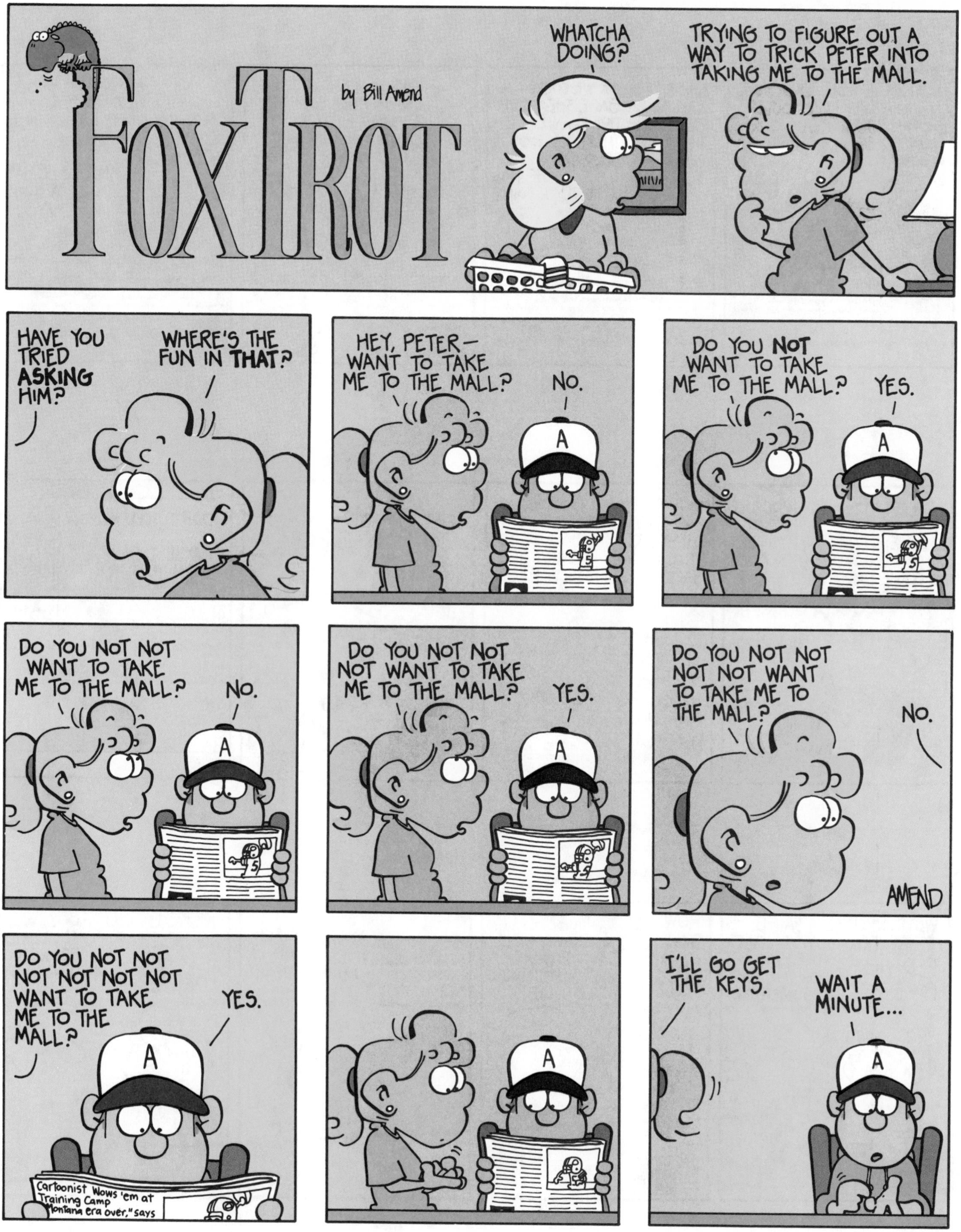
FoxTrot
by Bill Amend
WHATCHA DOING?
TRYING TO FIGURE OUT A WAY TO TRICK PETER INTO TAKING ME TO THE MALL.
HAVE YOU TRIED ASKING HIM?
WHERE'S THE FUN IN THAT?
HEY, PETER— WANT TO TAKE ME TO THE MALL?
NO.
DO YOU NOT WANT TO TAKE ME TO THE MALL?
YES.
DO YOU NOT NOT WANT TO TAKE ME TO THE MALL?
NO.
DO YOU NOT NOT NOT WANT TO TAKE ME TO THE MALL?
YES.
DO YOU NOT NOT NOT NOT WANT TO TAKE ME TO THE MALL?
NO.
AMEND
DO YOU NOT NOT NOT NOT NOT NOT WANT TO TAKE ME TO THE MALL?
YES.
Cartoonist Wows 'em at Training Camp
"Montana era over," says
I'LL GO GET THE KEYS.
WAIT A MINUTE...

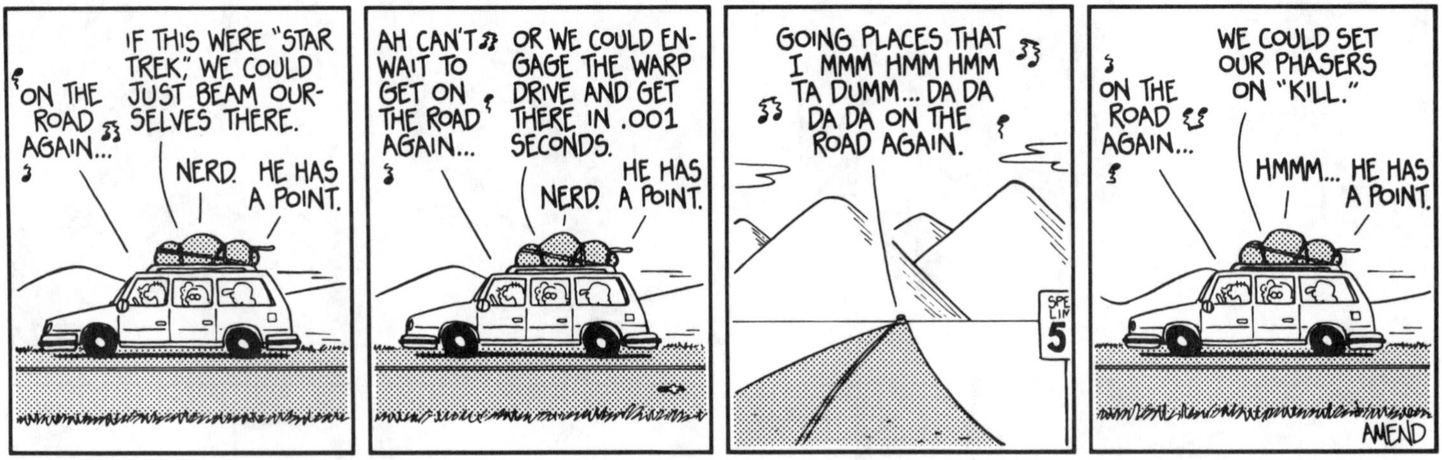
ON THE ROAD AGAIN...
IF THIS WERE "STAR TREK," WE COULD JUST BEAM OURSELVES THERE.
NERD.
HE HAS A POINT.
AH CAN'T WAIT TO GET ON THE ROAD AGAIN...
OR WE COULD ENGAGE THE WARP DRIVE AND GET THERE IN .001 SECONDS.
NERD.
HE HAS A POINT.
GOING PLACES THAT I MMM HMM HMM TA DUMM... DA DA DA DA ON THE ROAD AGAIN.
ON THE ROAD AGAIN...
WE COULD SET OUR PHASERS ON "KILL."
HMMM... HE HAS A POINT.
AMEND

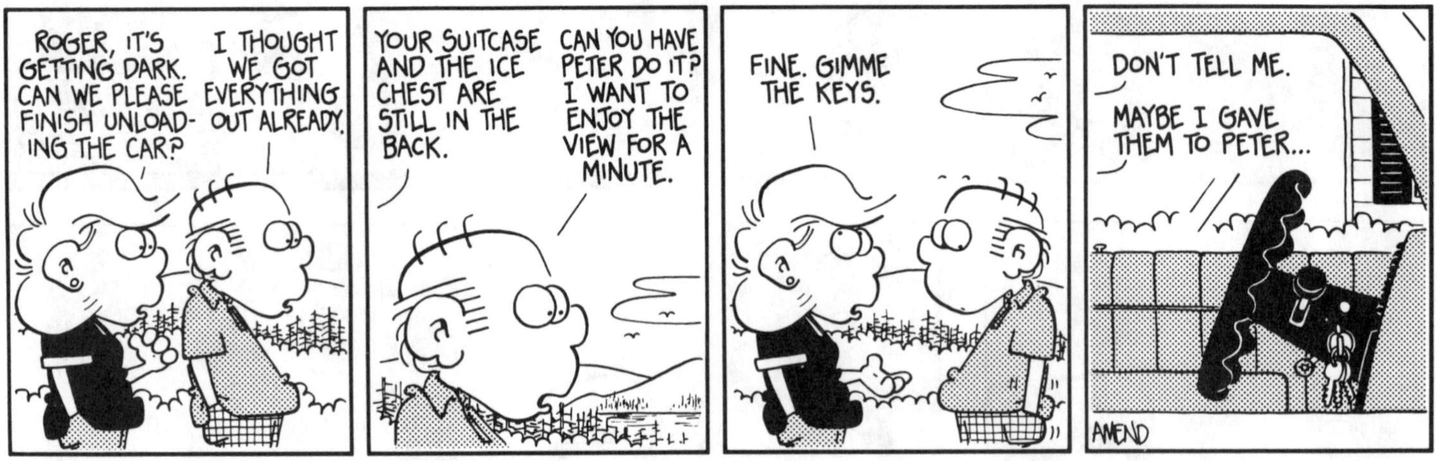
ROGER, IT'S GETTING DARK. CAN WE PLEASE FINISH UNLOADING THE CAR?
I THOUGHT WE GOT EVERYTHING OUT ALREADY.
YOUR SUITCASE AND THE ICE CHEST ARE STILL IN THE BACK.
CAN YOU HAVE PETER DO IT? I WANT TO ENJOY THE VIEW FOR A MINUTE.
FINE. GIMME THE KEYS.
DON'T TELL ME.
MAYBE I GAVE THEM TO PETER...
AMEND

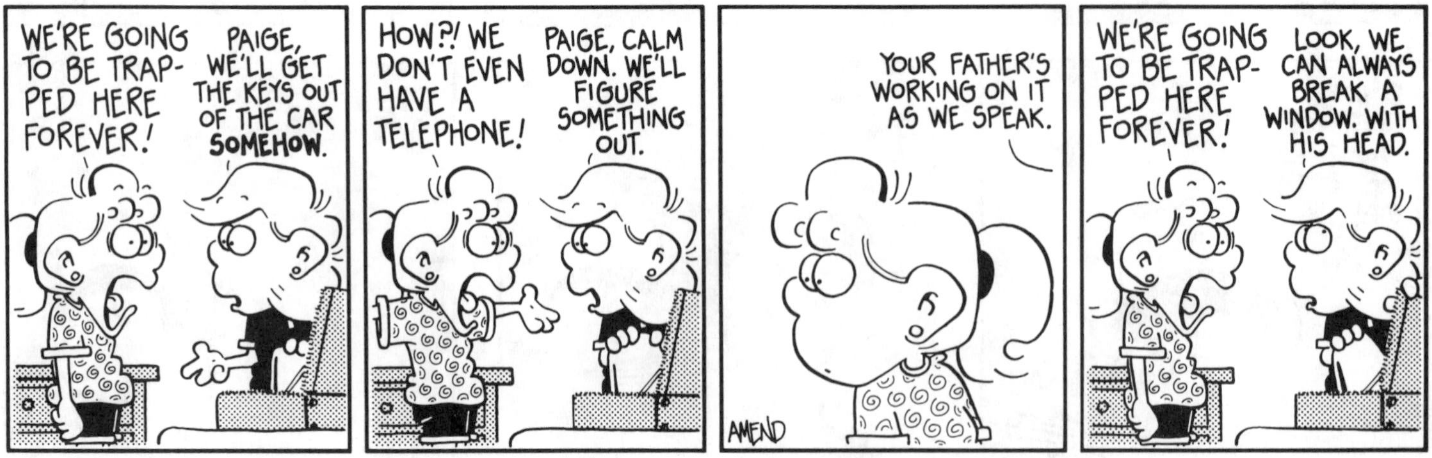
WE'RE GOING TO BE TRAPPED HERE FOREVER!
PAIGE, WE'LL GET THE KEYS OUT OF THE CAR SOMEHOW.
HOW?! WE DON'T EVEN HAVE A TELEPHONE!
PAIGE, CALM DOWN. WE'LL FIGURE SOMETHING OUT.
YOUR FATHER'S WORKING ON IT AS WE SPEAK.
AMEND
WE'RE GOING TO BE TRAPPED HERE FOREVER!
LOOK, WE CAN ALWAYS BREAK A WINDOW. WITH HIS HEAD.

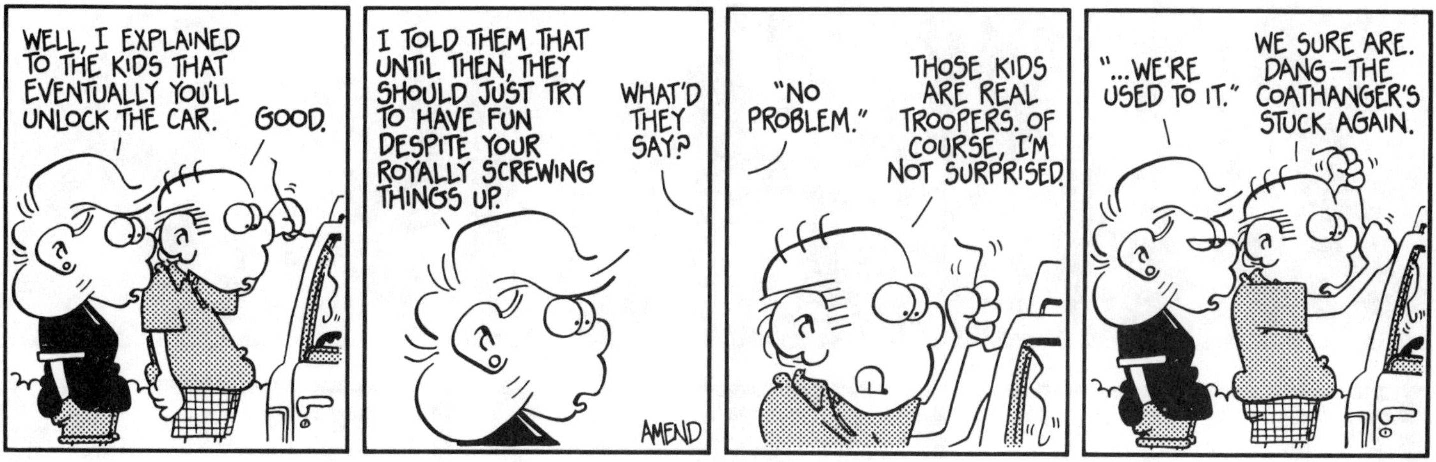
WELL, I EXPLAINED TO THE KIDS THAT EVENTUALLY YOU'LL UNLOCK THE CAR.
GOOD.
I TOLD THEM THAT UNTIL THEN, THEY SHOULD JUST TRY TO HAVE FUN DESPITE YOUR ROYALLY SCREWING THINGS UP.
WHAT'D THEY SAY?
AMEND
"NO PROBLEM."
THOSE KIDS ARE REAL TROOPERS. OF COURSE, I'M NOT SURPRISED.
"...WE'RE USED TO IT."
WE SURE ARE. DANG—THE COATHANGER'S STUCK AGAIN.

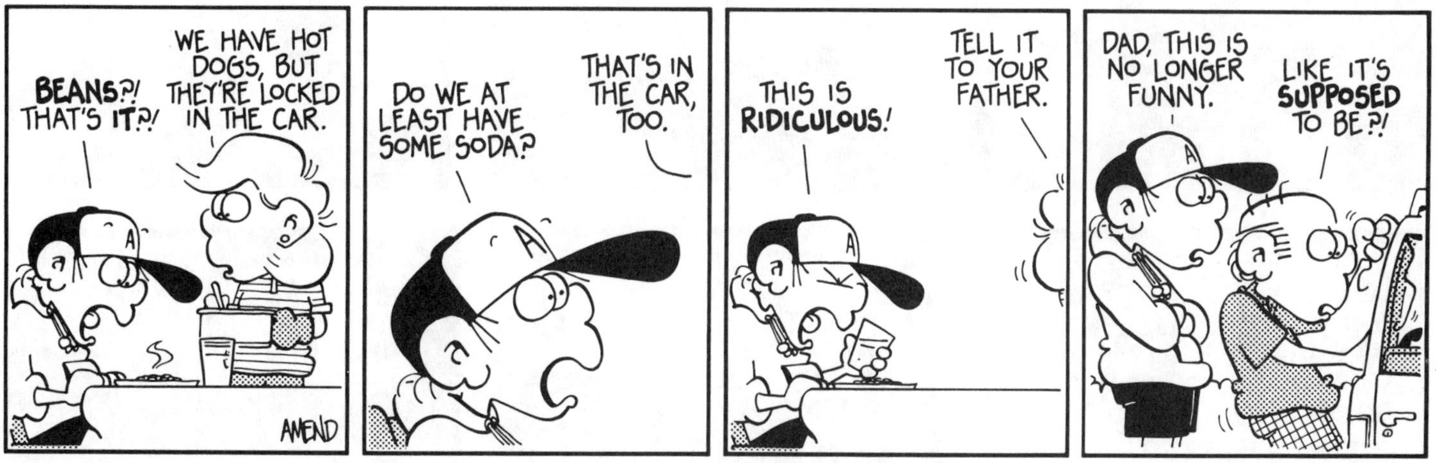
BEANS?! THAT'S **IT**?!
WE HAVE HOT DOGS, BUT THEY'RE LOCKED IN THE CAR.
AMEND
DO WE AT LEAST HAVE SOME SODA?
THAT'S IN THE CAR, TOO.
THIS IS **RIDICULOUS**!
TELL IT TO YOUR FATHER.
DAD, THIS IS NO LONGER FUNNY.
LIKE IT'S **SUPPOSED** TO BE?!

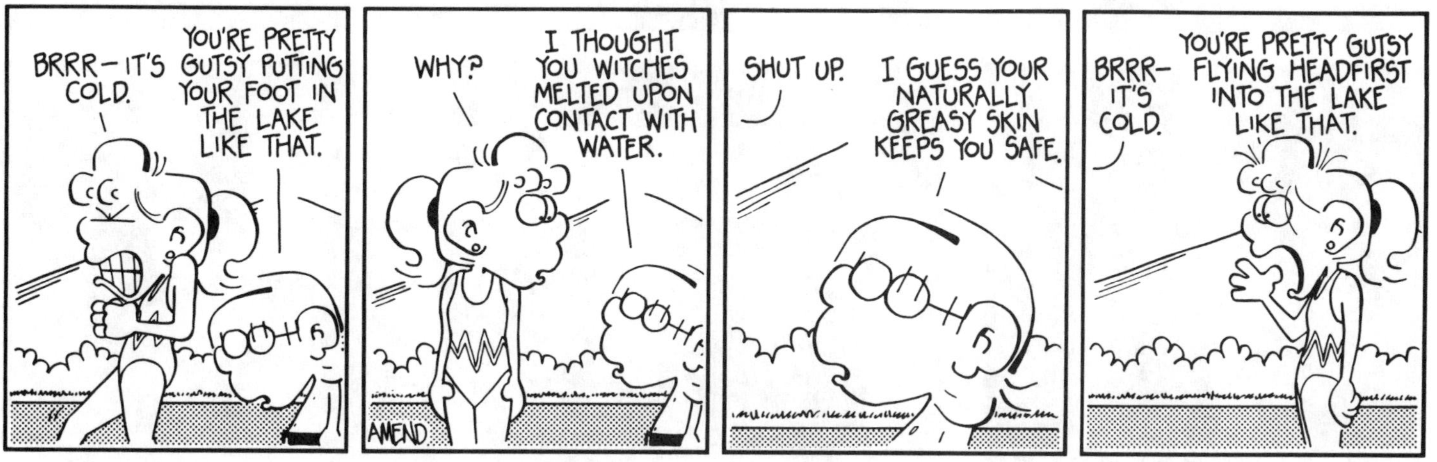
BRRR—IT'S COLD.
YOU'RE PRETTY GUTSY PUTTING YOUR FOOT IN THE LAKE LIKE THAT.
WHY?
I THOUGHT YOU WITCHES MELTED UPON CONTACT WITH WATER.
AMEND
SHUT UP.
I GUESS YOUR NATURALLY GREASY SKIN KEEPS YOU SAFE.
BRRR—IT'S COLD.
YOU'RE PRETTY GUTSY FLYING HEADFIRST INTO THE LAKE LIKE THAT.

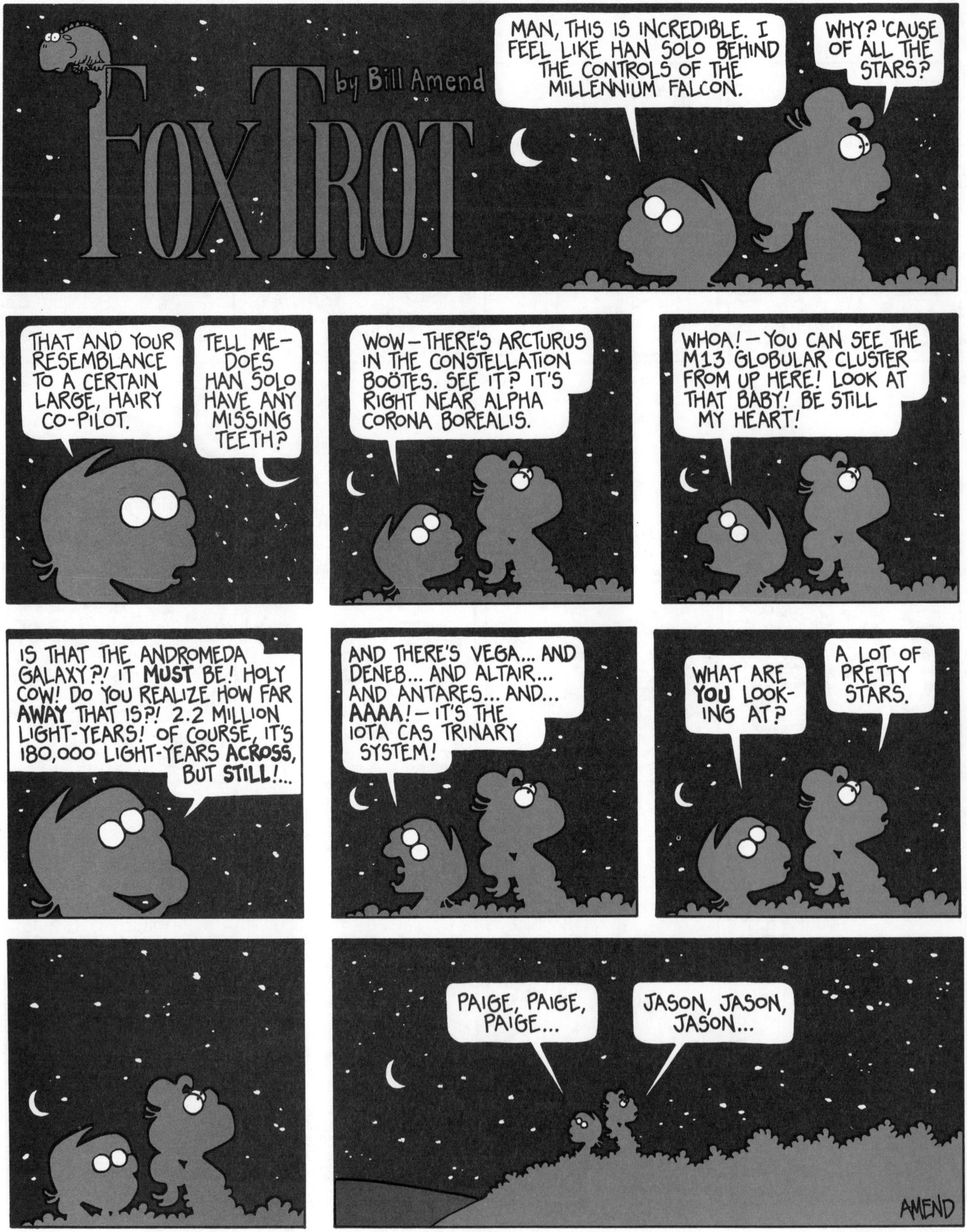
FoxTrot
by Bill Amend
MAN, THIS IS INCREDIBLE. I FEEL LIKE HAN SOLO BEHIND THE CONTROLS OF THE MILLENNIUM FALCON.
WHY? 'CAUSE OF ALL THE STARS?
THAT AND YOUR RESEMBLANCE TO A CERTAIN LARGE, HAIRY CO-PILOT.
TELL ME- DOES HAN SOLO HAVE ANY MISSING TEETH?
WOW—THERE'S ARCTURUS IN THE CONSTELLATION BOÖTES. SEE IT? IT'S RIGHT NEAR ALPHA CORONA BOREALIS.
WHOA!—YOU CAN SEE THE M13 GLOBULAR CLUSTER FROM UP HERE! LOOK AT THAT BABY! BE STILL MY HEART!
IS THAT THE ANDROMEDA GALAXY?! IT **MUST** BE! HOLY COW! DO YOU REALIZE HOW FAR **AWAY** THAT IS?! 2.2 MILLION LIGHT-YEARS! OF COURSE, IT'S 180,000 LIGHT-YEARS **ACROSS**, BUT **STILL**!...
AND THERE'S VEGA... AND DENEB... AND ALTAIR... AND ANTARES... AND... **AAAA!**—IT'S THE IOTA CAS TRINARY SYSTEM!
WHAT ARE **YOU** LOOK-ING AT?
A LOT OF PRETTY STARS.
PAIGE, PAIGE, PAIGE...
JASON, JASON, JASON...
AMEND

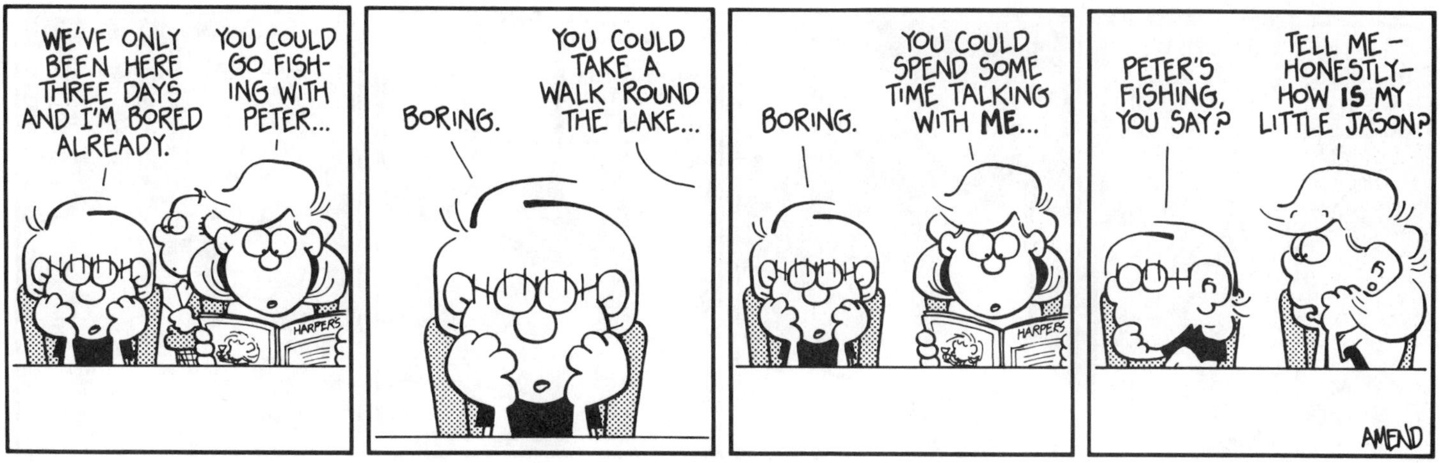
WE'VE ONLY BEEN HERE THREE DAYS AND I'M BORED ALREADY.
YOU COULD GO FISH-ING WITH PETER...
BORING.
YOU COULD TAKE A WALK 'ROUND THE LAKE...
BORING.
YOU COULD SPEND SOME TIME TALKING WITH ME...
PETER'S FISHING, YOU SAY?
TELL ME — HONESTLY — HOW IS MY LITTLE JASON?
HARPERS
AMEND

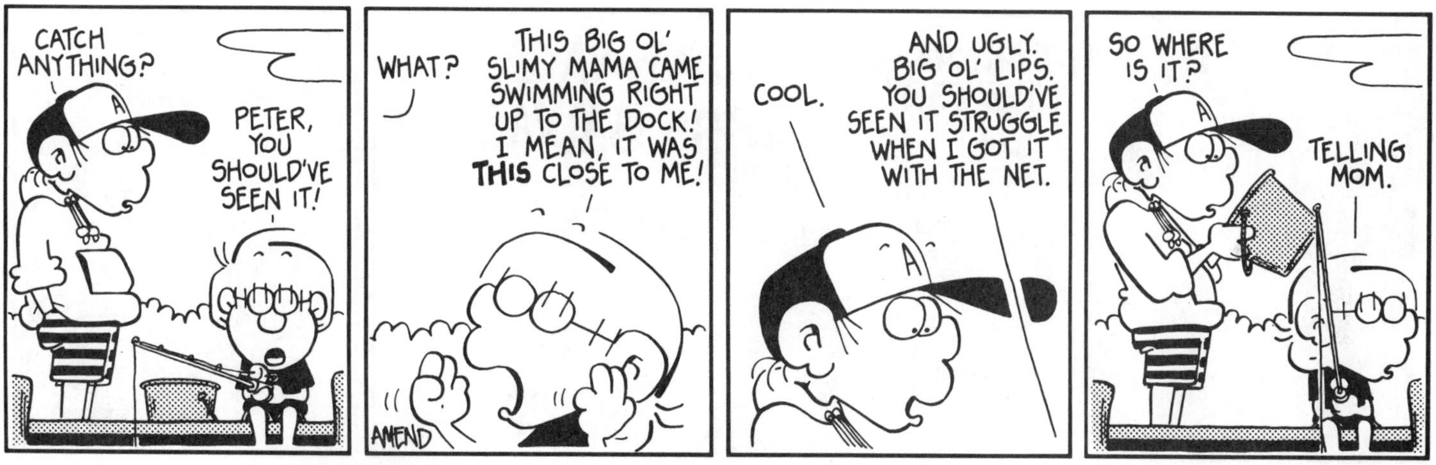
CATCH ANYTHING?
PETER, YOU SHOULD'VE SEEN IT!
WHAT?
THIS BIG OL' SLIMY MAMA CAME SWIMMING RIGHT UP TO THE DOCK! I MEAN, IT WAS THIS CLOSE TO ME!
AMEND
COOL.
AND UGLY. BIG OL' LIPS. YOU SHOULD'VE SEEN IT STRUGGLE WHEN I GOT IT WITH THE NET.
SO WHERE IS IT?
TELLING MOM.

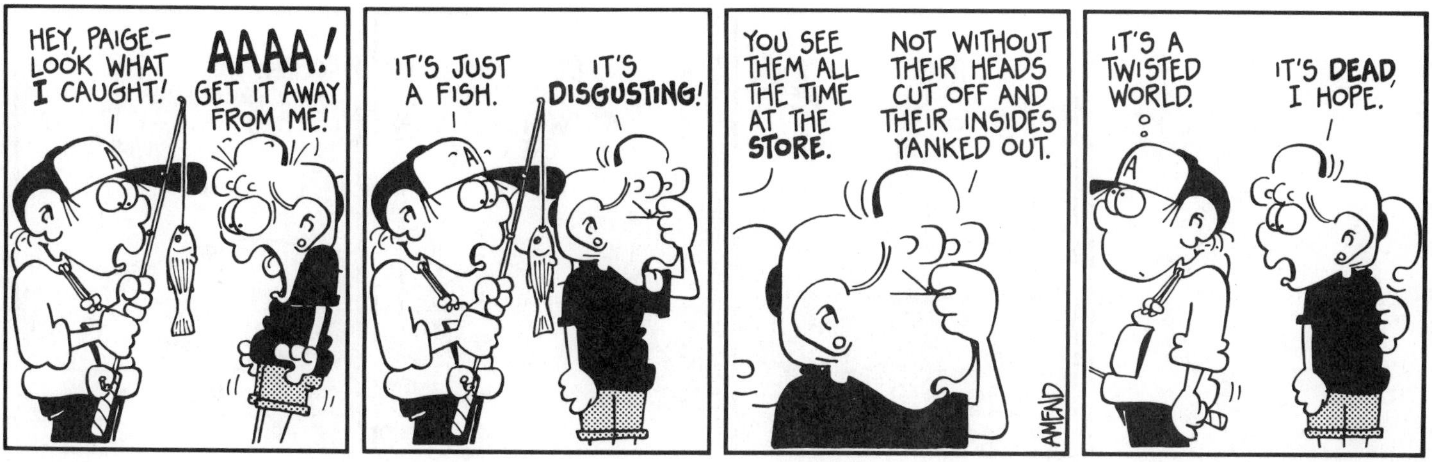
HEY, PAIGE — LOOK WHAT I CAUGHT!
AAAA! GET IT AWAY FROM ME!
IT'S JUST A FISH.
IT'S DISGUSTING!
YOU SEE THEM ALL THE TIME AT THE STORE.
NOT WITHOUT THEIR HEADS CUT OFF AND THEIR INSIDES YANKED OUT.
AMEND
IT'S A TWISTED WORLD.
IT'S DEAD, I HOPE.

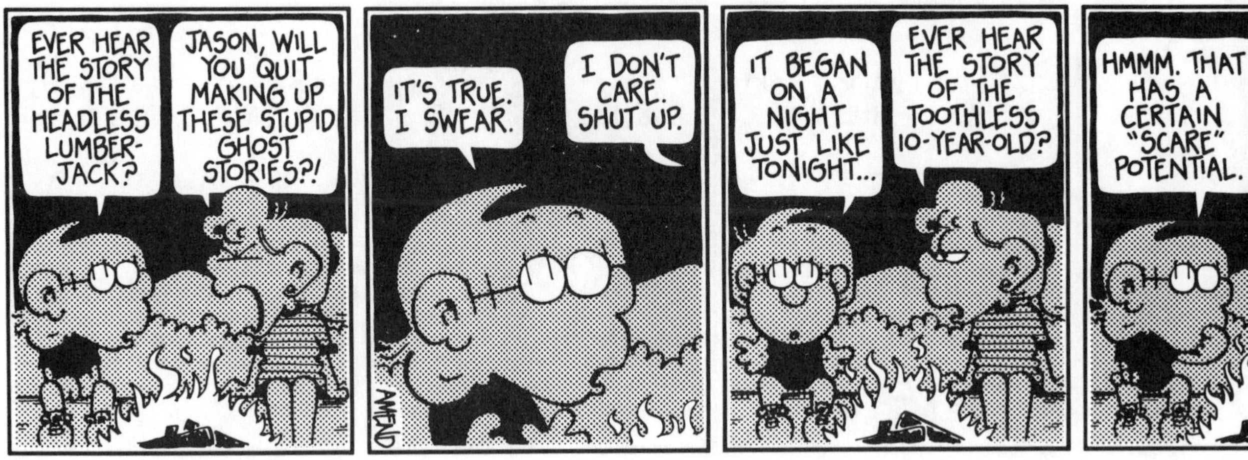
EVER HEAR THE STORY OF THE HEADLESS LUMBER-JACK?
JASON, WILL YOU QUIT MAKING UP THESE STUPID GHOST STORIES?!
IT'S TRUE. I SWEAR.
I DON'T CARE. SHUT UP.
AMEND
IT BEGAN ON A NIGHT JUST LIKE TONIGHT...
EVER HEAR THE STORY OF THE TOOTHLESS 10-YEAR-OLD?
HMMM. THAT HAS A CERTAIN "SCARE" POTENTIAL.
SOON TO BE TRUE. I SWEAR.

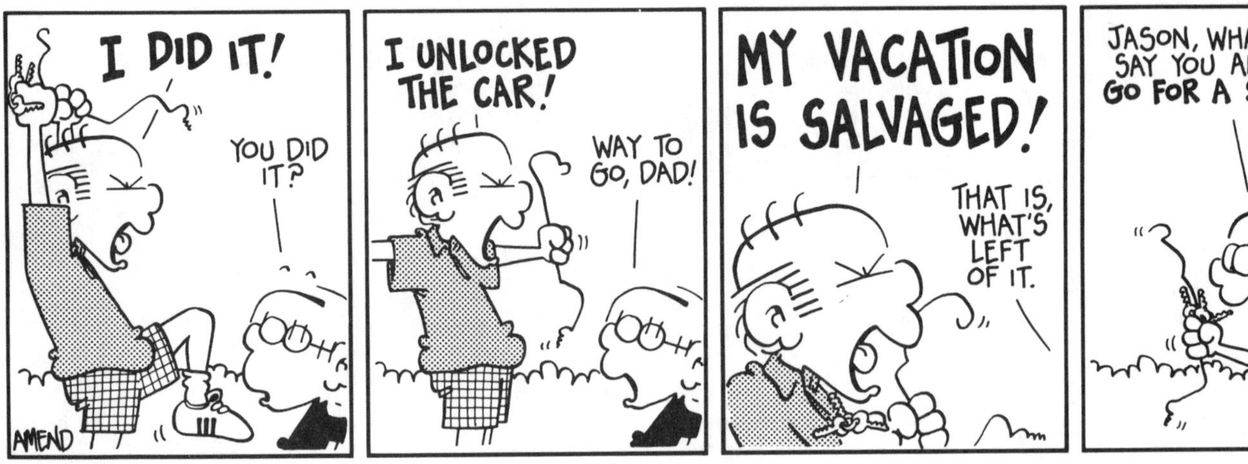
I DID IT!
YOU DID IT?
AMEND
I UNLOCKED THE CAR!
WAY TO GO, DAD!
MY VACATION IS SALVAGED!
THAT IS, WHAT'S LEFT OF IT.
JASON, WHADDYA SAY YOU AND I GO FOR A SWIM!
MOM SAYS I HAVE TO PACK.

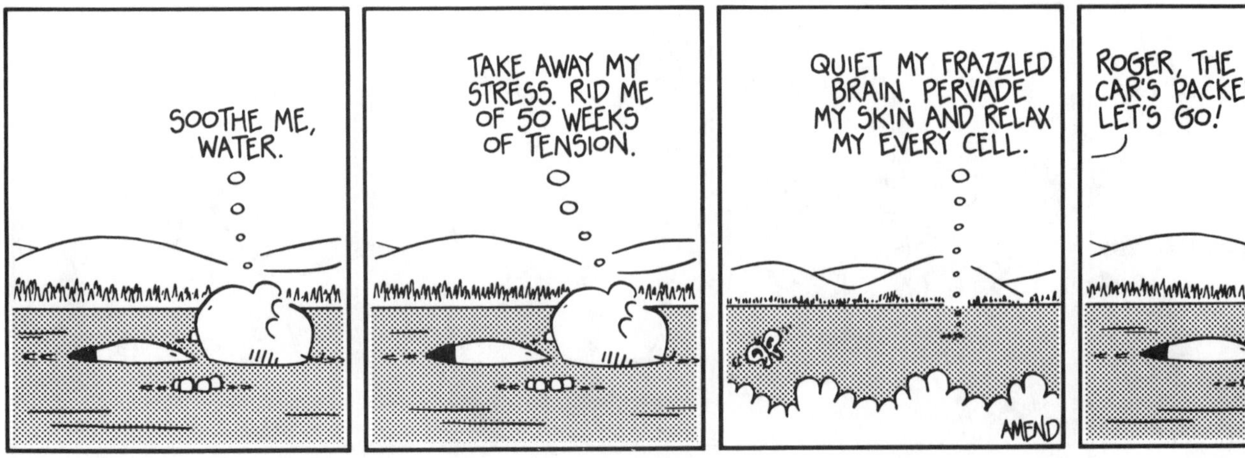
SOOTHE ME, WATER.
TAKE AWAY MY STRESS. RID ME OF 50 WEEKS OF TENSION.
QUIET MY FRAZZLED BRAIN. PERVADE MY SKIN AND RELAX MY EVERY CELL.
AMEND
ROGER, THE CAR'S PACKED. LET'S GO!
HURRY UP, WATER...

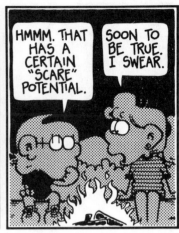

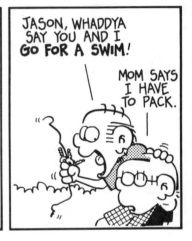

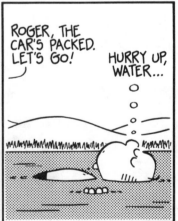

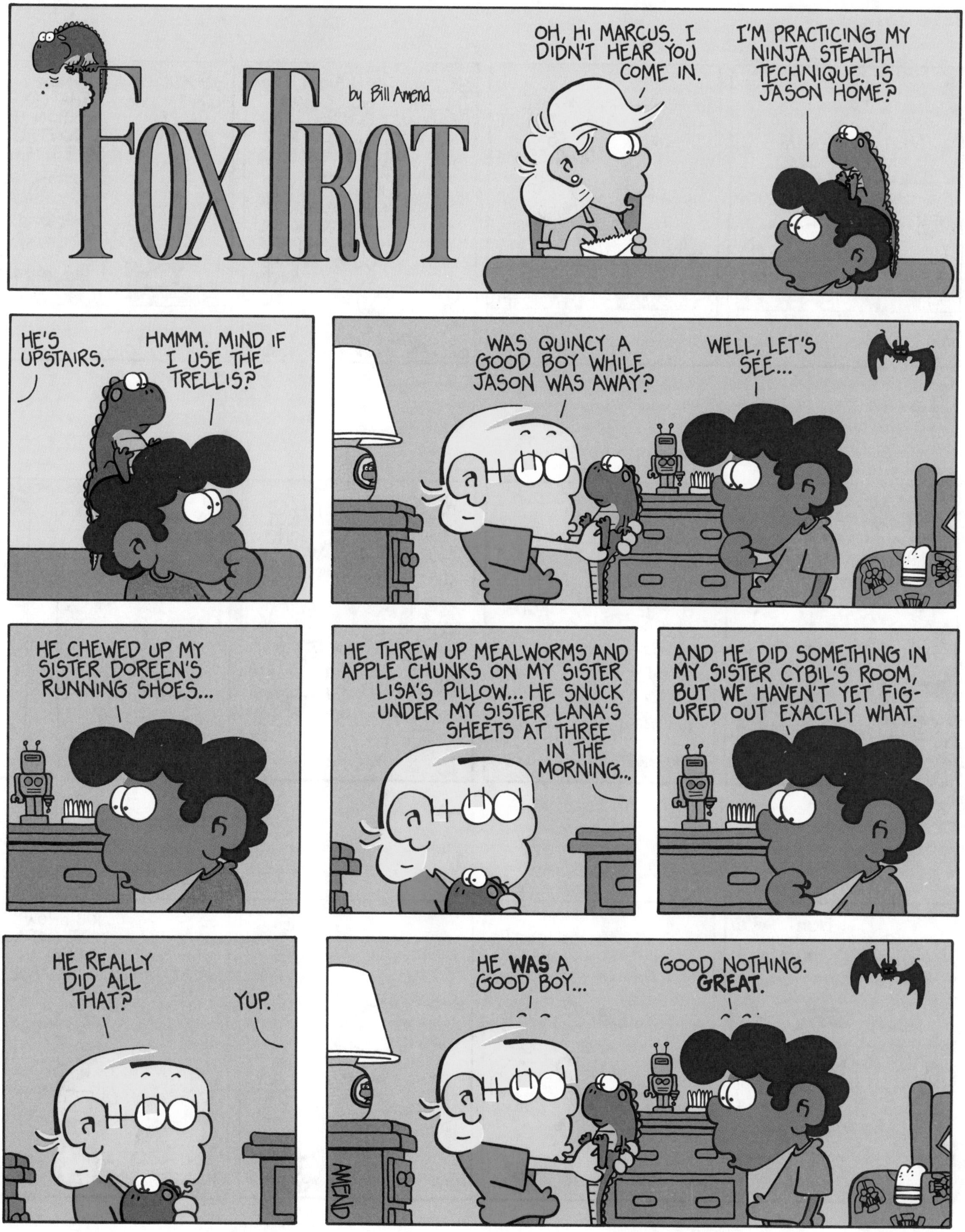
FoxTrot
by Bill Amend
OH, HI MARCUS. I DIDN'T HEAR YOU COME IN.
I'M PRACTICING MY NINJA STEALTH TECHNIQUE. IS JASON HOME?
HE'S UPSTAIRS.
HMMM. MIND IF I USE THE TRELLIS?
WAS QUINCY A GOOD BOY WHILE JASON WAS AWAY?
WELL, LET'S SEE...
HE CHEWED UP MY SISTER DOREEN'S RUNNING SHOES...
HE THREW UP MEALWORMS AND APPLE CHUNKS ON MY SISTER LISA'S PILLOW... HE SNUCK UNDER MY SISTER LANA'S SHEETS AT THREE IN THE MORNING...
AND HE DID SOMETHING IN MY SISTER CYBIL'S ROOM, BUT WE HAVEN'T YET FIGURED OUT EXACTLY WHAT.
HE REALLY DID ALL THAT?
YUP.
HE **WAS** A GOOD BOY...
GOOD NOTHING. **GREAT.**
AMEND

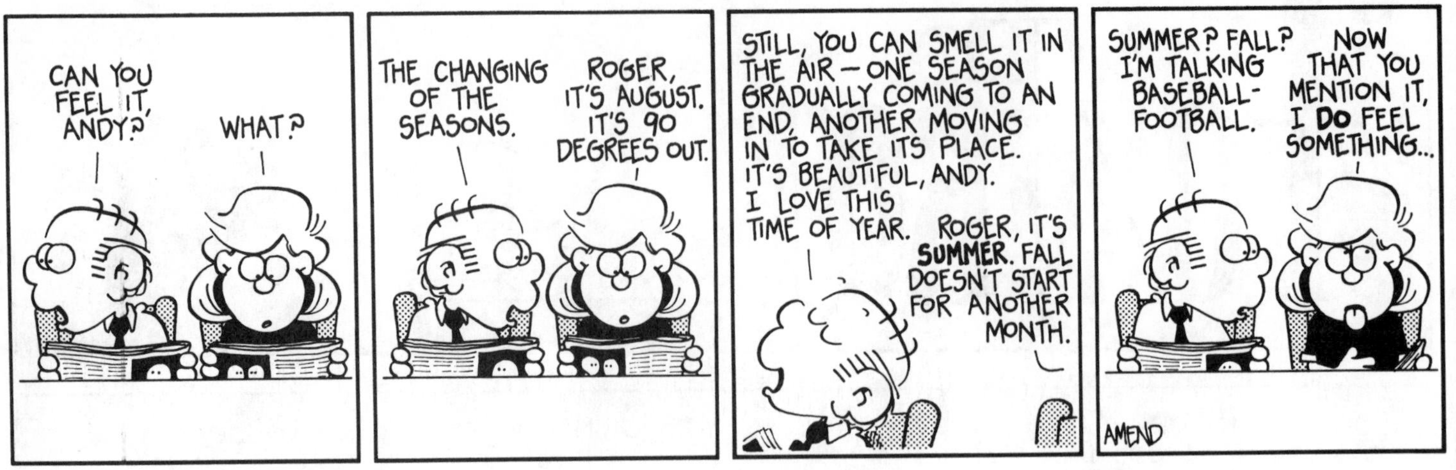
CAN YOU FEEL IT, ANDY?
WHAT?
THE CHANGING OF THE SEASONS.
ROGER, IT'S AUGUST. IT'S 90 DEGREES OUT.
STILL, YOU CAN SMELL IT IN THE AIR—ONE SEASON GRADUALLY COMING TO AN END, ANOTHER MOVING IN TO TAKE ITS PLACE. IT'S BEAUTIFUL, ANDY. I LOVE THIS TIME OF YEAR.
ROGER, IT'S SUMMER. FALL DOESN'T START FOR ANOTHER MONTH.
SUMMER? FALL? I'M TALKING BASEBALL-FOOTBALL.
NOW THAT YOU MENTION IT, I DO FEEL SOMETHING...
AMEND

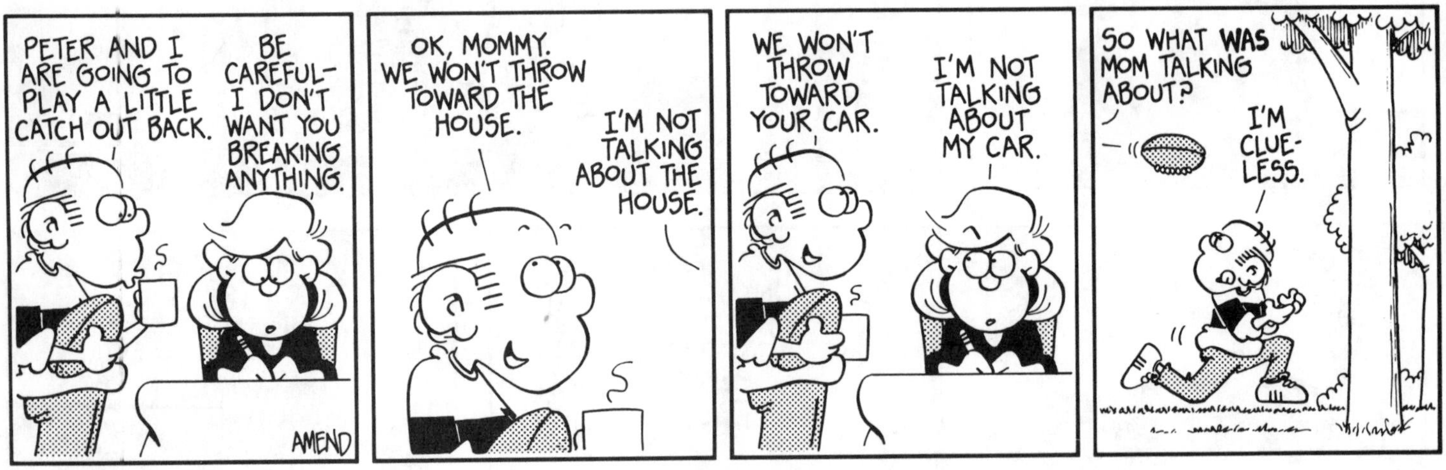
PETER AND I ARE GOING TO PLAY A LITTLE CATCH OUT BACK.
BE CAREFUL-I DON'T WANT YOU BREAKING ANYTHING.
AMEND
OK, MOMMY. WE WON'T THROW TOWARD THE HOUSE.
I'M NOT TALKING ABOUT THE HOUSE.
WE WON'T THROW TOWARD YOUR CAR.
I'M NOT TALKING ABOUT MY CAR.
SO WHAT WAS MOM TALKING ABOUT?
I'M CLUE-LESS.

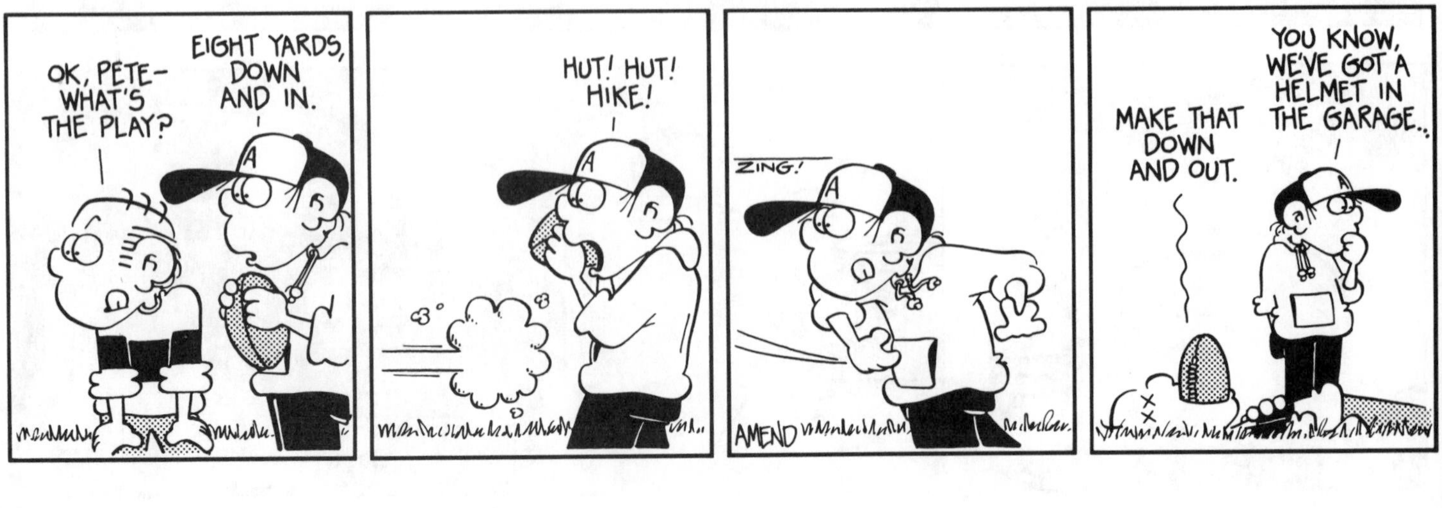
OK, PETE-WHAT'S THE PLAY?
EIGHT YARDS, DOWN AND IN.
HUT! HUT! HIKE!
ZING!
AMEND
MAKE THAT DOWN AND OUT.
YOU KNOW, WE'VE GOT A HELMET IN THE GARAGE...

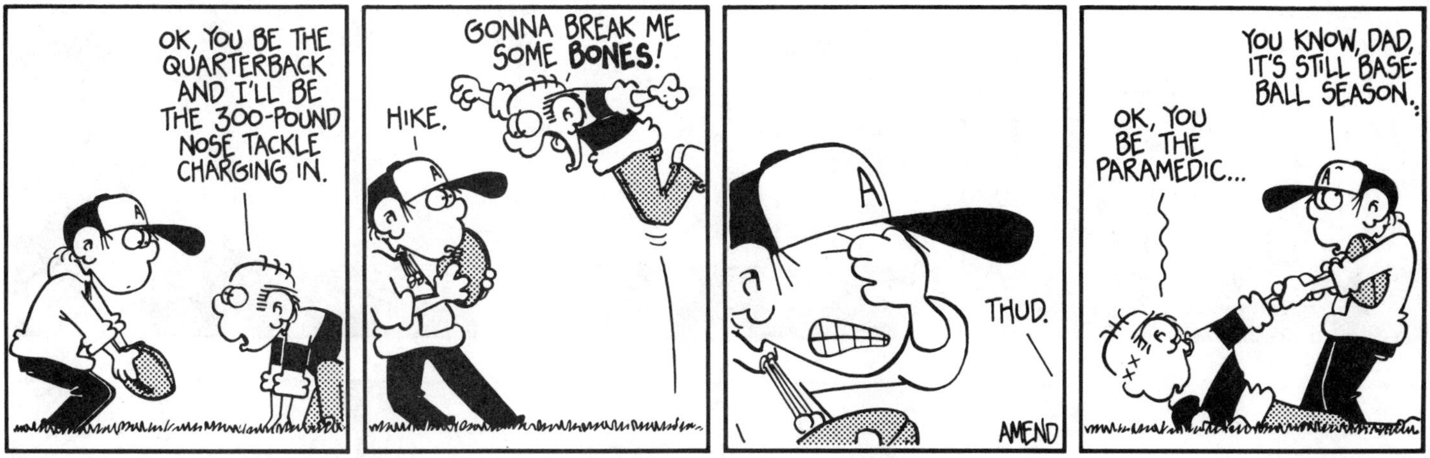
OK, YOU BE THE QUARTERBACK AND I'LL BE THE 300-POUND NOSE TACKLE CHARGING IN.
HIKE.
GONNA BREAK ME SOME **BONES**!
THUD.
AMEND
YOU KNOW, DAD, IT'S STILL BASEBALL SEASON.
OK, YOU BE THE PARAMEDIC...

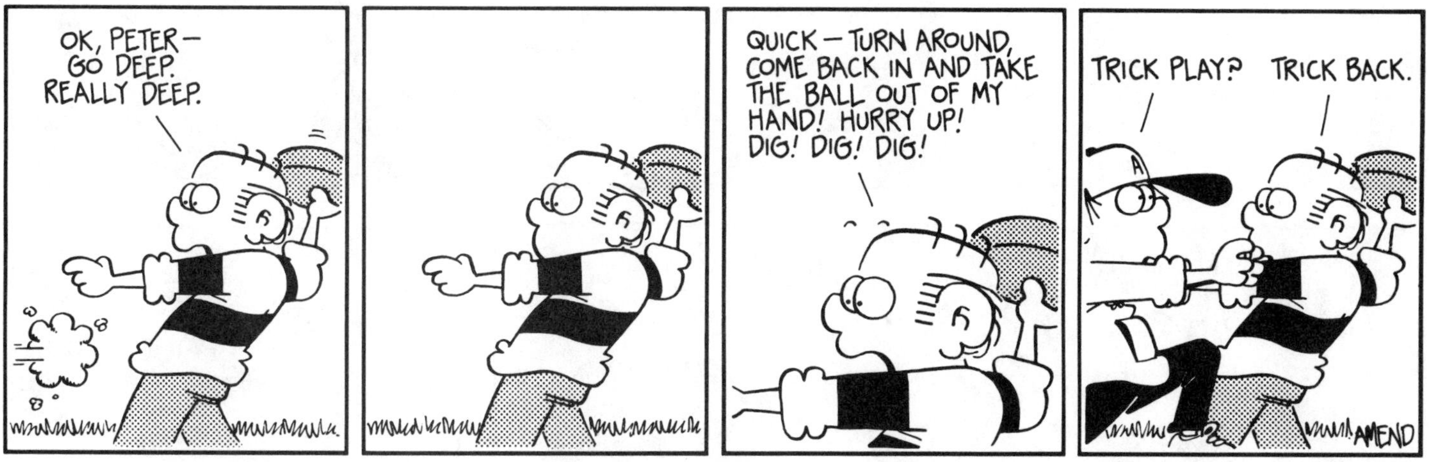
OK, PETER— GO DEEP. REALLY DEEP.
QUICK—TURN AROUND, COME BACK IN AND TAKE THE BALL OUT OF MY HAND! HURRY UP! DIG! DIG! DIG!
TRICK PLAY?
TRICK BACK.
AMEND

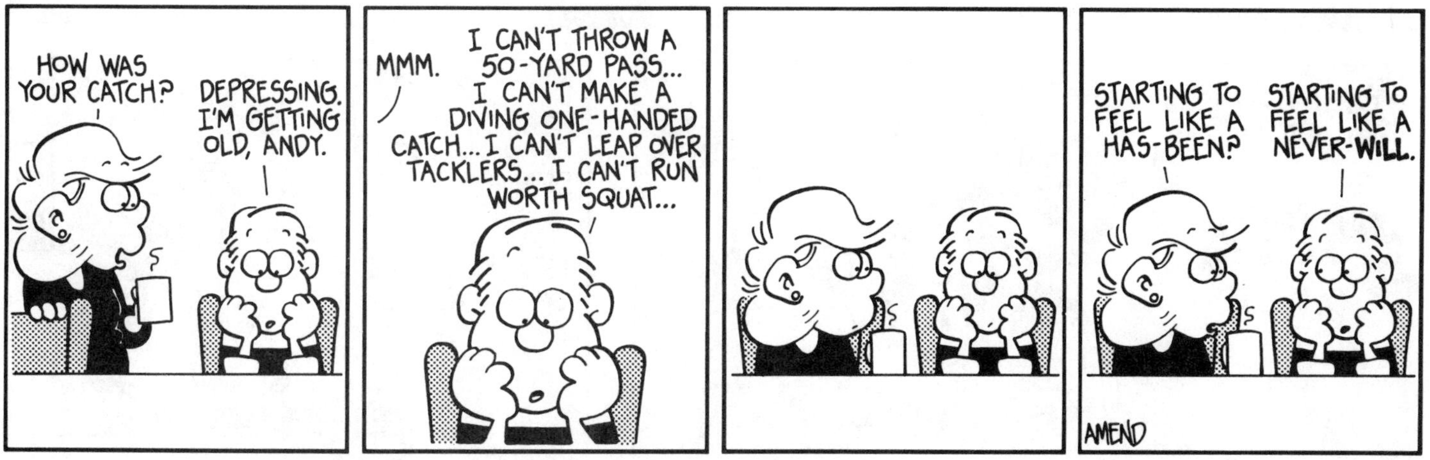
HOW WAS YOUR CATCH?
DEPRESSING. I'M GETTING OLD, ANDY.
MMM.
I CAN'T THROW A 50-YARD PASS... I CAN'T MAKE A DIVING ONE-HANDED CATCH... I CAN'T LEAP OVER TACKLERS... I CAN'T RUN WORTH SQUAT...
STARTING TO FEEL LIKE A HAS-BEEN?
STARTING TO FEEL LIKE A NEVER-**WILL**.
AMEND

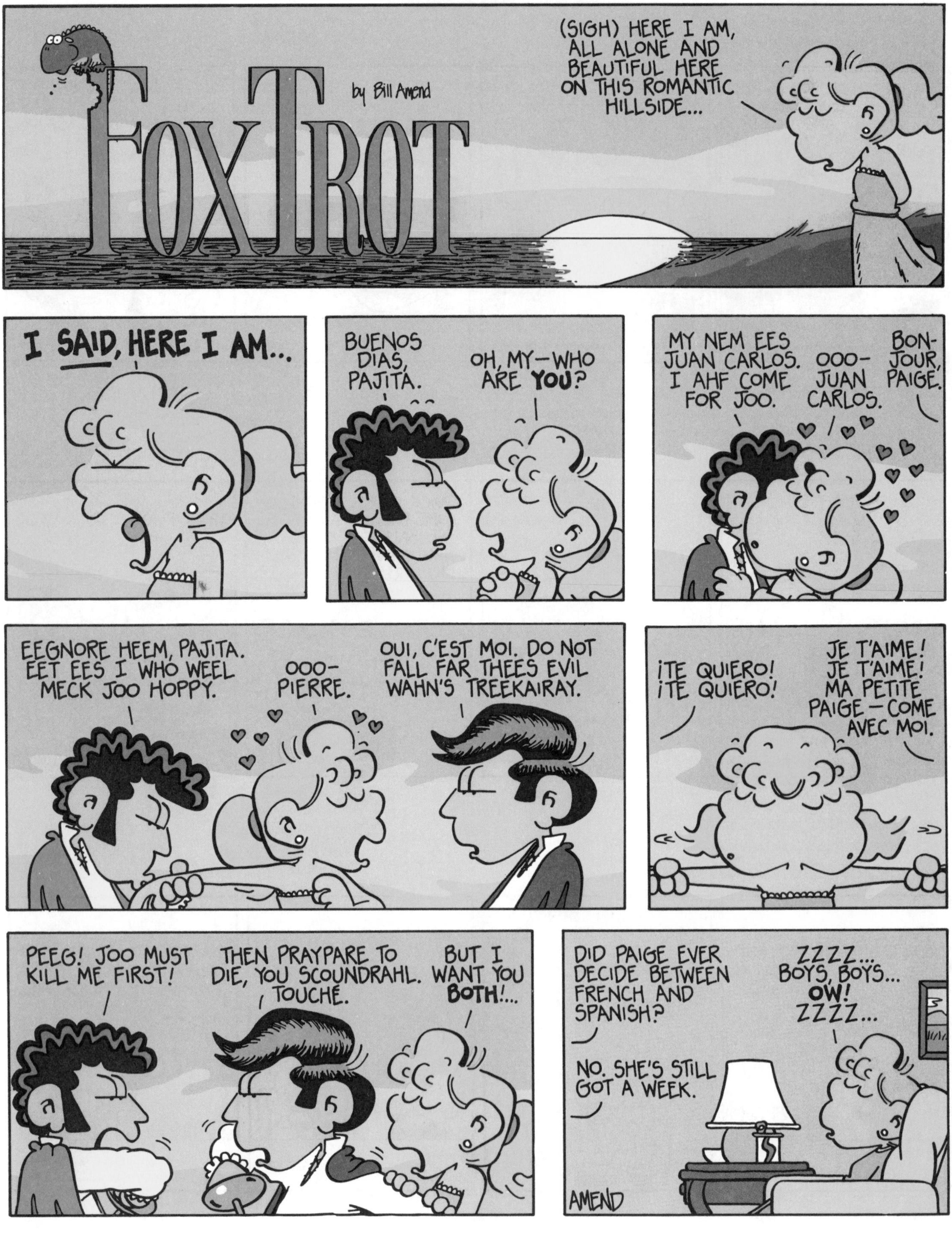
FoxTrot
by Bill Amend
(SIGH) HERE I AM, ALL ALONE AND BEAUTIFUL HERE ON THIS ROMANTIC HILLSIDE...
I SAID, HERE I AM...
BUENOS DIAS, PAJITA.
OH, MY—WHO ARE YOU?
MY NEM EES JUAN CARLOS. I AHF COME FOR JOO.
OOO- JUAN CARLOS.
BON-JOUR, PAIGE.
EEGNORE HEEM, PAJITA. EET EES I WHO WEEL MECK JOO HOPPY.
OOO- PIERRE.
OUI, C'EST MOI. DO NOT FALL FAR THEES EVIL WAHN'S TREEKAIRAY.
¡TE QUIERO! ¡TE QUIERO!
JE T'AIME! JE T'AIME! MA PETITE PAIGE—COME AVEC MOI.
PEEG! JOO MUST KILL ME FIRST!
THEN PRAYPARE TO DIE, YOU SCOUNDRAHL. TOUCHÉ.
BUT I WANT YOU BOTH!...
DID PAIGE EVER DECIDE BETWEEN FRENCH AND SPANISH?
ZZZZ... BOYS, BOYS... OW! ZZZZ...
NO. SHE'S STILL GOT A WEEK.
AMEND

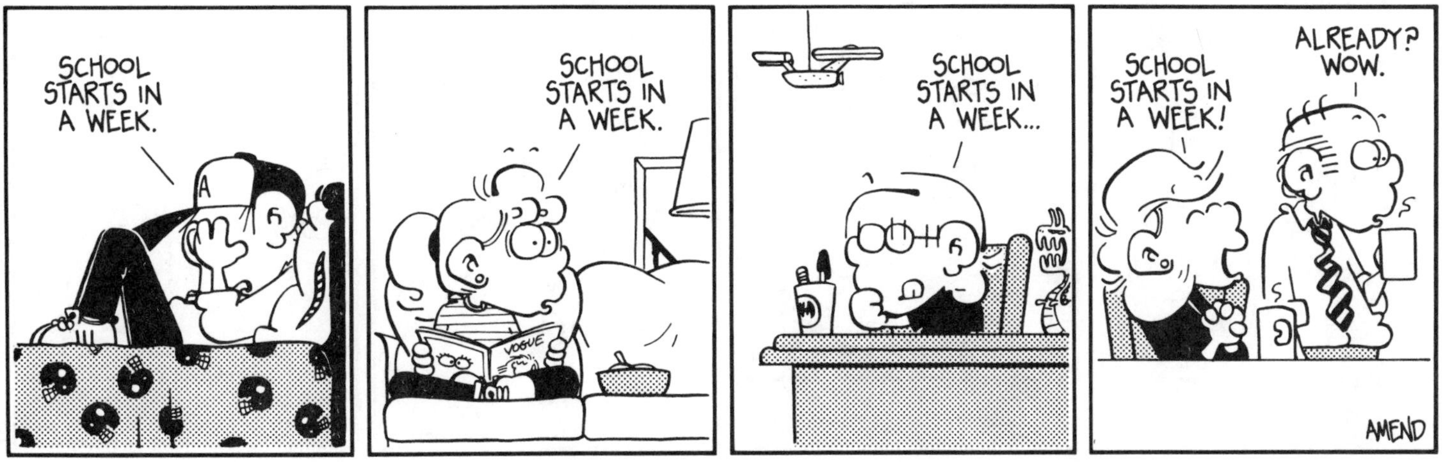
SCHOOL STARTS IN A WEEK.
SCHOOL STARTS IN A WEEK.
SCHOOL STARTS IN A WEEK...
SCHOOL STARTS IN A WEEK!
ALREADY? WOW.
AMEND

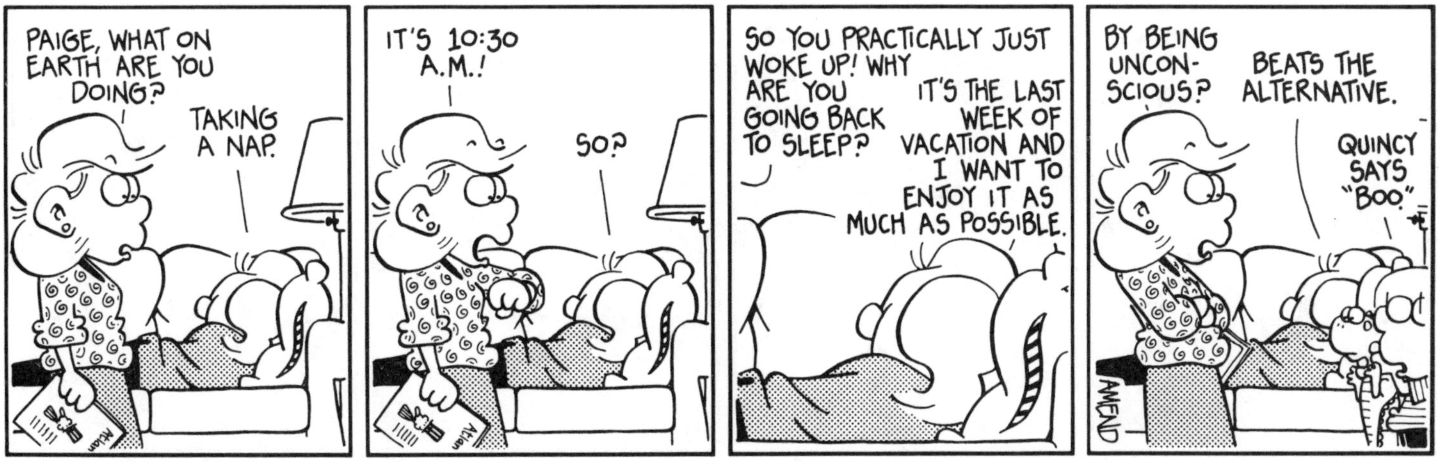
PAIGE, WHAT ON EARTH ARE YOU DOING?
TAKING A NAP.
IT'S 10:30 A.M.!
SO?
SO YOU PRACTICALLY JUST WOKE UP! WHY ARE YOU GOING BACK TO SLEEP?
IT'S THE LAST WEEK OF VACATION AND I WANT TO ENJOY IT AS MUCH AS POSSIBLE.
BY BEING UNCON-SCIOUS?
BEATS THE ALTERNATIVE.
QUINCY SAYS "BOO."
AMEND

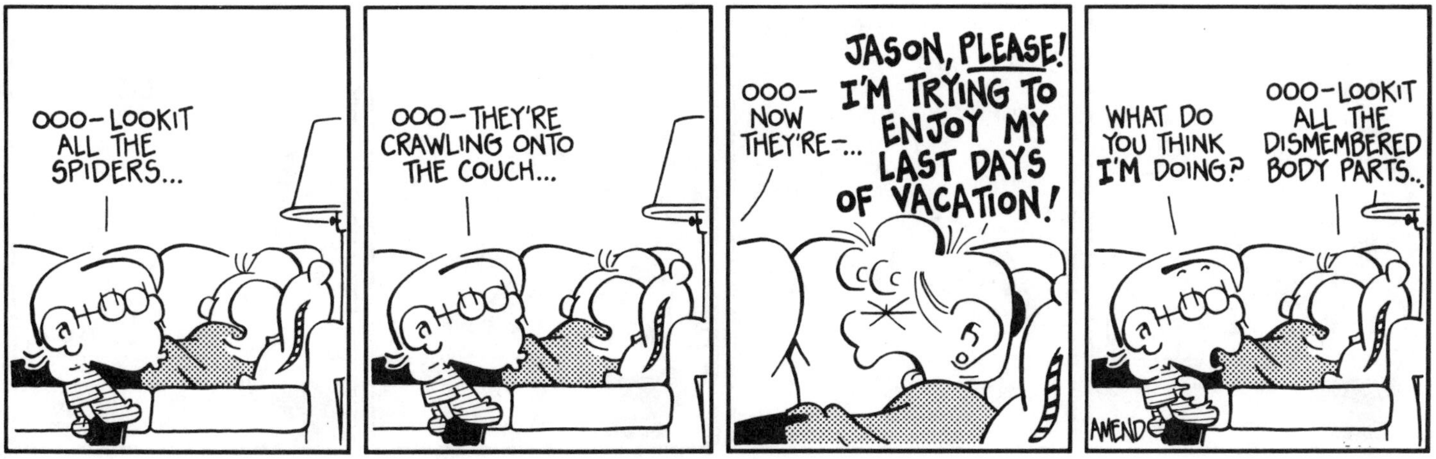
OOO-LOOKIT ALL THE SPIDERS...
OOO-THEY'RE CRAWLING ONTO THE COUCH...
OOO-NOW THEY'RE-...
JASON, PLEASE! I'M TRYING TO ENJOY MY LAST DAYS OF VACATION!
WHAT DO YOU THINK I'M DOING?
OOO-LOOKIT ALL THE DISMEMBERED BODY PARTS...
AMEND

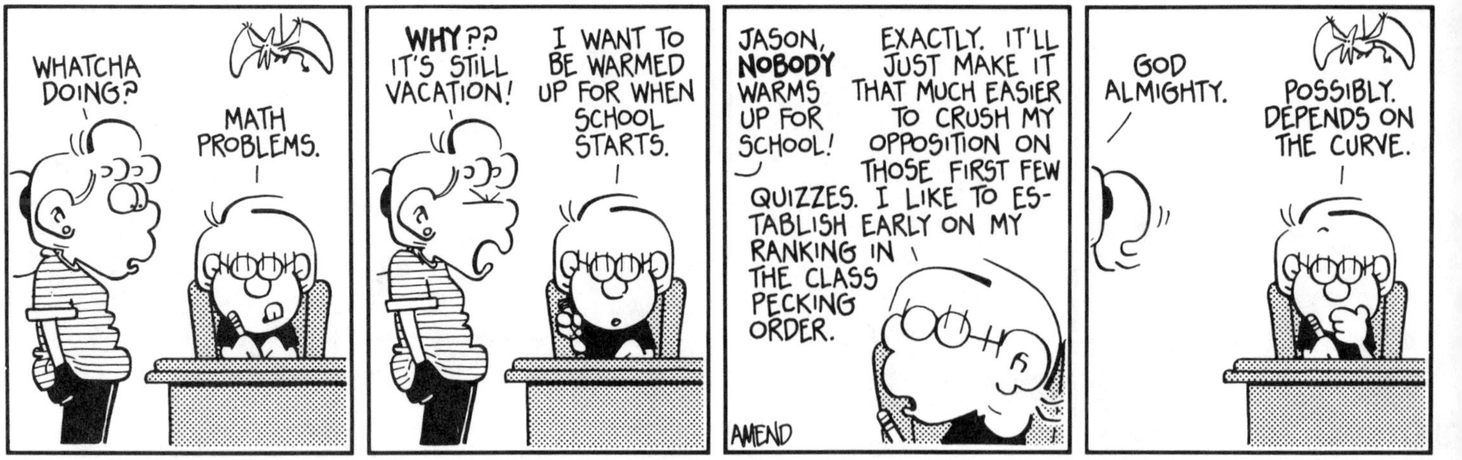
WHATCHA DOING?
MATH PROBLEMS.
WHY?? IT'S STILL VACATION!
I WANT TO BE WARMED UP FOR WHEN SCHOOL STARTS.
JASON, NOBODY WARMS UP FOR SCHOOL!
EXACTLY. IT'LL JUST MAKE IT THAT MUCH EASIER TO CRUSH MY OPPOSITION ON THOSE FIRST FEW QUIZZES. I LIKE TO ESTABLISH EARLY ON MY RANKING IN THE CLASS PECKING ORDER.
AMEND
GOD ALMIGHTY.
POSSIBLY. DEPENDS ON THE CURVE.

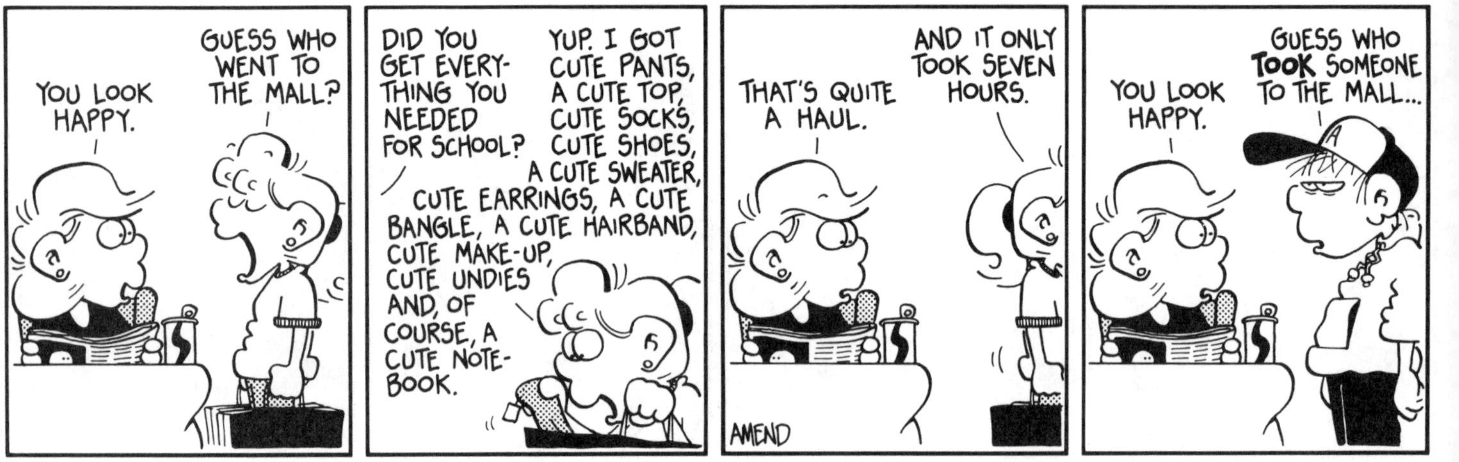
YOU LOOK HAPPY.
GUESS WHO WENT TO THE MALL?
DID YOU GET EVERYTHING YOU NEEDED FOR SCHOOL?
YUP. I GOT CUTE PANTS, A CUTE TOP, CUTE SOCKS, CUTE SHOES, A CUTE SWEATER, CUTE EARRINGS, A CUTE BANGLE, A CUTE HAIRBAND, CUTE MAKE-UP, CUTE UNDIES AND, OF COURSE, A CUTE NOTEBOOK.
THAT'S QUITE A HAUL.
AND IT ONLY TOOK SEVEN HOURS.
AMEND
YOU LOOK HAPPY.
GUESS WHO TOOK SOMEONE TO THE MALL...

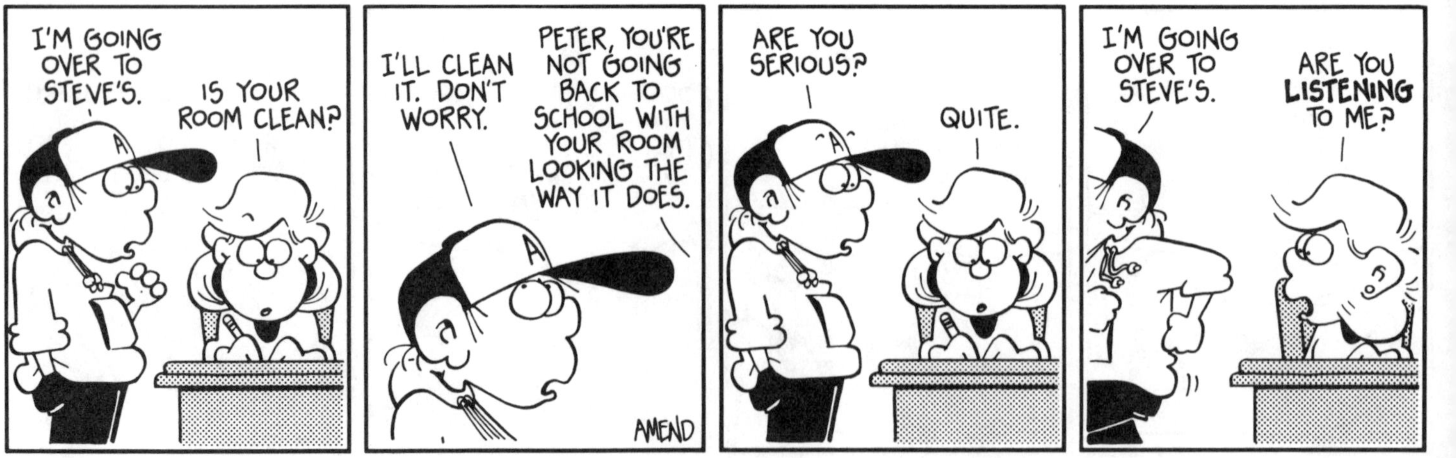
I'M GOING OVER TO STEVE'S.
IS YOUR ROOM CLEAN?
I'LL CLEAN IT. DON'T WORRY.
PETER, YOU'RE NOT GOING BACK TO SCHOOL WITH YOUR ROOM LOOKING THE WAY IT DOES.
AMEND
ARE YOU SERIOUS?
QUITE.
I'M GOING OVER TO STEVE'S.
ARE YOU LISTENING TO ME?

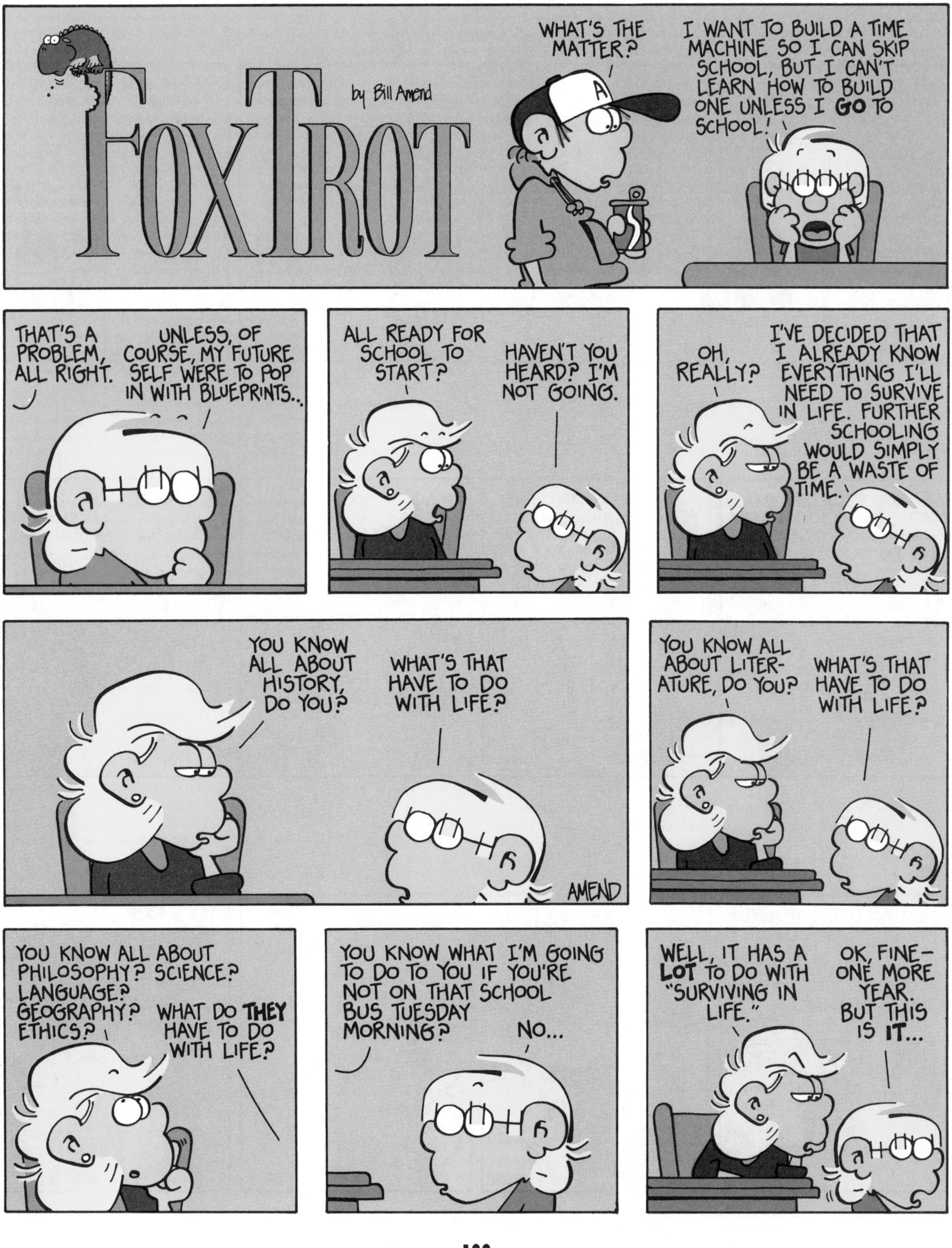
FoxTrot
by Bill Amend
WHAT'S THE MATTER?
I WANT TO BUILD A TIME MACHINE SO I CAN SKIP SCHOOL, BUT I CAN'T LEARN HOW TO BUILD ONE UNLESS I GO TO SCHOOL!
THAT'S A PROBLEM, ALL RIGHT.
UNLESS, OF COURSE, MY FUTURE SELF WERE TO POP IN WITH BLUEPRINTS...
ALL READY FOR SCHOOL TO START?
HAVEN'T YOU HEARD? I'M NOT GOING.
OH, REALLY?
I'VE DECIDED THAT I ALREADY KNOW EVERYTHING I'LL NEED TO SURVIVE IN LIFE. FURTHER SCHOOLING WOULD SIMPLY BE A WASTE OF TIME.
YOU KNOW ALL ABOUT HISTORY, DO YOU?
WHAT'S THAT HAVE TO DO WITH LIFE?
AMEND
YOU KNOW ALL ABOUT LITERATURE, DO YOU?
WHAT'S THAT HAVE TO DO WITH LIFE?
YOU KNOW ALL ABOUT PHILOSOPHY? SCIENCE? LANGUAGE? GEOGRAPHY? ETHICS?
WHAT DO THEY HAVE TO DO WITH LIFE?
YOU KNOW WHAT I'M GOING TO DO TO YOU IF YOU'RE NOT ON THAT SCHOOL BUS TUESDAY MORNING?
NO...
WELL, IT HAS A LOT TO DO WITH "SURVIVING IN LIFE."
OK, FINE- ONE MORE YEAR. BUT THIS IS IT...

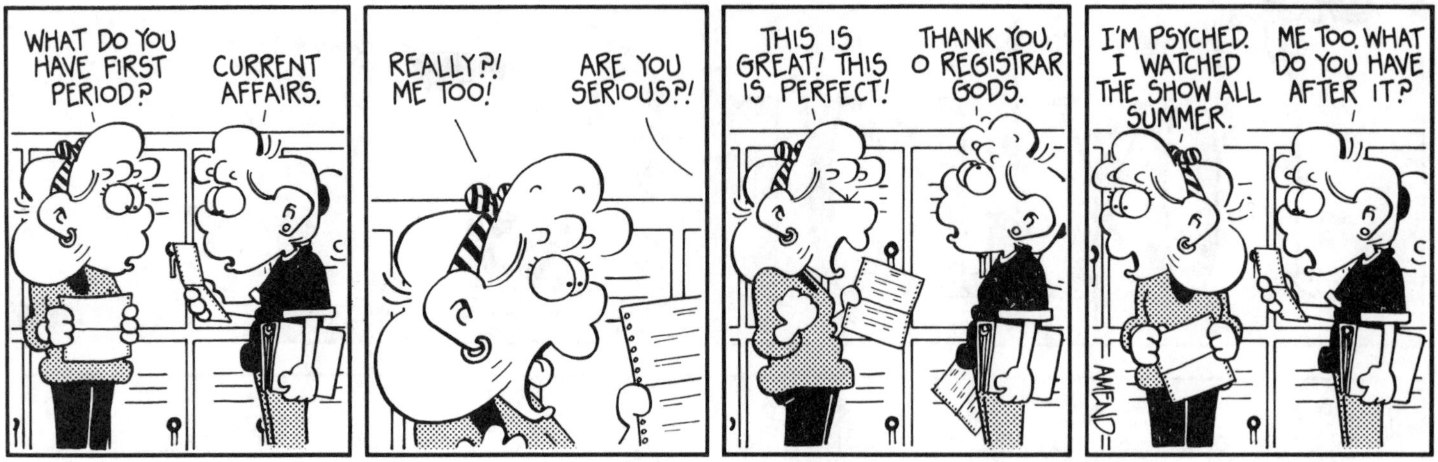
WHAT DO YOU HAVE FIRST PERIOD?
CURRENT AFFAIRS.
REALLY?! ME TOO!
ARE YOU SERIOUS?!
THIS IS GREAT! THIS IS PERFECT!
THANK YOU, O REGISTRAR GODS.
I'M PSYCHED. I WATCHED THE SHOW ALL SUMMER.
ME TOO. WHAT DO YOU HAVE AFTER IT?
AMEND

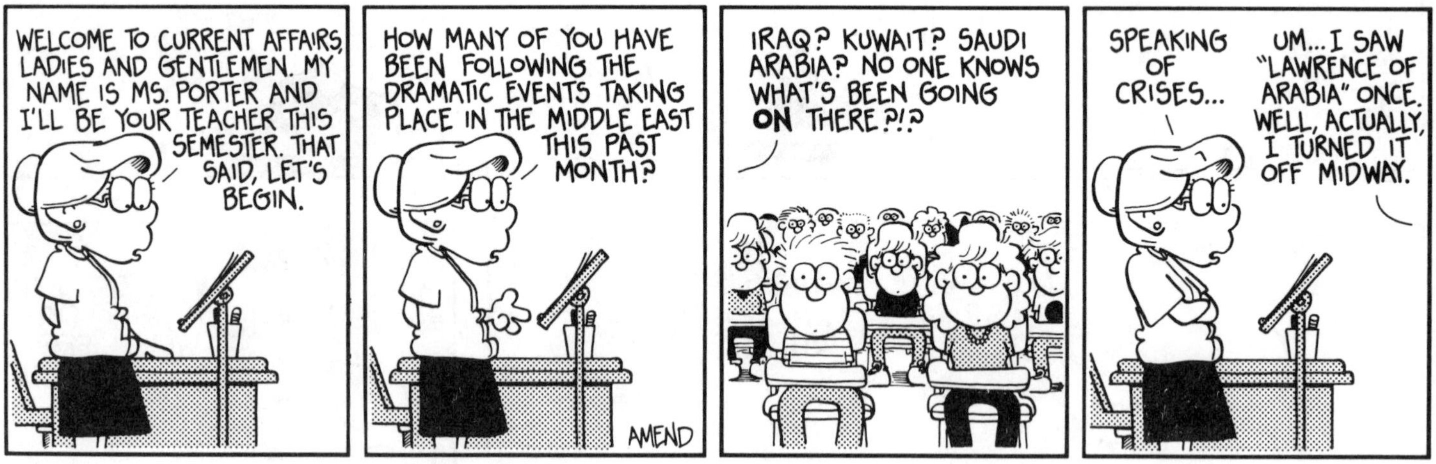
WELCOME TO CURRENT AFFAIRS, LADIES AND GENTLEMEN. MY NAME IS MS. PORTER AND I'LL BE YOUR TEACHER THIS SEMESTER. THAT SAID, LET'S BEGIN.
HOW MANY OF YOU HAVE BEEN FOLLOWING THE DRAMATIC EVENTS TAKING PLACE IN THE MIDDLE EAST THIS PAST MONTH?
AMEND
IRAQ? KUWAIT? SAUDI ARABIA? NO ONE KNOWS WHAT'S BEEN GOING **ON** THERE?!?
SPEAKING OF CRISES...
UM... I SAW "LAWRENCE OF ARABIA" ONCE. WELL, ACTUALLY, I TURNED IT OFF MIDWAY.

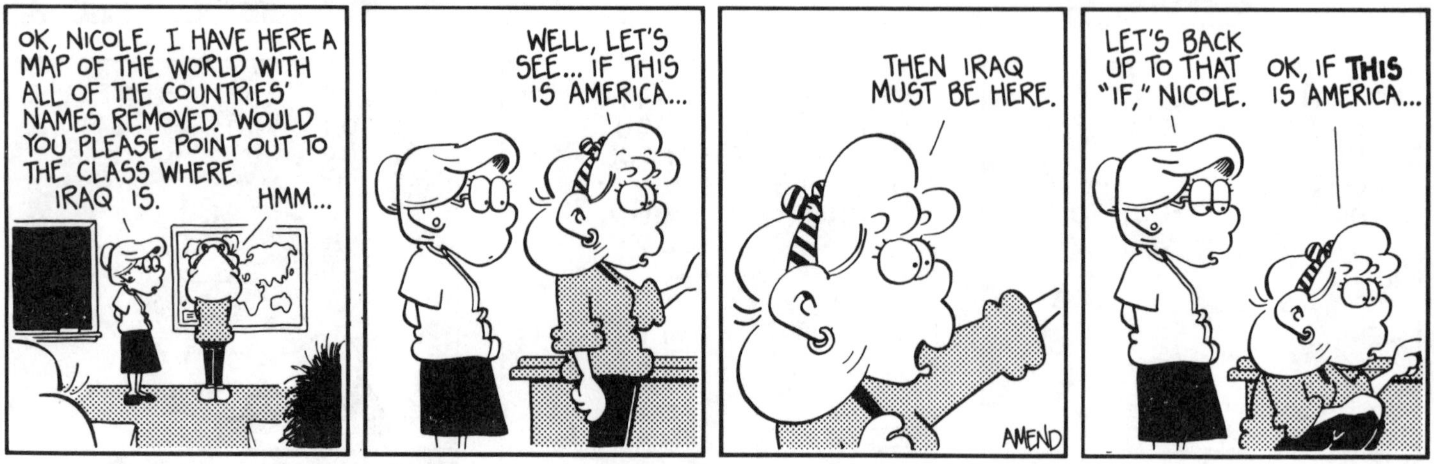
OK, NICOLE, I HAVE HERE A MAP OF THE WORLD WITH ALL OF THE COUNTRIES' NAMES REMOVED. WOULD YOU PLEASE POINT OUT TO THE CLASS WHERE IRAQ IS.
HMM...
WELL, LET'S SEE... IF THIS IS AMERICA...
THEN IRAQ MUST BE HERE.
AMEND
LET'S BACK UP TO THAT "IF," NICOLE.
OK, IF **THIS** IS AMERICA...

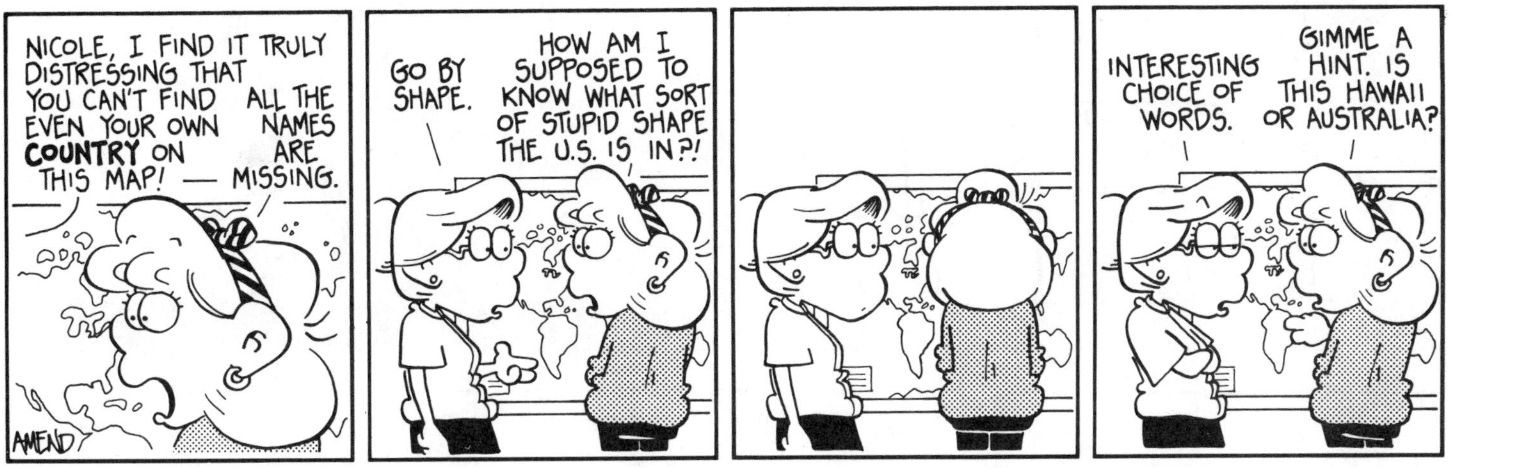
NICOLE, I FIND IT TRULY DISTRESSING THAT YOU CAN'T FIND EVEN YOUR OWN **COUNTRY** ON THIS MAP! —
ALL THE NAMES ARE MISSING.
AMEND
GO BY SHAPE.
HOW AM I SUPPOSED TO KNOW WHAT SORT OF STUPID SHAPE THE U.S. IS IN?!
INTERESTING CHOICE OF WORDS.
GIMME A HINT. IS THIS HAWAII OR AUSTRALIA?

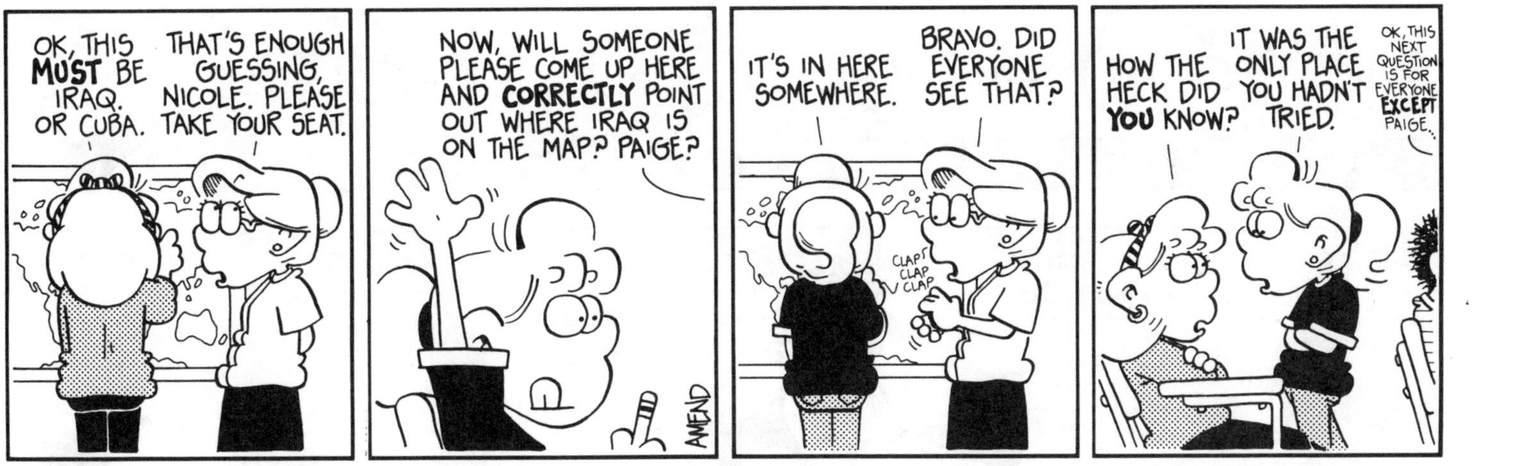
OK, THIS **MUST** BE IRAQ. OR CUBA.
THAT'S ENOUGH GUESSING, NICOLE. PLEASE TAKE YOUR SEAT.
NOW, WILL SOMEONE PLEASE COME UP HERE AND **CORRECTLY** POINT OUT WHERE IRAQ IS ON THE MAP? PAIGE?
AMEND
IT'S IN HERE SOMEWHERE.
BRAVO. DID EVERYONE SEE THAT?
CLAP CLAP CLAP
HOW THE HECK DID **YOU** KNOW?
IT WAS THE ONLY PLACE YOU HADN'T TRIED.
OK, THIS NEXT QUESTION IS FOR EVERYONE **EXCEPT** PAIGE...

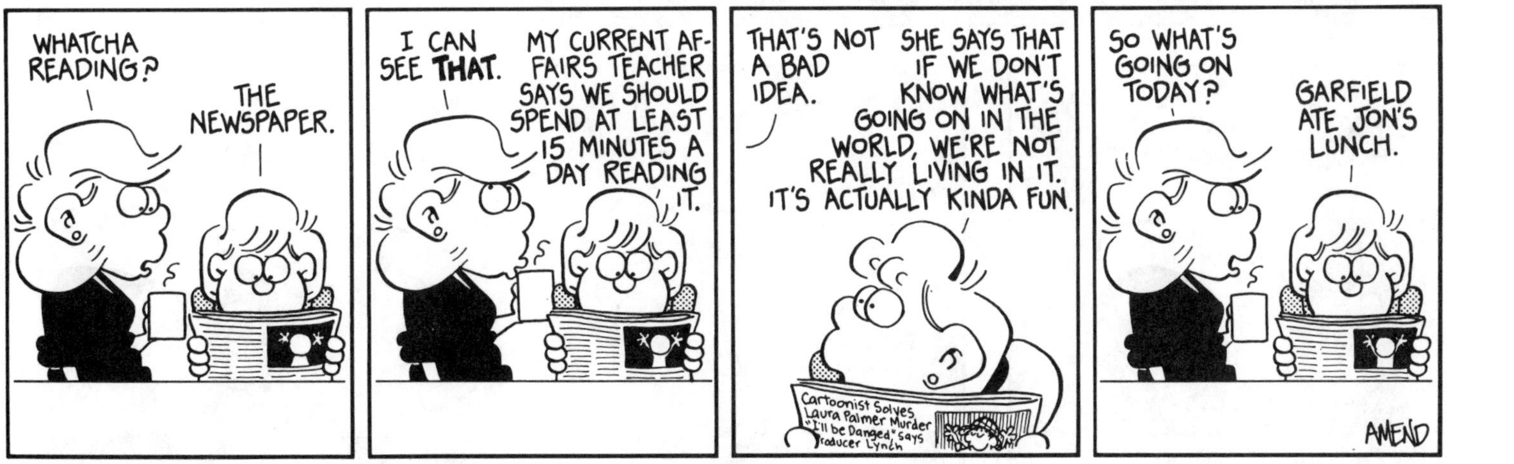
WHATCHA READING?
THE NEWSPAPER.
I CAN SEE **THAT**.
MY CURRENT AFFAIRS TEACHER SAYS WE SHOULD SPEND AT LEAST 15 MINUTES A DAY READING IT.
THAT'S NOT A BAD IDEA.
SHE SAYS THAT IF WE DON'T KNOW WHAT'S GOING ON IN THE WORLD, WE'RE NOT REALLY LIVING IN IT. IT'S ACTUALLY KINDA FUN.
Cartoonist Solves Laura Palmer Murder "I'll be Danged," says roducer Lynch
SO WHAT'S GOING ON TODAY?
GARFIELD ATE JON'S LUNCH.
AMEND

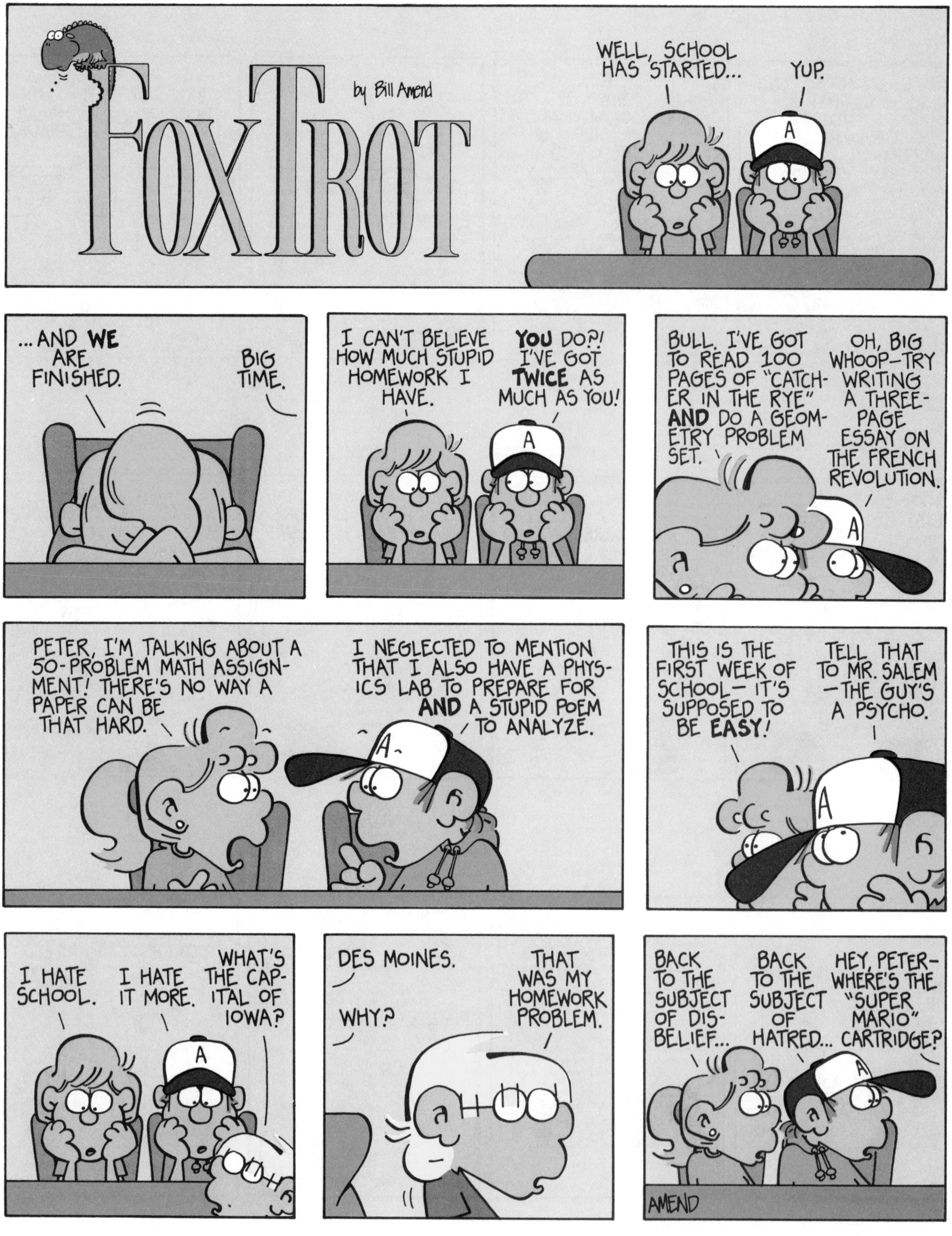
FoxTrot
by Bill Amend
WELL, SCHOOL HAS STARTED...
YUP.
...AND **WE** ARE FINISHED.
BIG TIME.
I CAN'T BELIEVE HOW MUCH STUPID HOMEWORK I HAVE.
YOU DO?! I'VE GOT **TWICE** AS MUCH AS YOU!
BULL. I'VE GOT TO READ 100 PAGES OF "CATCHER IN THE RYE" **AND** DO A GEOMETRY PROBLEM SET.
OH, BIG WHOOP–TRY WRITING A THREE-PAGE ESSAY ON THE FRENCH REVOLUTION.
PETER, I'M TALKING ABOUT A 50-PROBLEM MATH ASSIGNMENT! THERE'S NO WAY A PAPER CAN BE THAT HARD.
I NEGLECTED TO MENTION THAT I ALSO HAVE A PHYSICS LAB TO PREPARE FOR **AND** A STUPID POEM TO ANALYZE.
THIS IS THE FIRST WEEK OF SCHOOL– IT'S SUPPOSED TO BE **EASY**!
TELL THAT TO MR. SALEM –THE GUY'S A PSYCHO.
I HATE SCHOOL.
I HATE IT MORE.
WHAT'S THE CAPITAL OF IOWA?
DES MOINES.
WHY?
THAT WAS MY HOMEWORK PROBLEM.
BACK TO THE SUBJECT OF DISBELIEF...
BACK TO THE SUBJECT OF HATRED...
HEY, PETER– WHERE'S THE "SUPER MARIO" CARTRIDGE?
AMEND

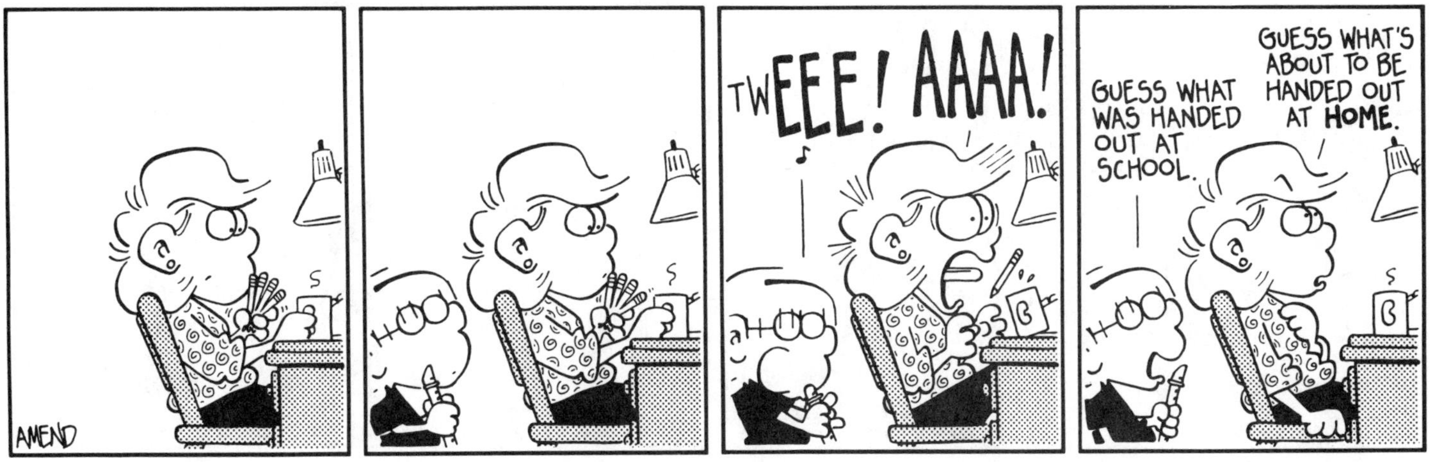
AMEND
TWEEE! AAAA!
GUESS WHAT WAS HANDED OUT AT SCHOOL.
GUESS WHAT'S ABOUT TO BE HANDED OUT AT **HOME**.

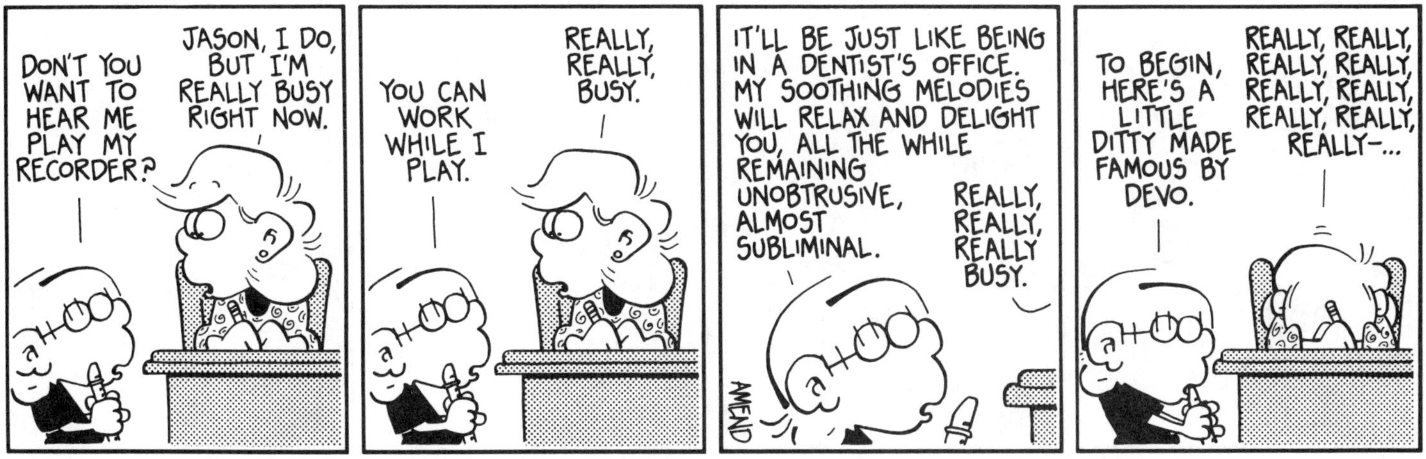
DON'T YOU WANT TO HEAR ME PLAY MY RECORDER?
JASON, I DO, BUT I'M REALLY BUSY RIGHT NOW.
YOU CAN WORK WHILE I PLAY.
REALLY, REALLY, BUSY.
IT'LL BE JUST LIKE BEING IN A DENTIST'S OFFICE. MY SOOTHING MELODIES WILL RELAX AND DELIGHT YOU, ALL THE WHILE REMAINING UNOBTRUSIVE, ALMOST SUBLIMINAL.
REALLY, REALLY, REALLY BUSY.
AMEND
TO BEGIN, HERE'S A LITTLE DITTY MADE FAMOUS BY DEVO.
REALLY, REALLY, REALLY, REALLY, REALLY, REALLY, REALLY, REALLY, REALLY–...

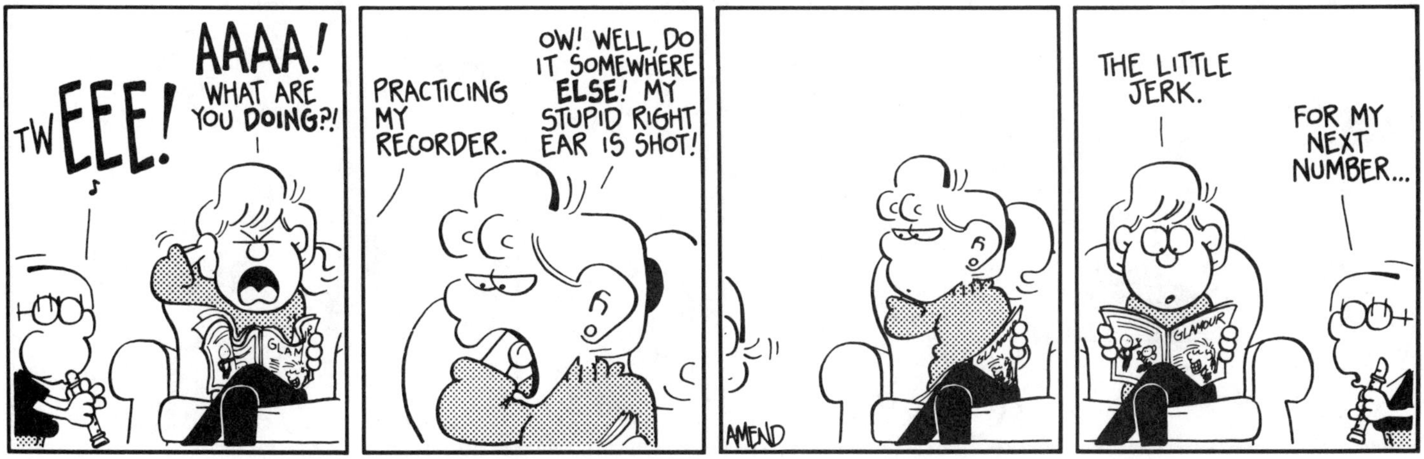
TWEEE!
AAAA! WHAT ARE YOU **DOING**?!
PRACTICING MY RECORDER.
OW! WELL, DO IT SOMEWHERE **ELSE**! MY STUPID RIGHT EAR IS SHOT!
AMEND
THE LITTLE JERK.
FOR MY NEXT NUMBER...

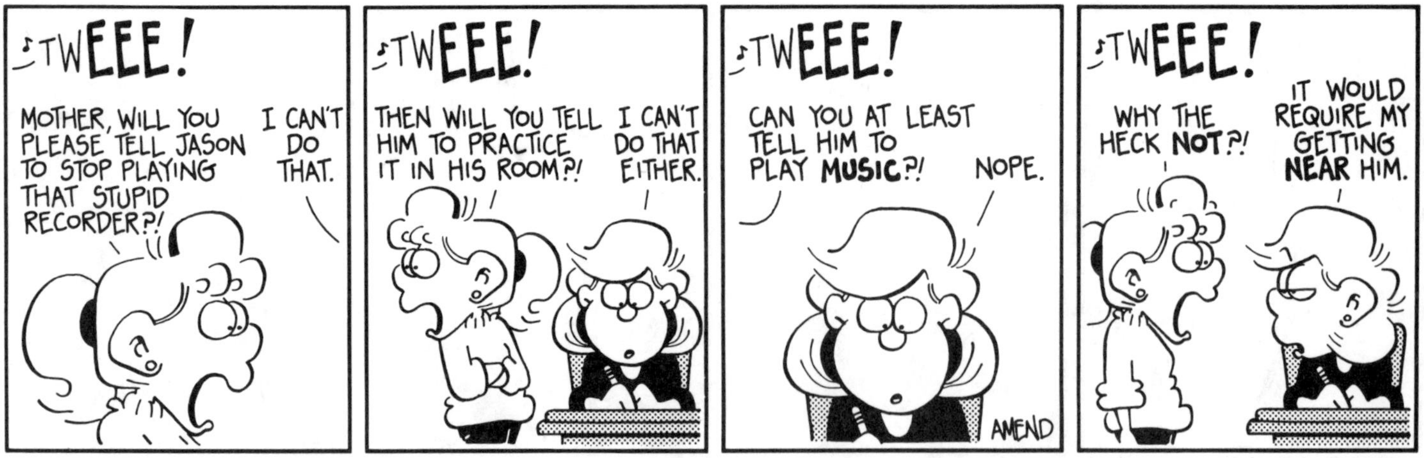
TWEEE!
MOTHER, WILL YOU PLEASE TELL JASON TO STOP PLAYING THAT STUPID RECORDER?!
I CAN'T DO THAT.
TWEEE!
THEN WILL YOU TELL HIM TO PRACTICE IT IN HIS ROOM?!
I CAN'T DO THAT EITHER.
TWEEE!
CAN YOU AT LEAST TELL HIM TO PLAY **MUSIC**?!
NOPE.
AMEND
TWEEE!
WHY THE HECK **NOT**?!
IT WOULD REQUIRE MY GETTING **NEAR** HIM.

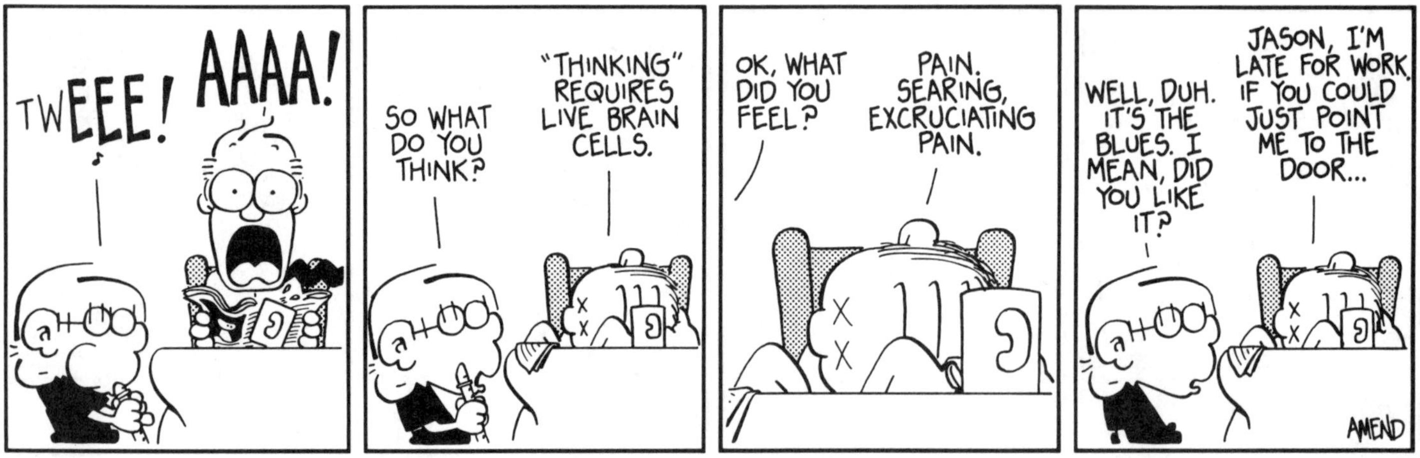
TWEEE!
AAAA!
SO WHAT DO YOU THINK?
"THINKING" REQUIRES LIVE BRAIN CELLS.
OK, WHAT DID YOU FEEL?
PAIN. SEARING, EXCRUCIATING PAIN.
WELL, DUH. IT'S THE BLUES. I MEAN, DID YOU LIKE IT?
JASON, I'M LATE FOR WORK. IF YOU COULD JUST POINT ME TO THE DOOR...
AMEND

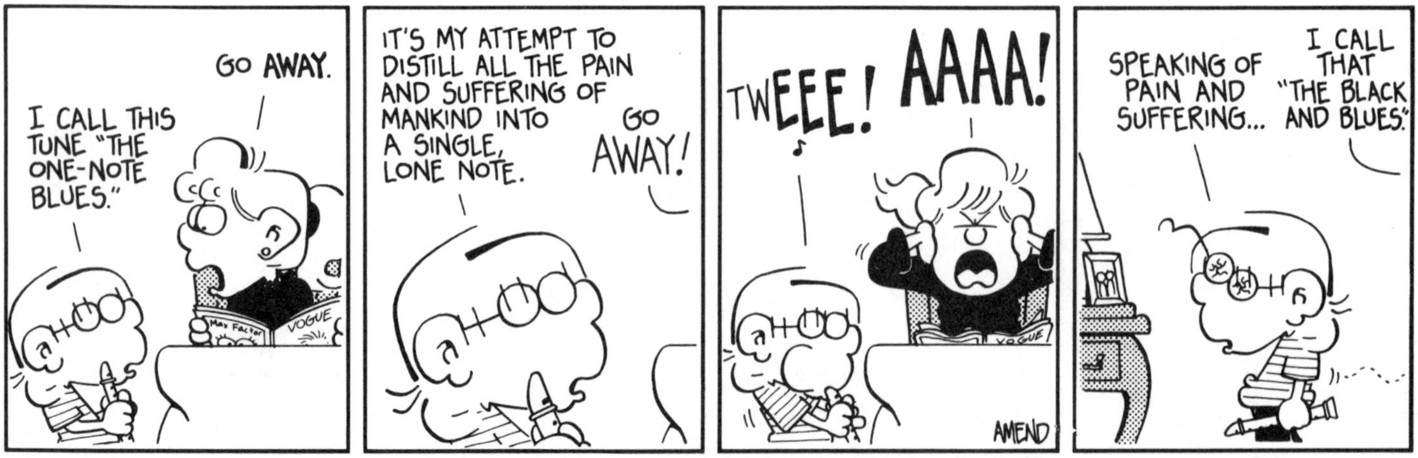
I CALL THIS TUNE "THE ONE-NOTE BLUES."
GO **AWAY**.
VOGUE
IT'S MY ATTEMPT TO DISTILL ALL THE PAIN AND SUFFERING OF MANKIND INTO A SINGLE, LONE NOTE.
GO AWAY!
TWEEE!
AAAA!
AMEND
SPEAKING OF PAIN AND SUFFERING...
I CALL THAT "THE BLACK AND BLUES."

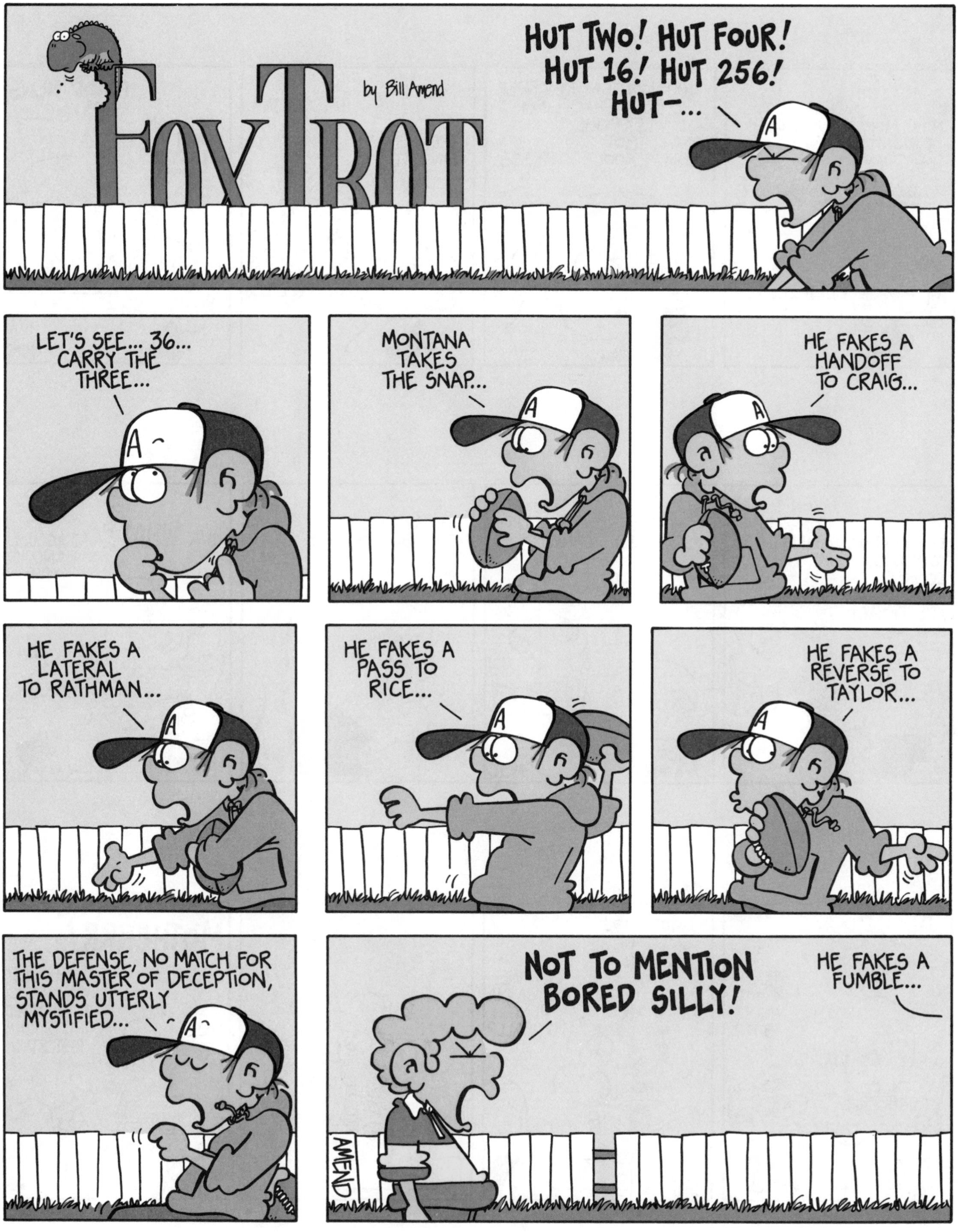
FoxTrot
by Bill Amend
HUT TWO! HUT FOUR! HUT 16! HUT 256! HUT-...
LET'S SEE... 36... CARRY THE THREE...
MONTANA TAKES THE SNAP...
HE FAKES A HANDOFF TO CRAIG...
HE FAKES A LATERAL TO RATHMAN...
HE FAKES A PASS TO RICE...
HE FAKES A REVERSE TO TAYLOR...
THE DEFENSE, NO MATCH FOR THIS MASTER OF DECEPTION, STANDS UTTERLY MYSTIFIED...
NOT TO MENTION BORED SILLY!
HE FAKES A FUMBLE...
AMEND

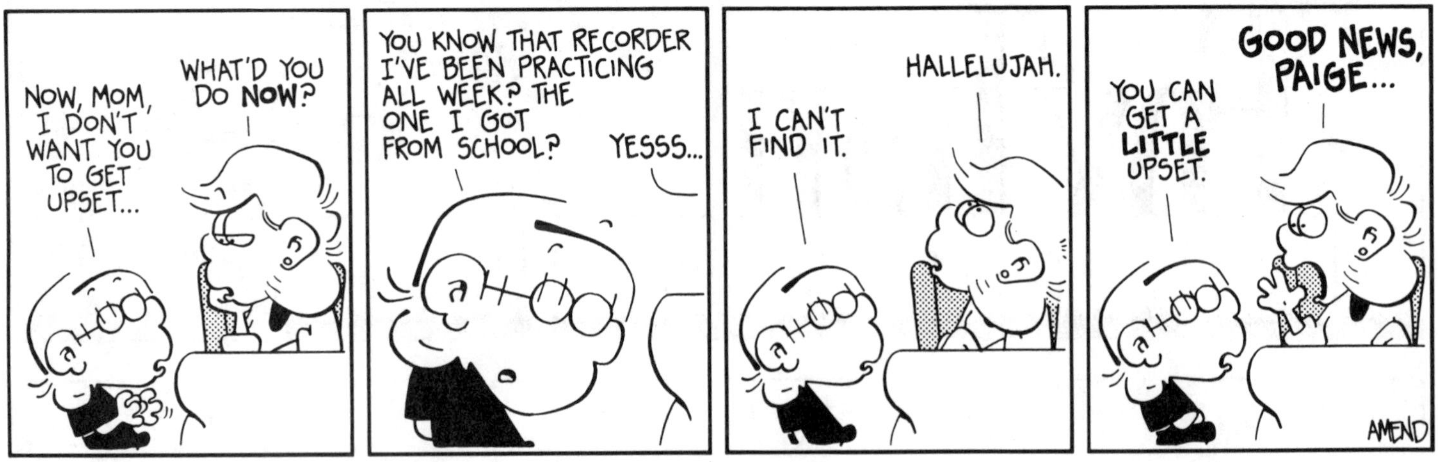

NOW, MOM, I DON'T WANT YOU TO GET UPSET...
WHAT'D YOU DO NOW?
YOU KNOW THAT RECORDER I'VE BEEN PRACTICING ALL WEEK? THE ONE I GOT FROM SCHOOL?
YESSS...
I CAN'T FIND IT.
HALLELUJAH.
YOU CAN GET A LITTLE UPSET.
GOOD NEWS, PAIGE...
AMEND

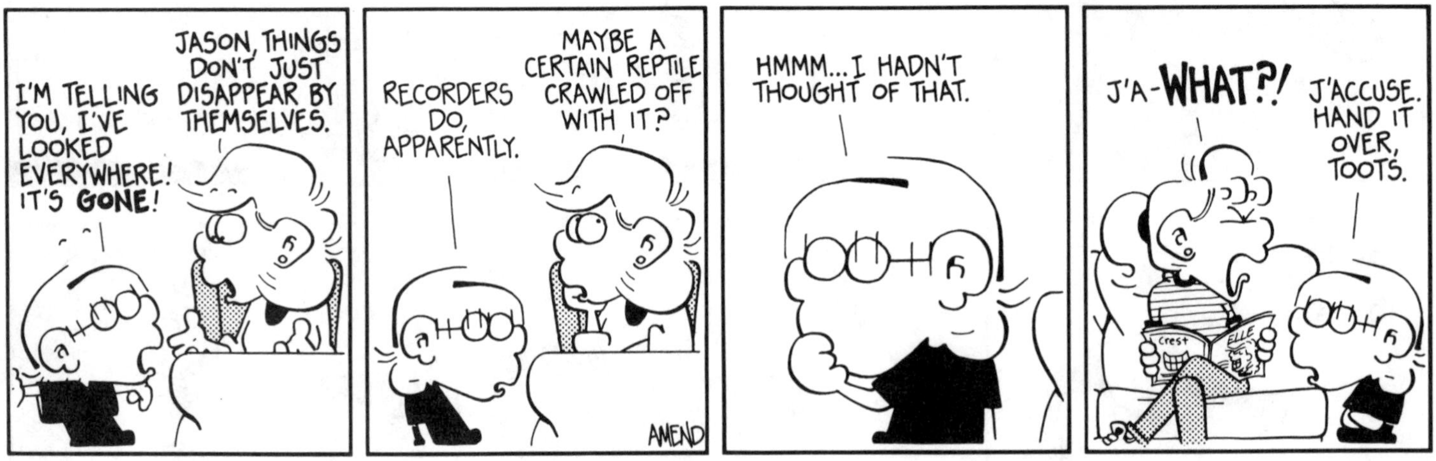

I'M TELLING YOU, I'VE LOOKED EVERYWHERE! IT'S GONE!
JASON, THINGS DON'T JUST DISAPPEAR BY THEMSELVES.
RECORDERS DO, APPARENTLY.
MAYBE A CERTAIN REPTILE CRAWLED OFF WITH IT?
AMEND
HMMM...I HADN'T THOUGHT OF THAT.
J'ACCUSE. HAND IT OVER, TOOTS.
J'A-WHAT?!
Crest
ELLE

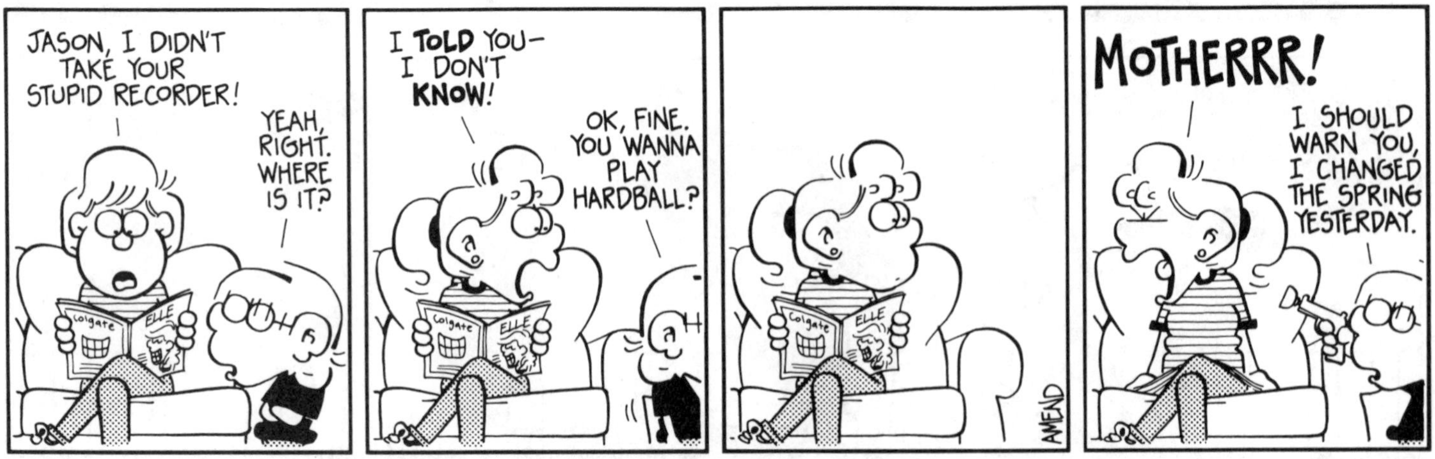

JASON, I DIDN'T TAKE YOUR STUPID RECORDER!
YEAH, RIGHT. WHERE IS IT?
Colgate
ELLE
I TOLD YOU-I DON'T KNOW!
OK, FINE. YOU WANNA PLAY HARDBALL?
AMEND
MOTHERRR!
I SHOULD WARN YOU, I CHANGED THE SPRING YESTERDAY.

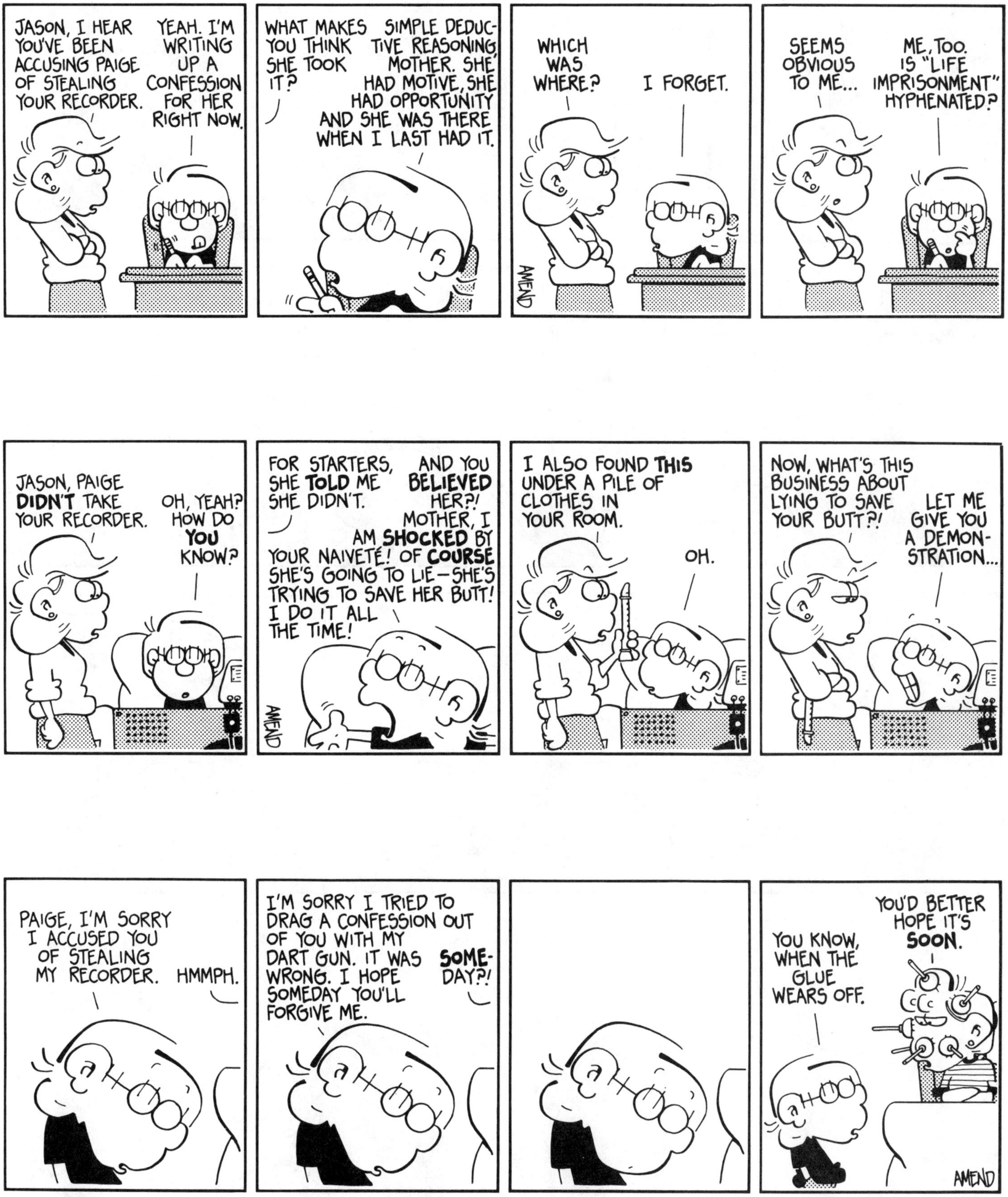
JASON, I HEAR YOU'VE BEEN ACCUSING PAIGE OF STEALING YOUR RECORDER.
YEAH. I'M WRITING UP A CONFESSION FOR HER RIGHT NOW.
WHAT MAKES YOU THINK SHE TOOK IT?
SIMPLE DEDUCTIVE REASONING, MOTHER. SHE HAD MOTIVE, SHE HAD OPPORTUNITY AND SHE WAS THERE WHEN I LAST HAD IT.
WHICH WAS WHERE?
I FORGET.
AMEND
SEEMS OBVIOUS TO ME...
ME, TOO. IS "LIFE IMPRISONMENT" HYPHENATED?
JASON, PAIGE DIDN'T TAKE YOUR RECORDER.
OH, YEAH? HOW DO YOU KNOW?
FOR STARTERS, SHE TOLD ME SHE DIDN'T.
AND YOU BELIEVED HER?! MOTHER, I AM SHOCKED BY YOUR NAIVETÉ! OF COURSE SHE'S GOING TO LIE—SHE'S TRYING TO SAVE HER BUTT! I DO IT ALL THE TIME!
AMEND
I ALSO FOUND THIS UNDER A PILE OF CLOTHES IN YOUR ROOM.
OH.
NOW, WHAT'S THIS BUSINESS ABOUT LYING TO SAVE YOUR BUTT?!
LET ME GIVE YOU A DEMONSTRATION...
PAIGE, I'M SORRY I ACCUSED YOU OF STEALING MY RECORDER.
HMMPH.
I'M SORRY I TRIED TO DRAG A CONFESSION OUT OF YOU WITH MY DART GUN. IT WAS WRONG. I HOPE SOMEDAY YOU'LL FORGIVE ME.
SOMEDAY?!
YOU KNOW, WHEN THE GLUE WEARS OFF.
YOU'D BETTER HOPE IT'S SOON.
AMEND

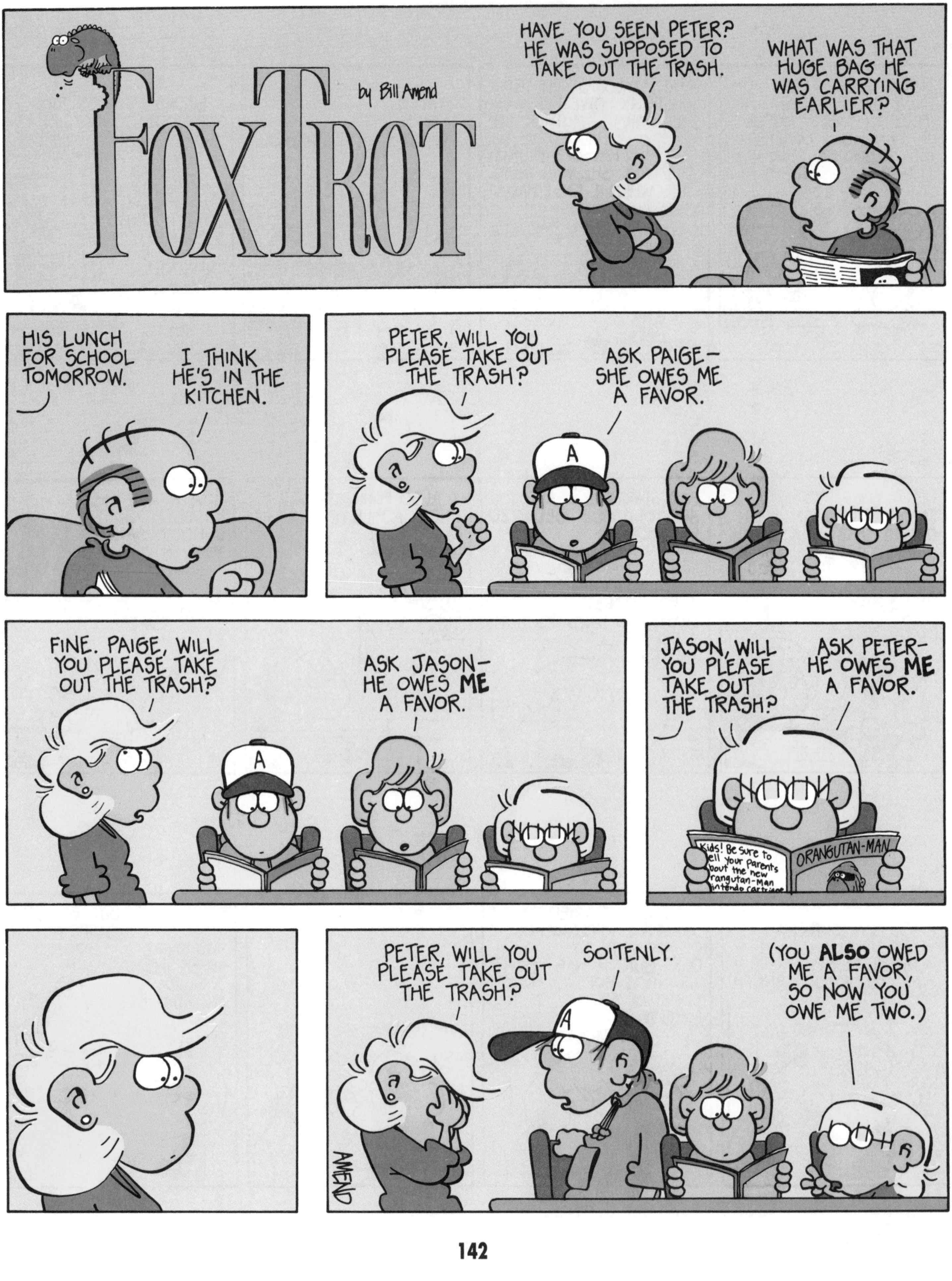
FoxTrot
by Bill Amend
HAVE YOU SEEN PETER? HE WAS SUPPOSED TO TAKE OUT THE TRASH.
WHAT WAS THAT HUGE BAG HE WAS CARRYING EARLIER?
HIS LUNCH FOR SCHOOL TOMORROW.
I THINK HE'S IN THE KITCHEN.
PETER, WILL YOU PLEASE TAKE OUT THE TRASH?
ASK PAIGE– SHE OWES ME A FAVOR.
FINE. PAIGE, WILL YOU PLEASE TAKE OUT THE TRASH?
ASK JASON– HE OWES **ME** A FAVOR.
JASON, WILL YOU PLEASE TAKE OUT THE TRASH?
ASK PETER– HE OWES **ME** A FAVOR.
Kids! Be sure to
ORANGUTAN-MAN
PETER, WILL YOU PLEASE TAKE OUT THE TRASH?
SOITENLY.
(YOU **ALSO** OWED ME A FAVOR, SO NOW YOU OWE ME TWO.)
AMEND

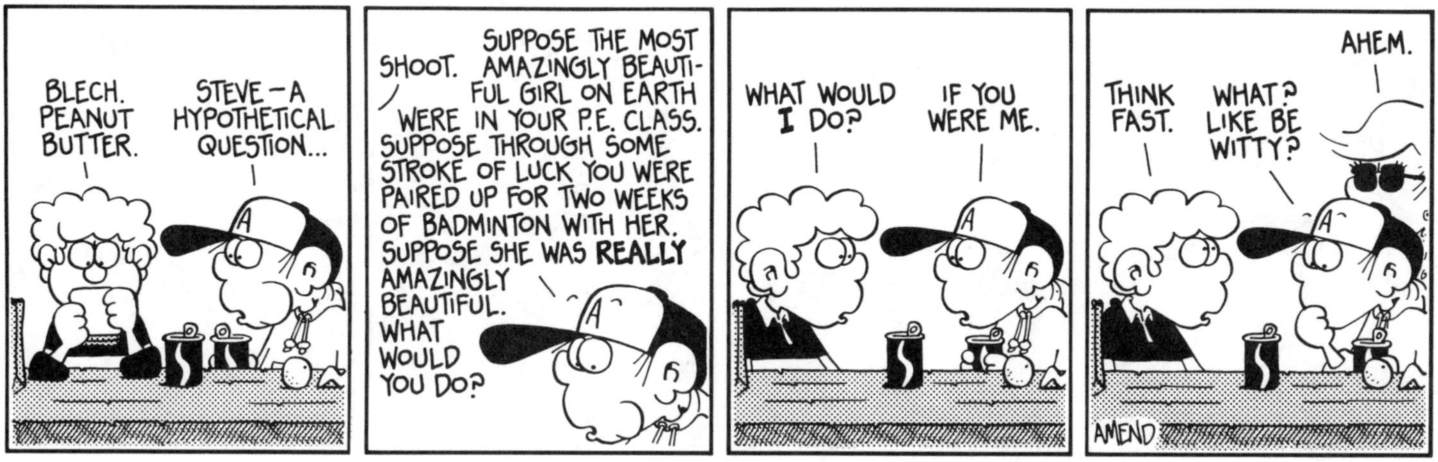
BLECH. PEANUT BUTTER.
STEVE — A HYPOTHETICAL QUESTION...
SHOOT.
SUPPOSE THE MOST AMAZINGLY BEAUTIFUL GIRL ON EARTH WERE IN YOUR P.E. CLASS. SUPPOSE THROUGH SOME STROKE OF LUCK YOU WERE PAIRED UP FOR TWO WEEKS OF BADMINTON WITH HER. SUPPOSE SHE WAS **REALLY** AMAZINGLY BEAUTIFUL. WHAT WOULD YOU DO?
WHAT WOULD **I** DO?
IF YOU WERE ME.
THINK FAST.
WHAT? LIKE BE WITTY?
AHEM.
AMEND

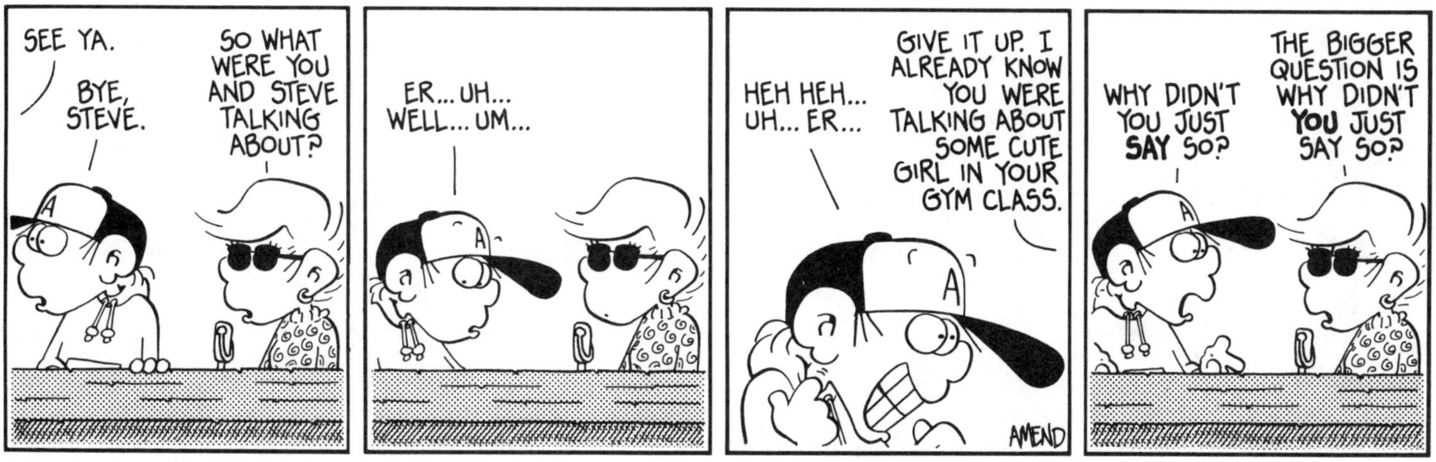
SEE YA.
BYE, STEVE.
SO WHAT WERE YOU AND STEVE TALKING ABOUT?
ER... UH... WELL... UM...
HEH HEH... UH... ER...
GIVE IT UP. I ALREADY KNOW YOU WERE TALKING ABOUT SOME CUTE GIRL IN YOUR GYM CLASS.
AMEND
WHY DIDN'T YOU JUST **SAY** SO?
THE BIGGER QUESTION IS WHY DIDN'T **YOU** JUST SAY SO?

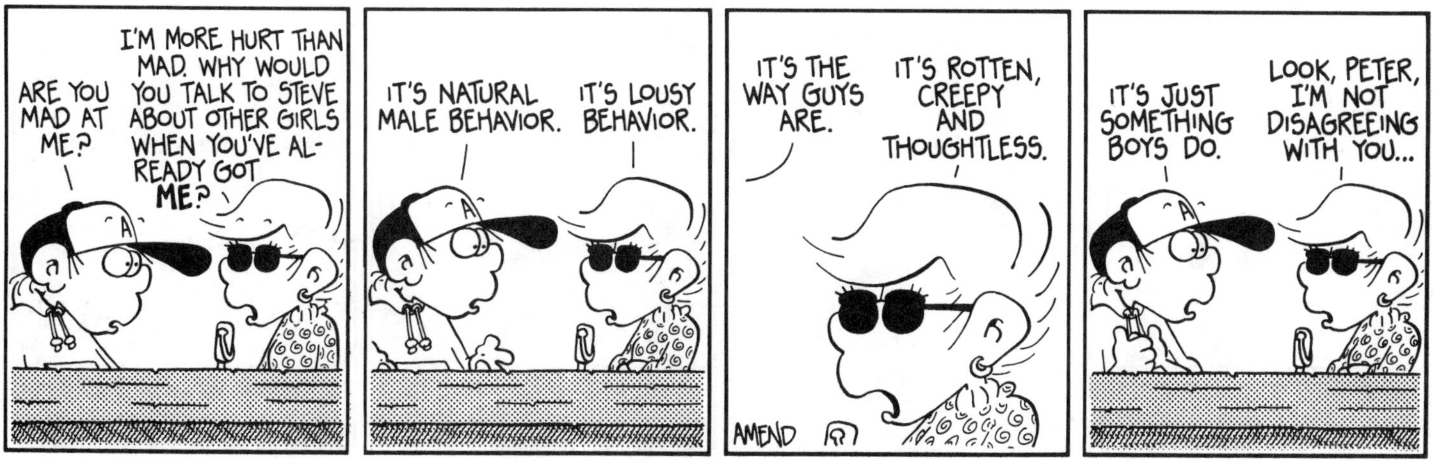
ARE YOU MAD AT ME?
I'M MORE HURT THAN MAD. WHY WOULD YOU TALK TO STEVE ABOUT OTHER GIRLS WHEN YOU'VE ALREADY GOT **ME**?
IT'S NATURAL MALE BEHAVIOR.
IT'S LOUSY BEHAVIOR.
IT'S THE WAY GUYS ARE.
IT'S ROTTEN, CREEPY AND THOUGHTLESS.
AMEND
IT'S JUST SOMETHING BOYS DO.
LOOK, PETER, I'M NOT DISAGREEING WITH YOU...

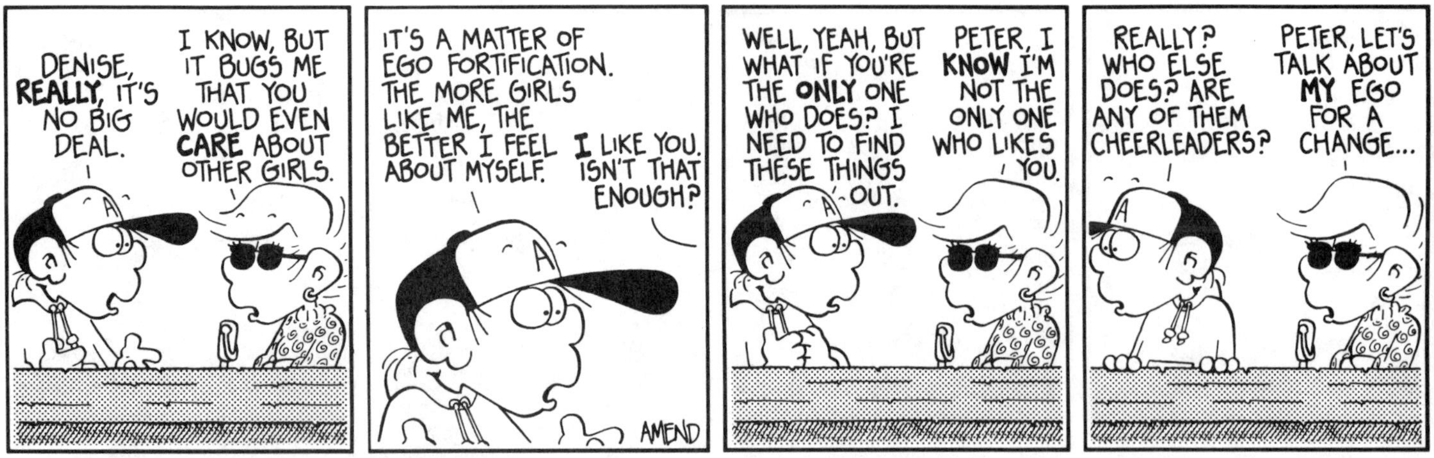
DENISE, **REALLY**, IT'S NO BIG DEAL.
I KNOW, BUT IT BUGS ME THAT YOU WOULD EVEN **CARE** ABOUT OTHER GIRLS.
IT'S A MATTER OF EGO FORTIFICATION. THE MORE GIRLS LIKE ME, THE BETTER I FEEL ABOUT MYSELF.
I LIKE YOU. ISN'T THAT ENOUGH?
AMEND
WELL, YEAH, BUT WHAT IF YOU'RE THE **ONLY** ONE WHO DOES? I NEED TO FIND THESE THINGS OUT.
PETER, I **KNOW** I'M NOT THE ONLY ONE WHO LIKES YOU.
REALLY? WHO ELSE DOES? ARE ANY OF THEM CHEERLEADERS?
PETER, LET'S TALK ABOUT **MY** EGO FOR A CHANGE...

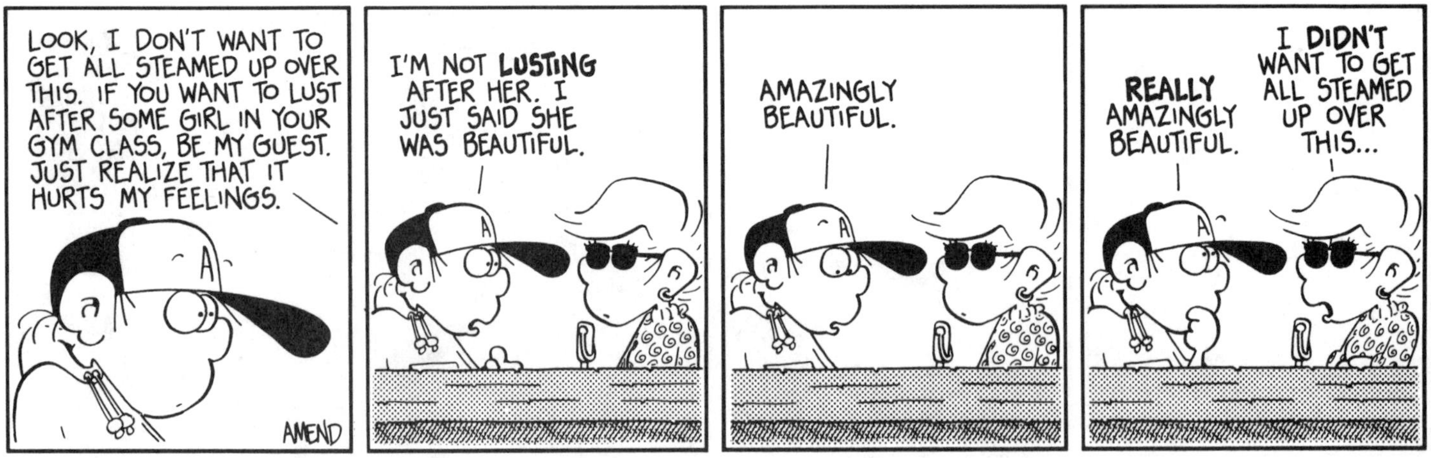
LOOK, I DON'T WANT TO GET ALL STEAMED UP OVER THIS. IF YOU WANT TO LUST AFTER SOME GIRL IN YOUR GYM CLASS, BE MY GUEST. JUST REALIZE THAT IT HURTS MY FEELINGS.
AMEND
I'M NOT **LUSTING** AFTER HER. I JUST SAID SHE WAS BEAUTIFUL.
AMAZINGLY BEAUTIFUL.
REALLY AMAZINGLY BEAUTIFUL.
I **DIDN'T** WANT TO GET ALL STEAMED UP OVER THIS...

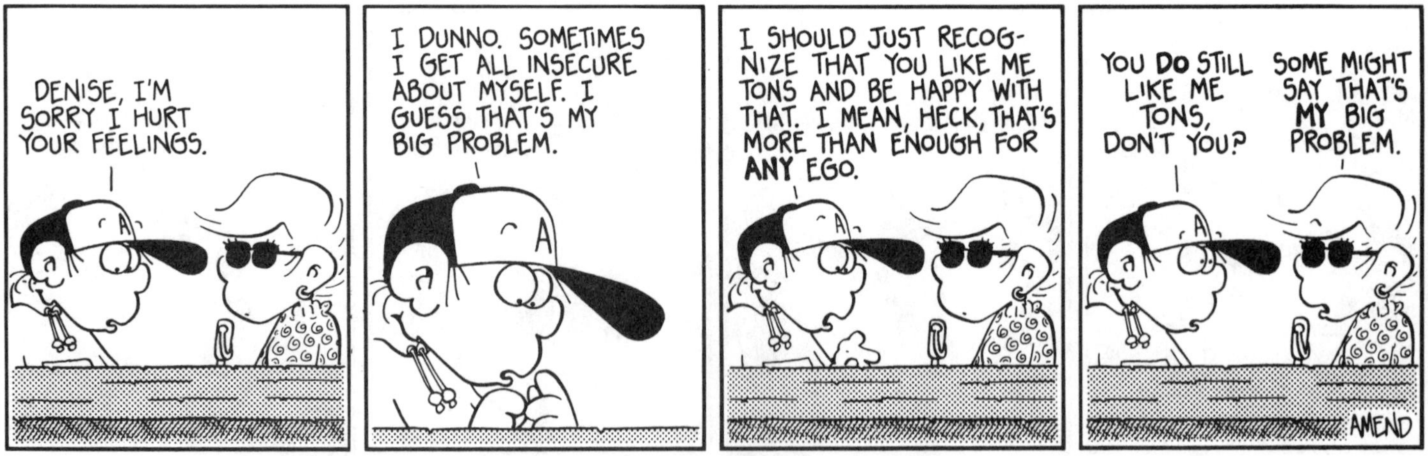
DENISE, I'M SORRY I HURT YOUR FEELINGS.
I DUNNO. SOMETIMES I GET ALL INSECURE ABOUT MYSELF. I GUESS THAT'S MY BIG PROBLEM.
I SHOULD JUST RECOG-NIZE THAT YOU LIKE ME TONS AND BE HAPPY WITH THAT. I MEAN, HECK, THAT'S MORE THAN ENOUGH FOR **ANY** EGO.
YOU **DO** STILL LIKE ME TONS, DON'T YOU?
SOME MIGHT SAY THAT'S **MY** BIG PROBLEM.
AMEND

by Bill Amend

FoxTrot

WHAT WOULD **YOU** DO IF THIS WERE YOUR ASSIGNMENT?

BESIDES EAT IT...

WHATCHA DOING?

PONDERING.

ANYTHING IN PARTICULAR?

THIS CARDBOARD DIORAMA I'M SUPPOSED TO MAKE FOR SCHOOL.

OH? WHAT'S IT OF?

THAT'S THE PROBLEM. I'VE NARROWED IT DOWN TO EITHER CUSTER'S LAST STAND OR THE FRENCH REVOLUTION. I'M HAVING A HARD TIME CHOOSING.

AMEND

WHY DON'T YOU DO WHAT **I** DO WHEN I HAVE A TOUGH DECISION TO MAKE. WRITE UP A LIST OF THE PROS AND CONS.

I DID. IT'S STILL A TOUGH CALL.

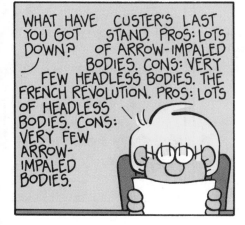

WHAT HAVE YOU GOT DOWN?

CUSTER'S LAST STAND. PROS: LOTS OF ARROW-IMPALED BODIES. CONS: VERY FEW HEADLESS BODIES. THE FRENCH REVOLUTION. PROS: LOTS OF HEADLESS BODIES. CONS: VERY FEW ARROW-IMPALED BODIES.

LET ME ASK YOU THIS. DO WE HAVE A LOT OF TOOTHPICKS?

WHATCHA DOING?

PONDERING.

YOU LOOK EXCITED.
YOU BET I AM. MISS GRINCHLEY GAVE US AN EXTRA CREDIT HOMEWORK PROBLEM.
OH?
IT'S WORTH 10 QUIZ POINTS, ASSUMING ONE GETS IT RIGHT, WHICH I WILL.
WHY? IS IT EASY?
MOM, PLEASE. IT'S A MATH PROBLEM. THEY'RE ALL EASY FOR JASON FOX, HUMAN SUPERCOMPUTER.
AMEND
UNLIKE, SAY... MODESTY?
HEY, LET'S HAVE SOME FUN— READ ME THE QUESTION AND I'LL DO IT IN MY HEAD.

FIGURE IT OUT YET?
HMMMM...
JASON, YOU DON'T HAVE TO DO THIS PROBLEM IN YOUR HEAD.
OF COURSE I DO. OTHERWISE IT WOULDN'T BE A CHALLENGE.
AMEND
YOU'RE CHALLENGING MY PATIENCE. HERE— TAKE THE PROBLEM AND GO DO IT IN YOUR ROOM.
AAAA! DON'T SHOW IT TO ME! THAT CONSTITUTES A SECOND READING! I NEVER READ MATH QUESTIONS TWICE!
NEVER?!
WELL, MY MEMORY BEFORE AGE FIVE IS A LITTLE SHAKY, BUT...

JASON, I HAVE TO GET DINNER READY. TAKE THE PROBLEM AND DO IT IN YOUR ROOM.
BUT IF I DO IT IN MY ROOM, NO ONE'LL SEE ME DO IT!
NO ONE'LL KNOW HOW EASY IT WAS FOR ME! NO ONE'LL KNOW HOW ASSUREDLY I ARRIVED AT THE SOLUTION!
AMEND
NO ONE'LL KNOW HOW QUICKLY I DID IT!
TREK
BY THE SAME TOKEN...

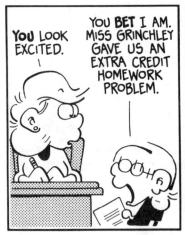

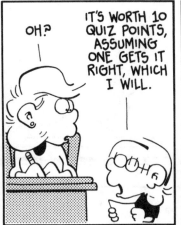

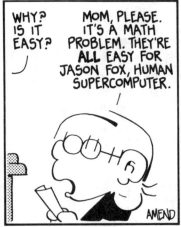

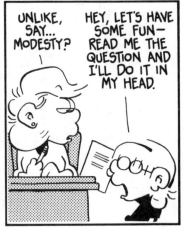

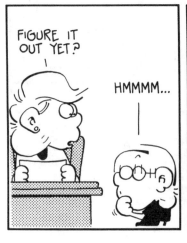

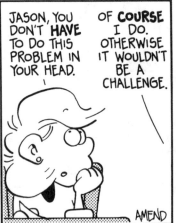

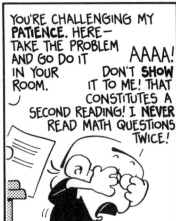

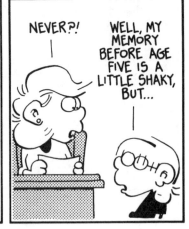

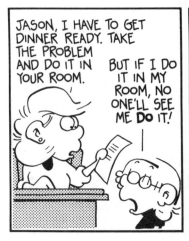

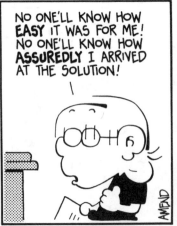

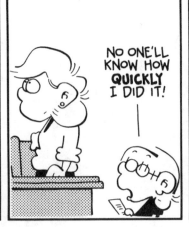

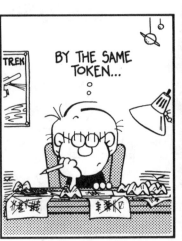

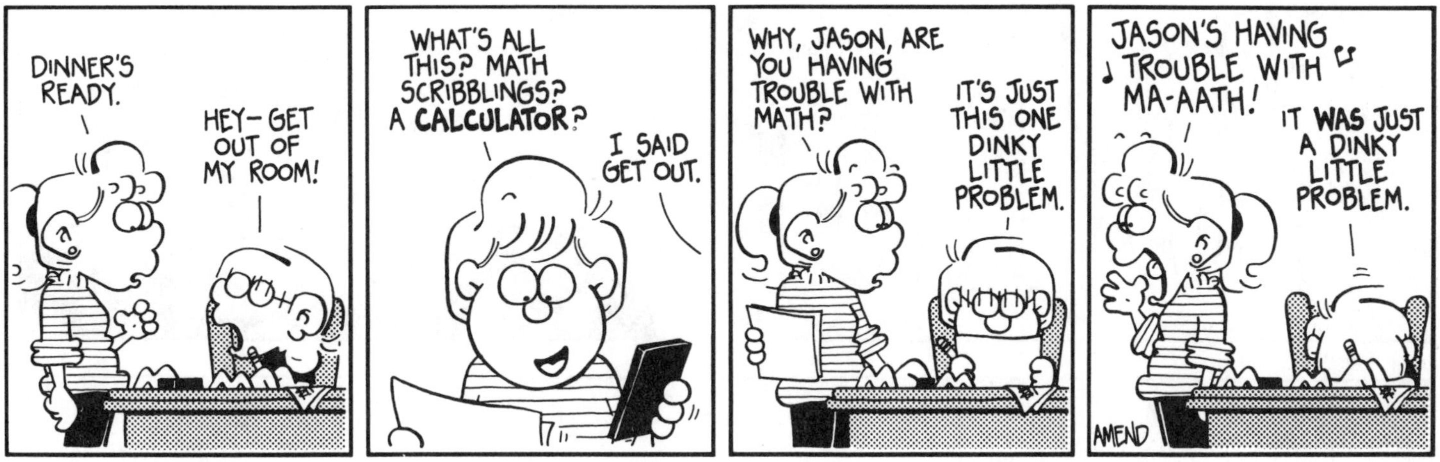
DINNER'S READY.
HEY— GET OUT OF MY ROOM!
WHAT'S ALL THIS? MATH SCRIBBLINGS? A **CALCULATOR**?
I SAID GET OUT.
WHY, JASON, ARE YOU HAVING TROUBLE WITH MATH?
IT'S JUST THIS ONE DINKY LITTLE PROBLEM.
♪ JASON'S HAVING TROUBLE WITH MA-AATH! ♫
IT **WAS** JUST A DINKY LITTLE PROBLEM.
AMEND

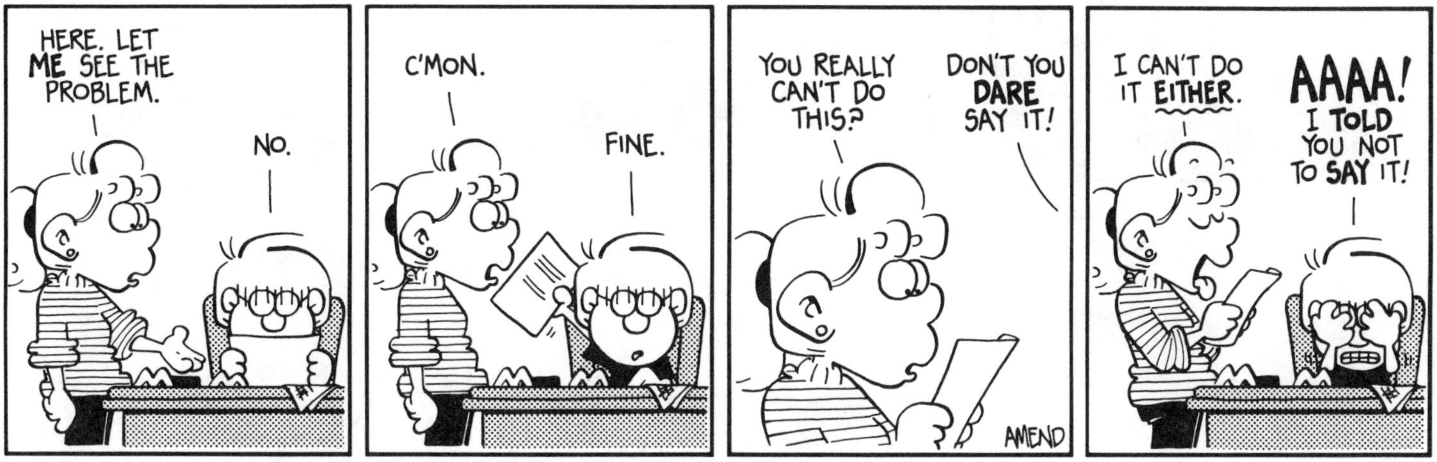
HERE. LET **ME** SEE THE PROBLEM.
NO.
C'MON.
FINE.
YOU REALLY CAN'T DO THIS?
DON'T YOU **DARE** SAY IT!
AMEND
I CAN'T DO IT **EITHER**.
AAAA! I **TOLD** YOU NOT TO **SAY** IT!

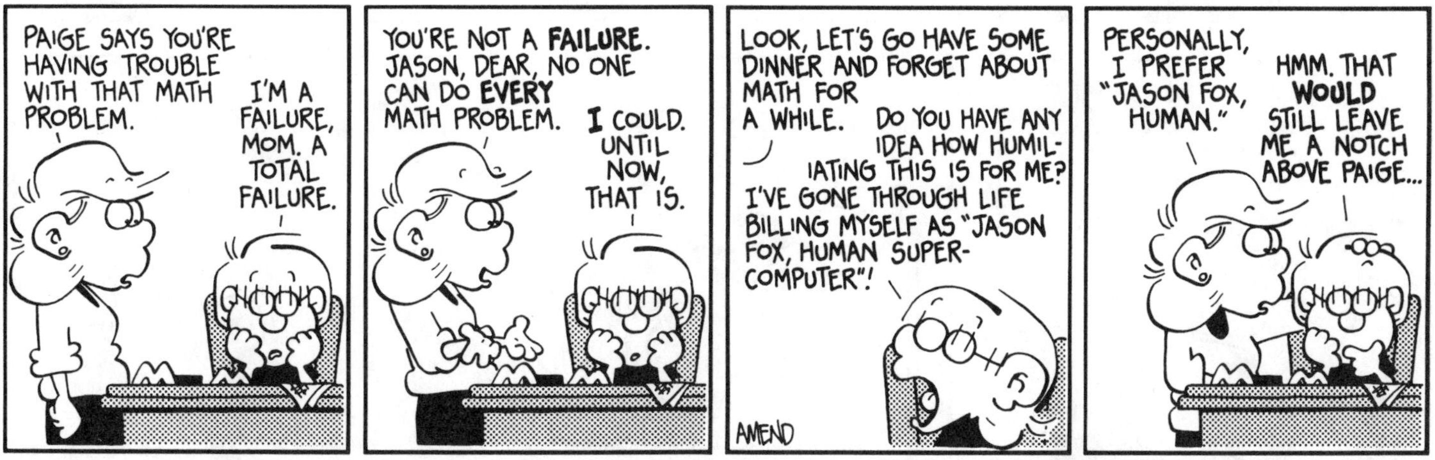
PAIGE SAYS YOU'RE HAVING TROUBLE WITH THAT MATH PROBLEM.
I'M A FAILURE, MOM. A TOTAL FAILURE.
YOU'RE NOT A **FAILURE**. JASON, DEAR, NO ONE CAN DO **EVERY** MATH PROBLEM.
I COULD. UNTIL NOW, THAT IS.
LOOK, LET'S GO HAVE SOME DINNER AND FORGET ABOUT MATH FOR A WHILE.
DO YOU HAVE ANY IDEA HOW HUMILIATING THIS IS FOR ME? I'VE GONE THROUGH LIFE BILLING MYSELF AS "JASON FOX, HUMAN SUPER-COMPUTER"!
AMEND
PERSONALLY, I PREFER "JASON FOX, HUMAN."
HMM. THAT **WOULD** STILL LEAVE ME A NOTCH ABOVE PAIGE...

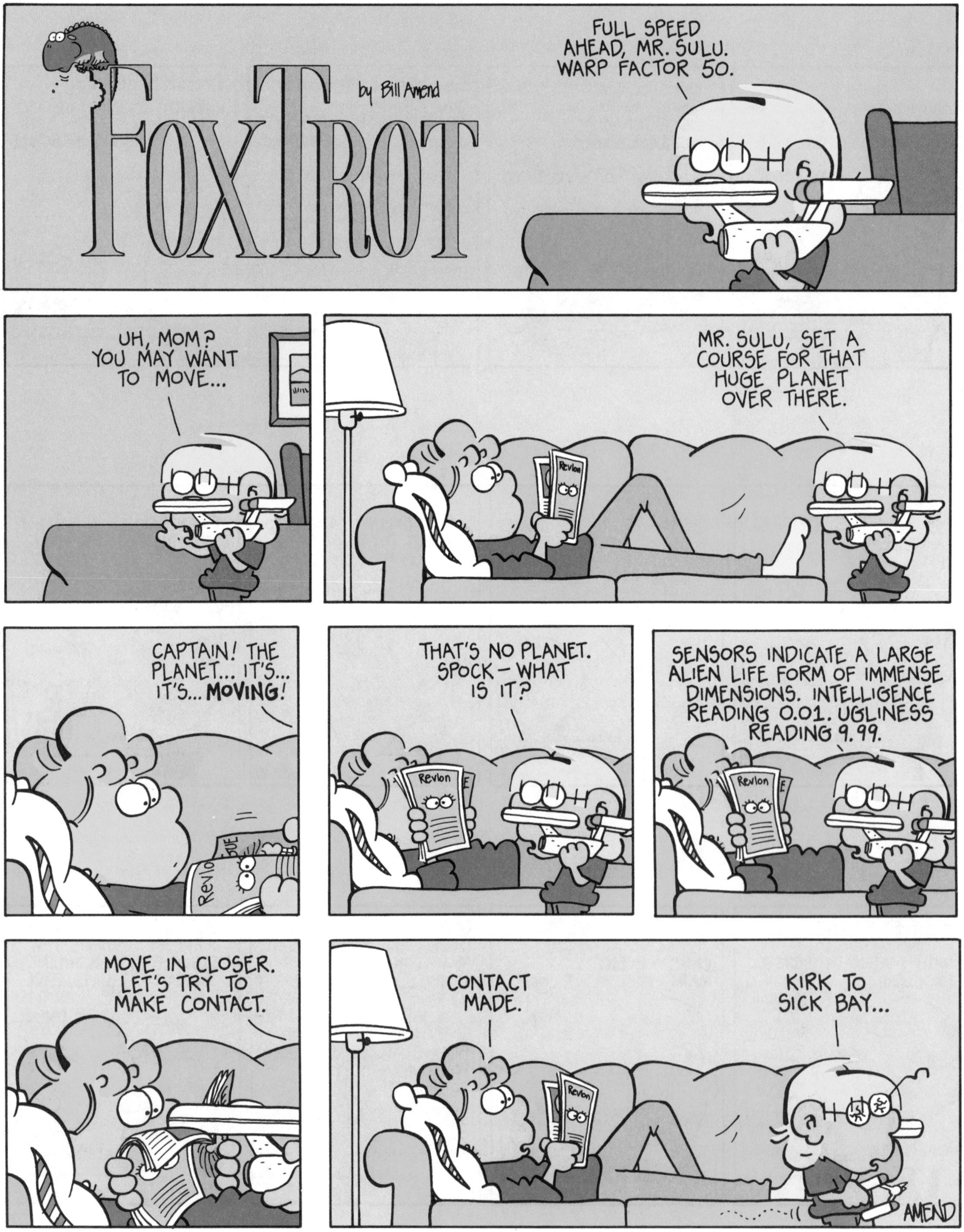

FoxTrot
by Bill Amend
FULL SPEED AHEAD, MR. SULU. WARP FACTOR 50.
UH, MOM? YOU MAY WANT TO MOVE...
MR. SULU, SET A COURSE FOR THAT HUGE PLANET OVER THERE.
CAPTAIN! THE PLANET... IT'S... IT'S... **MOVING**!
THAT'S NO PLANET. SPOCK — WHAT IS IT?
SENSORS INDICATE A LARGE ALIEN LIFE FORM OF IMMENSE DIMENSIONS. INTELLIGENCE READING 0.01. UGLINESS READING 9.99.
MOVE IN CLOSER. LET'S TRY TO MAKE CONTACT.
CONTACT MADE.
KIRK TO SICK BAY...
AMEND

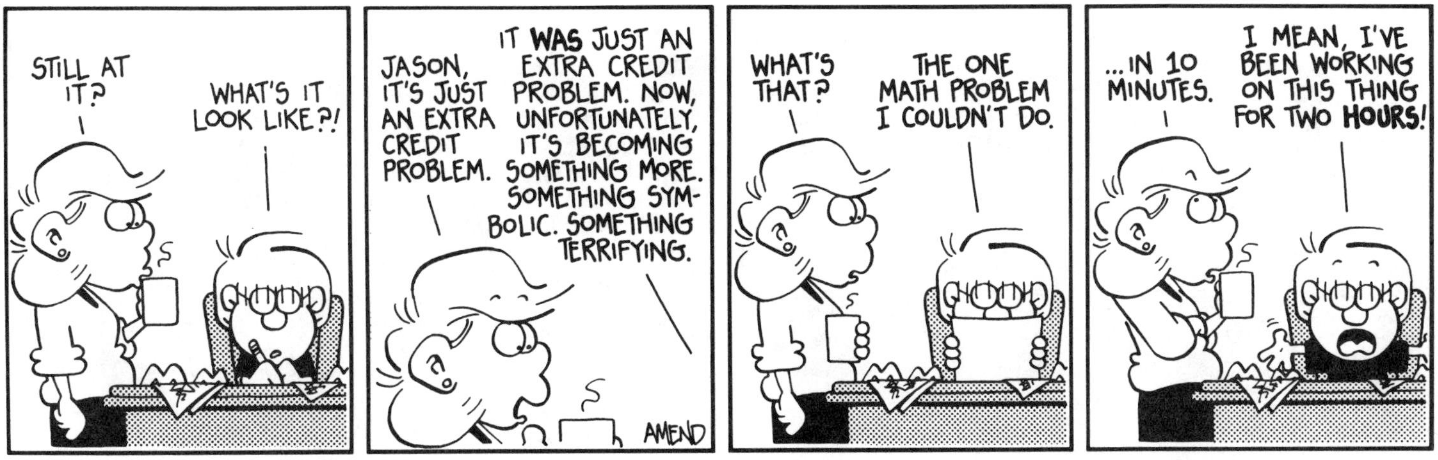
STILL AT IT?
WHAT'S IT LOOK LIKE?!
JASON, IT'S JUST AN EXTRA CREDIT PROBLEM.
IT **WAS** JUST AN EXTRA CREDIT PROBLEM. NOW, UNFORTUNATELY, IT'S BECOMING SOMETHING MORE. SOMETHING SYMBOLIC. SOMETHING TERRIFYING.
AMEND
WHAT'S THAT?
THE ONE MATH PROBLEM I COULDN'T DO.
...IN 10 MINUTES.
I MEAN, I'VE BEEN WORKING ON THIS THING FOR TWO **HOURS**!

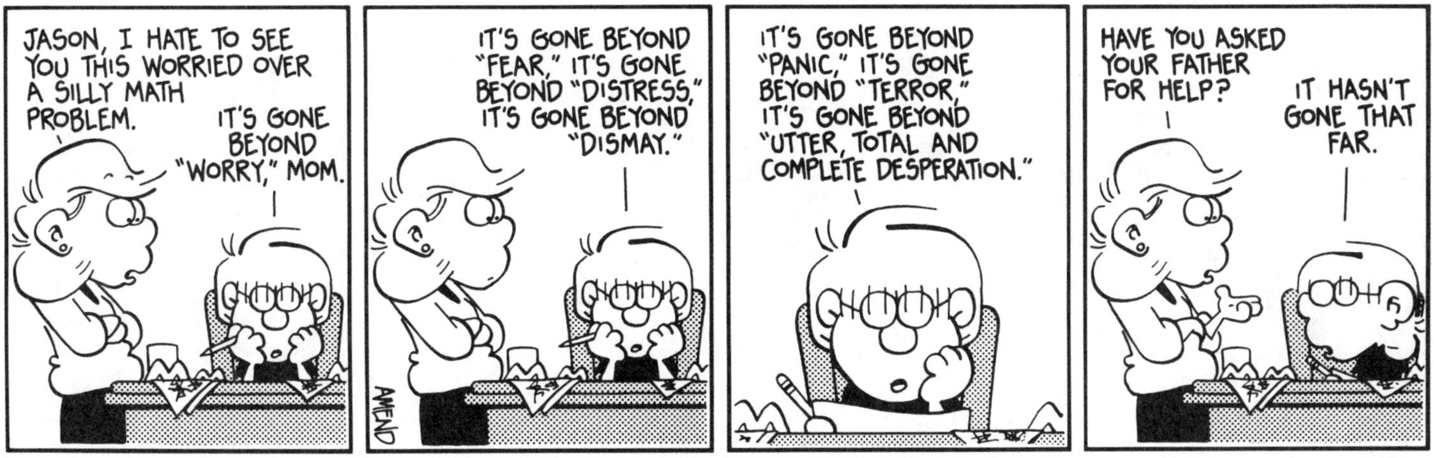
JASON, I HATE TO SEE YOU THIS WORRIED OVER A SILLY MATH PROBLEM.
IT'S GONE BEYOND "WORRY," MOM.
AMEND
IT'S GONE BEYOND "FEAR," IT'S GONE BEYOND "DISTRESS," IT'S GONE BEYOND "DISMAY."
IT'S GONE BEYOND "PANIC," IT'S GONE BEYOND "TERROR," IT'S GONE BEYOND "UTTER, TOTAL AND COMPLETE DESPERATION."
HAVE YOU ASKED YOUR FATHER FOR HELP?
IT HASN'T GONE THAT FAR.

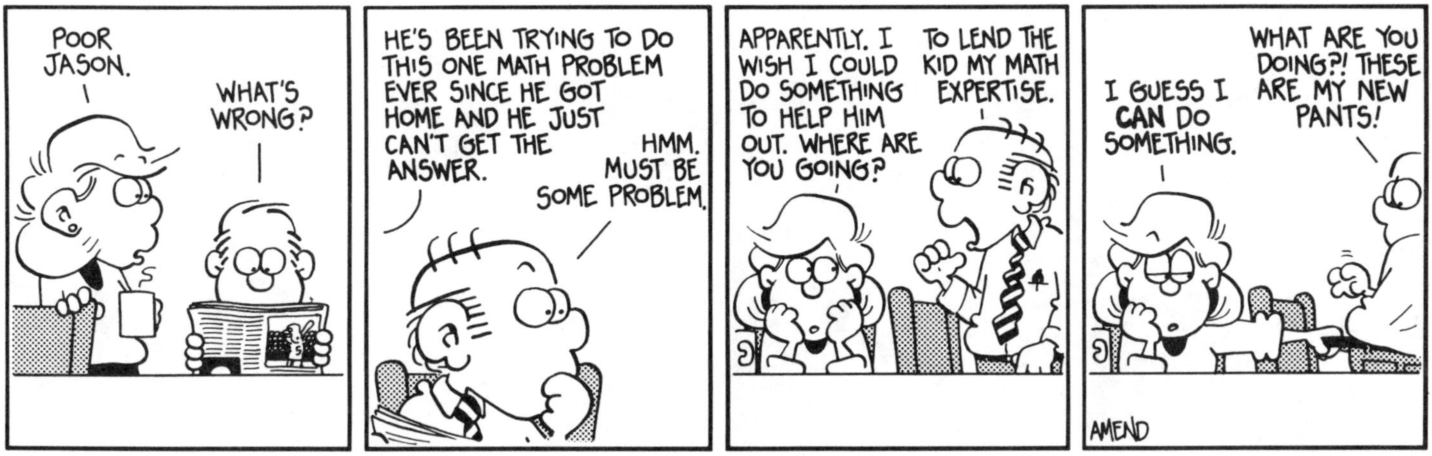
POOR JASON.
WHAT'S WRONG?
HE'S BEEN TRYING TO DO THIS ONE MATH PROBLEM EVER SINCE HE GOT HOME AND HE JUST CAN'T GET THE ANSWER.
HMM. MUST BE SOME PROBLEM.
APPARENTLY. I WISH I COULD DO SOMETHING TO HELP HIM OUT. WHERE ARE YOU GOING?
TO LEND THE KID MY MATH EXPERTISE.
I GUESS I **CAN** DO SOMETHING.
WHAT ARE YOU DOING?! THESE ARE MY NEW PANTS!
AMEND

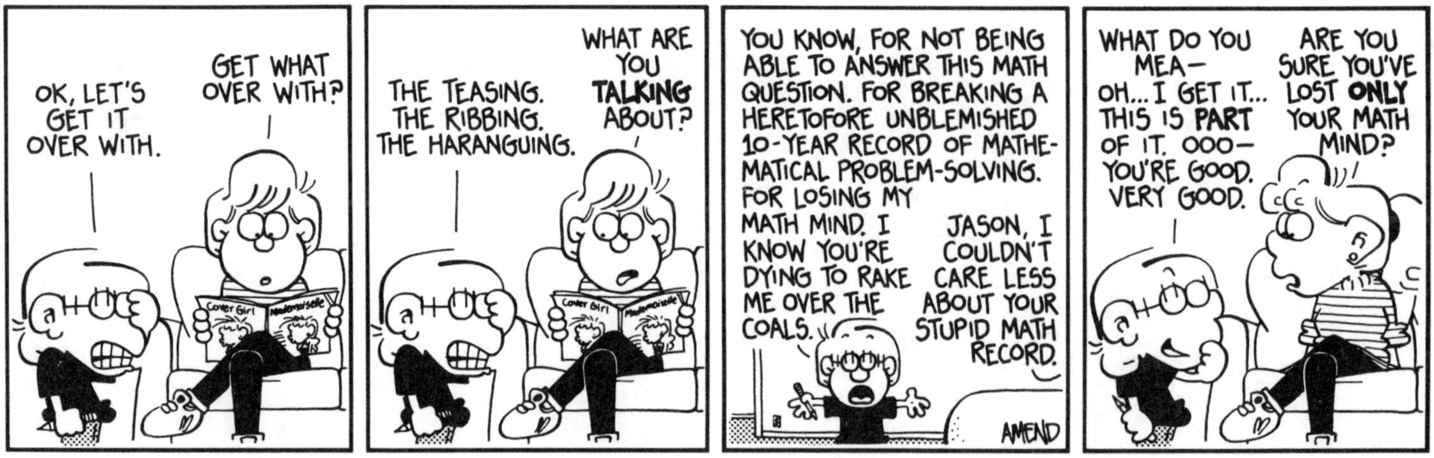
OK, LET'S GET IT OVER WITH.
GET WHAT OVER WITH?
THE TEASING. THE RIBBING. THE HARANGUING.
WHAT ARE YOU **TALKING** ABOUT?
YOU KNOW, FOR NOT BEING ABLE TO ANSWER THIS MATH QUESTION. FOR BREAKING A HERETOFORE UNBLEMISHED 10-YEAR RECORD OF MATHEMATICAL PROBLEM-SOLVING. FOR LOSING MY MATH MIND. I KNOW YOU'RE DYING TO RAKE ME OVER THE COALS.
JASON, I COULDN'T CARE LESS ABOUT YOUR STUPID MATH RECORD.
Cover Girl
Mademoiselle
AMEND
WHAT DO YOU MEA— OH... I GET IT... THIS IS **PART** OF IT. OOO— YOU'RE GOOD. VERY GOOD.
ARE YOU SURE YOU'VE LOST **ONLY** YOUR MATH MIND?

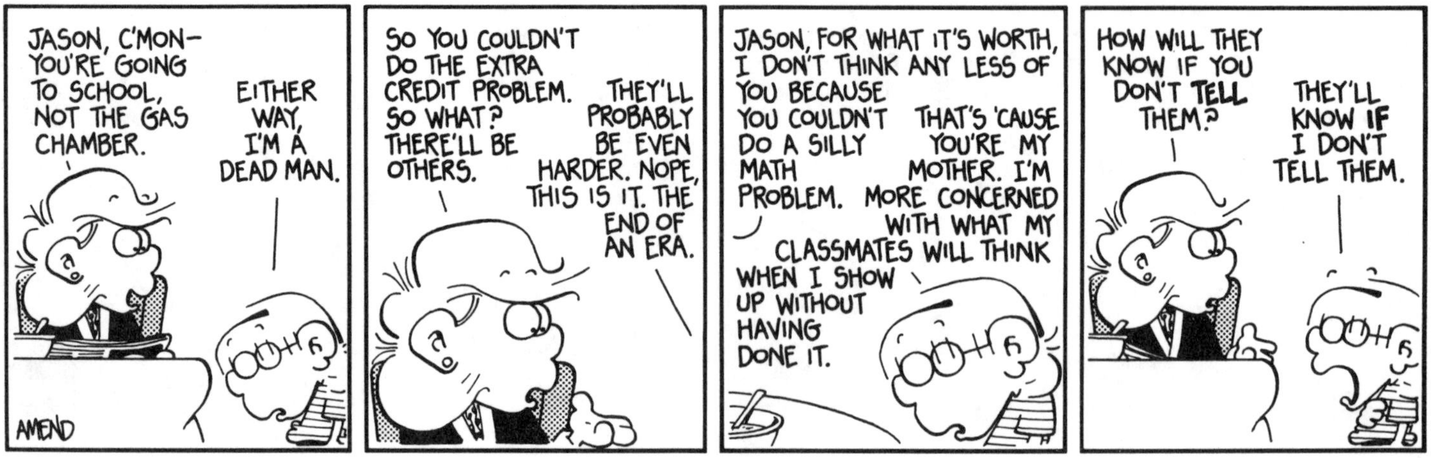
JASON, C'MON— YOU'RE GOING TO SCHOOL, NOT THE GAS CHAMBER.
EITHER WAY, I'M A DEAD MAN.
AMEND
SO YOU COULDN'T DO THE EXTRA CREDIT PROBLEM. SO WHAT? THERE'LL BE OTHERS.
THEY'LL PROBABLY BE EVEN HARDER. NOPE, THIS IS IT. THE END OF AN ERA.
JASON, FOR WHAT IT'S WORTH, I DON'T THINK ANY LESS OF YOU BECAUSE YOU COULDN'T DO A SILLY MATH PROBLEM.
THAT'S 'CAUSE YOU'RE MY MOTHER. I'M MORE CONCERNED WITH WHAT MY CLASSMATES WILL THINK WHEN I SHOW UP WITHOUT HAVING DONE IT.
HOW WILL THEY KNOW IF YOU DON'T **TELL** THEM?
THEY'LL KNOW **IF** I DON'T TELL THEM.

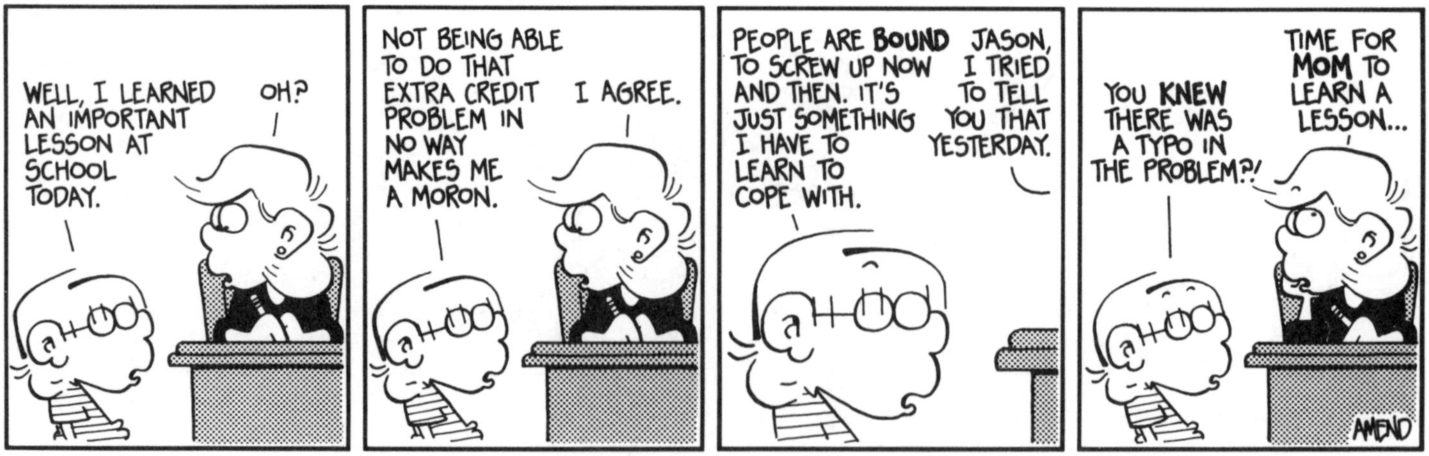
WELL, I LEARNED AN IMPORTANT LESSON AT SCHOOL TODAY.
OH?
NOT BEING ABLE TO DO THAT EXTRA CREDIT PROBLEM IN NO WAY MAKES ME A MORON.
I AGREE.
PEOPLE ARE **BOUND** TO SCREW UP NOW AND THEN. IT'S JUST SOMETHING I HAVE TO LEARN TO COPE WITH.
JASON, I TRIED TO TELL YOU THAT YESTERDAY.
YOU **KNEW** THERE WAS A TYPO IN THE PROBLEM?!
TIME FOR **MOM** TO LEARN A LESSON...
AMEND

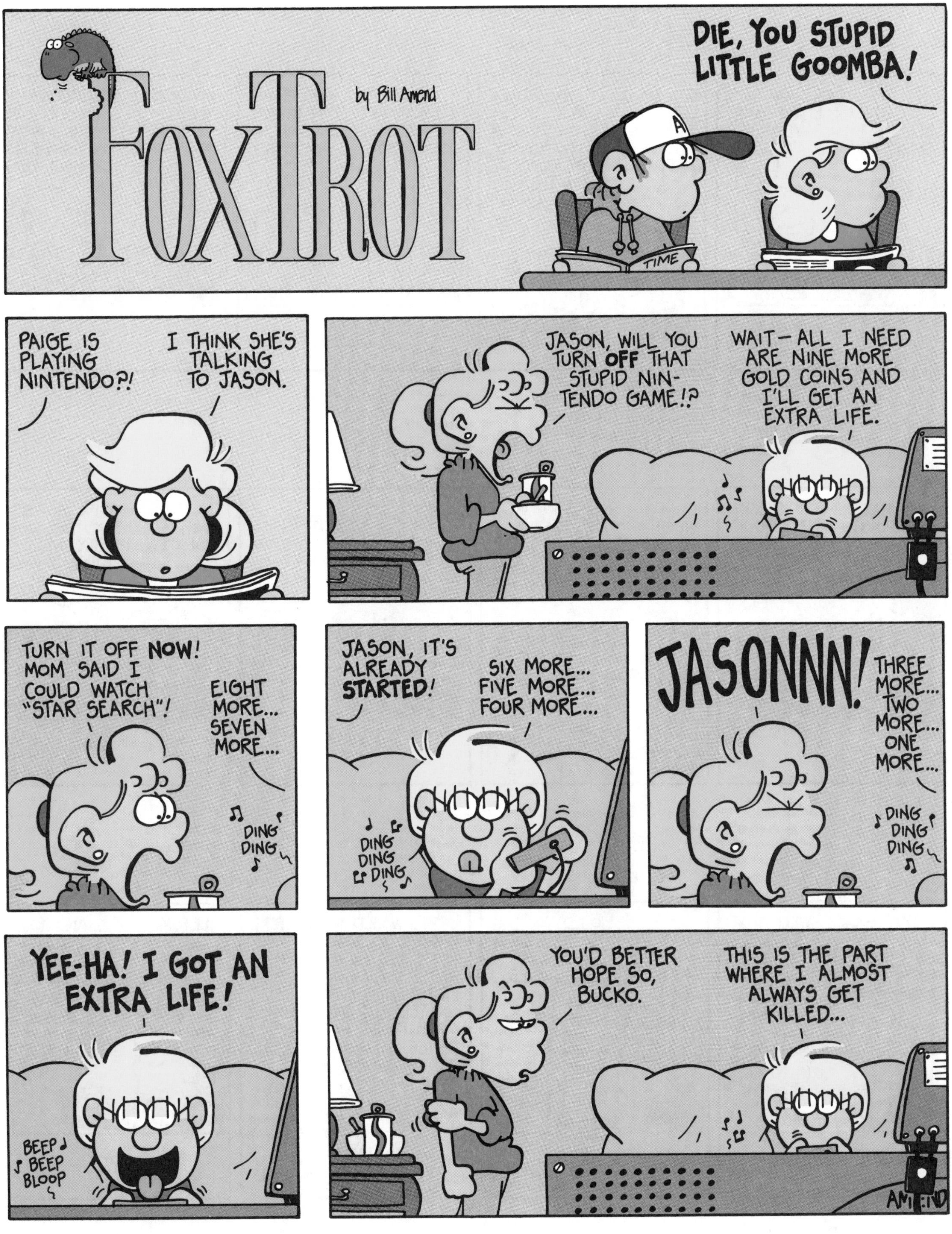

FoxTrot
by Bill Amend
DIE, YOU STUPID LITTLE GOOMBA!
TIME
PAIGE IS PLAYING NINTENDO?!
I THINK SHE'S TALKING TO JASON.
JASON, WILL YOU TURN OFF THAT STUPID NINTENDO GAME!?
WAIT— ALL I NEED ARE NINE MORE GOLD COINS AND I'LL GET AN EXTRA LIFE.
TURN IT OFF NOW! MOM SAID I COULD WATCH "STAR SEARCH"!
EIGHT MORE... SEVEN MORE...
DING DING
JASON, IT'S ALREADY STARTED!
SIX MORE... FIVE MORE... FOUR MORE...
DING DING DING
JASONNN!
THREE MORE... TWO MORE... ONE MORE...
DING DING DING
YEE-HA! I GOT AN EXTRA LIFE!
BEEP BEEP BLOOP
YOU'D BETTER HOPE SO, BUCKO.
THIS IS THE PART WHERE I ALMOST ALWAYS GET KILLED...
AMEND

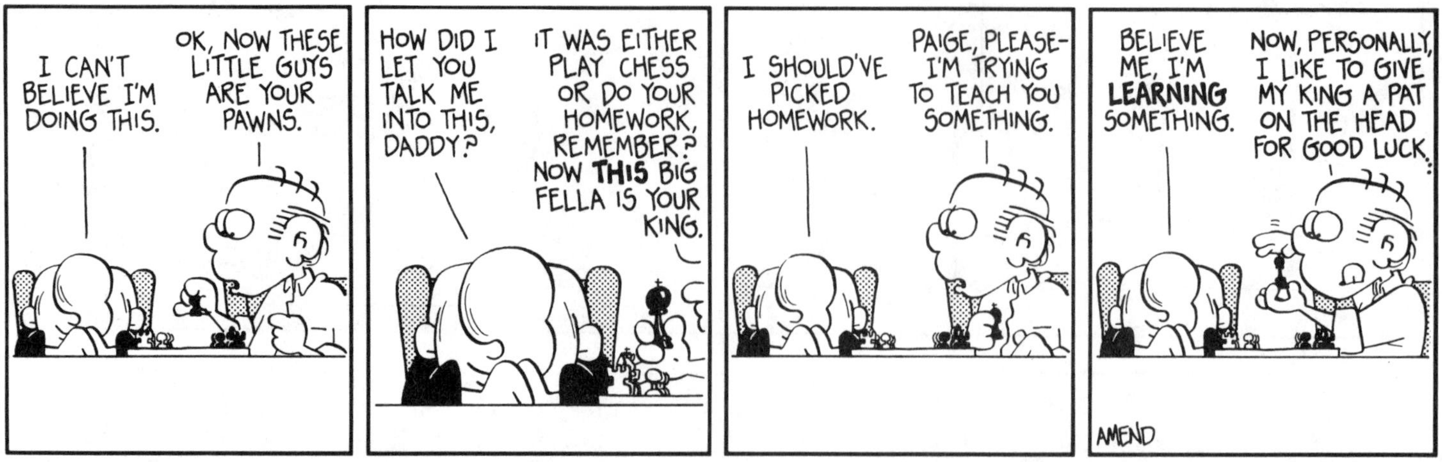
I CAN'T BELIEVE I'M DOING THIS.
OK, NOW THESE LITTLE GUYS ARE YOUR PAWNS.
HOW DID I LET YOU TALK ME INTO THIS, DADDY?
IT WAS EITHER PLAY CHESS OR DO YOUR HOMEWORK, REMEMBER? NOW **THIS** BIG FELLA IS YOUR KING.
I SHOULD'VE PICKED HOMEWORK.
PAIGE, PLEASE- I'M TRYING TO TEACH YOU SOMETHING.
BELIEVE ME, I'M **LEARNING** SOMETHING.
NOW, PERSONALLY, I LIKE TO GIVE MY KING A PAT ON THE HEAD FOR GOOD LUCK...
AMEND

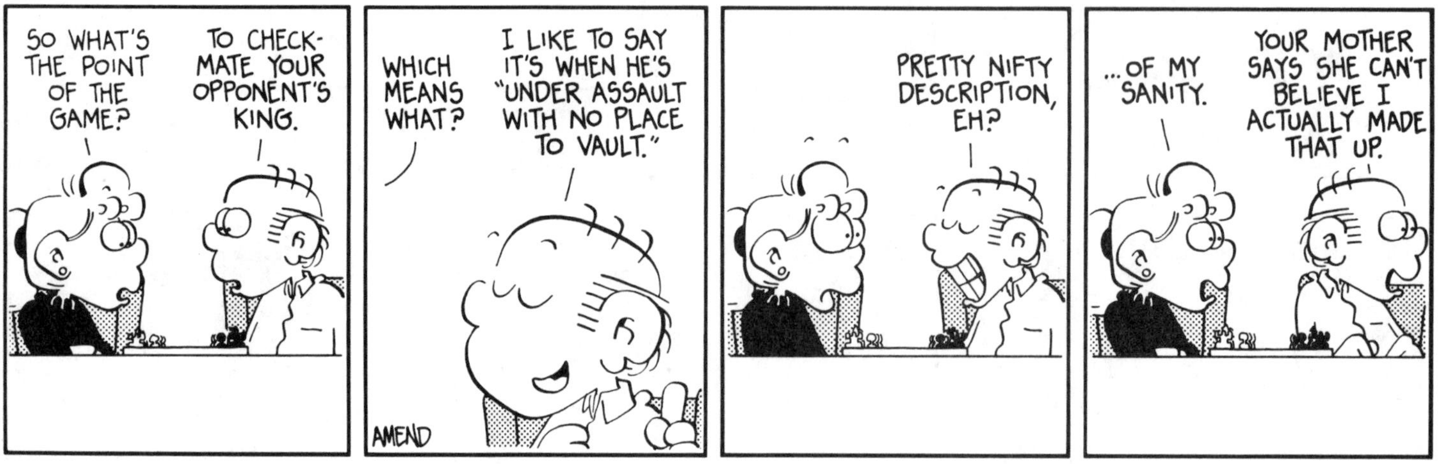
SO WHAT'S THE POINT OF THE GAME?
TO CHECK-MATE YOUR OPPONENT'S KING.
WHICH MEANS WHAT?
I LIKE TO SAY IT'S WHEN HE'S "UNDER ASSAULT WITH NO PLACE TO VAULT."
AMEND
PRETTY NIFTY DESCRIPTION, EH?
...OF MY SANITY.
YOUR MOTHER SAYS SHE CAN'T BELIEVE I ACTUALLY MADE THAT UP.

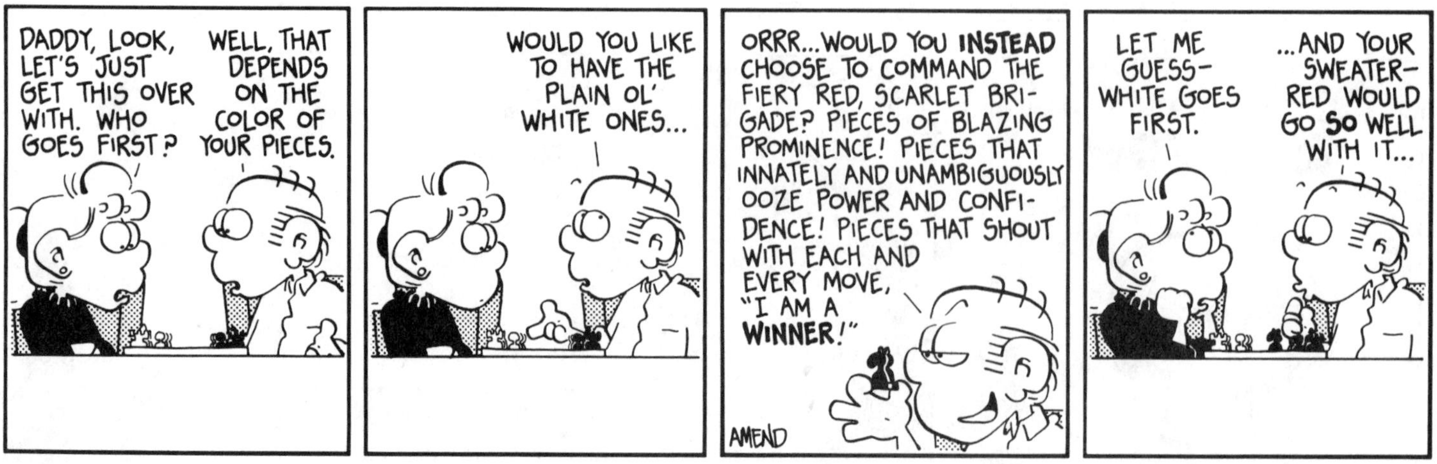
DADDY, LOOK, LET'S JUST GET THIS OVER WITH. WHO GOES FIRST?
WELL, THAT DEPENDS ON THE COLOR OF YOUR PIECES.
WOULD YOU LIKE TO HAVE THE PLAIN OL' WHITE ONES...
ORRR...WOULD YOU **INSTEAD** CHOOSE TO COMMAND THE FIERY RED, SCARLET BRI-GADE? PIECES OF BLAZING PROMINENCE! PIECES THAT INNATELY AND UNAMBIGUOUSLY OOZE POWER AND CONFI-DENCE! PIECES THAT SHOUT WITH EACH AND EVERY MOVE, "I AM A **WINNER**!"
AMEND
LET ME GUESS- WHITE GOES FIRST.
...AND YOUR SWEATER- RED WOULD GO **SO** WELL WITH IT...

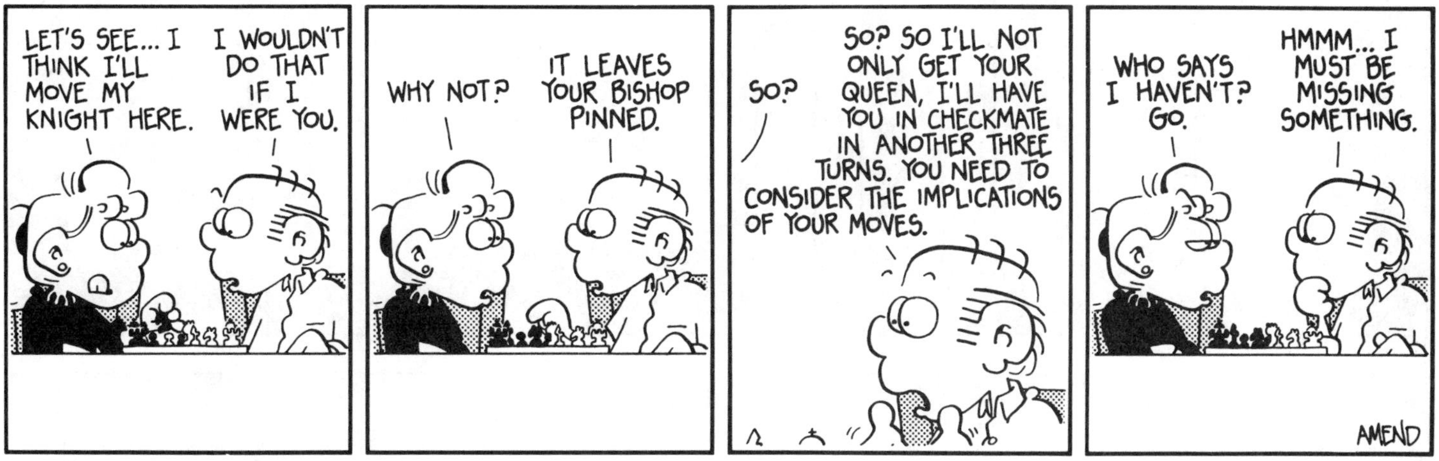
LET'S SEE... I THINK I'LL MOVE MY KNIGHT HERE.
I WOULDN'T DO THAT IF I WERE YOU.
WHY NOT?
IT LEAVES YOUR BISHOP PINNED.
SO?
SO? SO I'LL NOT ONLY GET YOUR QUEEN, I'LL HAVE YOU IN CHECKMATE IN ANOTHER THREE TURNS. YOU NEED TO CONSIDER THE IMPLICATIONS OF YOUR MOVES.
WHO SAYS I HAVEN'T? GO.
HMMM... I MUST BE MISSING SOMETHING.
AMEND

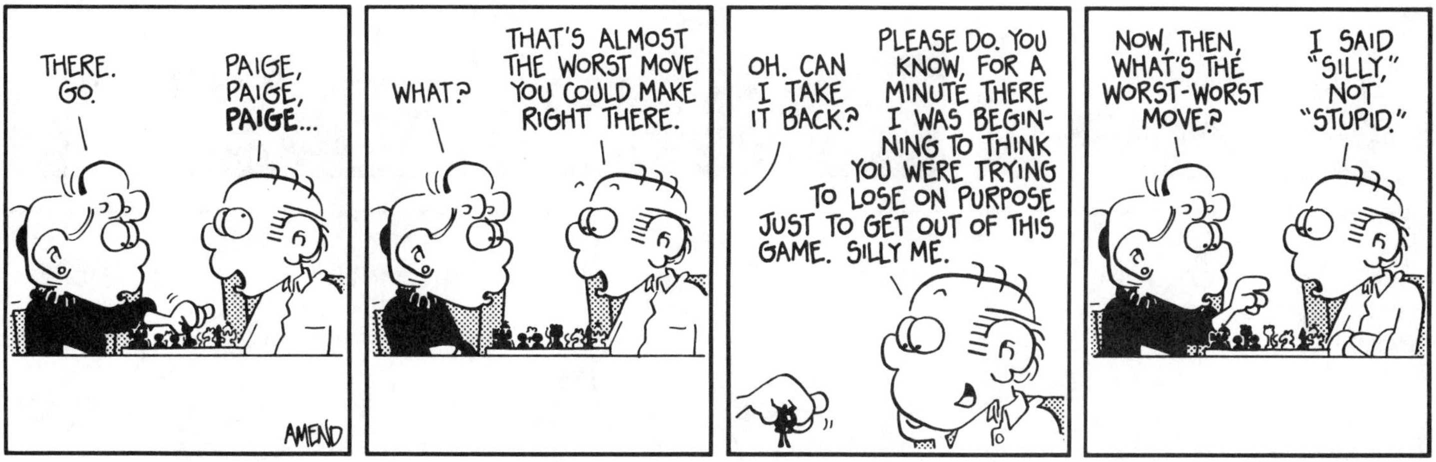
THERE. GO.
PAIGE, PAIGE, **PAIGE**...
AMEND
WHAT?
THAT'S ALMOST THE WORST MOVE YOU COULD MAKE RIGHT THERE.
OH. CAN I TAKE IT BACK?
PLEASE DO. YOU KNOW, FOR A MINUTE THERE I WAS BEGINNING TO THINK YOU WERE TRYING TO LOSE ON PURPOSE JUST TO GET OUT OF THIS GAME. SILLY ME.
NOW, THEN, WHAT'S THE WORST-WORST MOVE?
I SAID "SILLY," NOT "STUPID."

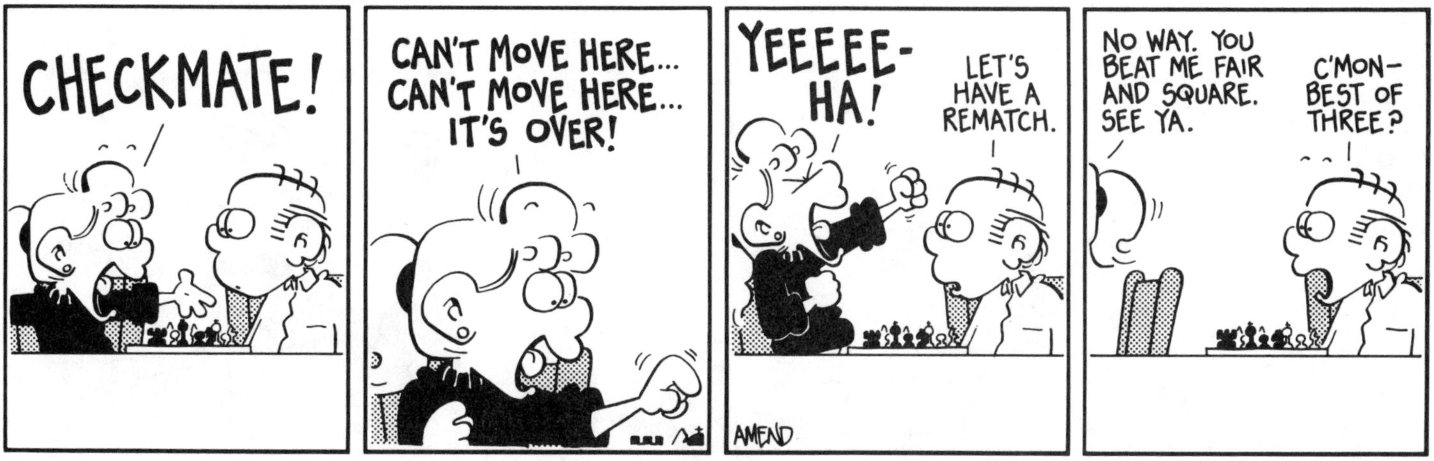
CHECKMATE!
CAN'T MOVE HERE... CAN'T MOVE HERE... IT'S OVER!
YEEEEE-HA!
LET'S HAVE A REMATCH.
AMEND
NO WAY. YOU BEAT ME FAIR AND SQUARE. SEE YA.
C'MON-BEST OF THREE?

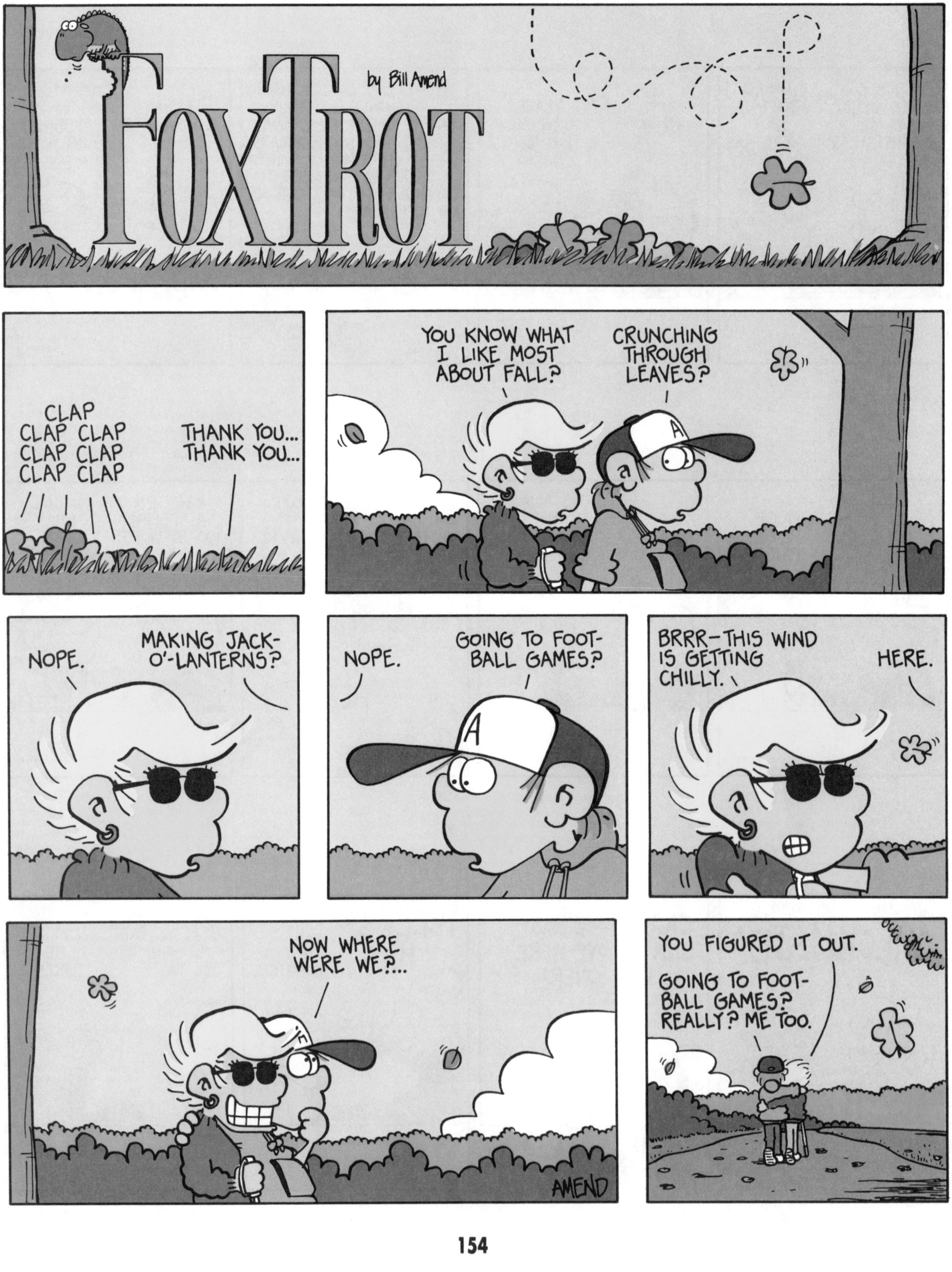

FOXTROT
by Bill Amend
CLAP
CLAP CLAP
CLAP CLAP
CLAP CLAP
THANK YOU... THANK YOU...
YOU KNOW WHAT I LIKE MOST ABOUT FALL?
CRUNCHING THROUGH LEAVES?
NOPE.
MAKING JACK-O'-LANTERNS?
NOPE.
GOING TO FOOT-BALL GAMES?
BRRR—THIS WIND IS GETTING CHILLY.
HERE.
NOW WHERE WERE WE?...
AMEND
YOU FIGURED IT OUT.
GOING TO FOOT-BALL GAMES? REALLY? ME TOO.

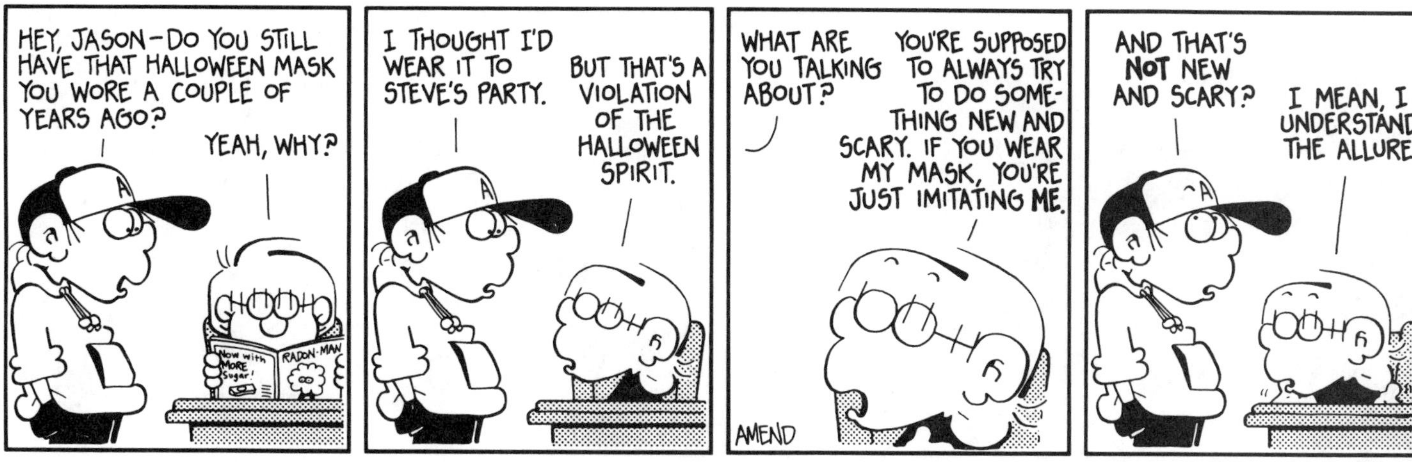
HEY, JASON—DO YOU STILL HAVE THAT HALLOWEEN MASK YOU WORE A COUPLE OF YEARS AGO?
YEAH, WHY?
I THOUGHT I'D WEAR IT TO STEVE'S PARTY.
BUT THAT'S A VIOLATION OF THE HALLOWEEN SPIRIT.
WHAT ARE YOU TALKING ABOUT?
YOU'RE SUPPOSED TO ALWAYS TRY TO DO SOMETHING NEW AND SCARY. IF YOU WEAR MY MASK, YOU'RE JUST IMITATING **ME**.
AMEND
AND THAT'S **NOT** NEW AND SCARY?
I MEAN, I UNDERSTAND THE ALLURE...
NOW with MORE Sugar!
RADON-MAN

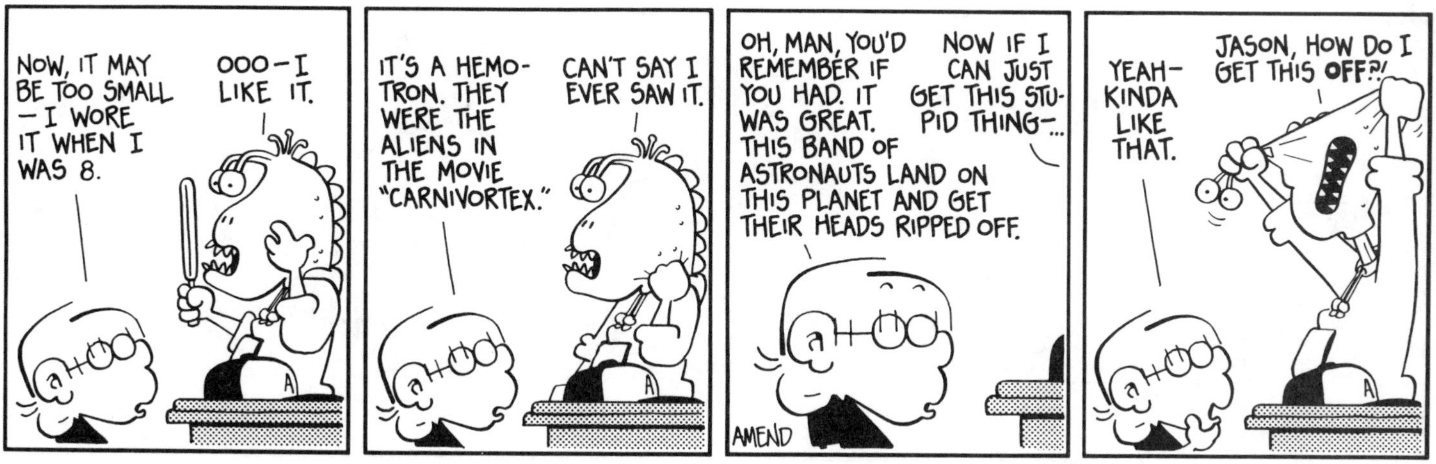
NOW, IT MAY BE TOO SMALL—I WORE IT WHEN I WAS 8.
OOO—I LIKE IT.
IT'S A HEMOTRON. THEY WERE THE ALIENS IN THE MOVIE "CARNIVORTEX."
CAN'T SAY I EVER SAW IT.
OH, MAN, YOU'D REMEMBER IF YOU HAD. IT WAS GREAT. THIS BAND OF ASTRONAUTS LAND ON THIS PLANET AND GET THEIR HEADS RIPPED OFF.
NOW IF I CAN JUST GET THIS STUPID THING—...
AMEND
YEAH—KINDA LIKE THAT.
JASON, HOW DO I GET THIS **OFF**?!

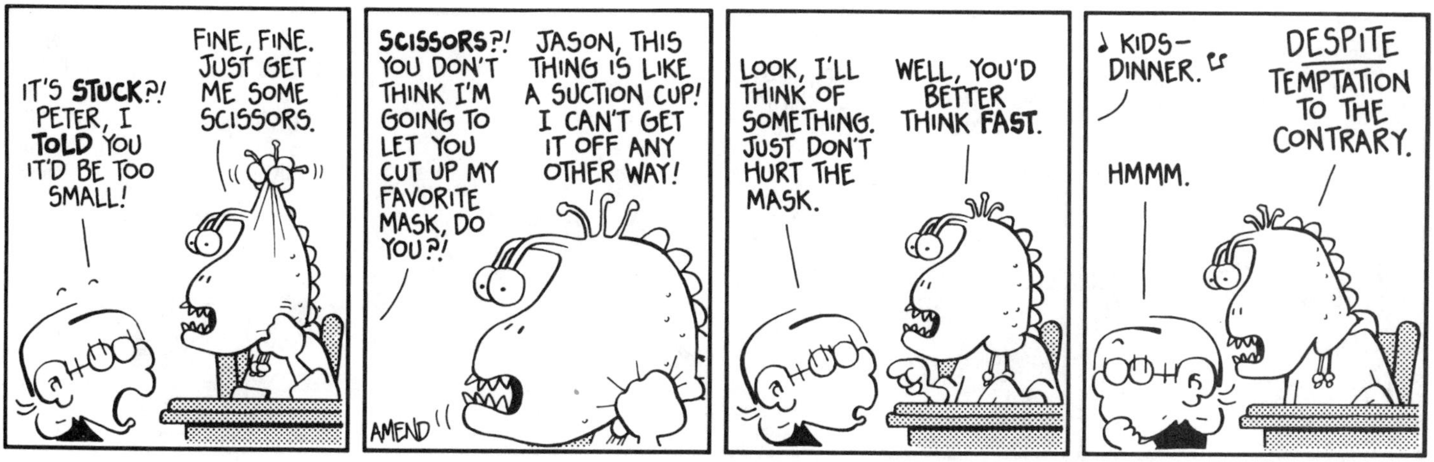
IT'S **STUCK**?! PETER, I **TOLD** YOU IT'D BE TOO SMALL!
FINE, FINE. JUST GET ME SOME SCISSORS.
SCISSORS?! YOU DON'T THINK I'M GOING TO LET YOU CUT UP MY FAVORITE MASK, DO YOU?!
JASON, THIS THING IS LIKE A SUCTION CUP! I CAN'T GET IT OFF ANY OTHER WAY!
AMEND
LOOK, I'LL THINK OF SOMETHING. JUST DON'T HURT THE MASK.
WELL, YOU'D BETTER THINK **FAST**.
♪ KIDS—DINNER.
HMMM.
DESPITE TEMPTATION TO THE CONTRARY.

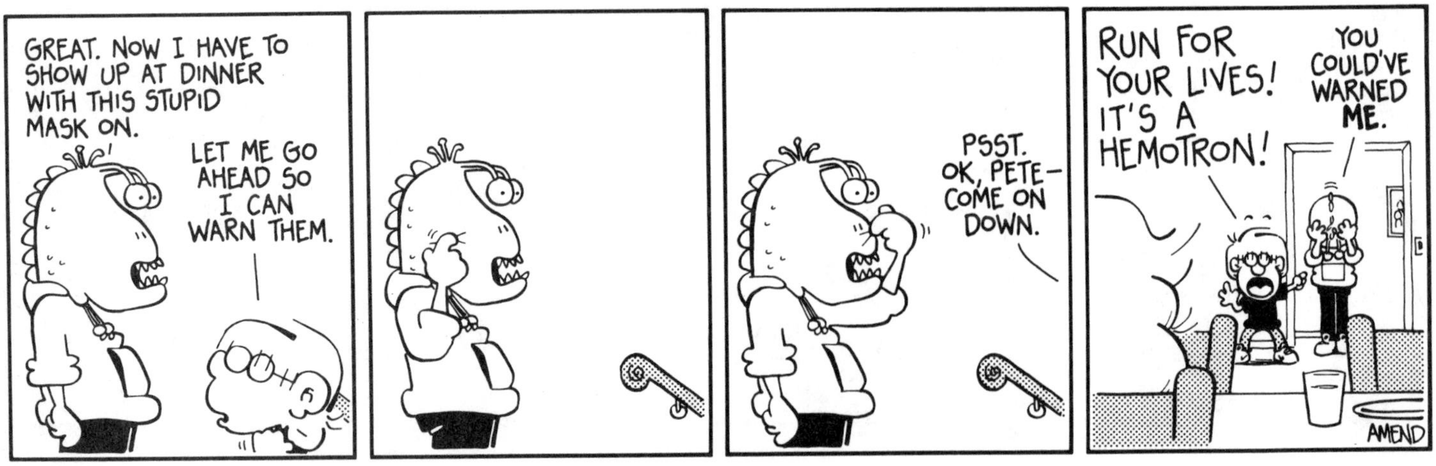
GREAT. NOW I HAVE TO SHOW UP AT DINNER WITH THIS STUPID MASK ON.
LET ME GO AHEAD SO I CAN WARN THEM.
PSST. OK, PETE– COME ON DOWN.
RUN FOR YOUR LIVES! IT'S A HEMOTRON!
YOU COULD'VE WARNED **ME.**
AMEND

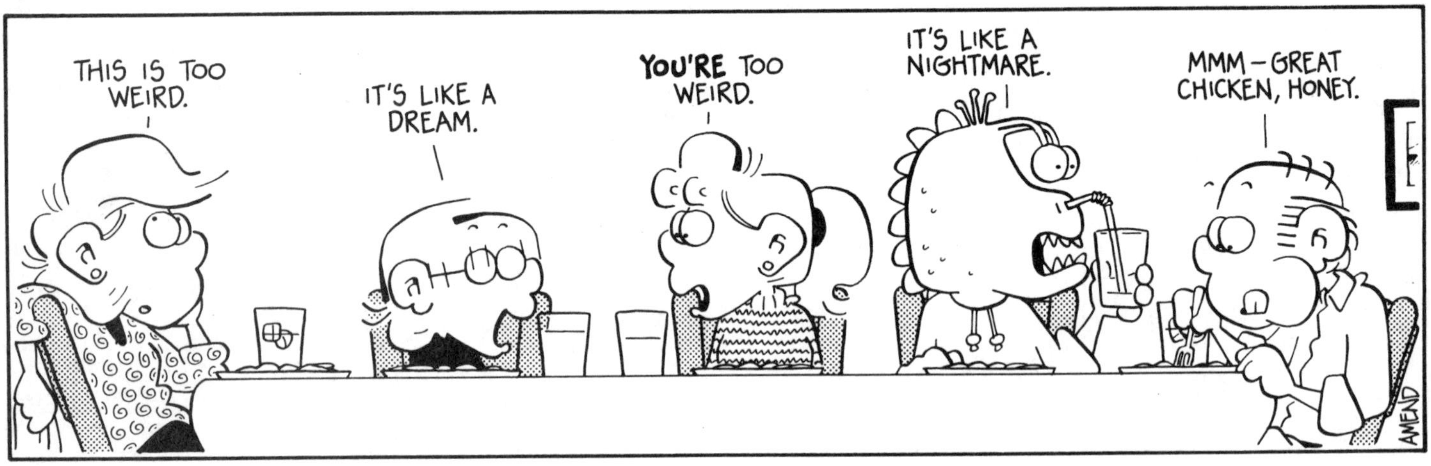
THIS IS TOO WEIRD.
IT'S LIKE A DREAM.
YOU'RE TOO WEIRD.
IT'S LIKE A NIGHTMARE.
MMM–GREAT CHICKEN, HONEY.
AMEND

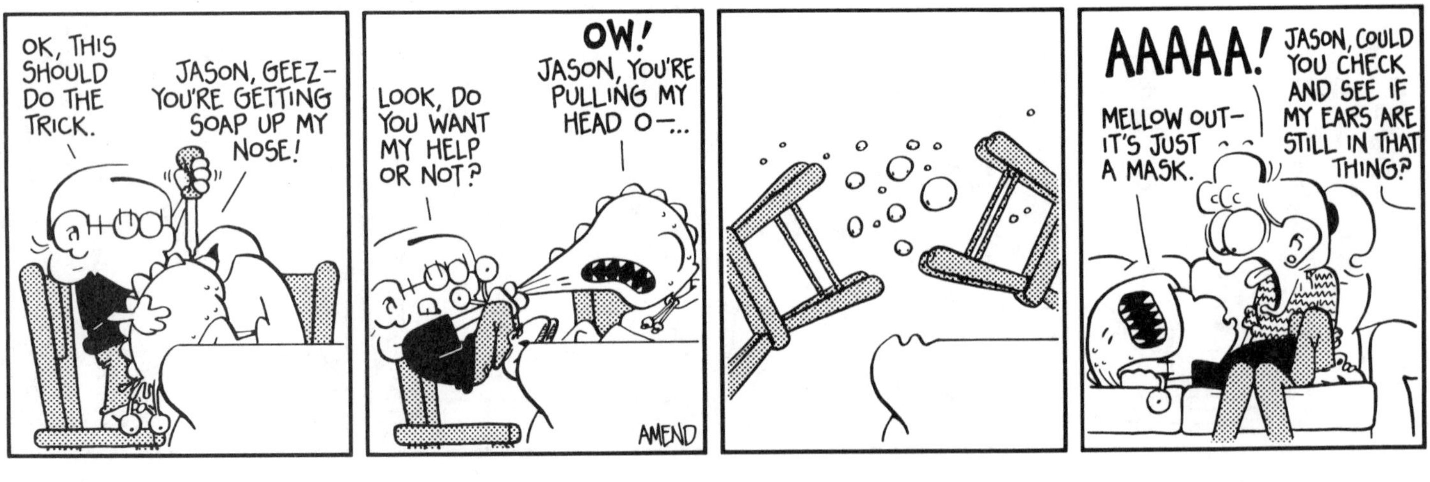
OK, THIS SHOULD DO THE TRICK.
JASON, GEEZ– YOU'RE GETTING SOAP UP MY NOSE!
LOOK, DO YOU WANT MY HELP OR NOT?
OW! JASON, YOU'RE PULLING MY HEAD O–...
AMEND
AAAAA!
MELLOW OUT– IT'S JUST A MASK.
JASON, COULD YOU CHECK AND SEE IF MY EARS ARE STILL IN THAT THING?

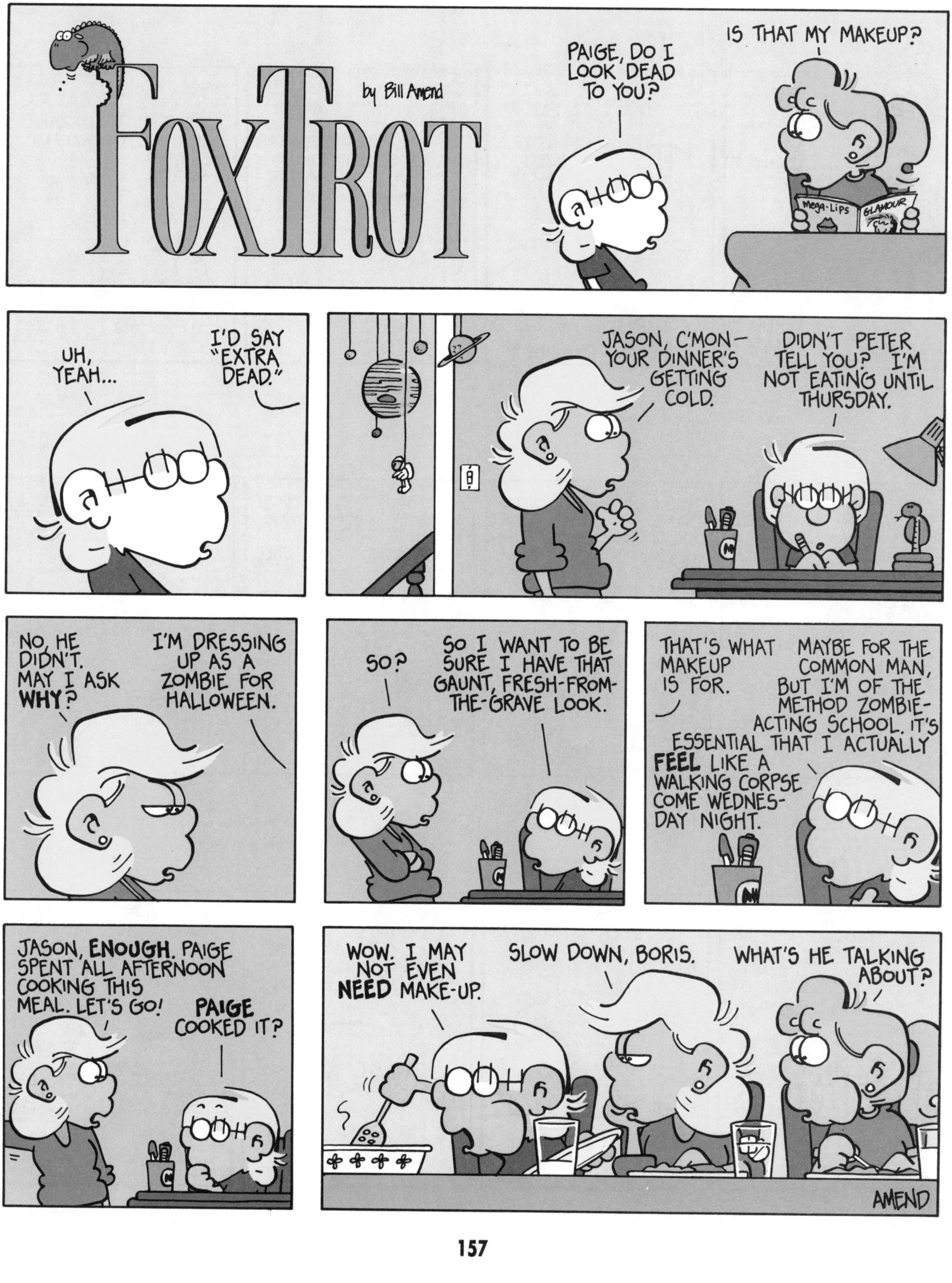
FoxTrot
by Bill Amend
PAIGE, DO I LOOK DEAD TO YOU?
IS THAT MY MAKEUP?
Mega-Lips
GLAMOUR
UH, YEAH...
I'D SAY "EXTRA DEAD."
JASON, C'MON— YOUR DINNER'S GETTING COLD.
DIDN'T PETER TELL YOU? I'M NOT EATING UNTIL THURSDAY.
NO, HE DIDN'T. MAY I ASK **WHY**?
I'M DRESSING UP AS A ZOMBIE FOR HALLOWEEN.
SO?
SO I WANT TO BE SURE I HAVE THAT GAUNT, FRESH-FROM-THE-GRAVE LOOK.
THAT'S WHAT MAKEUP IS FOR.
MAYBE FOR THE COMMON MAN, BUT I'M OF THE METHOD ZOMBIE-ACTING SCHOOL. IT'S ESSENTIAL THAT I ACTUALLY **FEEL** LIKE A WALKING CORPSE COME WEDNES-DAY NIGHT.
JASON, **ENOUGH**. PAIGE SPENT ALL AFTERNOON COOKING THIS MEAL. LET'S GO!
PAIGE COOKED IT?
WOW. I MAY NOT EVEN **NEED** MAKE-UP.
SLOW DOWN, BORIS.
WHAT'S HE TALKING ABOUT?
AMEND

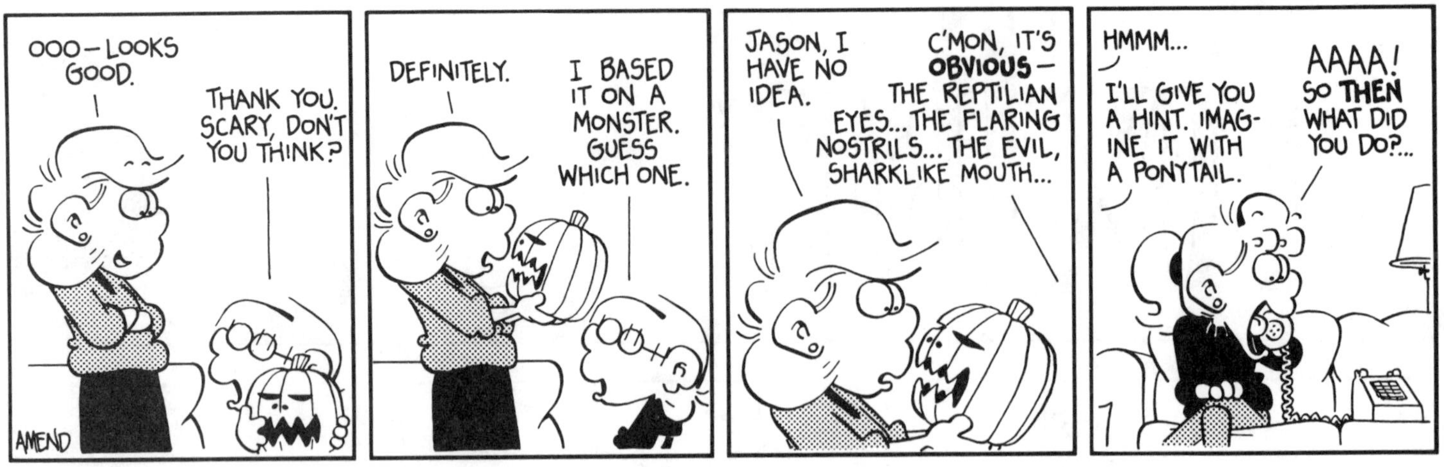
OOO—LOOKS GOOD.
THANK YOU. SCARY, DON'T YOU THINK?
AMEND
DEFINITELY.
I BASED IT ON A MONSTER. GUESS WHICH ONE.
JASON, I HAVE NO IDEA.
C'MON, IT'S **OBVIOUS**—THE REPTILIAN EYES... THE FLARING NOSTRILS... THE EVIL, SHARKLIKE MOUTH...
HMMM...
I'LL GIVE YOU A HINT. IMAGINE IT WITH A PONYTAIL.
AAAA! SO **THEN** WHAT DID YOU DO?...

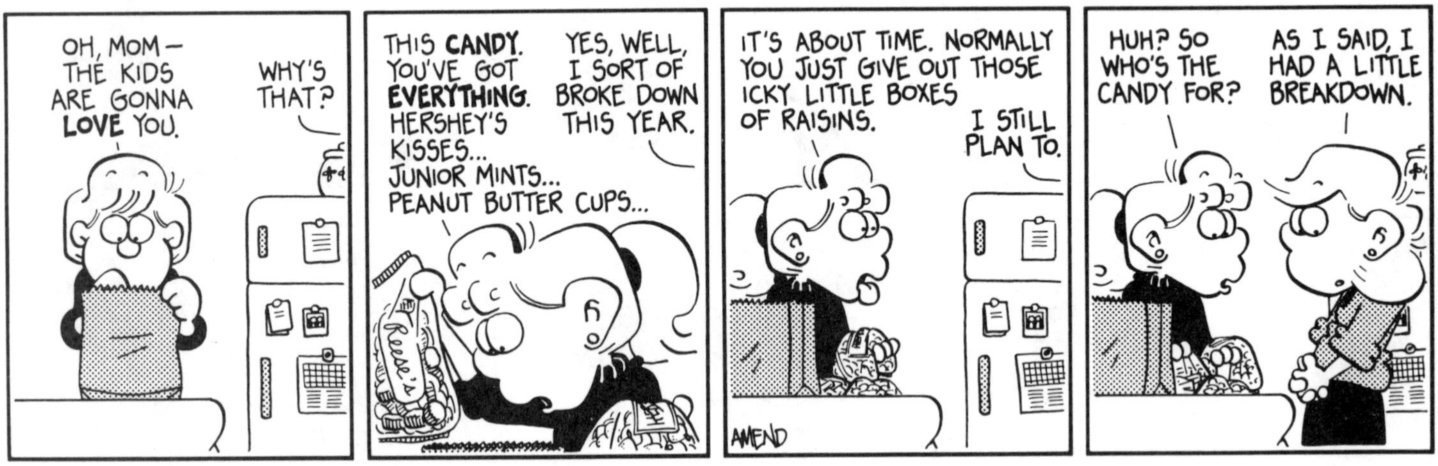
OH, MOM—THE KIDS ARE GONNA **LOVE** YOU.
WHY'S THAT?
THIS **CANDY**. YOU'VE GOT **EVERYTHING**. HERSHEY'S KISSES... JUNIOR MINTS... PEANUT BUTTER CUPS...
YES, WELL, I SORT OF BROKE DOWN THIS YEAR.
IT'S ABOUT TIME. NORMALLY YOU JUST GIVE OUT THOSE ICKY LITTLE BOXES OF RAISINS.
I STILL PLAN TO.
AMEND
HUH? SO WHO'S THE CANDY FOR?
AS I SAID, I HAD A LITTLE BREAKDOWN.

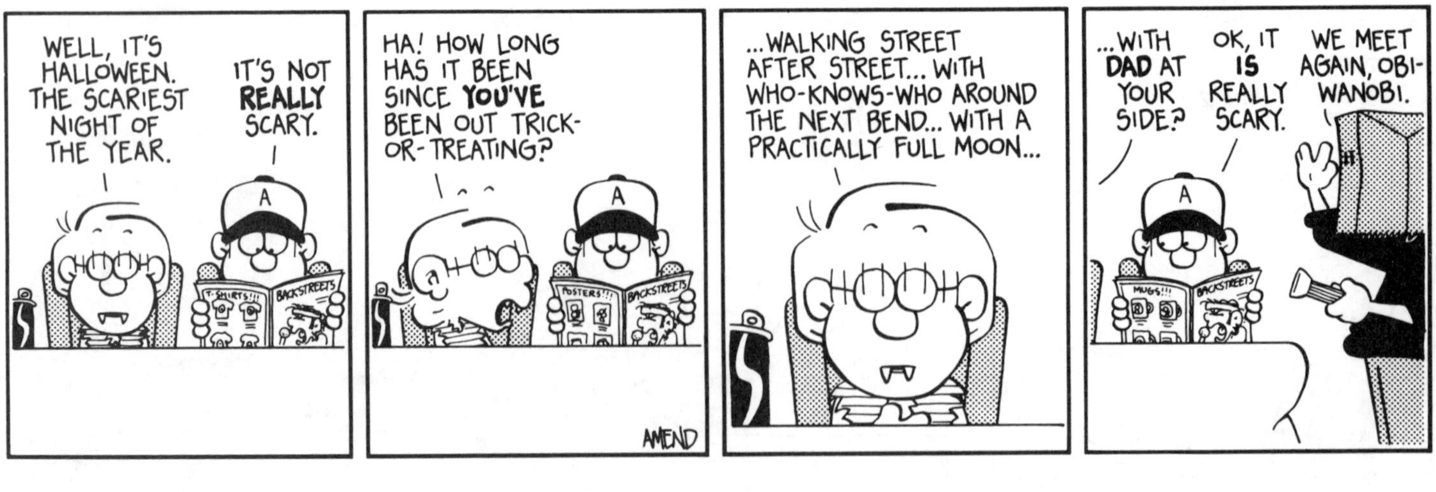
WELL, IT'S HALLOWEEN. THE SCARIEST NIGHT OF THE YEAR.
IT'S NOT **REALLY** SCARY.
BACKSTREETS
HA! HOW LONG HAS IT BEEN SINCE **YOU'VE** BEEN OUT TRICK-OR-TREATING?
AMEND
...WALKING STREET AFTER STREET... WITH WHO-KNOWS-WHO AROUND THE NEXT BEND... WITH A PRACTICALLY FULL MOON...
...WITH **DAD** AT YOUR SIDE?
OK, IT **IS** REALLY SCARY.
WE MEET AGAIN, OBI-WANOBI.

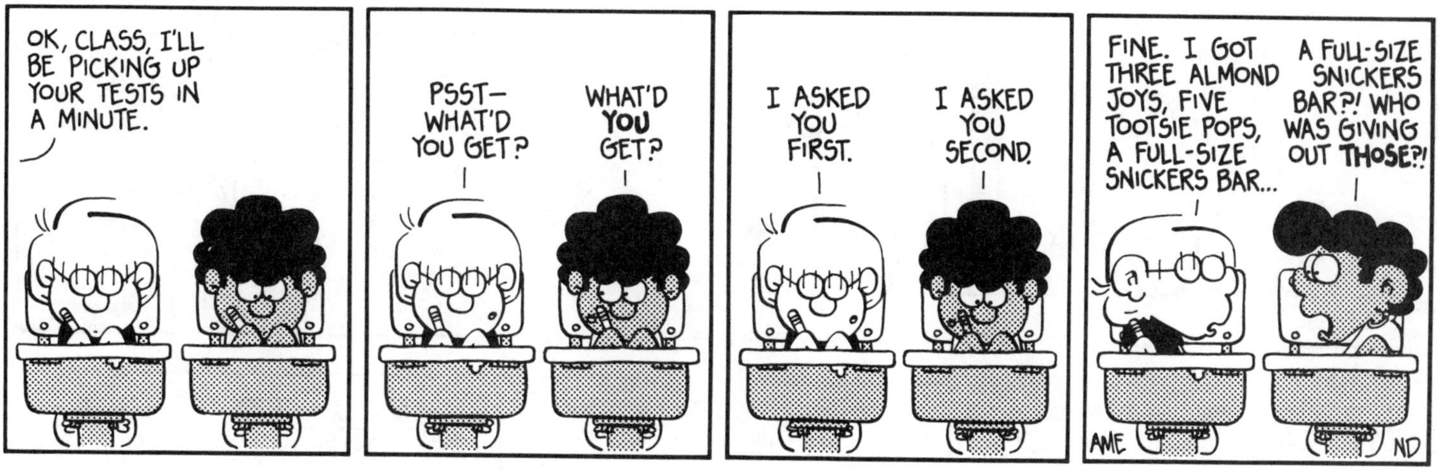
OK, CLASS, I'LL BE PICKING UP YOUR TESTS IN A MINUTE.
PSST— WHAT'D YOU GET?
WHAT'D **YOU** GET?
I ASKED YOU FIRST.
I ASKED YOU SECOND.
FINE. I GOT THREE ALMOND JOYS, FIVE TOOTSIE POPS, A FULL-SIZE SNICKERS BAR...
A FULL-SIZE SNICKERS BAR?! WHO WAS GIVING OUT **THOSE**?!
AME ND

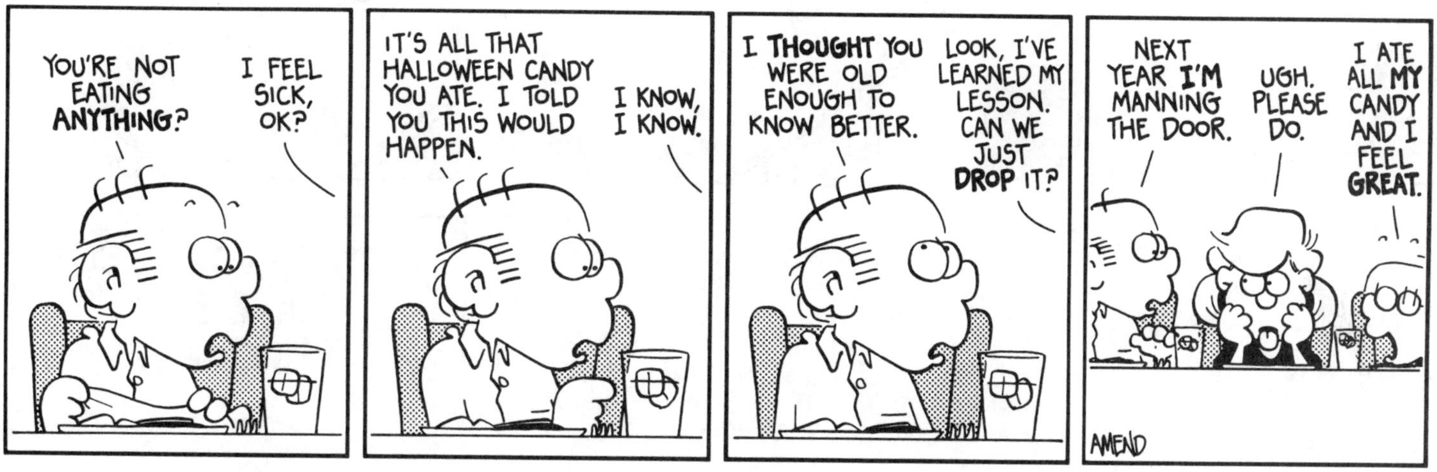
YOU'RE NOT EATING **ANYTHING**?
I FEEL SICK, OK?
IT'S ALL THAT HALLOWEEN CANDY YOU ATE. I TOLD YOU THIS WOULD HAPPEN.
I KNOW, I KNOW.
I **THOUGHT** YOU WERE OLD ENOUGH TO KNOW BETTER.
LOOK, I'VE LEARNED MY LESSON. CAN WE JUST **DROP** IT?
NEXT YEAR **I'M** MANNING THE DOOR.
UGH. PLEASE DO.
I ATE ALL **MY** CANDY AND I FEEL **GREAT**.
AMEND

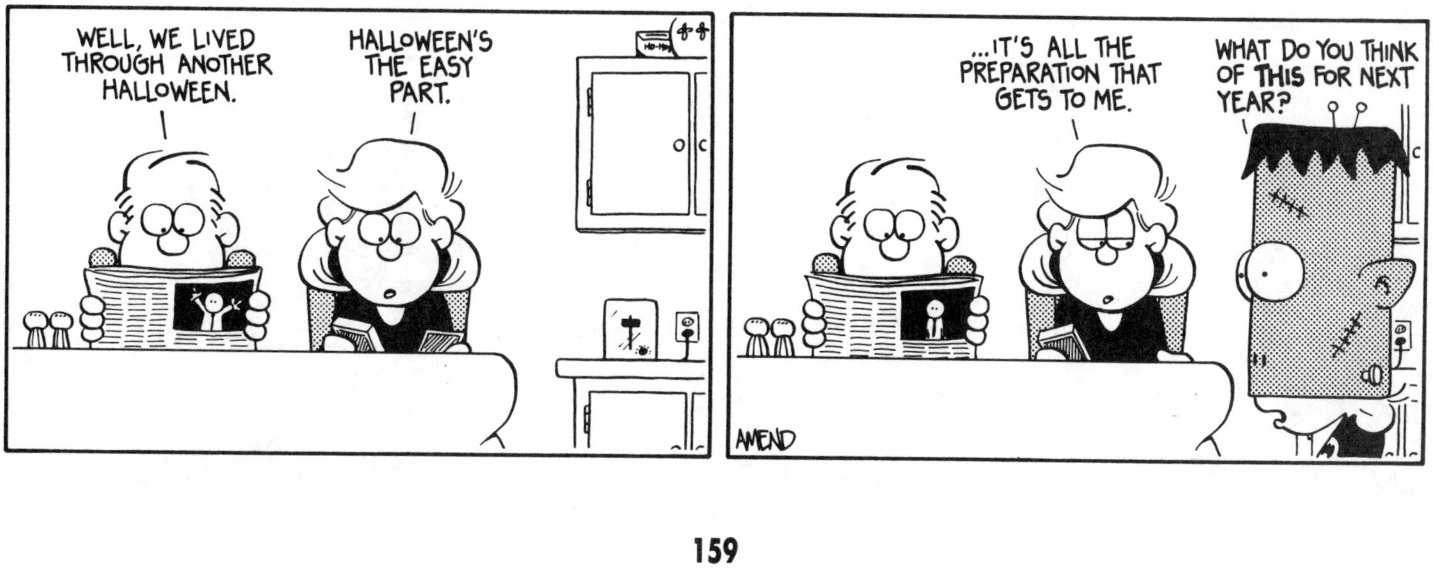
WELL, WE LIVED THROUGH ANOTHER HALLOWEEN.
HALLOWEEN'S THE EASY PART.
...IT'S ALL THE PREPARATION THAT GETS TO ME.
WHAT DO YOU THINK OF **THIS** FOR NEXT YEAR?
AMEND

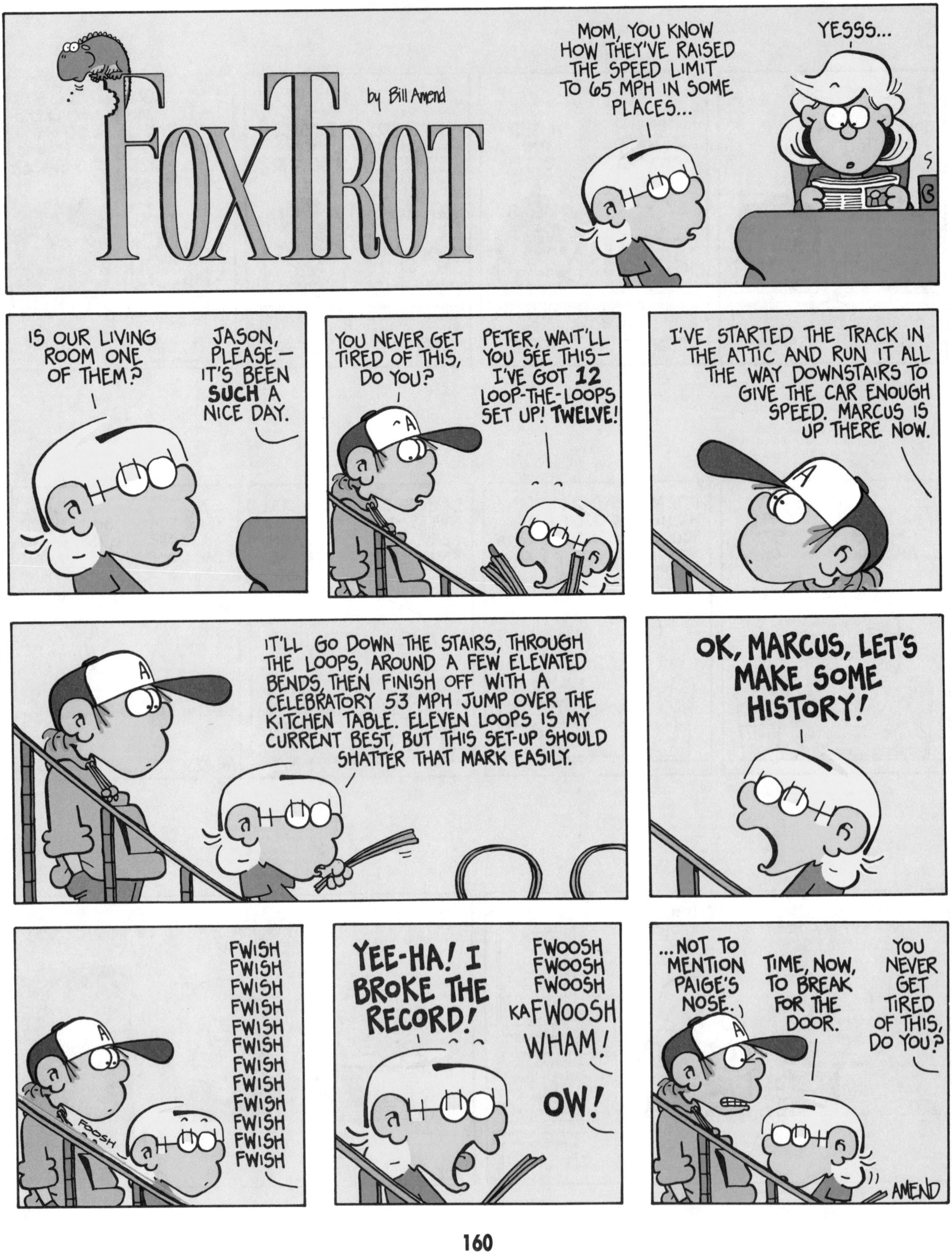
FoxTrot
by Bill Amend
MOM, YOU KNOW HOW THEY'VE RAISED THE SPEED LIMIT TO 65 MPH IN SOME PLACES...
YESSS...
IS OUR LIVING ROOM ONE OF THEM?
JASON, PLEASE— IT'S BEEN SUCH A NICE DAY.
YOU NEVER GET TIRED OF THIS, DO YOU?
PETER, WAIT'LL YOU SEE THIS— I'VE GOT 12 LOOP-THE-LOOPS SET UP! TWELVE!
I'VE STARTED THE TRACK IN THE ATTIC AND RUN IT ALL THE WAY DOWNSTAIRS TO GIVE THE CAR ENOUGH SPEED. MARCUS IS UP THERE NOW.
IT'LL GO DOWN THE STAIRS, THROUGH THE LOOPS, AROUND A FEW ELEVATED BENDS, THEN FINISH OFF WITH A CELEBRATORY 53 MPH JUMP OVER THE KITCHEN TABLE. ELEVEN LOOPS IS MY CURRENT BEST, BUT THIS SET-UP SHOULD SHATTER THAT MARK EASILY.
OK, MARCUS, LET'S MAKE SOME HISTORY!
FOOSH
FWISH FWISH FWISH FWISH FWISH FWISH FWISH FWISH FWISH FWISH FWISH FWISH
YEE-HA! I BROKE THE RECORD!
FWOOSH FWOOSH FWOOSH
KAFWOOSH
WHAM!
OW!
...NOT TO MENTION PAIGE'S NOSE.
TIME, NOW, TO BREAK FOR THE DOOR.
YOU NEVER GET TIRED OF THIS, DO YOU?
AMEND

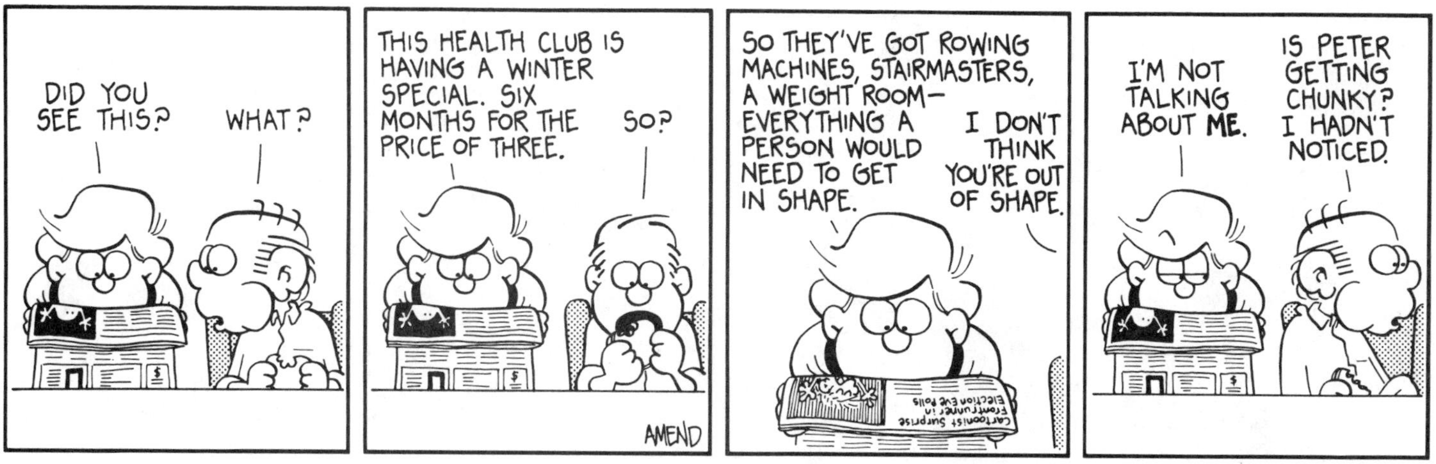
DID YOU SEE THIS?
WHAT?
THIS HEALTH CLUB IS HAVING A WINTER SPECIAL. SIX MONTHS FOR THE PRICE OF THREE.
SO?
AMEND
SO THEY'VE GOT ROWING MACHINES, STAIRMASTERS, A WEIGHT ROOM— EVERYTHING A PERSON WOULD NEED TO GET IN SHAPE.
I DON'T THINK YOU'RE OUT OF SHAPE.
Cartoonist Surprise Frontrunner in Election Eve Polls
I'M NOT TALKING ABOUT **ME**.
IS PETER GETTING CHUNKY? I HADN'T NOTICED.

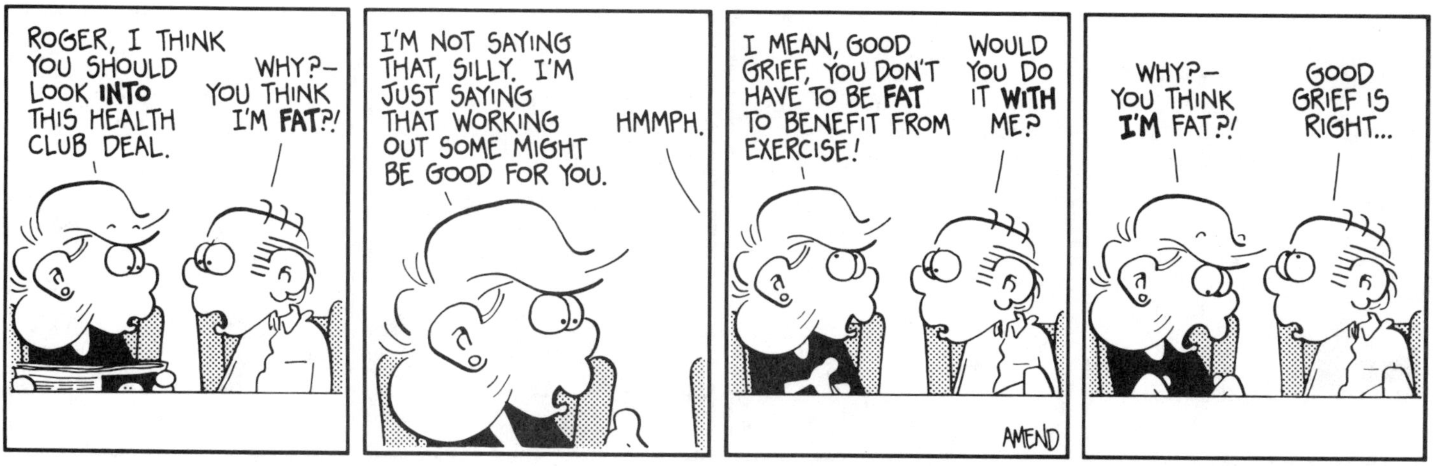
ROGER, I THINK YOU SHOULD LOOK **INTO** THIS HEALTH CLUB DEAL.
WHY?— YOU THINK I'M **FAT**?!
I'M NOT SAYING THAT, SILLY. I'M JUST SAYING THAT WORKING OUT SOME MIGHT BE GOOD FOR YOU.
HMMPH.
I MEAN, GOOD GRIEF, YOU DON'T HAVE TO BE **FAT** TO BENEFIT FROM EXERCISE!
WOULD YOU DO IT **WITH** ME?
AMEND
WHY?— YOU THINK **I'M** FAT?!
GOOD GRIEF IS RIGHT...

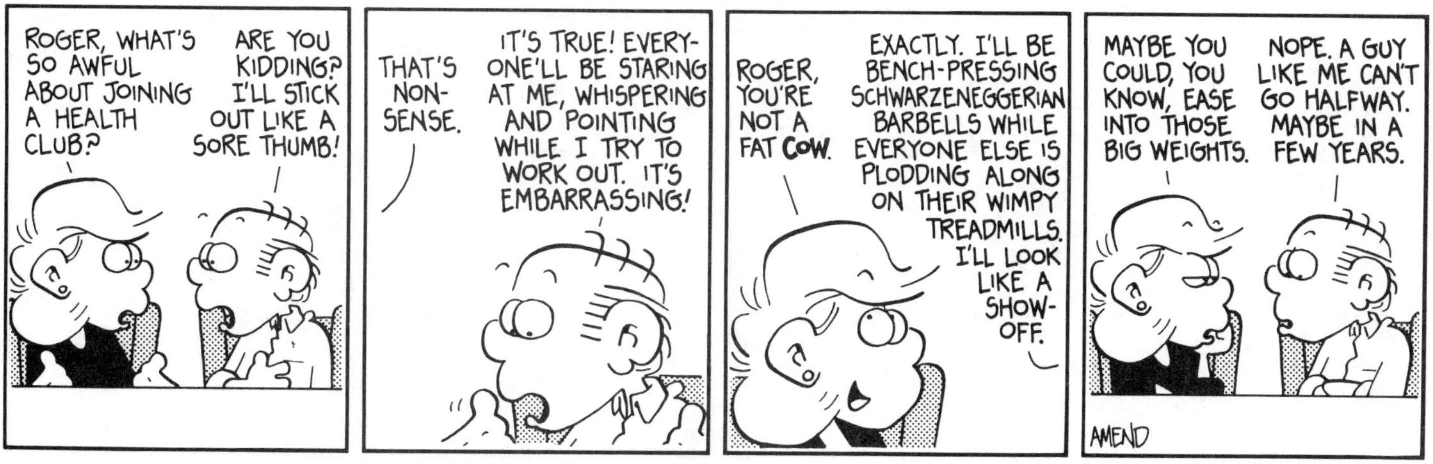
ROGER, WHAT'S SO AWFUL ABOUT JOINING A HEALTH CLUB?
ARE YOU KIDDING? I'LL STICK OUT LIKE A SORE THUMB!
THAT'S NON-SENSE.
IT'S TRUE! EVERY-ONE'LL BE STARING AT ME, WHISPERING AND POINTING WHILE I TRY TO WORK OUT. IT'S EMBARRASSING!
ROGER, YOU'RE NOT A FAT **COW**.
EXACTLY. I'LL BE BENCH-PRESSING SCHWARZENEGGERIAN BARBELLS WHILE EVERYONE ELSE IS PLODDING ALONG ON THEIR WIMPY TREADMILLS. I'LL LOOK LIKE A SHOW-OFF.
MAYBE YOU COULD, YOU KNOW, EASE INTO THOSE BIG WEIGHTS.
NOPE. A GUY LIKE ME CAN'T GO HALFWAY. MAYBE IN A FEW YEARS.
AMEND

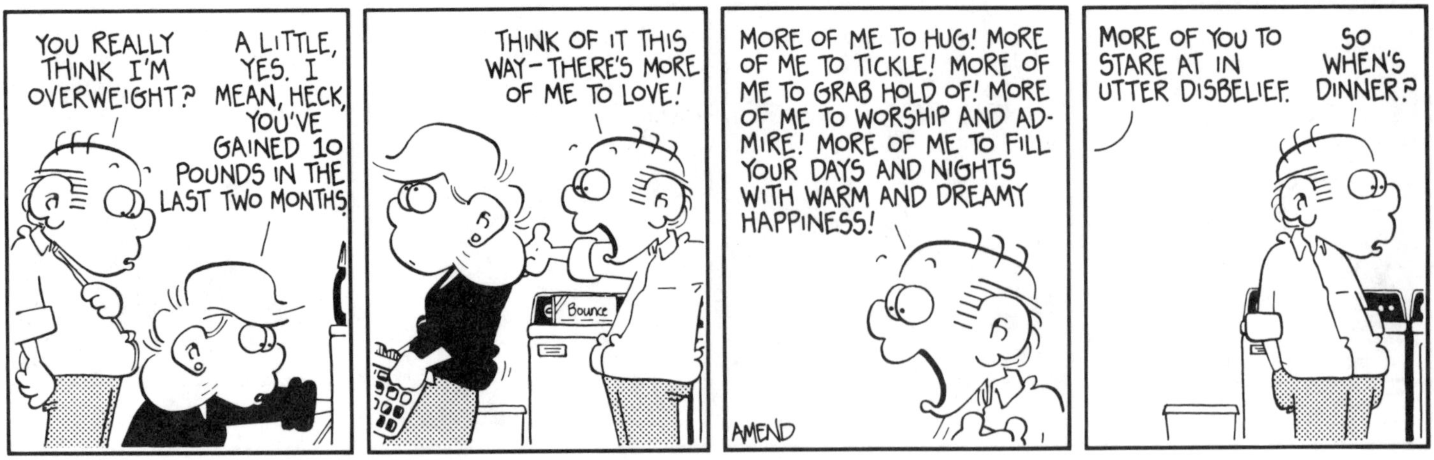
YOU REALLY THINK I'M OVERWEIGHT?
A LITTLE, YES. I MEAN, HECK, YOU'VE GAINED 10 POUNDS IN THE LAST TWO MONTHS.
THINK OF IT THIS WAY–THERE'S MORE OF ME TO LOVE!
Bounce
MORE OF ME TO HUG! MORE OF ME TO TICKLE! MORE OF ME TO GRAB HOLD OF! MORE OF ME TO WORSHIP AND ADMIRE! MORE OF ME TO FILL YOUR DAYS AND NIGHTS WITH WARM AND DREAMY HAPPINESS!
AMEND
MORE OF YOU TO STARE AT IN UTTER DISBELIEF.
SO WHEN'S DINNER?

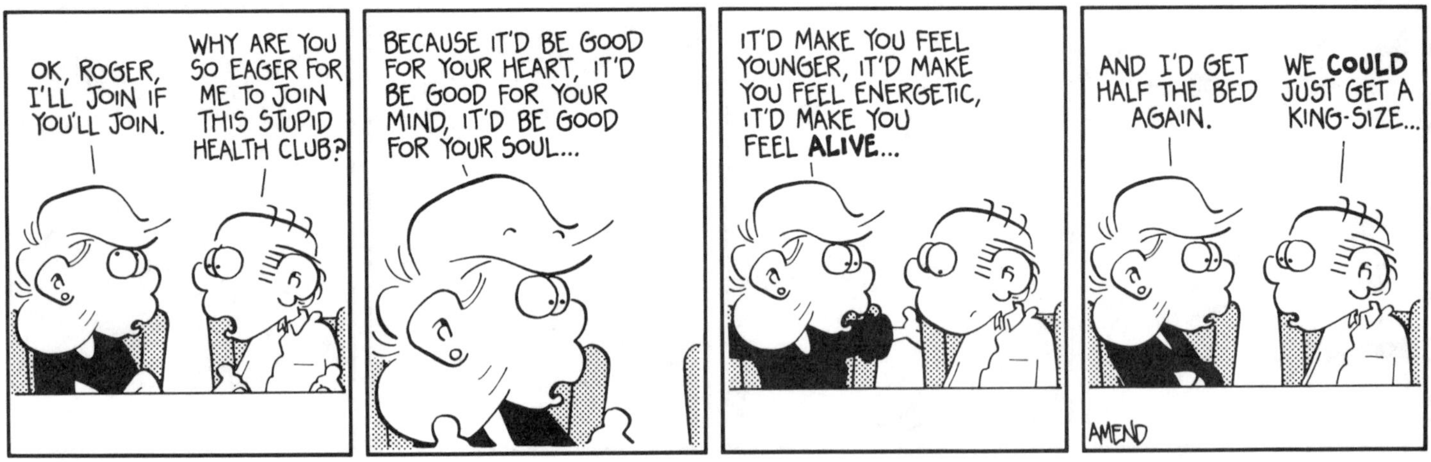
OK, ROGER, I'LL JOIN IF YOU'LL JOIN.
WHY ARE YOU SO EAGER FOR ME TO JOIN THIS STUPID HEALTH CLUB?
BECAUSE IT'D BE GOOD FOR YOUR HEART, IT'D BE GOOD FOR YOUR MIND, IT'D BE GOOD FOR YOUR SOUL...
IT'D MAKE YOU FEEL YOUNGER, IT'D MAKE YOU FEEL ENERGETIC, IT'D MAKE YOU FEEL **ALIVE**...
AND I'D GET HALF THE BED AGAIN.
WE **COULD** JUST GET A KING-SIZE...
AMEND

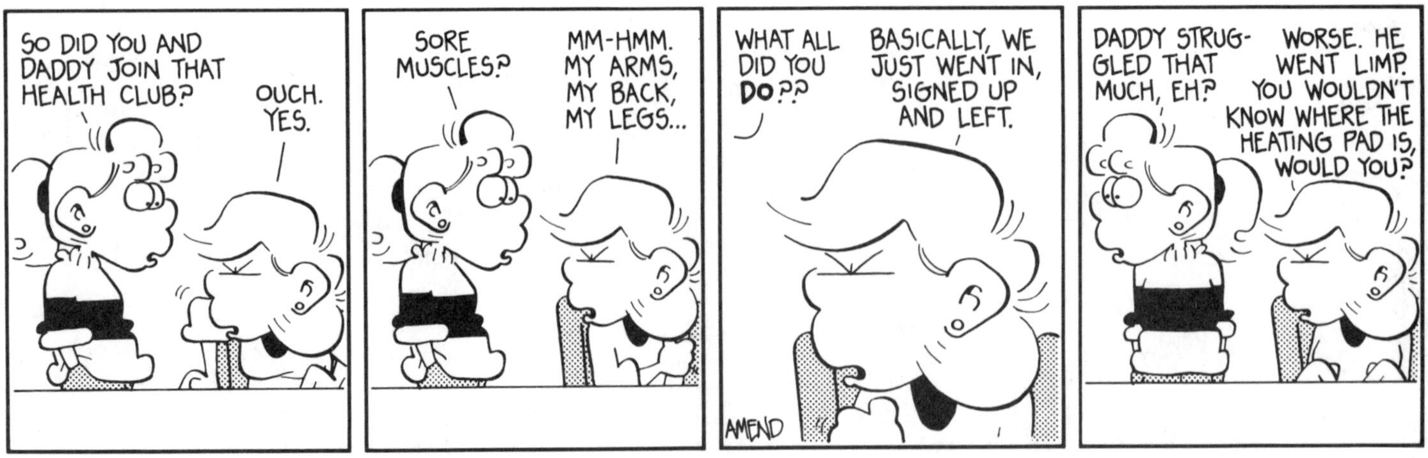
SO DID YOU AND DADDY JOIN THAT HEALTH CLUB?
OUCH. YES.
SORE MUSCLES?
MM-HMM. MY ARMS, MY BACK, MY LEGS...
WHAT ALL DID YOU **DO**??
BASICALLY, WE JUST WENT IN, SIGNED UP AND LEFT.
AMEND
DADDY STRUGGLED THAT MUCH, EH?
WORSE. HE WENT LIMP. YOU WOULDN'T KNOW WHERE THE HEATING PAD IS, WOULD YOU?

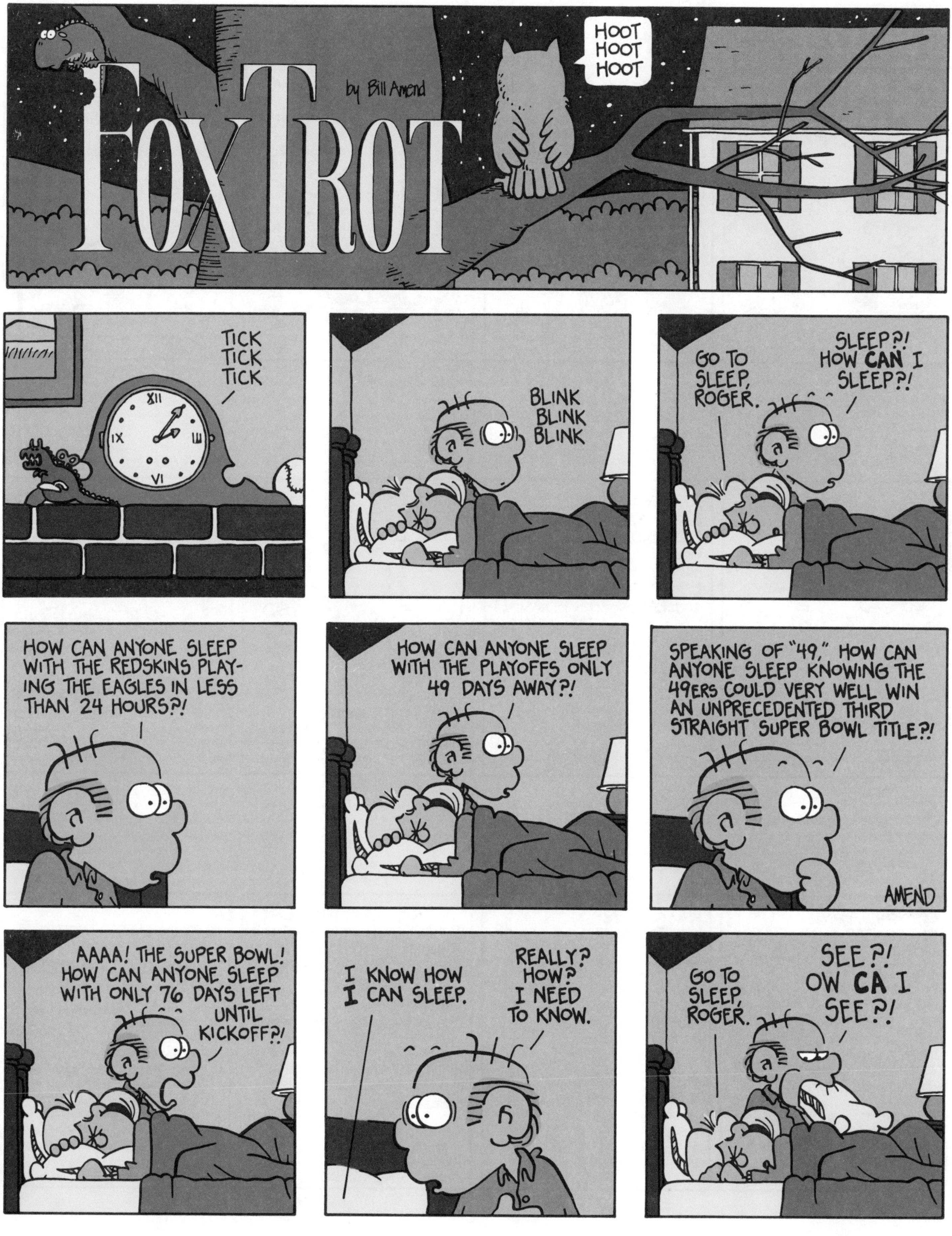
FOXTROT
by Bill Amend
HOOT HOOT HOOT
TICK TICK TICK
BLINK BLINK BLINK
GO TO SLEEP, ROGER.
SLEEP?! HOW **CAN** I SLEEP?!
HOW CAN ANYONE SLEEP WITH THE REDSKINS PLAYING THE EAGLES IN LESS THAN 24 HOURS?!
HOW CAN ANYONE SLEEP WITH THE PLAYOFFS ONLY 49 DAYS AWAY?!
SPEAKING OF "49," HOW CAN ANYONE SLEEP KNOWING THE 49ERS COULD VERY WELL WIN AN UNPRECEDENTED THIRD STRAIGHT SUPER BOWL TITLE?!
AMEND
AAAA! THE SUPER BOWL! HOW CAN ANYONE SLEEP WITH ONLY 76 DAYS LEFT UNTIL KICKOFF?!
I KNOW HOW **I** CAN SLEEP.
REALLY? HOW? I NEED TO KNOW.
GO TO SLEEP, ROGER.
SEE?! OW **CA** I SEE?!

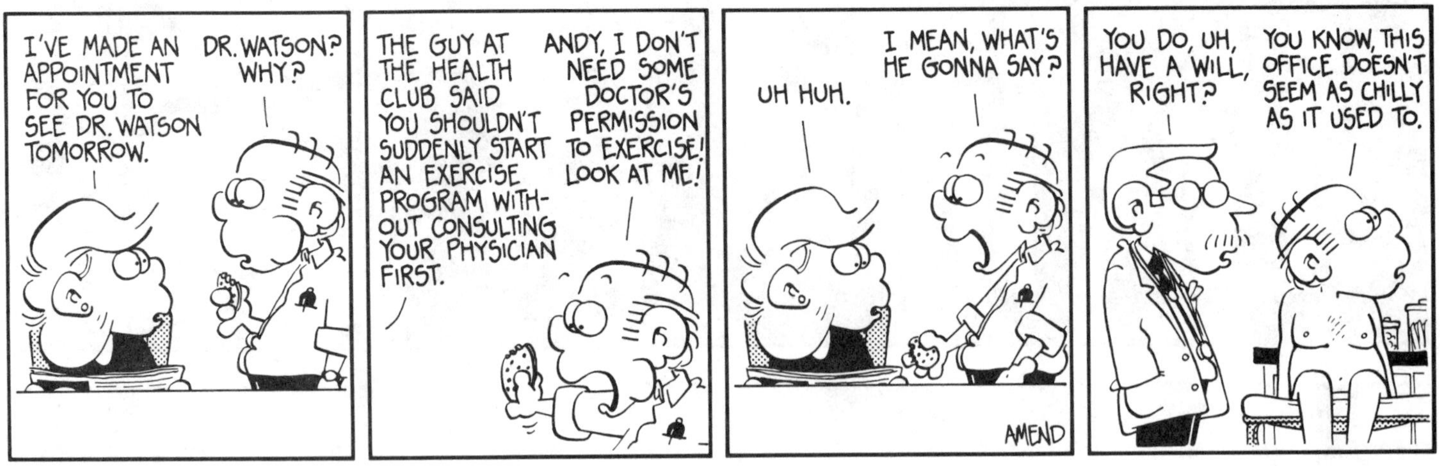
I'VE MADE AN APPOINTMENT FOR YOU TO SEE DR. WATSON TOMORROW.
DR. WATSON? WHY?
THE GUY AT THE HEALTH CLUB SAID YOU SHOULDN'T SUDDENLY START AN EXERCISE PROGRAM WITH-OUT CONSULTING YOUR PHYSICIAN FIRST.
ANDY, I DON'T NEED SOME DOCTOR'S PERMISSION TO EXERCISE! LOOK AT ME!
UH HUH.
I MEAN, WHAT'S HE GONNA SAY?
AMEND
YOU DO, UH, HAVE A WILL, RIGHT?
YOU KNOW, THIS OFFICE DOESN'T SEEM AS CHILLY AS IT USED TO.

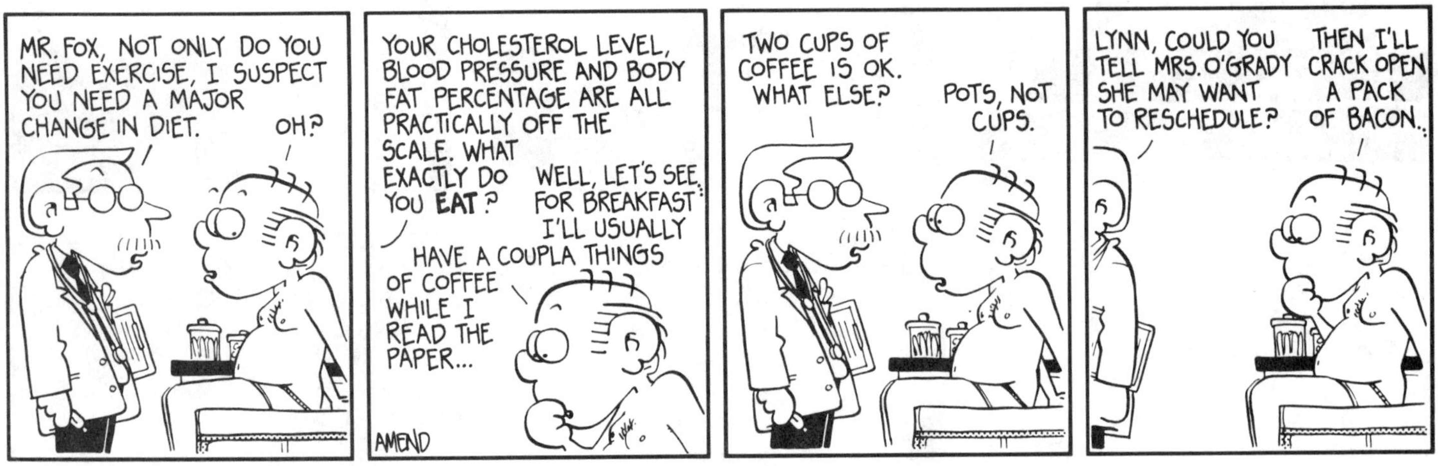
MR. FOX, NOT ONLY DO YOU NEED EXERCISE, I SUSPECT YOU NEED A MAJOR CHANGE IN DIET.
OH?
YOUR CHOLESTEROL LEVEL, BLOOD PRESSURE AND BODY FAT PERCENTAGE ARE ALL PRACTICALLY OFF THE SCALE. WHAT EXACTLY DO YOU EAT?
WELL, LET'S SEE... FOR BREAKFAST I'LL USUALLY HAVE A COUPLA THINGS OF COFFEE WHILE I READ THE PAPER...
AMEND
TWO CUPS OF COFFEE IS OK. WHAT ELSE?
POTS, NOT CUPS.
LYNN, COULD YOU TELL MRS. O'GRADY SHE MAY WANT TO RESCHEDULE?
THEN I'LL CRACK OPEN A PACK OF BACON...

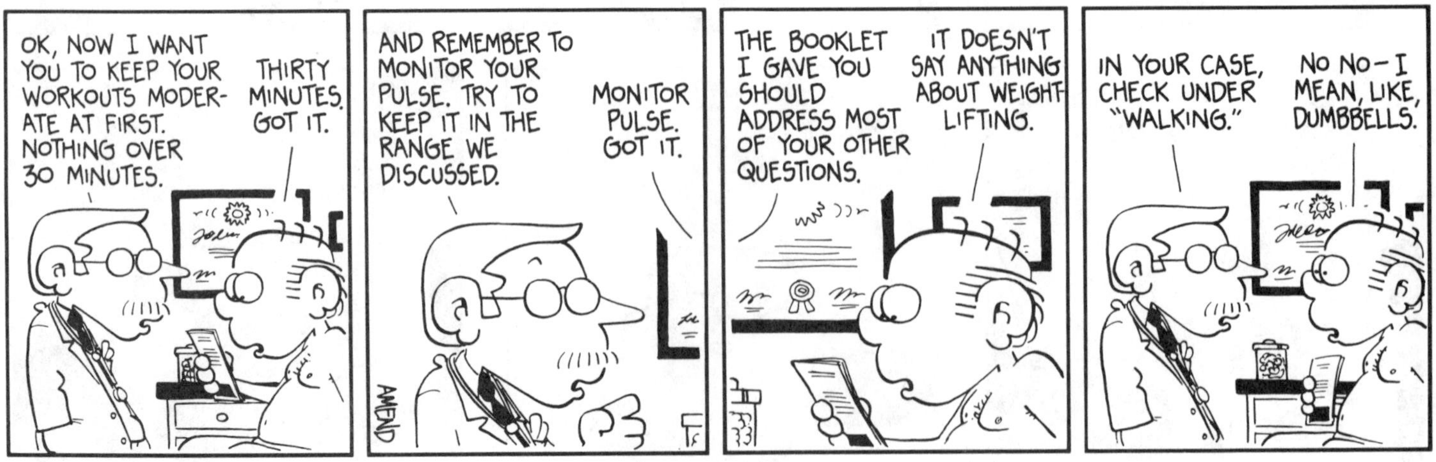
OK, NOW I WANT YOU TO KEEP YOUR WORKOUTS MODER-ATE AT FIRST. NOTHING OVER 30 MINUTES.
THIRTY MINUTES. GOT IT.
AND REMEMBER TO MONITOR YOUR PULSE. TRY TO KEEP IT IN THE RANGE WE DISCUSSED.
MONITOR PULSE. GOT IT.
AMEND
THE BOOKLET I GAVE YOU SHOULD ADDRESS MOST OF YOUR OTHER QUESTIONS.
IT DOESN'T SAY ANYTHING ABOUT WEIGHT-LIFTING.
IN YOUR CASE, CHECK UNDER "WALKING."
NO NO—I MEAN, LIKE, DUMBBELLS.

So what'd the doctor say? / **He said everything I DIDN'T want to hear.**

Oh? / **He said I'm overweight. He said my blood pressure's too high. He said my cholesterol level was practically off the scale. He said I have to completely rethink my lifestyle and stop eating half the foods I live for. This is all YOUR fault!**

MY FAULT?! / **YOU'RE the one who made me go SEE him!**

Gosh, what WAS I thinking? / **Did it ever occur to you that maybe I LIKED my life?!**

AMEND

OK, set the resistance level to "moderate." / **No sweat.** TIME LIMIT 30 Mi

Now set the timer for 20 minutes. / **No sweat.** TIME LIMIT 30 Mi

Now pedal. / **Pedal?**

AMEND

As in sweat. / **You know, I think I could use a little more stretching...** TIME LIMIT 30 Mi

Uggh. I feel like death incarnate. / **Roger, what did you expect?**

I didn't expect THIS. My throat's all dry... I feel nauseated... weak... I think I've gone through 12 glasses of water... / **It's your first time. It'll get easier.**

It'd BETTER. / **I mean, when WAS the last time you did any exercise?**

Exercise? I'm talking about eating these stupid rice cakes. / **Oh. Well, here — sprinkle some wheat germ on it.**

AMEND

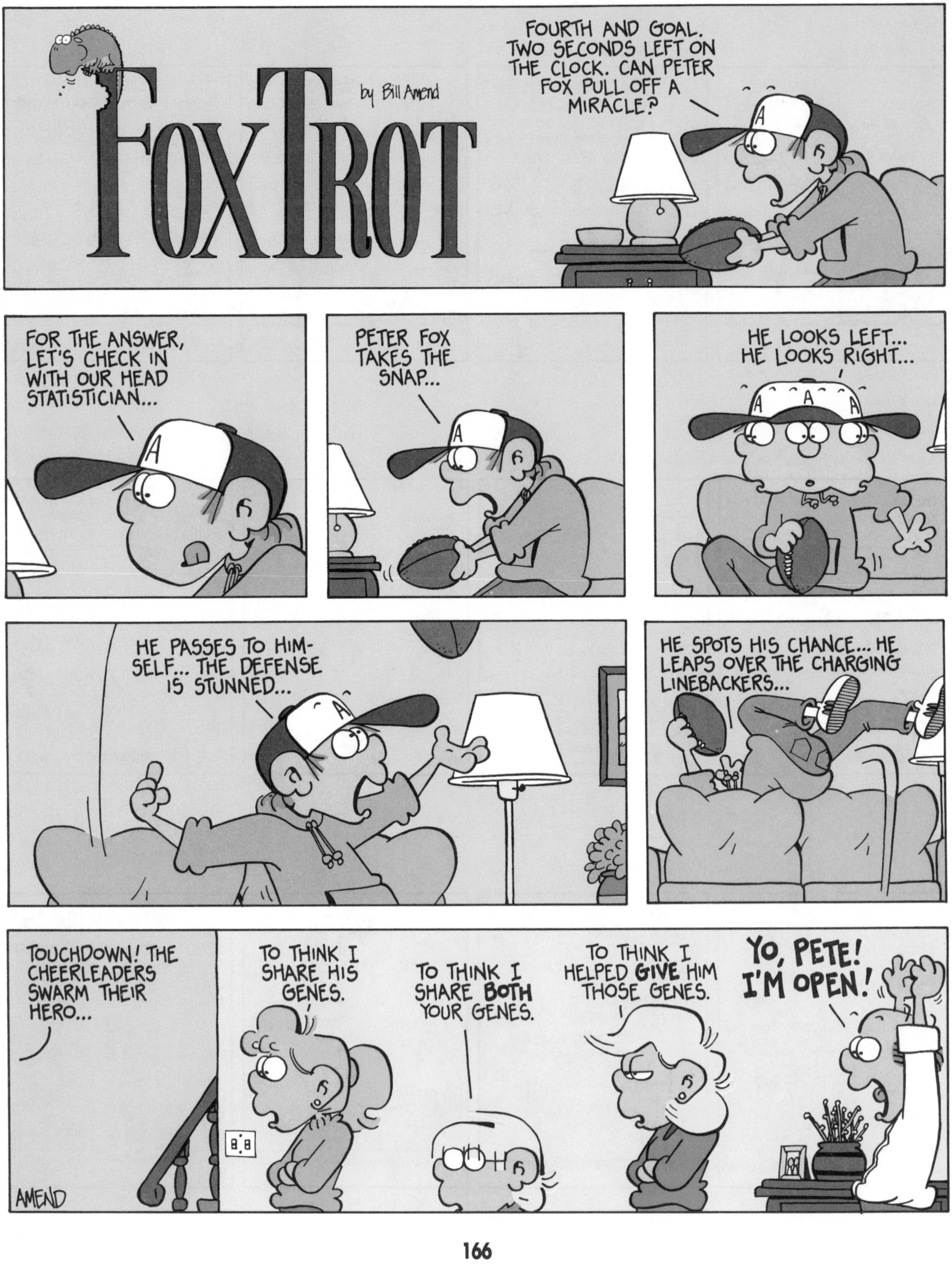

FoxTrot
by Bill Amend
FOURTH AND GOAL. TWO SECONDS LEFT ON THE CLOCK. CAN PETER FOX PULL OFF A MIRACLE?
FOR THE ANSWER, LET'S CHECK IN WITH OUR HEAD STATISTICIAN...
PETER FOX TAKES THE SNAP...
HE LOOKS LEFT... HE LOOKS RIGHT...
HE PASSES TO HIMSELF... THE DEFENSE IS STUNNED...
HE SPOTS HIS CHANCE... HE LEAPS OVER THE CHARGING LINEBACKERS...
TOUCHDOWN! THE CHEERLEADERS SWARM THEIR HERO...
TO THINK I SHARE HIS GENES.
TO THINK I SHARE **BOTH** YOUR GENES.
TO THINK I HELPED **GIVE** HIM THOSE GENES.
YO, PETE! I'M OPEN!
AMEND

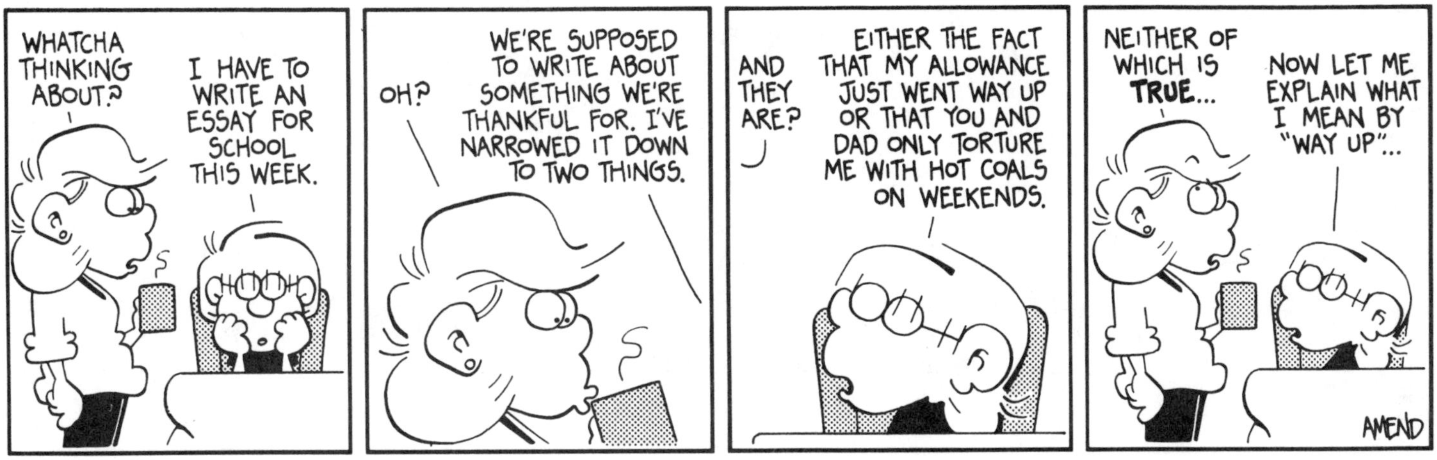
WHATCHA THINKING ABOUT?
I HAVE TO WRITE AN ESSAY FOR SCHOOL THIS WEEK.
OH?
WE'RE SUPPOSED TO WRITE ABOUT SOMETHING WE'RE THANKFUL FOR. I'VE NARROWED IT DOWN TO TWO THINGS.
AND THEY ARE?
EITHER THE FACT THAT MY ALLOWANCE JUST WENT WAY UP OR THAT YOU AND DAD ONLY TORTURE ME WITH HOT COALS ON WEEKENDS.
NEITHER OF WHICH IS **TRUE**...
NOW LET ME EXPLAIN WHAT I MEAN BY "WAY UP"...
AMEND

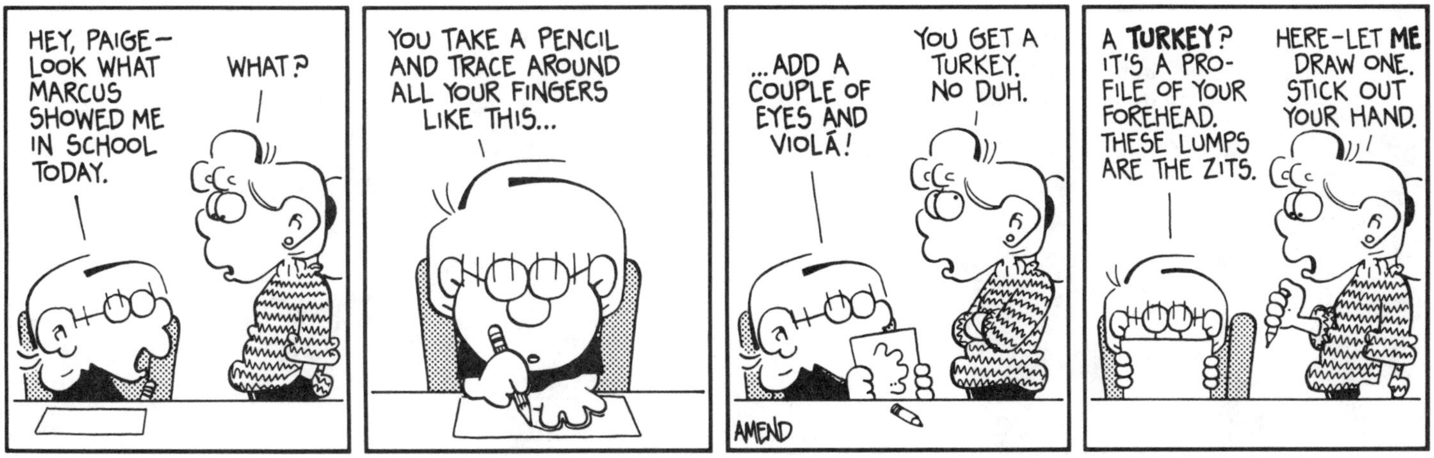
HEY, PAIGE— LOOK WHAT MARCUS SHOWED ME IN SCHOOL TODAY.
WHAT?
YOU TAKE A PENCIL AND TRACE AROUND ALL YOUR FINGERS LIKE THIS...
...ADD A COUPLE OF EYES AND VIOLÁ!
YOU GET A TURKEY. NO DUH.
AMEND
A **TURKEY**? IT'S A PRO-FILE OF YOUR FOREHEAD. THESE LUMPS ARE THE ZITS.
HERE—LET **ME** DRAW ONE. STICK OUT YOUR HAND.

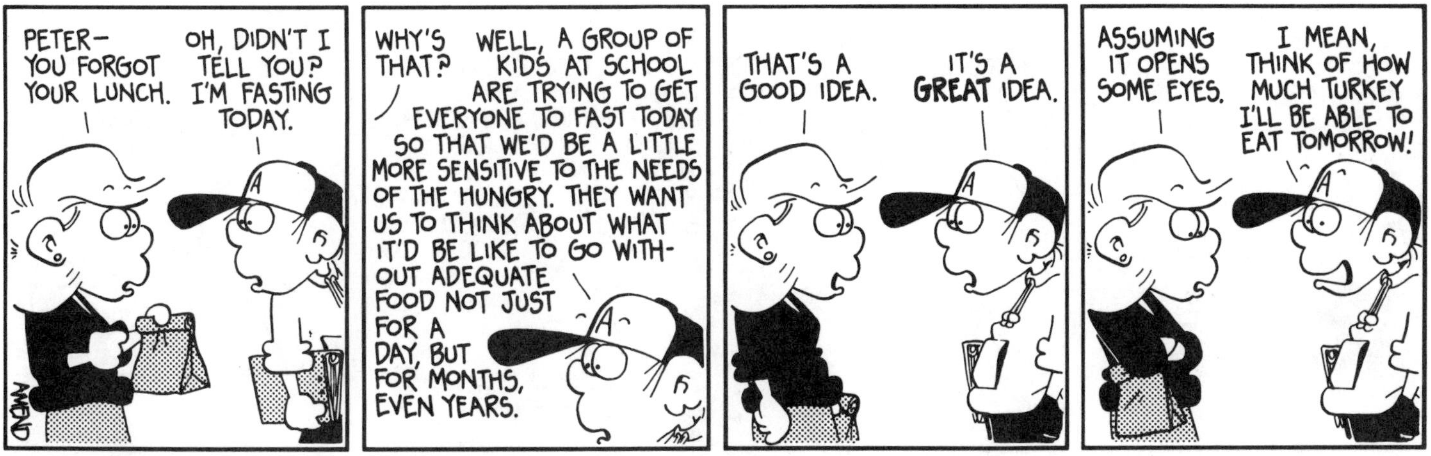
PETER— YOU FORGOT YOUR LUNCH.
OH, DIDN'T I TELL YOU? I'M FASTING TODAY.
AMEND
WHY'S THAT?
WELL, A GROUP OF KIDS AT SCHOOL ARE TRYING TO GET EVERYONE TO FAST TODAY SO THAT WE'D BE A LITTLE MORE SENSITIVE TO THE NEEDS OF THE HUNGRY. THEY WANT US TO THINK ABOUT WHAT IT'D BE LIKE TO GO WITH-OUT ADEQUATE FOOD NOT JUST FOR A DAY, BUT FOR MONTHS, EVEN YEARS.
THAT'S A GOOD IDEA.
IT'S A **GREAT** IDEA.
ASSUMING IT OPENS SOME EYES.
I MEAN, THINK OF HOW MUCH TURKEY I'LL BE ABLE TO EAT TOMORROW!

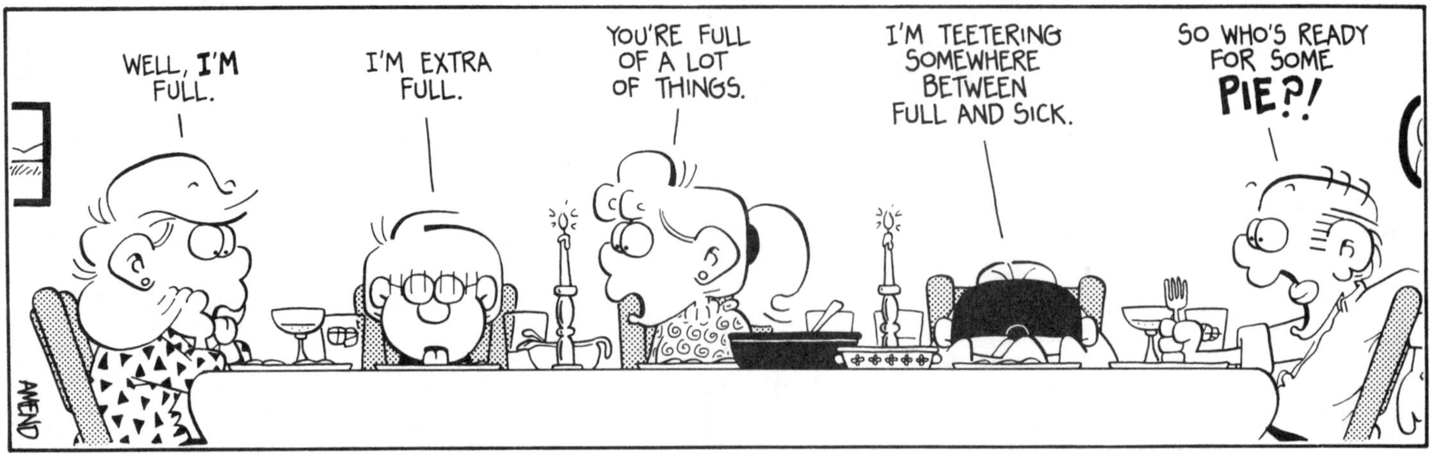
WELL, I'M FULL.
I'M EXTRA FULL.
YOU'RE FULL OF A LOT OF THINGS.
I'M TEETERING SOMEWHERE BETWEEN FULL AND SICK.
SO WHO'S READY FOR SOME PIE?!
AMEND

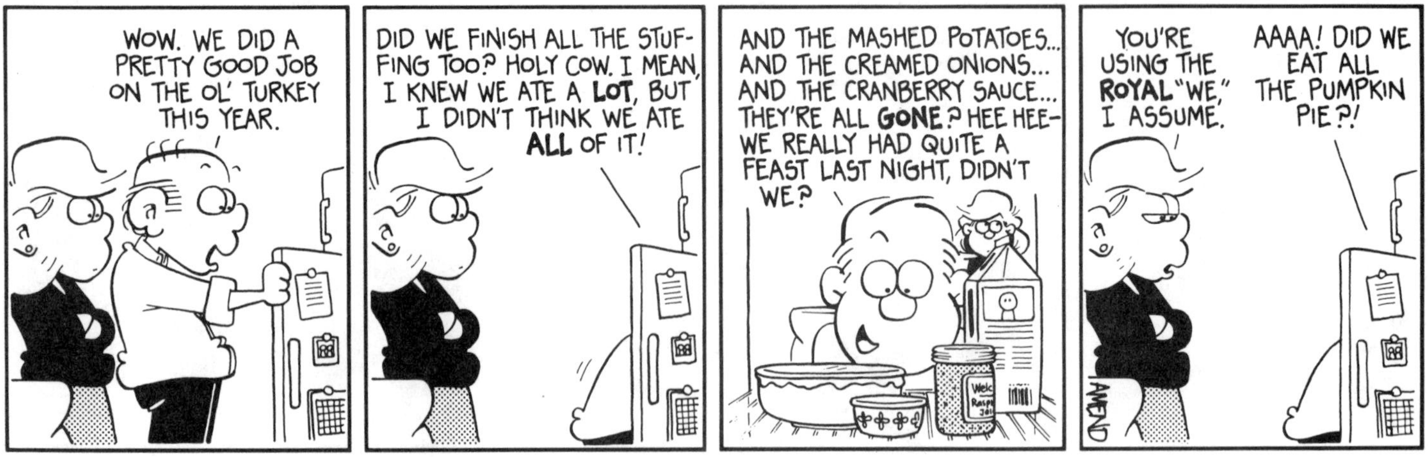
WOW. WE DID A PRETTY GOOD JOB ON THE OL' TURKEY THIS YEAR.
DID WE FINISH ALL THE STUFFING TOO? HOLY COW. I MEAN, I KNEW WE ATE A LOT, BUT I DIDN'T THINK WE ATE ALL OF IT!
AND THE MASHED POTATOES... AND THE CREAMED ONIONS... AND THE CRANBERRY SAUCE... THEY'RE ALL GONE? HEE HEE- WE REALLY HAD QUITE A FEAST LAST NIGHT, DIDN'T WE?
YOU'RE USING THE ROYAL "WE," I ASSUME.
AAAA! DID WE EAT ALL THE PUMPKIN PIE?!
AMEND

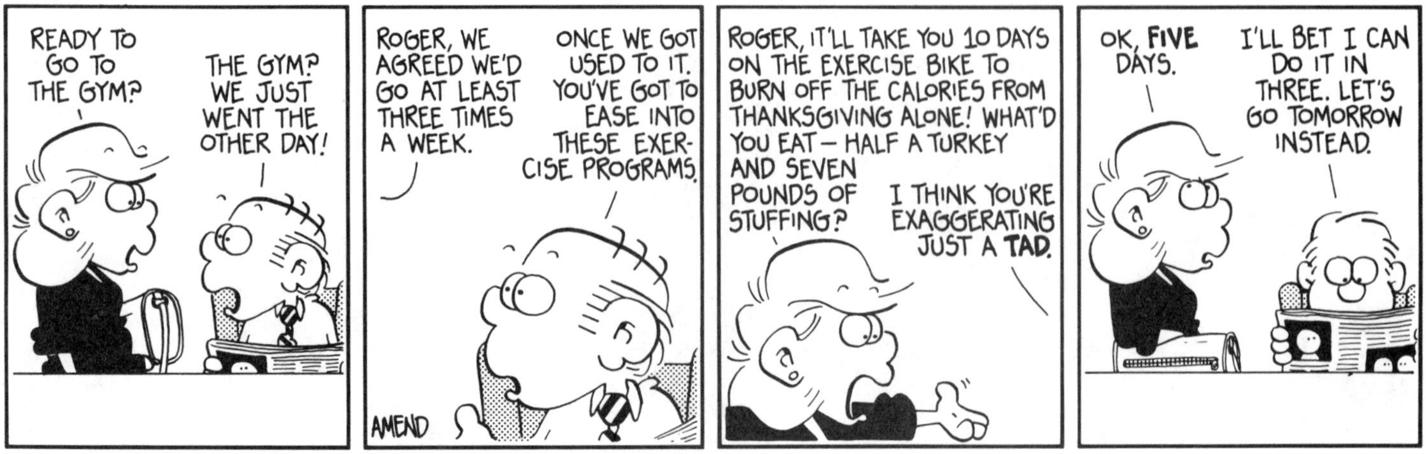
READY TO GO TO THE GYM?
THE GYM? WE JUST WENT THE OTHER DAY!
ROGER, WE AGREED WE'D GO AT LEAST THREE TIMES A WEEK.
ONCE WE GOT USED TO IT. YOU'VE GOT TO EASE INTO THESE EXERCISE PROGRAMS.
AMEND
ROGER, IT'LL TAKE YOU 10 DAYS ON THE EXERCISE BIKE TO BURN OFF THE CALORIES FROM THANKSGIVING ALONE! WHAT'D YOU EAT — HALF A TURKEY AND SEVEN POUNDS OF STUFFING?
I THINK YOU'RE EXAGGERATING JUST A TAD.
OK, FIVE DAYS.
I'LL BET I CAN DO IT IN THREE. LET'S GO TOMORROW INSTEAD.

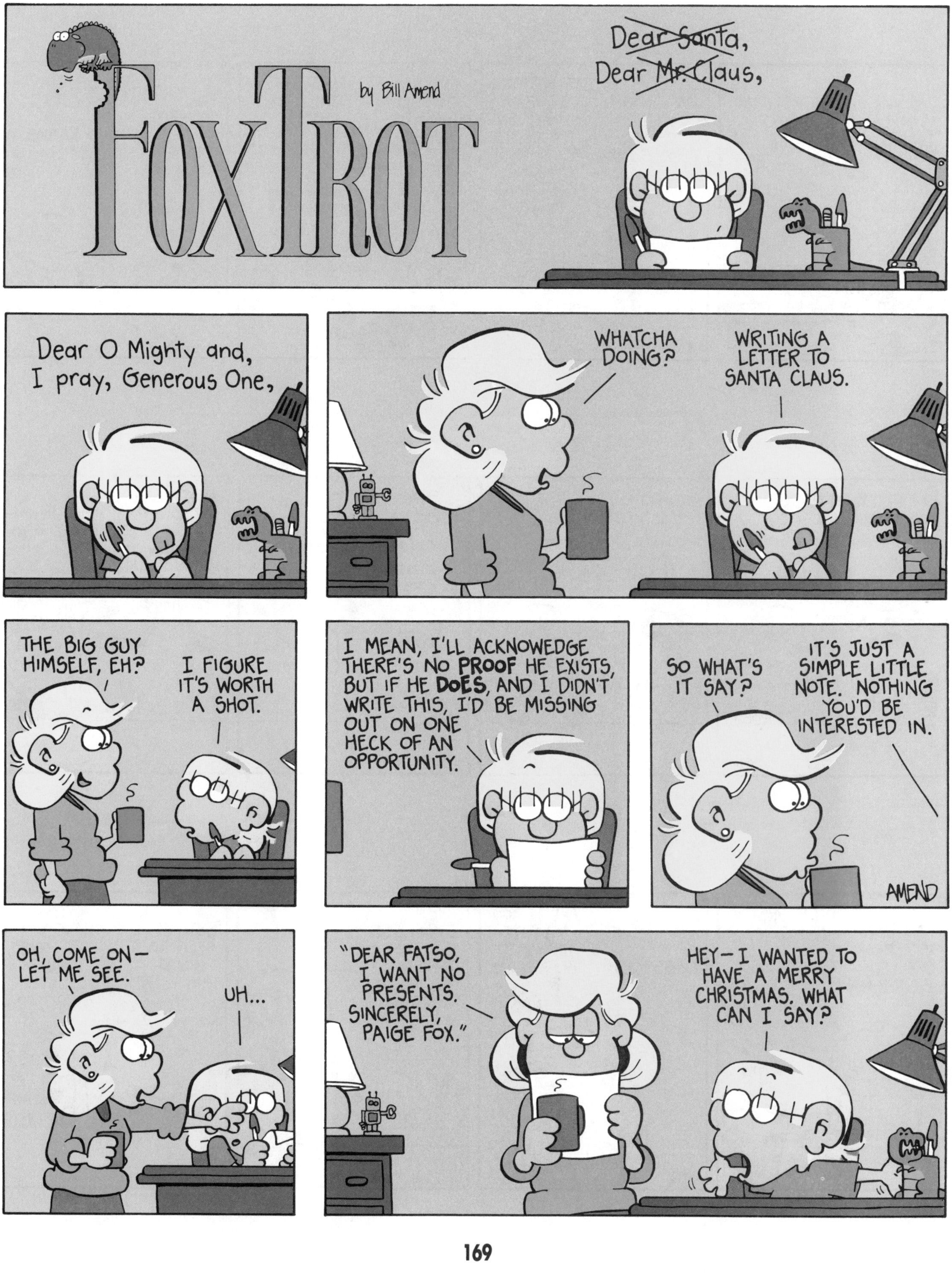
FoxTrot
by Bill Amend
Dear Santa,
Dear Mr. Claus,
Dear O Mighty and,
I pray, Generous One,
WHATCHA DOING?
WRITING A LETTER TO SANTA CLAUS.
THE BIG GUY HIMSELF, EH?
I FIGURE IT'S WORTH A SHOT.
I MEAN, I'LL ACKNOWEDGE THERE'S NO PROOF HE EXISTS, BUT IF HE DOES, AND I DIDN'T WRITE THIS, I'D BE MISSING OUT ON ONE HECK OF AN OPPORTUNITY.
SO WHAT'S IT SAY?
IT'S JUST A SIMPLE LITTLE NOTE. NOTHING YOU'D BE INTERESTED IN.
AMEND
OH, COME ON— LET ME SEE.
UH...
"DEAR FATSO, I WANT NO PRESENTS. SINCERELY, PAIGE FOX."
HEY— I WANTED TO HAVE A MERRY CHRISTMAS. WHAT CAN I SAY?

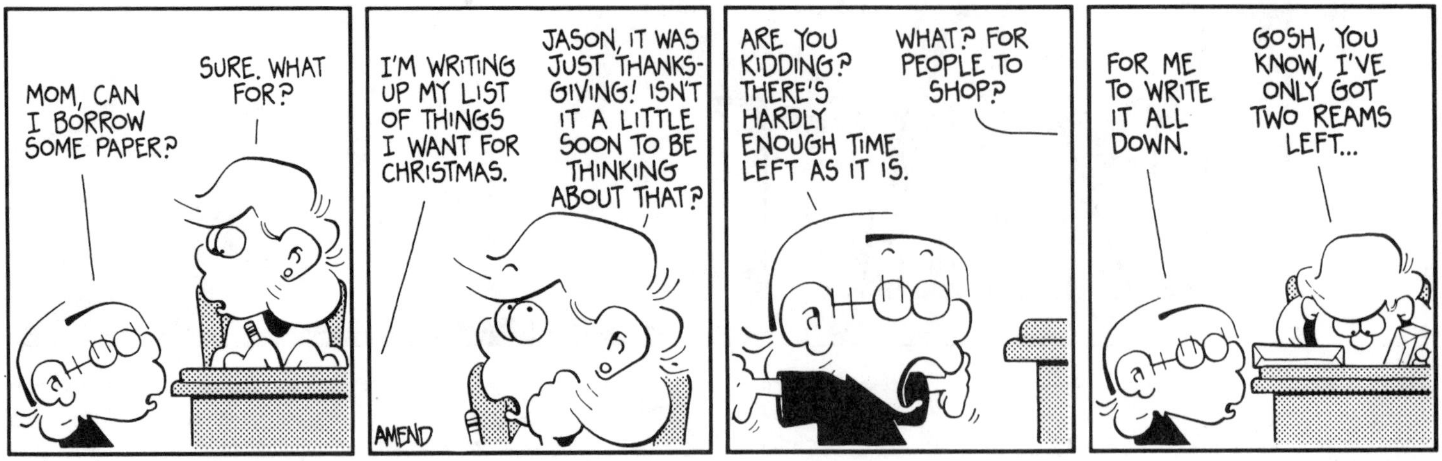

MOM, CAN I BORROW SOME PAPER?
SURE. WHAT FOR?
I'M WRITING UP MY LIST OF THINGS I WANT FOR CHRISTMAS.
JASON, IT WAS JUST THANKSGIVING! ISN'T IT A LITTLE SOON TO BE THINKING ABOUT THAT?
AMEND
ARE YOU KIDDING? THERE'S HARDLY ENOUGH TIME LEFT AS IT IS.
WHAT? FOR PEOPLE TO SHOP?
FOR ME TO WRITE IT ALL DOWN.
GOSH, YOU KNOW, I'VE ONLY GOT TWO REAMS LEFT...

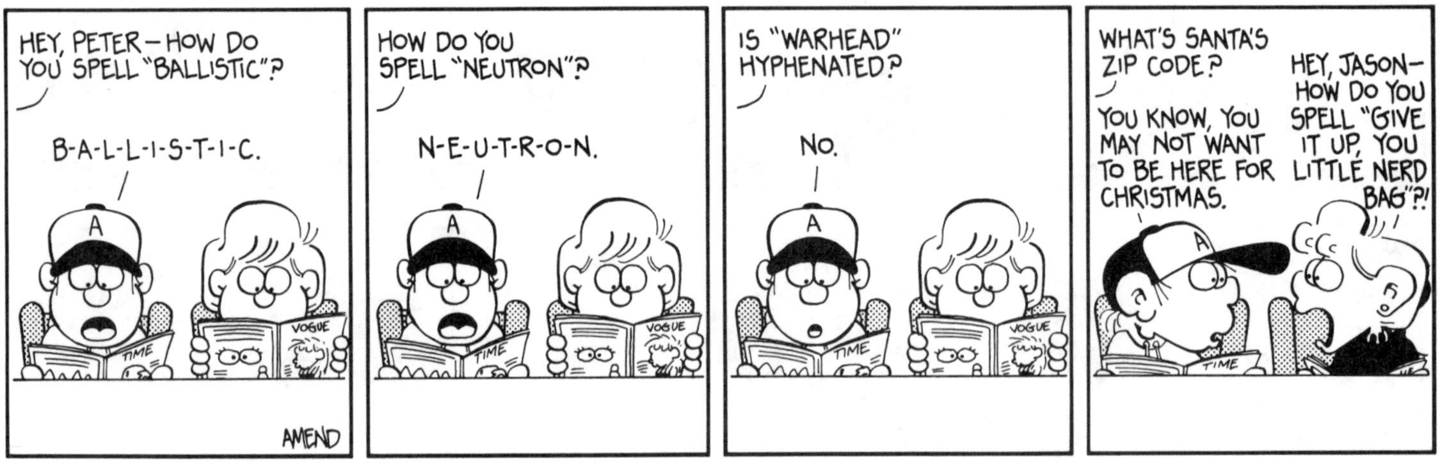

HEY, PETER—HOW DO YOU SPELL "BALLISTIC"?
B-A-L-L-I-S-T-I-C.
TIME
VOGUE
AMEND
HOW DO YOU SPELL "NEUTRON"?
N-E-U-T-R-O-N.
IS "WARHEAD" HYPHENATED?
NO.
WHAT'S SANTA'S ZIP CODE?
YOU KNOW, YOU MAY NOT WANT TO BE HERE FOR CHRISTMAS.
HEY, JASON—HOW DO YOU SPELL "GIVE IT UP, YOU LITTLE NERD BAG"?!

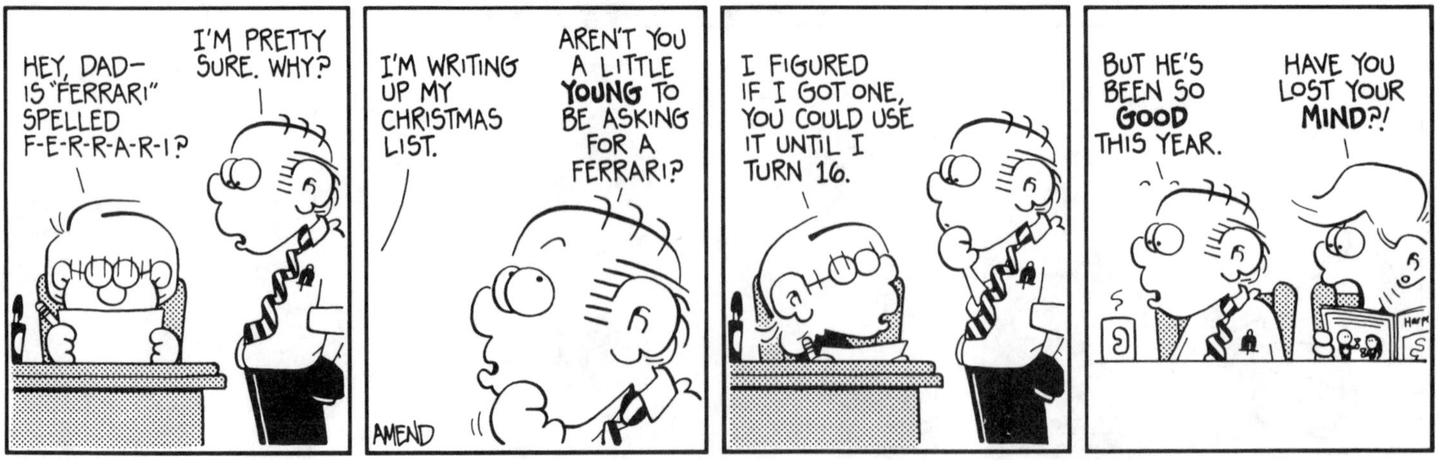

HEY, DAD—IS "FERRARI" SPELLED F-E-R-R-A-R-I?
I'M PRETTY SURE. WHY?
I'M WRITING UP MY CHRISTMAS LIST.
AREN'T YOU A LITTLE **YOUNG** TO BE ASKING FOR A FERRARI?
AMEND
I FIGURED IF I GOT ONE, YOU COULD USE IT UNTIL I TURN 16.
BUT HE'S BEEN SO **GOOD** THIS YEAR.
HAVE YOU LOST YOUR **MIND**?!

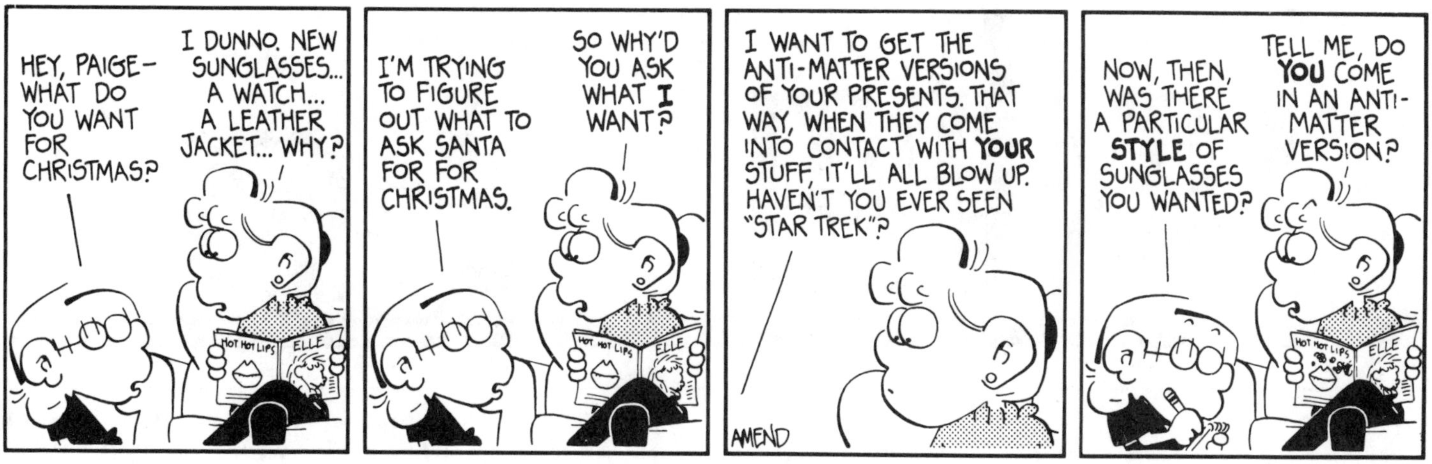
HEY, PAIGE– WHAT DO YOU WANT FOR CHRISTMAS?
I DUNNO. NEW SUNGLASSES... A WATCH... A LEATHER JACKET... WHY?
HOT HOT LIPS
ELLE
I'M TRYING TO FIGURE OUT WHAT TO ASK SANTA FOR FOR CHRISTMAS.
SO WHY'D YOU ASK WHAT **I** WANT?
HOT HOT LIPS
ELLE
I WANT TO GET THE ANTI-MATTER VERSIONS OF YOUR PRESENTS. THAT WAY, WHEN THEY COME INTO CONTACT WITH **YOUR** STUFF, IT'LL ALL BLOW UP. HAVEN'T YOU EVER SEEN "STAR TREK"?
AMEND
NOW, THEN, WAS THERE A PARTICULAR **STYLE** OF SUNGLASSES YOU WANTED?
TELL ME, DO **YOU** COME IN AN ANTI-MATTER VERSION?
HOT HOT LIPS
ELLE

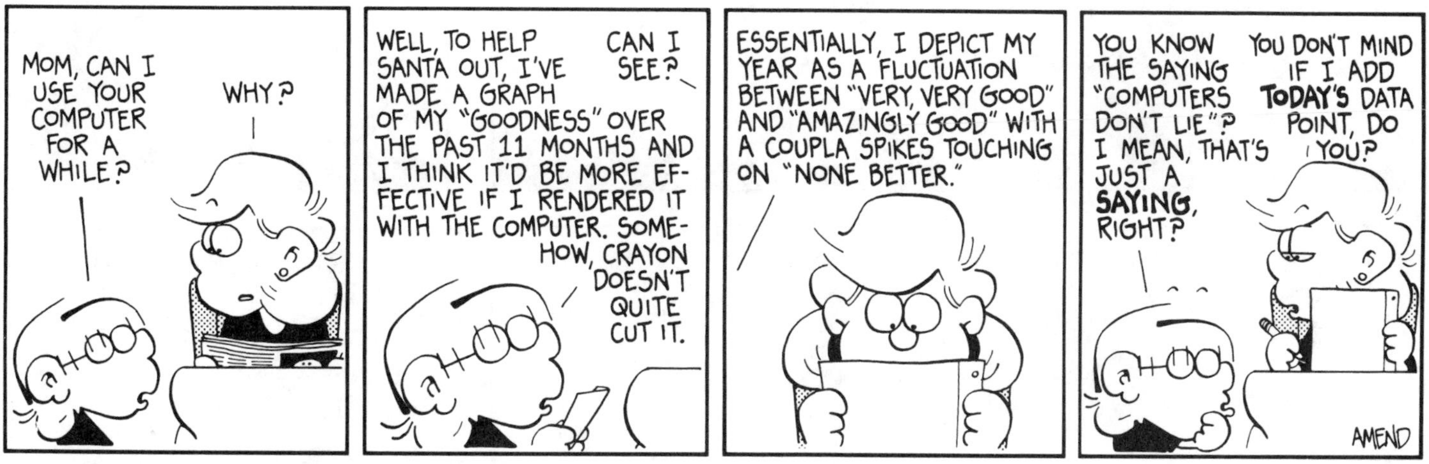
MOM, CAN I USE YOUR COMPUTER FOR A WHILE?
WHY?
WELL, TO HELP SANTA OUT, I'VE MADE A GRAPH OF MY "GOODNESS" OVER THE PAST 11 MONTHS AND I THINK IT'D BE MORE EFFECTIVE IF I RENDERED IT WITH THE COMPUTER. SOMEHOW, CRAYON DOESN'T QUITE CUT IT.
CAN I SEE?
ESSENTIALLY, I DEPICT MY YEAR AS A FLUCTUATION BETWEEN "VERY, VERY GOOD" AND "AMAZINGLY GOOD" WITH A COUPLA SPIKES TOUCHING ON "NONE BETTER."
YOU KNOW THE SAYING "COMPUTERS DON'T LIE"? I MEAN, THAT'S JUST A **SAYING**, RIGHT?
YOU DON'T MIND IF I ADD **TODAY'S** DATA POINT, DO YOU?
AMEND

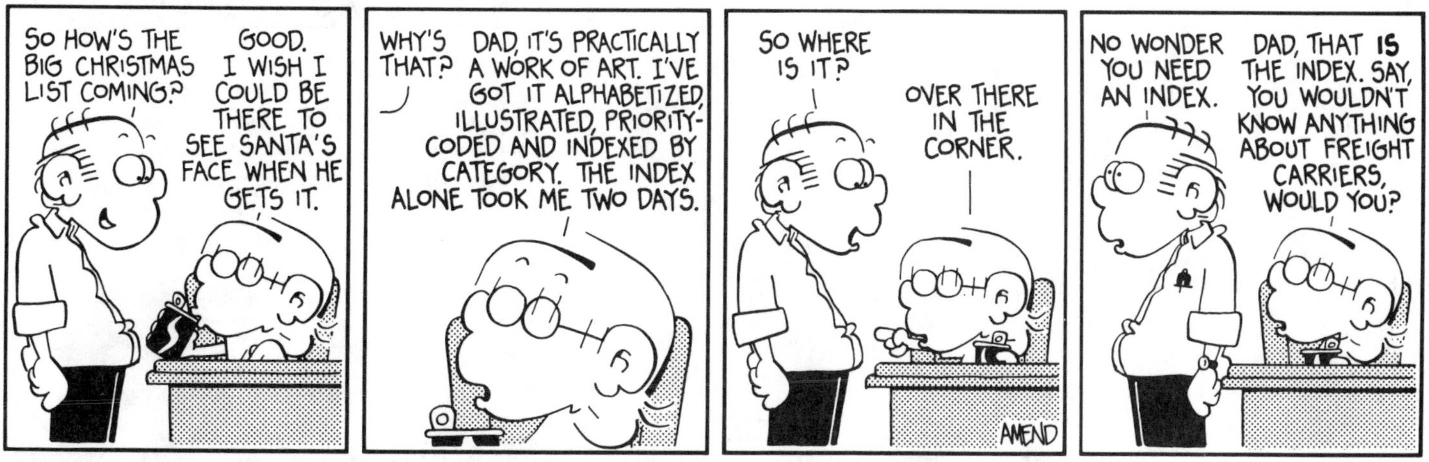
SO HOW'S THE BIG CHRISTMAS LIST COMING?
GOOD. I WISH I COULD BE THERE TO SEE SANTA'S FACE WHEN HE GETS IT.
WHY'S THAT?
DAD, IT'S PRACTICALLY A WORK OF ART. I'VE GOT IT ALPHABETIZED, ILLUSTRATED, PRIORITY-CODED AND INDEXED BY CATEGORY. THE INDEX ALONE TOOK ME TWO DAYS.
SO WHERE IS IT?
OVER THERE IN THE CORNER.
AMEND
NO WONDER YOU NEED AN INDEX.
DAD, THAT **IS** THE INDEX. SAY, YOU WOULDN'T KNOW ANYTHING ABOUT FREIGHT CARRIERS, WOULD YOU?

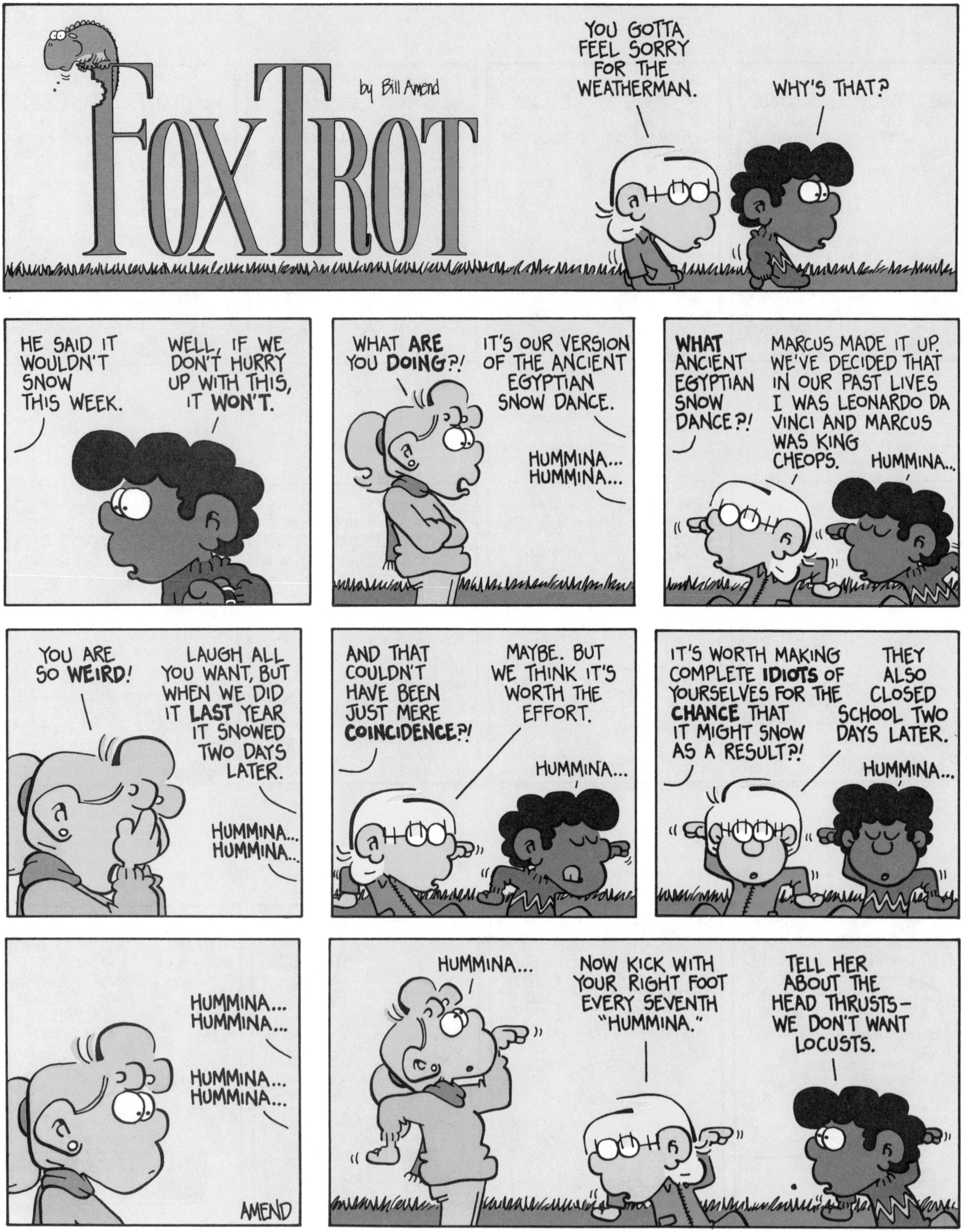
FOXTROT
by Bill Amend
YOU GOTTA FEEL SORRY FOR THE WEATHERMAN.
WHY'S THAT?
HE SAID IT WOULDN'T SNOW THIS WEEK.
WELL, IF WE DON'T HURRY UP WITH THIS, IT WON'T.
WHAT ARE YOU DOING?!
IT'S OUR VERSION OF THE ANCIENT EGYPTIAN SNOW DANCE.
HUMMINA... HUMMINA...
WHAT ANCIENT EGYPTIAN SNOW DANCE?!
MARCUS MADE IT UP. WE'VE DECIDED THAT IN OUR PAST LIVES I WAS LEONARDO DA VINCI AND MARCUS WAS KING CHEOPS.
HUMMINA...
YOU ARE SO WEIRD!
LAUGH ALL YOU WANT, BUT WHEN WE DID IT LAST YEAR IT SNOWED TWO DAYS LATER.
HUMMINA... HUMMINA...
AND THAT COULDN'T HAVE BEEN JUST MERE COINCIDENCE?!
MAYBE. BUT WE THINK IT'S WORTH THE EFFORT.
HUMMINA...
IT'S WORTH MAKING COMPLETE IDIOTS OF YOURSELVES FOR THE CHANCE THAT IT MIGHT SNOW AS A RESULT?!
THEY ALSO CLOSED SCHOOL TWO DAYS LATER.
HUMMINA...
HUMMINA... HUMMINA...
HUMMINA... HUMMINA...
AMEND
HUMMINA...
NOW KICK WITH YOUR RIGHT FOOT EVERY SEVENTH "HUMMINA."
TELL HER ABOUT THE HEAD THRUSTS— WE DON'T WANT LOCUSTS.

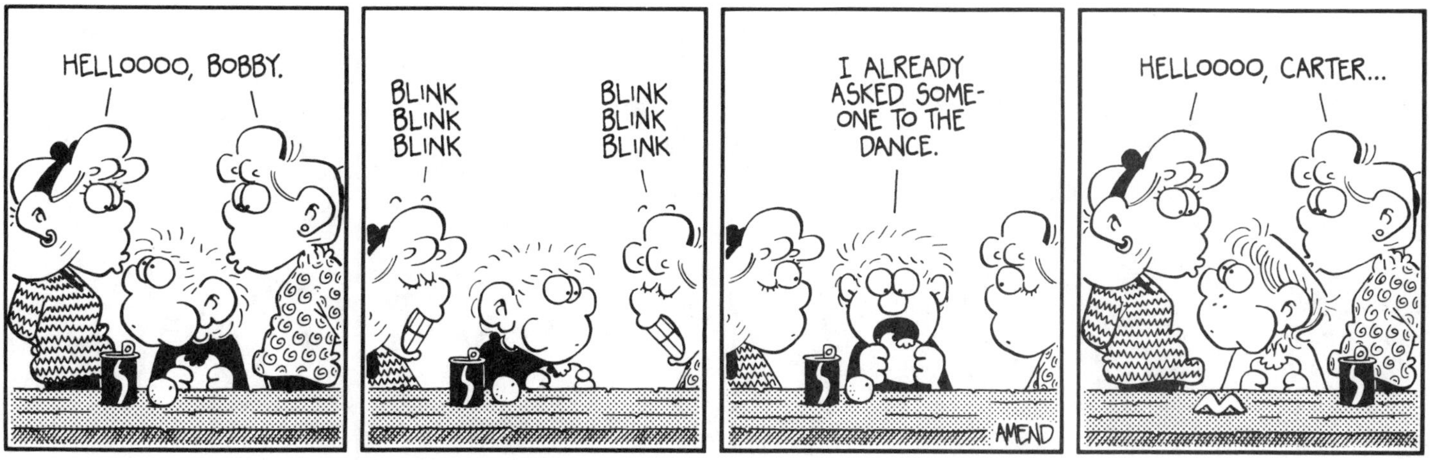
HELLOOOO, BOBBY.
BLINK BLINK BLINK
BLINK BLINK BLINK
I ALREADY ASKED SOME-ONE TO THE DANCE.
AMEND
HELLOOOO, CARTER...

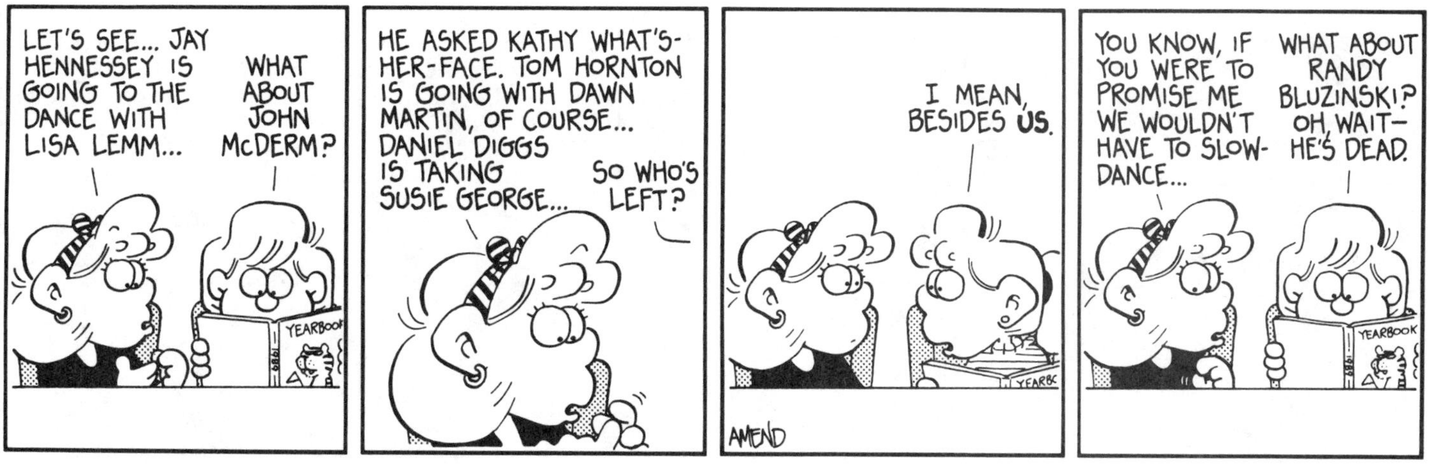
LET'S SEE... JAY HENNESSEY IS GOING TO THE DANCE WITH LISA LEMM...
WHAT ABOUT JOHN McDERM?
YEARBOOK
HE ASKED KATHY WHAT'S-HER-FACE. TOM HORNTON IS GOING WITH DAWN MARTIN, OF COURSE... DANIEL DIGGS IS TAKING SUSIE GEORGE...
SO WHO'S LEFT?
I MEAN, BESIDES US.
AMEND
YOU KNOW, IF YOU WERE TO PROMISE ME WE WOULDN'T HAVE TO SLOW-DANCE...
WHAT ABOUT RANDY BLUZINSKI? OH, WAIT– HE'S DEAD.
YEARBOOK

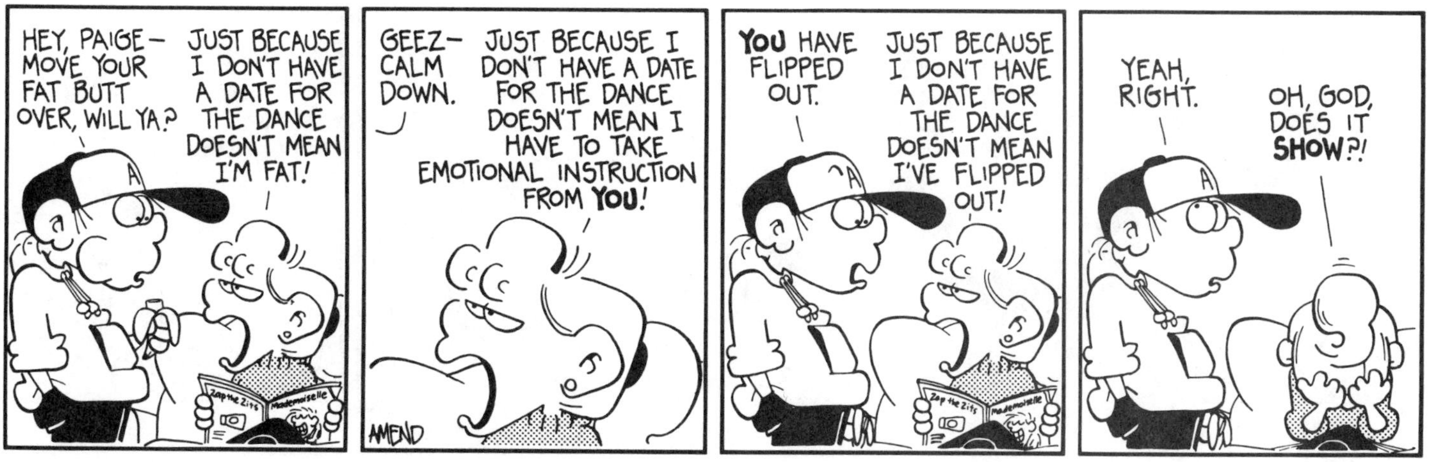
HEY, PAIGE– MOVE YOUR FAT BUTT OVER, WILL YA?
JUST BECAUSE I DON'T HAVE A DATE FOR THE DANCE DOESN'T MEAN I'M FAT!
GEEZ– CALM DOWN.
JUST BECAUSE I DON'T HAVE A DATE FOR THE DANCE DOESN'T MEAN I HAVE TO TAKE EMOTIONAL INSTRUCTION FROM YOU!
AMEND
YOU HAVE FLIPPED OUT.
JUST BECAUSE I DON'T HAVE A DATE FOR THE DANCE DOESN'T MEAN I'VE FLIPPED OUT!
YEAH, RIGHT.
OH, GOD, DOES IT SHOW?!

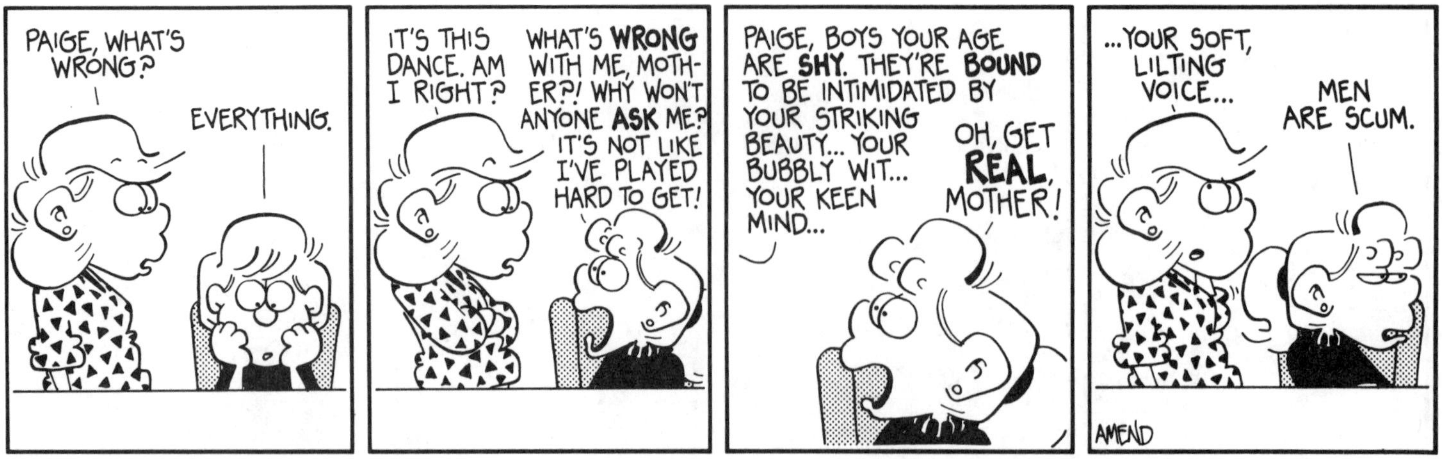
PAIGE, WHAT'S WRONG?
EVERYTHING.
IT'S THIS DANCE. AM I RIGHT?
WHAT'S WRONG WITH ME, MOTHER?! WHY WON'T ANYONE ASK ME? IT'S NOT LIKE I'VE PLAYED HARD TO GET!
PAIGE, BOYS YOUR AGE ARE SHY. THEY'RE BOUND TO BE INTIMIDATED BY YOUR STRIKING BEAUTY... YOUR BUBBLY WIT... YOUR KEEN MIND...
OH, GET REAL, MOTHER!
...YOUR SOFT, LILTING VOICE...
MEN ARE SCUM.
AMEND

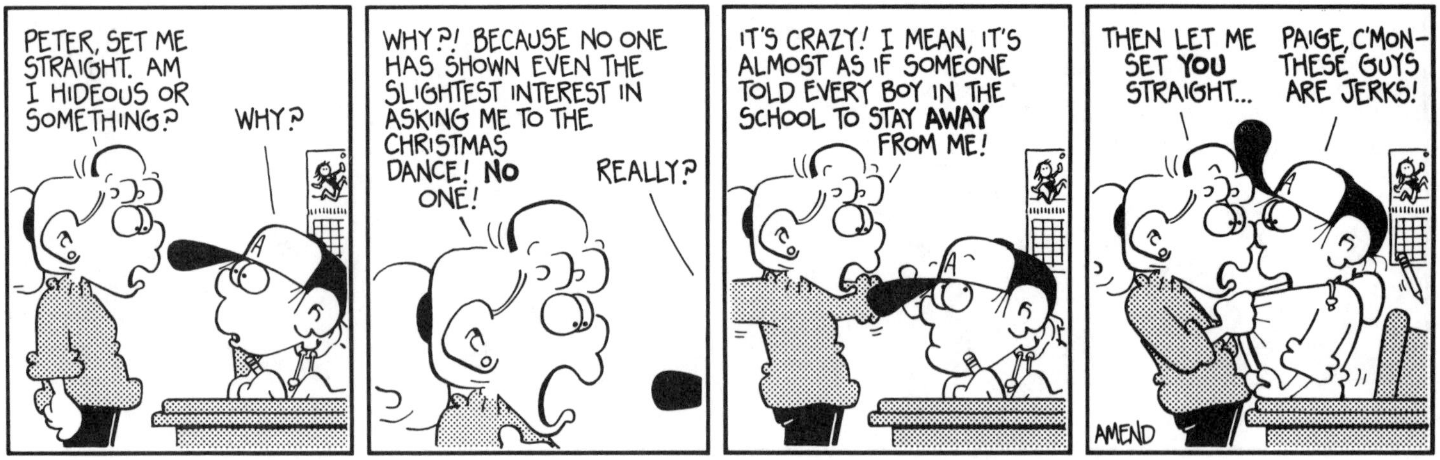
PETER, SET ME STRAIGHT. AM I HIDEOUS OR SOMETHING?
WHY?
WHY?! BECAUSE NO ONE HAS SHOWN EVEN THE SLIGHTEST INTEREST IN ASKING ME TO THE CHRISTMAS DANCE! NO ONE!
REALLY?
IT'S CRAZY! I MEAN, IT'S ALMOST AS IF SOMEONE TOLD EVERY BOY IN THE SCHOOL TO STAY AWAY FROM ME!
THEN LET ME SET YOU STRAIGHT...
PAIGE, C'MON— THESE GUYS ARE JERKS!
AMEND

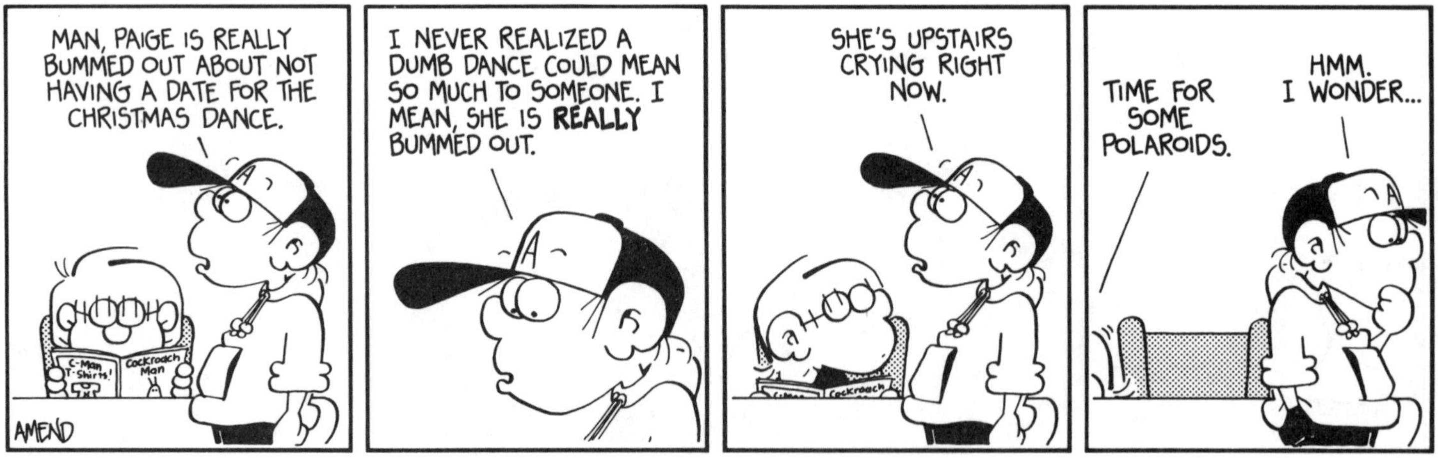
MAN, PAIGE IS REALLY BUMMED OUT ABOUT NOT HAVING A DATE FOR THE CHRISTMAS DANCE.
C-Man T-Shirts!
Cockroach Man
AMEND
I NEVER REALIZED A DUMB DANCE COULD MEAN SO MUCH TO SOMEONE. I MEAN, SHE IS REALLY BUMMED OUT.
SHE'S UPSTAIRS CRYING RIGHT NOW.
TIME FOR SOME POLAROIDS.
HMM. I WONDER...

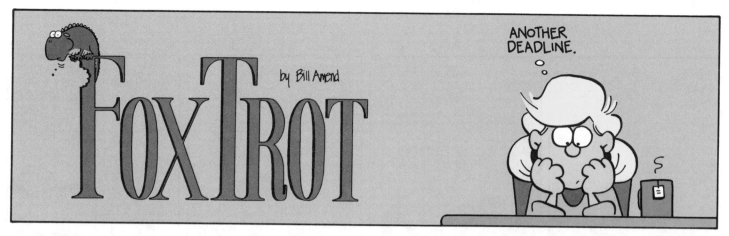

FoxTrot

by Bill Amend

ANOTHER DEADLINE.

ANOTHER DEAD WRITER.

WHAT'S THE MATTER?

I'M HAVING TROUBLE WRITING THIS WEEK'S COLUMN.

NEED A SUBJECT?

NO, I'VE GOT THAT.

NEED A CLEVER OPENING SENTENCE?

NO, I'VE GOT THAT, TOO.

NEED A UNIQUE ANGLE?

NO, I'VE GOT A PRETTY GOOD ONE.

NEED A STIRRING CONCLUSION?

NO, I'M ALL SET THERE.

AMEND

SO WHAT DO YOU NEED?

A CROWBAR.

BEEP. KLINGON WARSHIP DESTROYED.

ONLY 253 MORE FOR THE RECORD.

I WISH MY MOM HAD A COMPUTER.

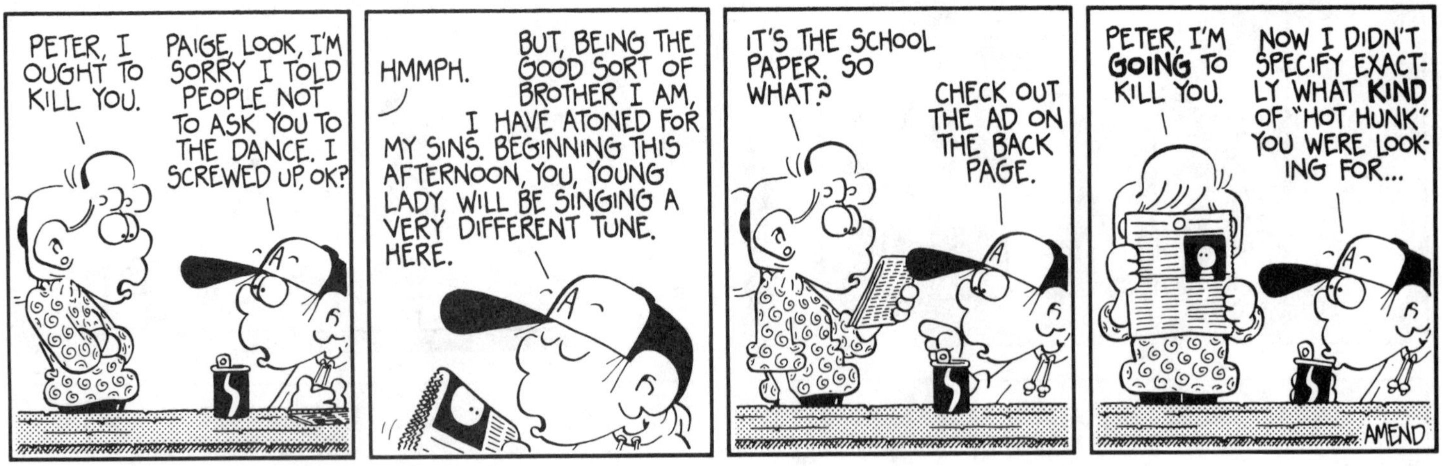
PETER, I OUGHT TO KILL YOU.
PAIGE, LOOK, I'M SORRY I TOLD PEOPLE NOT TO ASK YOU TO THE DANCE. I SCREWED UP, OK?
HMMPH.
BUT, BEING THE GOOD SORT OF BROTHER I AM, I HAVE ATONED FOR MY SINS. BEGINNING THIS AFTERNOON, YOU, YOUNG LADY, WILL BE SINGING A VERY DIFFERENT TUNE. HERE.
IT'S THE SCHOOL PAPER. SO WHAT?
CHECK OUT THE AD ON THE BACK PAGE.
PETER, I'M **GOING** TO KILL YOU.
NOW I DIDN'T SPECIFY EXACTLY WHAT **KIND** OF "HOT HUNK" YOU WERE LOOKING FOR...
AMEND

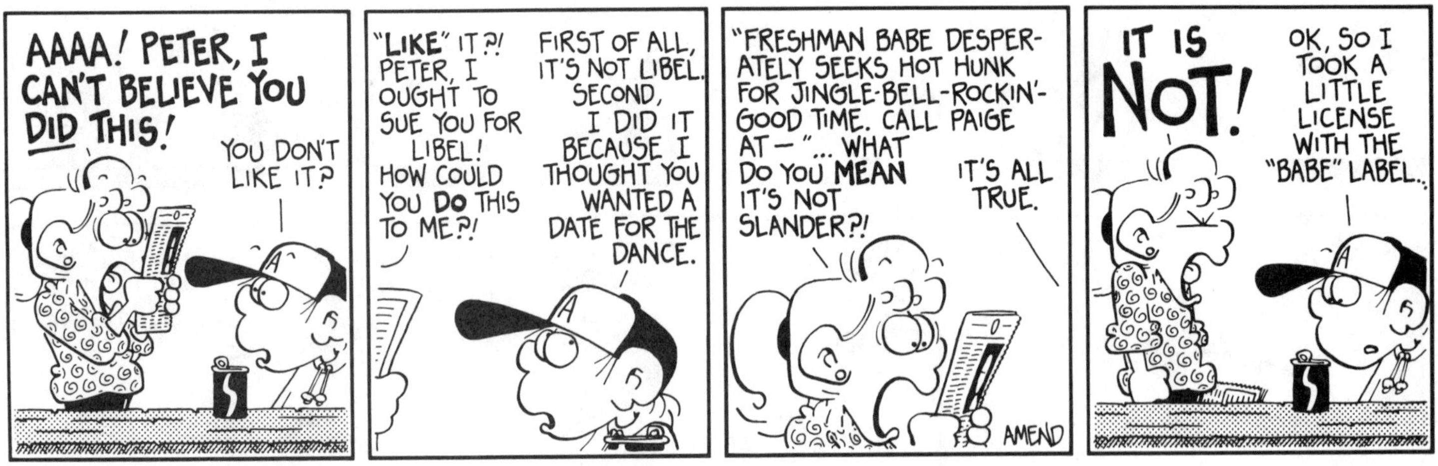
AAAA! PETER, I CAN'T BELIEVE YOU DID THIS!
YOU DON'T LIKE IT?
"**LIKE**" IT?! PETER, I OUGHT TO SUE YOU FOR LIBEL! HOW COULD YOU **DO** THIS TO ME?!
FIRST OF ALL, IT'S NOT LIBEL. SECOND, I DID IT BECAUSE I THOUGHT YOU WANTED A DATE FOR THE DANCE.
"FRESHMAN BABE DESPERATELY SEEKS HOT HUNK FOR JINGLE-BELL-ROCKIN'-GOOD TIME. CALL PAIGE AT—"... WHAT DO YOU **MEAN** IT'S NOT SLANDER?!
IT'S ALL TRUE.
AMEND
IT IS NOT!
OK, SO I TOOK A LITTLE LICENSE WITH THE "BABE" LABEL...

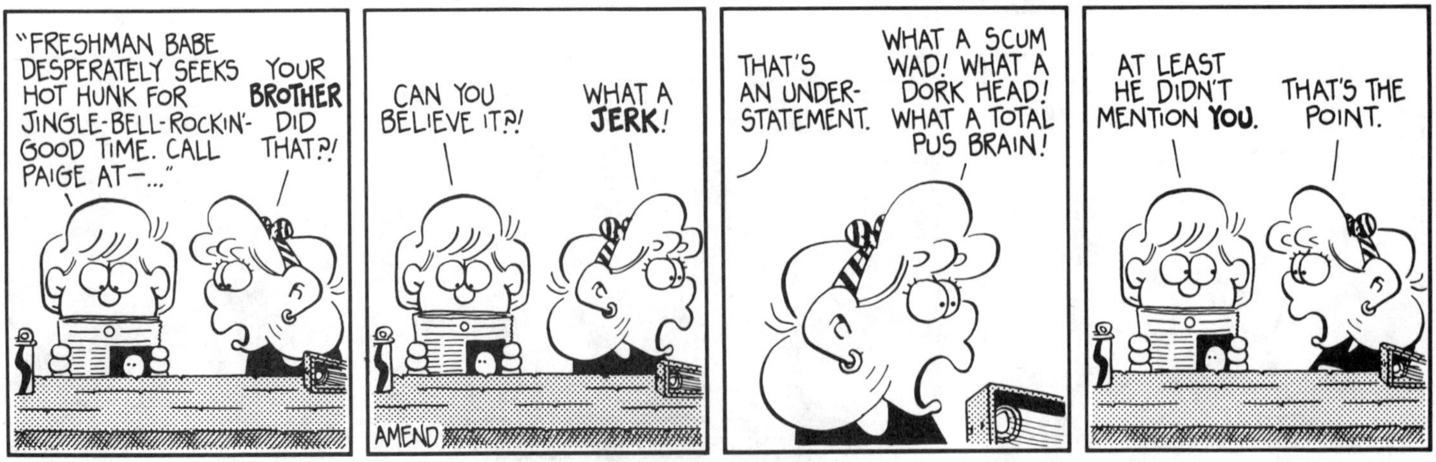
"FRESHMAN BABE DESPERATELY SEEKS HOT HUNK FOR JINGLE-BELL-ROCKIN'-GOOD TIME. CALL PAIGE AT—..."
YOUR **BROTHER** DID THAT?!
CAN YOU BELIEVE IT?!
WHAT A **JERK**!
AMEND
THAT'S AN UNDERSTATEMENT.
WHAT A SCUM WAD! WHAT A DORK HEAD! WHAT A TOTAL PUS BRAIN!
AT LEAST HE DIDN'T MENTION **YOU**.
THAT'S THE POINT.

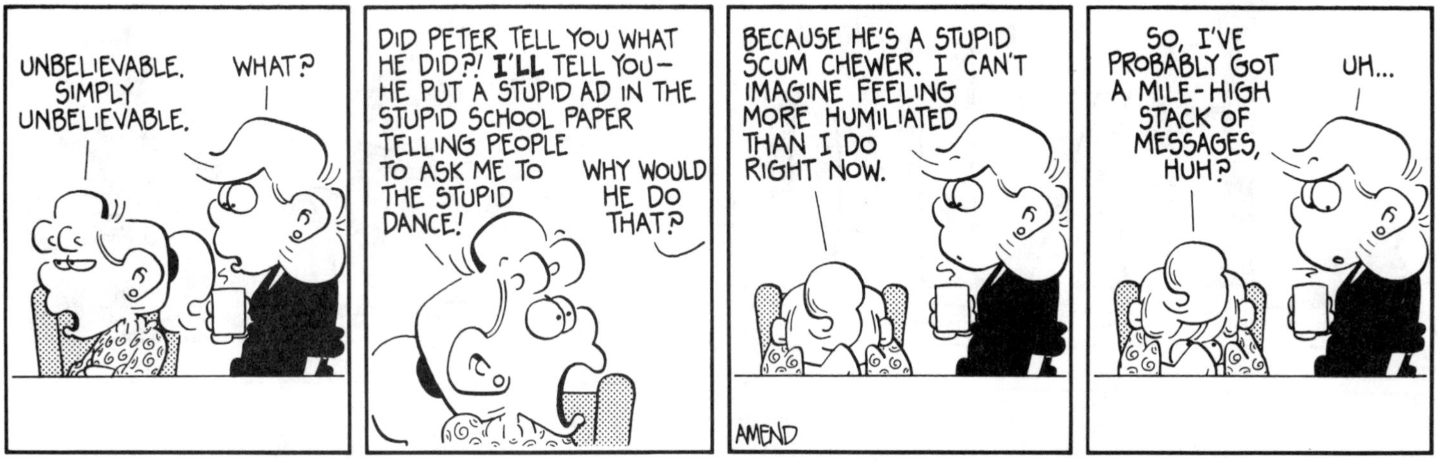
UNBELIEVABLE. SIMPLY UNBELIEVABLE.
WHAT?
DID PETER TELL YOU WHAT HE DID?! I'LL TELL YOU— HE PUT A STUPID AD IN THE STUPID SCHOOL PAPER TELLING PEOPLE TO ASK ME TO THE STUPID DANCE!
WHY WOULD HE DO THAT?
BECAUSE HE'S A STUPID SCUM CHEWER. I CAN'T IMAGINE FEELING MORE HUMILIATED THAN I DO RIGHT NOW.
AMEND
SO, I'VE PROBABLY GOT A MILE-HIGH STACK OF MESSAGES, HUH?
UH...

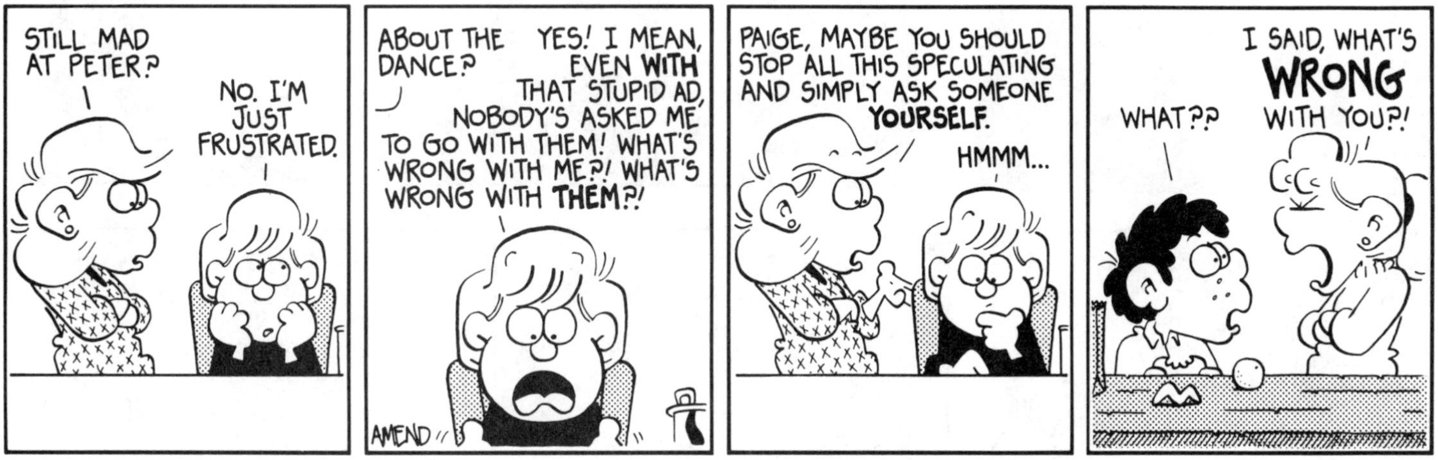
STILL MAD AT PETER?
NO. I'M JUST FRUSTRATED.
ABOUT THE DANCE?
YES! I MEAN, EVEN WITH THAT STUPID AD, NOBODY'S ASKED ME TO GO WITH THEM! WHAT'S WRONG WITH ME?! WHAT'S WRONG WITH THEM?!
AMEND
PAIGE, MAYBE YOU SHOULD STOP ALL THIS SPECULATING AND SIMPLY ASK SOMEONE YOURSELF.
HMMM...
WHAT??
I SAID, WHAT'S WRONG WITH YOU?!

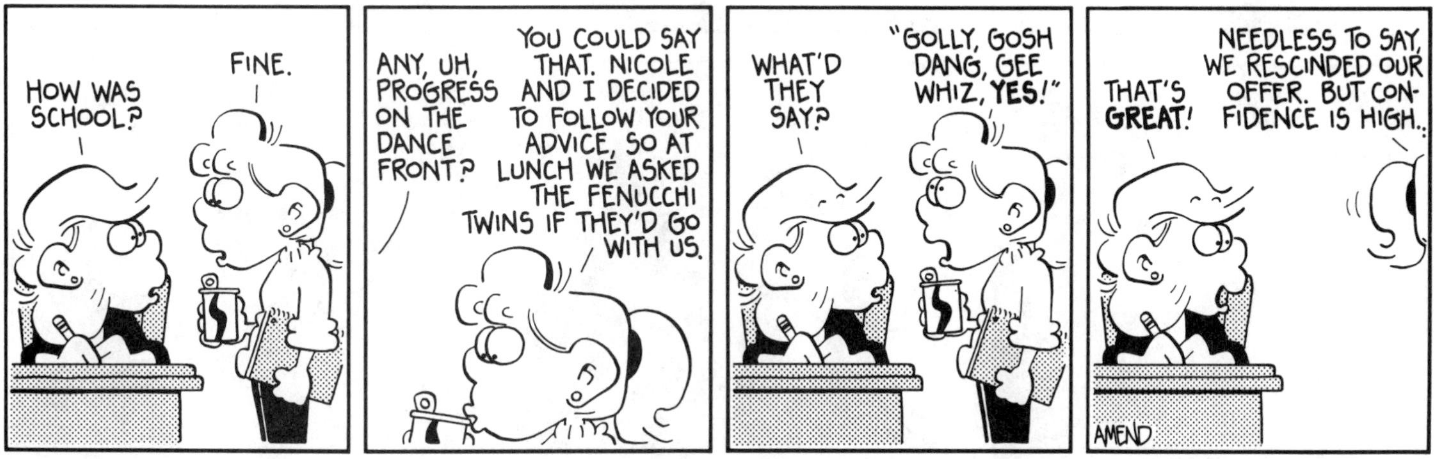
HOW WAS SCHOOL?
FINE.
ANY, UH, PROGRESS ON THE DANCE FRONT?
YOU COULD SAY THAT. NICOLE AND I DECIDED TO FOLLOW YOUR ADVICE, SO AT LUNCH WE ASKED THE FENUCCHI TWINS IF THEY'D GO WITH US.
WHAT'D THEY SAY?
"GOLLY, GOSH DANG, GEE WHIZ, YES!"
THAT'S GREAT!
NEEDLESS TO SAY, WE RESCINDED OUR OFFER. BUT CONFIDENCE IS HIGH.
AMEND

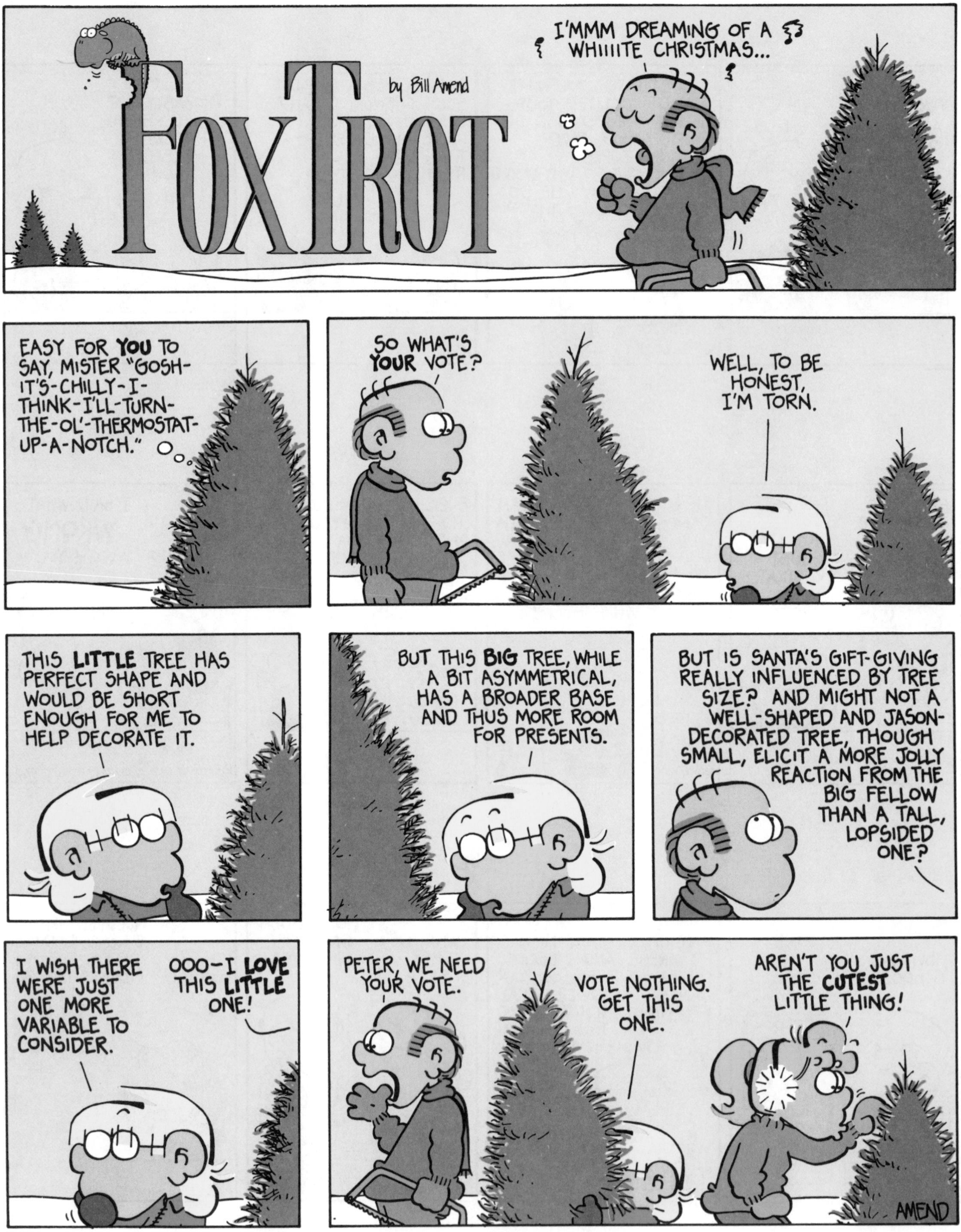
FoxTrot
by Bill Amend
I'MMM DREAMING OF A WHIIIIITE CHRISTMAS...
EASY FOR YOU TO SAY, MISTER "GOSH-IT'S-CHILLY-I-THINK-I'LL-TURN-THE-OL'-THERMOSTAT-UP-A-NOTCH."
SO WHAT'S YOUR VOTE?
WELL, TO BE HONEST, I'M TORN.
THIS LITTLE TREE HAS PERFECT SHAPE AND WOULD BE SHORT ENOUGH FOR ME TO HELP DECORATE IT.
BUT THIS BIG TREE, WHILE A BIT ASYMMETRICAL, HAS A BROADER BASE AND THUS MORE ROOM FOR PRESENTS.
BUT IS SANTA'S GIFT-GIVING REALLY INFLUENCED BY TREE SIZE? AND MIGHT NOT A WELL-SHAPED AND JASON-DECORATED TREE, THOUGH SMALL, ELICIT A MORE JOLLY REACTION FROM THE BIG FELLOW THAN A TALL, LOPSIDED ONE?
I WISH THERE WERE JUST ONE MORE VARIABLE TO CONSIDER.
OOO–I LOVE THIS LITTLE ONE!
PETER, WE NEED YOUR VOTE.
VOTE NOTHING. GET THIS ONE.
AREN'T YOU JUST THE CUTEST LITTLE THING!
AMEND

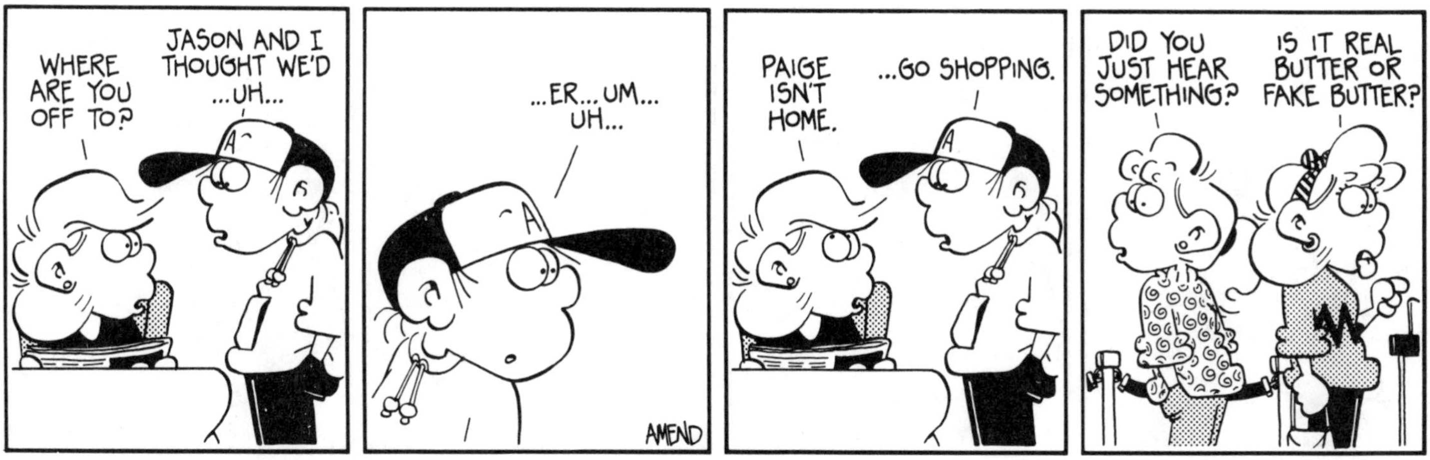
WHERE ARE YOU OFF TO?
JASON AND I THOUGHT WE'D ...UH...
...ER... UM... UH...
AMEND
PAIGE ISN'T HOME.
...GO SHOPPING.
DID YOU JUST HEAR SOMETHING?
IS IT REAL BUTTER OR FAKE BUTTER?

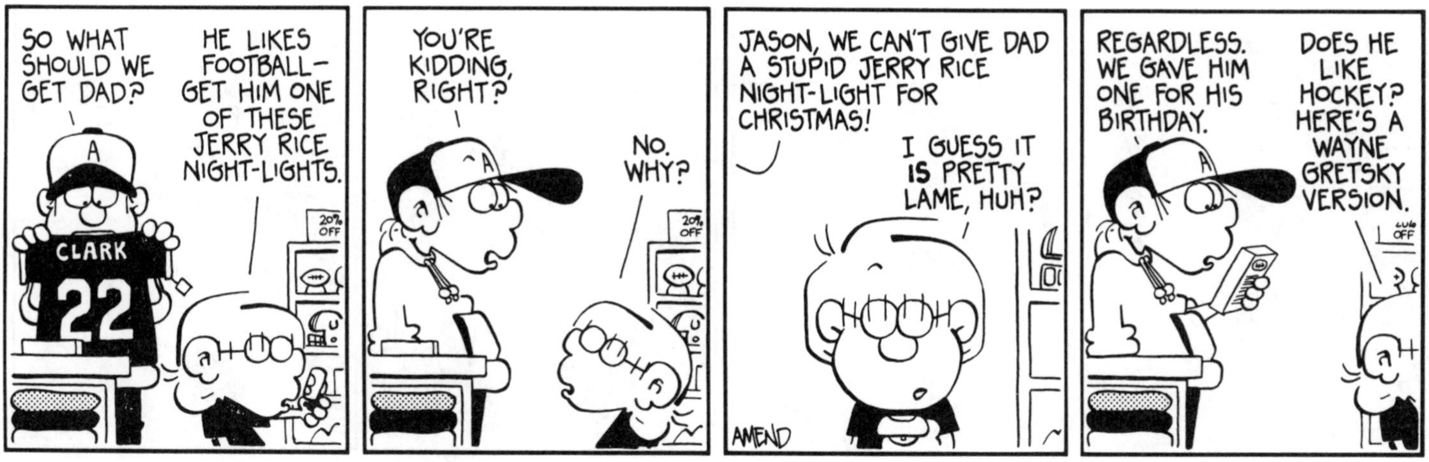
SO WHAT SHOULD WE GET DAD?
HE LIKES FOOTBALL– GET HIM ONE OF THESE JERRY RICE NIGHT-LIGHTS.
CLARK
22
20% OFF
YOU'RE KIDDING, RIGHT?
NO. WHY?
JASON, WE CAN'T GIVE DAD A STUPID JERRY RICE NIGHT-LIGHT FOR CHRISTMAS!
I GUESS IT **IS** PRETTY LAME, HUH?
AMEND
REGARDLESS. WE GAVE HIM ONE FOR HIS BIRTHDAY.
DOES HE LIKE HOCKEY? HERE'S A WAYNE GRETSKY VERSION.

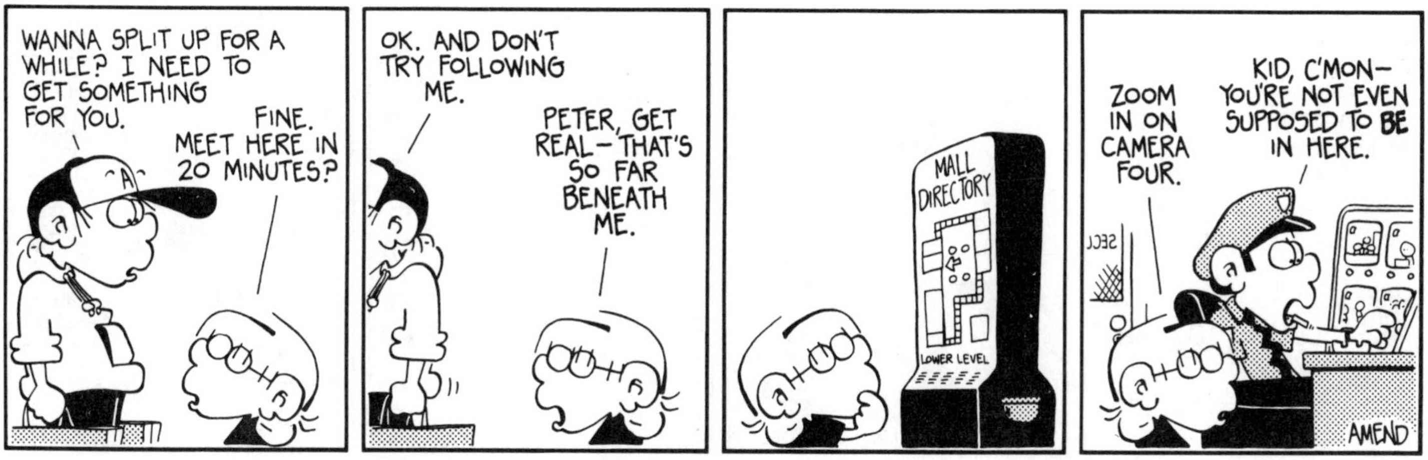
WANNA SPLIT UP FOR A WHILE? I NEED TO GET SOMETHING FOR YOU.
FINE. MEET HERE IN 20 MINUTES?
OK. AND DON'T TRY FOLLOWING ME.
PETER, GET REAL– THAT'S SO FAR BENEATH ME.
MALL DIRECTORY
LOWER LEVEL
ZOOM IN ON CAMERA FOUR.
KID, C'MON– YOU'RE NOT EVEN SUPPOSED TO **BE** IN HERE.
AMEND

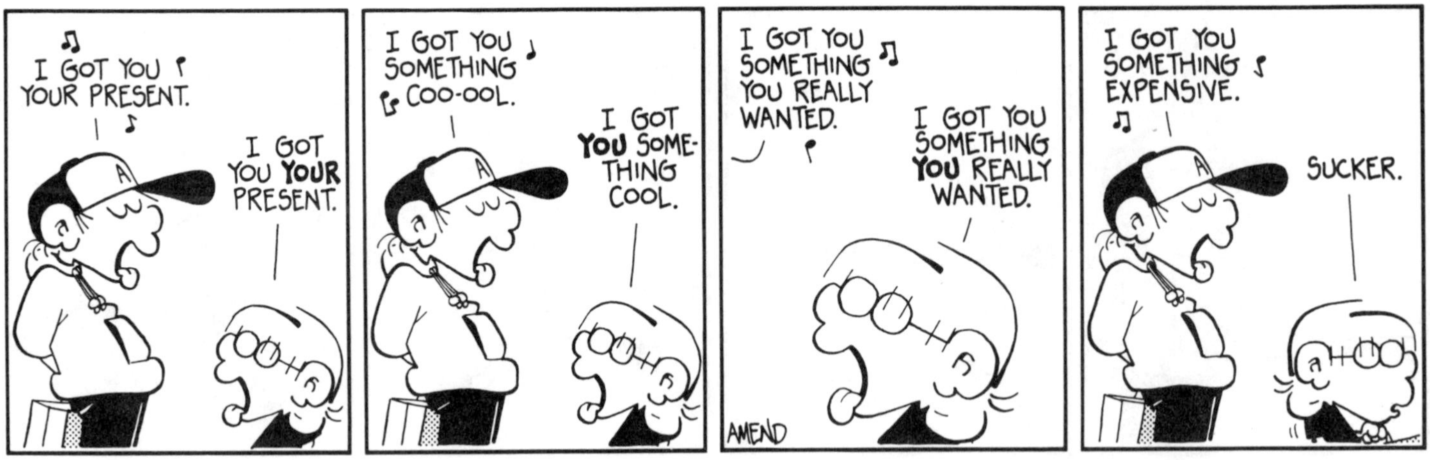
I GOT YOU YOUR PRESENT.
I GOT YOU **YOUR** PRESENT.
I GOT YOU SOMETHING COO-OOL.
I GOT **YOU** SOMETHING COOL.
I GOT YOU SOMETHING YOU REALLY WANTED.
I GOT YOU SOMETHING **YOU** REALLY WANTED.
AMEND
I GOT YOU SOMETHING EXPENSIVE.
SUCKER.

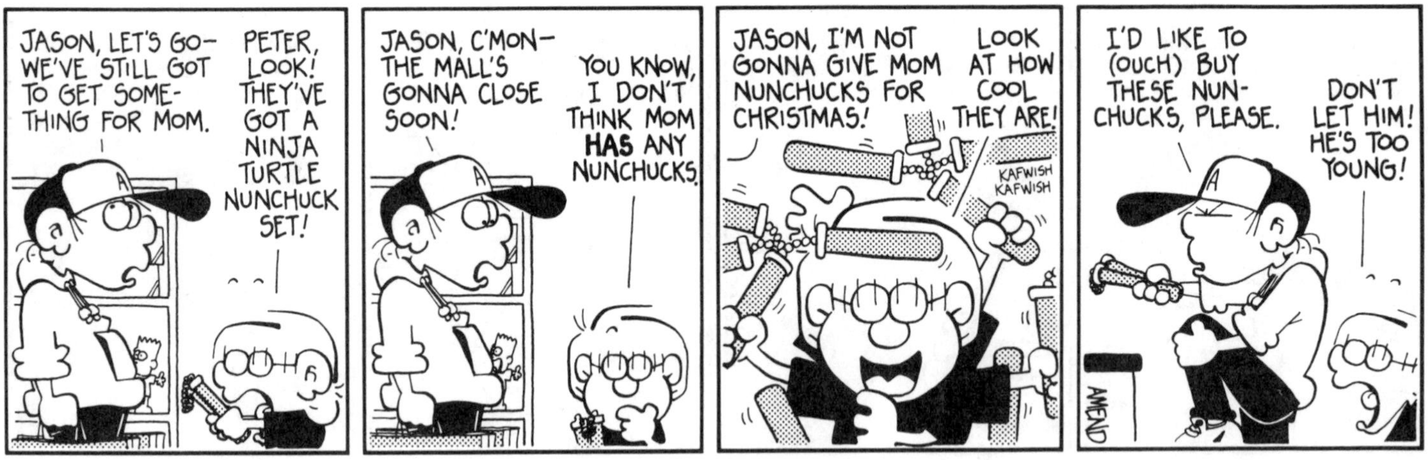
JASON, LET'S GO– WE'VE STILL GOT TO GET SOMETHING FOR MOM.
PETER, LOOK! THEY'VE GOT A NINJA TURTLE NUNCHUCK SET!
JASON, C'MON– THE MALL'S GONNA CLOSE SOON!
YOU KNOW, I DON'T THINK MOM **HAS** ANY NUNCHUCKS.
JASON, I'M NOT GONNA GIVE MOM NUNCHUCKS FOR CHRISTMAS!
LOOK AT HOW COOL THEY ARE!
KAFWISH KAFWISH
I'D LIKE TO (OUCH) BUY THESE NUNCHUCKS, PLEASE.
DON'T LET HIM! HE'S TOO YOUNG!
AMEND

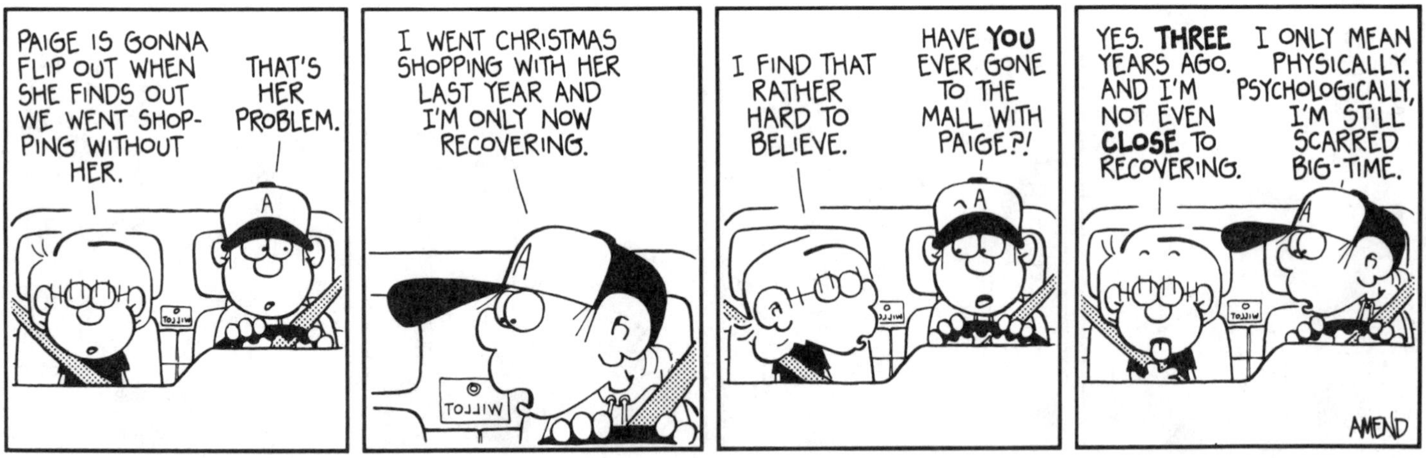
PAIGE IS GONNA FLIP OUT WHEN SHE FINDS OUT WE WENT SHOPPING WITHOUT HER.
THAT'S HER PROBLEM.
I WENT CHRISTMAS SHOPPING WITH HER LAST YEAR AND I'M ONLY NOW RECOVERING.
I FIND THAT RATHER HARD TO BELIEVE.
HAVE **YOU** EVER GONE TO THE MALL WITH PAIGE?!
YES. **THREE** YEARS AGO. AND I'M NOT EVEN **CLOSE** TO RECOVERING.
I ONLY MEAN PHYSICALLY. PSYCHOLOGICALLY, I'M STILL SCARRED BIG-TIME.
AMEND

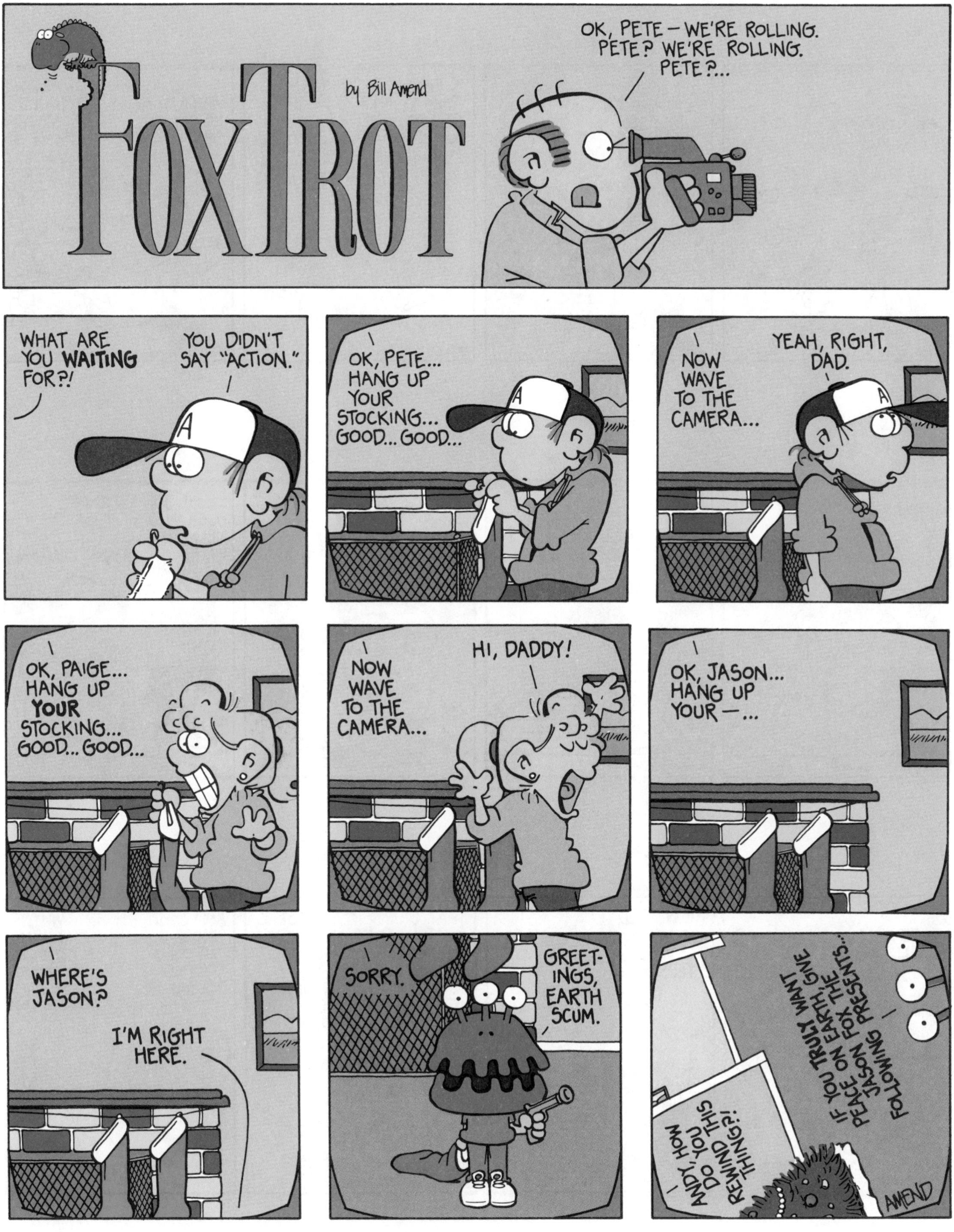
FoxTrot
by Bill Amend
OK, PETE — WE'RE ROLLING. PETE? WE'RE ROLLING. PETE?...
WHAT ARE YOU WAITING FOR?!
YOU DIDN'T SAY "ACTION."
OK, PETE... HANG UP YOUR STOCKING... GOOD... GOOD...
NOW WAVE TO THE CAMERA...
YEAH, RIGHT, DAD.
OK, PAIGE... HANG UP YOUR STOCKING... GOOD... GOOD...
NOW WAVE TO THE CAMERA...
HI, DADDY!
OK, JASON... HANG UP YOUR — ...
WHERE'S JASON?
I'M RIGHT HERE.
SORRY.
GREETINGS, EARTH SCUM.
IF YOU TRULY WANT PEACE ON EARTH, GIVE THE JASON FOX PRESENTS...
FOLLOWING
ANDY, HOW DO YOU REWIND THIS THING?!
AMEND

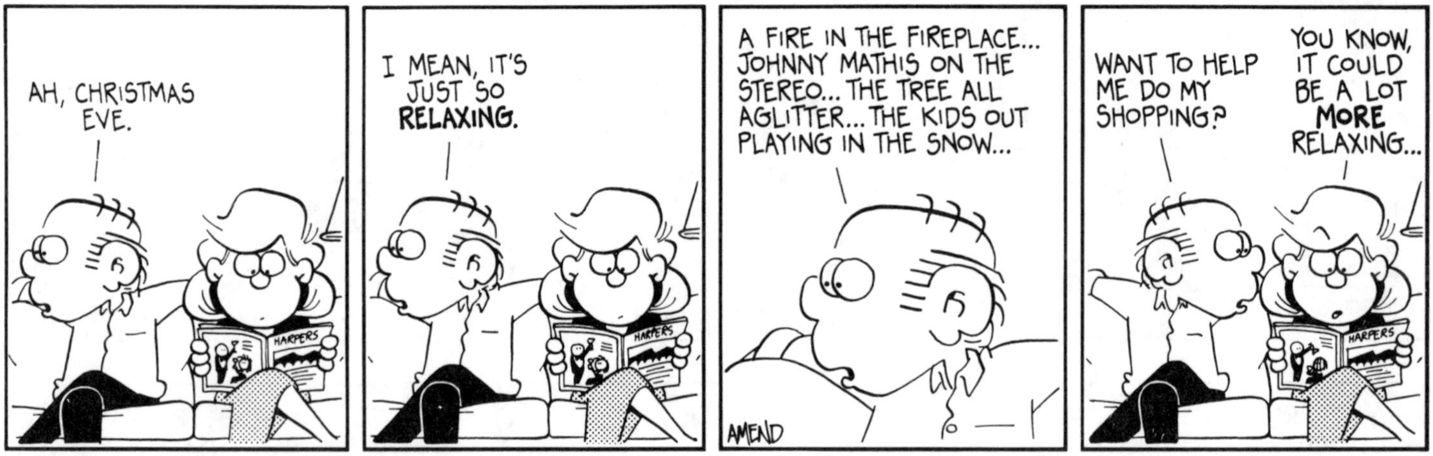
AH, CHRISTMAS EVE.
I MEAN, IT'S JUST SO **RELAXING**.
A FIRE IN THE FIREPLACE... JOHNNY MATHIS ON THE STEREO... THE TREE ALL AGLITTER... THE KIDS OUT PLAYING IN THE SNOW...
WANT TO HELP ME DO MY SHOPPING?
YOU KNOW, IT COULD BE A LOT **MORE** RELAXING...

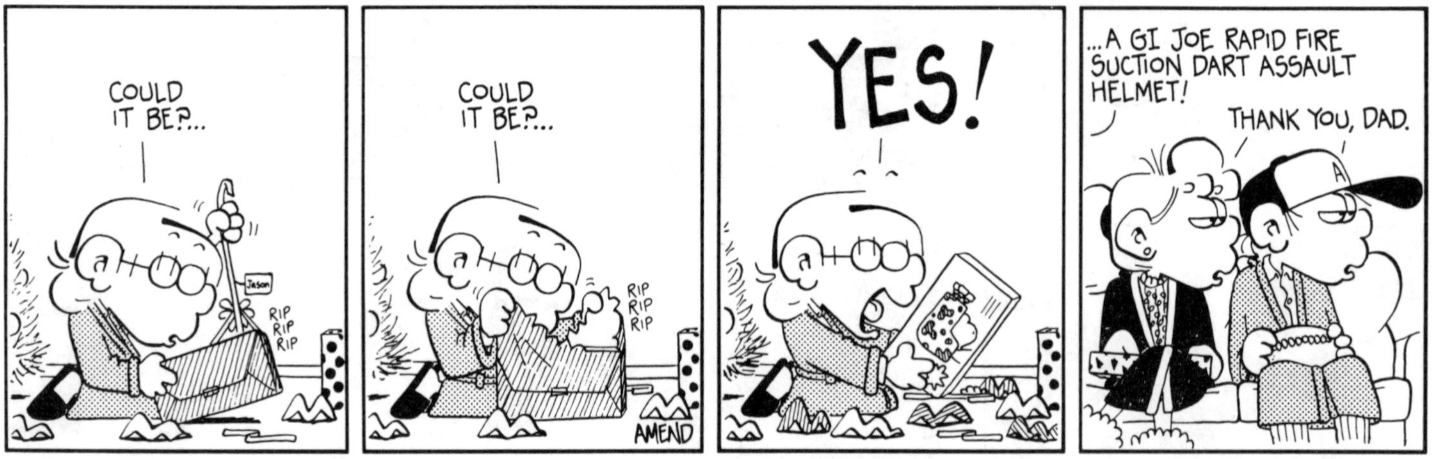
COULD IT BE?...
RIP RIP RIP
COULD IT BE?...
RIP RIP RIP
YES!
...A GI JOE RAPID FIRE SUCTION DART ASSAULT HELMET!
THANK YOU, DAD.

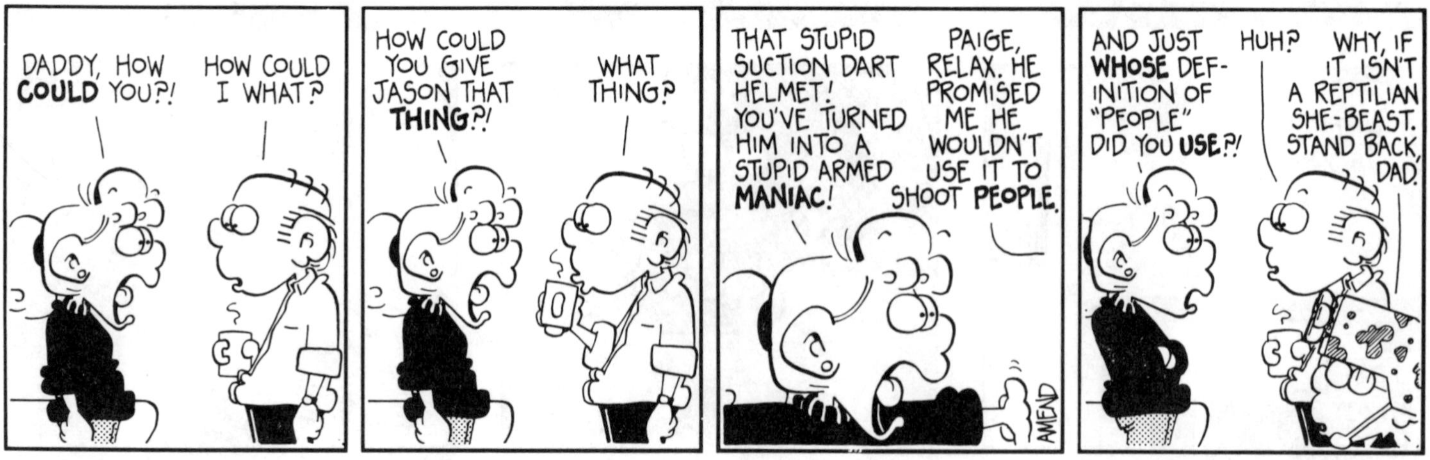
DADDY, HOW **COULD** YOU?!
HOW COULD I WHAT?
HOW COULD YOU GIVE JASON THAT **THING**?!
WHAT THING?
THAT STUPID SUCTION DART HELMET! YOU'VE TURNED HIM INTO A STUPID ARMED **MANIAC**!
PAIGE, RELAX. HE PROMISED ME HE WOULDN'T USE IT TO SHOOT **PEOPLE**.
AND JUST **WHOSE** DEFINITION OF "PEOPLE" DID YOU **USE**?!
HUH?
WHY, IF IT ISN'T A REPTILIAN SHE-BEAST. STAND BACK, DAD.

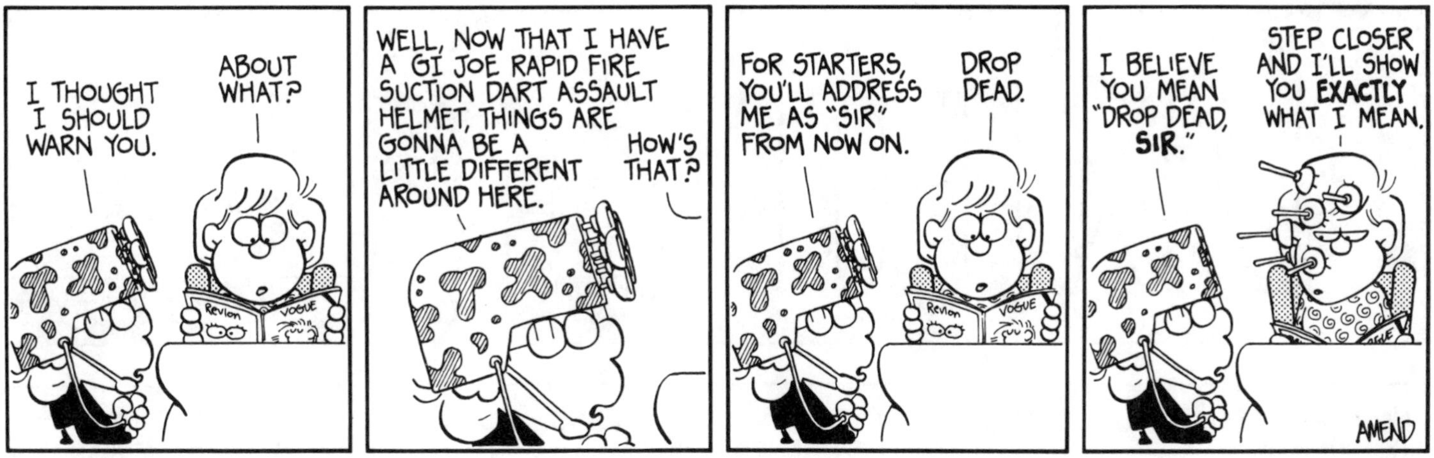
I THOUGHT I SHOULD WARN YOU.
ABOUT WHAT?
Revlon
VOGUE
WELL, NOW THAT I HAVE A GI JOE RAPID FIRE SUCTION DART ASSAULT HELMET, THINGS ARE GONNA BE A LITTLE DIFFERENT AROUND HERE.
HOW'S THAT?
FOR STARTERS, YOU'LL ADDRESS ME AS "SIR" FROM NOW ON.
DROP DEAD.
I BELIEVE YOU MEAN "DROP DEAD, **SIR**."
STEP CLOSER AND I'LL SHOW YOU **EXACTLY** WHAT I MEAN.
AMEND

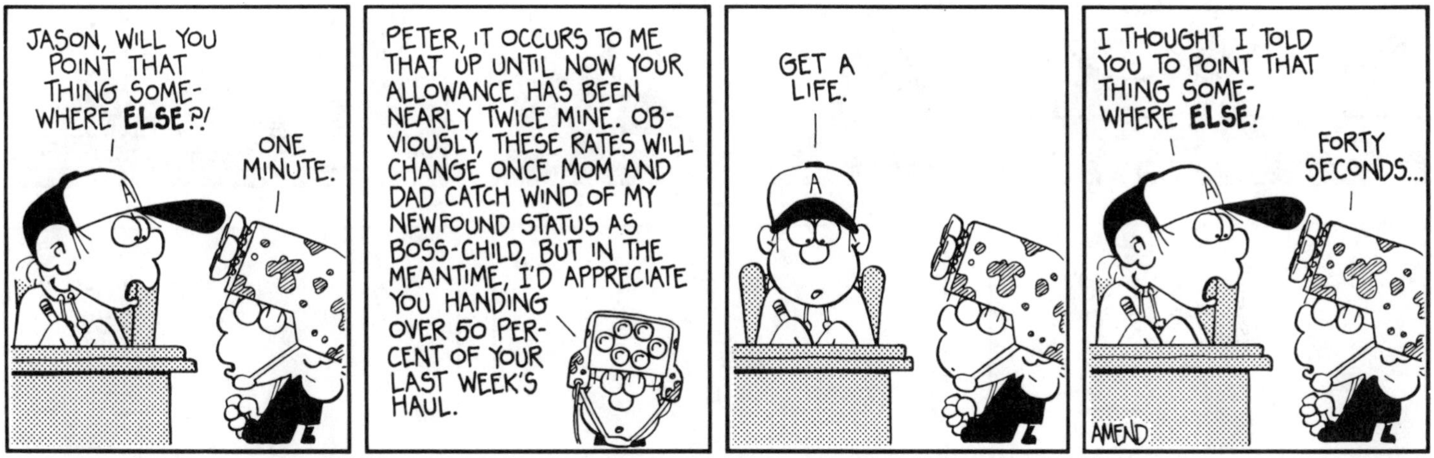
JASON, WILL YOU POINT THAT THING SOMEWHERE **ELSE**?!
ONE MINUTE.
PETER, IT OCCURS TO ME THAT UP UNTIL NOW YOUR ALLOWANCE HAS BEEN NEARLY TWICE MINE. OBVIOUSLY, THESE RATES WILL CHANGE ONCE MOM AND DAD CATCH WIND OF MY NEWFOUND STATUS AS BOSS-CHILD, BUT IN THE MEANTIME, I'D APPRECIATE YOU HANDING OVER 50 PERCENT OF YOUR LAST WEEK'S HAUL.
GET A LIFE.
I THOUGHT I TOLD YOU TO POINT THAT THING SOMEWHERE **ELSE**!
FORTY SECONDS...
AMEND

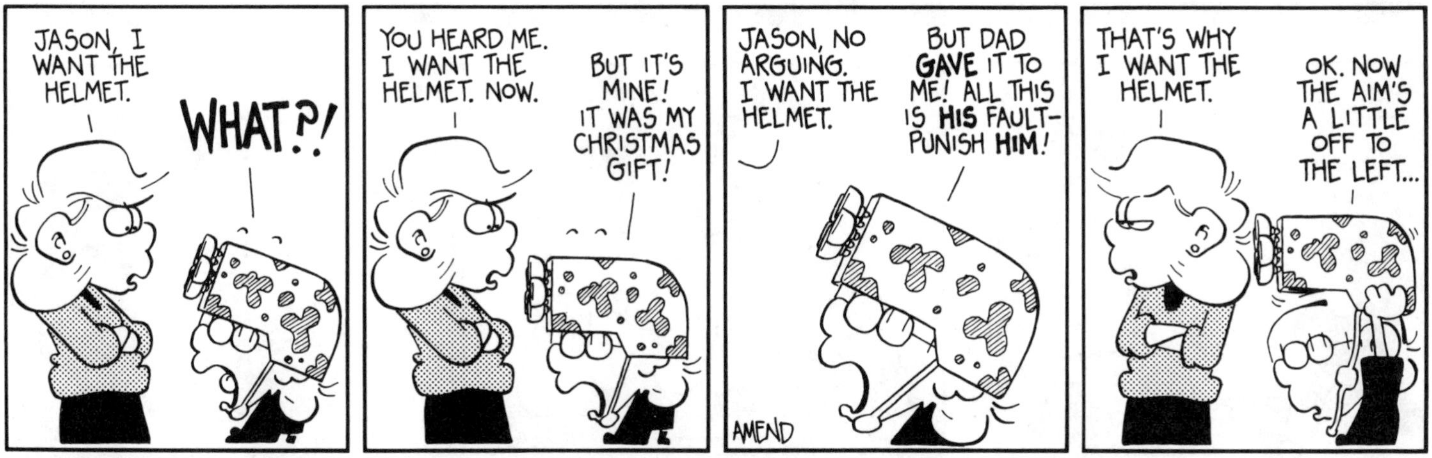
JASON, I WANT THE HELMET.
WHAT?!
YOU HEARD ME. I WANT THE HELMET. NOW.
BUT IT'S MINE! IT WAS MY CHRISTMAS GIFT!
JASON, NO ARGUING. I WANT THE HELMET.
BUT DAD **GAVE** IT TO ME! ALL THIS IS **HIS** FAULT- PUNISH **HIM**!
AMEND
THAT'S WHY I WANT THE HELMET.
OK. NOW THE AIM'S A LITTLE OFF TO THE LEFT...

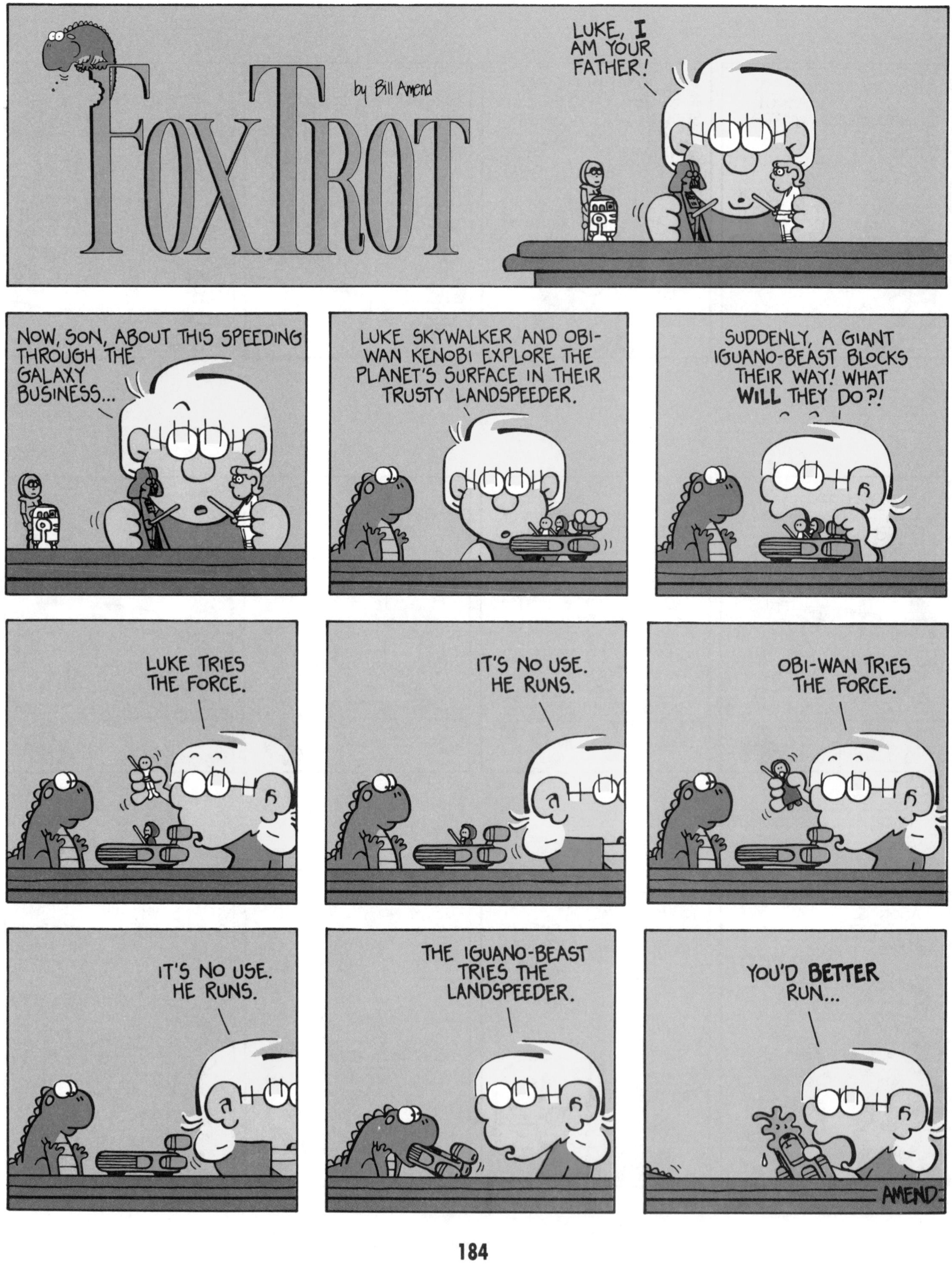
FOXTROT
by Bill Amend
LUKE, I AM YOUR FATHER!
NOW, SON, ABOUT THIS SPEEDING THROUGH THE GALAXY BUSINESS...
LUKE SKYWALKER AND OBI-WAN KENOBI EXPLORE THE PLANET'S SURFACE IN THEIR TRUSTY LANDSPEEDER.
SUDDENLY, A GIANT IGUANO-BEAST BLOCKS THEIR WAY! WHAT WILL THEY DO?!
LUKE TRIES THE FORCE.
IT'S NO USE. HE RUNS.
OBI-WAN TRIES THE FORCE.
IT'S NO USE. HE RUNS.
THE IGUANO-BEAST TRIES THE LANDSPEEDER.
YOU'D BETTER RUN...
AMEND

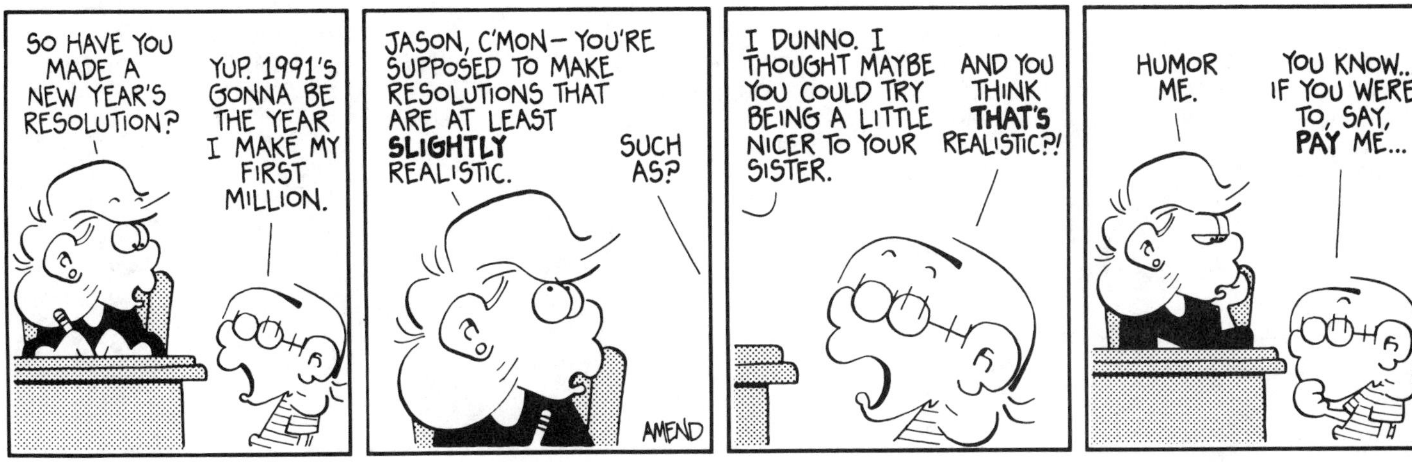
SO HAVE YOU MADE A NEW YEAR'S RESOLUTION?
YUP. 1991'S GONNA BE THE YEAR I MAKE MY FIRST MILLION.
JASON, C'MON — YOU'RE SUPPOSED TO MAKE RESOLUTIONS THAT ARE AT LEAST **SLIGHTLY** REALISTIC.
SUCH AS?
AMEND
I DUNNO. I THOUGHT MAYBE YOU COULD TRY BEING A LITTLE NICER TO YOUR SISTER.
AND YOU THINK **THAT'S** REALISTIC?!
HUMOR ME.
YOU KNOW... IF YOU WERE TO, SAY, **PAY** ME...

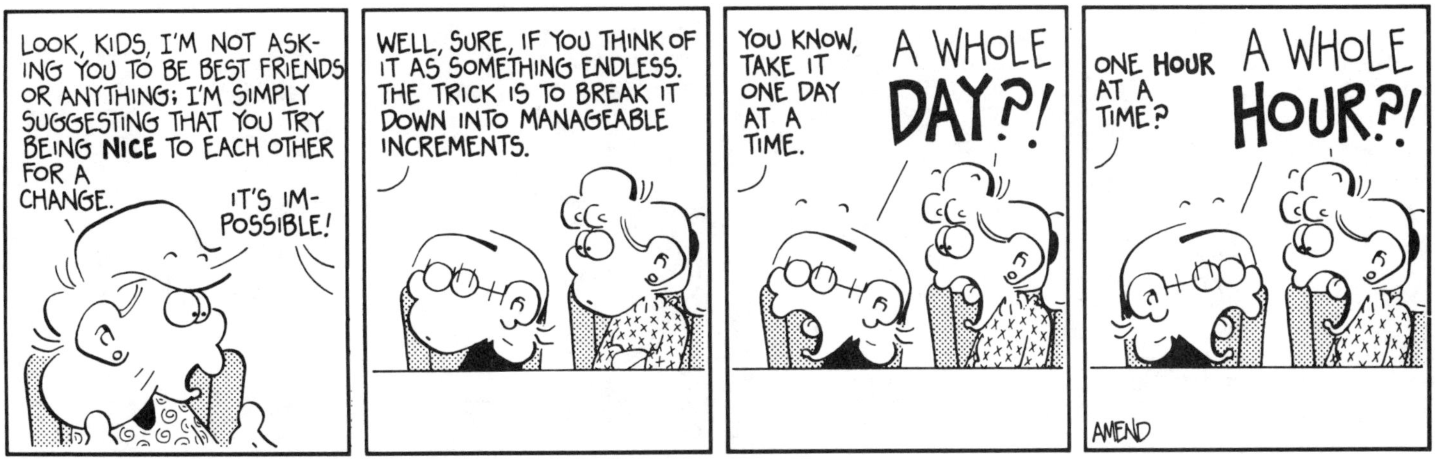
LOOK, KIDS, I'M NOT ASKING YOU TO BE BEST FRIENDS OR ANYTHING; I'M SIMPLY SUGGESTING THAT YOU TRY BEING **NICE** TO EACH OTHER FOR A CHANGE.
IT'S IMPOSSIBLE!
WELL, SURE, IF YOU THINK OF IT AS SOMETHING ENDLESS. THE TRICK IS TO BREAK IT DOWN INTO MANAGEABLE INCREMENTS.
YOU KNOW, TAKE IT ONE DAY AT A TIME.
A WHOLE **DAY?!**
ONE **HOUR** AT A TIME?
A WHOLE **HOUR?!**
AMEND

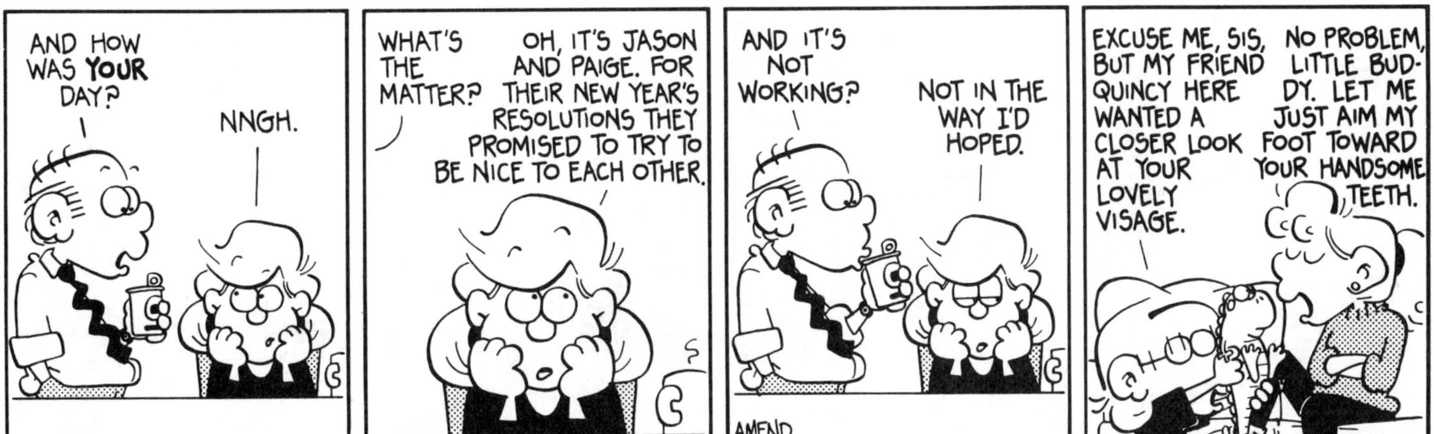
AND HOW WAS **YOUR** DAY?
NNGH.
WHAT'S THE MATTER?
OH, IT'S JASON AND PAIGE. FOR THEIR NEW YEAR'S RESOLUTIONS THEY PROMISED TO TRY TO BE NICE TO EACH OTHER.
AND IT'S NOT WORKING?
NOT IN THE WAY I'D HOPED.
AMEND
EXCUSE ME, SIS, BUT MY FRIEND QUINCY HERE WANTED A CLOSER LOOK AT YOUR LOVELY VISAGE.
NO PROBLEM, LITTLE BUDDY. LET ME JUST AIM MY FOOT TOWARD YOUR HANDSOME TEETH.

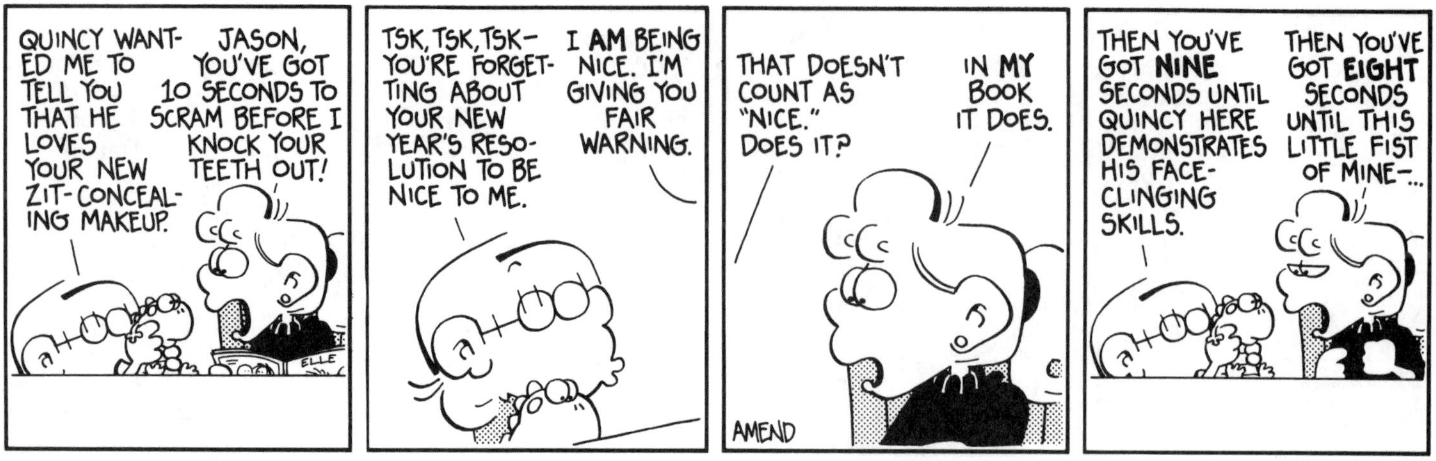
QUINCY WANTED ME TO TELL YOU THAT HE LOVES YOUR NEW ZIT-CONCEALING MAKEUP.
JASON, YOU'VE GOT 10 SECONDS TO SCRAM BEFORE I KNOCK YOUR TEETH OUT!
ELLE
TSK, TSK, TSK– YOU'RE FORGETTING ABOUT YOUR NEW YEAR'S RESOLUTION TO BE NICE TO ME.
I AM BEING NICE. I'M GIVING YOU FAIR WARNING.
THAT DOESN'T COUNT AS "NICE." DOES IT?
IN MY BOOK IT DOES.
AMEND
THEN YOU'VE GOT NINE SECONDS UNTIL QUINCY HERE DEMONSTRATES HIS FACE-CLINGING SKILLS.
THEN YOU'VE GOT EIGHT SECONDS UNTIL THIS LITTLE FIST OF MINE–...

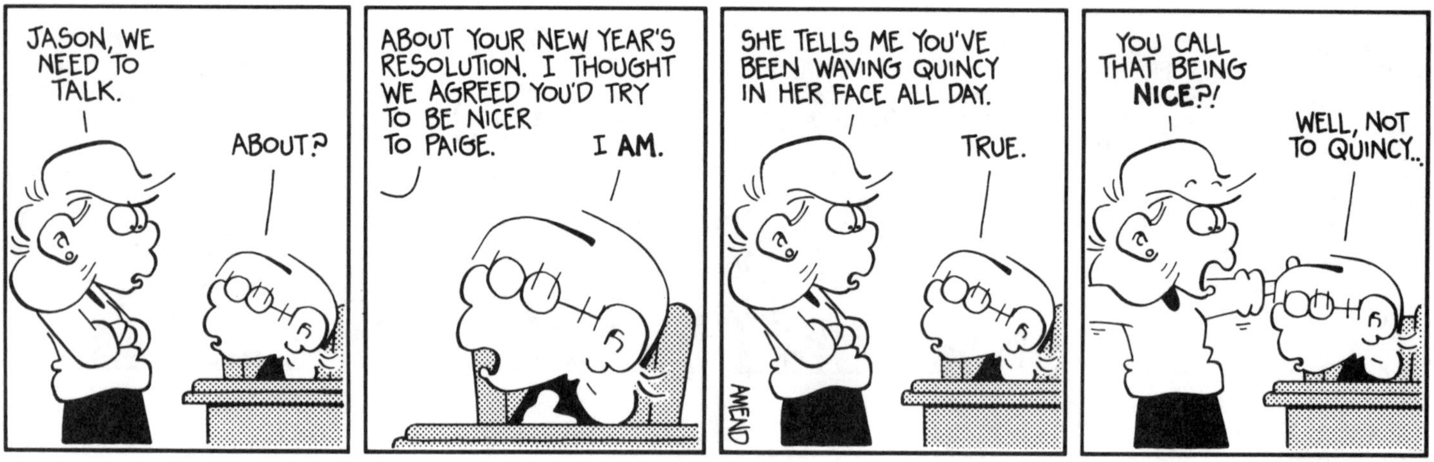
JASON, WE NEED TO TALK.
ABOUT?
ABOUT YOUR NEW YEAR'S RESOLUTION. I THOUGHT WE AGREED YOU'D TRY TO BE NICER TO PAIGE.
I AM.
AMEND
SHE TELLS ME YOU'VE BEEN WAVING QUINCY IN HER FACE ALL DAY.
TRUE.
YOU CALL THAT BEING NICE?!
WELL, NOT TO QUINCY...

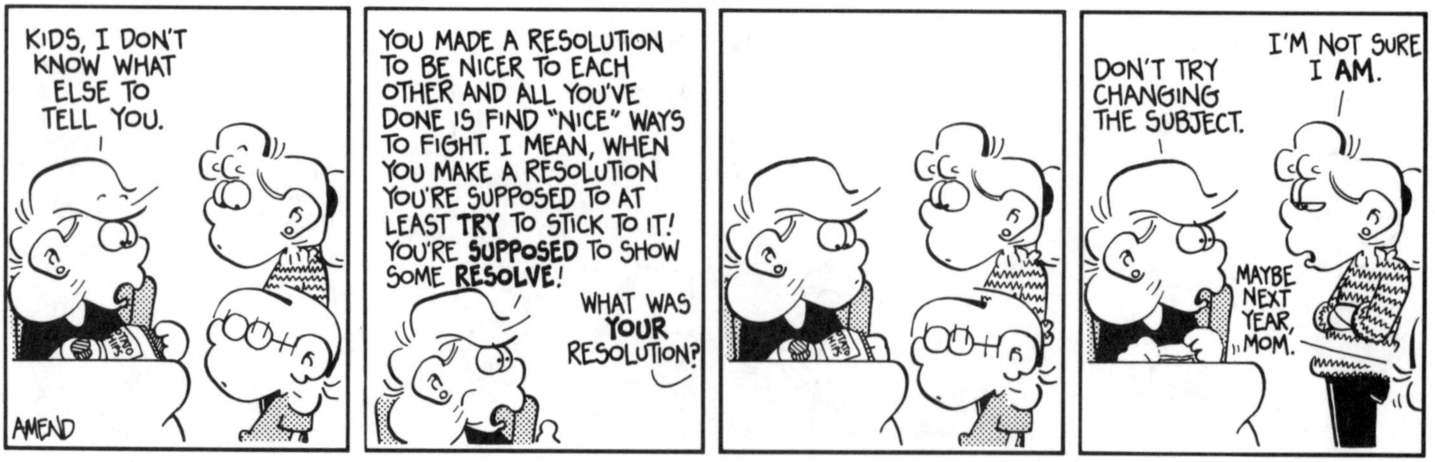
KIDS, I DON'T KNOW WHAT ELSE TO TELL YOU.
AMEND
YOU MADE A RESOLUTION TO BE NICER TO EACH OTHER AND ALL YOU'VE DONE IS FIND "NICE" WAYS TO FIGHT. I MEAN, WHEN YOU MAKE A RESOLUTION YOU'RE SUPPOSED TO AT LEAST TRY TO STICK TO IT! YOU'RE SUPPOSED TO SHOW SOME RESOLVE!
WHAT WAS YOUR RESOLUTION?
DON'T TRY CHANGING THE SUBJECT.
I'M NOT SURE I AM.
MAYBE NEXT YEAR, MOM.

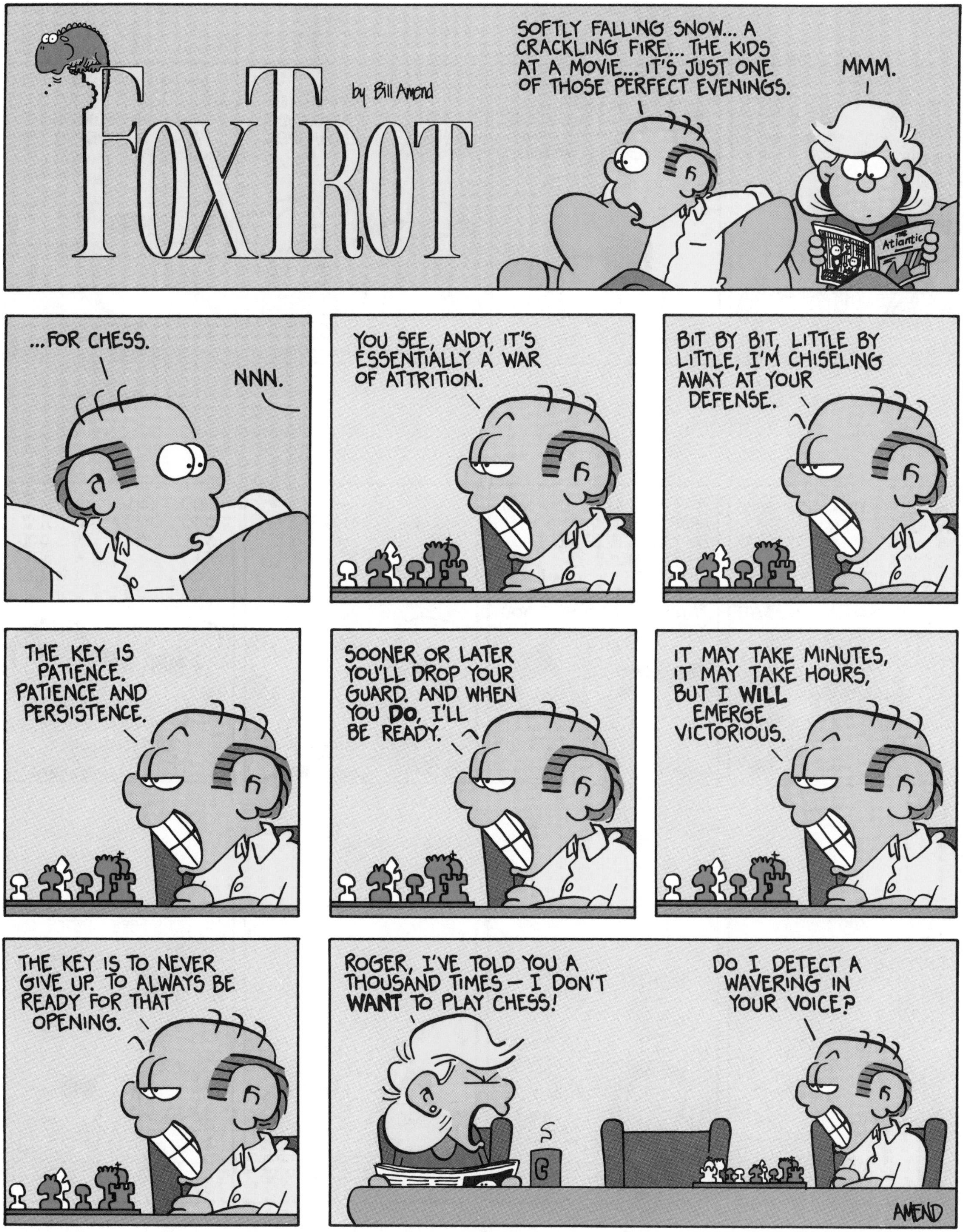
FoxTrot
by Bill Amend
SOFTLY FALLING SNOW... A CRACKLING FIRE... THE KIDS AT A MOVIE... IT'S JUST ONE OF THOSE PERFECT EVENINGS.
MMM.
The Atlantic
...FOR CHESS.
NNN.
YOU SEE, ANDY, IT'S ESSENTIALLY A WAR OF ATTRITION.
BIT BY BIT, LITTLE BY LITTLE, I'M CHISELING AWAY AT YOUR DEFENSE.
THE KEY IS PATIENCE. PATIENCE AND PERSISTENCE.
SOONER OR LATER YOU'LL DROP YOUR GUARD. AND WHEN YOU **DO**, I'LL BE READY.
IT MAY TAKE MINUTES, IT MAY TAKE HOURS, BUT I **WILL** EMERGE VICTORIOUS.
THE KEY IS TO NEVER GIVE UP. TO ALWAYS BE READY FOR THAT OPENING.
ROGER, I'VE TOLD YOU A THOUSAND TIMES — I DON'T **WANT** TO PLAY CHESS!
DO I DETECT A WAVERING IN YOUR VOICE?
AMEND

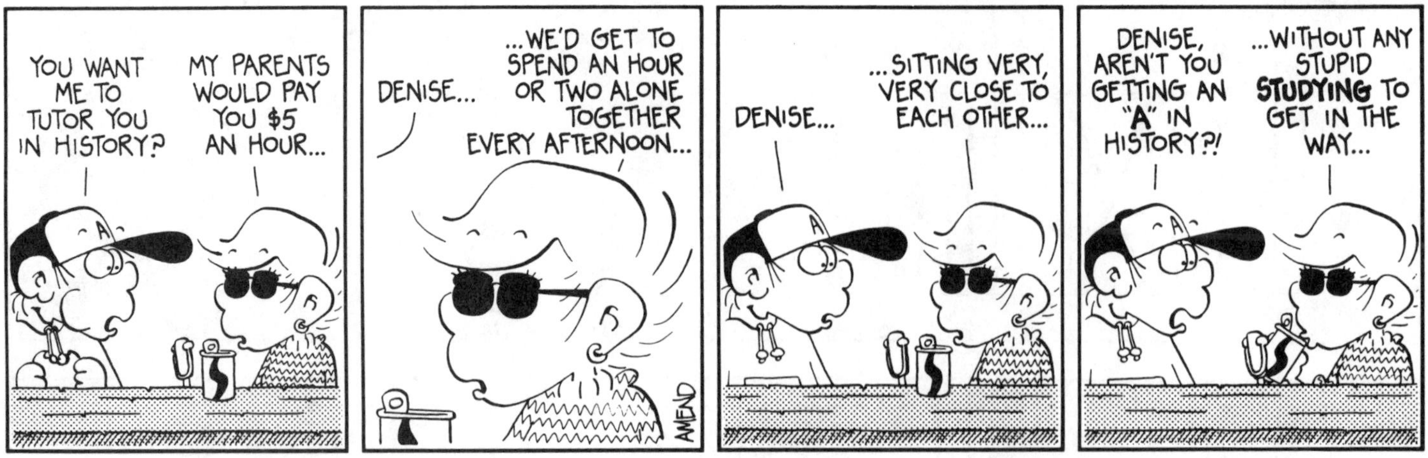
YOU WANT ME TO TUTOR YOU IN HISTORY?
MY PARENTS WOULD PAY YOU $5 AN HOUR...
DENISE...
...WE'D GET TO SPEND AN HOUR OR TWO ALONE TOGETHER EVERY AFTERNOON...
AMEND
DENISE...
...SITTING VERY, VERY CLOSE TO EACH OTHER...
DENISE, AREN'T YOU GETTING AN "A" IN HISTORY?!
...WITHOUT ANY STUPID STUDYING TO GET IN THE WAY...

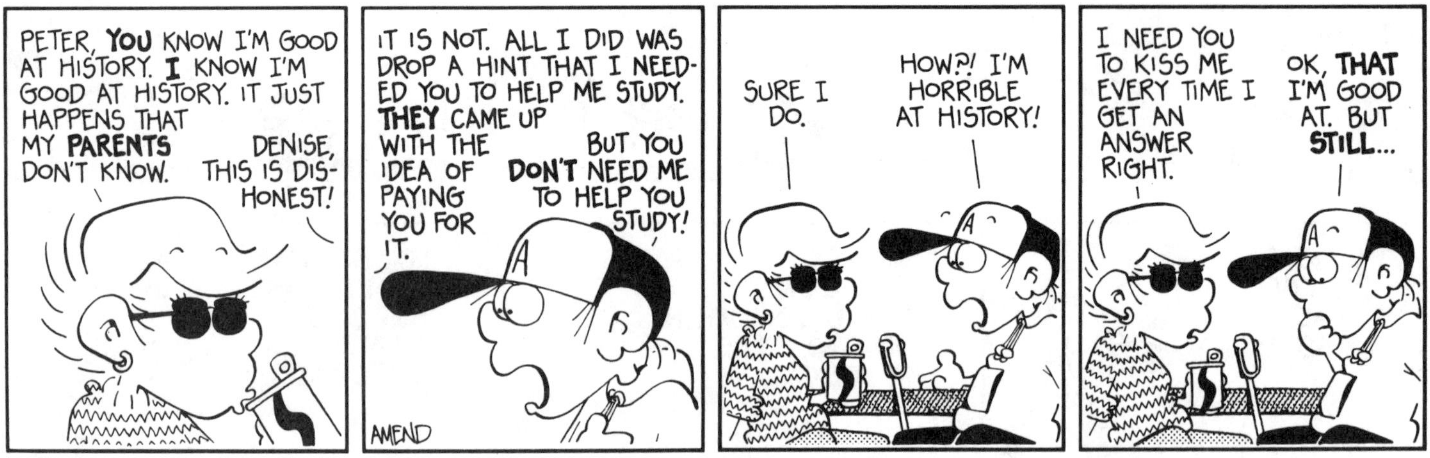
PETER, YOU KNOW I'M GOOD AT HISTORY. I KNOW I'M GOOD AT HISTORY. IT JUST HAPPENS THAT MY PARENTS DON'T KNOW.
DENISE, THIS IS DISHONEST!
IT IS NOT. ALL I DID WAS DROP A HINT THAT I NEEDED YOU TO HELP ME STUDY. THEY CAME UP WITH THE IDEA OF PAYING YOU FOR IT.
BUT YOU DON'T NEED ME TO HELP YOU STUDY!
AMEND
SURE I DO.
HOW?! I'M HORRIBLE AT HISTORY!
I NEED YOU TO KISS ME EVERY TIME I GET AN ANSWER RIGHT.
OK, THAT I'M GOOD AT. BUT STILL...

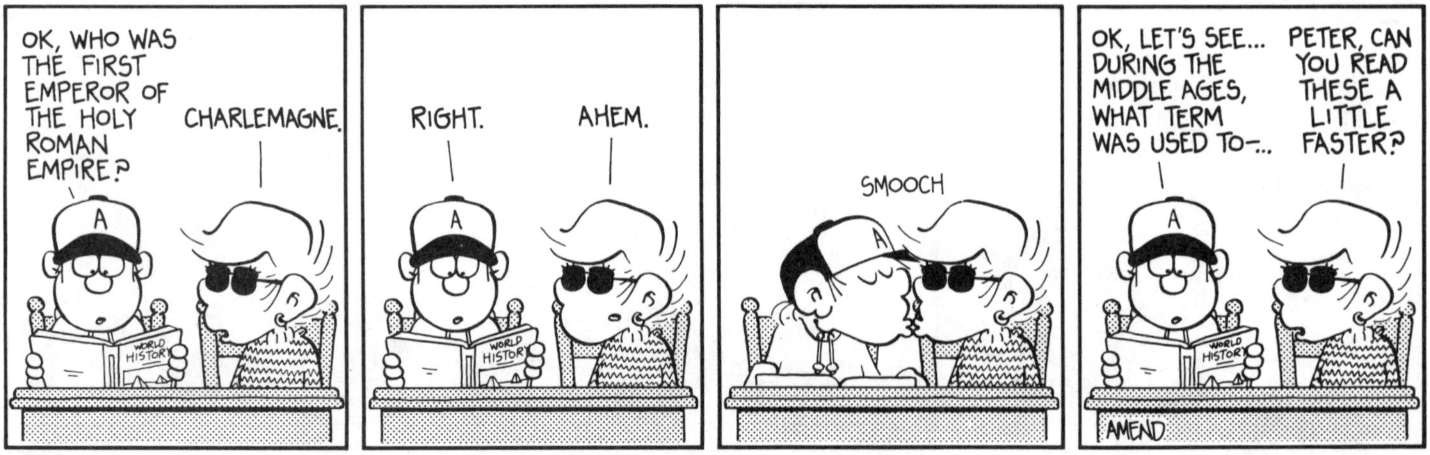
OK, WHO WAS THE FIRST EMPEROR OF THE HOLY ROMAN EMPIRE?
CHARLEMAGNE.
WORLD HISTORY
RIGHT.
AHEM.
SMOOCH
OK, LET'S SEE... DURING THE MIDDLE AGES, WHAT TERM WAS USED TO-...
PETER, CAN YOU READ THESE A LITTLE FASTER?
AMEND

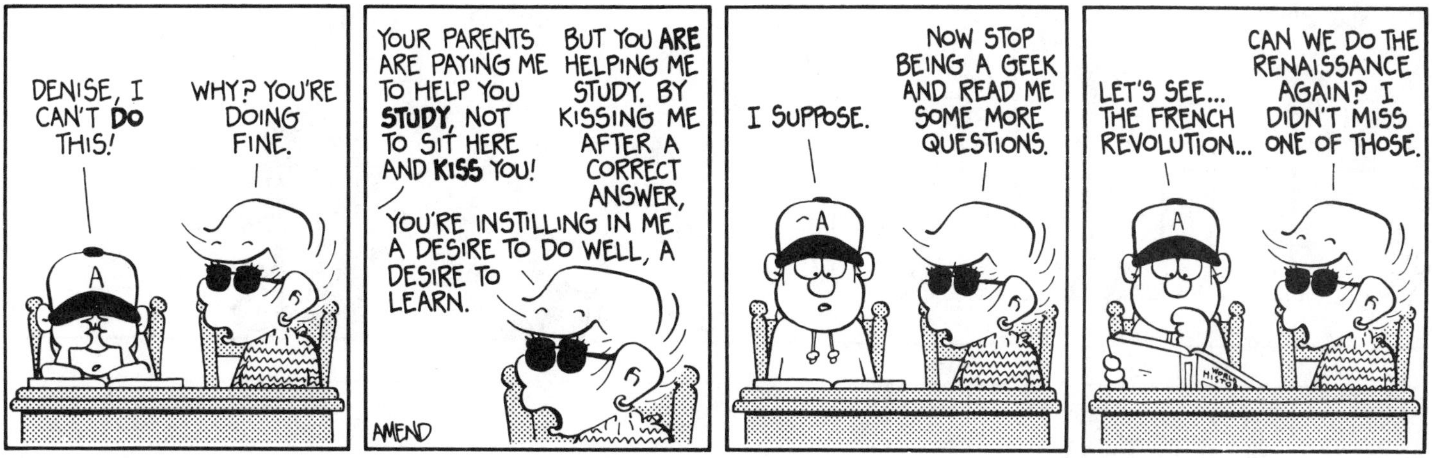
DENISE, I CAN'T **DO** THIS!
WHY? YOU'RE DOING FINE.
YOUR PARENTS ARE PAYING ME TO HELP YOU **STUDY**, NOT TO SIT HERE AND **KISS** YOU!
BUT YOU **ARE** HELPING ME STUDY. BY KISSING ME AFTER A CORRECT ANSWER, YOU'RE INSTILLING IN ME A DESIRE TO DO WELL, A DESIRE TO LEARN.
AMEND
I SUPPOSE.
NOW STOP BEING A GEEK AND READ ME SOME MORE QUESTIONS.
LET'S SEE... THE FRENCH REVOLUTION...
CAN WE DO THE RENAISSANCE AGAIN? I DIDN'T MISS ONE OF THOSE.

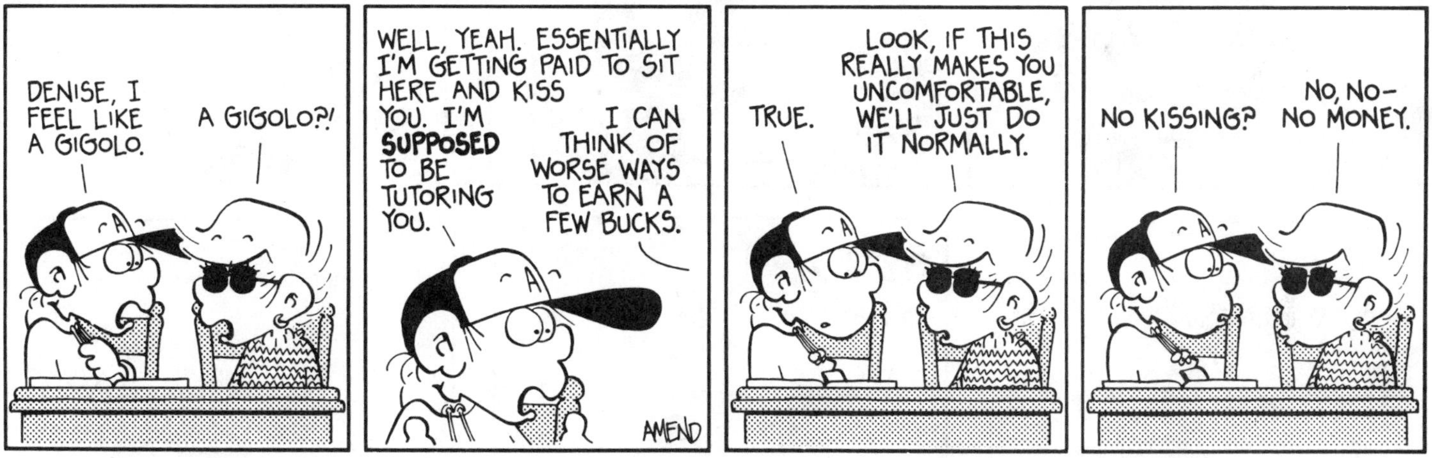
DENISE, I FEEL LIKE A GIGOLO.
A GIGOLO?!
WELL, YEAH. ESSENTIALLY I'M GETTING PAID TO SIT HERE AND KISS YOU. I'M **SUPPOSED** TO BE TUTORING YOU.
I CAN THINK OF WORSE WAYS TO EARN A FEW BUCKS.
AMEND
TRUE.
LOOK, IF THIS REALLY MAKES YOU UNCOMFORTABLE, WE'LL JUST DO IT NORMALLY.
NO KISSING?
NO, NO– NO MONEY.

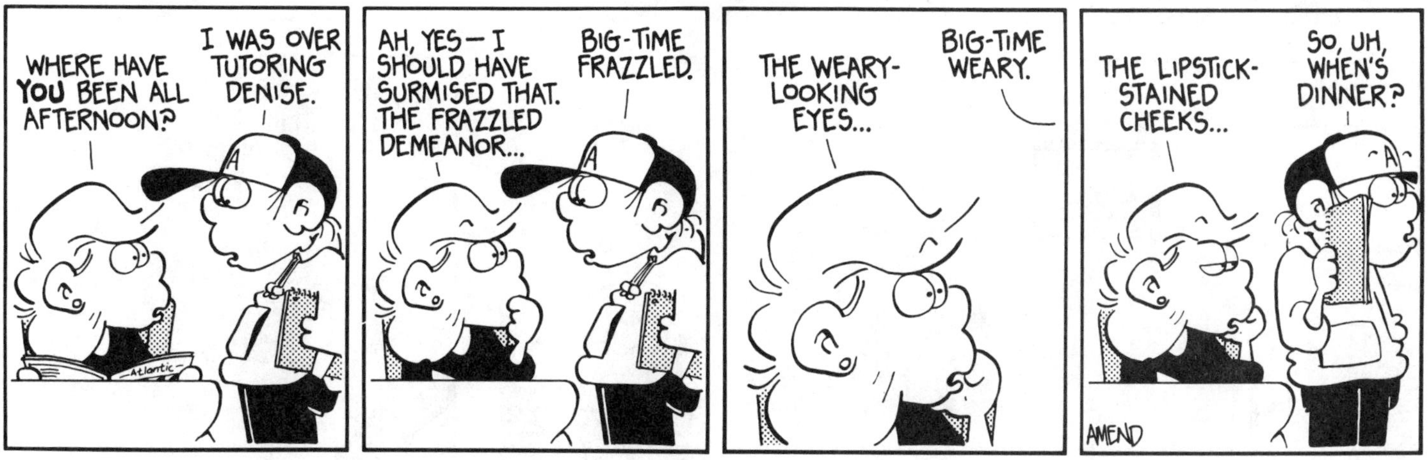
WHERE HAVE **YOU** BEEN ALL AFTERNOON?
I WAS OVER TUTORING DENISE.
Atlantic
AH, YES— I SHOULD HAVE SURMISED THAT. THE FRAZZLED DEMEANOR...
BIG-TIME FRAZZLED.
THE WEARY-LOOKING EYES...
BIG-TIME WEARY.
THE LIPSTICK-STAINED CHEEKS...
SO, UH, WHEN'S DINNER?
AMEND

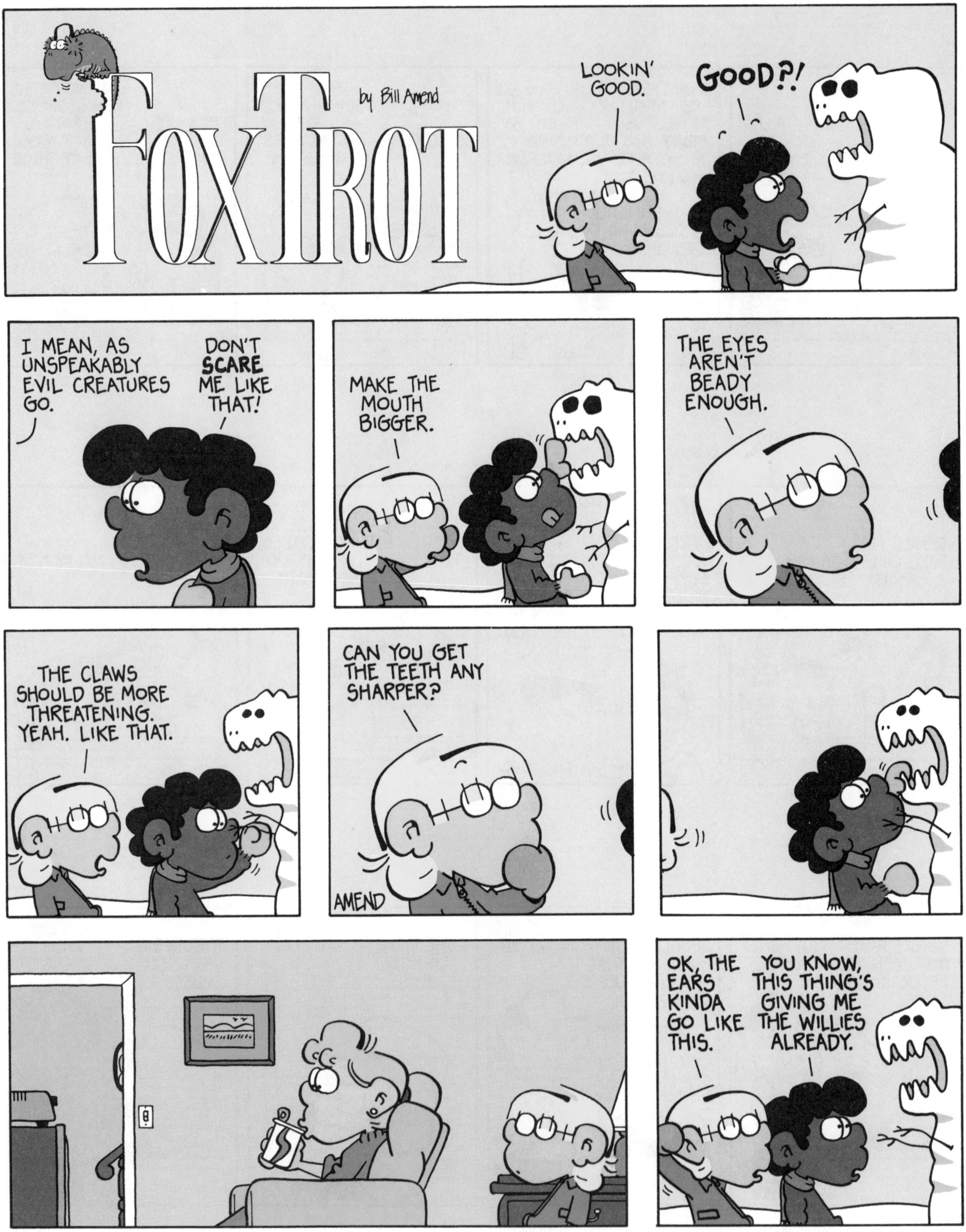
FoxTrot
by Bill Amend
LOOKIN' GOOD.
GOOD?!
I MEAN, AS UNSPEAKABLY EVIL CREATURES GO.
DON'T **SCARE** ME LIKE THAT!
MAKE THE MOUTH BIGGER.
THE EYES AREN'T BEADY ENOUGH.
THE CLAWS SHOULD BE MORE THREATENING. YEAH. LIKE THAT.
CAN YOU GET THE TEETH ANY SHARPER?
AMEND
OK, THE EARS KINDA GO LIKE THIS.
YOU KNOW, THIS THING'S GIVING ME THE WILLIES ALREADY.

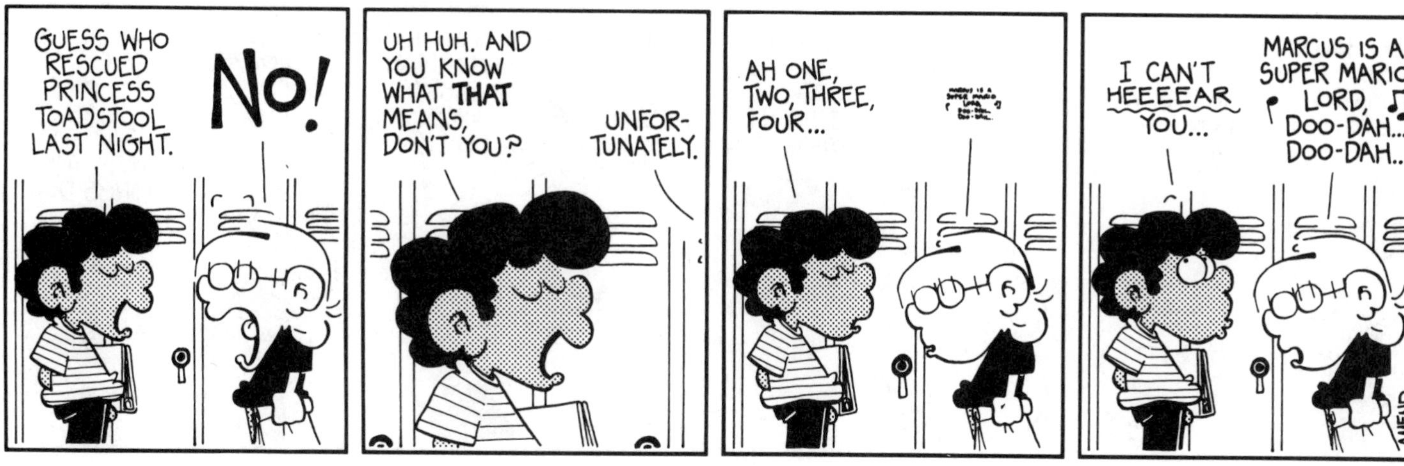
GUESS WHO RESCUED PRINCESS TOADSTOOL LAST NIGHT.
No!
UH HUH. AND YOU KNOW WHAT **THAT** MEANS, DON'T YOU?
UNFORTUNATELY.
AH ONE, TWO, THREE, FOUR...
I CAN'T HEEEEAR YOU...
MARCUS IS A SUPER MARIO LORD, DOO-DAH... DOO-DAH...
AMEND

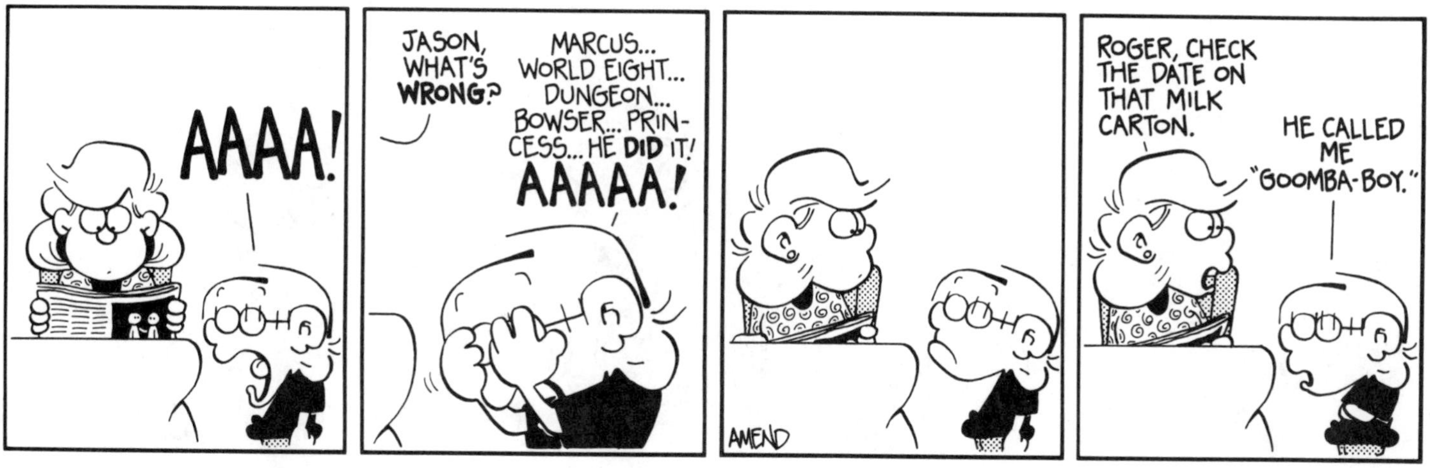
AAAA!
JASON, WHAT'S **WRONG**?
MARCUS... WORLD EIGHT... DUNGEON... BOWSER... PRINCESS... HE **DID** IT! AAAAA!
AMEND
ROGER, CHECK THE DATE ON THAT MILK CARTON.
HE CALLED ME "GOOMBA-BOY."

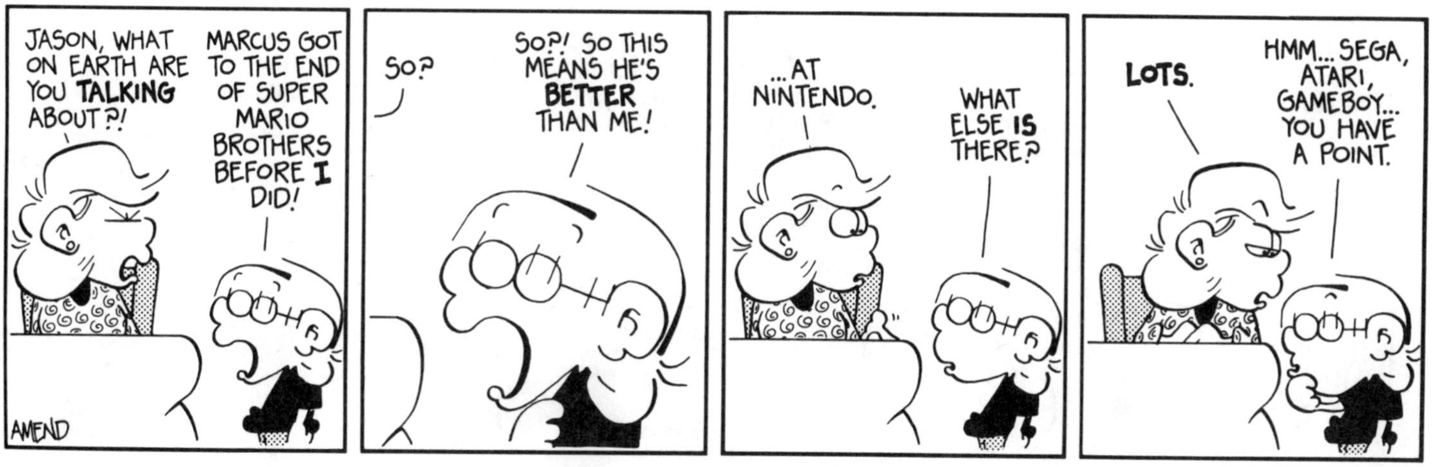
JASON, WHAT ON EARTH ARE YOU **TALKING** ABOUT?!
MARCUS GOT TO THE END OF SUPER MARIO BROTHERS BEFORE **I** DID!
AMEND
SO?
SO?! SO THIS MEANS HE'S **BETTER** THAN ME!
...AT NINTENDO.
WHAT ELSE **IS** THERE?
LOTS.
HMM... SEGA, ATARI, GAMEBOY... YOU HAVE A POINT.

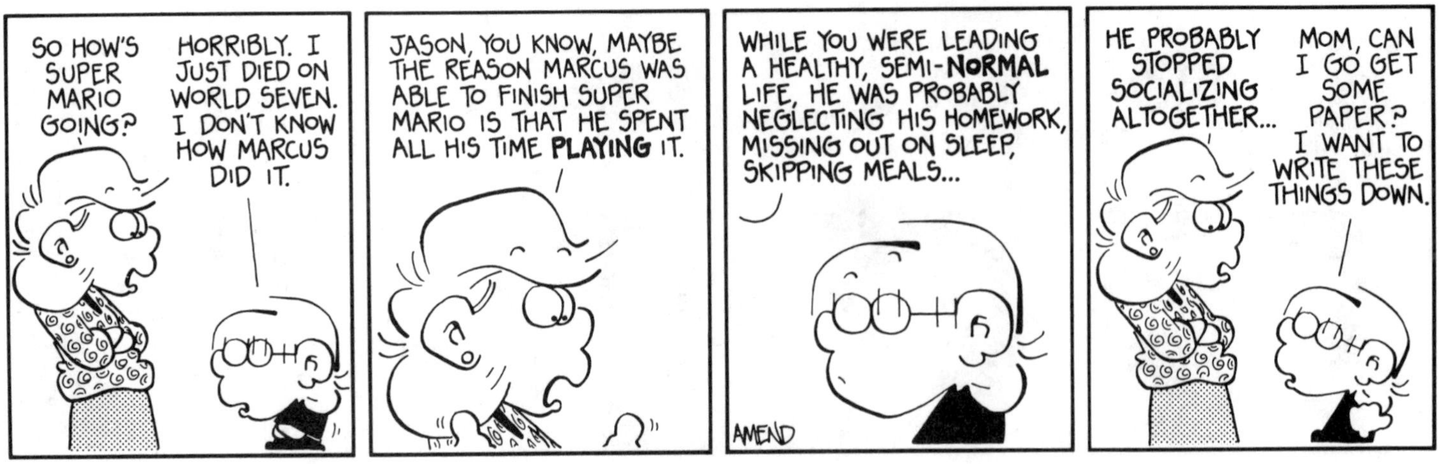

SO HOW'S SUPER MARIO GOING?
HORRIBLY. I JUST DIED ON WORLD SEVEN. I DON'T KNOW HOW MARCUS DID IT.
JASON, YOU KNOW, MAYBE THE REASON MARCUS WAS ABLE TO FINISH SUPER MARIO IS THAT HE SPENT ALL HIS TIME **PLAYING** IT.
WHILE YOU WERE LEADING A HEALTHY, SEMI-**NORMAL** LIFE, HE WAS PROBABLY NEGLECTING HIS HOMEWORK, MISSING OUT ON SLEEP, SKIPPING MEALS...
AMEND
HE PROBABLY STOPPED SOCIALIZING ALTOGETHER...
MOM, CAN I GO GET SOME PAPER? I WANT TO WRITE THESE THINGS DOWN.

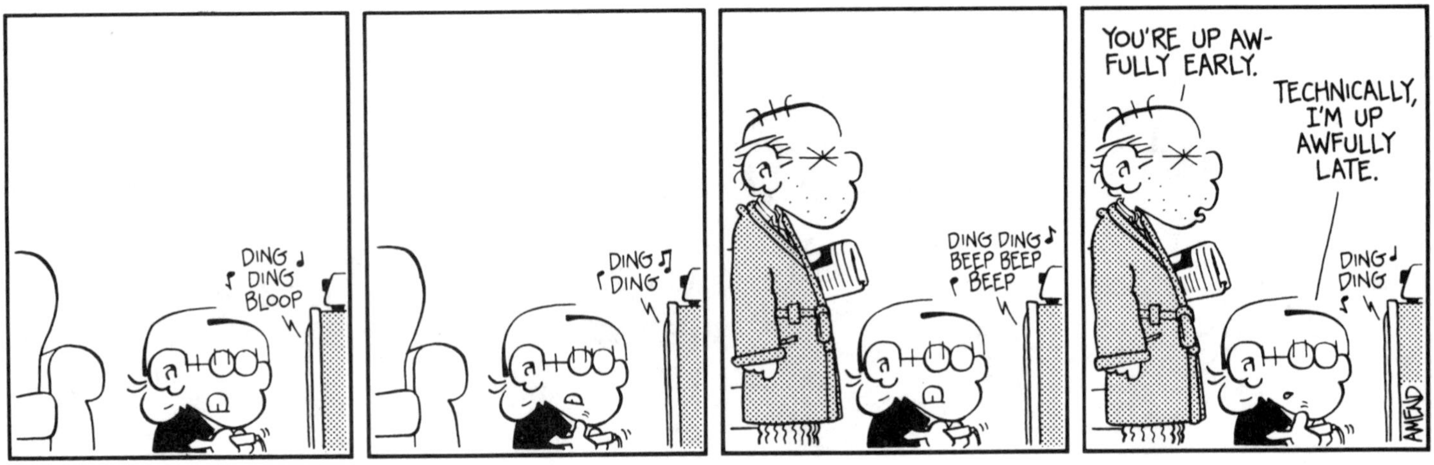

DING DING BLOOP
DING DING
DING DING BEEP BEEP BEEP
YOU'RE UP AWFULLY EARLY.
TECHNICALLY, I'M UP AWFULLY LATE.
DING DING
AMEND

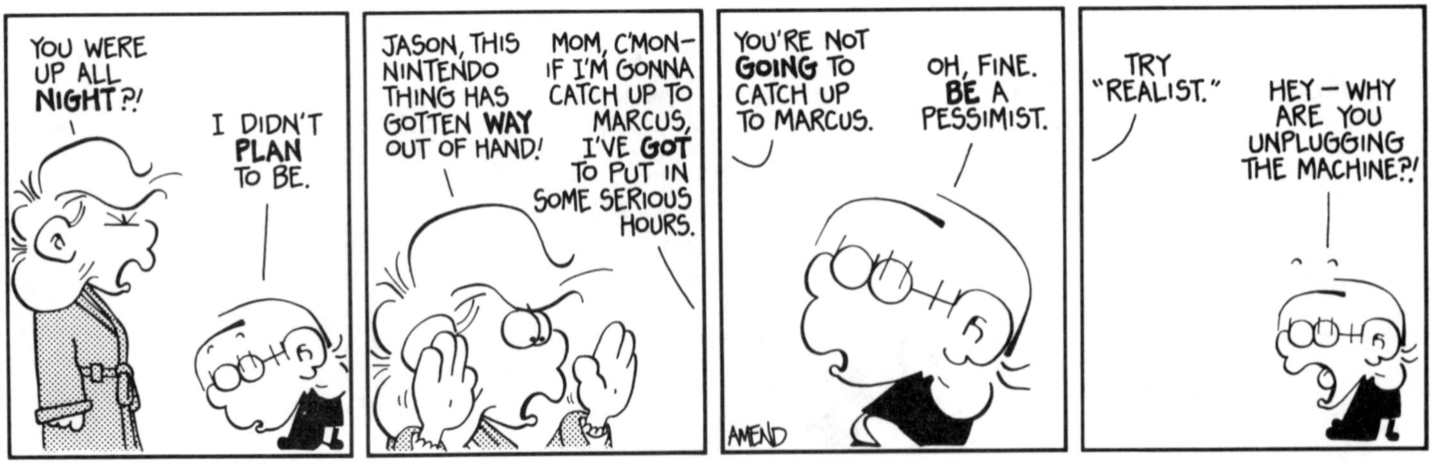

YOU WERE UP ALL **NIGHT**?!
I DIDN'T **PLAN** TO BE.
JASON, THIS NINTENDO THING HAS GOTTEN **WAY** OUT OF HAND!
MOM, C'MON- IF I'M GONNA CATCH UP TO MARCUS, I'VE **GOT** TO PUT IN SOME SERIOUS HOURS.
YOU'RE NOT **GOING** TO CATCH UP TO MARCUS.
OH, FINE. **BE** A PESSIMIST.
AMEND
TRY "REALIST."
HEY—WHY ARE YOU UNPLUGGING THE MACHINE?!

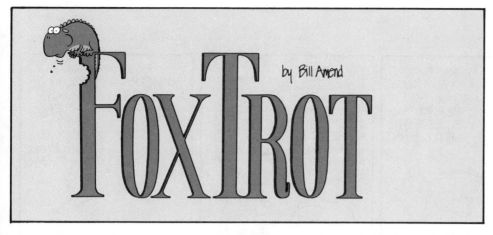

by Bill Amend

FoxTrot

Give Jason all your money

SO WHAT DO YOU THINK OF MY FLIP-BOOK? SAY... ISN'T THIS YOUR NEW **PURSE**?...

PROMISE ME YOU WON'T SHOW THIS THING TO YOUR FATHER.

FLIP FLIP FLIP

SON, I'VE BEEN THINKING...

AMEND

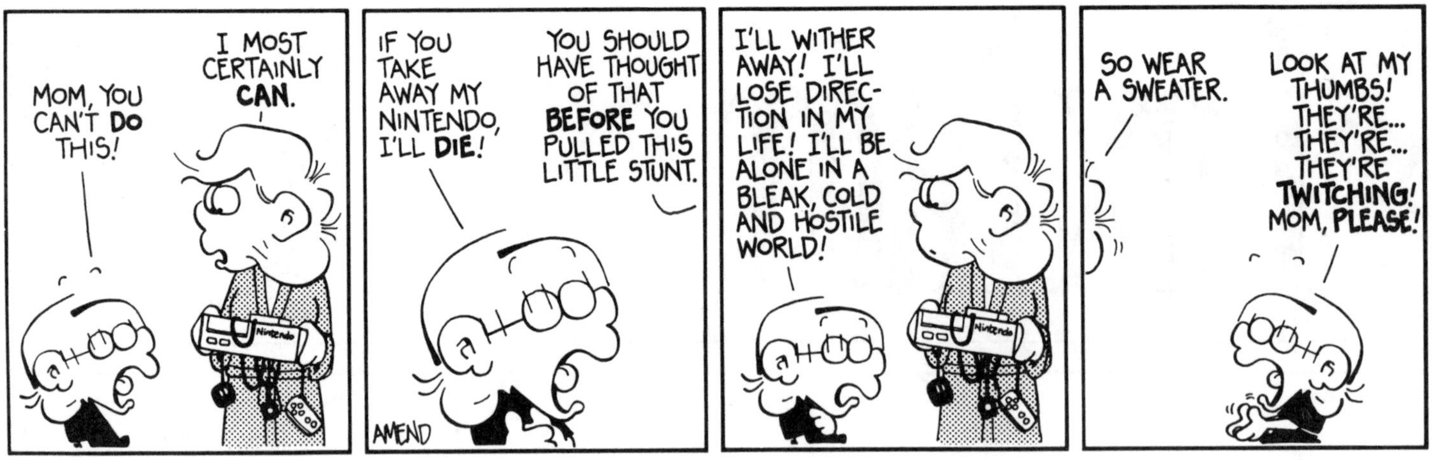
MOM, YOU CAN'T **DO** THIS!
I MOST CERTAINLY **CAN**.
IF YOU TAKE AWAY MY NINTENDO, I'LL **DIE**!
YOU SHOULD HAVE THOUGHT OF THAT **BEFORE** YOU PULLED THIS LITTLE STUNT.
AMEND
I'LL WITHER AWAY! I'LL LOSE DIRECTION IN MY LIFE! I'LL BE ALONE IN A BLEAK, COLD AND HOSTILE WORLD!
SO WEAR A SWEATER.
LOOK AT MY THUMBS! THEY'RE... THEY'RE... THEY'RE **TWITCHING**! MOM, **PLEASE**!

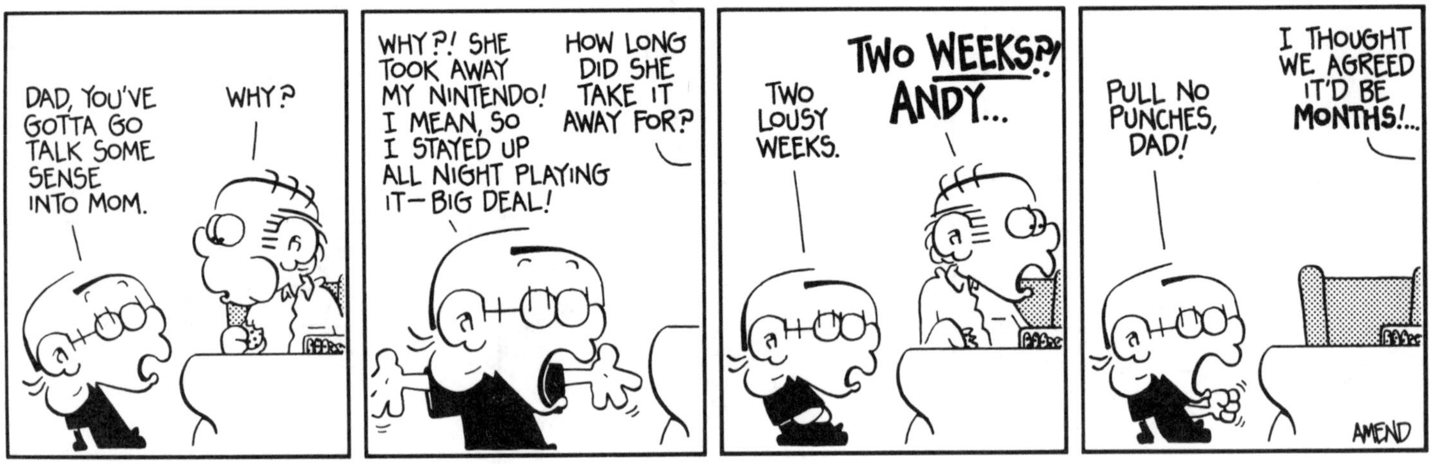
DAD, YOU'VE GOTTA GO TALK SOME SENSE INTO MOM.
WHY?
WHY?! SHE TOOK AWAY MY NINTENDO! I MEAN, SO I STAYED UP ALL NIGHT PLAYING IT—BIG DEAL!
HOW LONG DID SHE TAKE IT AWAY FOR?
TWO LOUSY WEEKS.
TWO WEEKS?! ANDY...
PULL NO PUNCHES, DAD!
I THOUGHT WE AGREED IT'D BE **MONTHS**!...
AMEND

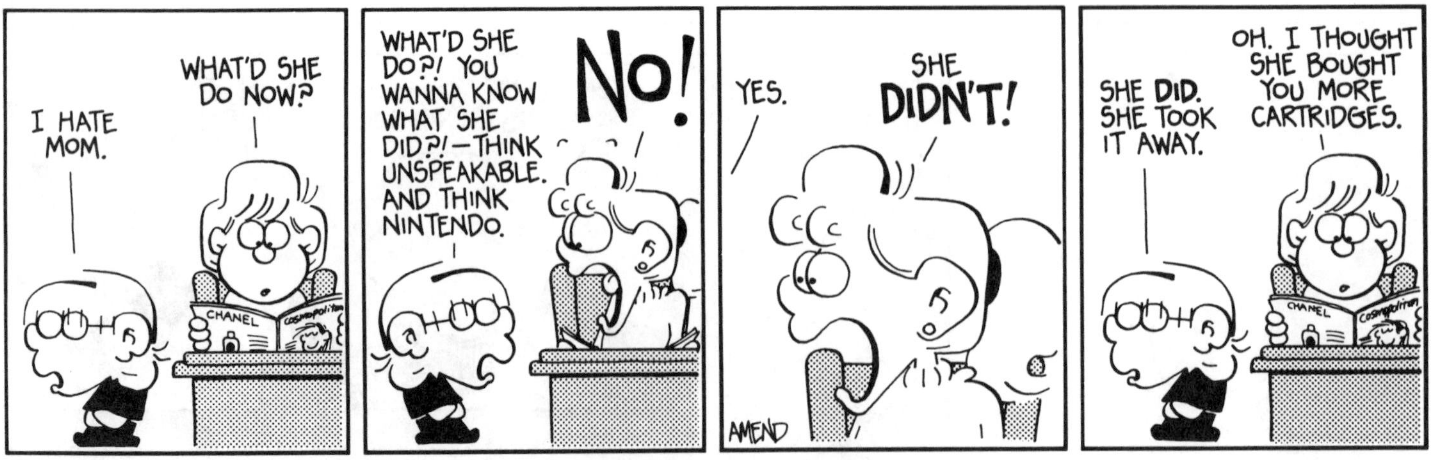
I HATE MOM.
WHAT'D SHE DO NOW?
WHAT'D SHE DO?! YOU WANNA KNOW WHAT SHE DID?!—THINK UNSPEAKABLE. AND THINK NINTENDO.
No!
YES.
SHE **DIDN'T**!
AMEND
SHE **DID**. SHE TOOK IT AWAY.
OH. I THOUGHT SHE BOUGHT YOU MORE CARTRIDGES.

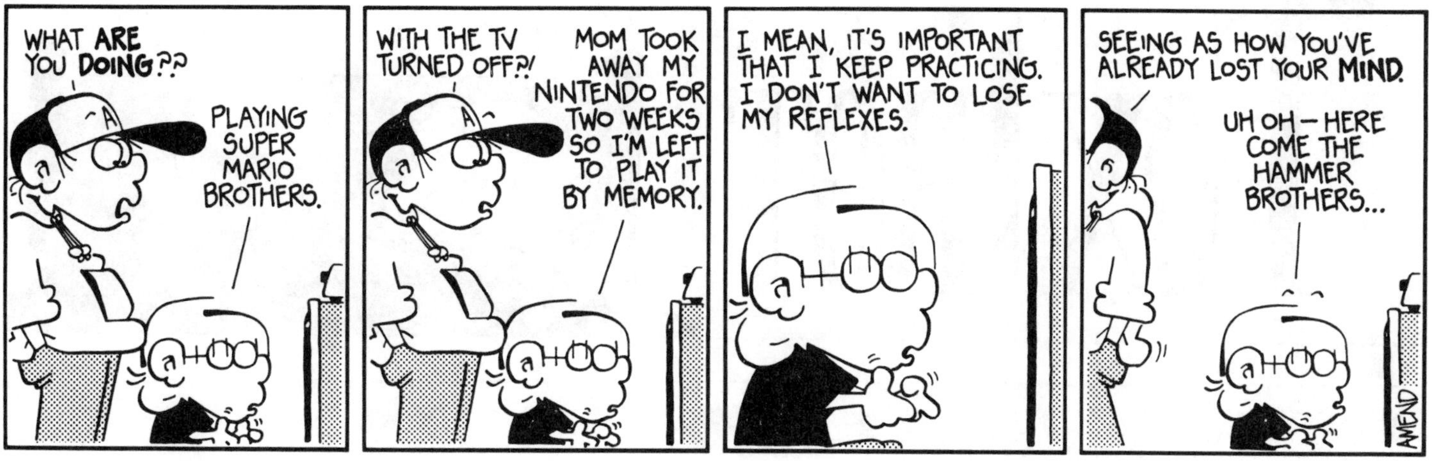
WHAT ARE YOU DOING?!?
PLAYING SUPER MARIO BROTHERS.
WITH THE TV TURNED OFF?!
MOM TOOK AWAY MY NINTENDO FOR TWO WEEKS SO I'M LEFT TO PLAY IT BY MEMORY.
I MEAN, IT'S IMPORTANT THAT I KEEP PRACTICING. I DON'T WANT TO LOSE MY REFLEXES.
SEEING AS HOW YOU'VE ALREADY LOST YOUR MIND.
UH OH — HERE COME THE HAMMER BROTHERS...
AMEND

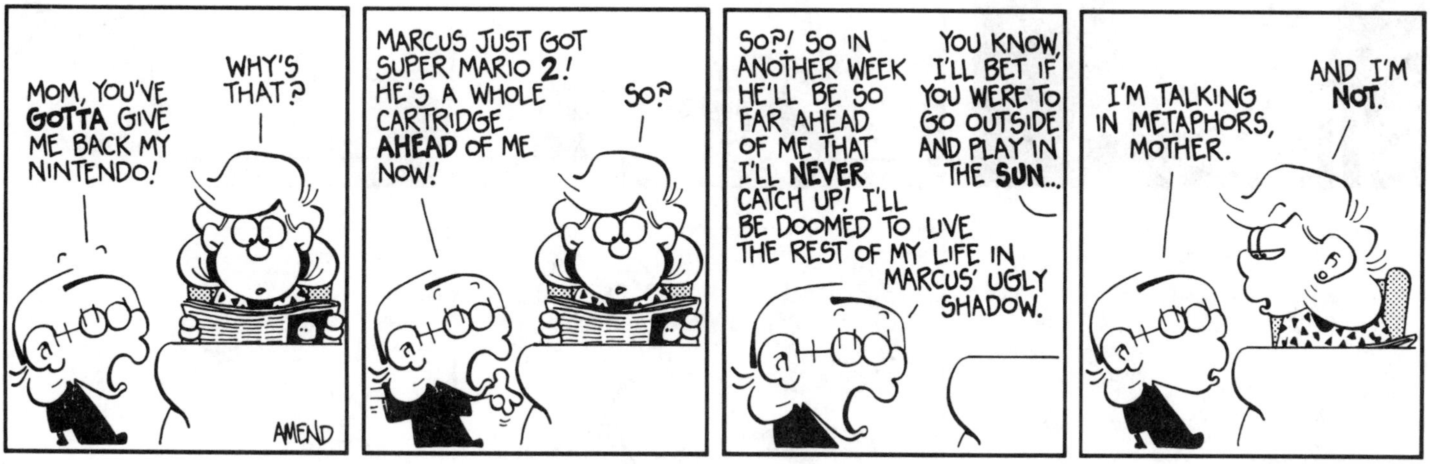
MOM, YOU'VE GOTTA GIVE ME BACK MY NINTENDO!
WHY'S THAT?
MARCUS JUST GOT SUPER MARIO 2! HE'S A WHOLE CARTRIDGE AHEAD OF ME NOW!
SO?
SO?! SO IN ANOTHER WEEK HE'LL BE SO FAR AHEAD OF ME THAT I'LL NEVER CATCH UP! I'LL BE DOOMED TO LIVE THE REST OF MY LIFE IN MARCUS' UGLY SHADOW.
YOU KNOW, I'LL BET IF YOU WERE TO GO OUTSIDE AND PLAY IN THE SUN...
I'M TALKING IN METAPHORS, MOTHER.
AND I'M NOT.
AMEND

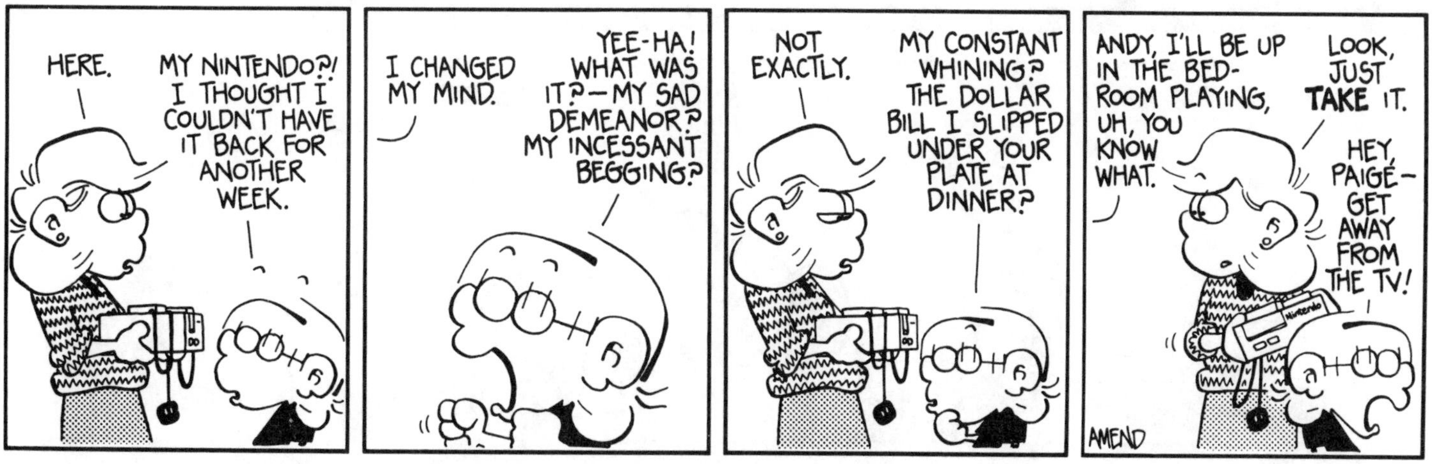
HERE.
MY NINTENDO?! I THOUGHT I COULDN'T HAVE IT BACK FOR ANOTHER WEEK.
I CHANGED MY MIND.
YEE-HA! WHAT WAS IT? — MY SAD DEMEANOR? MY INCESSANT BEGGING?
NOT EXACTLY.
MY CONSTANT WHINING? THE DOLLAR BILL I SLIPPED UNDER YOUR PLATE AT DINNER?
ANDY, I'LL BE UP IN THE BED-ROOM PLAYING, UH, YOU KNOW WHAT.
LOOK, JUST TAKE IT.
HEY, PAIGE — GET AWAY FROM THE TV!
AMEND

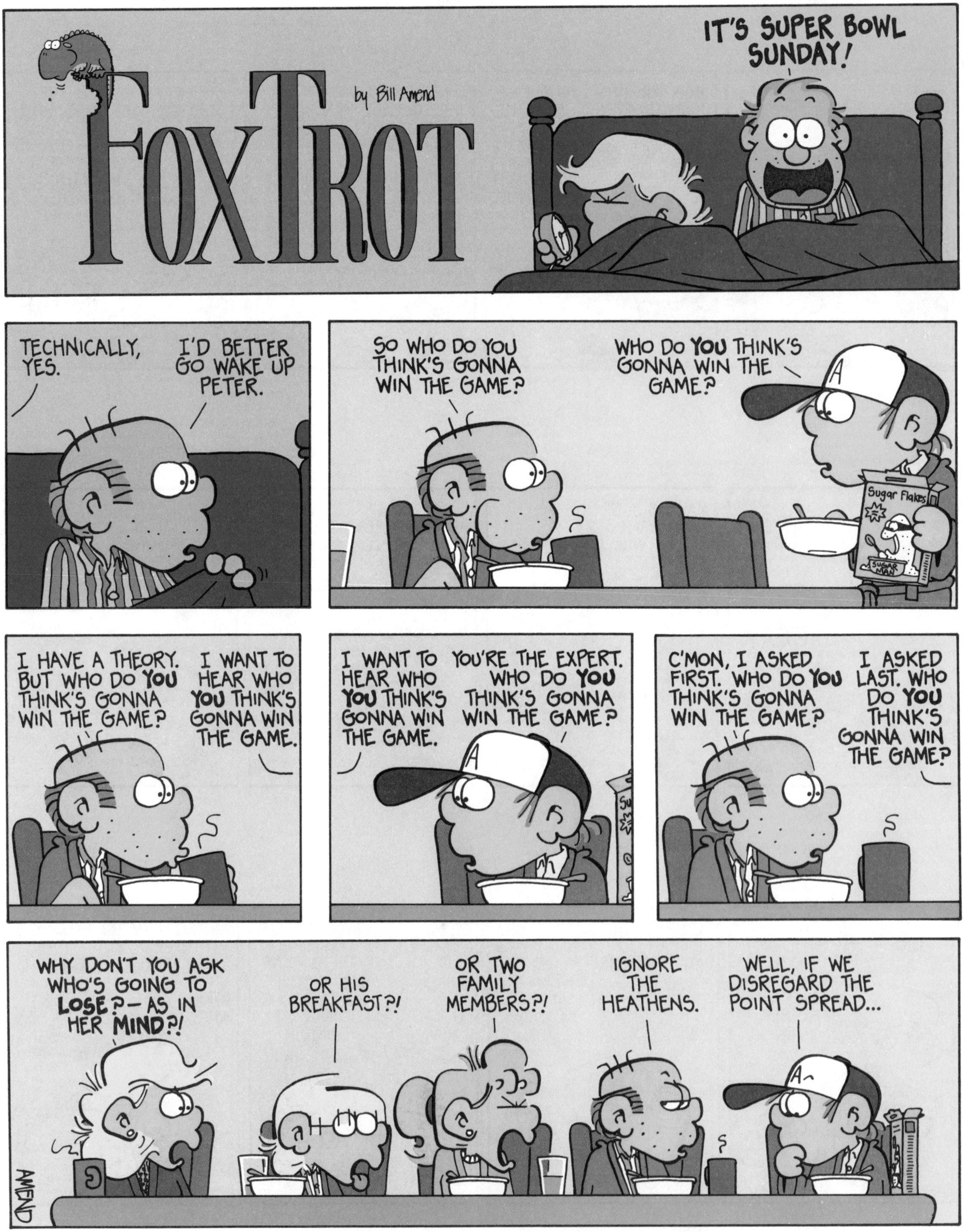
FoxTrot
by Bill Amend
IT'S SUPER BOWL SUNDAY!
TECHNICALLY, YES.
I'D BETTER GO WAKE UP PETER.
SO WHO DO YOU THINK'S GONNA WIN THE GAME?
WHO DO YOU THINK'S GONNA WIN THE GAME?
Sugar Flakes
SUGAR MAN
I HAVE A THEORY. BUT WHO DO YOU THINK'S GONNA WIN THE GAME?
I WANT TO HEAR WHO YOU THINK'S GONNA WIN THE GAME.
I WANT TO HEAR WHO YOU THINK'S GONNA WIN THE GAME.
YOU'RE THE EXPERT. WHO DO YOU THINK'S GONNA WIN THE GAME?
C'MON, I ASKED FIRST. WHO DO YOU THINK'S GONNA WIN THE GAME?
I ASKED LAST. WHO DO YOU THINK'S GONNA WIN THE GAME?
WHY DON'T YOU ASK WHO'S GOING TO LOSE?— AS IN HER MIND?!
OR HIS BREAKFAST?!
OR TWO FAMILY MEMBERS?!
IGNORE THE HEATHENS.
WELL, IF WE DISREGARD THE POINT SPREAD...
AMEND

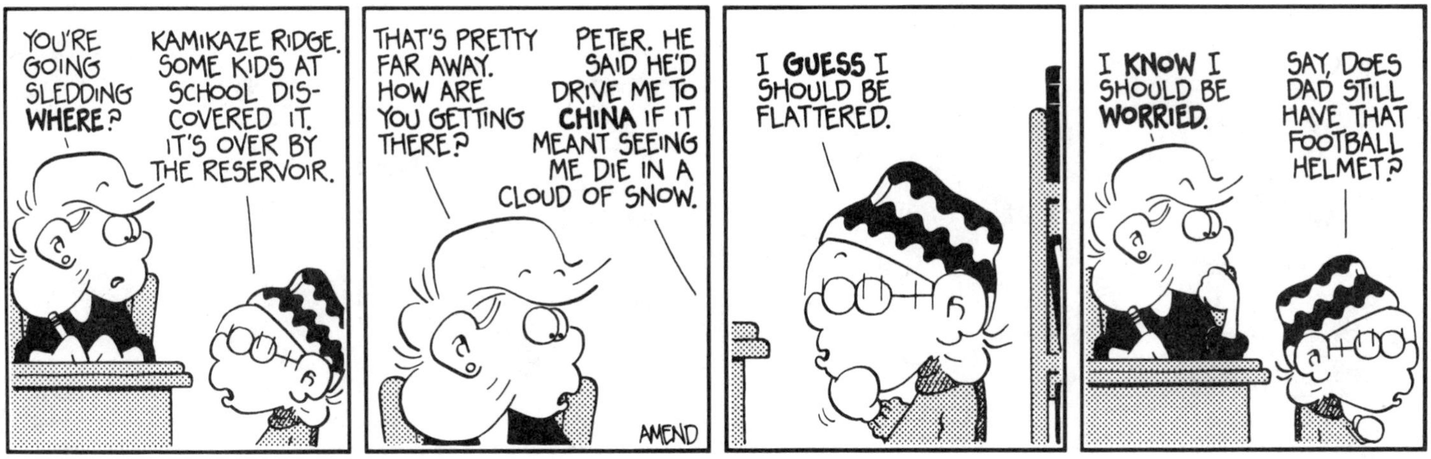
YOU'RE GOING SLEDDING WHERE?
KAMIKAZE RIDGE. SOME KIDS AT SCHOOL DISCOVERED IT. IT'S OVER BY THE RESERVOIR.
THAT'S PRETTY FAR AWAY. HOW ARE YOU GETTING THERE?
PETER. HE SAID HE'D DRIVE ME TO CHINA IF IT MEANT SEEING ME DIE IN A CLOUD OF SNOW.
AMEND
I GUESS I SHOULD BE FLATTERED.
I KNOW I SHOULD BE WORRIED.
SAY, DOES DAD STILL HAVE THAT FOOTBALL HELMET?

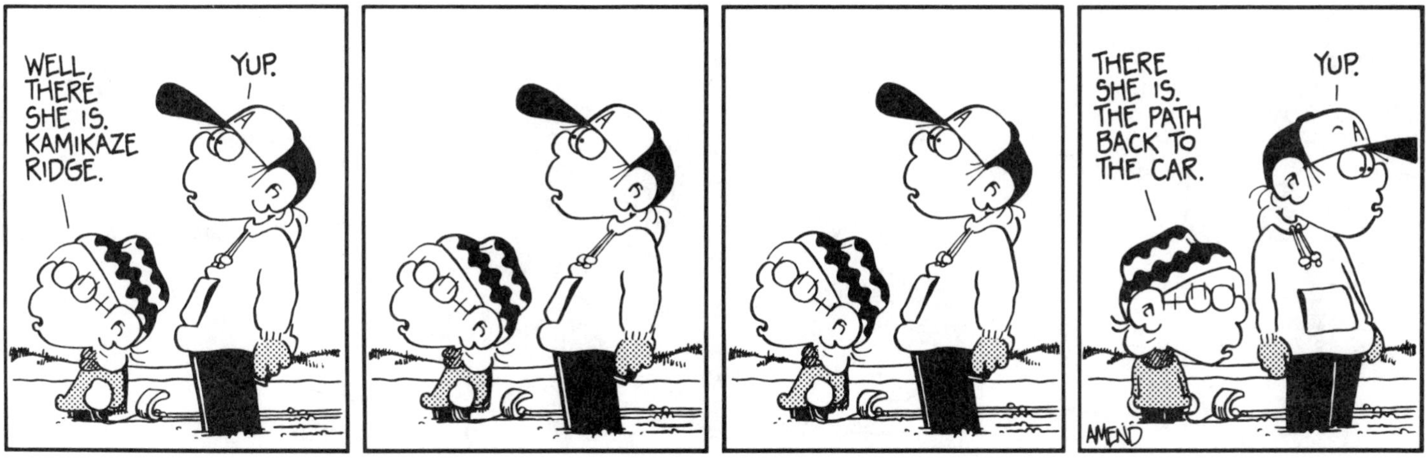
WELL, THERE SHE IS. KAMIKAZE RIDGE.
YUP.
THERE SHE IS. THE PATH BACK TO THE CAR.
YUP.
AMEND

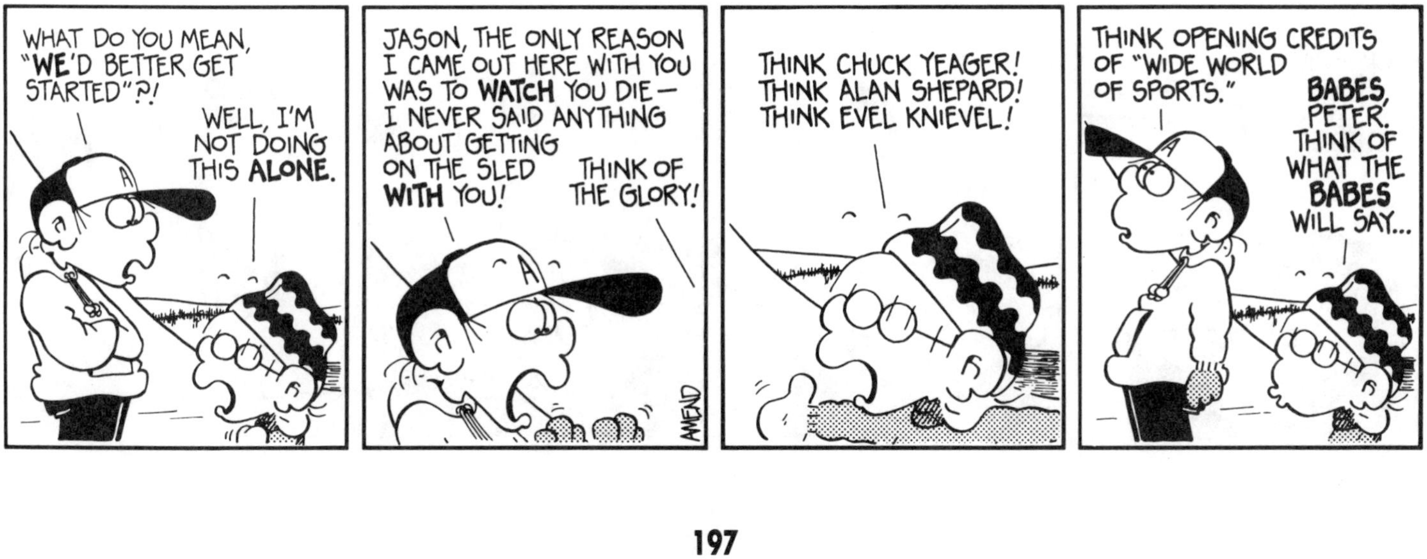
WHAT DO YOU MEAN, "WE'D BETTER GET STARTED"?!
WELL, I'M NOT DOING THIS ALONE.
JASON, THE ONLY REASON I CAME OUT HERE WITH YOU WAS TO WATCH YOU DIE— I NEVER SAID ANYTHING ABOUT GETTING ON THE SLED WITH YOU!
THINK OF THE GLORY!
AMEND
THINK CHUCK YEAGER! THINK ALAN SHEPARD! THINK EVEL KNIEVEL!
THINK OPENING CREDITS OF "WIDE WORLD OF SPORTS."
BABES, PETER. THINK OF WHAT THE BABES WILL SAY...

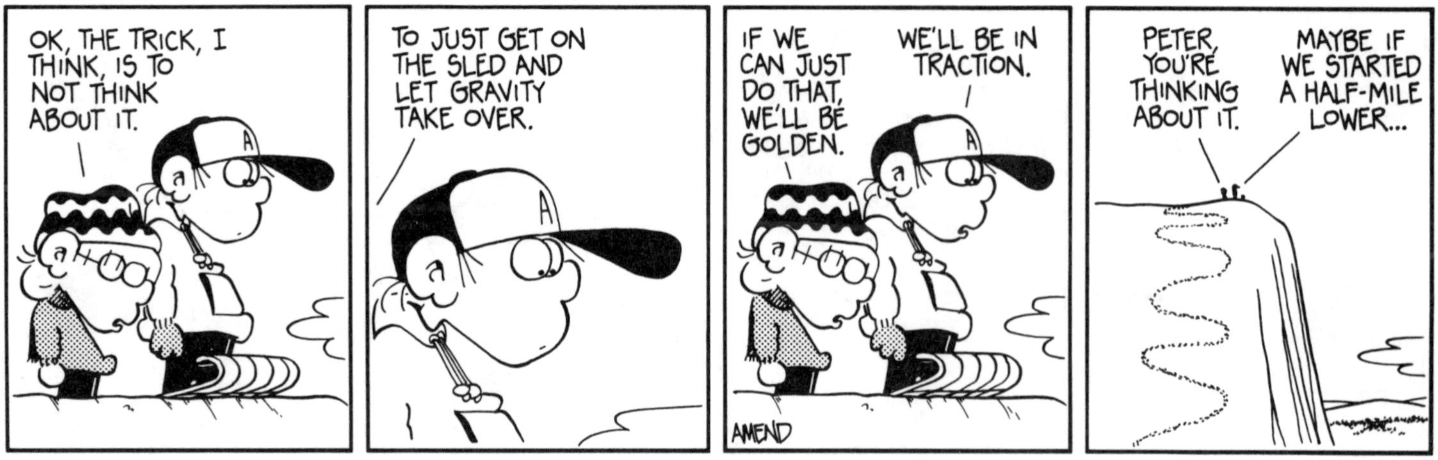
OK, THE TRICK, I THINK, IS TO NOT THINK ABOUT IT.
TO JUST GET ON THE SLED AND LET GRAVITY TAKE OVER.
IF WE CAN JUST DO THAT, WE'LL BE GOLDEN.
WE'LL BE IN TRACTION.
AMEND
PETER, YOU'RE THINKING ABOUT IT.
MAYBE IF WE STARTED A HALF-MILE LOWER...

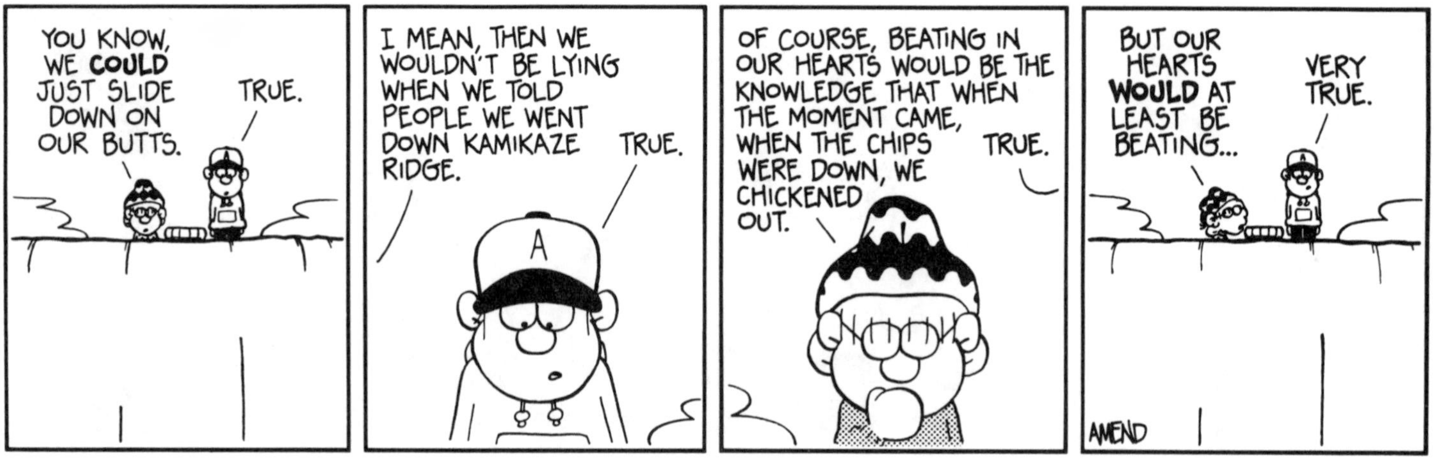
YOU KNOW, WE **COULD** JUST SLIDE DOWN ON OUR BUTTS.
TRUE.
I MEAN, THEN WE WOULDN'T BE LYING WHEN WE TOLD PEOPLE WE WENT DOWN KAMIKAZE RIDGE.
TRUE.
OF COURSE, BEATING IN OUR HEARTS WOULD BE THE KNOWLEDGE THAT WHEN THE MOMENT CAME, WHEN THE CHIPS WERE DOWN, WE CHICKENED OUT.
TRUE.
BUT OUR HEARTS **WOULD** AT LEAST BE BEATING...
VERY TRUE.
AMEND

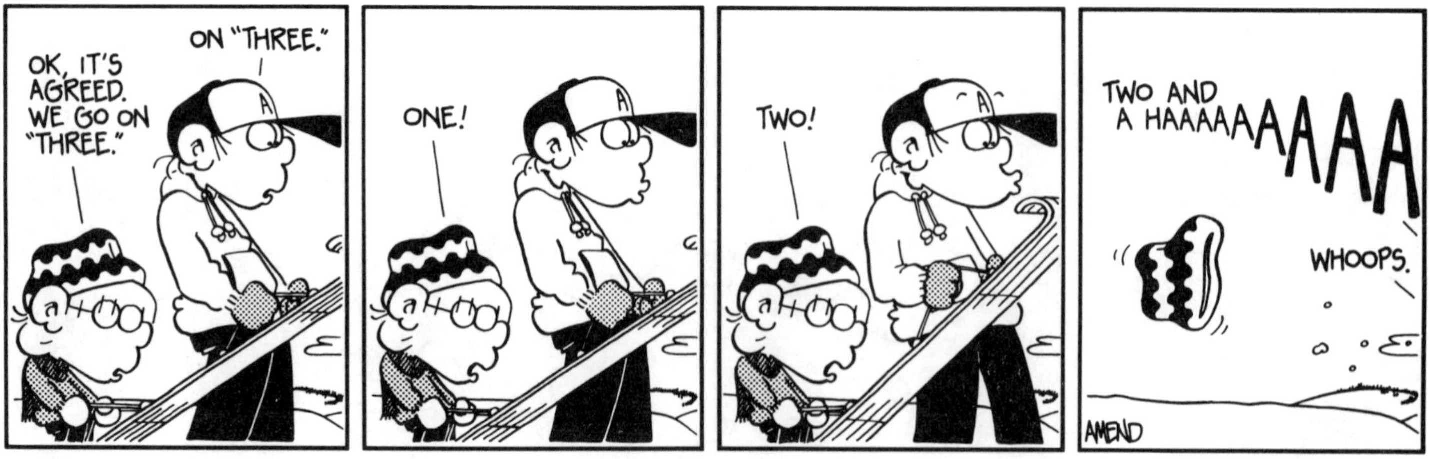
OK, IT'S AGREED. WE GO ON "THREE."
ON "THREE."
ONE!
TWO!
TWO AND A HAAAAAAAAA
WHOOPS.
AMEND

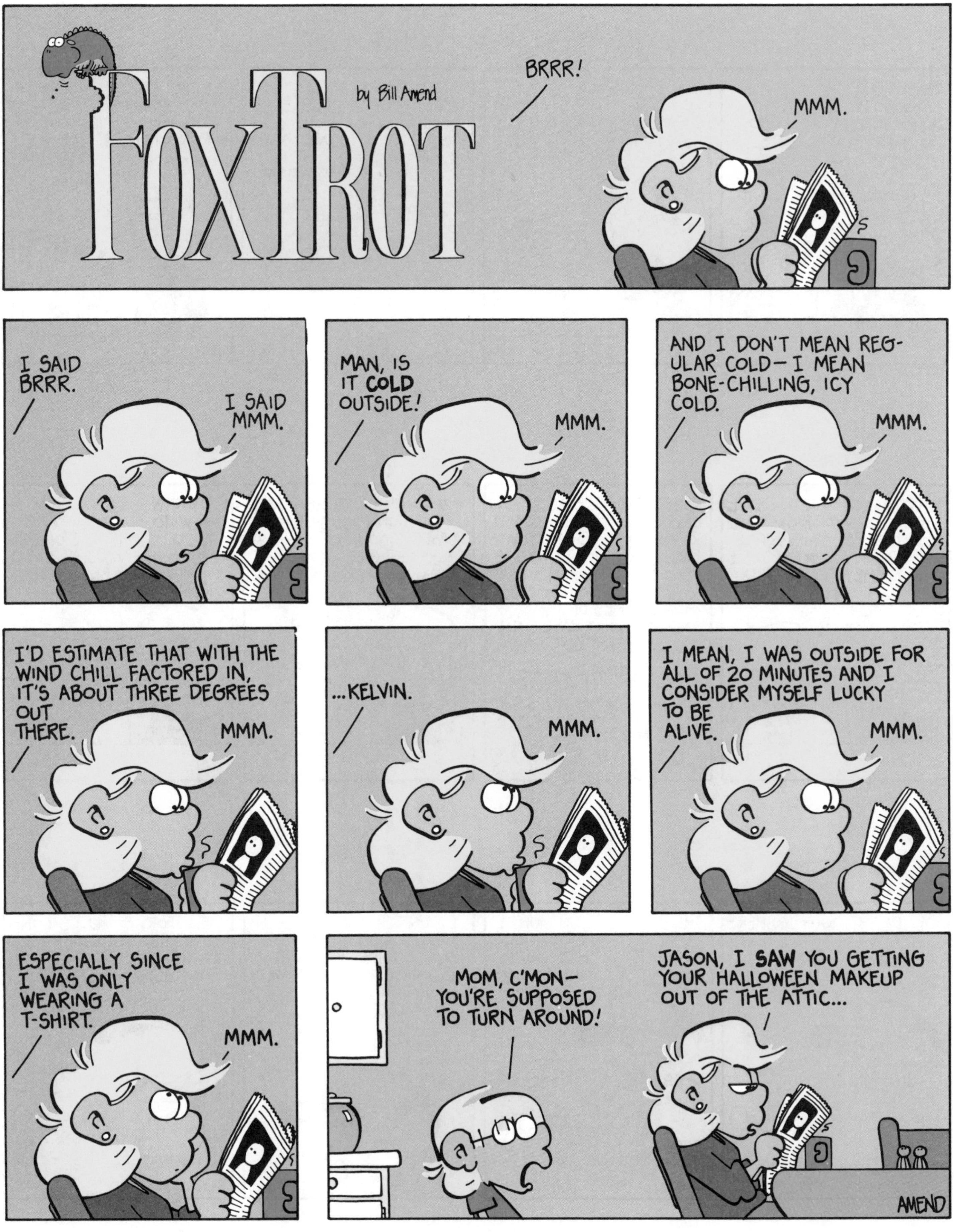
FoxTrot
by Bill Amend
BRRR!
MMM.
I SAID BRRR.
I SAID MMM.
MAN, IS IT COLD OUTSIDE!
MMM.
AND I DON'T MEAN REG-ULAR COLD—I MEAN BONE-CHILLING, ICY COLD.
MMM.
I'D ESTIMATE THAT WITH THE WIND CHILL FACTORED IN, IT'S ABOUT THREE DEGREES OUT THERE.
MMM.
...KELVIN.
MMM.
I MEAN, I WAS OUTSIDE FOR ALL OF 20 MINUTES AND I CONSIDER MYSELF LUCKY TO BE ALIVE.
MMM.
ESPECIALLY SINCE I WAS ONLY WEARING A T-SHIRT.
MMM.
MOM, C'MON—YOU'RE SUPPOSED TO TURN AROUND!
JASON, I SAW YOU GETTING YOUR HALLOWEEN MAKEUP OUT OF THE ATTIC...
AMEND

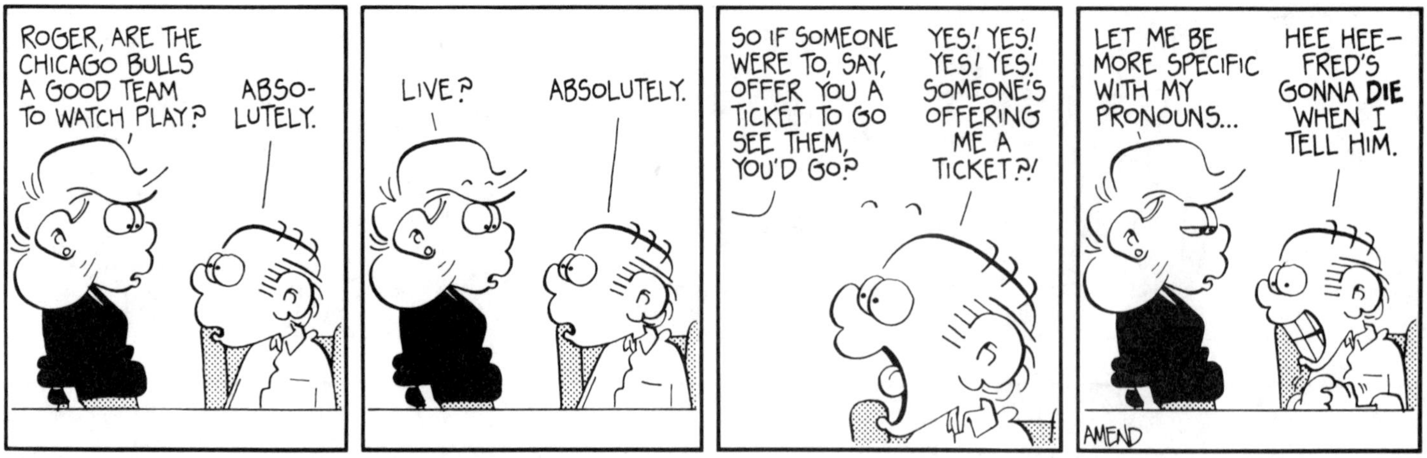
ROGER, ARE THE CHICAGO BULLS A GOOD TEAM TO WATCH PLAY?
ABSO-LUTELY.
LIVE?
ABSOLUTELY.
SO IF SOMEONE WERE TO, SAY, OFFER YOU A TICKET TO GO SEE THEM, YOU'D GO?
YES! YES! YES! YES! SOMEONE'S OFFERING ME A TICKET?!
LET ME BE MORE SPECIFIC WITH MY PRONOUNS...
HEE HEE– FRED'S GONNA **DIE** WHEN I TELL HIM.
AMEND

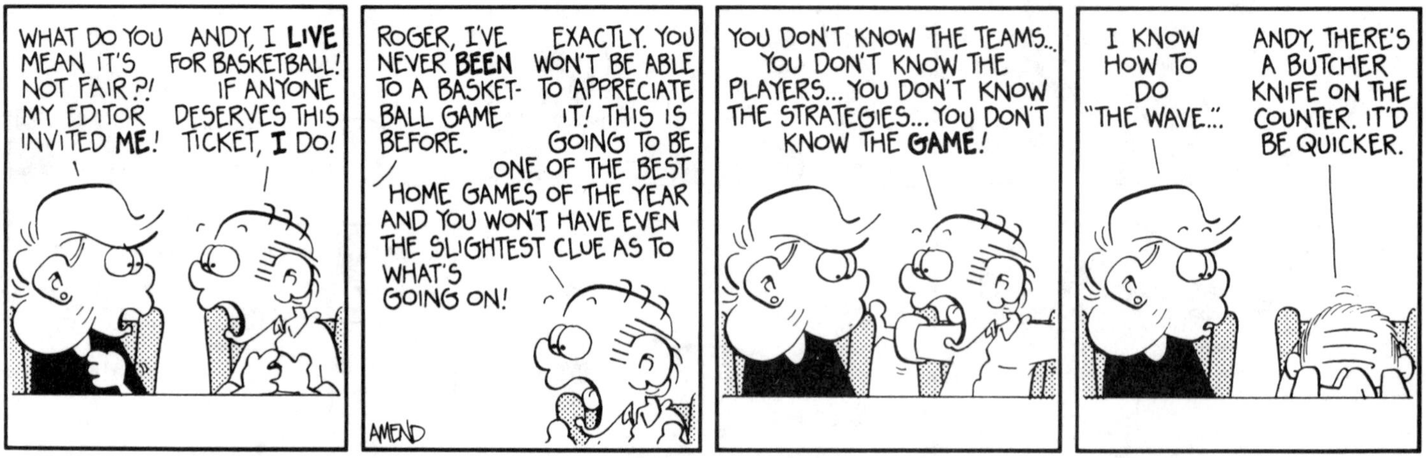
WHAT DO YOU MEAN IT'S NOT FAIR?! MY EDITOR INVITED **ME**!
ANDY, I **LIVE** FOR BASKETBALL! IF ANYONE DESERVES THIS TICKET, **I** DO!
ROGER, I'VE NEVER **BEEN** TO A BASKET-BALL GAME BEFORE.
EXACTLY. YOU WON'T BE ABLE TO APPRECIATE IT! THIS IS GOING TO BE ONE OF THE BEST HOME GAMES OF THE YEAR AND YOU WON'T HAVE EVEN THE SLIGHTEST CLUE AS TO WHAT'S GOING ON!
AMEND
YOU DON'T KNOW THE TEAMS... YOU DON'T KNOW THE PLAYERS... YOU DON'T KNOW THE STRATEGIES... YOU DON'T KNOW THE **GAME**!
I KNOW HOW TO DO "THE WAVE."
ANDY, THERE'S A BUTCHER KNIFE ON THE COUNTER. IT'D BE QUICKER.

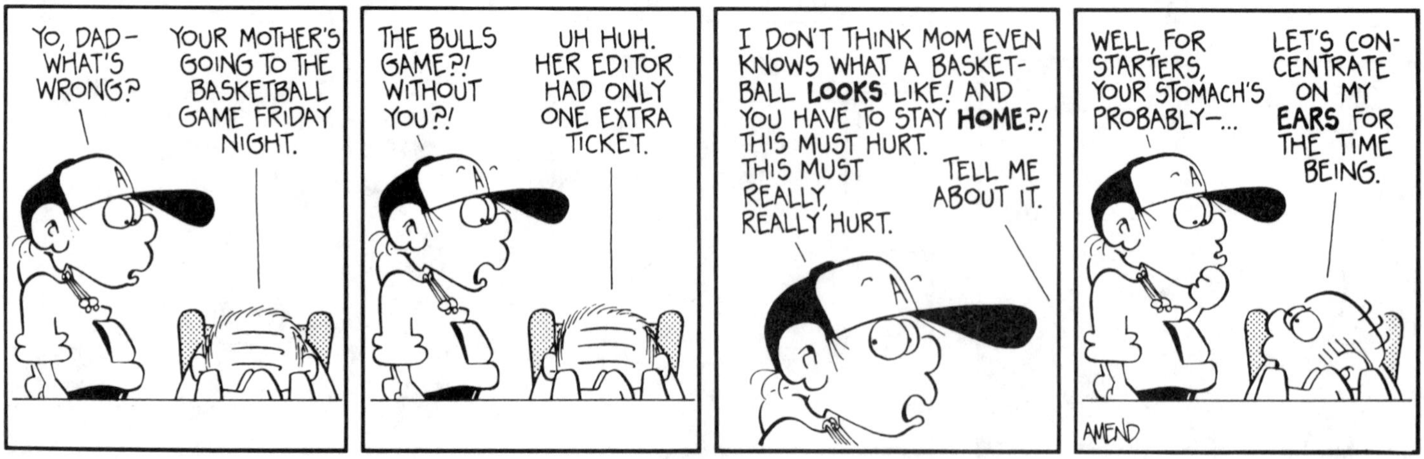
YO, DAD– WHAT'S WRONG?
YOUR MOTHER'S GOING TO THE BASKETBALL GAME FRIDAY NIGHT.
THE BULLS GAME?! WITHOUT YOU?!
UH HUH. HER EDITOR HAD ONLY ONE EXTRA TICKET.
I DON'T THINK MOM EVEN KNOWS WHAT A BASKET-BALL **LOOKS** LIKE! AND YOU HAVE TO STAY **HOME**?! THIS MUST HURT. THIS MUST REALLY, REALLY HURT.
TELL ME ABOUT IT.
WELL, FOR STARTERS, YOUR STOMACH'S PROBABLY–...
LET'S CON-CENTRATE ON MY **EARS** FOR THE TIME BEING.
AMEND

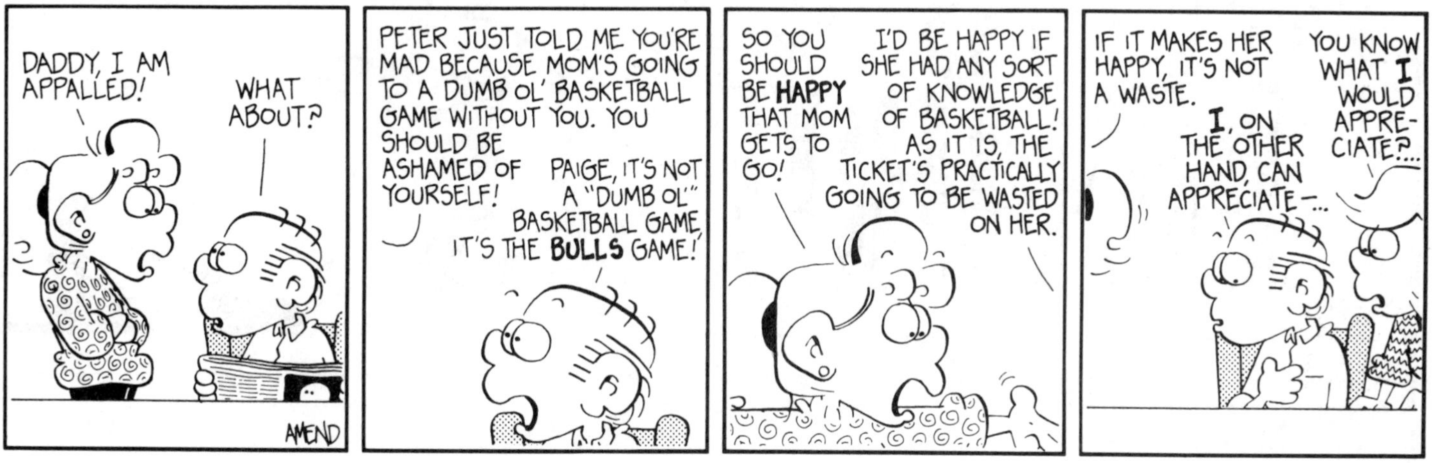
DADDY, I AM APPALLED!
WHAT ABOUT?
PETER JUST TOLD ME YOU'RE MAD BECAUSE MOM'S GOING TO A DUMB OL' BASKETBALL GAME WITHOUT YOU. YOU SHOULD BE ASHAMED OF YOURSELF!
PAIGE, IT'S NOT A "DUMB OL'" BASKETBALL GAME, IT'S THE BULLS GAME!
SO YOU SHOULD BE HAPPY THAT MOM GETS TO GO!
I'D BE HAPPY IF SHE HAD ANY SORT OF KNOWLEDGE OF BASKETBALL! AS IT IS, THE TICKET'S PRACTICALLY GOING TO BE WASTED ON HER.
IF IT MAKES HER HAPPY, IT'S NOT A WASTE.
I, ON THE OTHER HAND, CAN APPRECIATE–...
YOU KNOW WHAT I WOULD APPRECIATE?...
AMEND

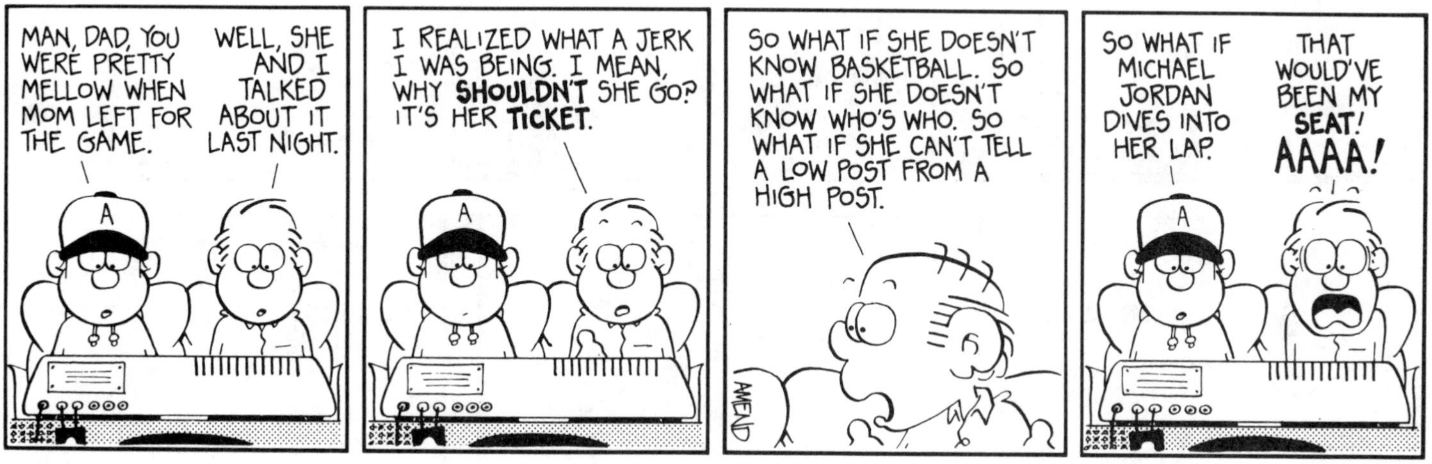
MAN, DAD, YOU WERE PRETTY MELLOW WHEN MOM LEFT FOR THE GAME.
WELL, SHE AND I TALKED ABOUT IT LAST NIGHT.
I REALIZED WHAT A JERK I WAS BEING. I MEAN, WHY SHOULDN'T SHE GO? IT'S HER TICKET.
SO WHAT IF SHE DOESN'T KNOW BASKETBALL. SO WHAT IF SHE DOESN'T KNOW WHO'S WHO. SO WHAT IF SHE CAN'T TELL A LOW POST FROM A HIGH POST.
AMEND
SO WHAT IF MICHAEL JORDAN DIVES INTO HER LAP.
THAT WOULD'VE BEEN MY SEAT! AAAA!

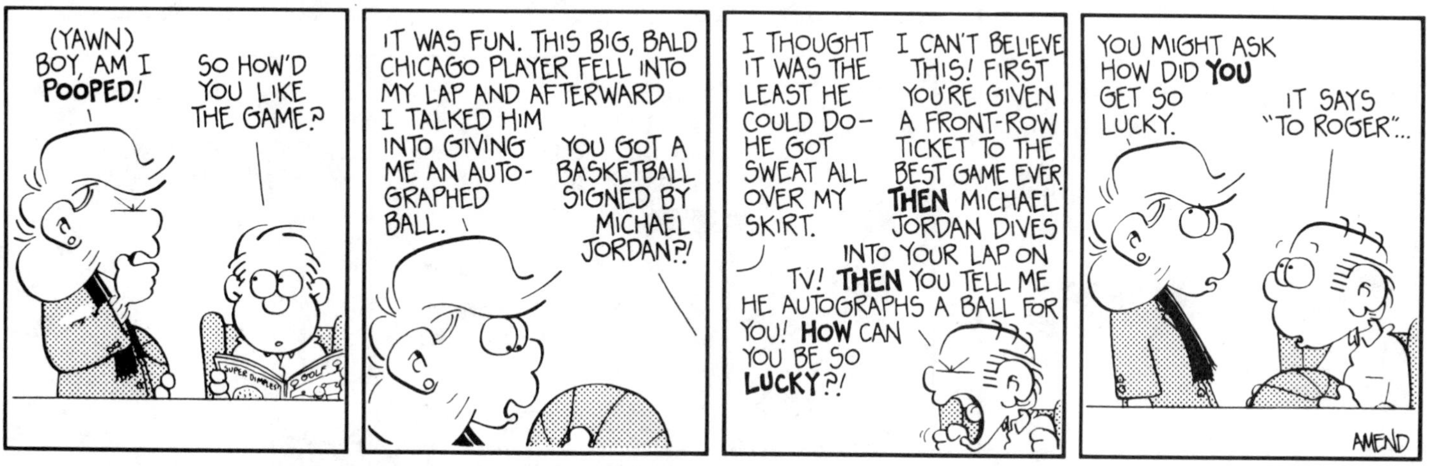
(YAWN) BOY, AM I POOPED!
SO HOW'D YOU LIKE THE GAME?
IT WAS FUN. THIS BIG, BALD CHICAGO PLAYER FELL INTO MY LAP AND AFTERWARD I TALKED HIM INTO GIVING ME AN AUTOGRAPHED BALL.
YOU GOT A BASKETBALL SIGNED BY MICHAEL JORDAN?!
I THOUGHT IT WAS THE LEAST HE COULD DO– HE GOT SWEAT ALL OVER MY SKIRT.
I CAN'T BELIEVE THIS! FIRST YOU'RE GIVEN A FRONT-ROW TICKET TO THE BEST GAME EVER. THEN MICHAEL JORDAN DIVES INTO YOUR LAP ON TV! THEN YOU TELL ME HE AUTOGRAPHS A BALL FOR YOU! HOW CAN YOU BE SO LUCKY?!
YOU MIGHT ASK HOW DID YOU GET SO LUCKY.
IT SAYS "TO ROGER"...
AMEND

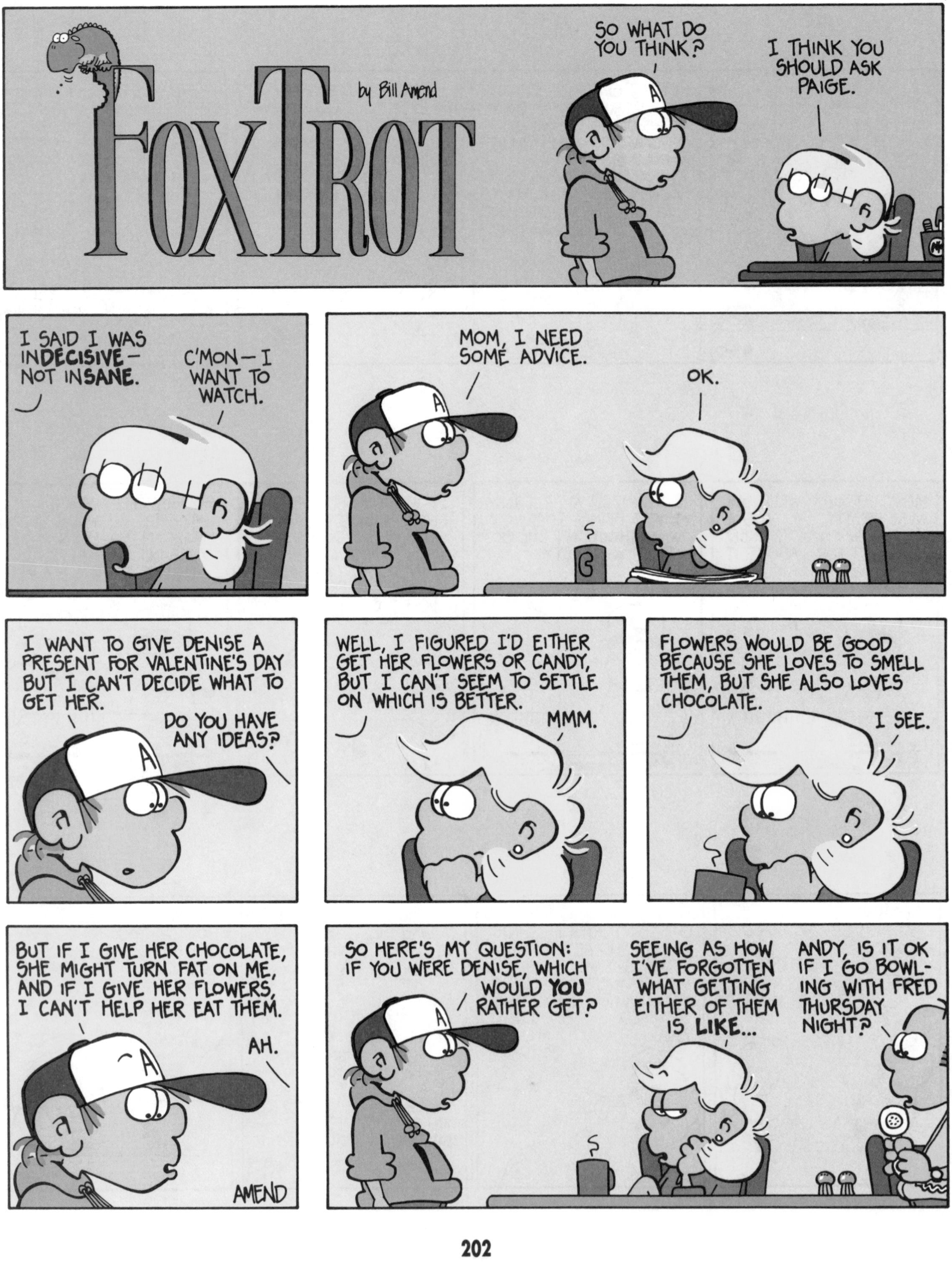

FOXTROT
by Bill Amend
SO WHAT DO YOU THINK?
I THINK YOU SHOULD ASK PAIGE.
I SAID I WAS INDECISIVE — NOT INSANE.
C'MON — I WANT TO WATCH.
MOM, I NEED SOME ADVICE.
OK.
I WANT TO GIVE DENISE A PRESENT FOR VALENTINE'S DAY BUT I CAN'T DECIDE WHAT TO GET HER.
DO YOU HAVE ANY IDEAS?
WELL, I FIGURED I'D EITHER GET HER FLOWERS OR CANDY, BUT I CAN'T SEEM TO SETTLE ON WHICH IS BETTER.
MMM.
FLOWERS WOULD BE GOOD BECAUSE SHE LOVES TO SMELL THEM, BUT SHE ALSO LOVES CHOCOLATE.
I SEE.
BUT IF I GIVE HER CHOCOLATE, SHE MIGHT TURN FAT ON ME, AND IF I GIVE HER FLOWERS, I CAN'T HELP HER EAT THEM.
AH.
AMEND
SO HERE'S MY QUESTION: IF YOU WERE DENISE, WHICH WOULD YOU RATHER GET?
SEEING AS HOW I'VE FORGOTTEN WHAT GETTING EITHER OF THEM IS LIKE...
ANDY, IS IT OK IF I GO BOWLING WITH FRED THURSDAY NIGHT?

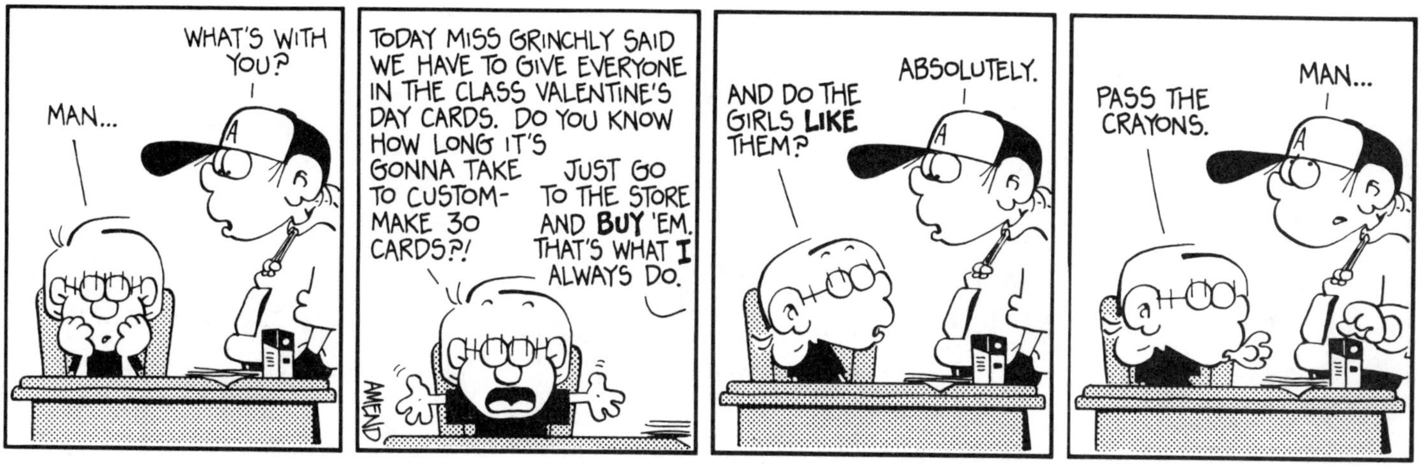
MAN...
WHAT'S WITH YOU?
TODAY MISS GRINCHLY SAID WE HAVE TO GIVE EVERYONE IN THE CLASS VALENTINE'S DAY CARDS. DO YOU KNOW HOW LONG IT'S GONNA TAKE TO CUSTOM-MAKE 30 CARDS?!
JUST GO TO THE STORE AND BUY 'EM. THAT'S WHAT I ALWAYS DO.
AMEND
AND DO THE GIRLS LIKE THEM?
ABSOLUTELY.
PASS THE CRAYONS.
MAN...

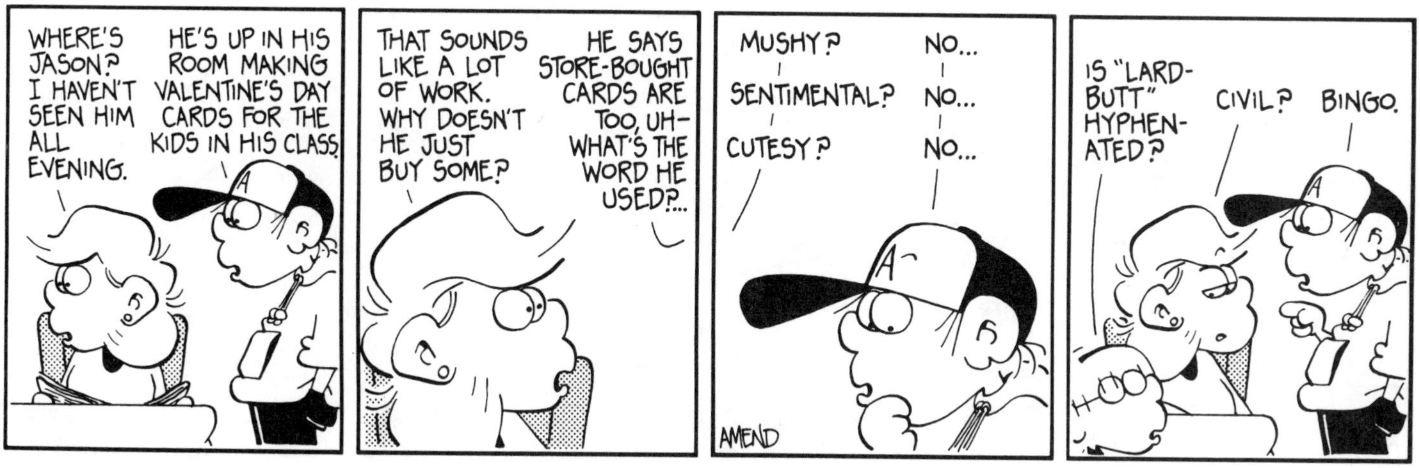
WHERE'S JASON? I HAVEN'T SEEN HIM ALL EVENING.
HE'S UP IN HIS ROOM MAKING VALENTINE'S DAY CARDS FOR THE KIDS IN HIS CLASS.
THAT SOUNDS LIKE A LOT OF WORK. WHY DOESN'T HE JUST BUY SOME?
HE SAYS STORE-BOUGHT CARDS ARE TOO, UH– WHAT'S THE WORD HE USED?...
MUSHY?
NO...
SENTIMENTAL?
NO...
CUTESY?
NO...
AMEND
IS "LARD-BUTT" HYPHENATED?
CIVIL?
BINGO.

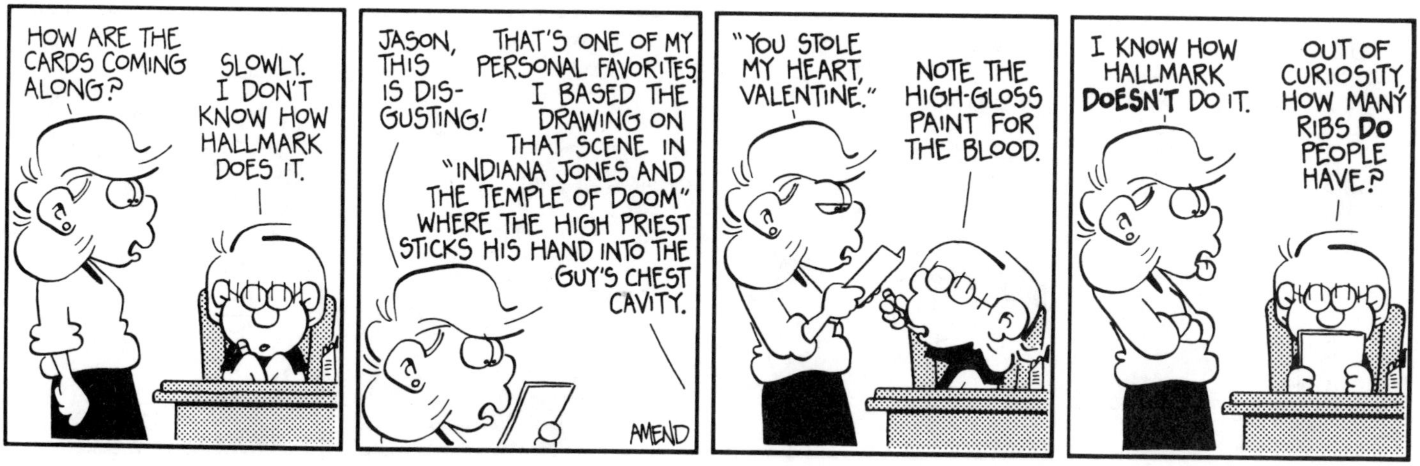
HOW ARE THE CARDS COMING ALONG?
SLOWLY. I DON'T KNOW HOW HALLMARK DOES IT.
JASON, THIS IS DISGUSTING!
THAT'S ONE OF MY PERSONAL FAVORITES. I BASED THE DRAWING ON THAT SCENE IN "INDIANA JONES AND THE TEMPLE OF DOOM" WHERE THE HIGH PRIEST STICKS HIS HAND INTO THE GUY'S CHEST CAVITY.
AMEND
"YOU STOLE MY HEART, VALENTINE."
NOTE THE HIGH-GLOSS PAINT FOR THE BLOOD.
I KNOW HOW HALLMARK DOESN'T DO IT.
OUT OF CURIOSITY, HOW MANY RIBS DO PEOPLE HAVE?

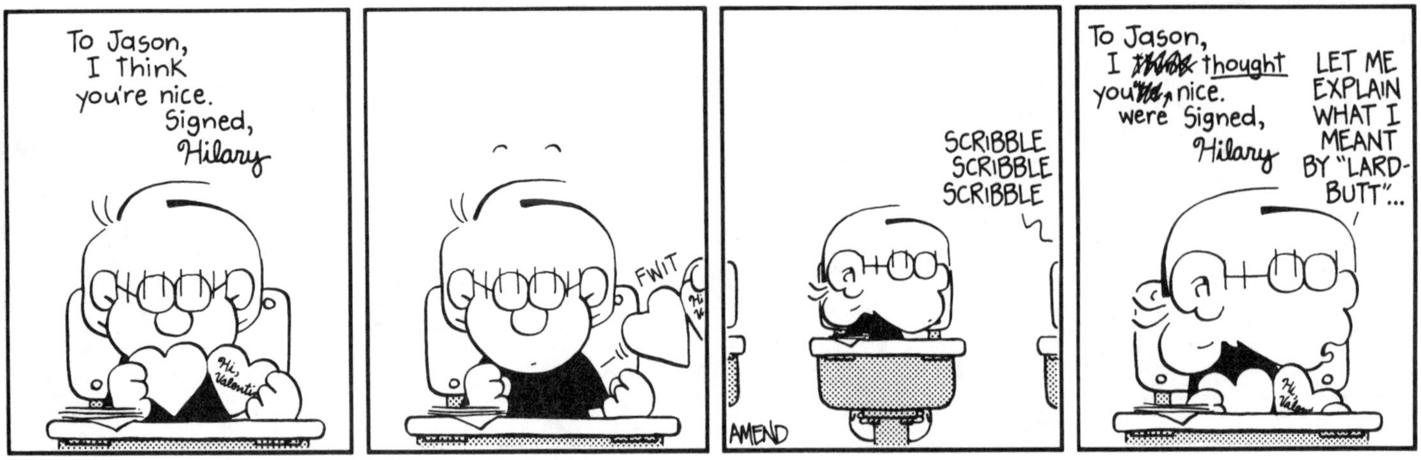
To Jason,
I think
you're nice.
Signed,
Hilary
Hi, Valentine
FWIT
SCRIBBLE
SCRIBBLE
SCRIBBLE
AMEND
To Jason,
I ~~think~~ thought
you~~'re~~ were nice.
Signed,
Hilary
LET ME EXPLAIN WHAT I MEANT BY "LARD-BUTT"...

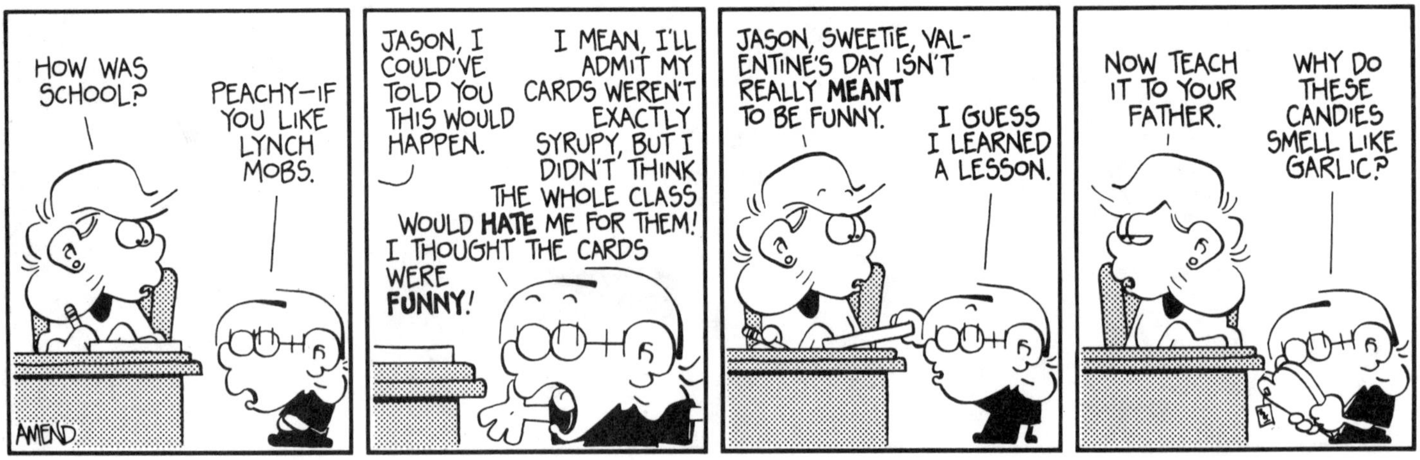
HOW WAS SCHOOL?
PEACHY—IF YOU LIKE LYNCH MOBS.
AMEND
JASON, I COULD'VE TOLD YOU THIS WOULD HAPPEN.
I MEAN, I'LL ADMIT MY CARDS WEREN'T EXACTLY SYRUPY, BUT I DIDN'T THINK THE WHOLE CLASS WOULD **HATE** ME FOR THEM! I THOUGHT THE CARDS WERE **FUNNY**!
JASON, SWEETIE, VALENTINE'S DAY ISN'T REALLY **MEANT** TO BE FUNNY.
I GUESS I LEARNED A LESSON.
NOW TEACH IT TO YOUR FATHER.
WHY DO THESE CANDIES SMELL LIKE GARLIC?

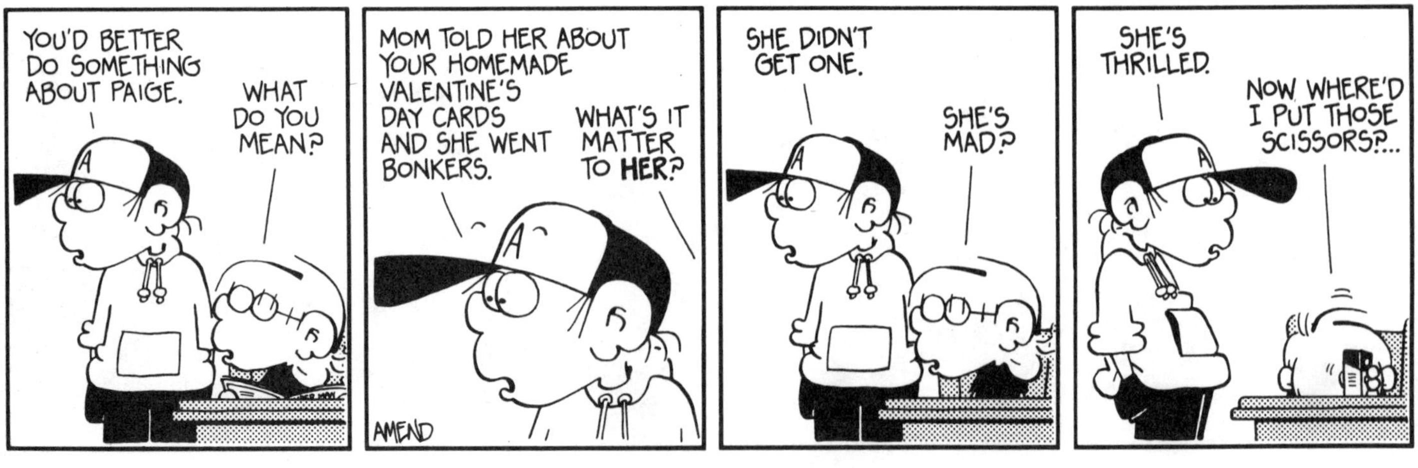
YOU'D BETTER DO SOMETHING ABOUT PAIGE.
WHAT DO YOU MEAN?
MOM TOLD HER ABOUT YOUR HOMEMADE VALENTINE'S DAY CARDS AND SHE WENT BONKERS.
WHAT'S IT MATTER TO **HER**?
AMEND
SHE DIDN'T GET ONE.
SHE'S MAD?
SHE'S THRILLED.
NOW WHERE'D I PUT THOSE SCISSORS?...

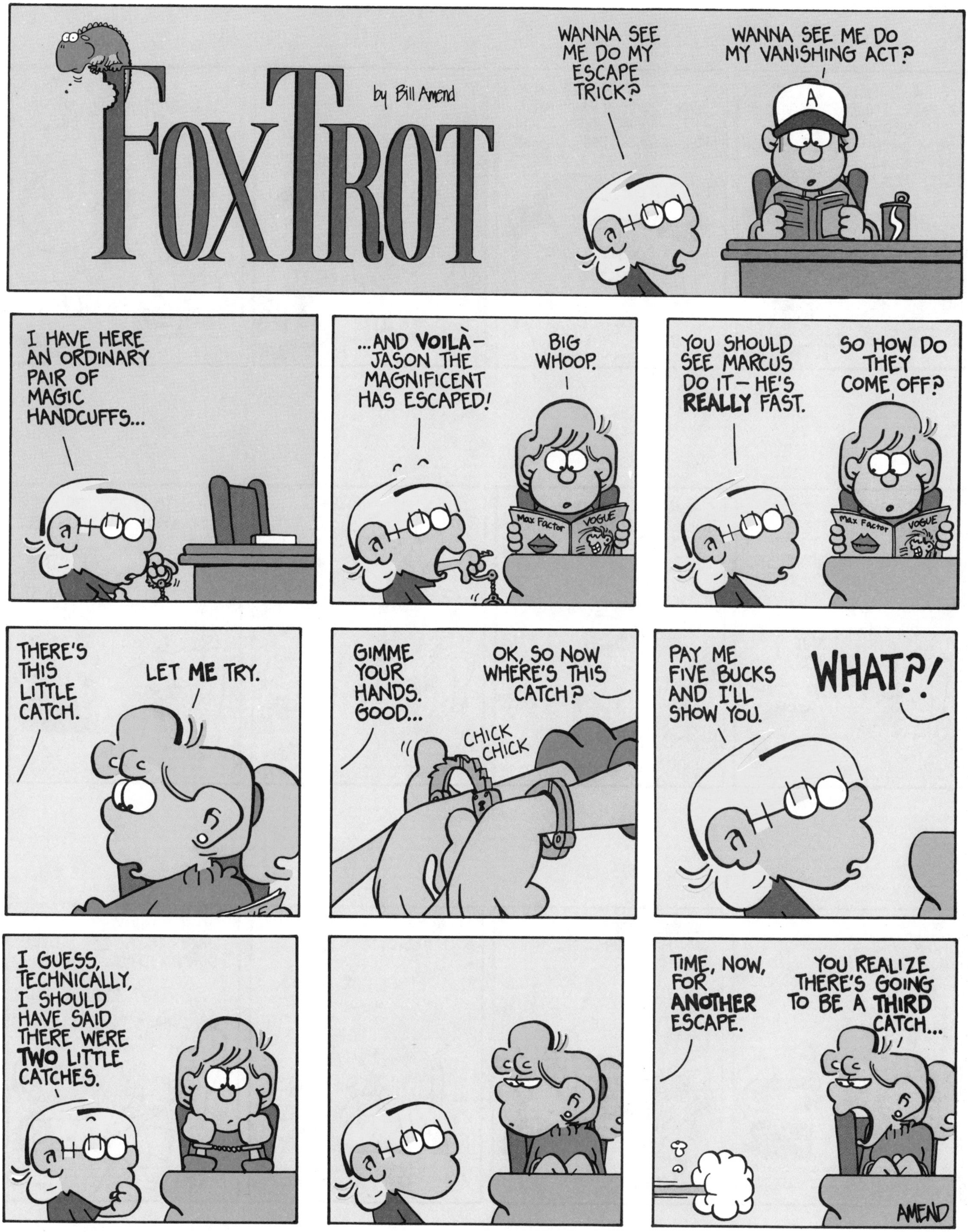
FoxTrot
by Bill Amend
WANNA SEE ME DO MY ESCAPE TRICK?
WANNA SEE ME DO MY VANISHING ACT?
I HAVE HERE AN ORDINARY PAIR OF MAGIC HANDCUFFS...
...AND **VOILÀ**— JASON THE MAGNIFICENT HAS ESCAPED!
BIG WHOOP.
Max Factor
VOGUE
YOU SHOULD SEE MARCUS DO IT—HE'S **REALLY** FAST.
SO HOW DO THEY COME OFF?
Max Factor
VOGUE
THERE'S THIS LITTLE CATCH.
LET **ME** TRY.
GIMME YOUR HANDS. GOOD...
CHICK CHICK
OK, SO NOW WHERE'S THIS CATCH?
PAY ME FIVE BUCKS AND I'LL SHOW YOU.
WHAT?!
I GUESS, TECHNICALLY, I SHOULD HAVE SAID THERE WERE **TWO** LITTLE CATCHES.
TIME, NOW, FOR **ANOTHER** ESCAPE.
YOU REALIZE THERE'S GOING TO BE A **THIRD** CATCH...
AMEND

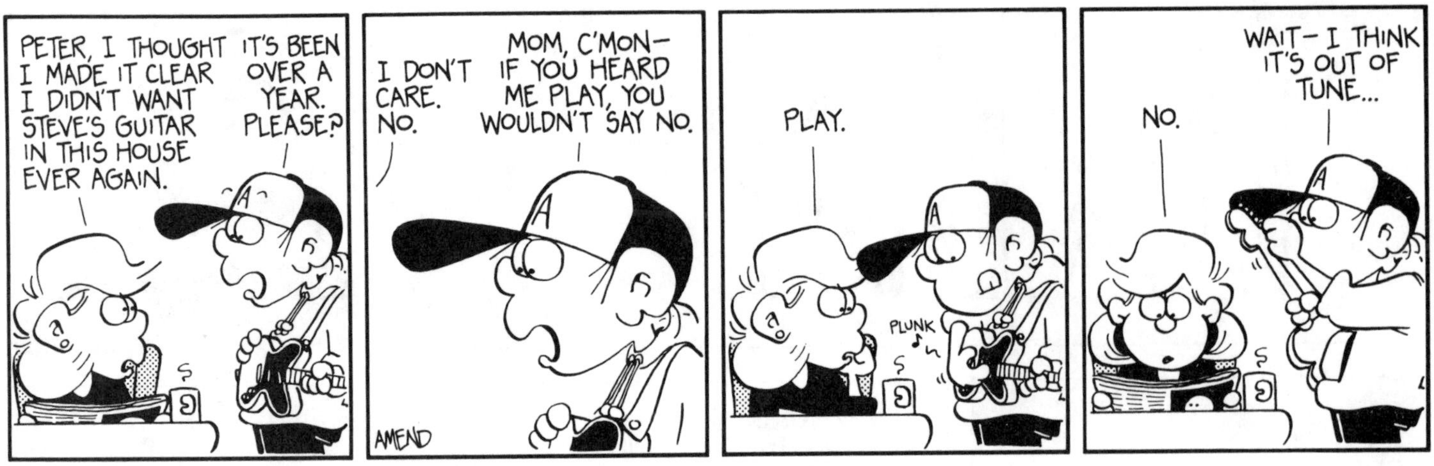
PETER, I THOUGHT I MADE IT CLEAR I DIDN'T WANT STEVE'S GUITAR IN THIS HOUSE EVER AGAIN.
IT'S BEEN OVER A YEAR. PLEASE?
I DON'T CARE. NO.
MOM, C'MON— IF YOU HEARD ME PLAY, YOU WOULDN'T SAY NO.
AMEND
PLAY.
PLUNK
NO.
WAIT— I THINK IT'S OUT OF TUNE...

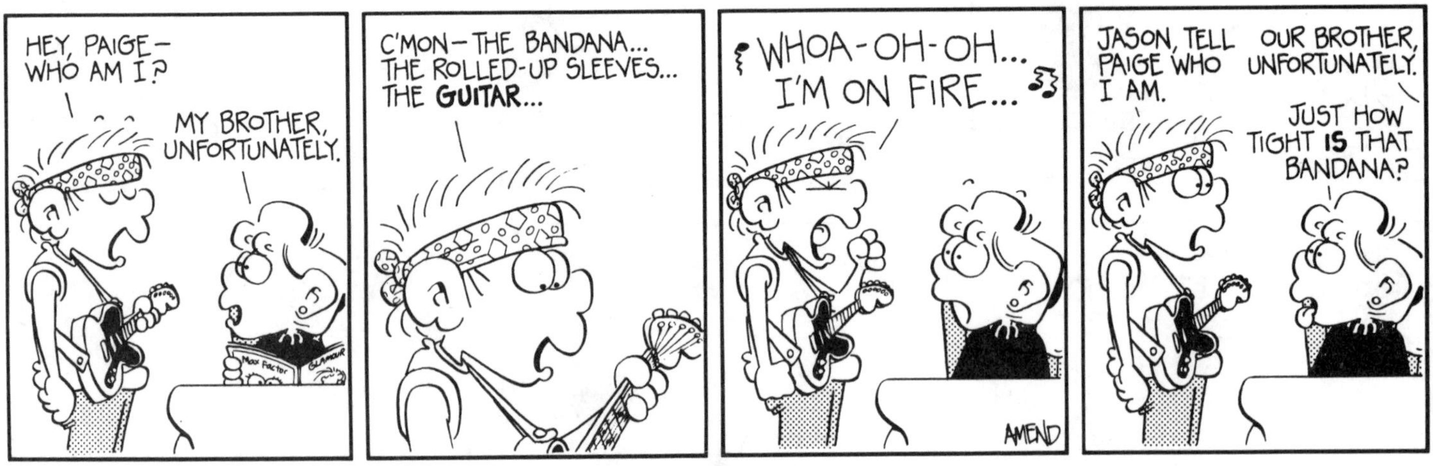
HEY, PAIGE— WHO AM I?
MY BROTHER, UNFORTUNATELY.
C'MON— THE BANDANA... THE ROLLED-UP SLEEVES... THE **GUITAR**...
WHOA-OH-OH... I'M ON FIRE...
AMEND
JASON, TELL PAIGE WHO I AM.
OUR BROTHER, UNFORTUNATELY.
JUST HOW TIGHT **IS** THAT BANDANA?

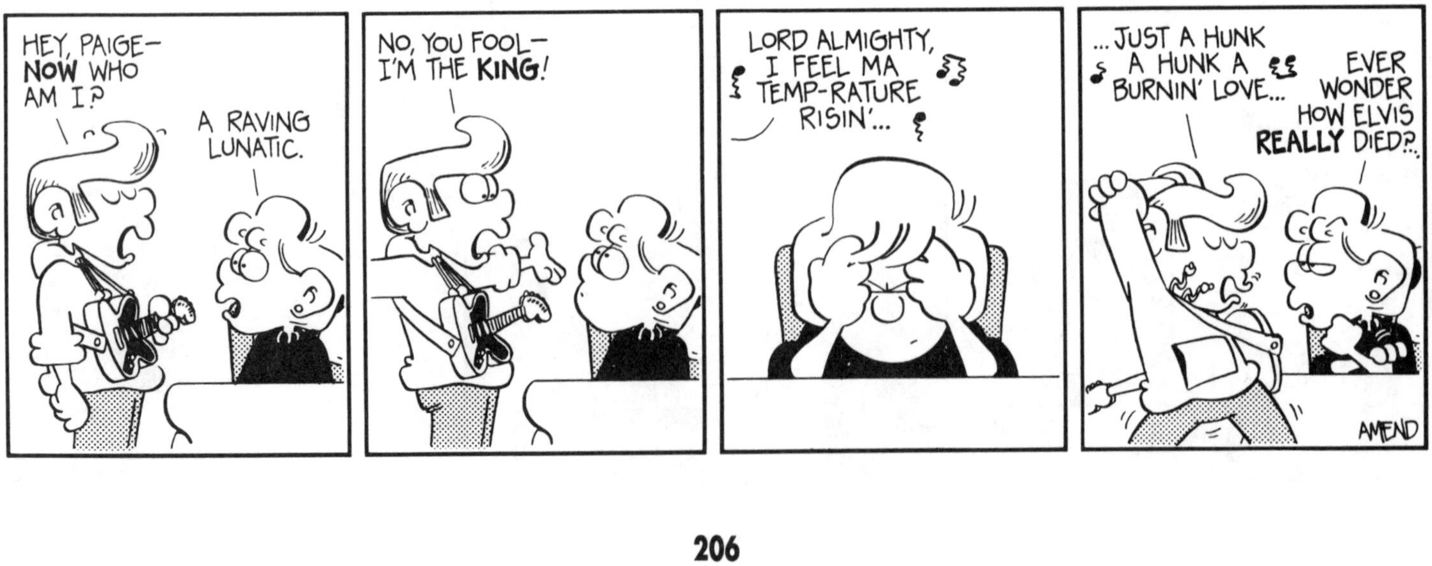
HEY, PAIGE— **NOW** WHO AM I?
A RAVING LUNATIC.
NO, YOU FOOL— I'M THE **KING**!
LORD ALMIGHTY, I FEEL MA TEMP-RATURE RISIN'...
...JUST A HUNK A HUNK A BURNIN' LOVE...
EVER WONDER HOW ELVIS **REALLY** DIED?
AMEND

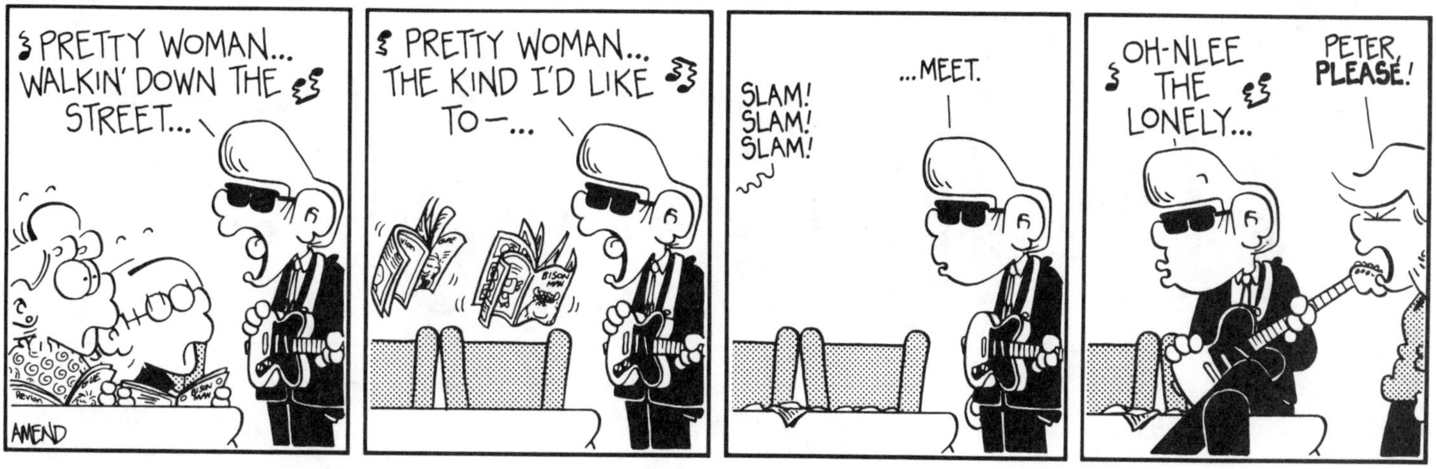
PRETTY WOMAN... WALKIN' DOWN THE STREET...
PRETTY WOMAN... THE KIND I'D LIKE TO—...
SLAM! SLAM! SLAM!
...MEET.
OH-NLEE THE LONELY...
PETER, **PLEASE**!
AMEND

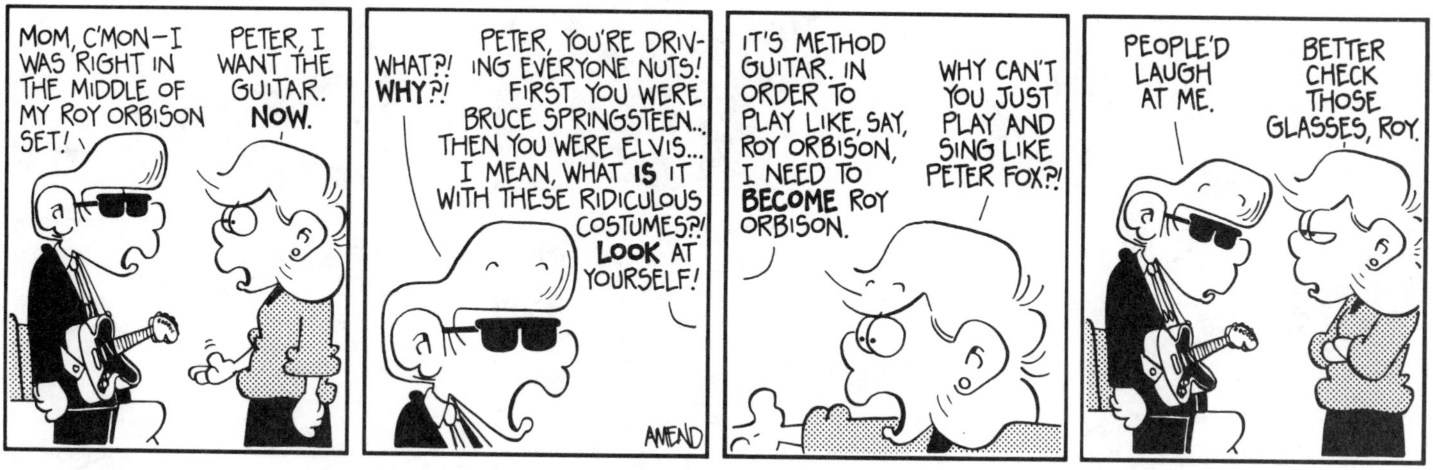
MOM, C'MON—I WAS RIGHT IN THE MIDDLE OF MY ROY ORBISON SET!
PETER, I WANT THE GUITAR. **NOW**.
WHAT?! **WHY**?!
PETER, YOU'RE DRIVING EVERYONE NUTS! FIRST YOU WERE BRUCE SPRINGSTEEN... THEN YOU WERE ELVIS... I MEAN, WHAT **IS** IT WITH THESE RIDICULOUS COSTUMES?! **LOOK** AT YOURSELF!
AMEND
IT'S METHOD GUITAR. IN ORDER TO PLAY LIKE, SAY, ROY ORBISON, I NEED TO **BECOME** ROY ORBISON.
WHY CAN'T YOU JUST PLAY AND SING LIKE PETER FOX?!
PEOPLE'D LAUGH AT ME.
BETTER CHECK THOSE GLASSES, ROY.

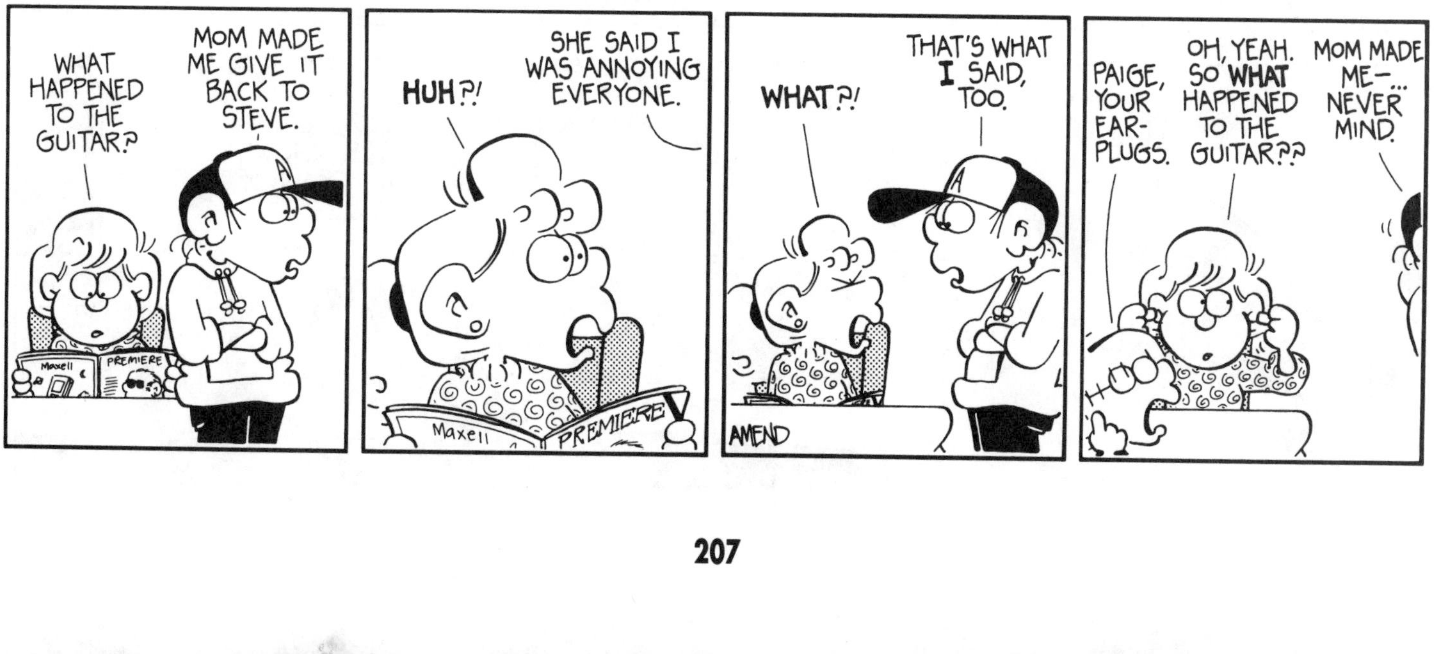
WHAT HAPPENED TO THE GUITAR?
MOM MADE ME GIVE IT BACK TO STEVE.
HUH?!
SHE SAID I WAS ANNOYING EVERYONE.
WHAT?!
THAT'S WHAT **I** SAID, TOO.
AMEND
PAIGE, YOUR EAR-PLUGS.
OH, YEAH. SO **WHAT** HAPPENED TO THE GUITAR??
MOM MADE ME—... NEVER MIND.

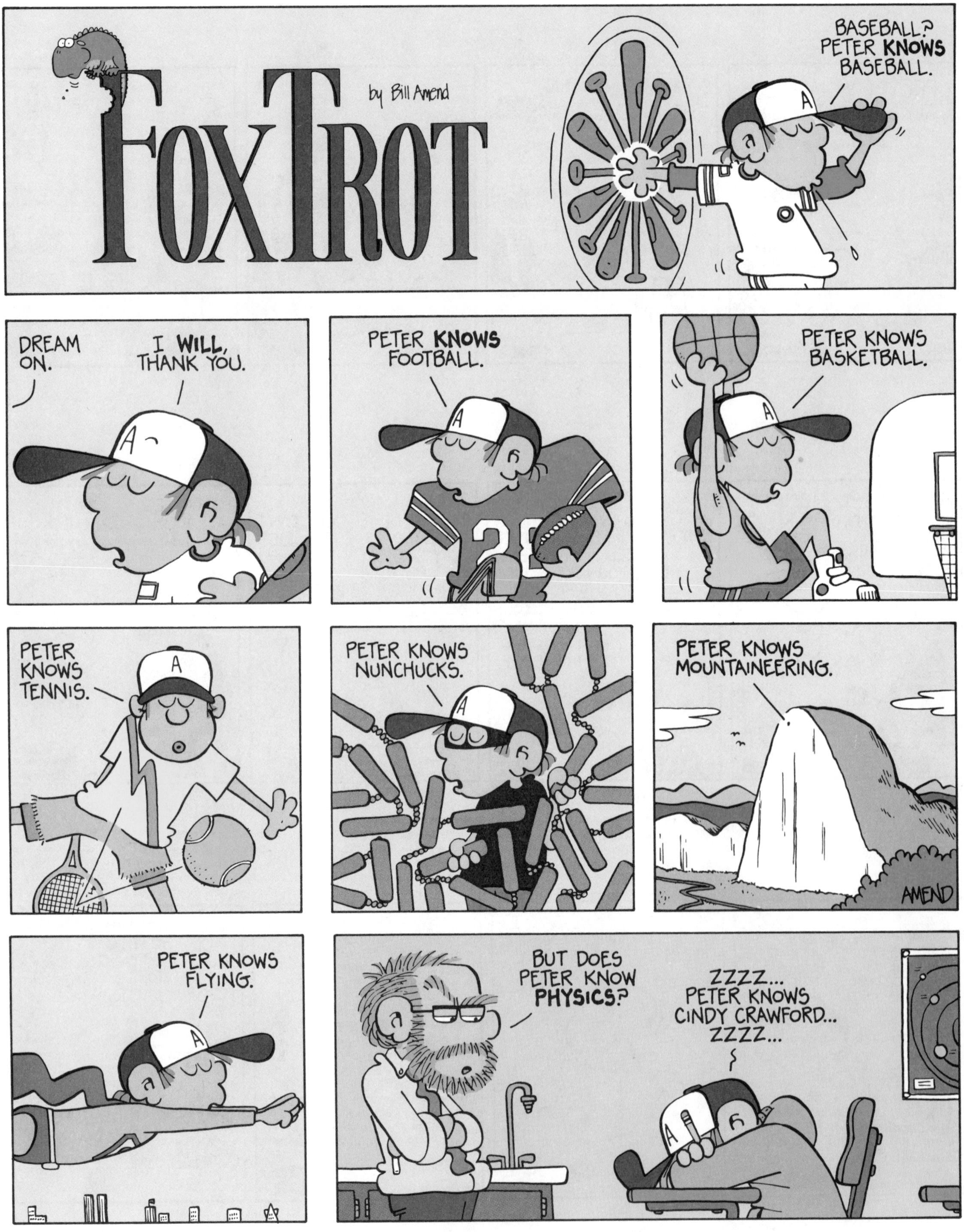
FoxTrot
by Bill Amend
BASEBALL? PETER **KNOWS** BASEBALL.
DREAM ON.
I **WILL**, THANK YOU.
PETER **KNOWS** FOOTBALL.
PETER KNOWS BASKETBALL.
PETER KNOWS TENNIS.
PETER KNOWS NUNCHUCKS.
PETER KNOWS MOUNTAINEERING.
AMEND
PETER KNOWS FLYING.
BUT DOES PETER KNOW **PHYSICS**?
ZZZZ... PETER KNOWS CINDY CRAWFORD... ZZZZ...

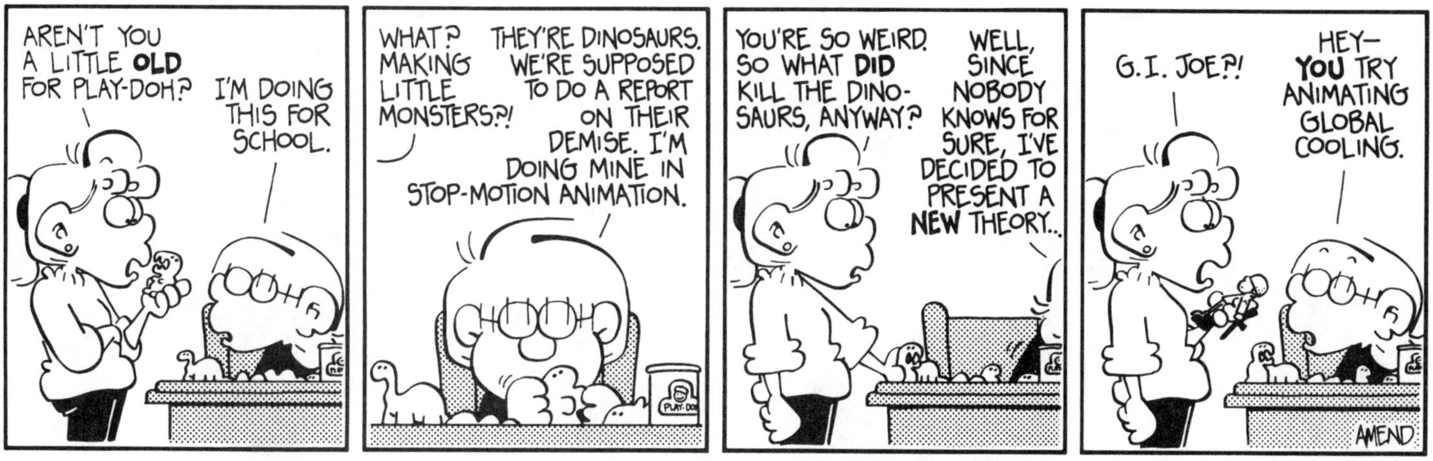
AREN'T YOU A LITTLE **OLD** FOR PLAY-DOH?
I'M DOING THIS FOR SCHOOL.
WHAT? MAKING LITTLE MONSTERS?!
THEY'RE DINOSAURS. WE'RE SUPPOSED TO DO A REPORT ON THEIR DEMISE. I'M DOING MINE IN STOP-MOTION ANIMATION.
YOU'RE SO WEIRD. SO WHAT **DID** KILL THE DINOSAURS, ANYWAY?
WELL, SINCE NOBODY KNOWS FOR SURE, I'VE DECIDED TO PRESENT A **NEW** THEORY...
G.I. JOE?!
HEY— **YOU** TRY ANIMATING GLOBAL COOLING.
AMEND

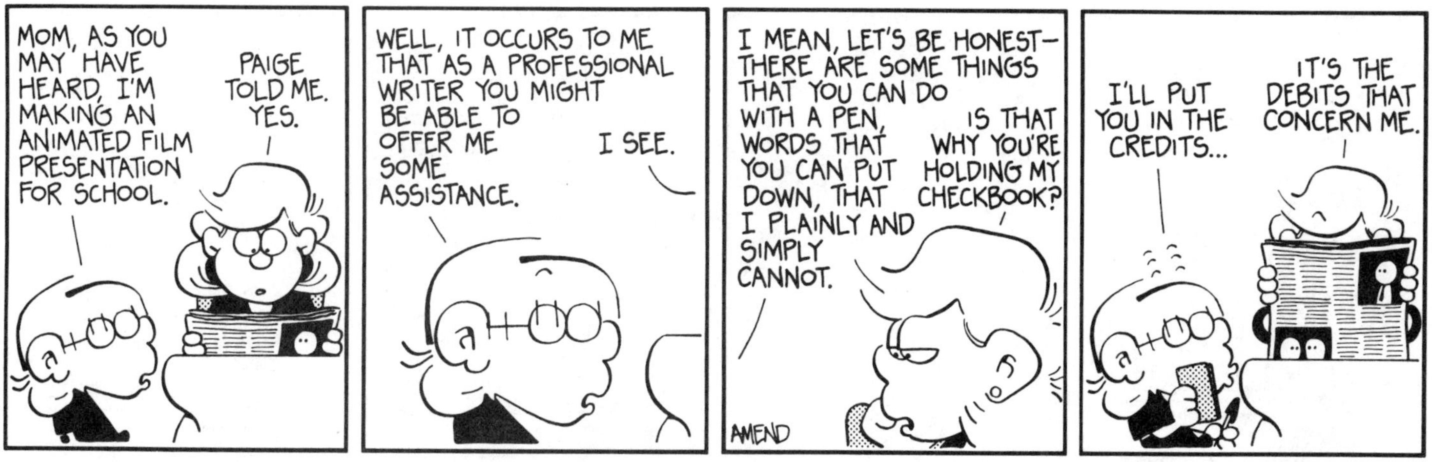
MOM, AS YOU MAY HAVE HEARD, I'M MAKING AN ANIMATED FILM PRESENTATION FOR SCHOOL.
PAIGE TOLD ME. YES.
WELL, IT OCCURS TO ME THAT AS A PROFESSIONAL WRITER YOU MIGHT BE ABLE TO OFFER ME SOME ASSISTANCE.
I SEE.
I MEAN, LET'S BE HONEST— THERE ARE SOME THINGS THAT YOU CAN DO WITH A PEN, WORDS THAT YOU CAN PUT DOWN, THAT I PLAINLY AND SIMPLY CANNOT.
IS THAT WHY YOU'RE HOLDING MY CHECKBOOK?
AMEND
I'LL PUT YOU IN THE CREDITS...
IT'S THE DEBITS THAT CONCERN ME.

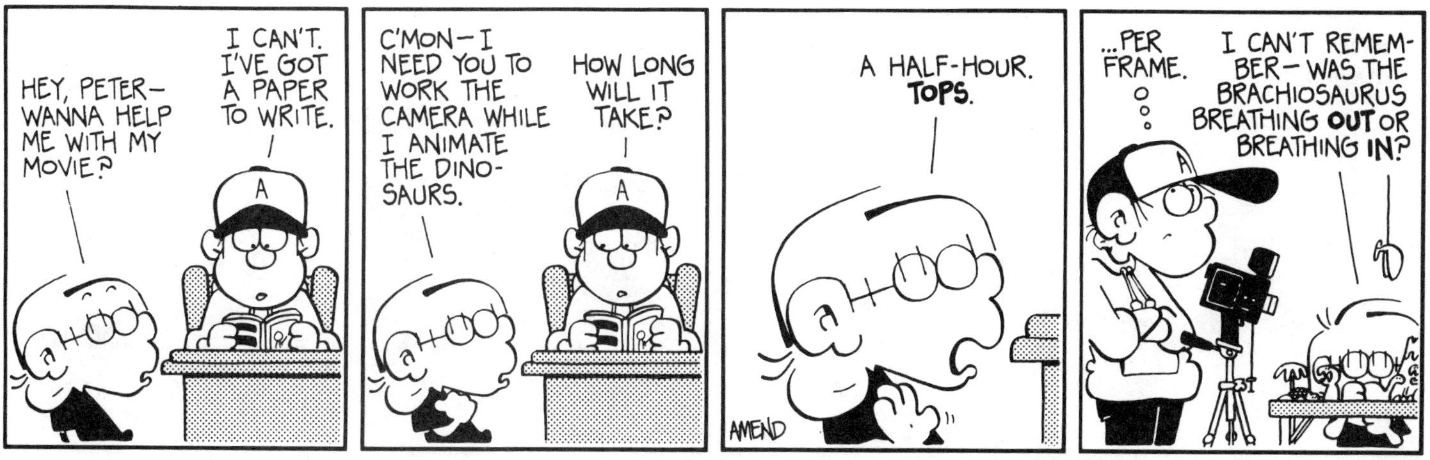
HEY, PETER— WANNA HELP ME WITH MY MOVIE?
I CAN'T. I'VE GOT A PAPER TO WRITE.
C'MON—I NEED YOU TO WORK THE CAMERA WHILE I ANIMATE THE DINOSAURS.
HOW LONG WILL IT TAKE?
A HALF-HOUR. **TOPS**.
AMEND
...PER FRAME.
I CAN'T REMEMBER— WAS THE BRACHIOSAURUS BREATHING **OUT** OR BREATHING **IN**?

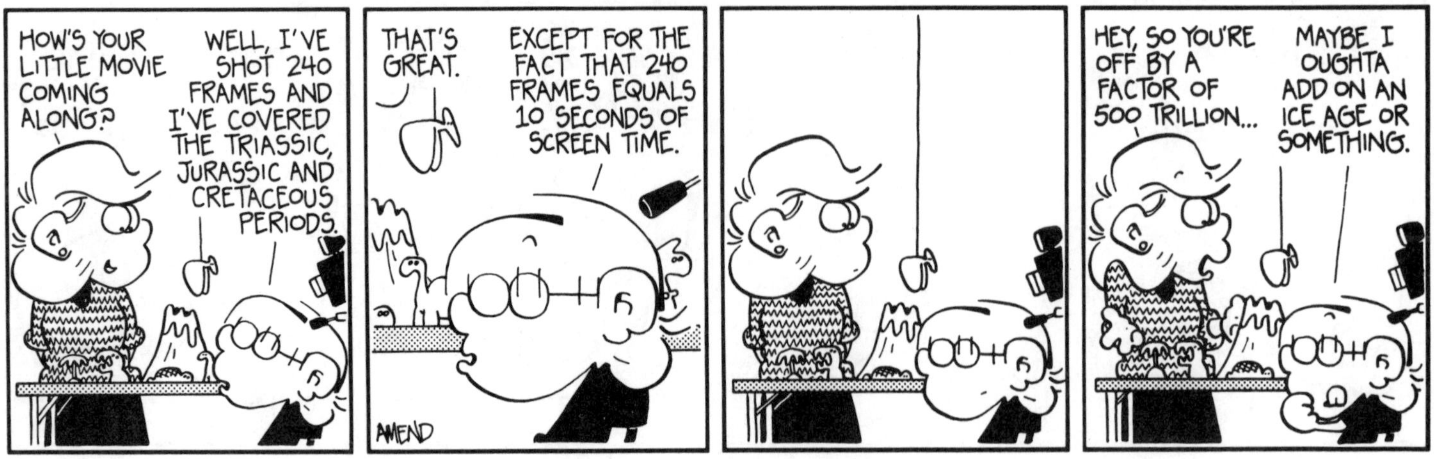
HOW'S YOUR LITTLE MOVIE COMING ALONG?
WELL, I'VE SHOT 240 FRAMES AND I'VE COVERED THE TRIASSIC, JURASSIC AND CRETACEOUS PERIODS.
THAT'S GREAT.
EXCEPT FOR THE FACT THAT 240 FRAMES EQUALS 10 SECONDS OF SCREEN TIME.
AMEND
HEY, SO YOU'RE OFF BY A FACTOR OF 500 TRILLION...
MAYBE I OUGHTA ADD ON AN ICE AGE OR SOMETHING.

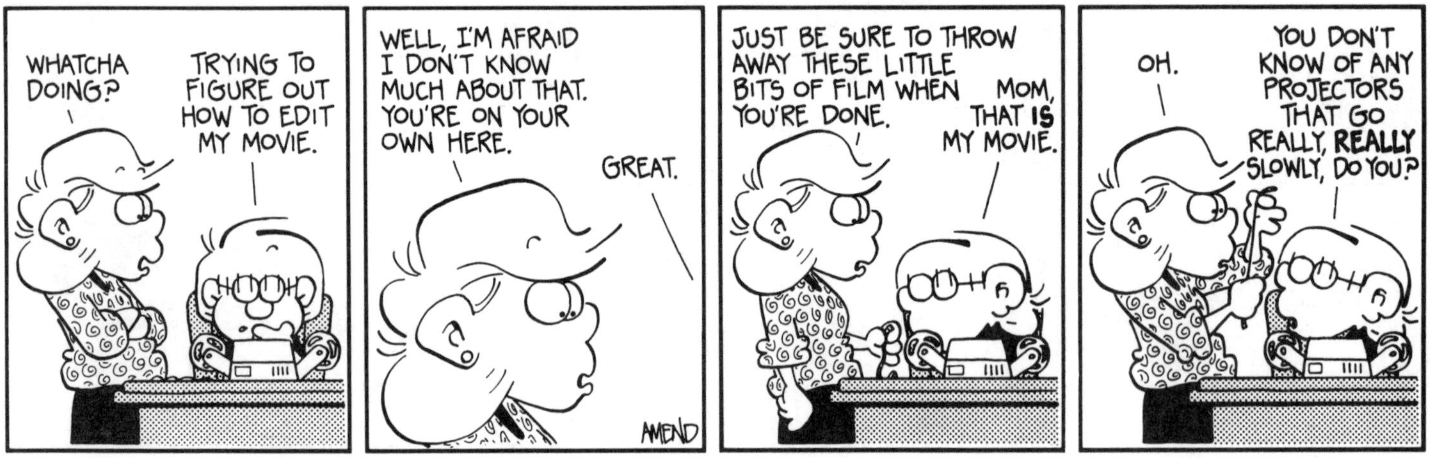
WHATCHA DOING?
TRYING TO FIGURE OUT HOW TO EDIT MY MOVIE.
WELL, I'M AFRAID I DON'T KNOW MUCH ABOUT THAT. YOU'RE ON YOUR OWN HERE.
GREAT.
AMEND
JUST BE SURE TO THROW AWAY THESE LITTLE BITS OF FILM WHEN YOU'RE DONE.
MOM, THAT **IS** MY MOVIE.
OH.
YOU DON'T KNOW OF ANY PROJECTORS THAT GO REALLY, **REALLY** SLOWLY, DO YOU?

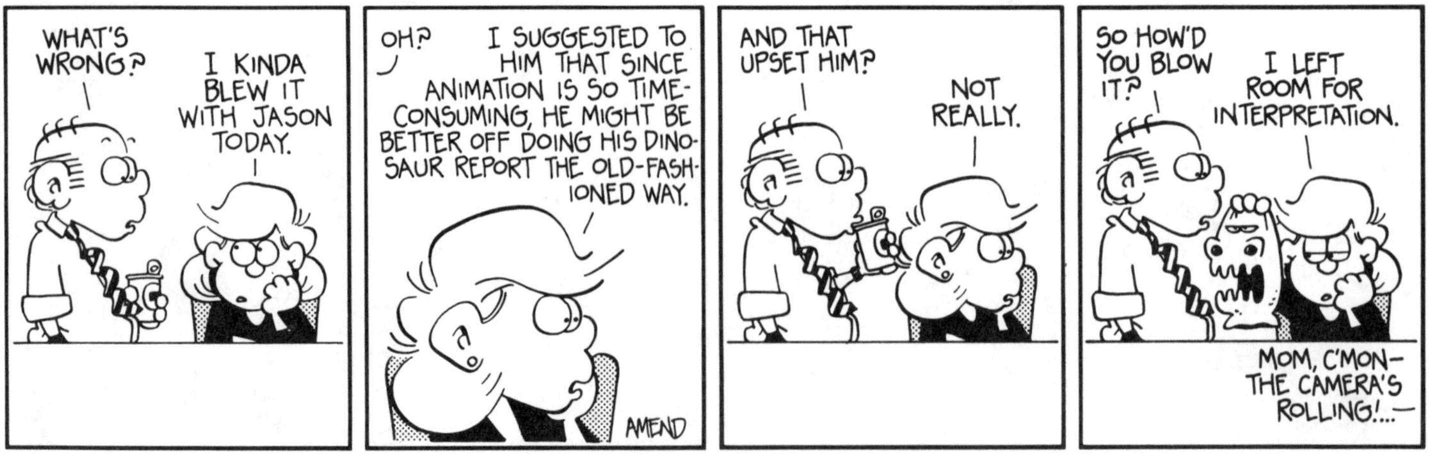
WHAT'S WRONG?
I KINDA BLEW IT WITH JASON TODAY.
OH?
I SUGGESTED TO HIM THAT SINCE ANIMATION IS SO TIME-CONSUMING, HE MIGHT BE BETTER OFF DOING HIS DINOSAUR REPORT THE OLD-FASHIONED WAY.
AMEND
AND THAT UPSET HIM?
NOT REALLY.
SO HOW'D YOU BLOW IT?
I LEFT ROOM FOR INTERPRETATION.
MOM, C'MON— THE CAMERA'S ROLLING!...

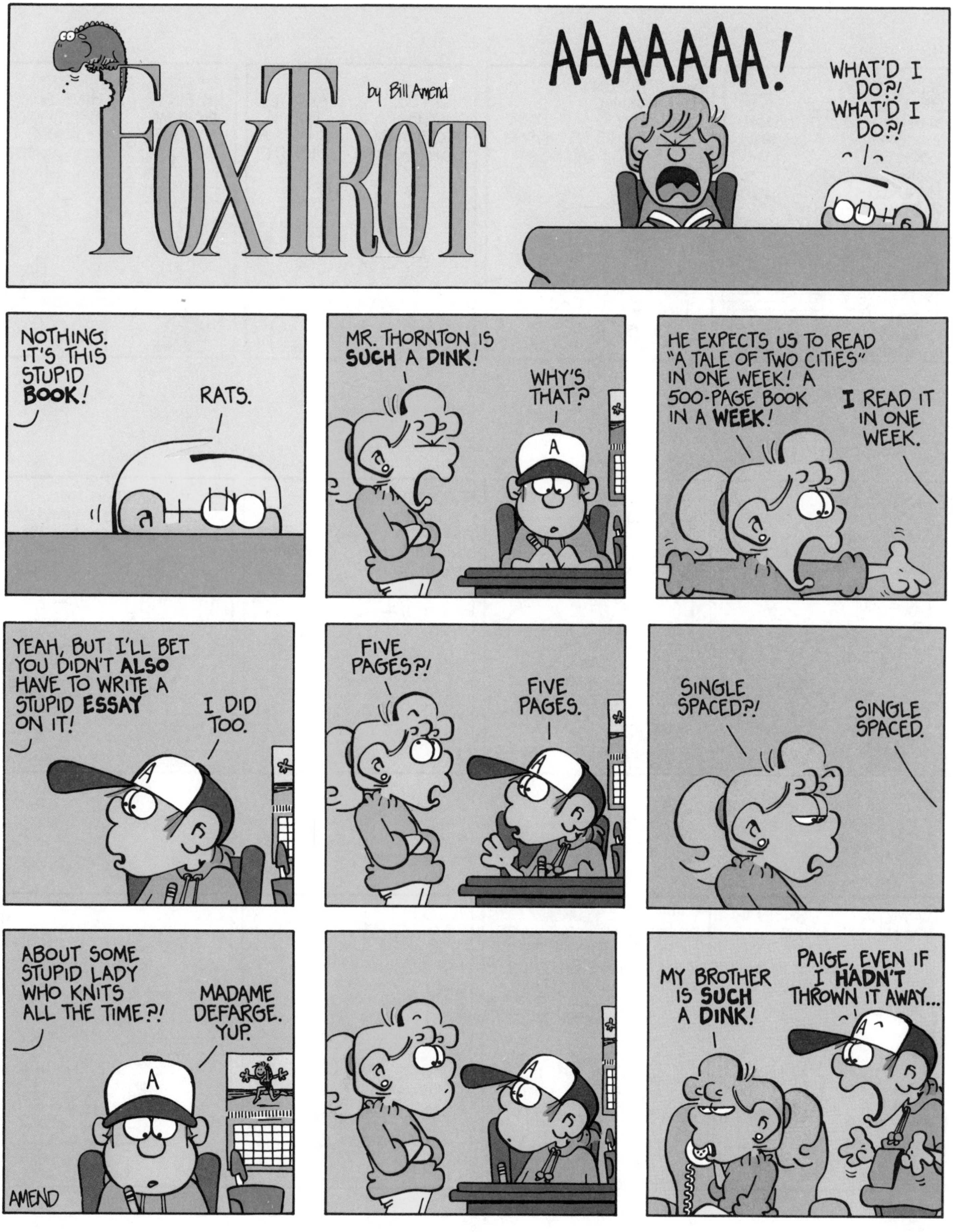
FoxTrot
by Bill Amend
AAAAAAA!
WHAT'D I DO?! WHAT'D I DO?!
NOTHING. IT'S THIS STUPID BOOK!
RATS.
MR. THORNTON IS SUCH A DINK!
WHY'S THAT?
HE EXPECTS US TO READ "A TALE OF TWO CITIES" IN ONE WEEK! A 500-PAGE BOOK IN A WEEK!
I READ IT IN ONE WEEK.
YEAH, BUT I'LL BET YOU DIDN'T ALSO HAVE TO WRITE A STUPID ESSAY ON IT!
I DID TOO.
FIVE PAGES?!
FIVE PAGES.
SINGLE SPACED?!
SINGLE SPACED.
ABOUT SOME STUPID LADY WHO KNITS ALL THE TIME?!
MADAME DEFARGE. YUP.
AMEND
MY BROTHER IS SUCH A DINK!
PAIGE, EVEN IF I HADN'T THROWN IT AWAY...

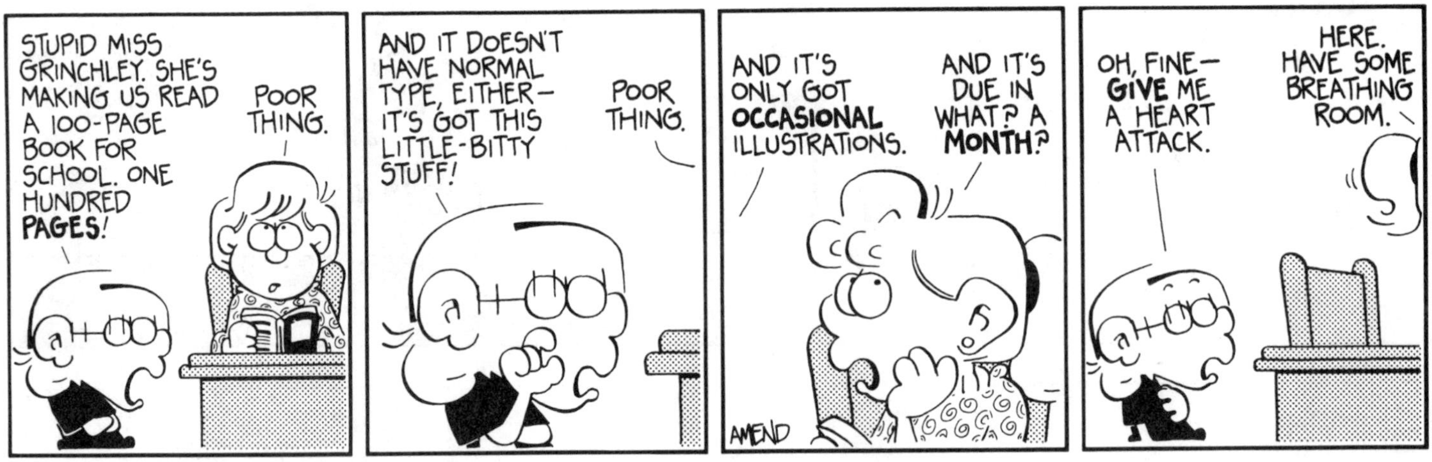
STUPID MISS GRINCHLEY. SHE'S MAKING US READ A 100-PAGE BOOK FOR SCHOOL. ONE HUNDRED **PAGES**!
POOR THING.
AND IT DOESN'T HAVE NORMAL TYPE, EITHER— IT'S GOT THIS LITTLE-BITTY STUFF!
POOR THING.
AND IT'S ONLY GOT **OCCASIONAL** ILLUSTRATIONS.
AND IT'S DUE IN WHAT? A **MONTH**?
AMEND
OH, FINE— **GIVE** ME A HEART ATTACK.
HERE. HAVE SOME BREATHING ROOM.

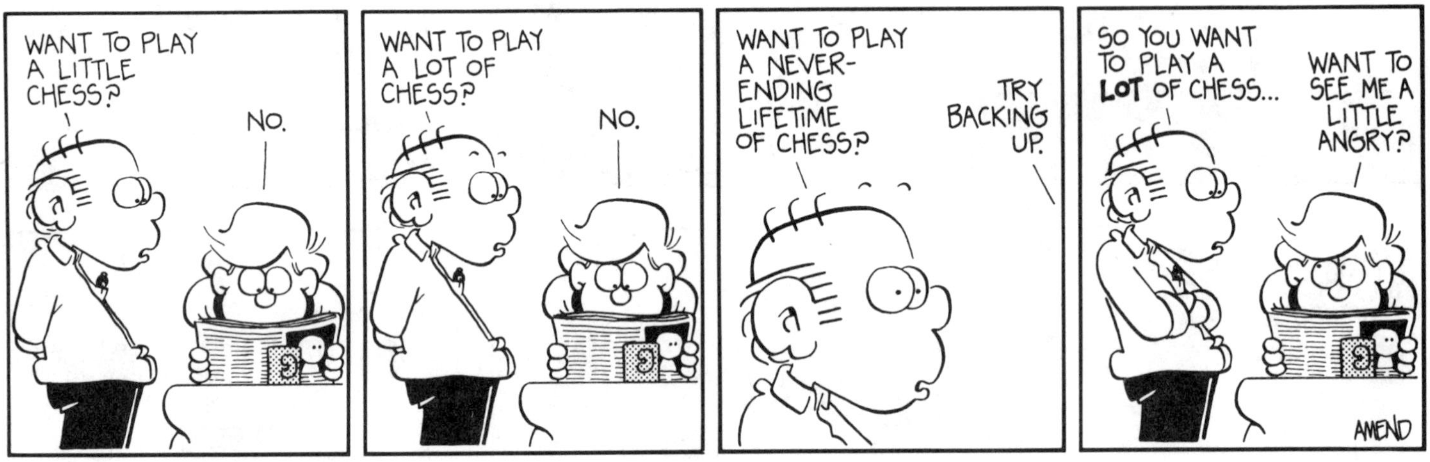
WANT TO PLAY A LITTLE CHESS?
NO.
WANT TO PLAY A LOT OF CHESS?
NO.
WANT TO PLAY A NEVER-ENDING LIFETIME OF CHESS?
TRY BACKING UP.
SO YOU WANT TO PLAY A **LOT** OF CHESS...
WANT TO SEE ME A LITTLE ANGRY?
AMEND

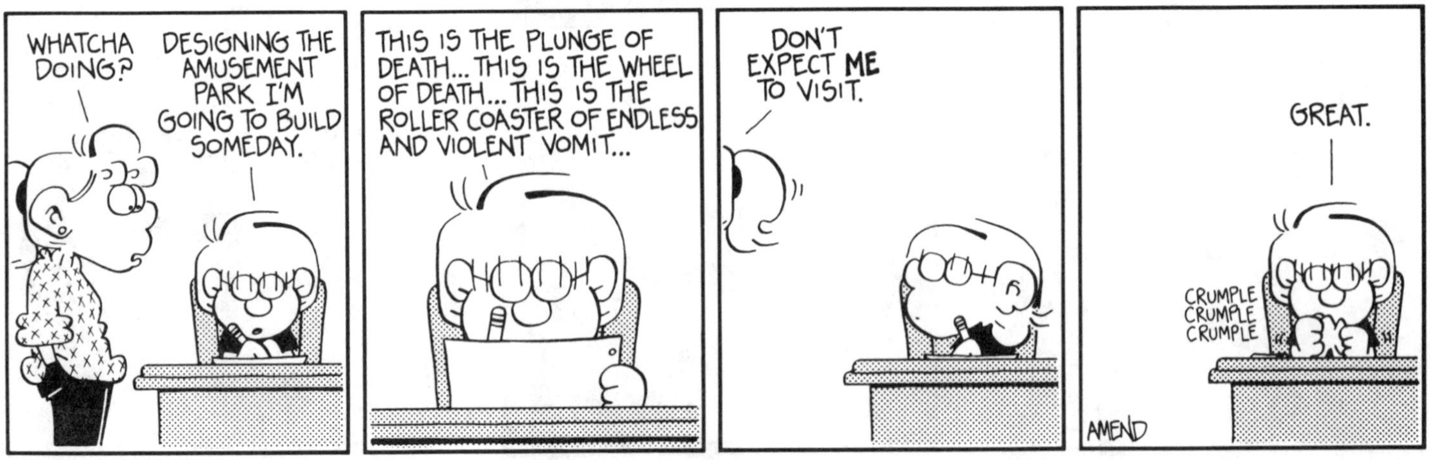
WHATCHA DOING?
DESIGNING THE AMUSEMENT PARK I'M GOING TO BUILD SOMEDAY.
THIS IS THE PLUNGE OF DEATH... THIS IS THE WHEEL OF DEATH... THIS IS THE ROLLER COASTER OF ENDLESS AND VIOLENT VOMIT...
DON'T EXPECT **ME** TO VISIT.
GREAT.
CRUMPLE CRUMPLE CRUMPLE
AMEND

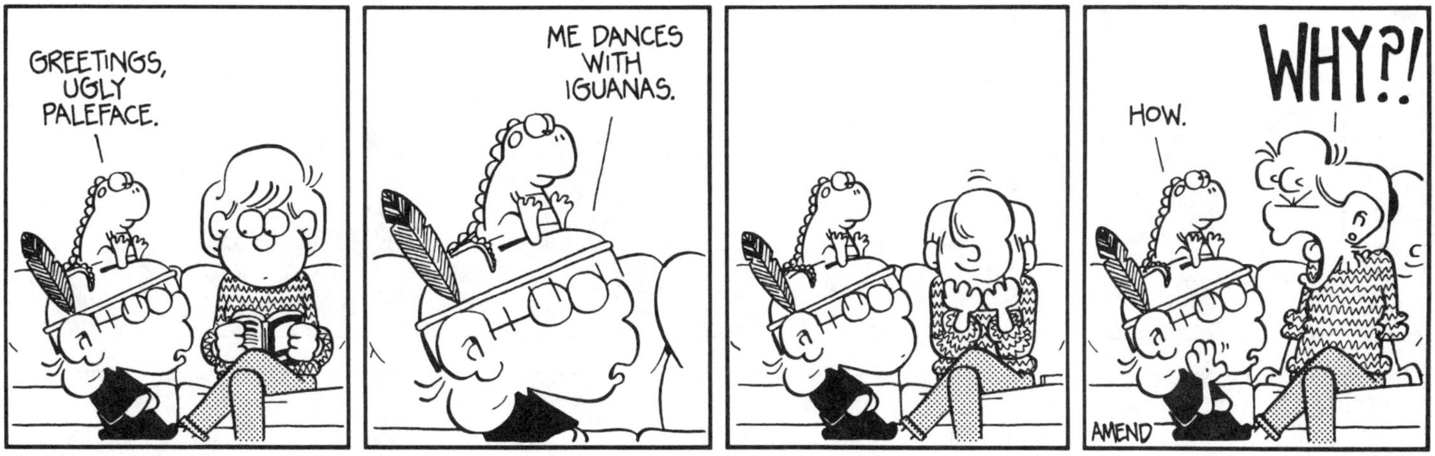
GREETINGS, UGLY PALEFACE.
ME DANCES WITH IGUANAS.
HOW.
WHY?!
AMEND

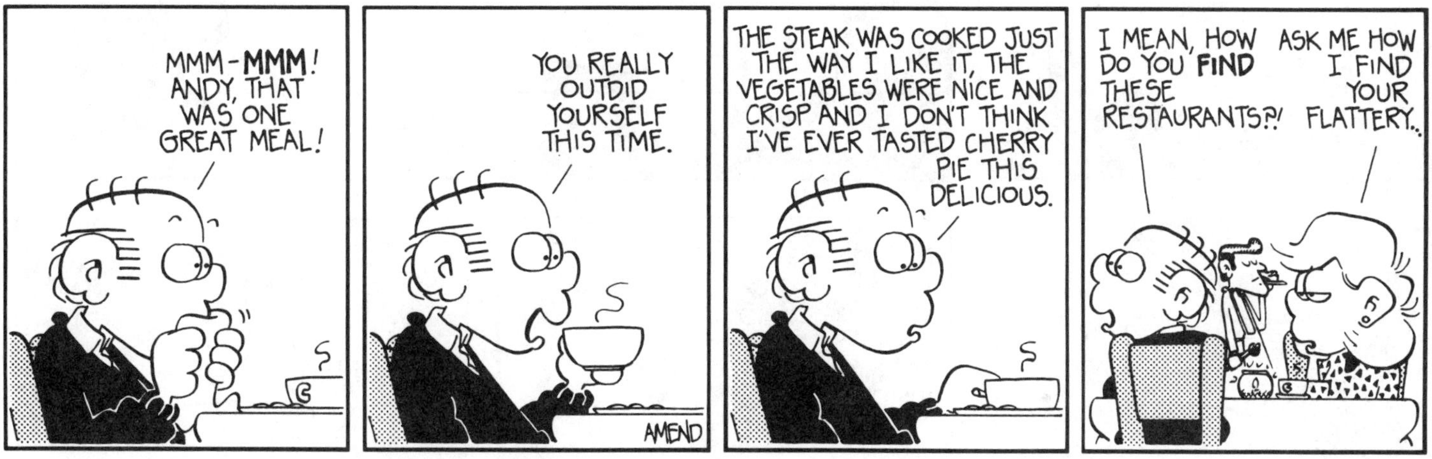
MMM-**MMM**! ANDY, THAT WAS ONE GREAT MEAL!
YOU REALLY OUTDID YOURSELF THIS TIME.
AMEND
THE STEAK WAS COOKED JUST THE WAY I LIKE IT, THE VEGETABLES WERE NICE AND CRISP AND I DON'T THINK I'VE EVER TASTED CHERRY PIE THIS DELICIOUS.
I MEAN, HOW DO YOU **FIND** THESE RESTAURANTS?!
ASK ME HOW I FIND YOUR FLATTERY...

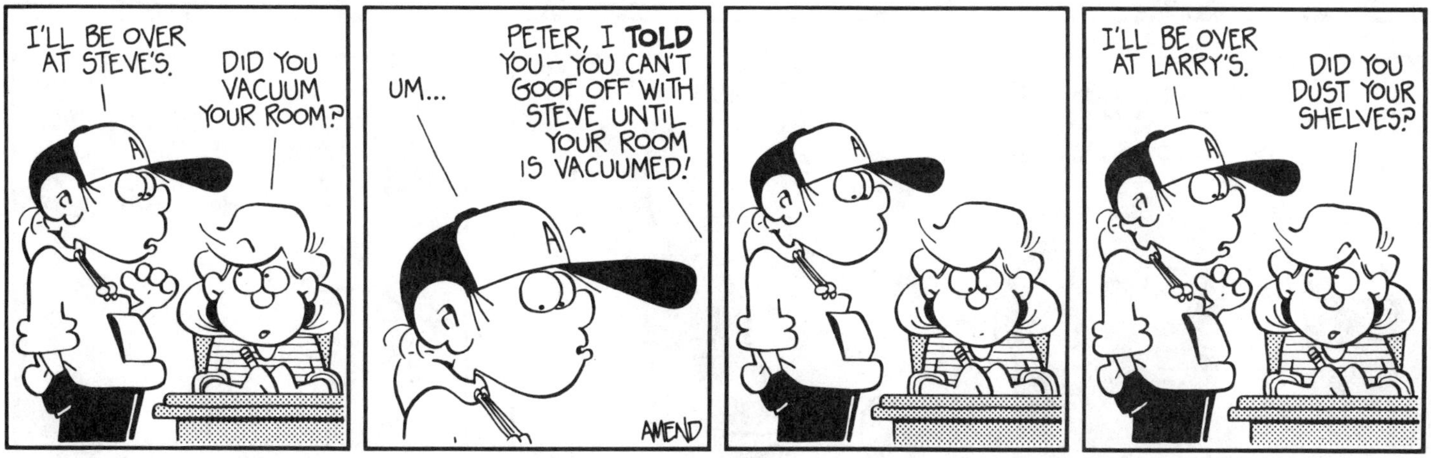
I'LL BE OVER AT STEVE'S.
DID YOU VACUUM YOUR ROOM?
UM...
PETER, I **TOLD** YOU— YOU CAN'T GOOF OFF WITH STEVE UNTIL YOUR ROOM IS VACUUMED!
AMEND
I'LL BE OVER AT LARRY'S.
DID YOU DUST YOUR SHELVES?

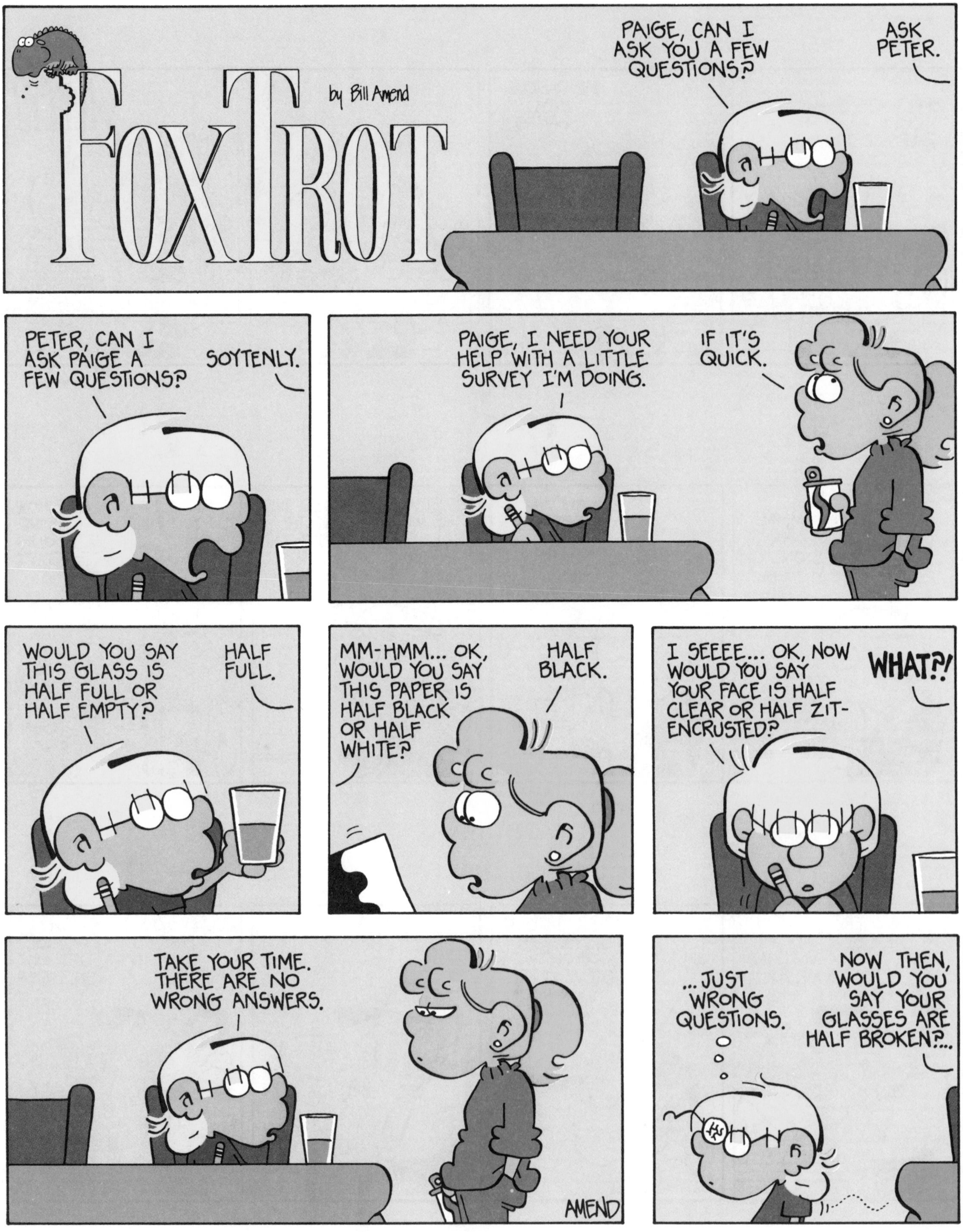
FOXTROT
by Bill Amend
PAIGE, CAN I ASK YOU A FEW QUESTIONS?
ASK PETER.
PETER, CAN I ASK PAIGE A FEW QUESTIONS?
SOYTENLY.
PAIGE, I NEED YOUR HELP WITH A LITTLE SURVEY I'M DOING.
IF IT'S QUICK.
WOULD YOU SAY THIS GLASS IS HALF FULL OR HALF EMPTY?
HALF FULL.
MM-HMM... OK, WOULD YOU SAY THIS PAPER IS HALF BLACK OR HALF WHITE?
HALF BLACK.
I SEEEE... OK, NOW WOULD YOU SAY YOUR FACE IS HALF CLEAR OR HALF ZIT-ENCRUSTED?
WHAT?!
TAKE YOUR TIME. THERE ARE NO WRONG ANSWERS.
AMEND
...JUST WRONG QUESTIONS.
NOW THEN, WOULD YOU SAY YOUR GLASSES ARE HALF BROKEN?...

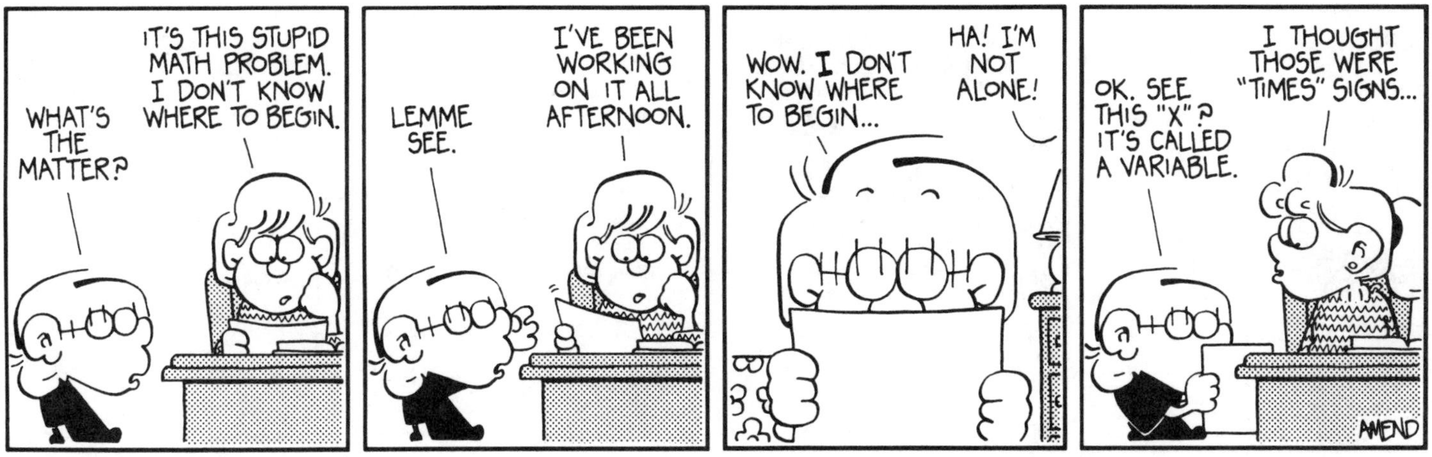
WHAT'S THE MATTER?
IT'S THIS STUPID MATH PROBLEM. I DON'T KNOW WHERE TO BEGIN.
LEMME SEE.
I'VE BEEN WORKING ON IT ALL AFTERNOON.
WOW. I DON'T KNOW WHERE TO BEGIN...
HA! I'M NOT ALONE!
OK. SEE THIS "X"? IT'S CALLED A VARIABLE.
I THOUGHT THOSE WERE "TIMES" SIGNS...
AMEND

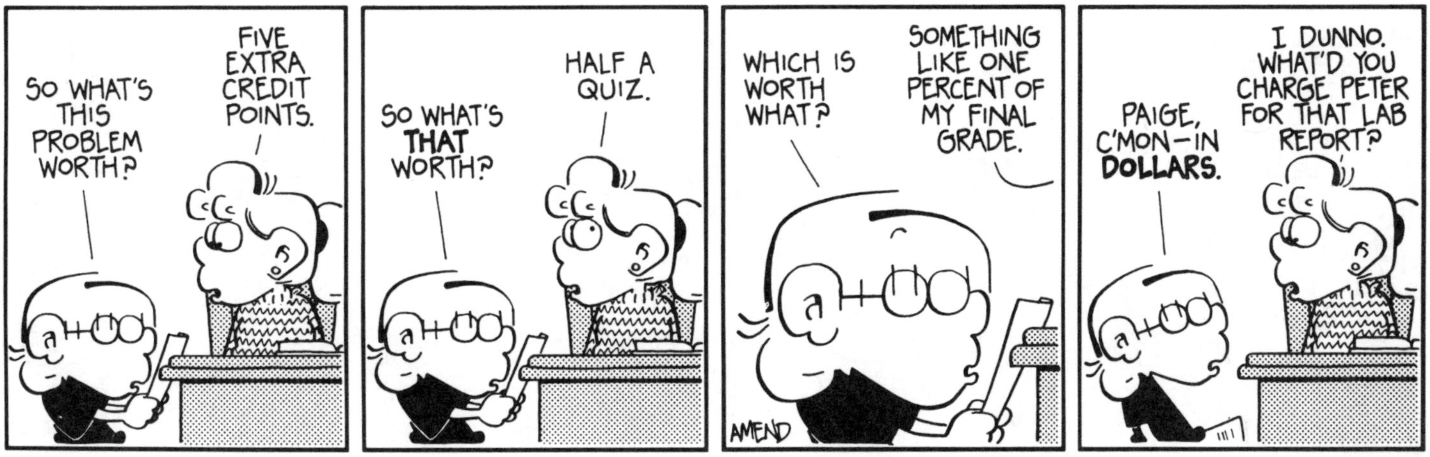
SO WHAT'S THIS PROBLEM WORTH?
FIVE EXTRA CREDIT POINTS.
SO WHAT'S THAT WORTH?
HALF A QUIZ.
WHICH IS WORTH WHAT?
SOMETHING LIKE ONE PERCENT OF MY FINAL GRADE.
AMEND
PAIGE, C'MON—IN DOLLARS.
I DUNNO. WHAT'D YOU CHARGE PETER FOR THAT LAB REPORT?

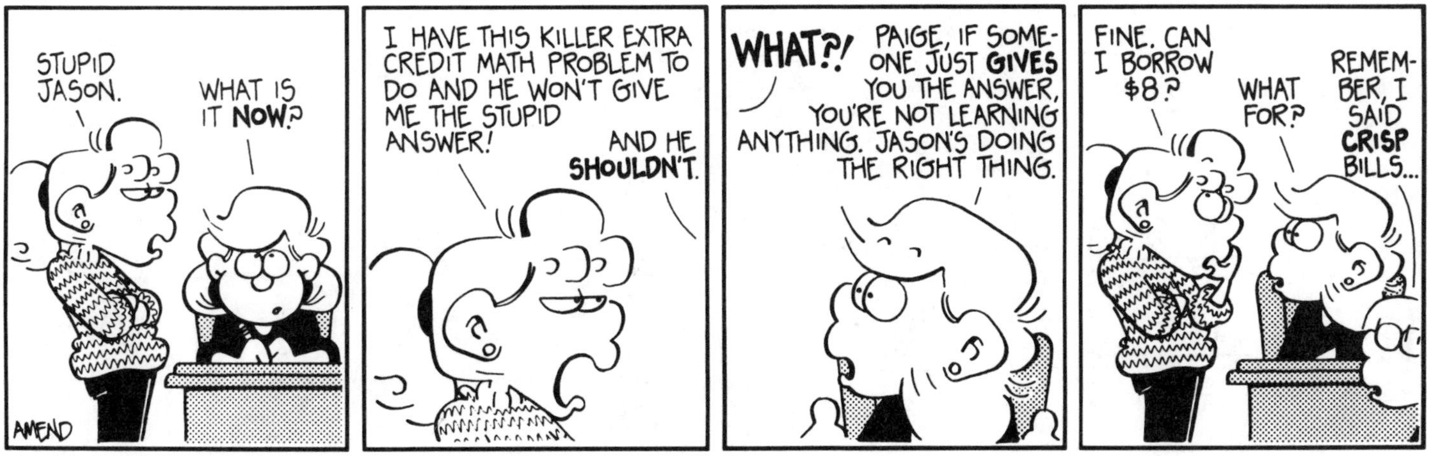
STUPID JASON.
WHAT IS IT NOW?
AMEND
I HAVE THIS KILLER EXTRA CREDIT MATH PROBLEM TO DO AND HE WON'T GIVE ME THE STUPID ANSWER!
AND HE SHOULDN'T.
WHAT?!
PAIGE, IF SOMEONE JUST GIVES YOU THE ANSWER, YOU'RE NOT LEARNING ANYTHING. JASON'S DOING THE RIGHT THING.
FINE. CAN I BORROW $8?
WHAT FOR?
REMEMBER, I SAID CRISP BILLS...

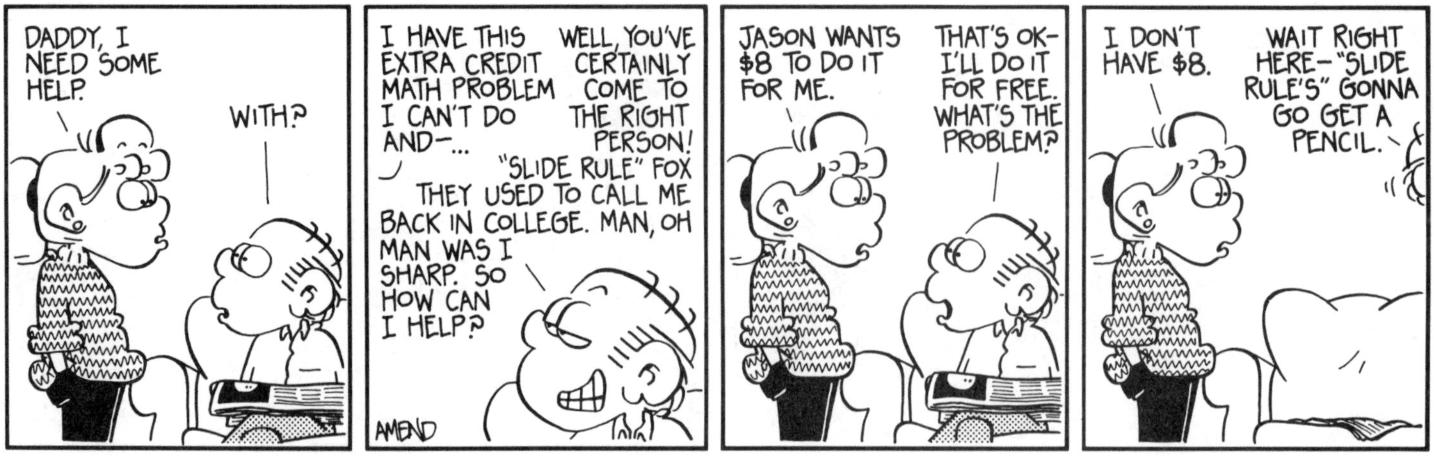
DADDY, I NEED SOME HELP.
WITH?
I HAVE THIS EXTRA CREDIT MATH PROBLEM I CAN'T DO AND–...
WELL, YOU'VE CERTAINLY COME TO THE RIGHT PERSON! "SLIDE RULE" FOX THEY USED TO CALL ME BACK IN COLLEGE. MAN, OH MAN WAS I SHARP. SO HOW CAN I HELP?
AMEND
JASON WANTS $8 TO DO IT FOR ME.
THAT'S OK– I'LL DO IT FOR FREE. WHAT'S THE PROBLEM?
I DON'T HAVE $8.
WAIT RIGHT HERE– "SLIDE RULE'S" GONNA GO GET A PENCIL.

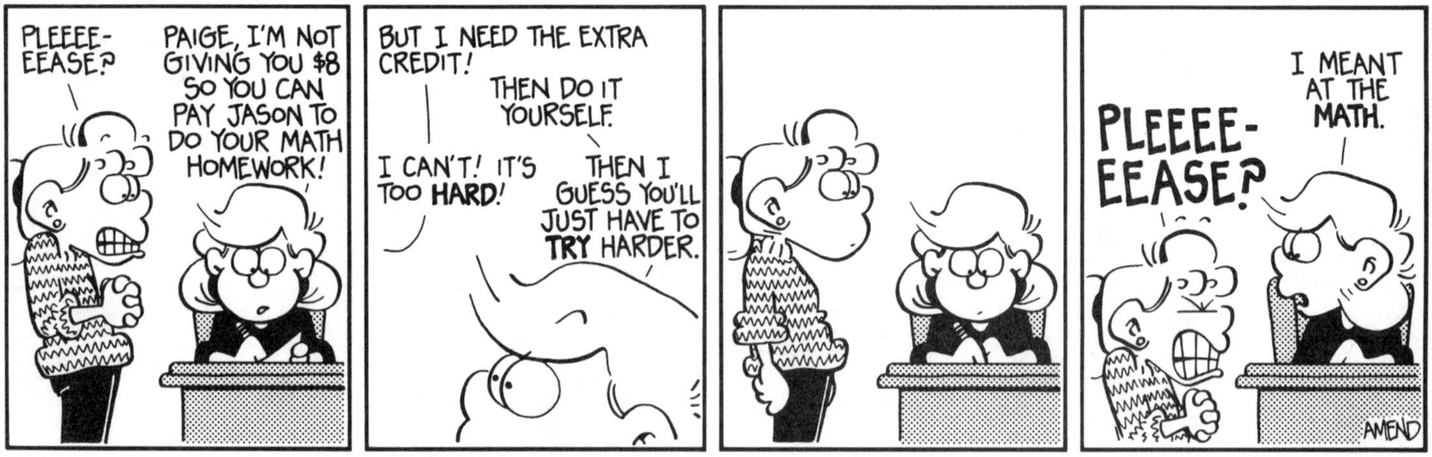
PLEEEEE-EEASE?
PAIGE, I'M NOT GIVING YOU $8 SO YOU CAN PAY JASON TO DO YOUR MATH HOMEWORK!
BUT I NEED THE EXTRA CREDIT!
THEN DO IT YOURSELF.
I CAN'T! IT'S TOO **HARD**!
THEN I GUESS YOU'LL JUST HAVE TO **TRY** HARDER.
PLEEEE-EEASE?
I MEANT AT THE **MATH**.
AMEND

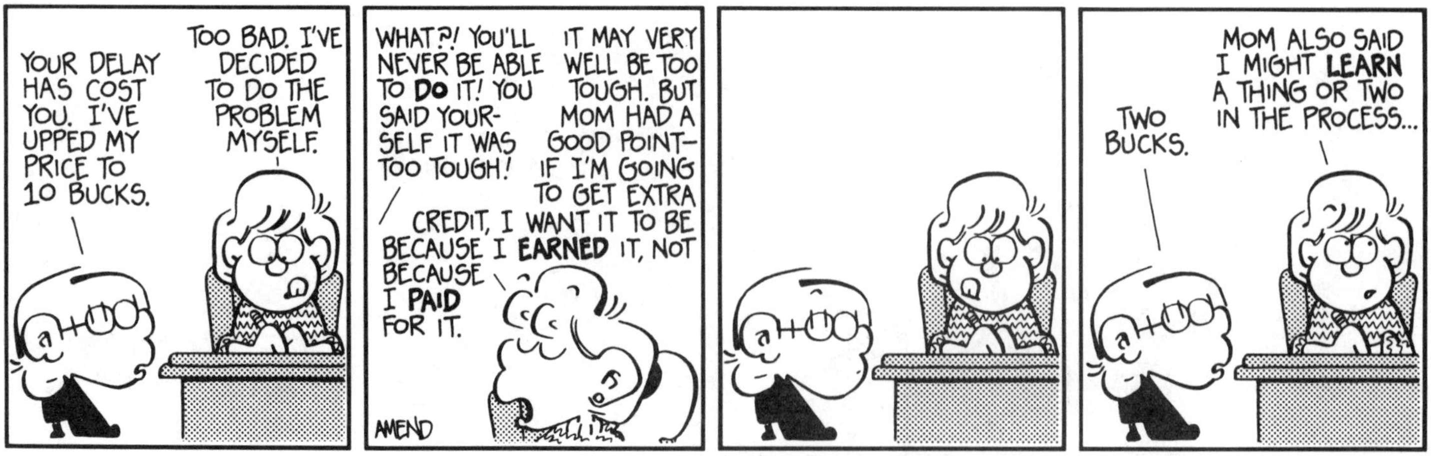
YOUR DELAY HAS COST YOU. I'VE UPPED MY PRICE TO 10 BUCKS.
TOO BAD. I'VE DECIDED TO DO THE PROBLEM MYSELF.
WHAT?! YOU'LL NEVER BE ABLE TO **DO** IT! YOU SAID YOURSELF IT WAS TOO TOUGH!
IT MAY VERY WELL BE TOO TOUGH. BUT MOM HAD A GOOD POINT– IF I'M GOING TO GET EXTRA CREDIT, I WANT IT TO BE BECAUSE I **EARNED** IT, NOT BECAUSE I **PAID** FOR IT.
AMEND
TWO BUCKS.
MOM ALSO SAID I MIGHT **LEARN** A THING OR TWO IN THE PROCESS...

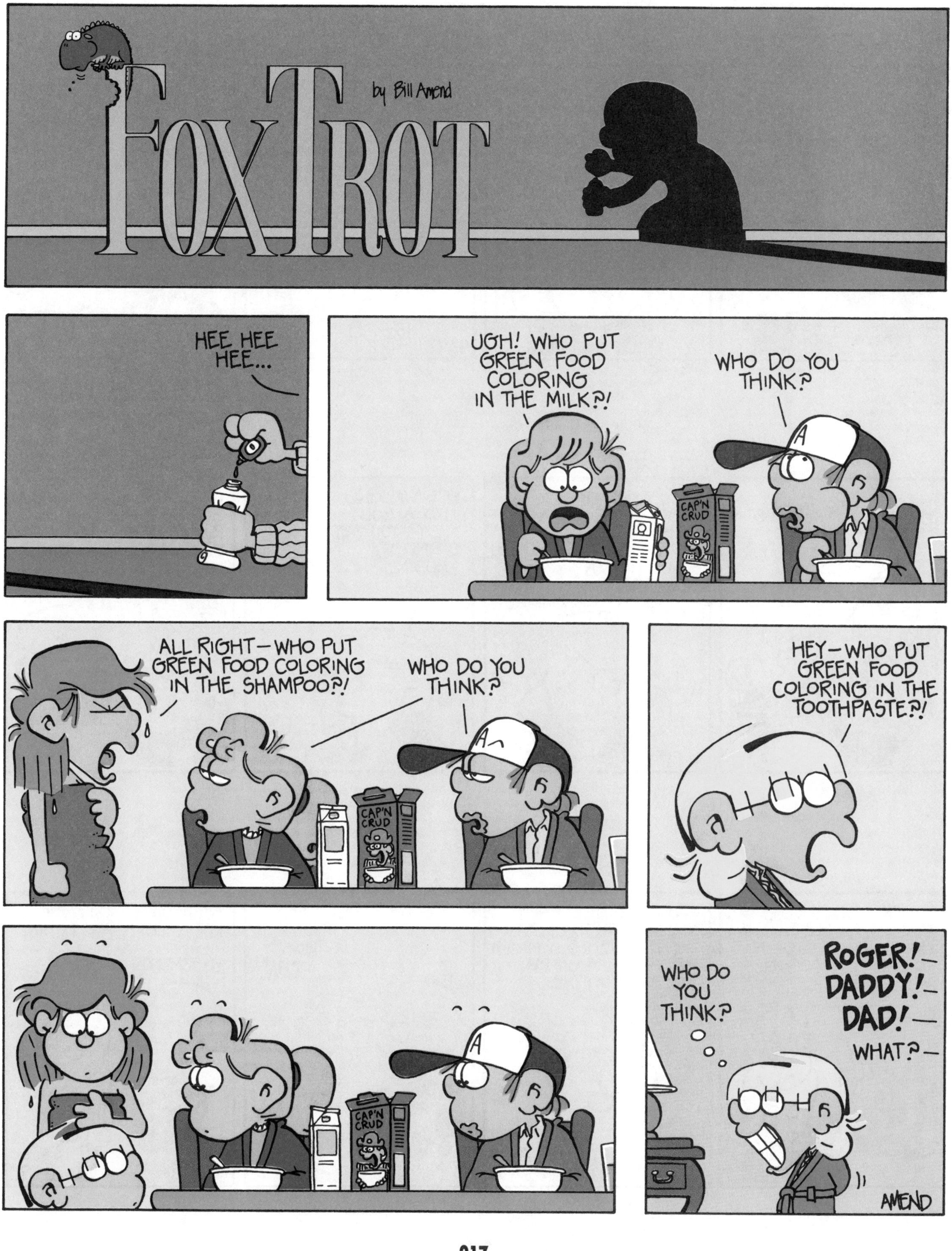
FoxTrot
by Bill Amend
HEE HEE HEE...
UGH! WHO PUT GREEN FOOD COLORING IN THE MILK?!
WHO DO YOU THINK?
CAP'N CRUD
ALL RIGHT—WHO PUT GREEN FOOD COLORING IN THE SHAMPOO?!
WHO DO YOU THINK?
CAP'N CRUD
HEY—WHO PUT GREEN FOOD COLORING IN THE TOOTHPASTE?!
CAP'N CRUD
WHO DO YOU THINK?
ROGER!—
DADDY!—
DAD!—
WHAT?—
AMEND

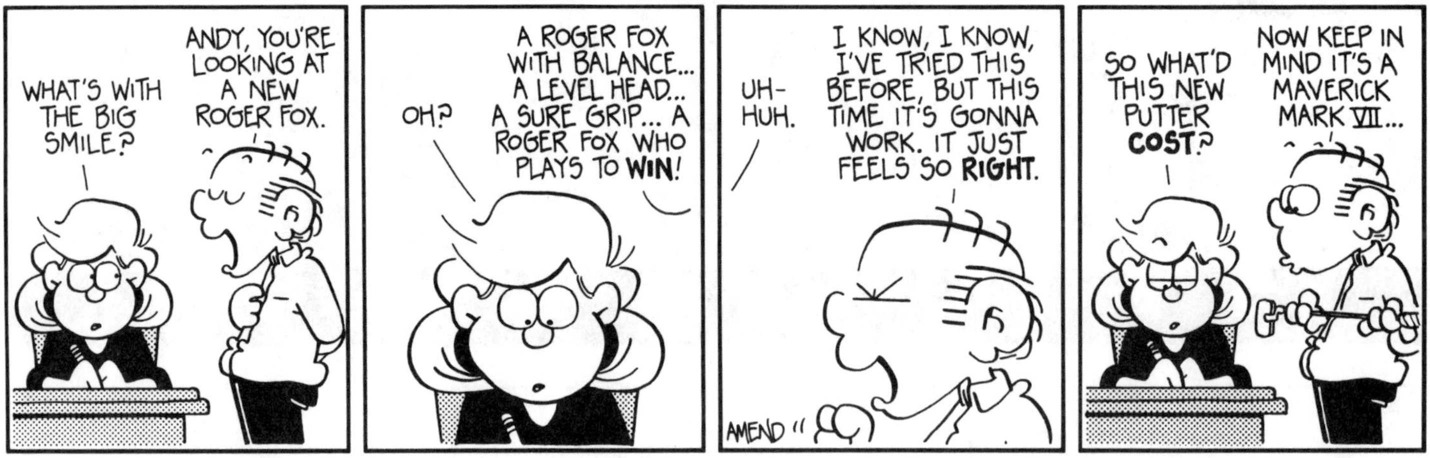
WHAT'S WITH THE BIG SMILE?
ANDY, YOU'RE LOOKING AT A NEW ROGER FOX.
OH?
A ROGER FOX WITH BALANCE... A LEVEL HEAD... A SURE GRIP... A ROGER FOX WHO PLAYS TO **WIN**!
UH-HUH.
I KNOW, I KNOW, I'VE TRIED THIS BEFORE, BUT THIS TIME IT'S GONNA WORK. IT JUST FEELS SO **RIGHT**.
AMEND
SO WHAT'D THIS NEW PUTTER **COST**?
NOW KEEP IN MIND IT'S A MAVERICK MARK VII...

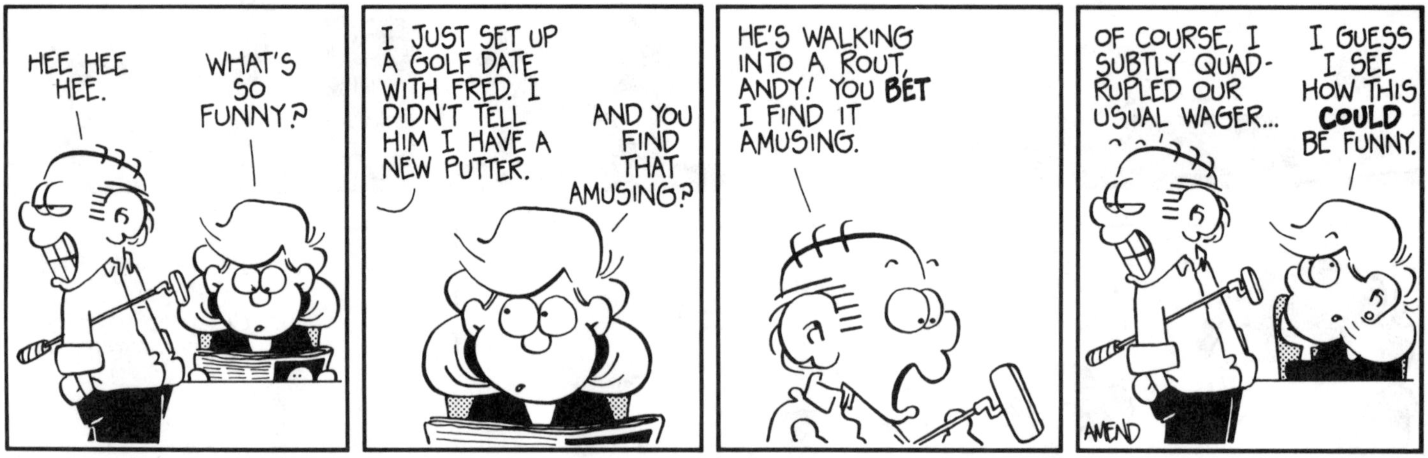
HEE HEE HEE.
WHAT'S SO FUNNY?
I JUST SET UP A GOLF DATE WITH FRED. I DIDN'T TELL HIM I HAVE A NEW PUTTER.
AND YOU FIND THAT AMUSING?
HE'S WALKING INTO A ROUT, ANDY! YOU **BET** I FIND IT AMUSING.
OF COURSE, I SUBTLY QUADRUPLED OUR USUAL WAGER...
I GUESS I SEE HOW THIS **COULD** BE FUNNY.
AMEND

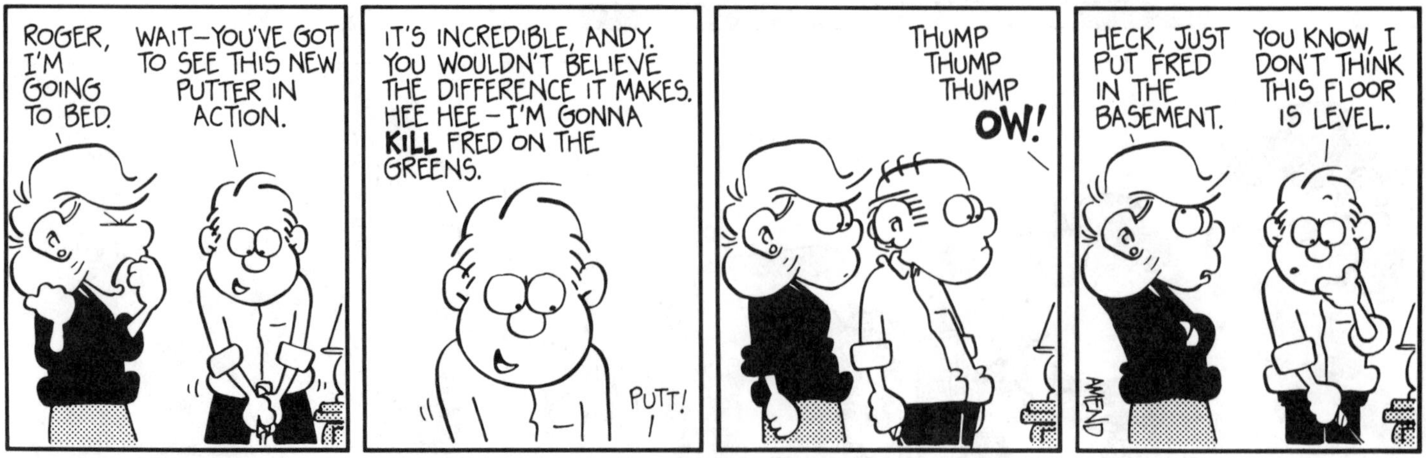
ROGER, I'M GOING TO BED.
WAIT—YOU'VE GOT TO SEE THIS NEW PUTTER IN ACTION.
IT'S INCREDIBLE, ANDY. YOU WOULDN'T BELIEVE THE DIFFERENCE IT MAKES. HEE HEE—I'M GONNA **KILL** FRED ON THE GREENS.
PUTT!
THUMP THUMP THUMP
OW!
HECK, JUST PUT FRED IN THE BASEMENT.
YOU KNOW, I DON'T THINK THIS FLOOR IS LEVEL.
AMEND

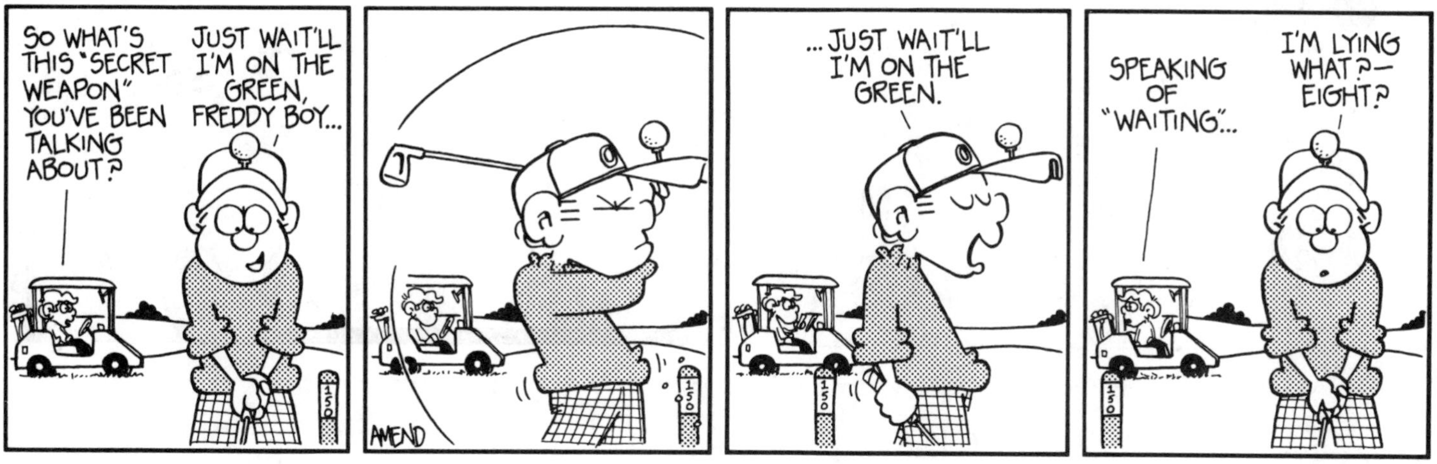
SO WHAT'S THIS "SECRET WEAPON" YOU'VE BEEN TALKING ABOUT?
JUST WAIT'LL I'M ON THE GREEN, FREDDY BOY...
AMEND
...JUST WAIT'LL I'M ON THE GREEN.
SPEAKING OF "WAITING"...
I'M LYING WHAT?— EIGHT?

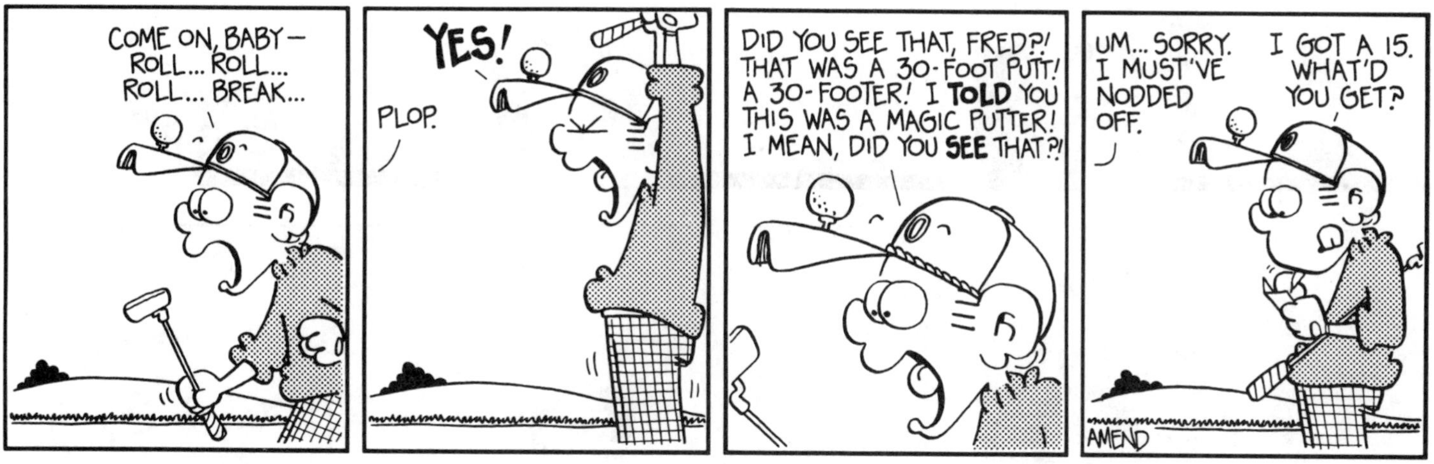
COME ON, BABY— ROLL... ROLL... ROLL... BREAK...
PLOP.
YES!
DID YOU SEE THAT, FRED?! THAT WAS A 30-FOOT PUTT! A 30-FOOTER! I TOLD YOU THIS WAS A MAGIC PUTTER! I MEAN, DID YOU SEE THAT?!
UM... SORRY. I MUST'VE NODDED OFF.
I GOT A 15. WHAT'D YOU GET?
AMEND

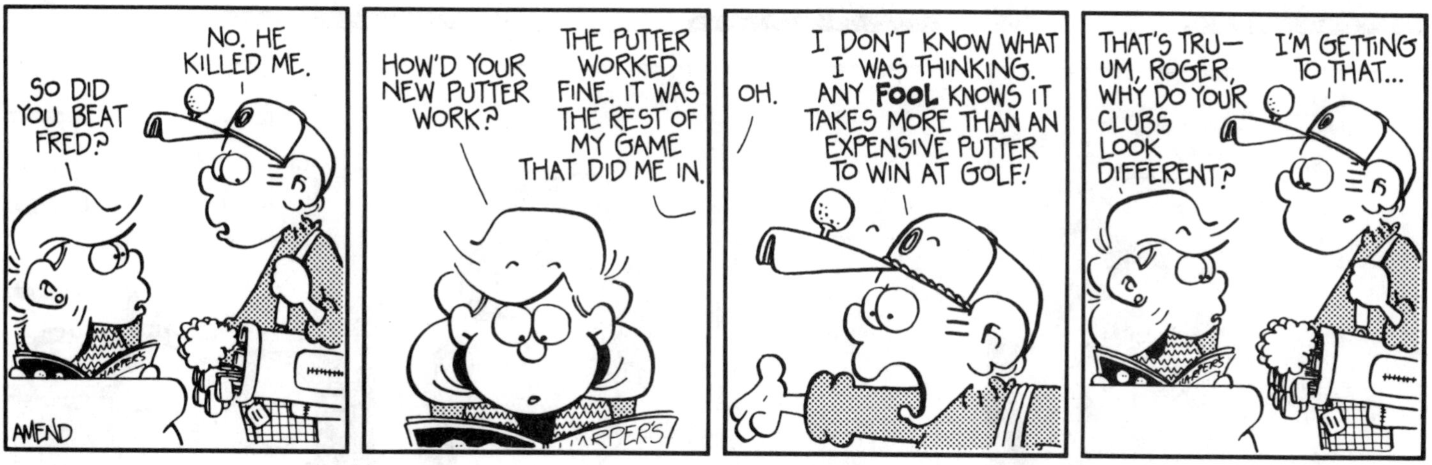
SO DID YOU BEAT FRED?
NO. HE KILLED ME.
AMEND
HOW'D YOUR NEW PUTTER WORK?
THE PUTTER WORKED FINE. IT WAS THE REST OF MY GAME THAT DID ME IN.
HARPER'S
OH.
I DON'T KNOW WHAT I WAS THINKING. ANY FOOL KNOWS IT TAKES MORE THAN AN EXPENSIVE PUTTER TO WIN AT GOLF!
THAT'S TRU— UM, ROGER, WHY DO YOUR CLUBS LOOK DIFFERENT?
I'M GETTING TO THAT...

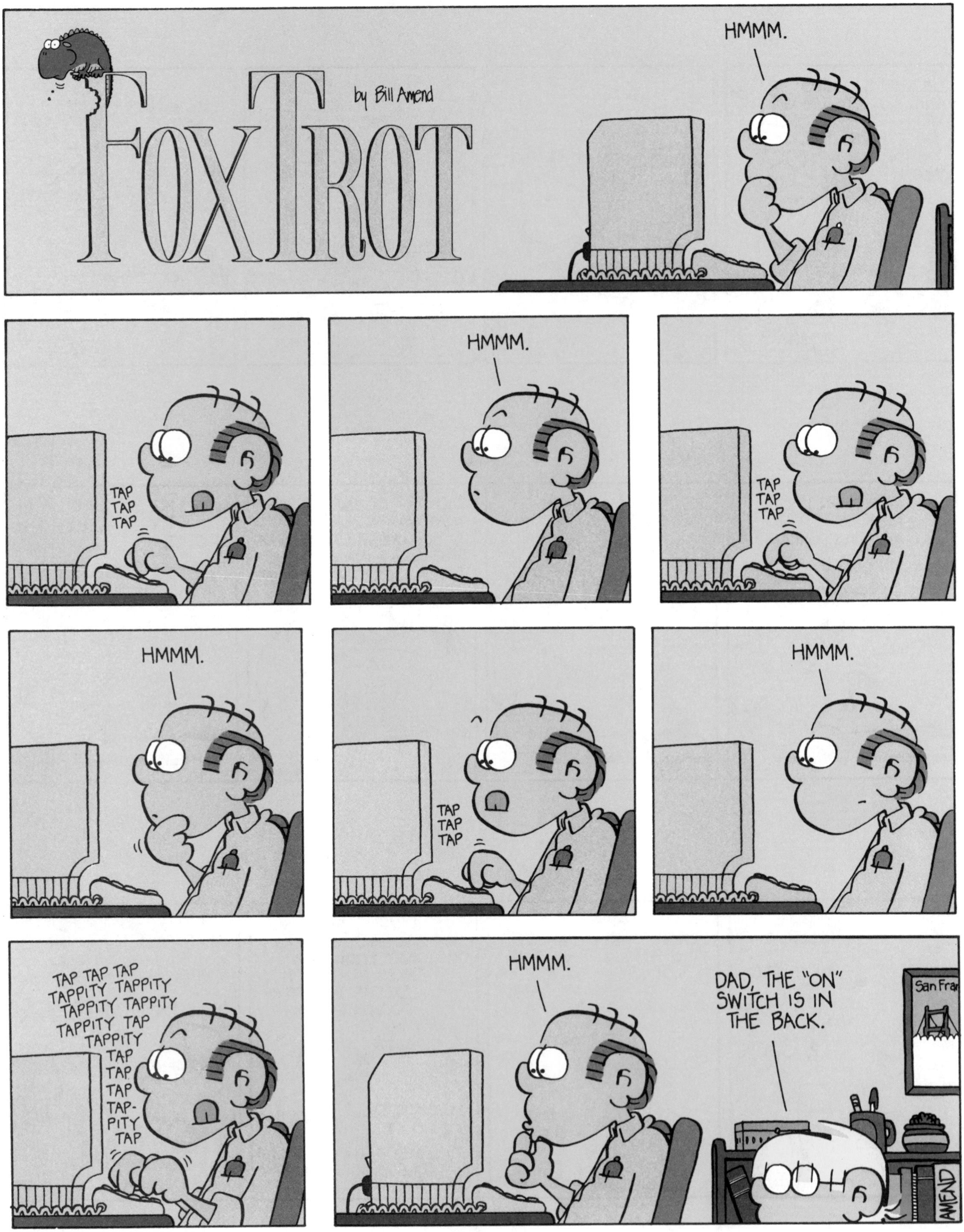
FoxTrot
by Bill Amend
HMMM.
TAP TAP TAP
HMMM.
TAP TAP TAP
HMMM.
TAP TAP TAP
HMMM.
TAP TAP TAP TAPPITY TAPPITY TAPPITY TAPPITY TAPPITY TAP TAPPITY TAP TAP TAP TAP-PITY TAP
HMMM.
DAD, THE "ON" SWITCH IS IN THE BACK.
San Fran
AMEND

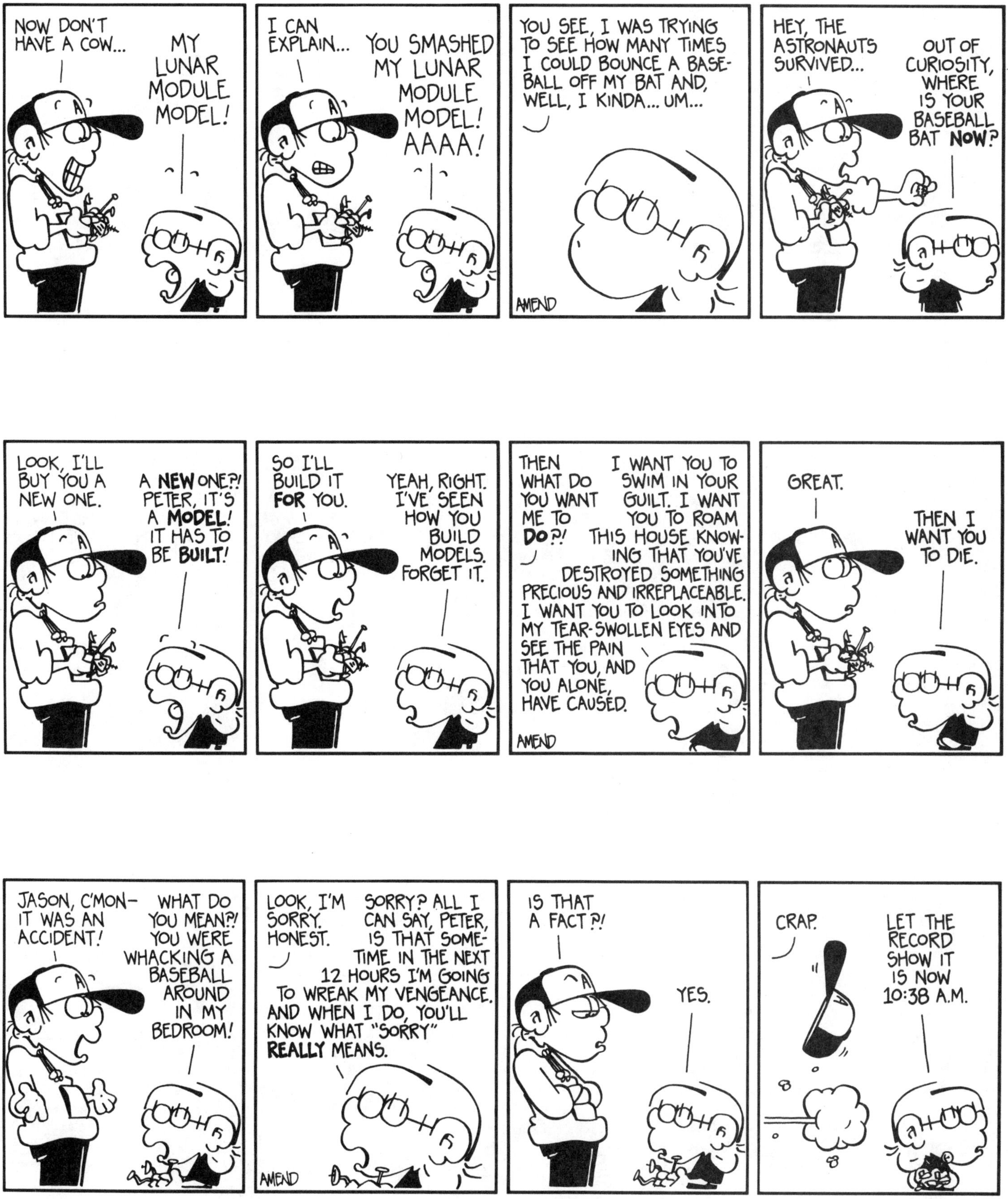
NOW DON'T HAVE A COW...
MY LUNAR MODULE MODEL!
I CAN EXPLAIN...
YOU SMASHED MY LUNAR MODULE MODEL! AAAA!
YOU SEE, I WAS TRYING TO SEE HOW MANY TIMES I COULD BOUNCE A BASE-BALL OFF MY BAT AND, WELL, I KINDA... UM...
AMEND
HEY, THE ASTRONAUTS SURVIVED...
OUT OF CURIOSITY, WHERE IS YOUR BASEBALL BAT NOW?
LOOK, I'LL BUY YOU A NEW ONE.
A NEW ONE?! PETER, IT'S A MODEL! IT HAS TO BE BUILT!
SO I'LL BUILD IT FOR YOU.
YEAH, RIGHT. I'VE SEEN HOW YOU BUILD MODELS. FORGET IT.
THEN WHAT DO YOU WANT ME TO DO?!
I WANT YOU TO SWIM IN YOUR GUILT. I WANT YOU TO ROAM THIS HOUSE KNOWING THAT YOU'VE DESTROYED SOMETHING PRECIOUS AND IRREPLACEABLE. I WANT YOU TO LOOK INTO MY TEAR-SWOLLEN EYES AND SEE THE PAIN THAT YOU, AND YOU ALONE, HAVE CAUSED.
AMEND
GREAT.
THEN I WANT YOU TO DIE.
JASON, C'MON– IT WAS AN ACCIDENT!
WHAT DO YOU MEAN?! YOU WERE WHACKING A BASEBALL AROUND IN MY BEDROOM!
LOOK, I'M SORRY. HONEST.
SORRY? ALL I CAN SAY, PETER, IS THAT SOMETIME IN THE NEXT 12 HOURS I'M GOING TO WREAK MY VENGEANCE. AND WHEN I DO, YOU'LL KNOW WHAT "SORRY" REALLY MEANS.
AMEND
IS THAT A FACT?!
YES.
CRAP.
LET THE RECORD SHOW IT IS NOW 10:38 A.M.

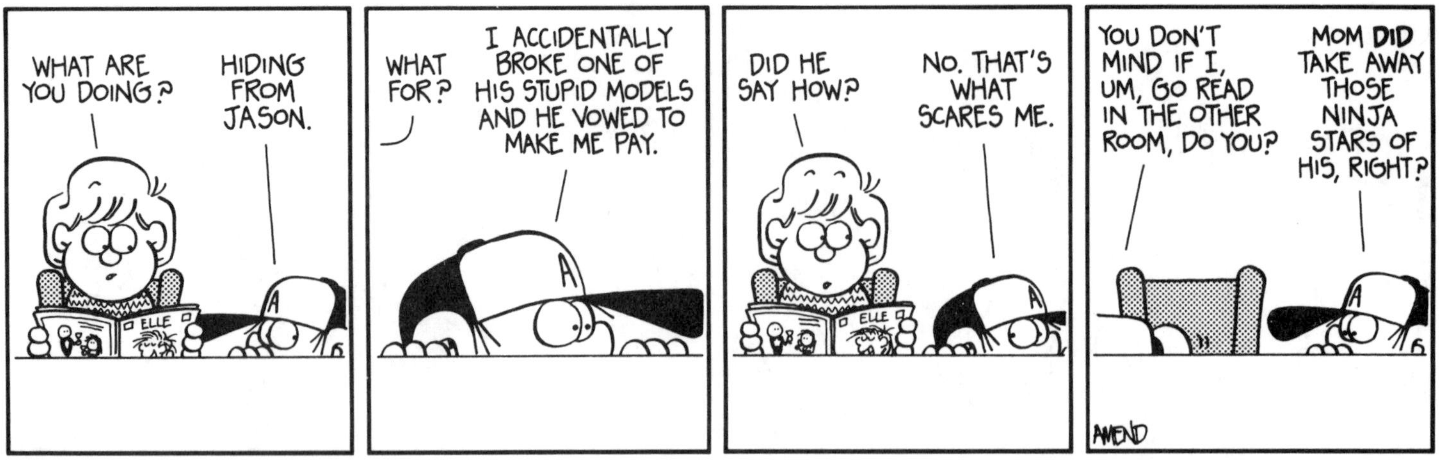
WHAT ARE YOU DOING?
HIDING FROM JASON.
WHAT FOR?
I ACCIDENTALLY BROKE ONE OF HIS STUPID MODELS AND HE VOWED TO MAKE ME PAY.
DID HE SAY HOW?
NO. THAT'S WHAT SCARES ME.
YOU DON'T MIND IF I, UM, GO READ IN THE OTHER ROOM, DO YOU?
MOM **DID** TAKE AWAY THOSE NINJA STARS OF HIS, RIGHT?
AMEND

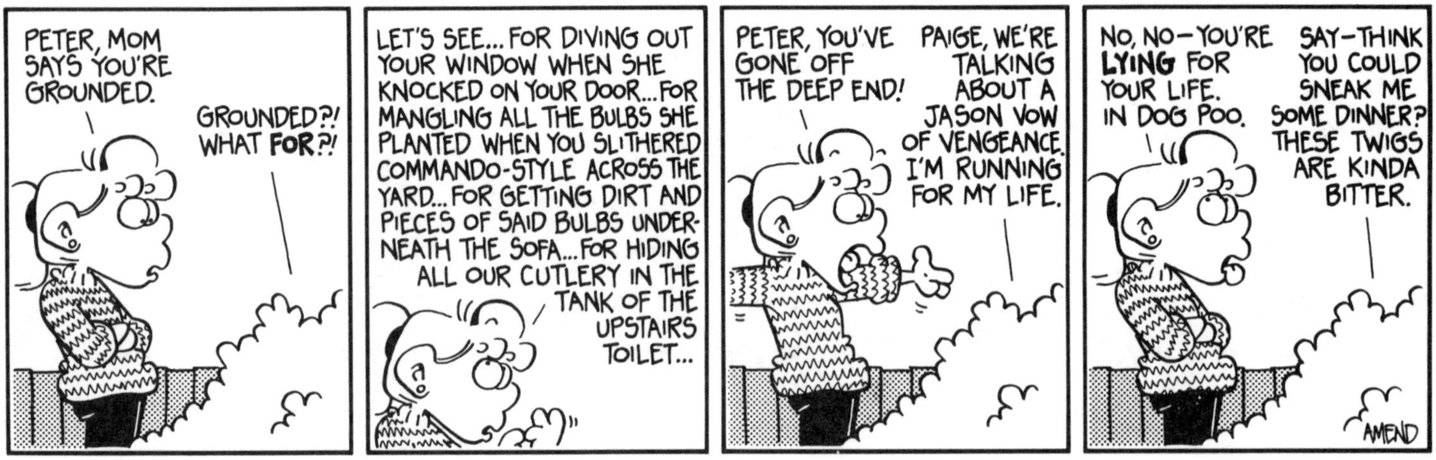
PETER, MOM SAYS YOU'RE GROUNDED.
GROUNDED?! WHAT **FOR**?!
LET'S SEE... FOR DIVING OUT YOUR WINDOW WHEN SHE KNOCKED ON YOUR DOOR... FOR MANGLING ALL THE BULBS SHE PLANTED WHEN YOU SLITHERED COMMANDO-STYLE ACROSS THE YARD... FOR GETTING DIRT AND PIECES OF SAID BULBS UNDERNEATH THE SOFA... FOR HIDING ALL OUR CUTLERY IN THE TANK OF THE UPSTAIRS TOILET...
PETER, YOU'VE GONE OFF THE DEEP END!
PAIGE, WE'RE TALKING ABOUT A JASON VOW OF VENGEANCE. I'M RUNNING FOR MY LIFE.
NO, NO—YOU'RE **LYING** FOR YOUR LIFE. IN DOG POO.
SAY—THINK YOU COULD SNEAK ME SOME DINNER? THESE TWIGS ARE KINDA BITTER.
AMEND

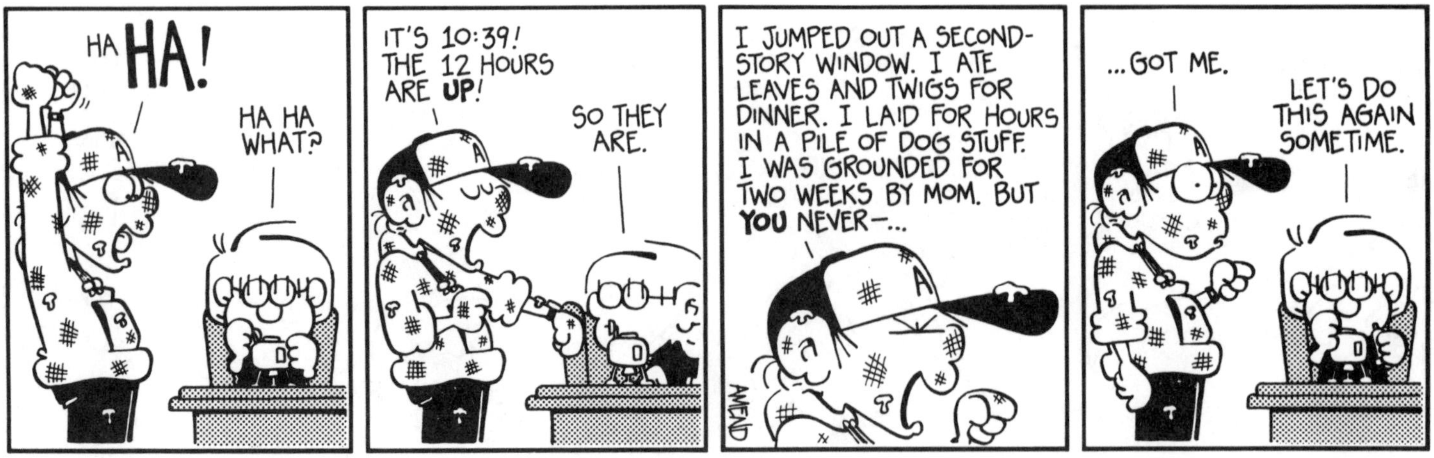
HA **HA!**
HA HA WHAT?
IT'S 10:39! THE 12 HOURS ARE **UP**!
SO THEY ARE.
I JUMPED OUT A SECOND-STORY WINDOW. I ATE LEAVES AND TWIGS FOR DINNER. I LAID FOR HOURS IN A PILE OF DOG STUFF. I WAS GROUNDED FOR TWO WEEKS BY MOM. BUT **YOU** NEVER—...
AMEND
...GOT ME.
LET'S DO THIS AGAIN SOMETIME.

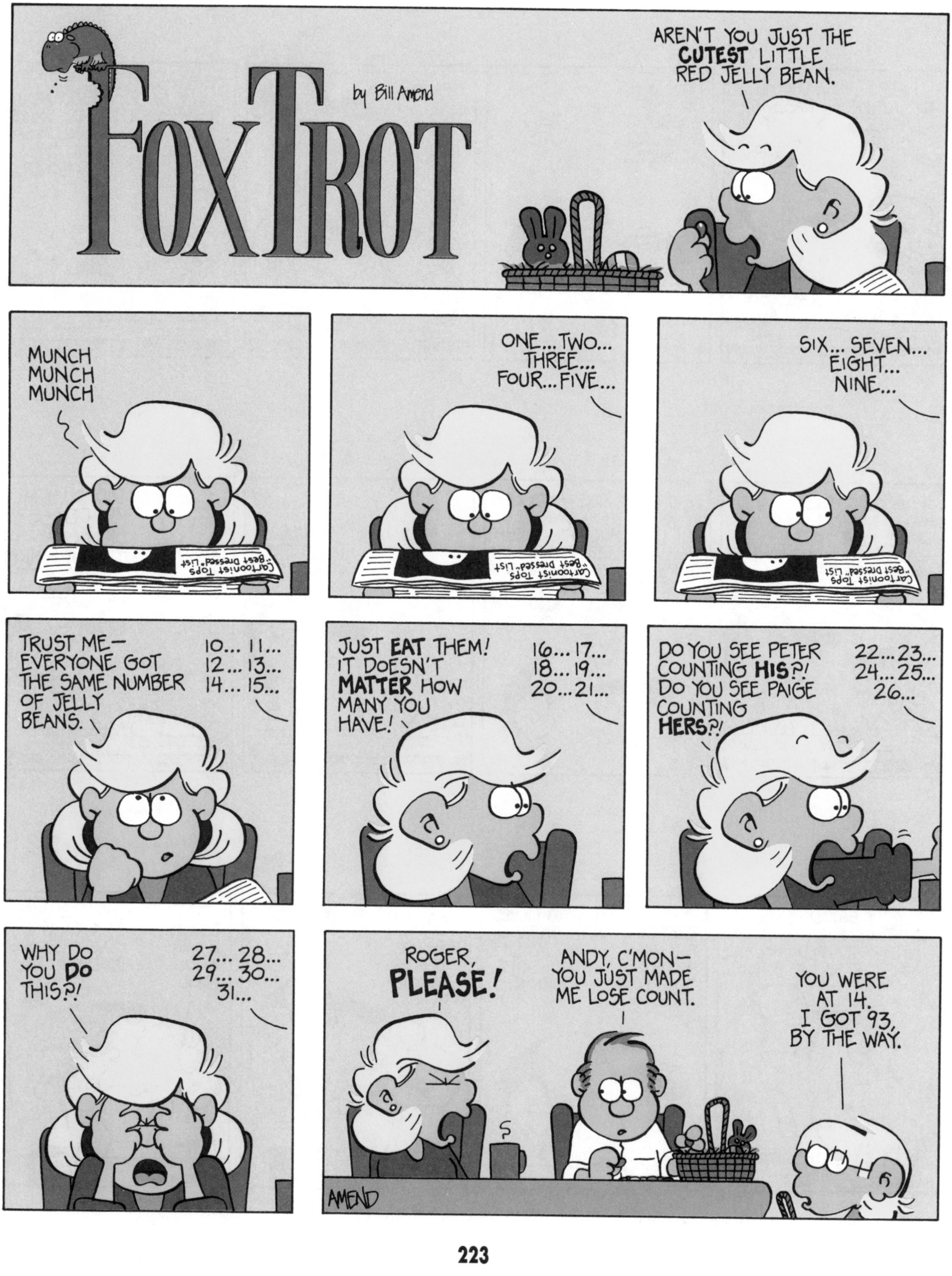
FoxTrot
by Bill Amend
AREN'T YOU JUST THE CUTEST LITTLE RED JELLY BEAN.
MUNCH MUNCH MUNCH
Cartoonist Tops "Best Dressed" List
ONE... TWO... THREE... FOUR... FIVE...
SIX... SEVEN... EIGHT... NINE...
TRUST ME— EVERYONE GOT THE SAME NUMBER OF JELLY BEANS.
10... 11... 12... 13... 14... 15...
JUST EAT THEM! IT DOESN'T MATTER HOW MANY YOU HAVE!
16... 17... 18... 19... 20... 21...
DO YOU SEE PETER COUNTING HIS?! DO YOU SEE PAIGE COUNTING HERS?!
22... 23... 24... 25... 26...
WHY DO YOU DO THIS?!
27... 28... 29... 30... 31...
ROGER, PLEASE!
ANDY, C'MON— YOU JUST MADE ME LOSE COUNT.
YOU WERE AT 14. I GOT 93, BY THE WAY.
AMEND

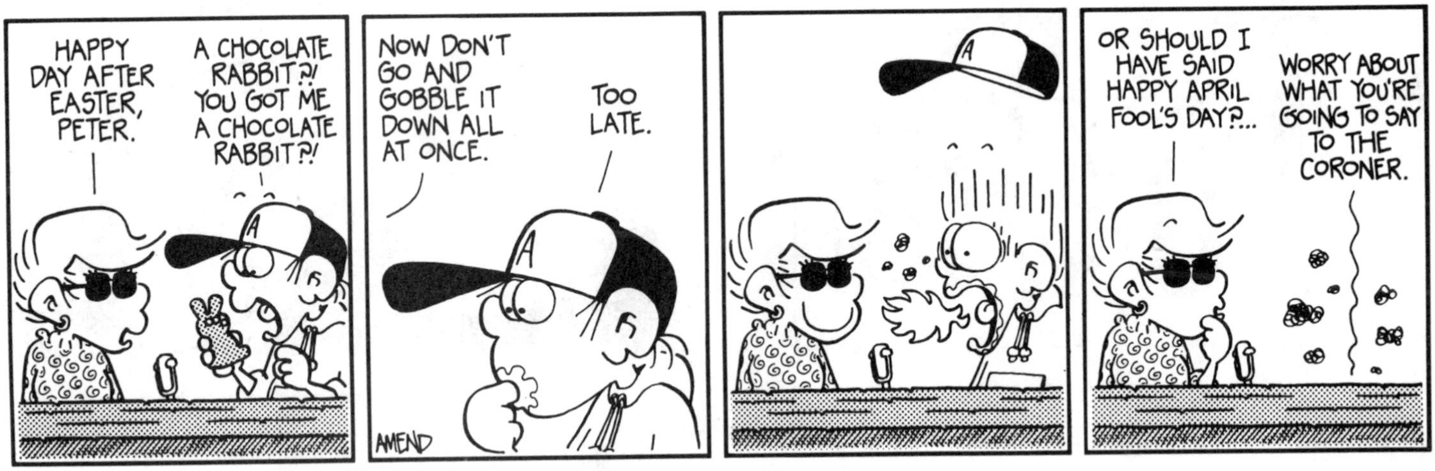
HAPPY DAY AFTER EASTER, PETER.
A CHOCOLATE RABBIT?! YOU GOT ME A CHOCOLATE RABBIT?!
NOW DON'T GO AND GOBBLE IT DOWN ALL AT ONCE.
TOO LATE.
AMEND
OR SHOULD I HAVE SAID HAPPY APRIL FOOL'S DAY?...
WORRY ABOUT WHAT YOU'RE GOING TO SAY TO THE CORONER.

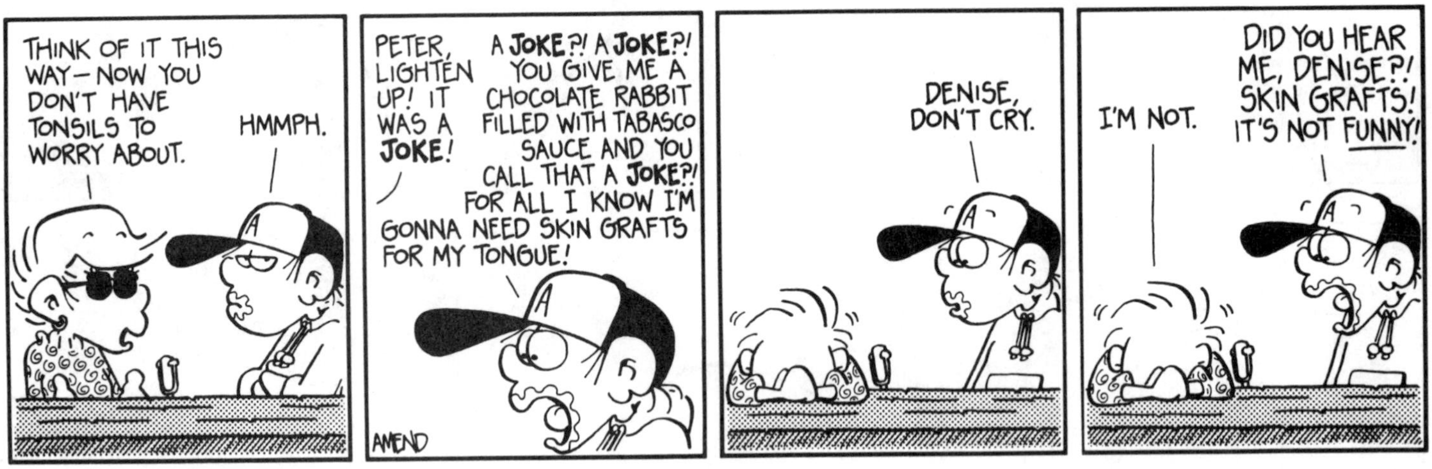
THINK OF IT THIS WAY—NOW YOU DON'T HAVE TONSILS TO WORRY ABOUT.
HMMPH.
PETER, LIGHTEN UP! IT WAS A **JOKE**!
A **JOKE**?! A **JOKE**?! YOU GIVE ME A CHOCOLATE RABBIT FILLED WITH TABASCO SAUCE AND YOU CALL THAT A **JOKE**?! FOR ALL I KNOW I'M GONNA NEED SKIN GRAFTS FOR MY TONGUE!
AMEND
DENISE, DON'T CRY.
I'M NOT.
DID YOU HEAR ME, DENISE?! SKIN GRAFTS! IT'S NOT FUNNY!

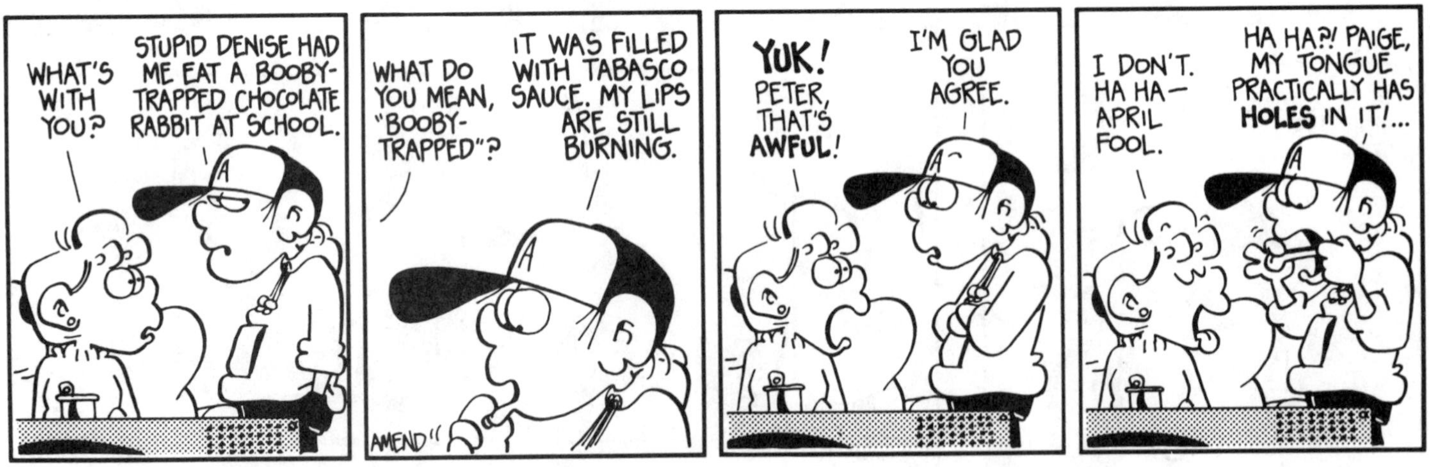
WHAT'S WITH YOU?
STUPID DENISE HAD ME EAT A BOOBY-TRAPPED CHOCOLATE RABBIT AT SCHOOL.
WHAT DO YOU MEAN, "BOOBY-TRAPPED"?
IT WAS FILLED WITH TABASCO SAUCE. MY LIPS ARE STILL BURNING.
AMEND
YUK! PETER, THAT'S **AWFUL**!
I'M GLAD YOU AGREE.
I DON'T. HA HA—APRIL FOOL.
HA HA?! PAIGE, MY TONGUE PRACTICALLY HAS **HOLES** IN IT!...

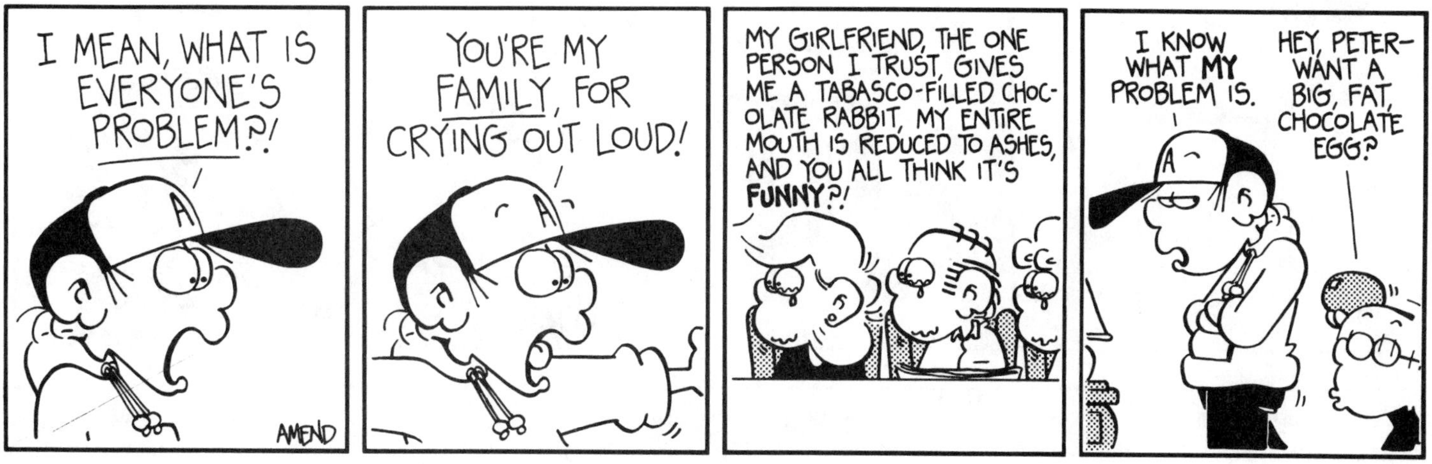
I MEAN, WHAT IS EVERYONE'S PROBLEM?!
YOU'RE MY FAMILY, FOR CRYING OUT LOUD!
MY GIRLFRIEND, THE ONE PERSON I TRUST, GIVES ME A TABASCO-FILLED CHOCOLATE RABBIT, MY ENTIRE MOUTH IS REDUCED TO ASHES, AND YOU ALL THINK IT'S **FUNNY**?!
I KNOW WHAT **MY** PROBLEM IS.
HEY, PETER– WANT A BIG, FAT, CHOCOLATE EGG?
AMEND

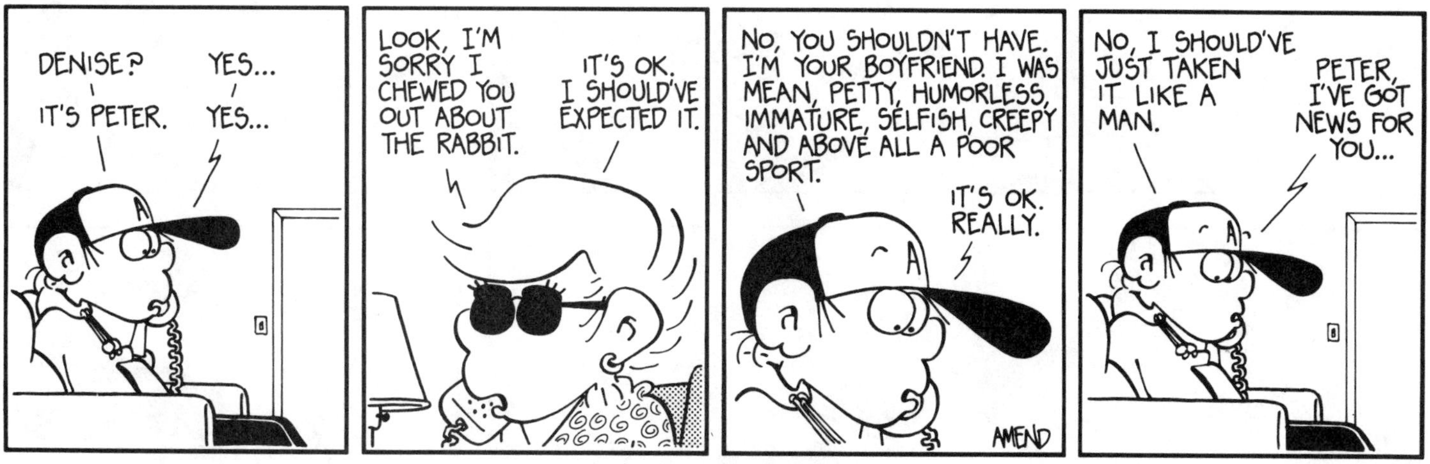
DENISE?
YES...
IT'S PETER.
YES...
LOOK, I'M SORRY I CHEWED YOU OUT ABOUT THE RABBIT.
IT'S OK. I SHOULD'VE EXPECTED IT.
NO, YOU SHOULDN'T HAVE. I'M YOUR BOYFRIEND. I WAS MEAN, PETTY, HUMORLESS, IMMATURE, SELFISH, CREEPY AND ABOVE ALL A POOR SPORT.
IT'S OK. REALLY.
NO, I SHOULD'VE JUST TAKEN IT LIKE A MAN.
PETER, I'VE GOT NEWS FOR YOU...
AMEND

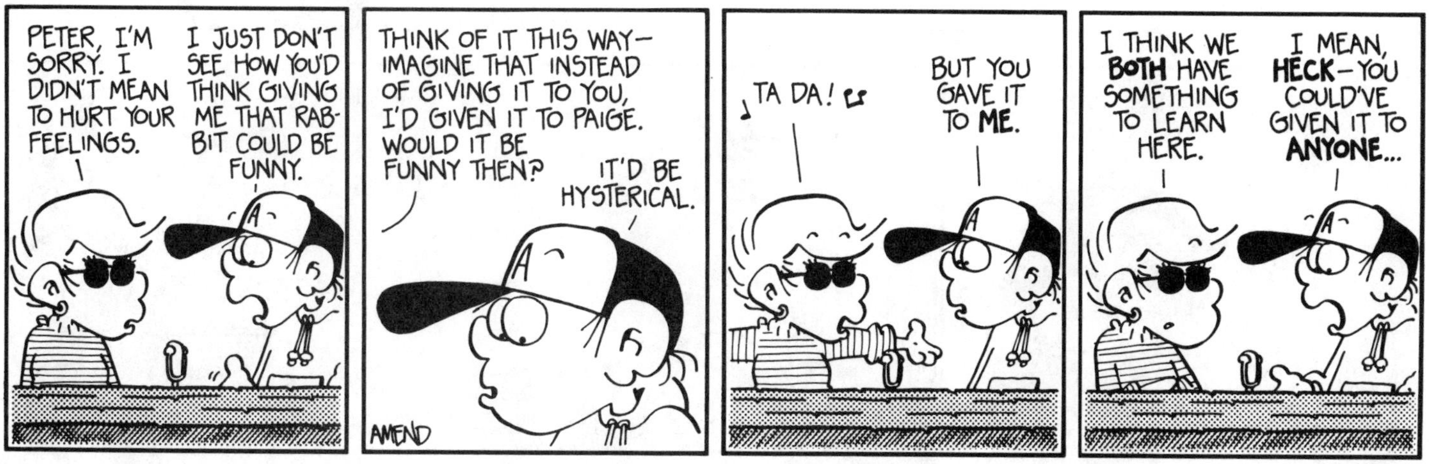
PETER, I'M SORRY. I DIDN'T MEAN TO HURT YOUR FEELINGS.
I JUST DON'T SEE HOW YOU'D THINK GIVING ME THAT RABBIT COULD BE FUNNY.
THINK OF IT THIS WAY– IMAGINE THAT INSTEAD OF GIVING IT TO YOU, I'D GIVEN IT TO PAIGE. WOULD IT BE FUNNY THEN?
IT'D BE HYSTERICAL.
TA DA!
BUT YOU GAVE IT TO **ME**.
I THINK WE **BOTH** HAVE SOMETHING TO LEARN HERE.
I MEAN, **HECK**–YOU COULD'VE GIVEN IT TO **ANYONE**...
AMEND

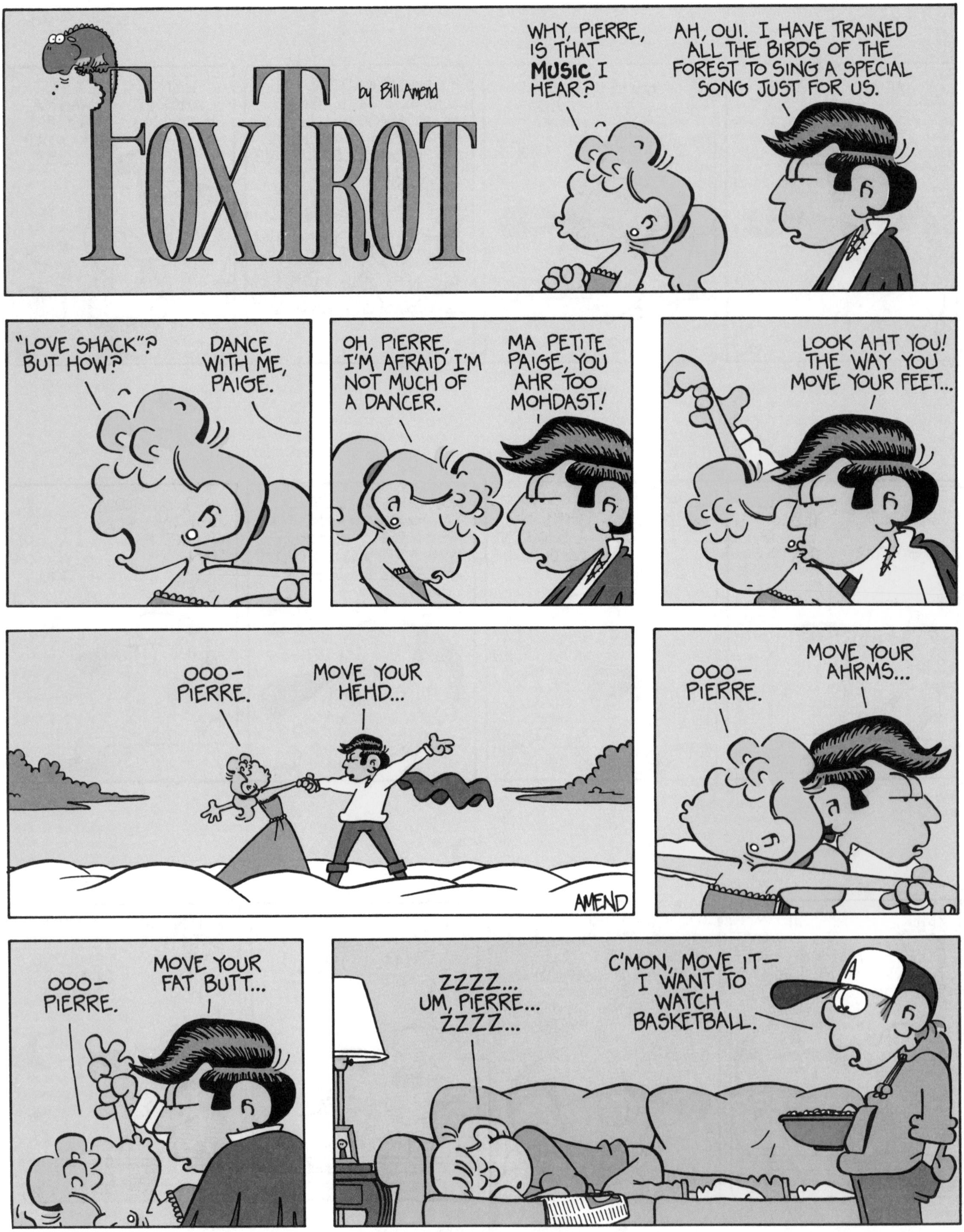
FoxTrot
by Bill Amend
WHY, PIERRE, IS THAT MUSIC I HEAR?
AH, OUI. I HAVE TRAINED ALL THE BIRDS OF THE FOREST TO SING A SPECIAL SONG JUST FOR US.
"LOVE SHACK"? BUT HOW?
DANCE WITH ME, PAIGE.
OH, PIERRE, I'M AFRAID I'M NOT MUCH OF A DANCER.
MA PETITE PAIGE, YOU AHR TOO MOHDAST!
LOOK AHT YOU! THE WAY YOU MOVE YOUR FEET...
OOO-PIERRE.
MOVE YOUR HEHD...
AMEND
OOO-PIERRE.
MOVE YOUR AHRMS...
OOO-PIERRE.
MOVE YOUR FAT BUTT...
ZZZZ... UM, PIERRE... ZZZZ...
C'MON, MOVE IT— I WANT TO WATCH BASKETBALL.

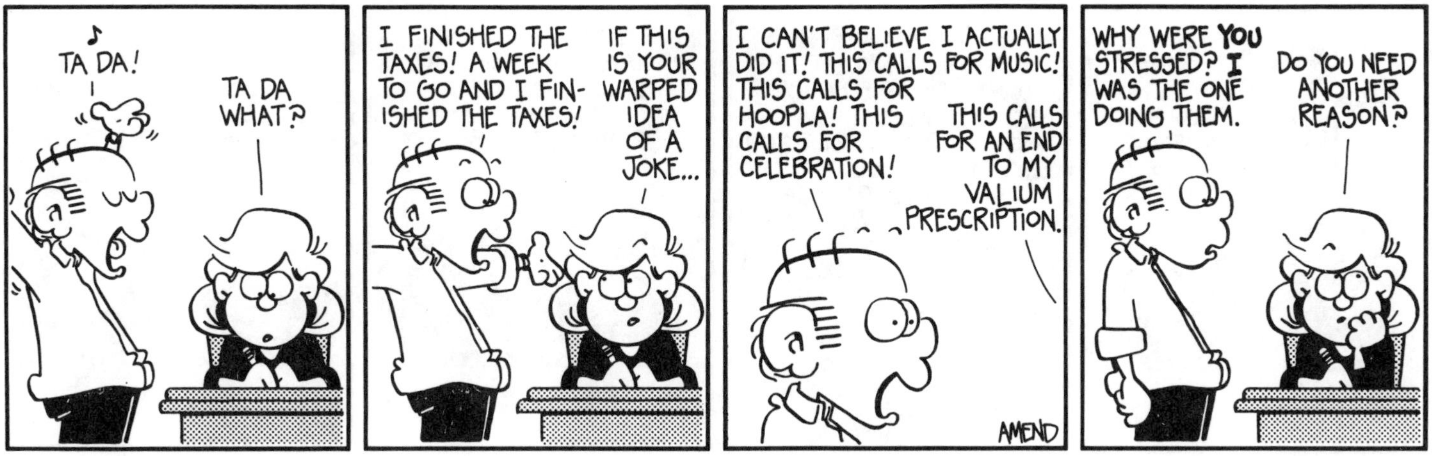
♪ TA DA!
TA DA WHAT?
I FINISHED THE TAXES! A WEEK TO GO AND I FIN-ISHED THE TAXES!
IF THIS IS YOUR WARPED IDEA OF A JOKE...
I CAN'T BELIEVE I ACTUALLY DID IT! THIS CALLS FOR MUSIC! THIS CALLS FOR HOOPLA! THIS CALLS FOR CELEBRATION!
THIS CALLS FOR AN END TO MY VALIUM PRESCRIPTION.
AMEND
WHY WERE **YOU** STRESSED? **I** WAS THE ONE DOING THEM.
DO YOU NEED ANOTHER REASON?

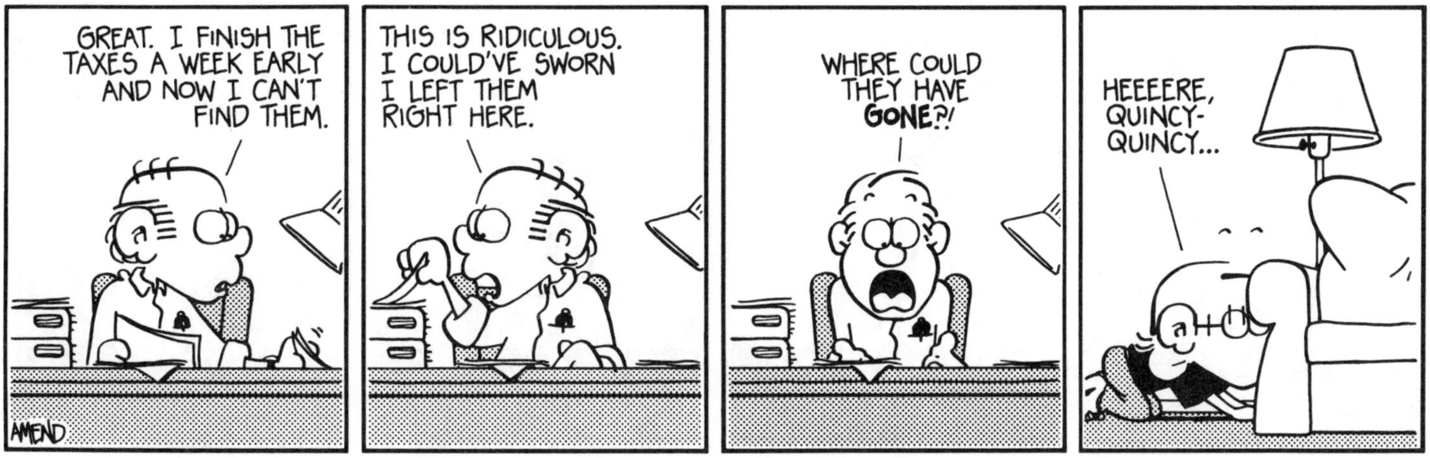
GREAT. I FINISH THE TAXES A WEEK EARLY AND NOW I CAN'T FIND THEM.
AMEND
THIS IS RIDICULOUS. I COULD'VE SWORN I LEFT THEM RIGHT HERE.
WHERE COULD THEY HAVE **GONE**?!
HEEEERE, QUINCY-QUINCY...

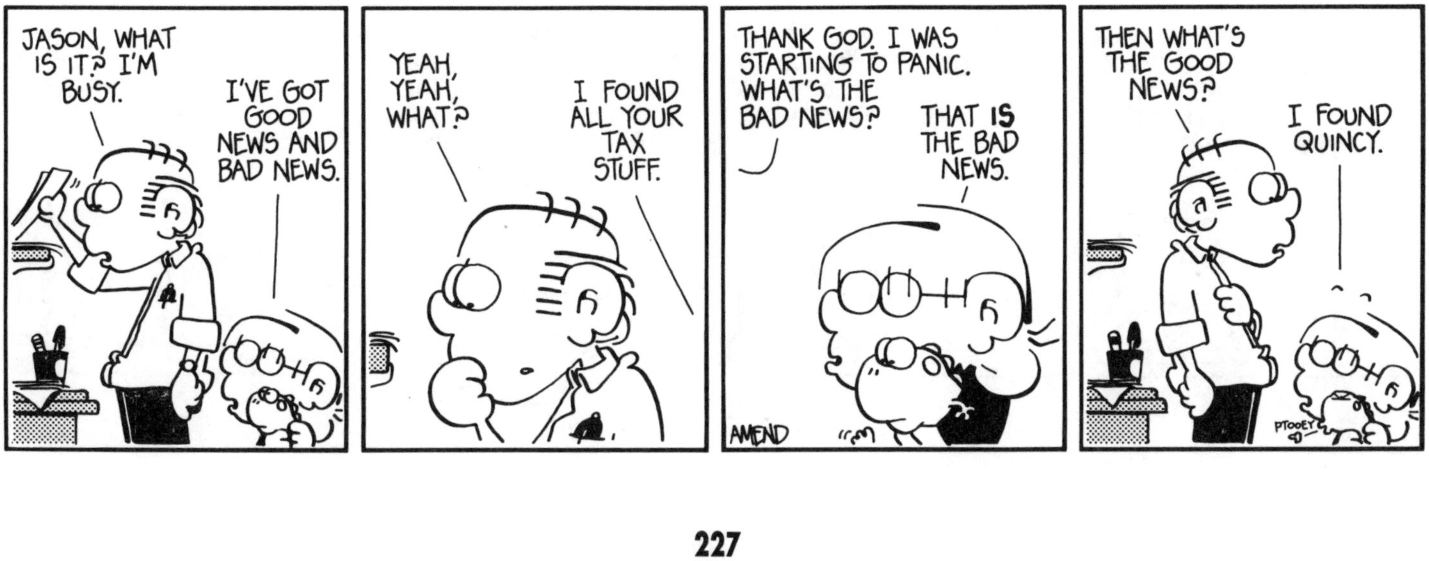
JASON, WHAT IS IT? I'M BUSY.
I'VE GOT GOOD NEWS AND BAD NEWS.
YEAH, YEAH, WHAT?
I FOUND ALL YOUR TAX STUFF.
THANK GOD. I WAS STARTING TO PANIC. WHAT'S THE BAD NEWS?
THAT **IS** THE BAD NEWS.
AMEND
THEN WHAT'S THE GOOD NEWS?
I FOUND QUINCY.
PTOOEY

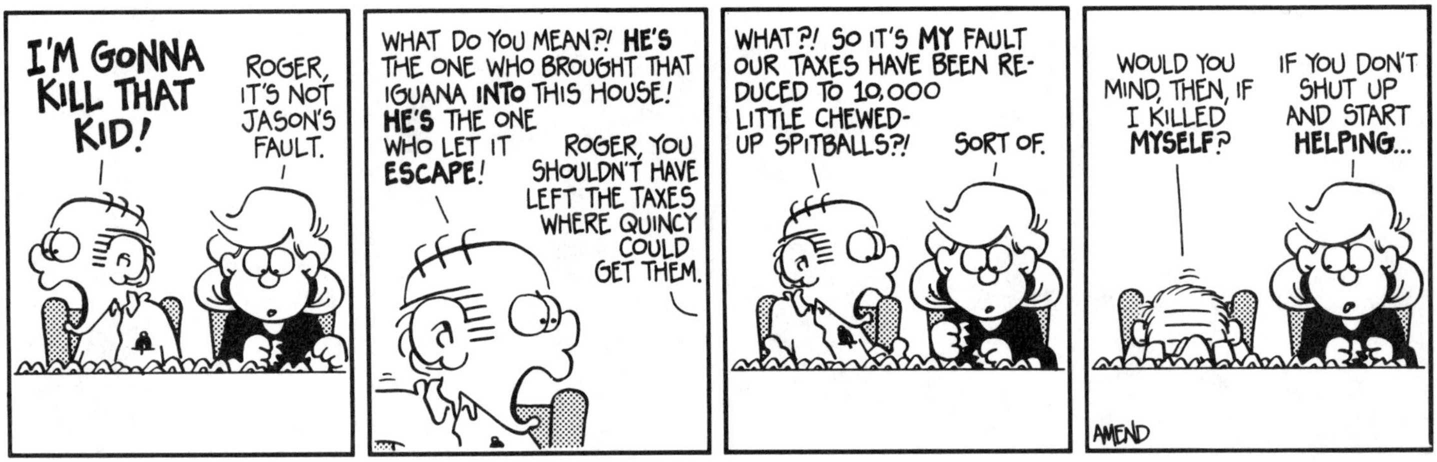
I'M GONNA KILL THAT KID!
ROGER, IT'S NOT JASON'S FAULT.
WHAT DO YOU MEAN?! HE'S THE ONE WHO BROUGHT THAT IGUANA INTO THIS HOUSE! HE'S THE ONE WHO LET IT ESCAPE!
ROGER, YOU SHOULDN'T HAVE LEFT THE TAXES WHERE QUINCY COULD GET THEM.
WHAT?! SO IT'S MY FAULT OUR TAXES HAVE BEEN REDUCED TO 10,000 LITTLE CHEWED-UP SPITBALLS?!
SORT OF.
WOULD YOU MIND, THEN, IF I KILLED MYSELF?
IF YOU DON'T SHUT UP AND START HELPING...
AMEND

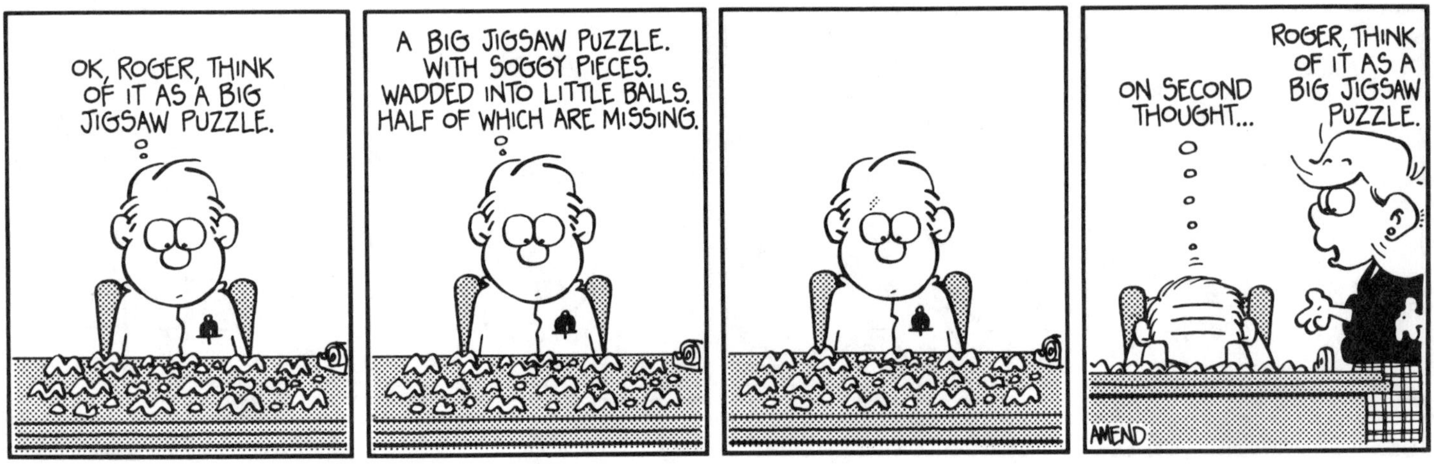
OK, ROGER, THINK OF IT AS A BIG JIGSAW PUZZLE.
A BIG JIGSAW PUZZLE. WITH SOGGY PIECES. WADDED INTO LITTLE BALLS. HALF OF WHICH ARE MISSING.
ON SECOND THOUGHT...
ROGER, THINK OF IT AS A BIG JIGSAW PUZZLE.
AMEND

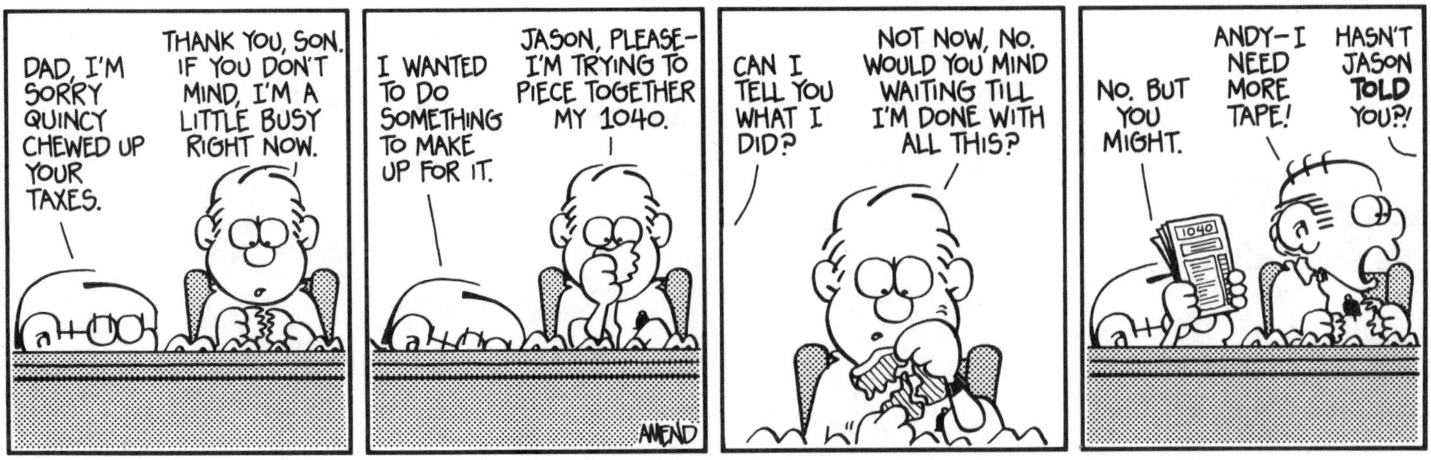
DAD, I'M SORRY QUINCY CHEWED UP YOUR TAXES.
THANK YOU, SON. IF YOU DON'T MIND, I'M A LITTLE BUSY RIGHT NOW.
I WANTED TO DO SOMETHING TO MAKE UP FOR IT.
JASON, PLEASE-I'M TRYING TO PIECE TOGETHER MY 1040.
AMEND
CAN I TELL YOU WHAT I DID?
NOT NOW, NO. WOULD YOU MIND WAITING TILL I'M DONE WITH ALL THIS?
NO. BUT YOU MIGHT.
1040
ANDY—I NEED MORE TAPE!
HASN'T JASON TOLD YOU?!

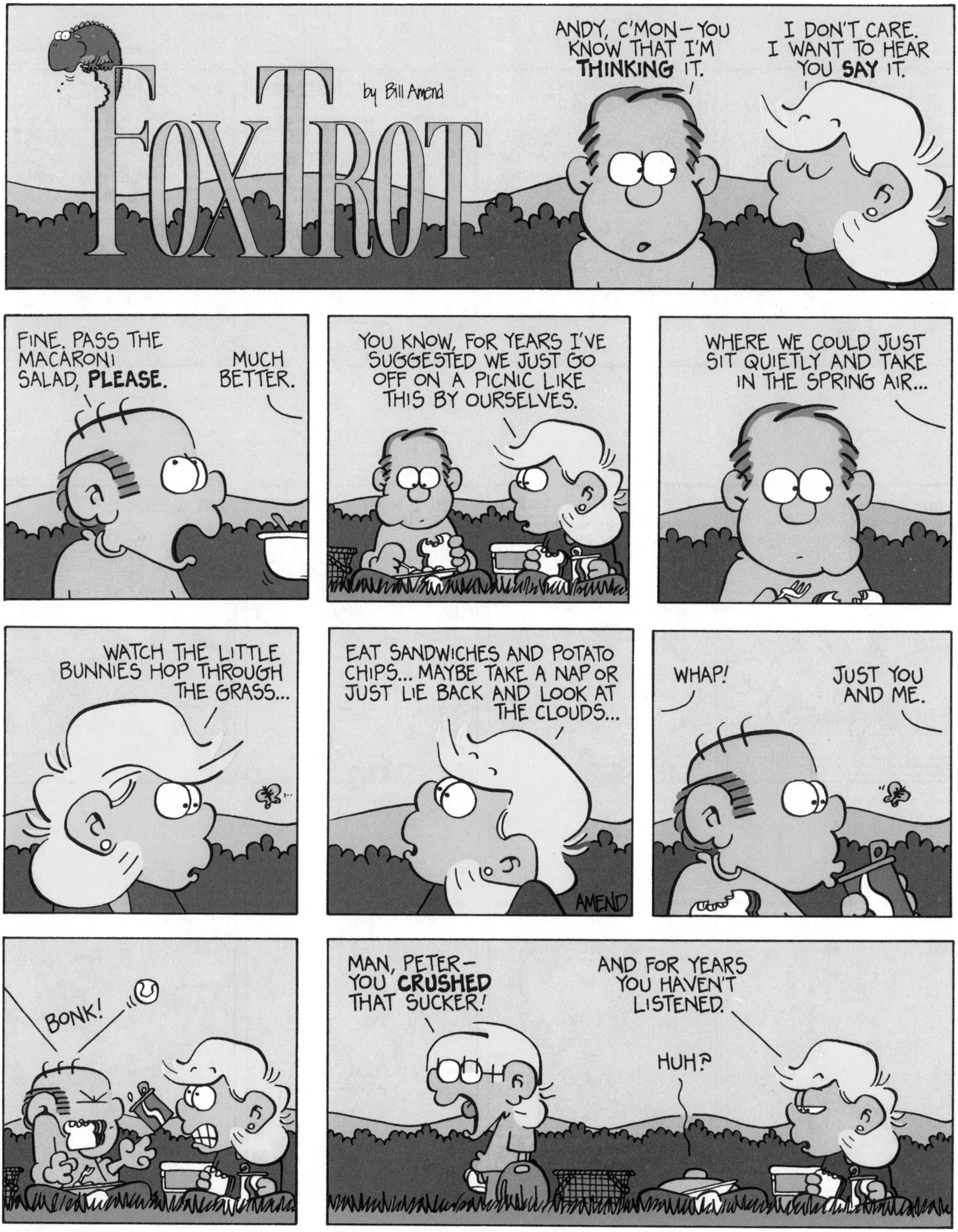
FoxTrot
by Bill Amend
ANDY, C'MON—YOU KNOW THAT I'M **THINKING** IT.
I DON'T CARE. I WANT TO HEAR YOU **SAY** IT.
FINE. PASS THE MACARONI SALAD, **PLEASE.**
MUCH BETTER.
YOU KNOW, FOR YEARS I'VE SUGGESTED WE JUST GO OFF ON A PICNIC LIKE THIS BY OURSELVES.
WHERE WE COULD JUST SIT QUIETLY AND TAKE IN THE SPRING AIR...
WATCH THE LITTLE BUNNIES HOP THROUGH THE GRASS...
EAT SANDWICHES AND POTATO CHIPS... MAYBE TAKE A NAP OR JUST LIE BACK AND LOOK AT THE CLOUDS...
AMEND
WHAP!
JUST YOU AND ME.
BONK!
MAN, PETER—YOU **CRUSHED** THAT SUCKER!
AND FOR YEARS YOU HAVEN'T LISTENED.
HUH?

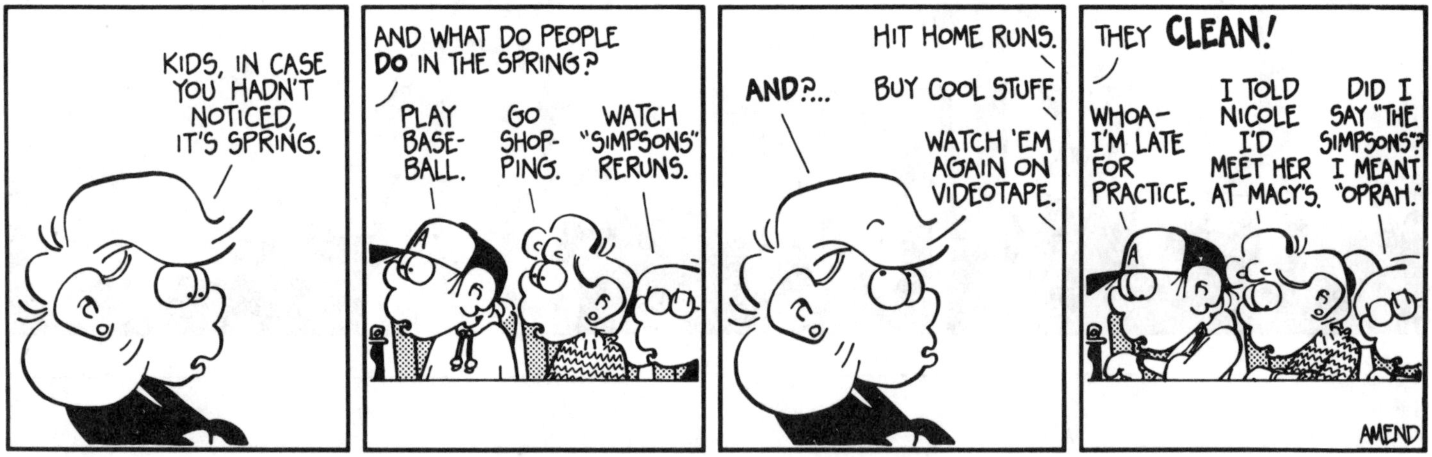
KIDS, IN CASE YOU HADN'T NOTICED, IT'S SPRING.
AND WHAT DO PEOPLE **DO** IN THE SPRING?
PLAY BASE-BALL.
GO SHOP-PING.
WATCH "SIMPSONS" RERUNS.
AND?...
HIT HOME RUNS.
BUY COOL STUFF.
WATCH 'EM AGAIN ON VIDEOTAPE.
THEY **CLEAN!**
WHOA– I'M LATE FOR PRACTICE.
I TOLD NICOLE I'D MEET HER AT MACY'S.
DID I SAY "THE SIMPSONS"? I MEANT "OPRAH."
AMEND

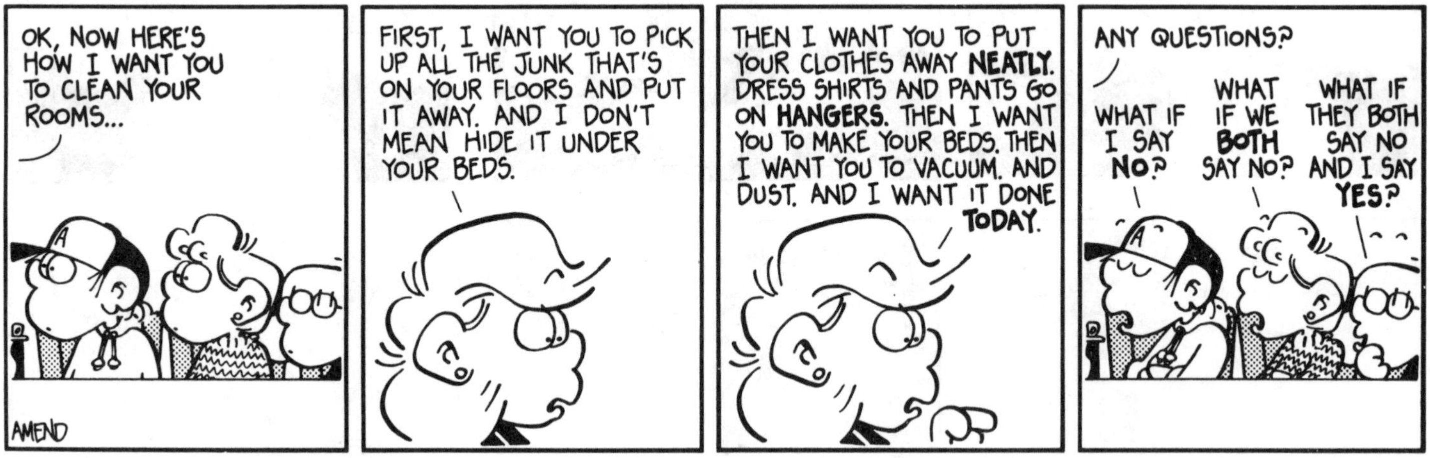
OK, NOW HERE'S HOW I WANT YOU TO CLEAN YOUR ROOMS...
AMEND
FIRST, I WANT YOU TO PICK UP ALL THE JUNK THAT'S ON YOUR FLOORS AND PUT IT AWAY. AND I DON'T MEAN HIDE IT UNDER YOUR BEDS.
THEN I WANT YOU TO PUT YOUR CLOTHES AWAY **NEATLY**. DRESS SHIRTS AND PANTS GO ON **HANGERS**. THEN I WANT YOU TO MAKE YOUR BEDS. THEN I WANT YOU TO VACUUM. AND DUST. AND I WANT IT DONE **TODAY**.
ANY QUESTIONS?
WHAT IF I SAY **NO**?
WHAT IF WE **BOTH** SAY NO?
WHAT IF THEY BOTH SAY NO AND I SAY **YES**?

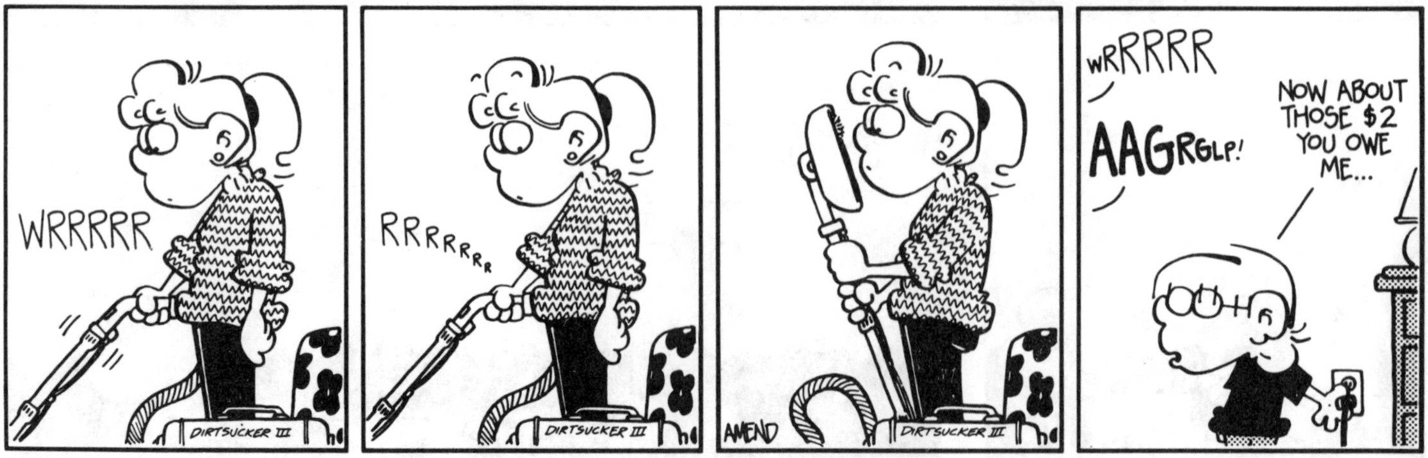
WRRRRR
DIRTSUCKER III
RRRRRRR
DIRTSUCKER III
AMEND
DIRTSUCKER III
WRRRRR
AAGRGLP!
NOW ABOUT THOSE $2 YOU OWE ME...

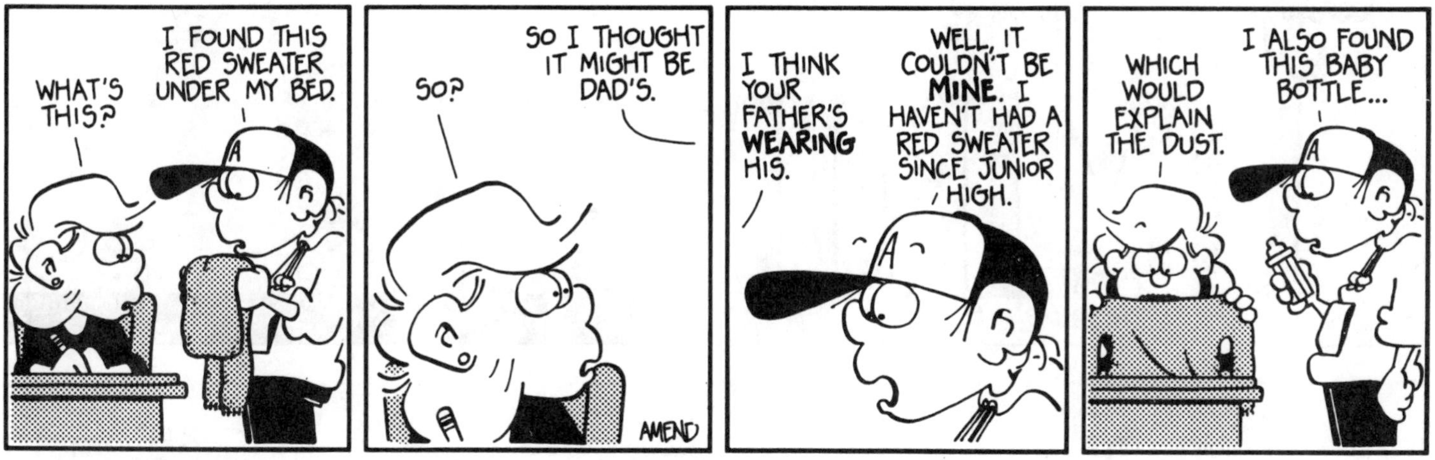
WHAT'S THIS?
I FOUND THIS RED SWEATER UNDER MY BED.
SO?
SO I THOUGHT IT MIGHT BE DAD'S.
I THINK YOUR FATHER'S **WEARING** HIS.
WELL, IT COULDN'T BE **MINE**. I HAVEN'T HAD A RED SWEATER SINCE JUNIOR HIGH.
WHICH WOULD EXPLAIN THE DUST.
I ALSO FOUND THIS BABY BOTTLE...
AMEND

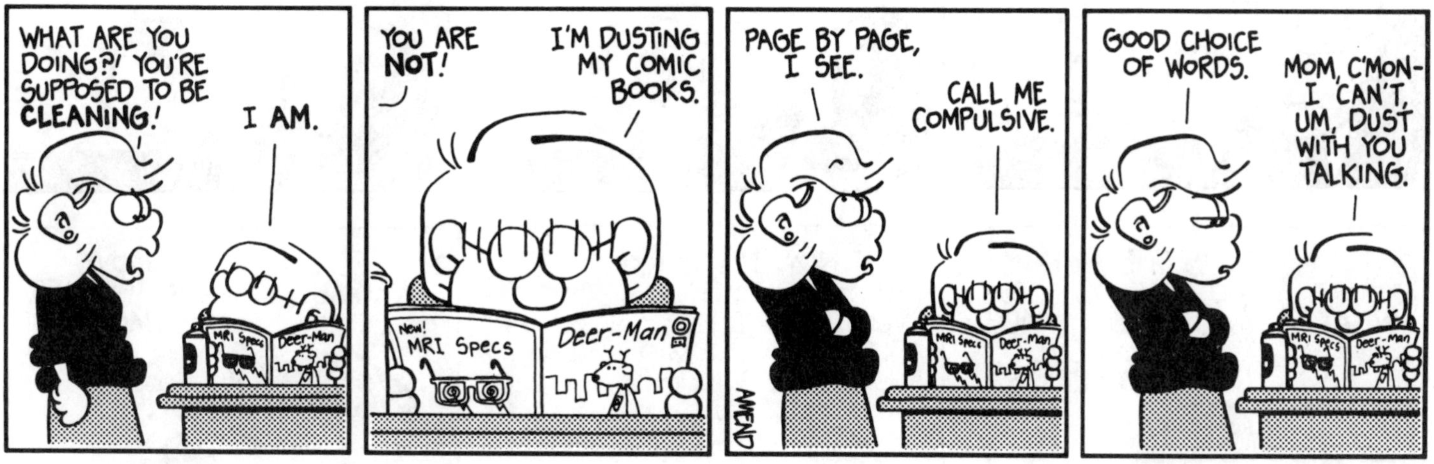
WHAT ARE YOU DOING?! YOU'RE SUPPOSED TO BE **CLEANING**!
I AM.
YOU ARE **NOT**!
I'M DUSTING MY COMIC BOOKS.
New! MRI Specs
Deer-Man
PAGE BY PAGE, I SEE.
CALL ME COMPULSIVE.
GOOD CHOICE OF WORDS.
MOM, C'MON- I CAN'T, UM, DUST WITH YOU TALKING.
AMEND

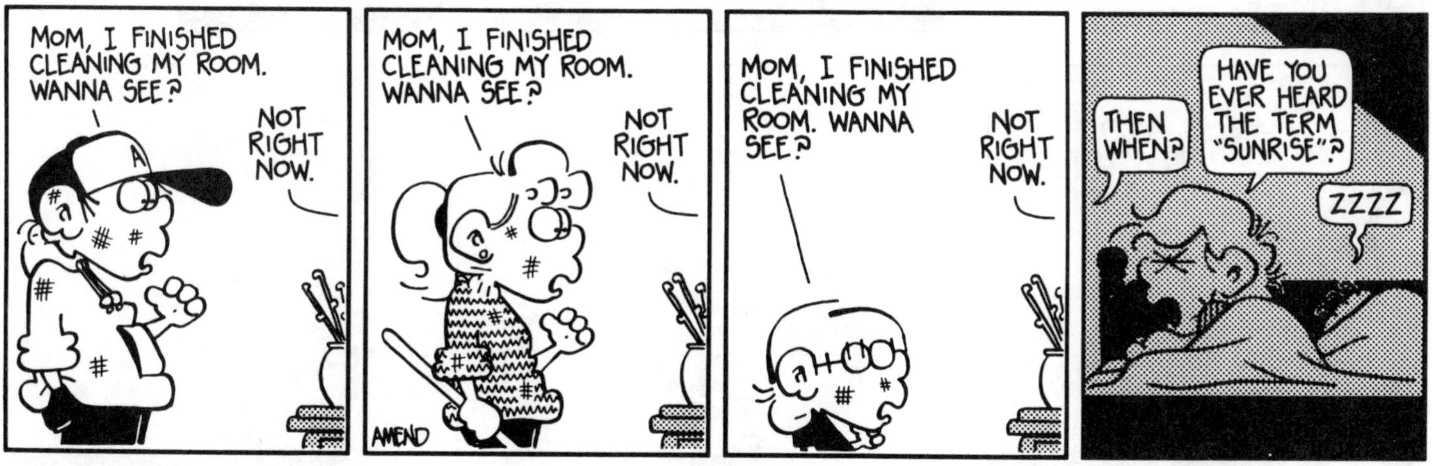
MOM, I FINISHED CLEANING MY ROOM. WANNA SEE?
NOT RIGHT NOW.
MOM, I FINISHED CLEANING MY ROOM. WANNA SEE?
NOT RIGHT NOW.
MOM, I FINISHED CLEANING MY ROOM. WANNA SEE?
NOT RIGHT NOW.
THEN WHEN?
HAVE YOU EVER HEARD THE TERM "SUNRISE"?
ZZZZ
AMEND

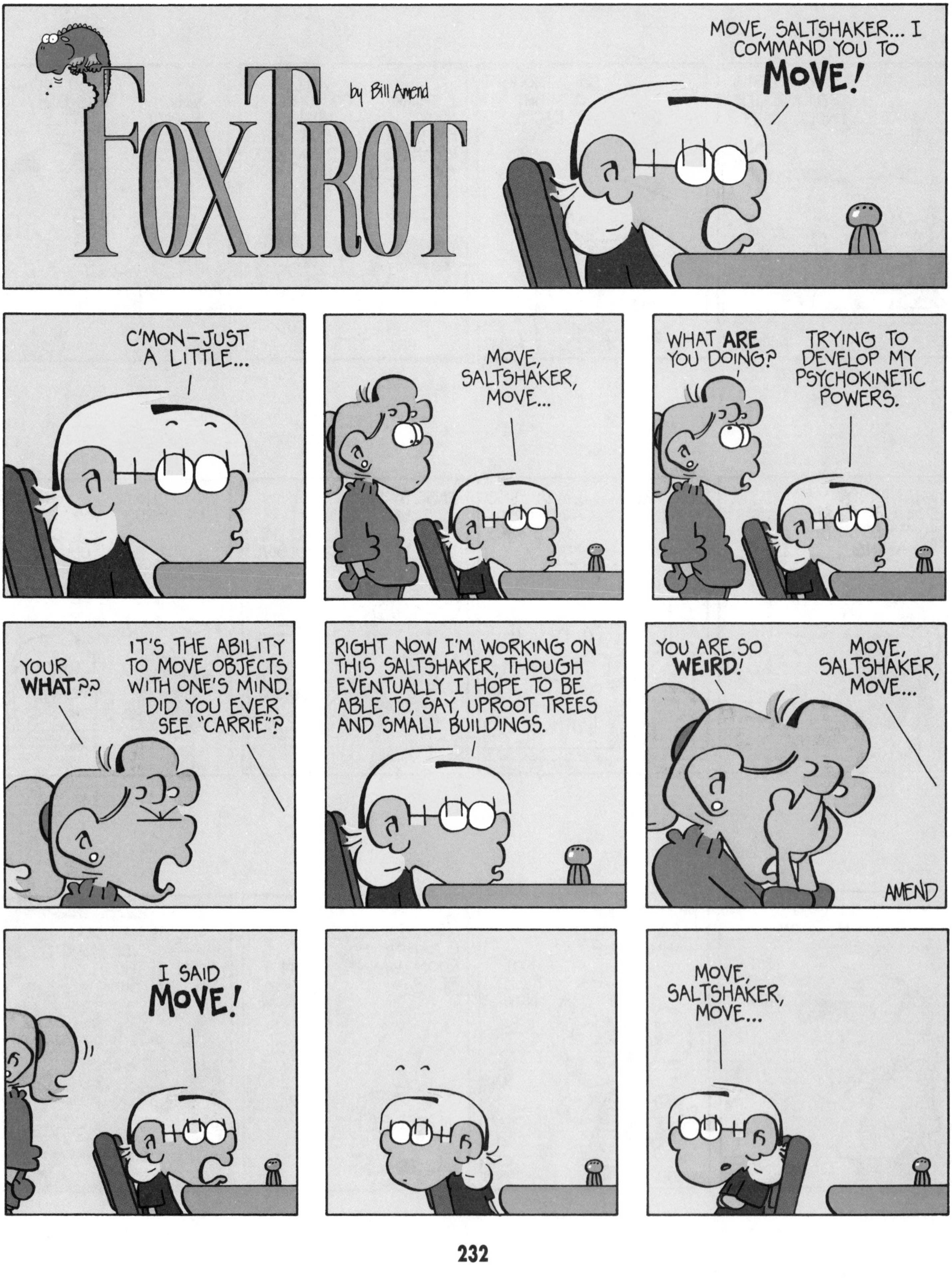

FOXTROT
by Bill Amend
MOVE, SALTSHAKER... I COMMAND YOU TO **MOVE!**
C'MON—JUST A LITTLE...
MOVE, SALTSHAKER, MOVE...
WHAT **ARE** YOU DOING?
TRYING TO DEVELOP MY PSYCHOKINETIC POWERS.
YOUR **WHAT**??
IT'S THE ABILITY TO MOVE OBJECTS WITH ONE'S MIND. DID YOU EVER SEE "CARRIE"?
RIGHT NOW I'M WORKING ON THIS SALTSHAKER, THOUGH EVENTUALLY I HOPE TO BE ABLE TO, SAY, UPROOT TREES AND SMALL BUILDINGS.
YOU ARE SO **WEIRD!**
MOVE, SALTSHAKER, MOVE...
AMEND
I SAID **MOVE!**
MOVE, SALTSHAKER, MOVE...

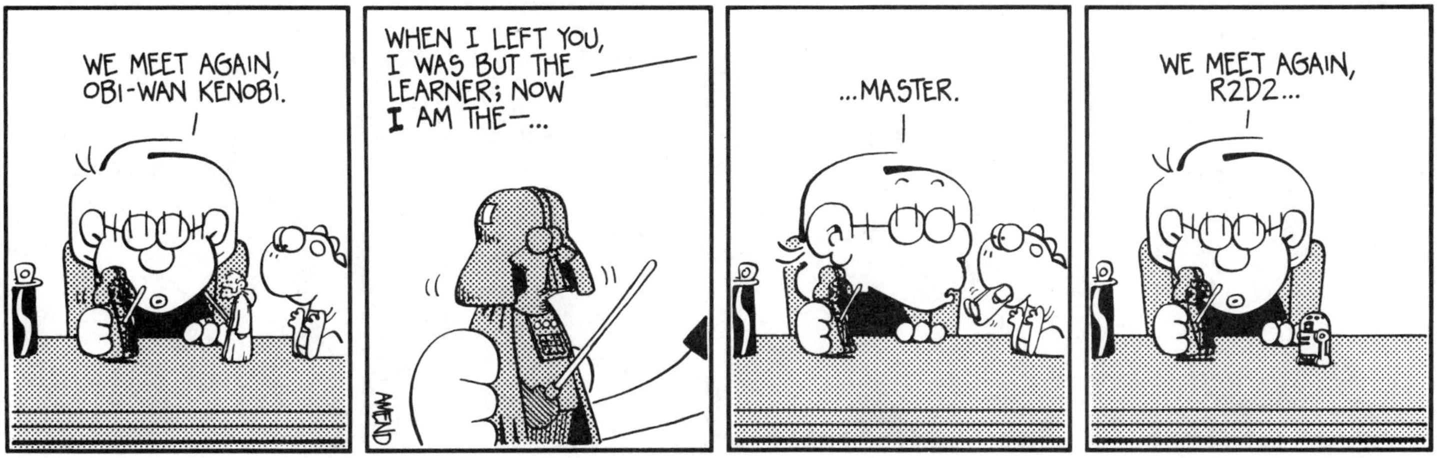

WE MEET AGAIN, OBI-WAN KENOBI.
WHEN I LEFT YOU, I WAS BUT THE LEARNER; NOW **I** AM THE—...
AMEND
...MASTER.
WE MEET AGAIN, R2D2...

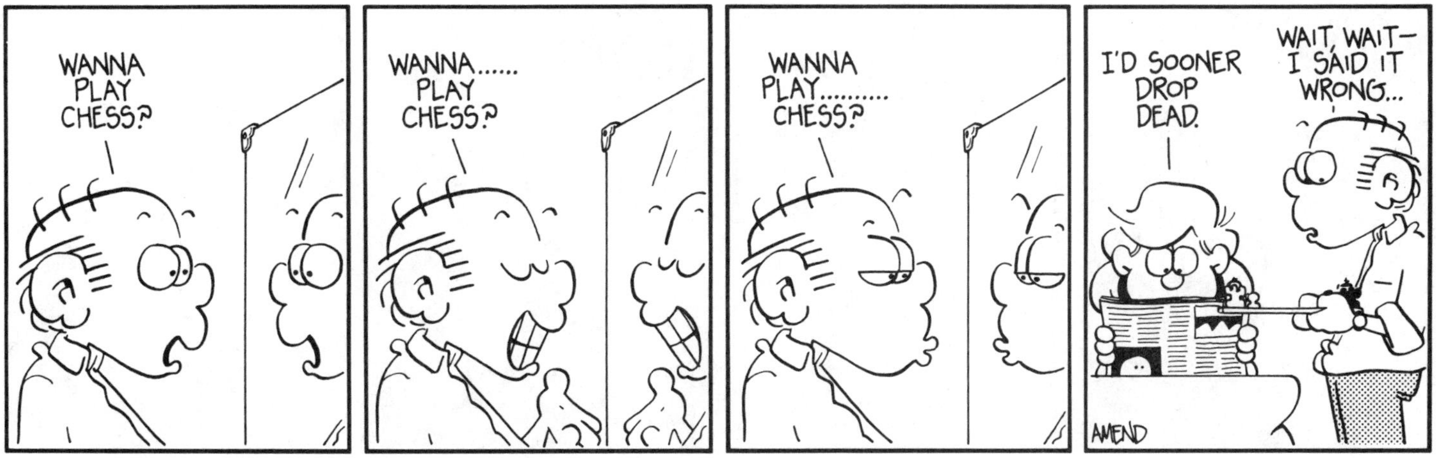

WANNA PLAY CHESS?
WANNA...... PLAY CHESS?
WANNA PLAY.......... CHESS?
I'D SOONER DROP DEAD.
WAIT, WAIT— I SAID IT WRONG...
AMEND

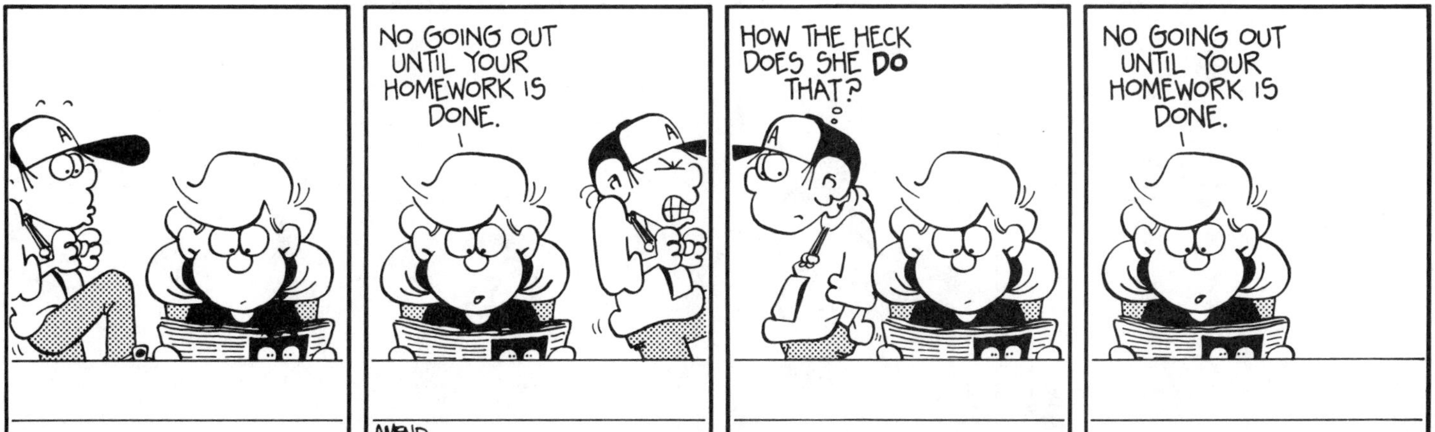

NO GOING OUT UNTIL YOUR HOMEWORK IS DONE.
AMEND
HOW THE HECK DOES SHE **DO** THAT?
NO GOING OUT UNTIL YOUR HOMEWORK IS DONE.

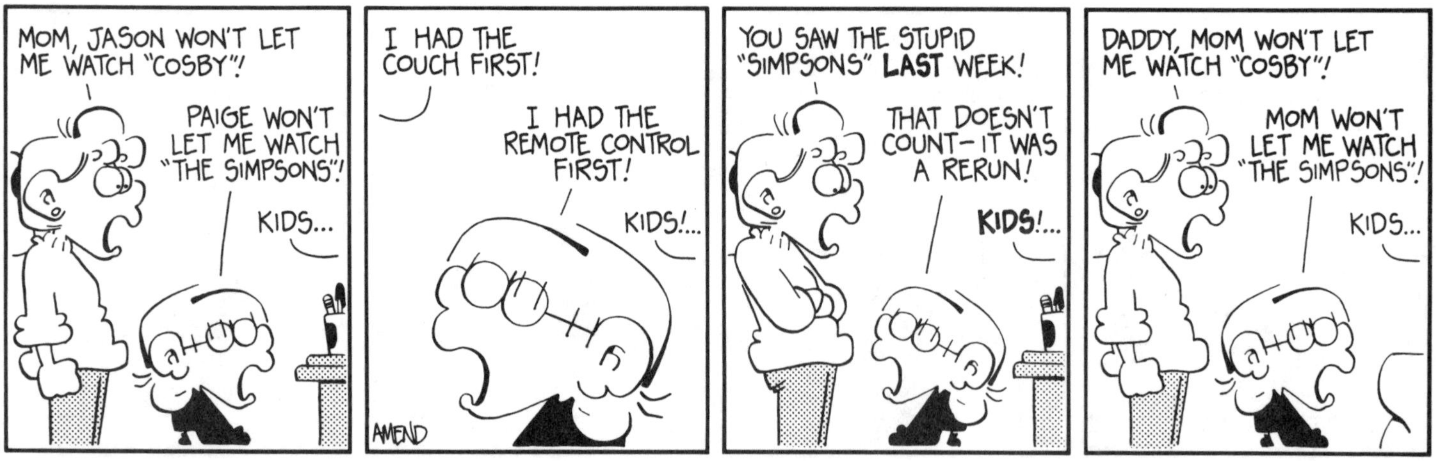
MOM, JASON WON'T LET ME WATCH "COSBY"!
PAIGE WON'T LET ME WATCH "THE SIMPSONS"!
KIDS...
I HAD THE COUCH FIRST!
I HAD THE REMOTE CONTROL FIRST!
KIDS!...
AMEND
YOU SAW THE STUPID "SIMPSONS" **LAST** WEEK!
THAT DOESN'T COUNT– IT WAS A RERUN!
KIDS!...
DADDY, MOM WON'T LET ME WATCH "COSBY"!
MOM WON'T LET ME WATCH "THE SIMPSONS"!
KIDS...

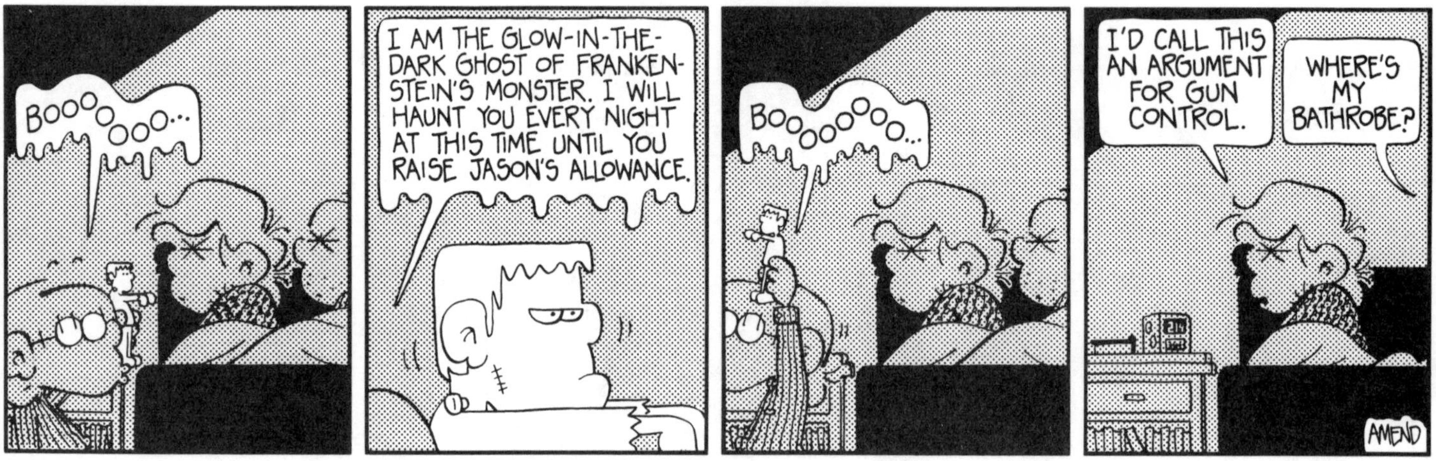
BOOOOOOO...
I AM THE GLOW-IN-THE-DARK GHOST OF FRANKENSTEIN'S MONSTER. I WILL HAUNT YOU EVERY NIGHT AT THIS TIME UNTIL YOU RAISE JASON'S ALLOWANCE.
BOOOOOOOO...
I'D CALL THIS AN ARGUMENT FOR GUN CONTROL.
WHERE'S MY BATHROBE?
AMEND

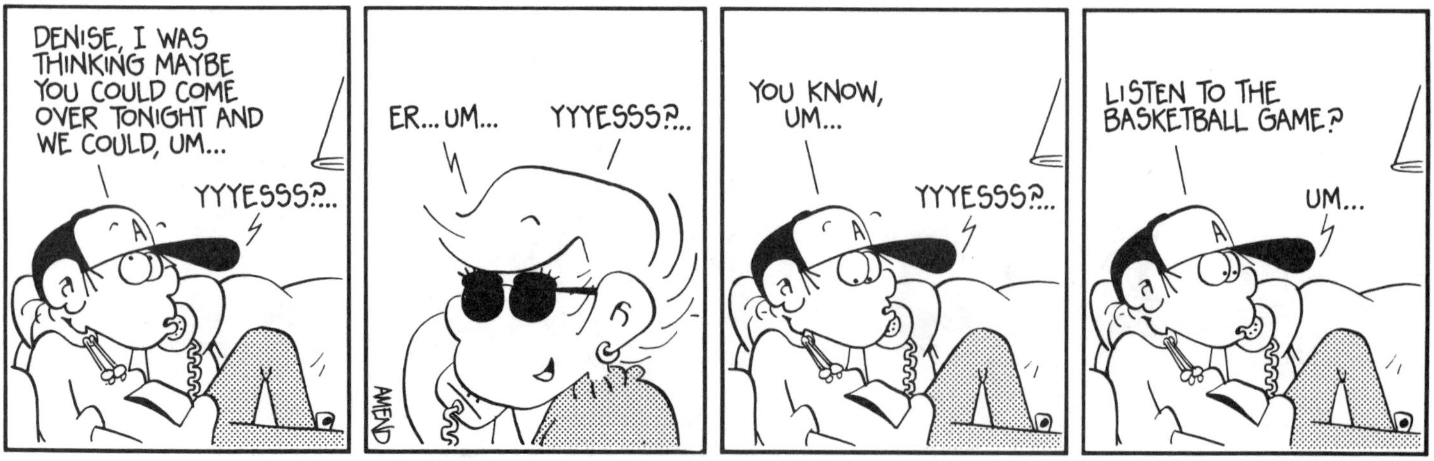
DENISE, I WAS THINKING MAYBE YOU COULD COME OVER TONIGHT AND WE COULD, UM...
YYYESSS?...
ER... UM...
YYYESSS?...
AMEND
YOU KNOW, UM...
YYYESSS?...
LISTEN TO THE BASKETBALL GAME?
UM...

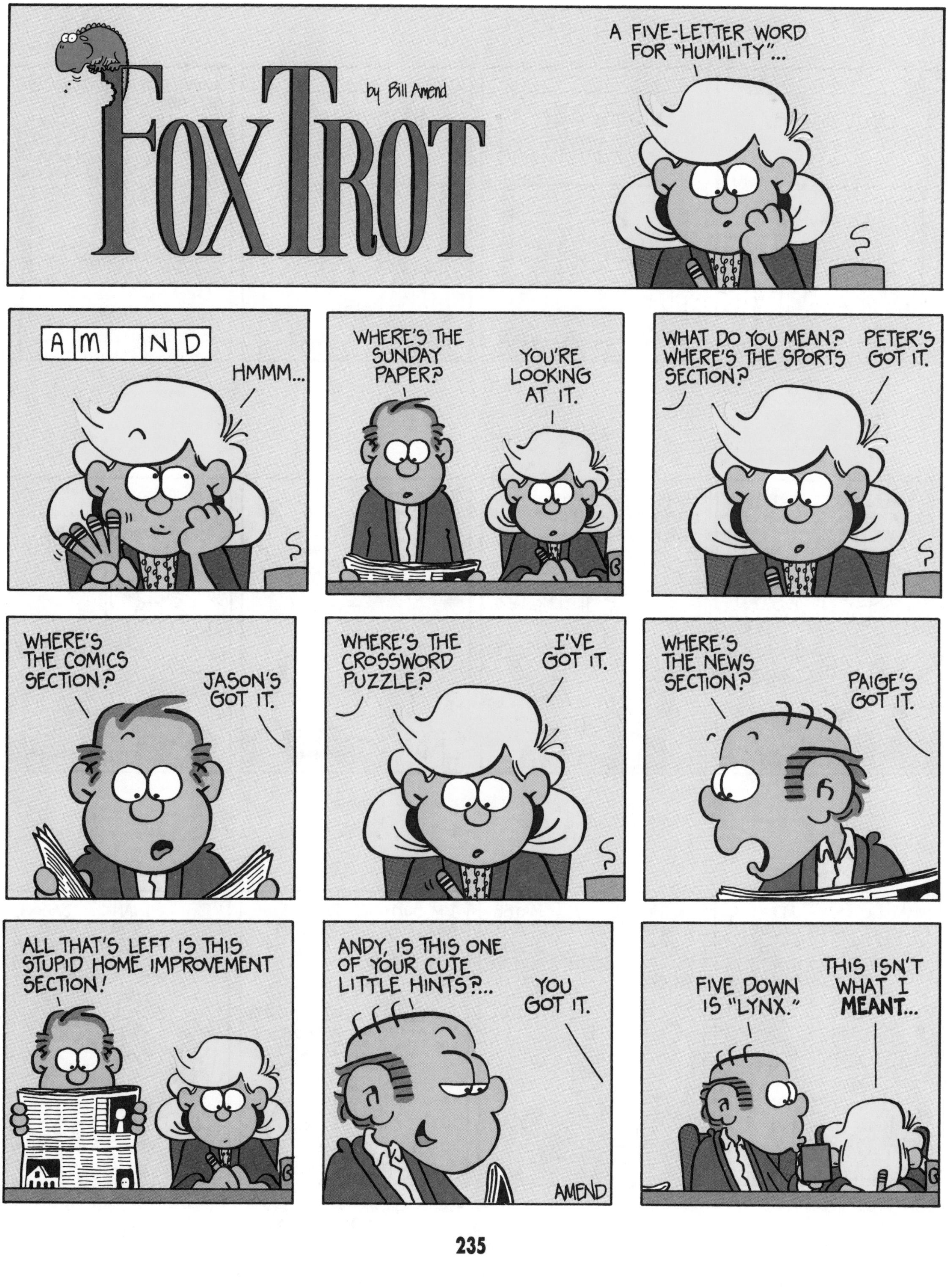
FoxTrot
by Bill Amend
A FIVE-LETTER WORD FOR "HUMILITY"...
A M N D
HMMM...
WHERE'S THE SUNDAY PAPER?
YOU'RE LOOKING AT IT.
WHAT DO YOU MEAN? WHERE'S THE SPORTS SECTION?
PETER'S GOT IT.
WHERE'S THE COMICS SECTION?
JASON'S GOT IT.
WHERE'S THE CROSSWORD PUZZLE?
I'VE GOT IT.
WHERE'S THE NEWS SECTION?
PAIGE'S GOT IT.
ALL THAT'S LEFT IS THIS STUPID HOME IMPROVEMENT SECTION!
ANDY, IS THIS ONE OF YOUR CUTE LITTLE HINTS?...
YOU GOT IT.
AMEND
FIVE DOWN IS "LYNX."
THIS ISN'T WHAT I **MEANT**...

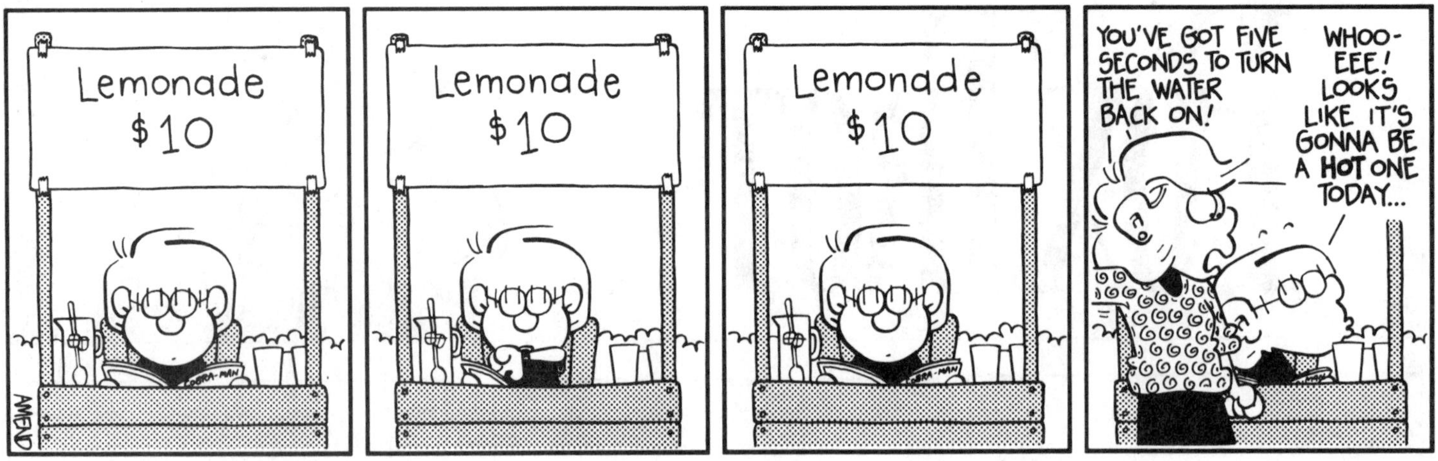
Lemonade $10
AMEND
Lemonade $10
Lemonade $10
YOU'VE GOT FIVE SECONDS TO TURN THE WATER BACK ON!
WHOO-EEE! LOOKS LIKE IT'S GONNA BE A **HOT** ONE TODAY...

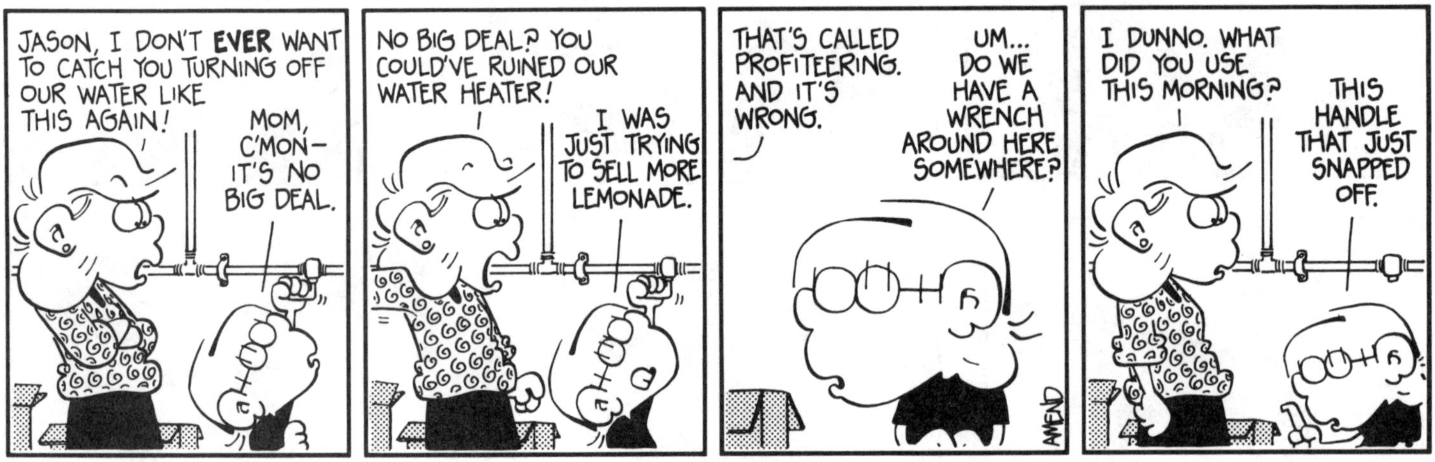
JASON, I DON'T **EVER** WANT TO CATCH YOU TURNING OFF OUR WATER LIKE THIS AGAIN!
MOM, C'MON– IT'S NO BIG DEAL.
NO BIG DEAL? YOU COULD'VE RUINED OUR WATER HEATER!
I WAS JUST TRYING TO SELL MORE LEMONADE.
THAT'S CALLED PROFITEERING. AND IT'S WRONG.
UM... DO WE HAVE A WRENCH AROUND HERE SOMEWHERE?
AMEND
I DUNNO. WHAT DID YOU USE THIS MORNING?
THIS HANDLE THAT JUST SNAPPED OFF.

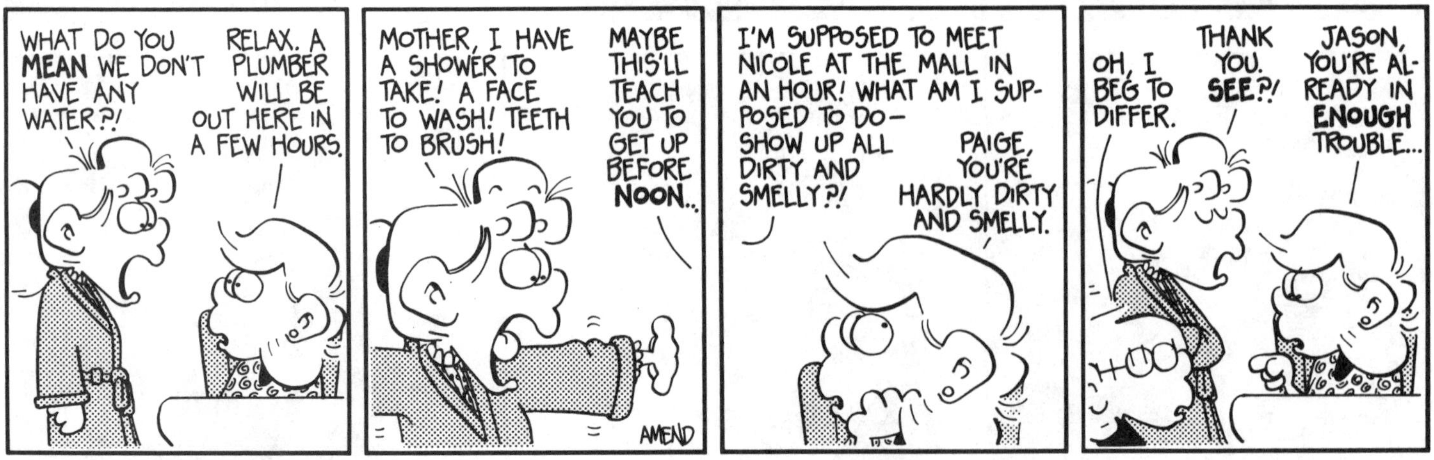
WHAT DO YOU **MEAN** WE DON'T HAVE ANY WATER?!
RELAX. A PLUMBER WILL BE OUT HERE IN A FEW HOURS.
MOTHER, I HAVE A SHOWER TO TAKE! A FACE TO WASH! TEETH TO BRUSH!
MAYBE THIS'LL TEACH YOU TO GET UP BEFORE **NOON**...
AMEND
I'M SUPPOSED TO MEET NICOLE AT THE MALL IN AN HOUR! WHAT AM I SUPPOSED TO DO– SHOW UP ALL DIRTY AND SMELLY?!
PAIGE, YOU'RE HARDLY DIRTY AND SMELLY.
OH, I BEG TO DIFFER.
THANK YOU. **SEE**?!
JASON, YOU'RE ALREADY IN **ENOUGH** TROUBLE...

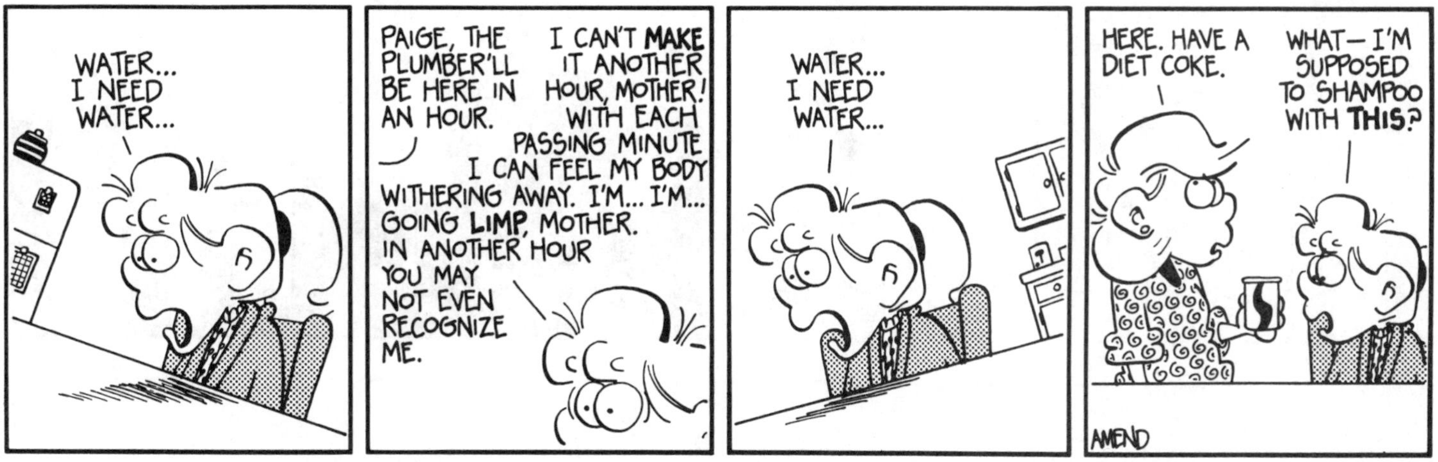
WATER... I NEED WATER...
PAIGE, THE PLUMBER'LL BE HERE IN AN HOUR.
I CAN'T **MAKE** IT ANOTHER HOUR, MOTHER! WITH EACH PASSING MINUTE I CAN FEEL MY BODY WITHERING AWAY. I'M... I'M... GOING **LIMP**, MOTHER. IN ANOTHER HOUR YOU MAY NOT EVEN RECOGNIZE ME.
WATER... I NEED WATER...
HERE. HAVE A DIET COKE.
WHAT— I'M SUPPOSED TO SHAMPOO WITH **THIS**?
AMEND

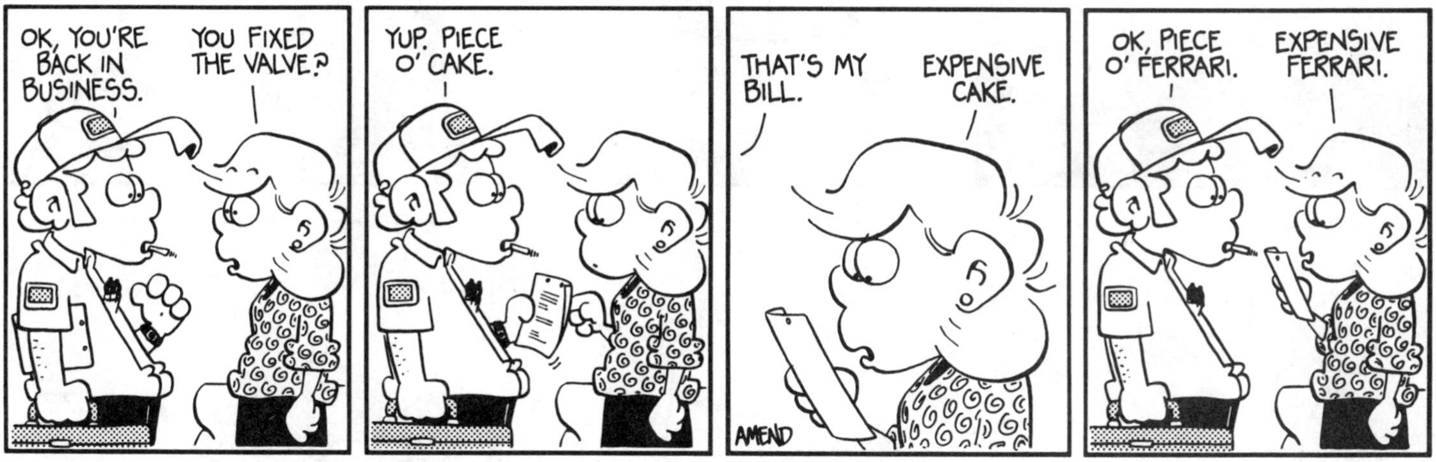
OK, YOU'RE BACK IN BUSINESS.
YOU FIXED THE VALVE?
YUP. PIECE O' CAKE.
THAT'S MY BILL.
EXPENSIVE CAKE.
AMEND
OK, PIECE O' FERRARI.
EXPENSIVE FERRARI.

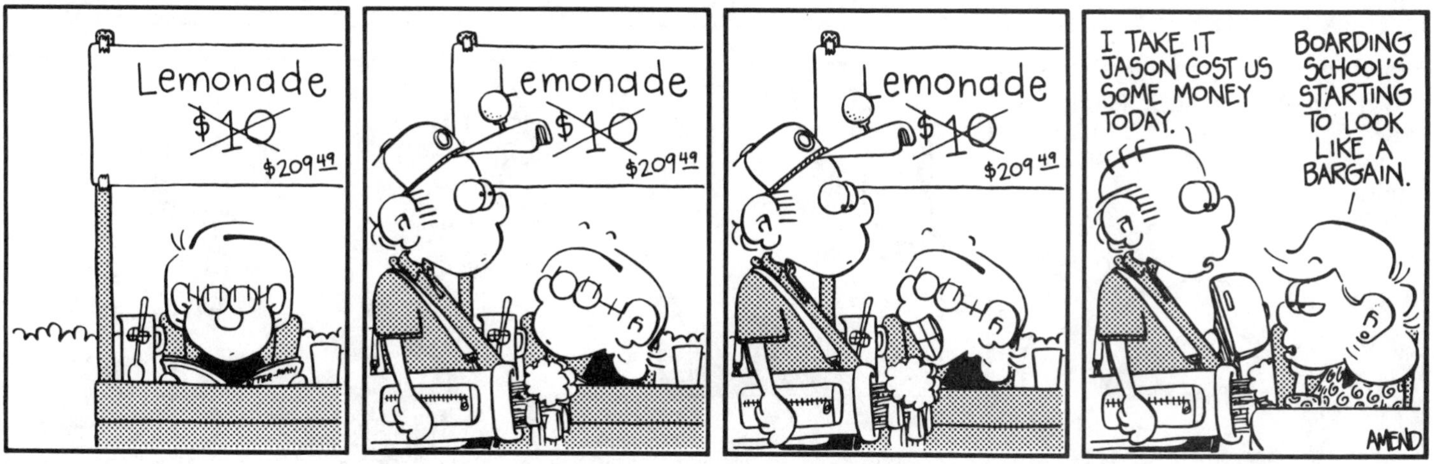
Lemonade
$10
$209 49
I TAKE IT JASON COST US SOME MONEY TODAY.
BOARDING SCHOOL'S STARTING TO LOOK LIKE A BARGAIN.
AMEND

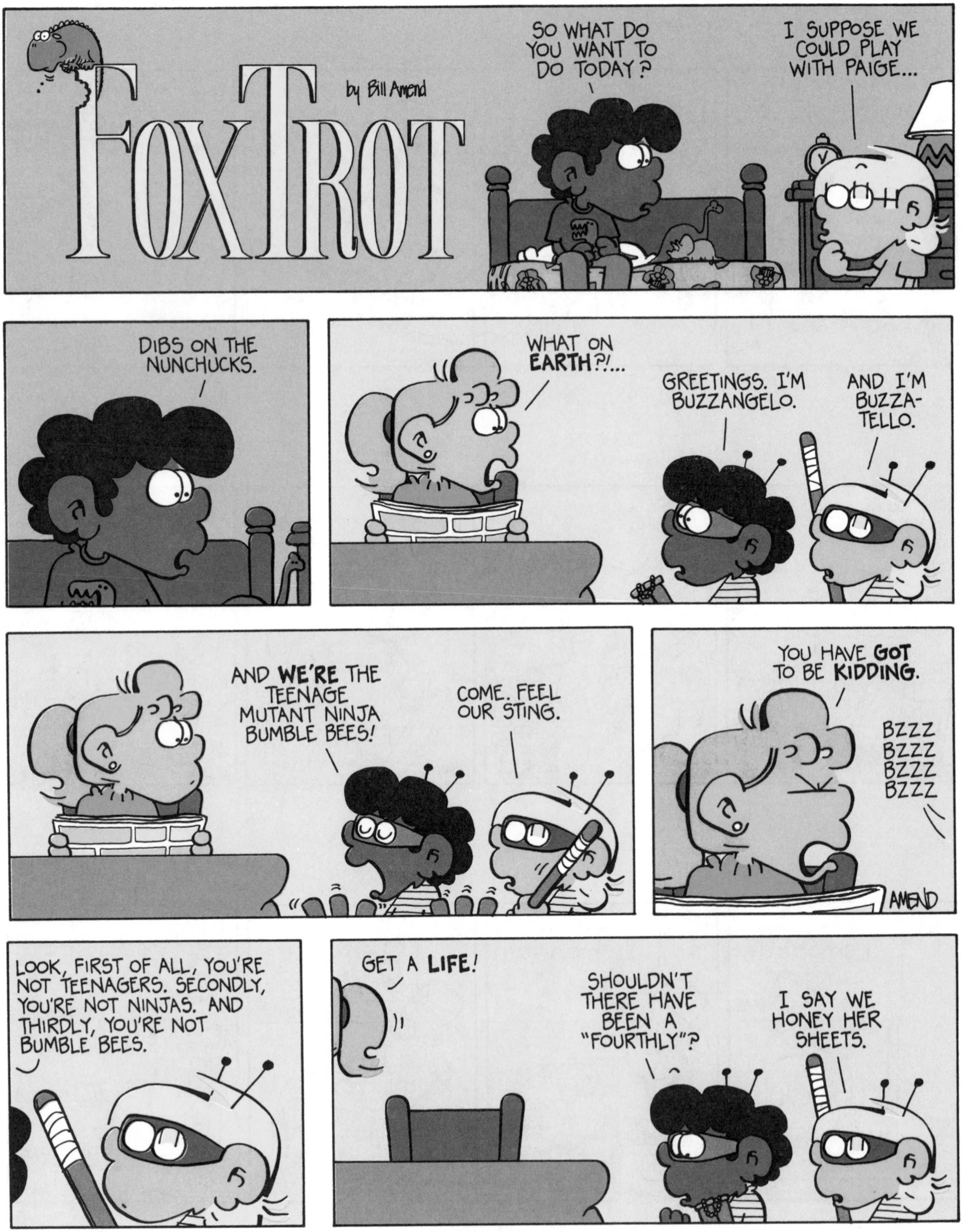
FoxTrot
by Bill Amend
SO WHAT DO YOU WANT TO DO TODAY?
I SUPPOSE WE COULD PLAY WITH PAIGE...
DIBS ON THE NUNCHUCKS.
WHAT ON EARTH?!...
GREETINGS. I'M BUZZANGELO.
AND I'M BUZZA-TELLO.
AND WE'RE THE TEENAGE MUTANT NINJA BUMBLE BEES!
COME. FEEL OUR STING.
YOU HAVE GOT TO BE KIDDING.
BZZZ BZZZ BZZZ BZZZ
AMEND
LOOK, FIRST OF ALL, YOU'RE NOT TEENAGERS. SECONDLY, YOU'RE NOT NINJAS. AND THIRDLY, YOU'RE NOT BUMBLE BEES.
GET A LIFE!
SHOULDN'T THERE HAVE BEEN A "FOURTHLY"?
I SAY WE HONEY HER SHEETS.

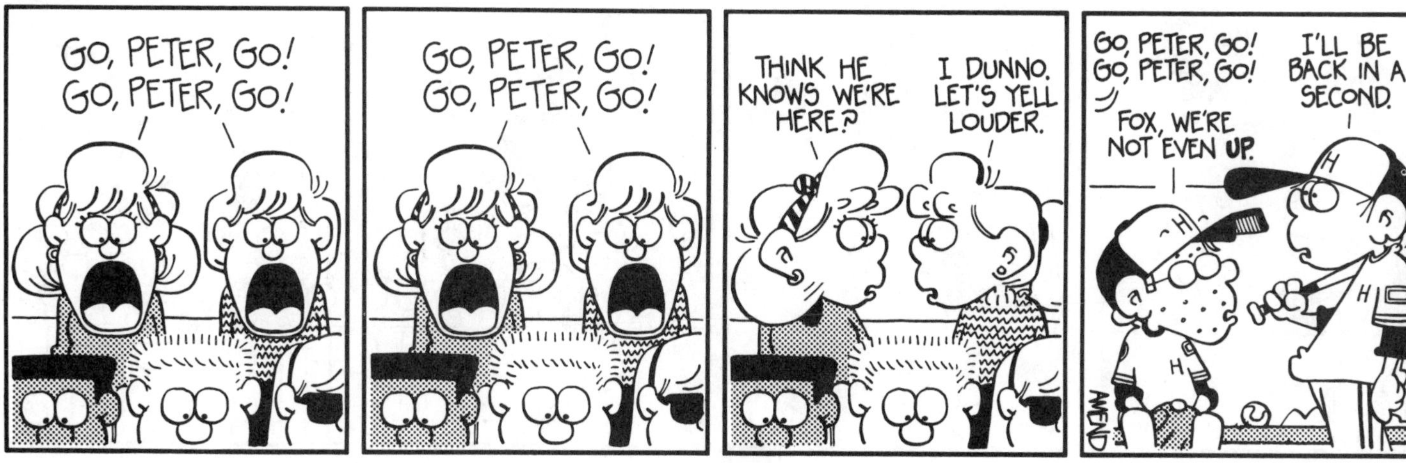
GO, PETER, GO! GO, PETER, GO!
GO, PETER, GO! GO, PETER, GO!
THINK HE KNOWS WE'RE HERE?
I DUNNO. LET'S YELL LOUDER.
GO, PETER, GO! GO, PETER, GO!
I'LL BE BACK IN A SECOND.
FOX, WE'RE NOT EVEN UP.
AMEND

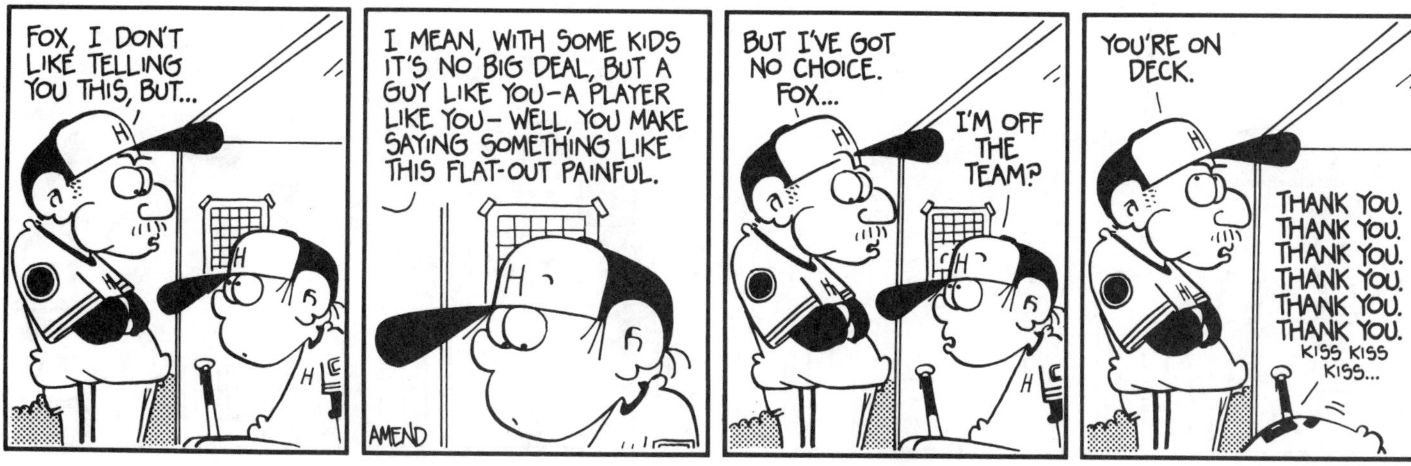
FOX, I DON'T LIKE TELLING YOU THIS, BUT...
I MEAN, WITH SOME KIDS IT'S NO BIG DEAL, BUT A GUY LIKE YOU—A PLAYER LIKE YOU— WELL, YOU MAKE SAYING SOMETHING LIKE THIS FLAT-OUT PAINFUL.
AMEND
BUT I'VE GOT NO CHOICE. FOX...
I'M OFF THE TEAM?
YOU'RE ON DECK.
THANK YOU. THANK YOU. THANK YOU. THANK YOU. THANK YOU. THANK YOU.
KISS KISS KISS...

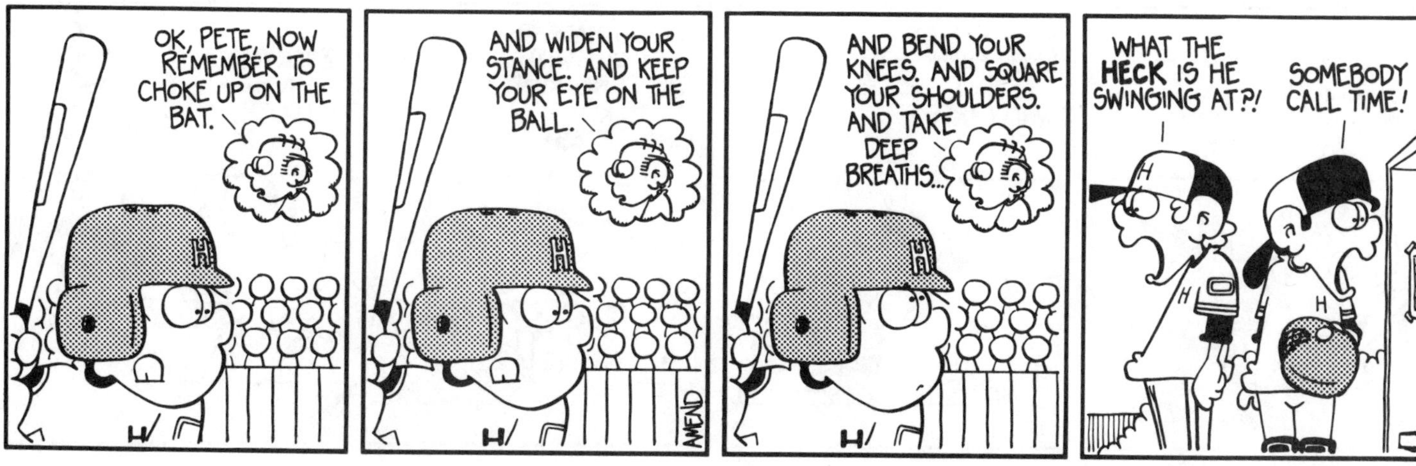
OK, PETE, NOW REMEMBER TO CHOKE UP ON THE BAT.
AND WIDEN YOUR STANCE. AND KEEP YOUR EYE ON THE BALL.
AMEND
AND BEND YOUR KNEES. AND SQUARE YOUR SHOULDERS. AND TAKE DEEP BREATHS...
WHAT THE **HECK** IS HE SWINGING AT?!
SOMEBODY CALL TIME!

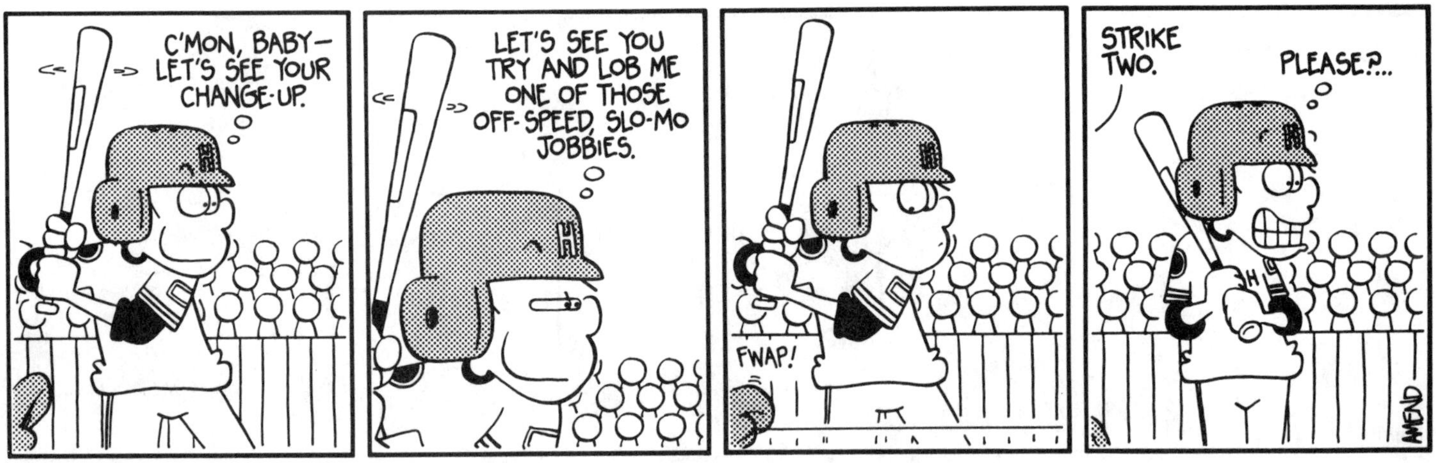
C'MON, BABY— LET'S SEE YOUR CHANGE-UP.
LET'S SEE YOU TRY AND LOB ME ONE OF THOSE OFF-SPEED, SLO-MO JOBBIES.
FWAP!
STRIKE TWO.
PLEASE?...
AMEND

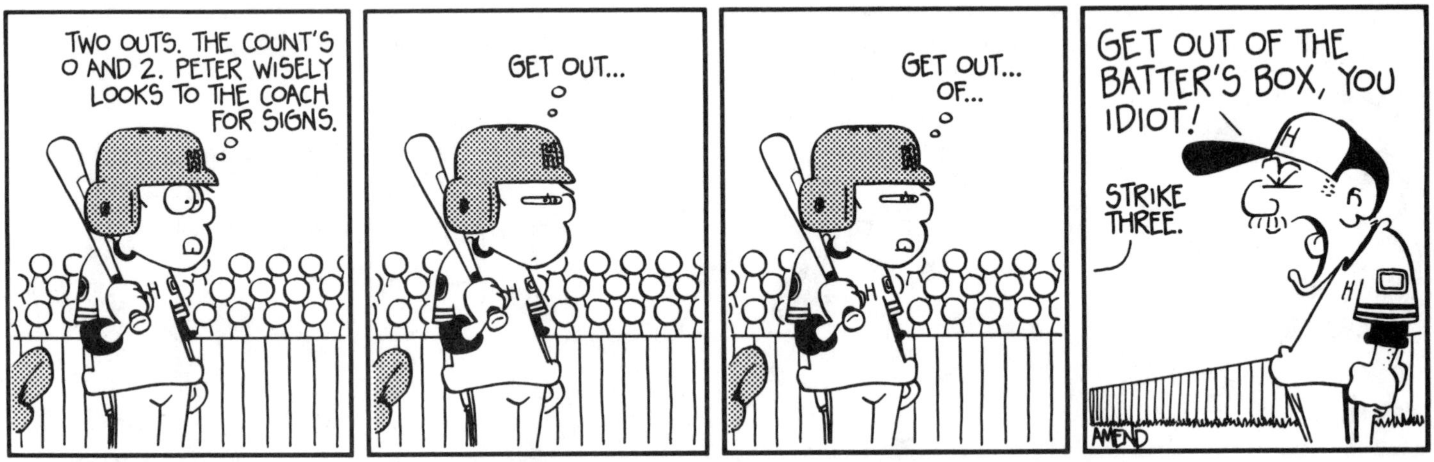
TWO OUTS. THE COUNT'S 0 AND 2. PETER WISELY LOOKS TO THE COACH FOR SIGNS.
GET OUT...
GET OUT... OF...
GET OUT OF THE BATTER'S BOX, YOU IDIOT!
STRIKE THREE.
AMEND

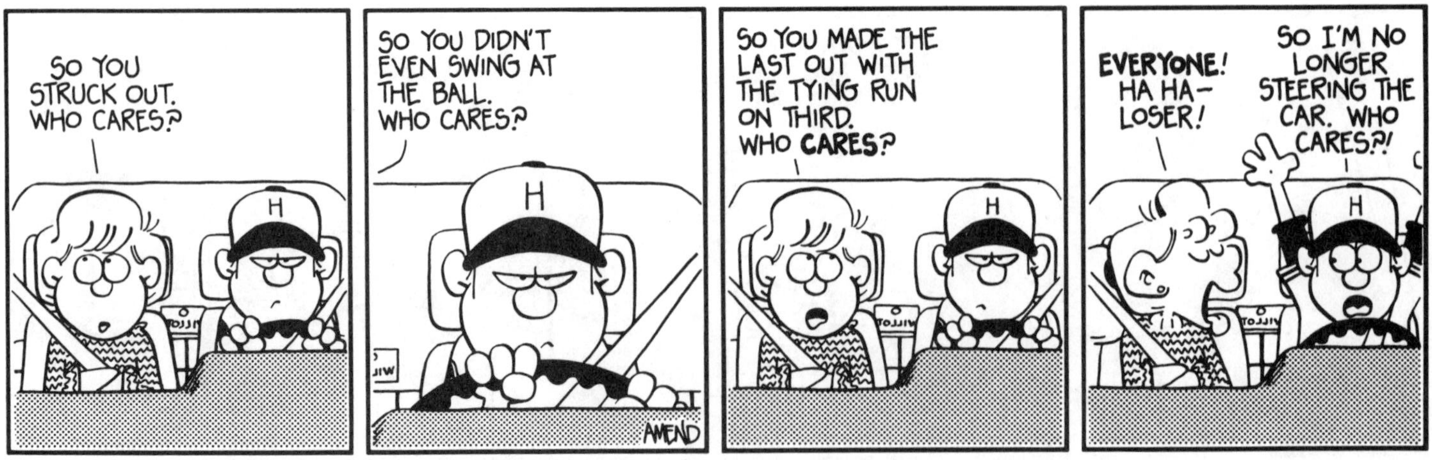
SO YOU STRUCK OUT. WHO CARES?
SO YOU DIDN'T EVEN SWING AT THE BALL. WHO CARES?
AMEND
SO YOU MADE THE LAST OUT WITH THE TYING RUN ON THIRD. WHO **CARES**?
EVERYONE! HA HA—LOSER!
SO I'M NO LONGER STEERING THE CAR. WHO CARES?!

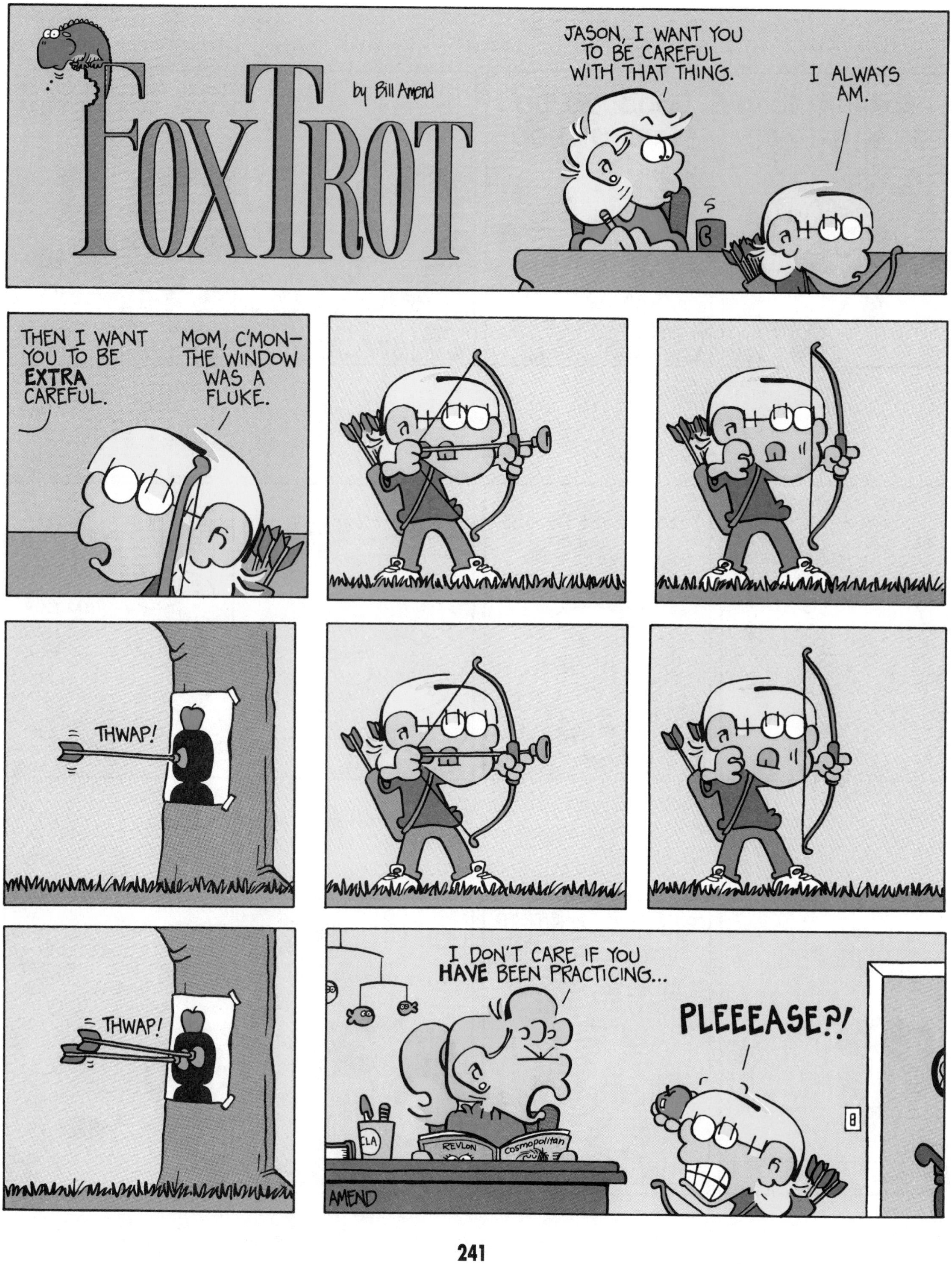
FoxTrot
by Bill Amend
JASON, I WANT YOU TO BE CAREFUL WITH THAT THING.
I ALWAYS AM.
THEN I WANT YOU TO BE **EXTRA** CAREFUL.
MOM, C'MON– THE WINDOW WAS A FLUKE.
THWAP!
THWAP!
I DON'T CARE IF YOU **HAVE** BEEN PRACTICING...
PLEEEASE?!
REVLON
Cosmopolitan
AMEND

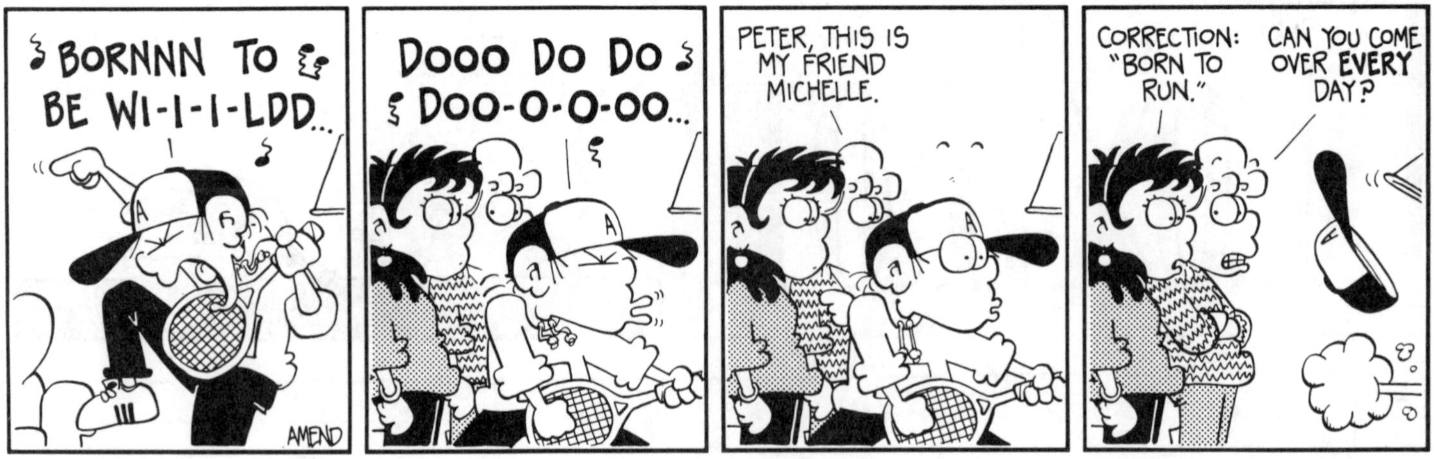
BORNNN TO BE WI-I-I-LDD...
DOOO DO DO DOO-O-O-OO...
PETER, THIS IS MY FRIEND MICHELLE.
CORRECTION: "BORN TO RUN."
CAN YOU COME OVER EVERY DAY?
AMEND

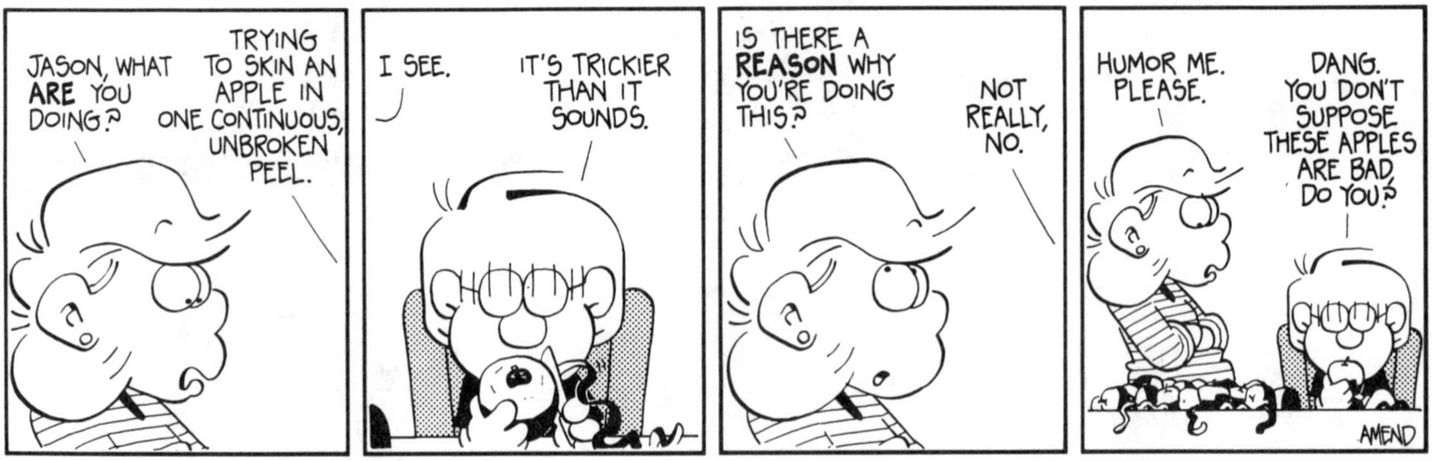
JASON, WHAT ARE YOU DOING?
TRYING TO SKIN AN APPLE IN ONE CONTINUOUS, UNBROKEN PEEL.
I SEE.
IT'S TRICKIER THAN IT SOUNDS.
IS THERE A REASON WHY YOU'RE DOING THIS?
NOT REALLY, NO.
HUMOR ME. PLEASE.
DANG. YOU DON'T SUPPOSE THESE APPLES ARE BAD, DO YOU?
AMEND

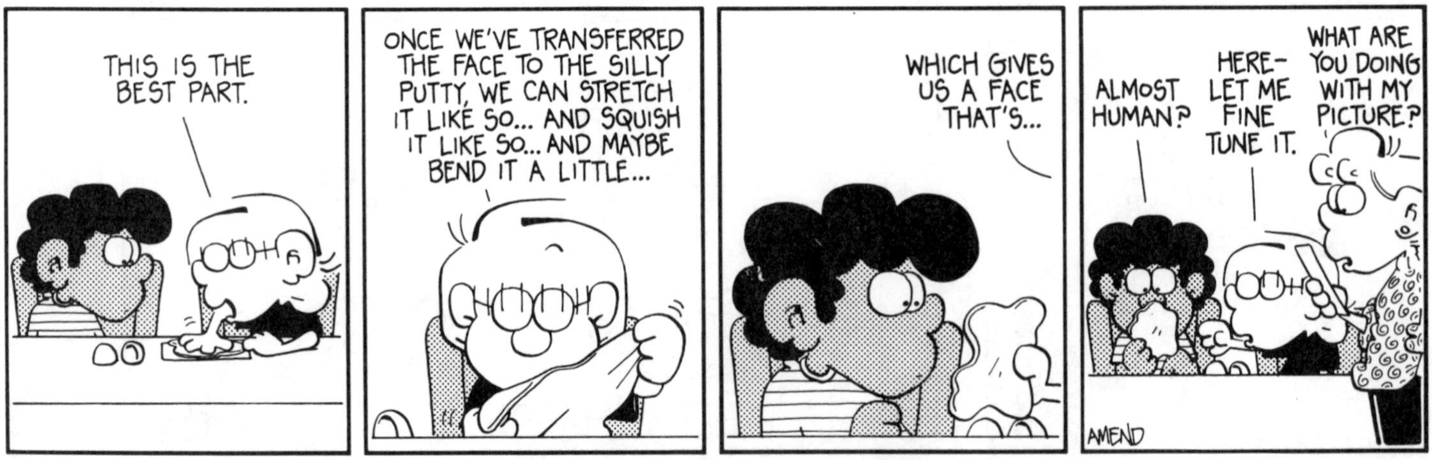
THIS IS THE BEST PART.
ONCE WE'VE TRANSFERRED THE FACE TO THE SILLY PUTTY, WE CAN STRETCH IT LIKE SO... AND SQUISH IT LIKE SO... AND MAYBE BEND IT A LITTLE...
WHICH GIVES US A FACE THAT'S...
ALMOST HUMAN?
HERE- LET ME FINE TUNE IT.
WHAT ARE YOU DOING WITH MY PICTURE?
AMEND

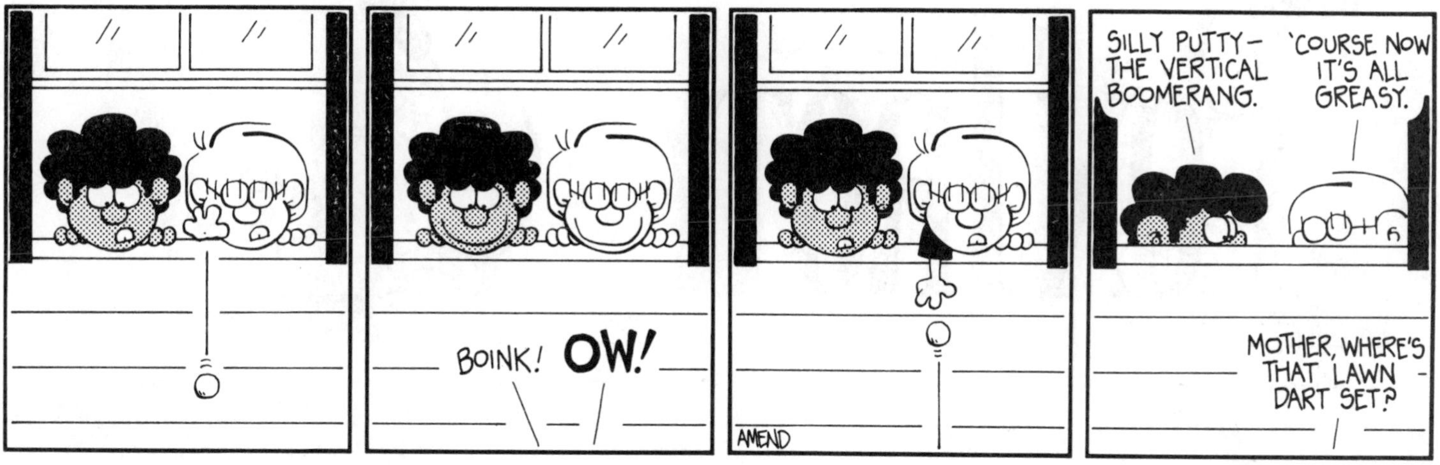
BOINK!
OW!
AMEND
SILLY PUTTY– THE VERTICAL BOOMERANG.
'COURSE NOW IT'S ALL GREASY.
MOTHER, WHERE'S THAT LAWN DART SET?

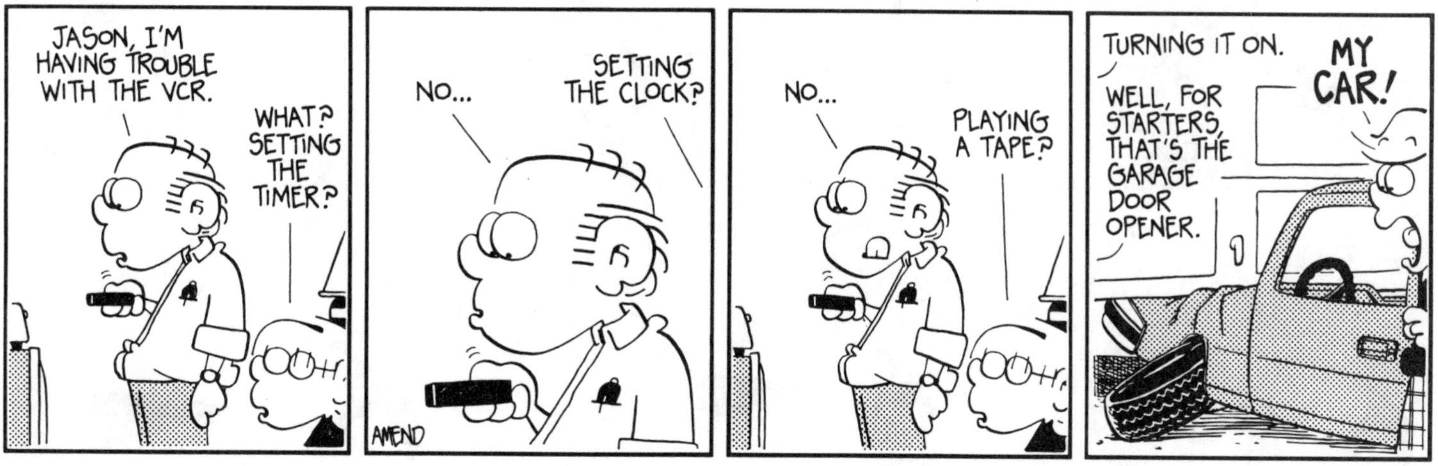
JASON, I'M HAVING TROUBLE WITH THE VCR.
WHAT? SETTING THE TIMER?
NO...
SETTING THE CLOCK?
AMEND
NO...
PLAYING A TAPE?
TURNING IT ON.
WELL, FOR STARTERS, THAT'S THE GARAGE DOOR OPENER.
MY CAR!

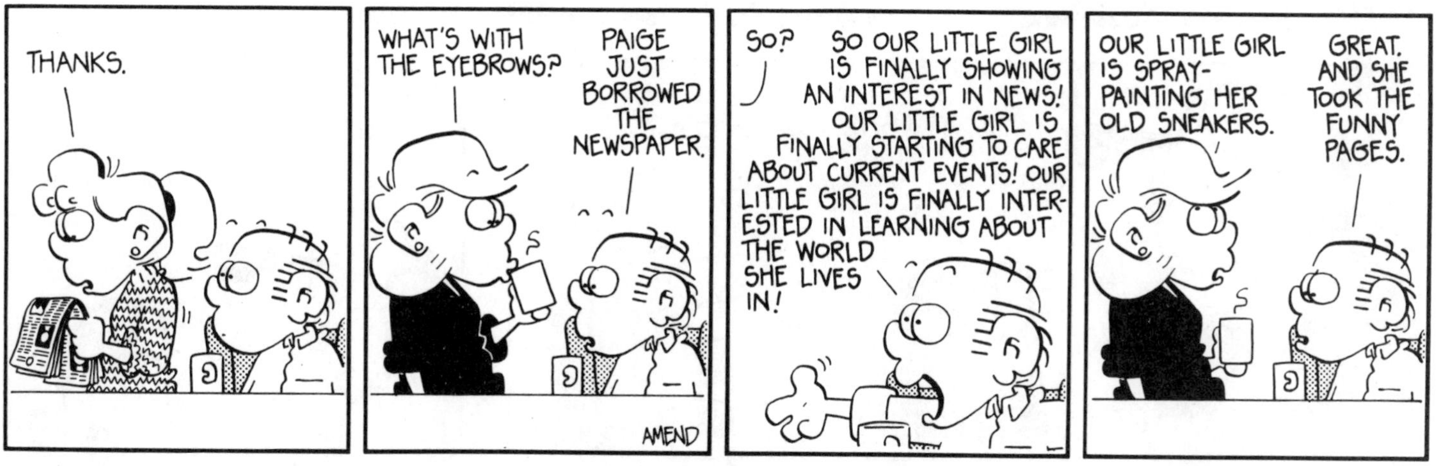
THANKS.
WHAT'S WITH THE EYEBROWS?
PAIGE JUST BORROWED THE NEWSPAPER.
AMEND
SO?
SO OUR LITTLE GIRL IS FINALLY SHOWING AN INTEREST IN NEWS! OUR LITTLE GIRL IS FINALLY STARTING TO CARE ABOUT CURRENT EVENTS! OUR LITTLE GIRL IS FINALLY INTERESTED IN LEARNING ABOUT THE WORLD SHE LIVES IN!
OUR LITTLE GIRL IS SPRAY-PAINTING HER OLD SNEAKERS.
GREAT. AND SHE TOOK THE FUNNY PAGES.

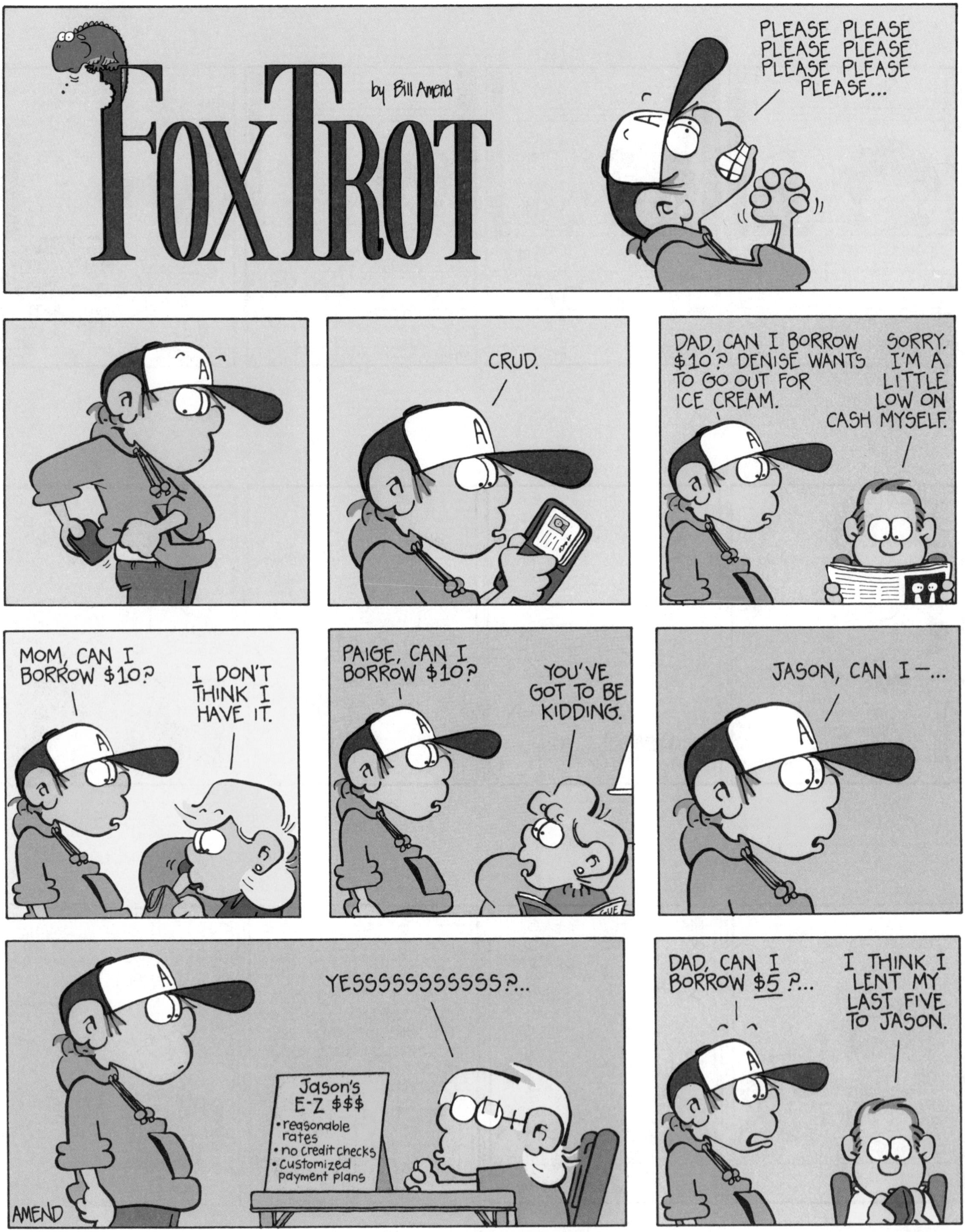
FoxTrot
by Bill Amend
PLEASE PLEASE PLEASE PLEASE PLEASE PLEASE PLEASE...
CRUD.
DAD, CAN I BORROW $10? DENISE WANTS TO GO OUT FOR ICE CREAM.
SORRY. I'M A LITTLE LOW ON CASH MYSELF.
MOM, CAN I BORROW $10?
I DON'T THINK I HAVE IT.
PAIGE, CAN I BORROW $10?
YOU'VE GOT TO BE KIDDING.
JASON, CAN I —...
YESSSSSSSSSSS?...
Jason's E-Z $$$
• reasonable rates
• no credit checks
• customized payment plans
AMEND
DAD, CAN I BORROW $5?...
I THINK I LENT MY LAST FIVE TO JASON.

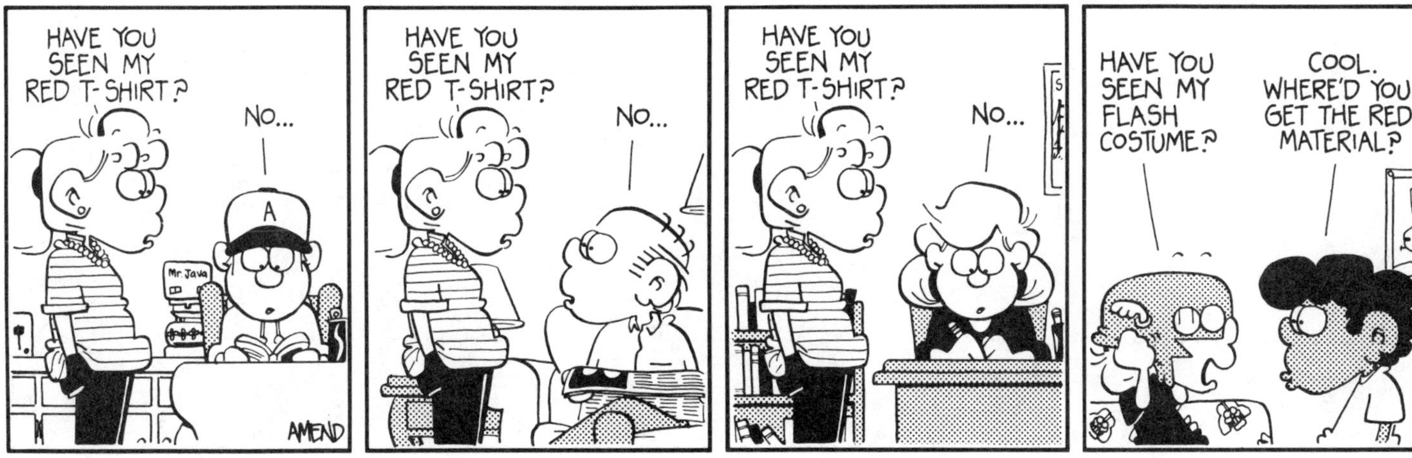
HAVE YOU SEEN MY RED T-SHIRT?
NO...
Mr. Java
HAVE YOU SEEN MY RED T-SHIRT?
NO...
HAVE YOU SEEN MY RED T-SHIRT?
NO...
HAVE YOU SEEN MY FLASH COSTUME?
COOL. WHERE'D YOU GET THE RED MATERIAL?
AMEND

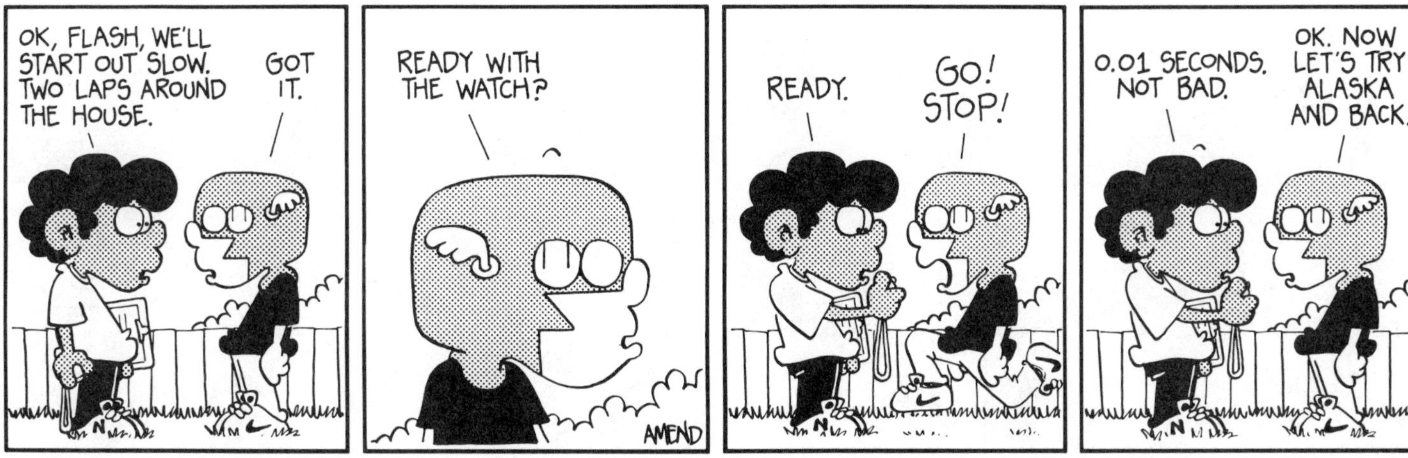
OK, FLASH, WE'LL START OUT SLOW. TWO LAPS AROUND THE HOUSE.
GOT IT.
READY WITH THE WATCH?
READY.
GO! STOP!
0.01 SECONDS. NOT BAD.
OK. NOW LET'S TRY ALASKA AND BACK.
AMEND

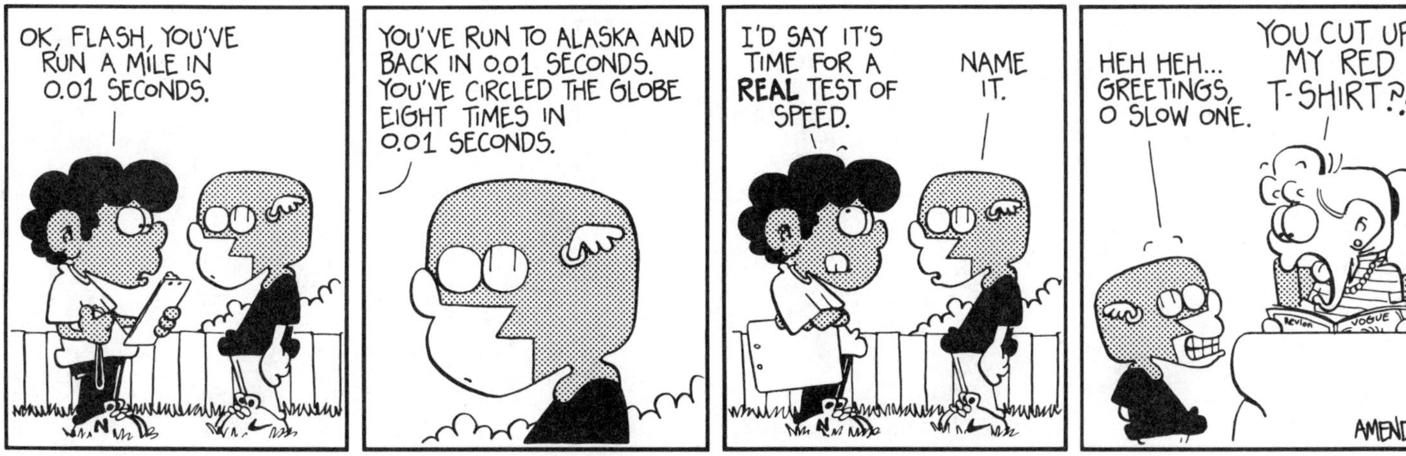
OK, FLASH, YOU'VE RUN A MILE IN 0.01 SECONDS.
YOU'VE RUN TO ALASKA AND BACK IN 0.01 SECONDS. YOU'VE CIRCLED THE GLOBE EIGHT TIMES IN 0.01 SECONDS.
I'D SAY IT'S TIME FOR A REAL TEST OF SPEED.
NAME IT.
HEH HEH... GREETINGS, O SLOW ONE.
YOU CUT UP MY RED T-SHIRT?!
Revlon
VOGUE
AMEND

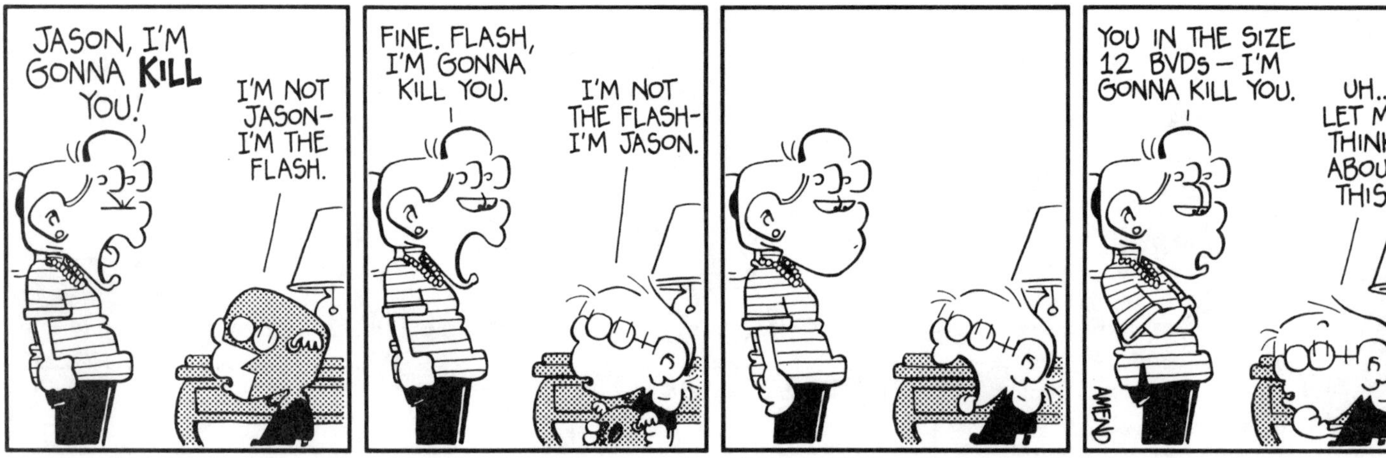
JASON, I'M GONNA **KILL** YOU!
I'M NOT JASON- I'M THE FLASH.
FINE. FLASH, I'M GONNA KILL YOU.
I'M NOT THE FLASH- I'M JASON.
YOU IN THE SIZE 12 BVDs – I'M GONNA KILL YOU.
UH... LET ME THINK ABOUT THIS.
AMEND

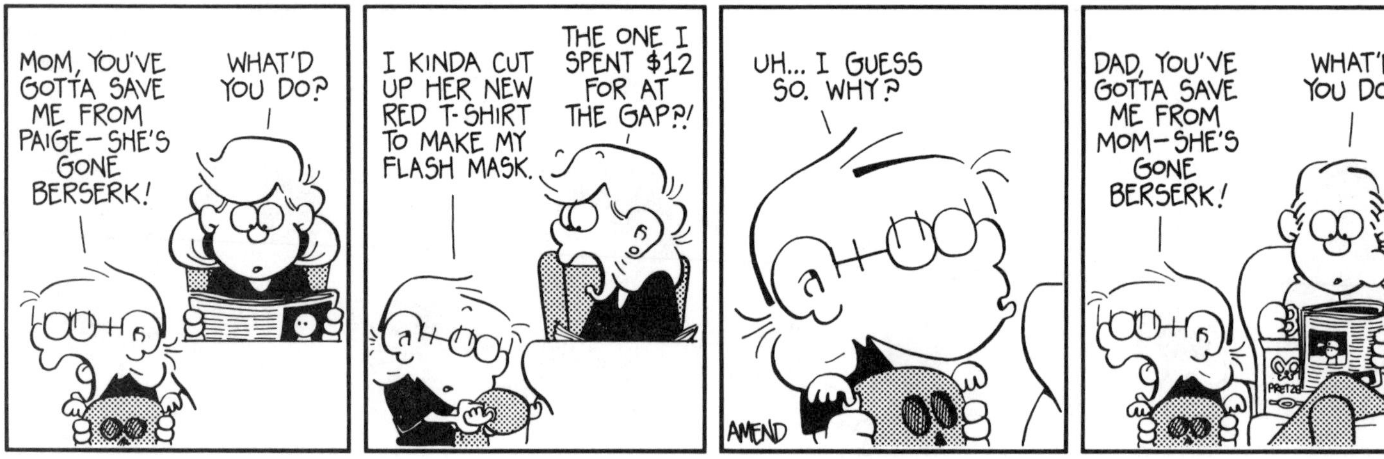
MOM, YOU'VE GOTTA SAVE ME FROM PAIGE – SHE'S GONE BERSERK!
WHAT'D YOU DO?
I KINDA CUT UP HER NEW RED T-SHIRT TO MAKE MY FLASH MASK.
THE ONE I SPENT $12 FOR AT THE GAP?!
UH... I GUESS SO. WHY?
AMEND
DAD, YOU'VE GOTTA SAVE ME FROM MOM – SHE'S GONE BERSERK!
WHAT'D YOU DO?

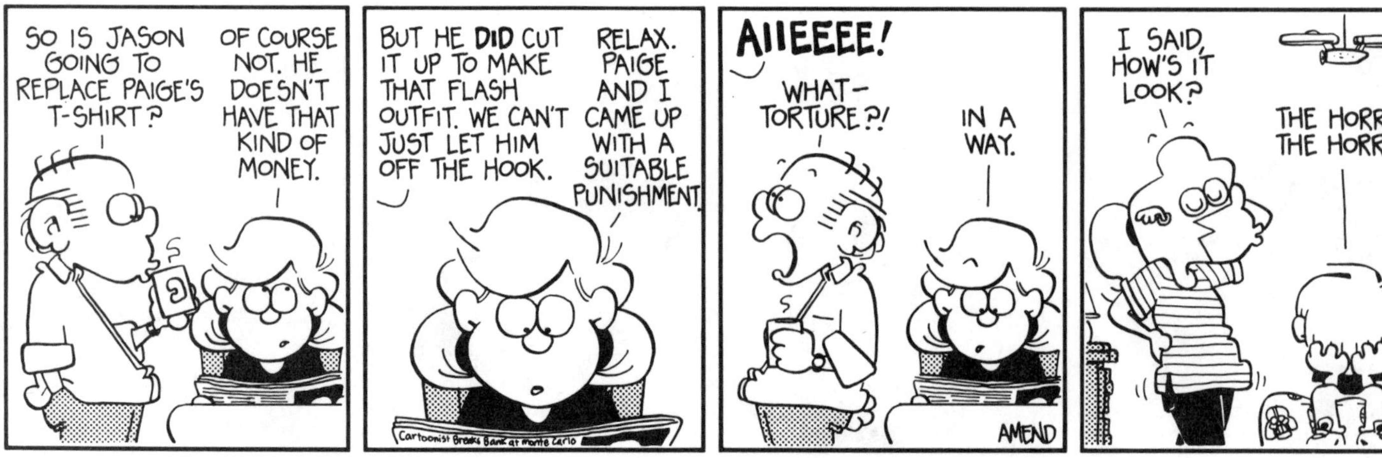
SO IS JASON GOING TO REPLACE PAIGE'S T-SHIRT?
OF COURSE NOT. HE DOESN'T HAVE THAT KIND OF MONEY.
BUT HE **DID** CUT IT UP TO MAKE THAT FLASH OUTFIT. WE CAN'T JUST LET HIM OFF THE HOOK.
RELAX. PAIGE AND I CAME UP WITH A SUITABLE PUNISHMENT.
Cartoonist Breaks Bank at Monte Carlo
AIIEEEE!
WHAT- TORTURE?!
IN A WAY.
AMEND
I SAID, HOW'S IT LOOK?
THE HORROR. THE HORROR.

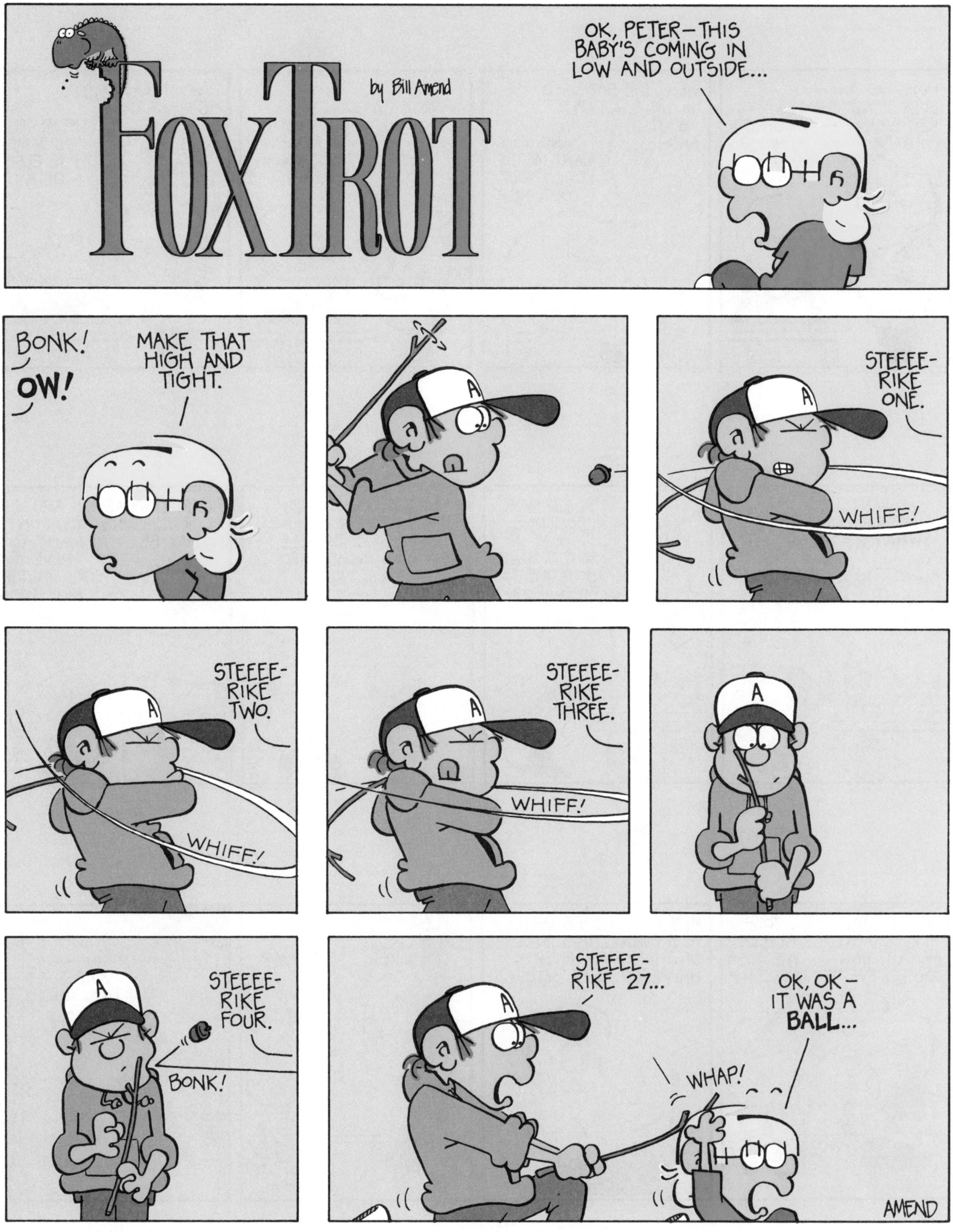
FOXTROT
by Bill Amend
OK, PETER—THIS BABY'S COMING IN LOW AND OUTSIDE...
BONK!
OW!
MAKE THAT HIGH AND TIGHT.
STEEEE-RIKE ONE.
WHIFF!
STEEEE-RIKE TWO.
WHIFF!
STEEEE-RIKE THREE.
WHIFF!
STEEEE-RIKE FOUR.
BONK!
STEEEE-RIKE 27...
WHAP!
OK, OK—IT WAS A BALL...
AMEND

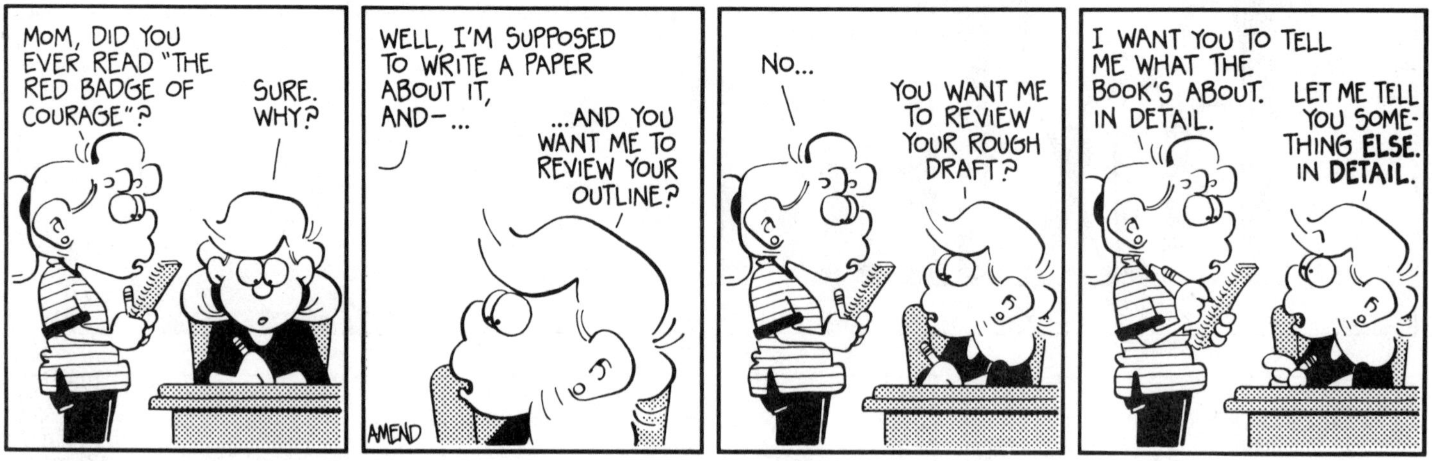
MOM, DID YOU EVER READ "THE RED BADGE OF COURAGE"?
SURE. WHY?
WELL, I'M SUPPOSED TO WRITE A PAPER ABOUT IT, AND— ...
...AND YOU WANT ME TO REVIEW YOUR OUTLINE?
AMEND
NO...
YOU WANT ME TO REVIEW YOUR ROUGH DRAFT?
I WANT YOU TO TELL ME WHAT THE BOOK'S ABOUT. IN DETAIL.
LET ME TELL YOU SOMETHING **ELSE**. IN **DETAIL**.

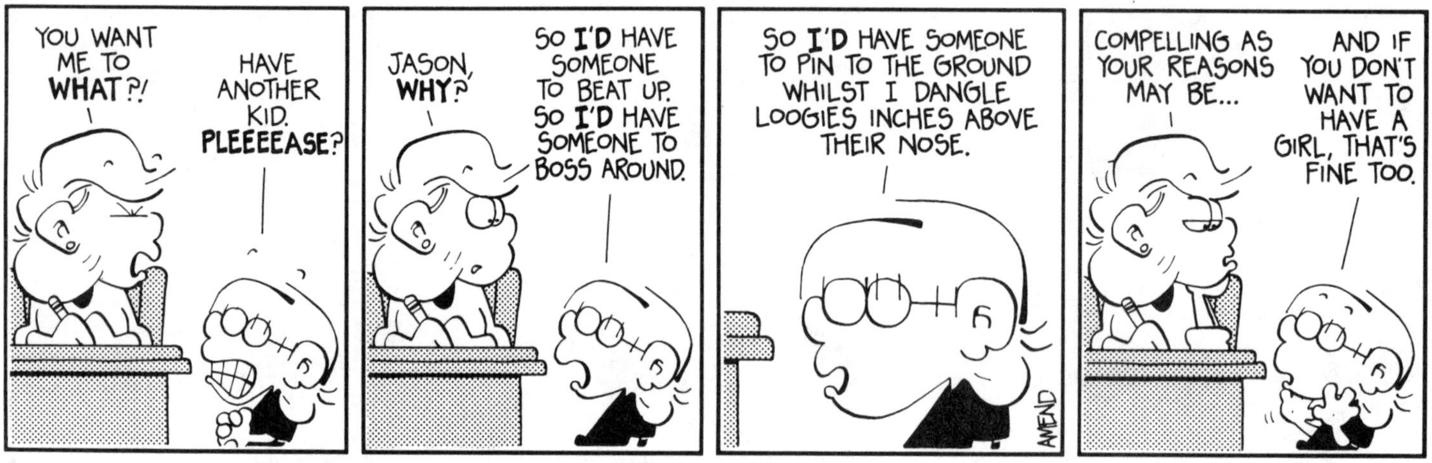
YOU WANT ME TO **WHAT**?!
HAVE ANOTHER KID. **PLEEEEASE**?
JASON, **WHY**?
SO **I'D** HAVE SOMEONE TO BEAT UP. SO **I'D** HAVE SOMEONE TO BOSS AROUND.
SO **I'D** HAVE SOMEONE TO PIN TO THE GROUND WHILST I DANGLE LOOGIES INCHES ABOVE THEIR NOSE.
AMEND
COMPELLING AS YOUR REASONS MAY BE...
AND IF YOU DON'T WANT TO HAVE A GIRL, THAT'S FINE TOO.

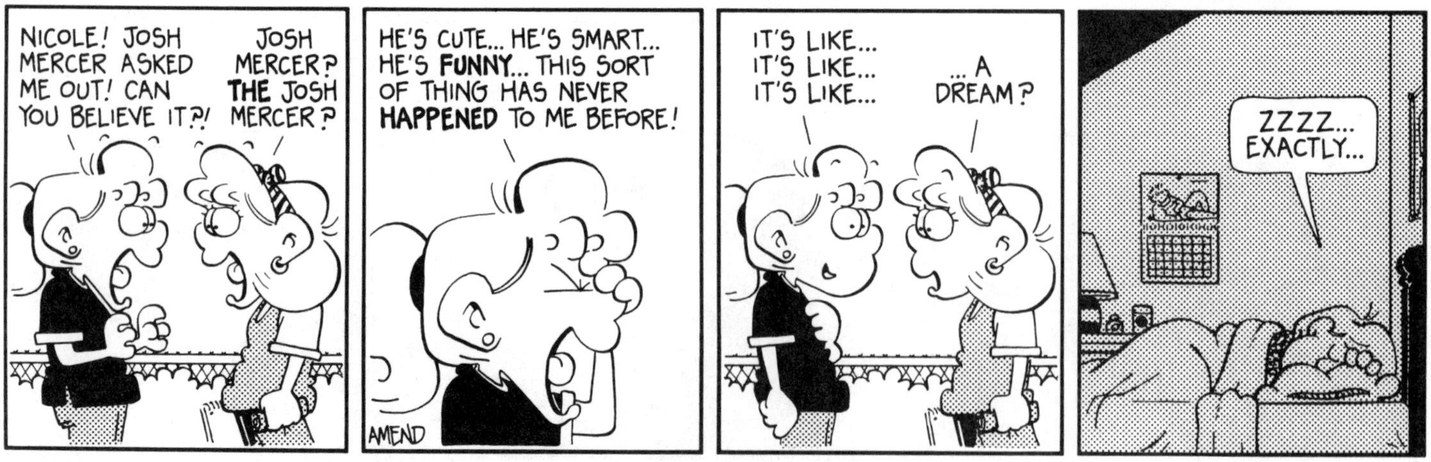
NICOLE! JOSH MERCER ASKED ME OUT! CAN YOU BELIEVE IT?!
JOSH MERCER? **THE** JOSH MERCER?
HE'S CUTE... HE'S SMART... HE'S **FUNNY**... THIS SORT OF THING HAS NEVER **HAPPENED** TO ME BEFORE!
AMEND
IT'S LIKE... IT'S LIKE... IT'S LIKE...
... A DREAM?
ZZZZ... EXACTLY...

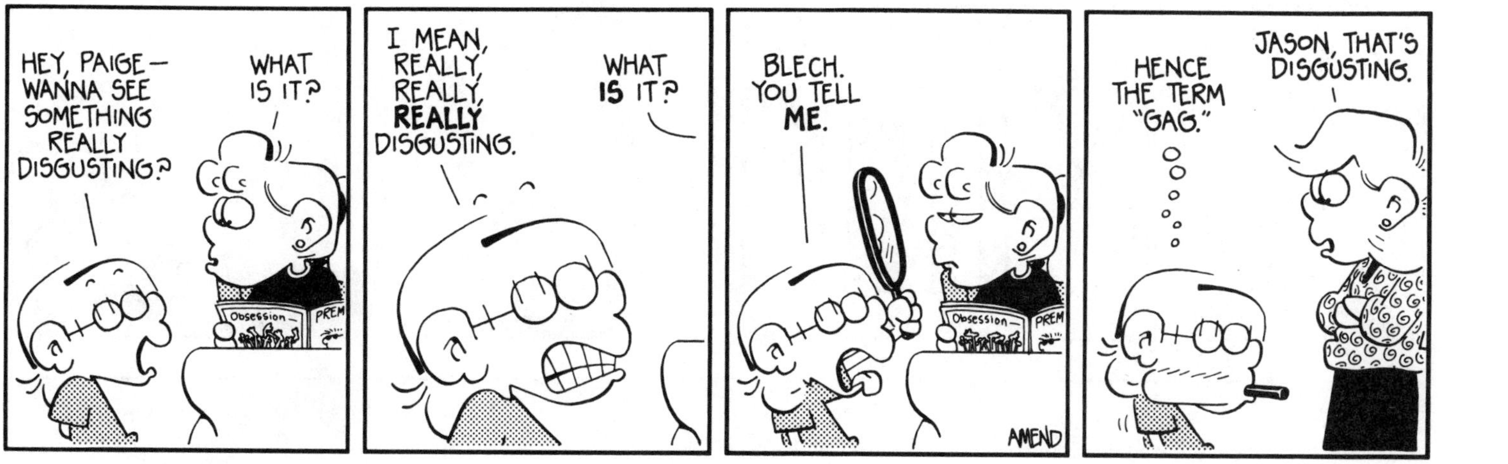
HEY, PAIGE— WANNA SEE SOMETHING REALLY DISGUSTING?
WHAT IS IT?
Obsession
PREM
I MEAN, REALLY, REALLY, **REALLY** DISGUSTING.
WHAT **IS** IT?
BLECH. YOU TELL **ME**.
AMEND
HENCE THE TERM "GAG."
JASON, THAT'S DISGUSTING.

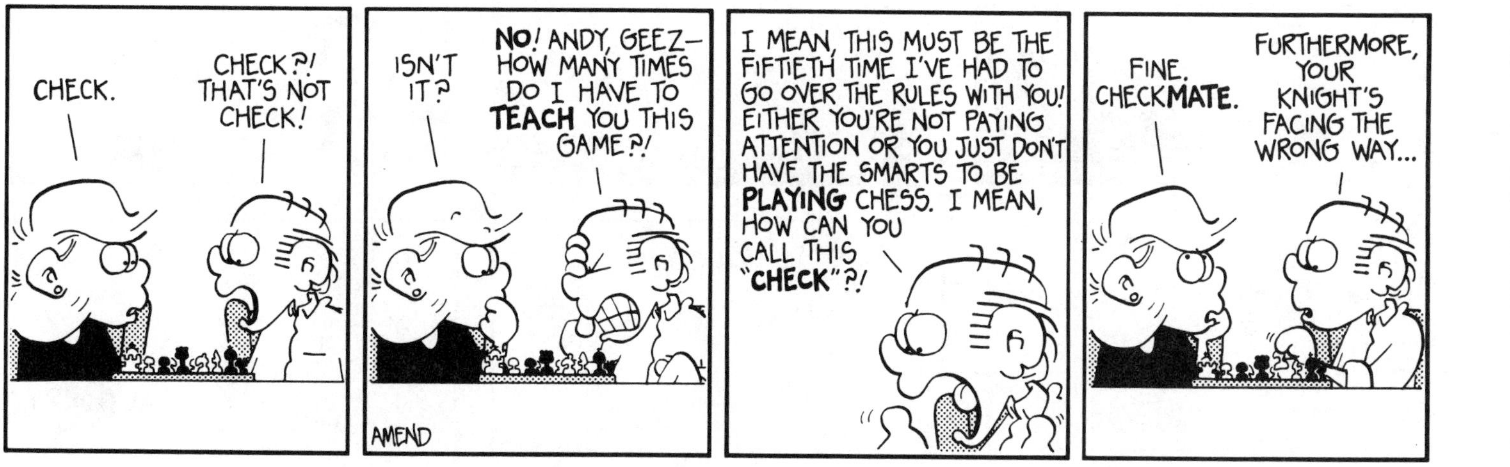
CHECK.
CHECK?! THAT'S NOT CHECK!
ISN'T IT?
NO! ANDY, GEEZ— HOW MANY TIMES DO I HAVE TO **TEACH** YOU THIS GAME?!
AMEND
I MEAN, THIS MUST BE THE FIFTIETH TIME I'VE HAD TO GO OVER THE RULES WITH YOU! EITHER YOU'RE NOT PAYING ATTENTION OR YOU JUST DON'T HAVE THE SMARTS TO BE **PLAYING** CHESS. I MEAN, HOW CAN YOU CALL THIS "**CHECK**"?!
FINE. CHECK**MATE**.
FURTHERMORE, YOUR KNIGHT'S FACING THE WRONG WAY...

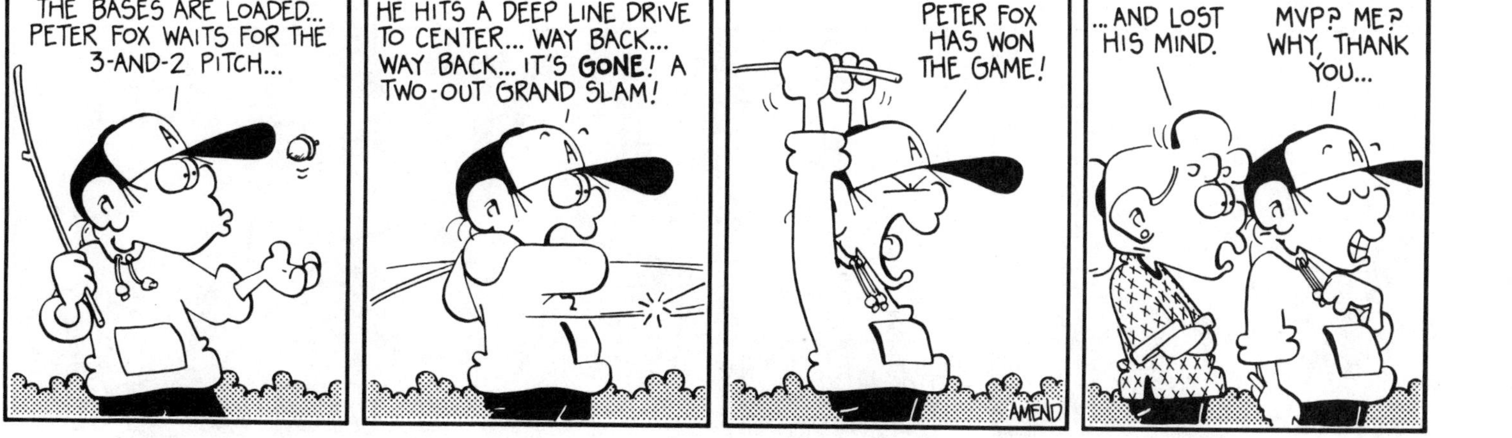
THE BASES ARE LOADED... PETER FOX WAITS FOR THE 3-AND-2 PITCH...
HE HITS A DEEP LINE DRIVE TO CENTER... WAY BACK... WAY BACK... IT'S **GONE**! A TWO-OUT GRAND SLAM!
PETER FOX HAS WON THE GAME!
AMEND
...AND LOST HIS MIND.
MVP? ME? WHY, THANK YOU...

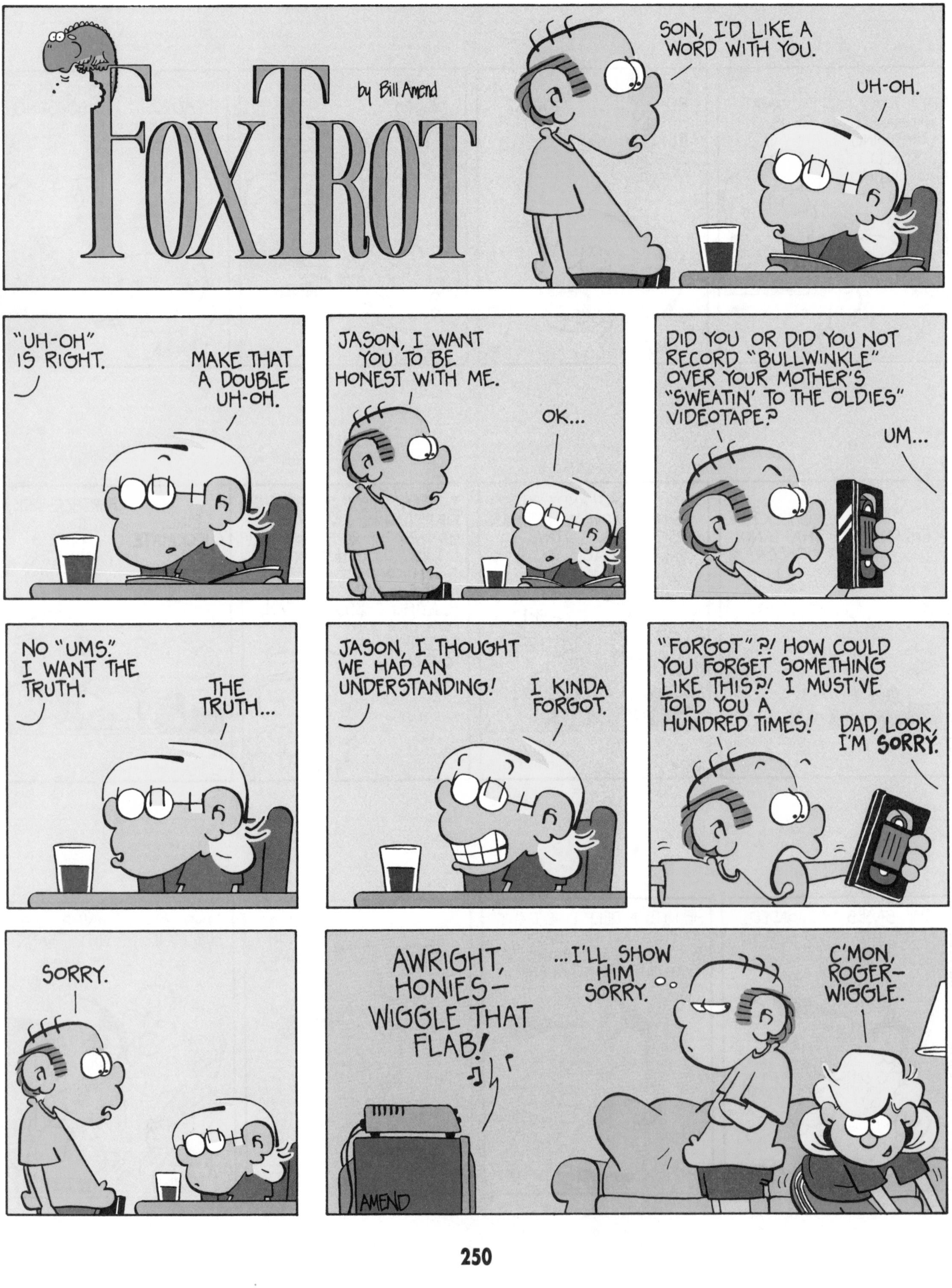
FoxTrot
by Bill Amend
SON, I'D LIKE A WORD WITH YOU.
UH-OH.
"UH-OH" IS RIGHT.
MAKE THAT A DOUBLE UH-OH.
JASON, I WANT YOU TO BE HONEST WITH ME.
OK...
DID YOU OR DID YOU NOT RECORD "BULLWINKLE" OVER YOUR MOTHER'S "SWEATIN' TO THE OLDIES" VIDEOTAPE?
UM...
NO "UMS." I WANT THE TRUTH.
THE TRUTH...
JASON, I THOUGHT WE HAD AN UNDERSTANDING!
I KINDA FORGOT.
"FORGOT"?! HOW COULD YOU FORGET SOMETHING LIKE THIS?! I MUST'VE TOLD YOU A HUNDRED TIMES!
DAD, LOOK, I'M SORRY.
SORRY.
AWRIGHT, HONIES— WIGGLE THAT FLAB!
...I'LL SHOW HIM SORRY.
C'MON, ROGER— WIGGLE.
AMEND

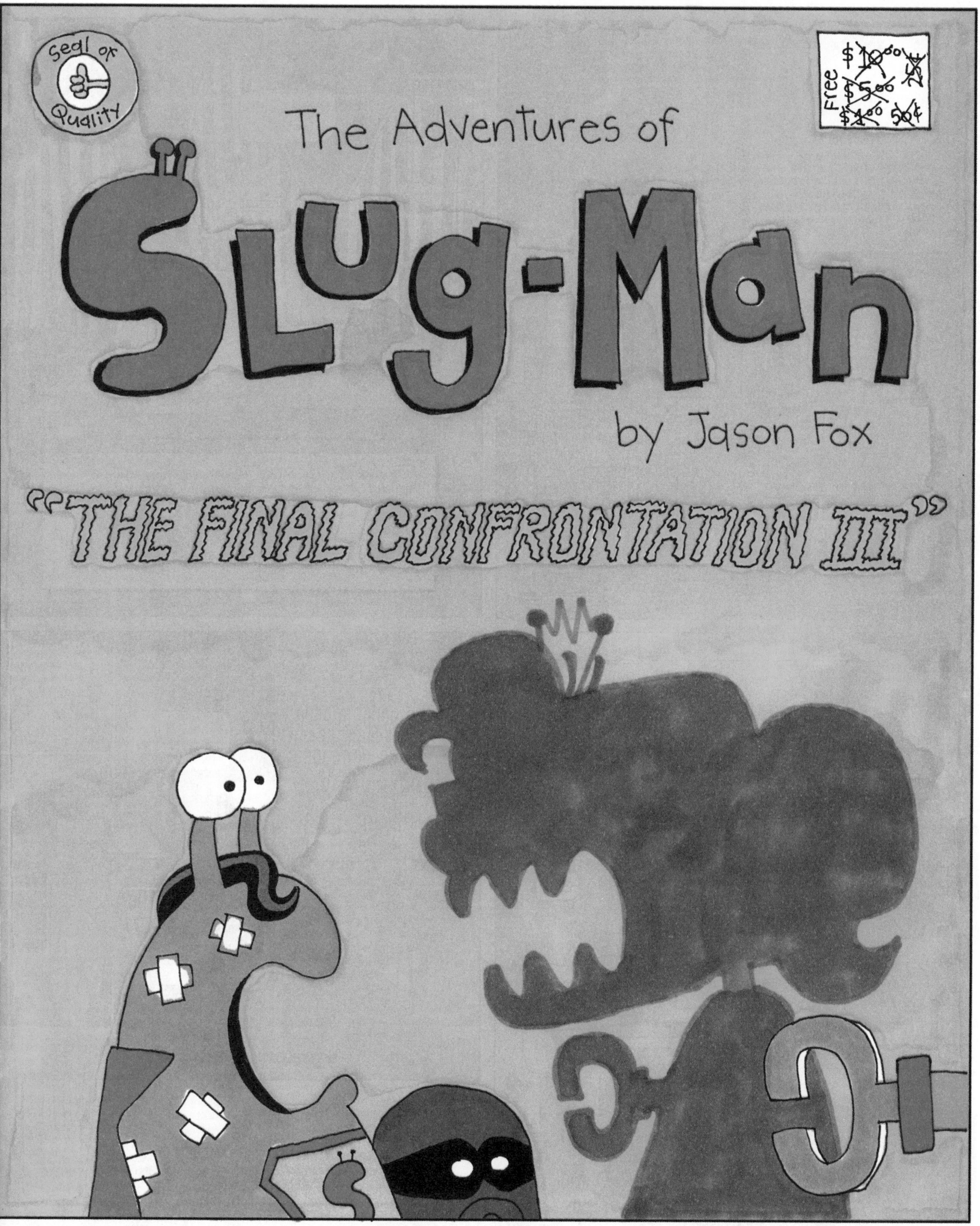
Seal of Quality
Free
$10.00
$5.00
$1.00
25¢
50¢
The Adventures of
Slug-Man
by Jason Fox
"THE FINAL CONFRONTATION III"

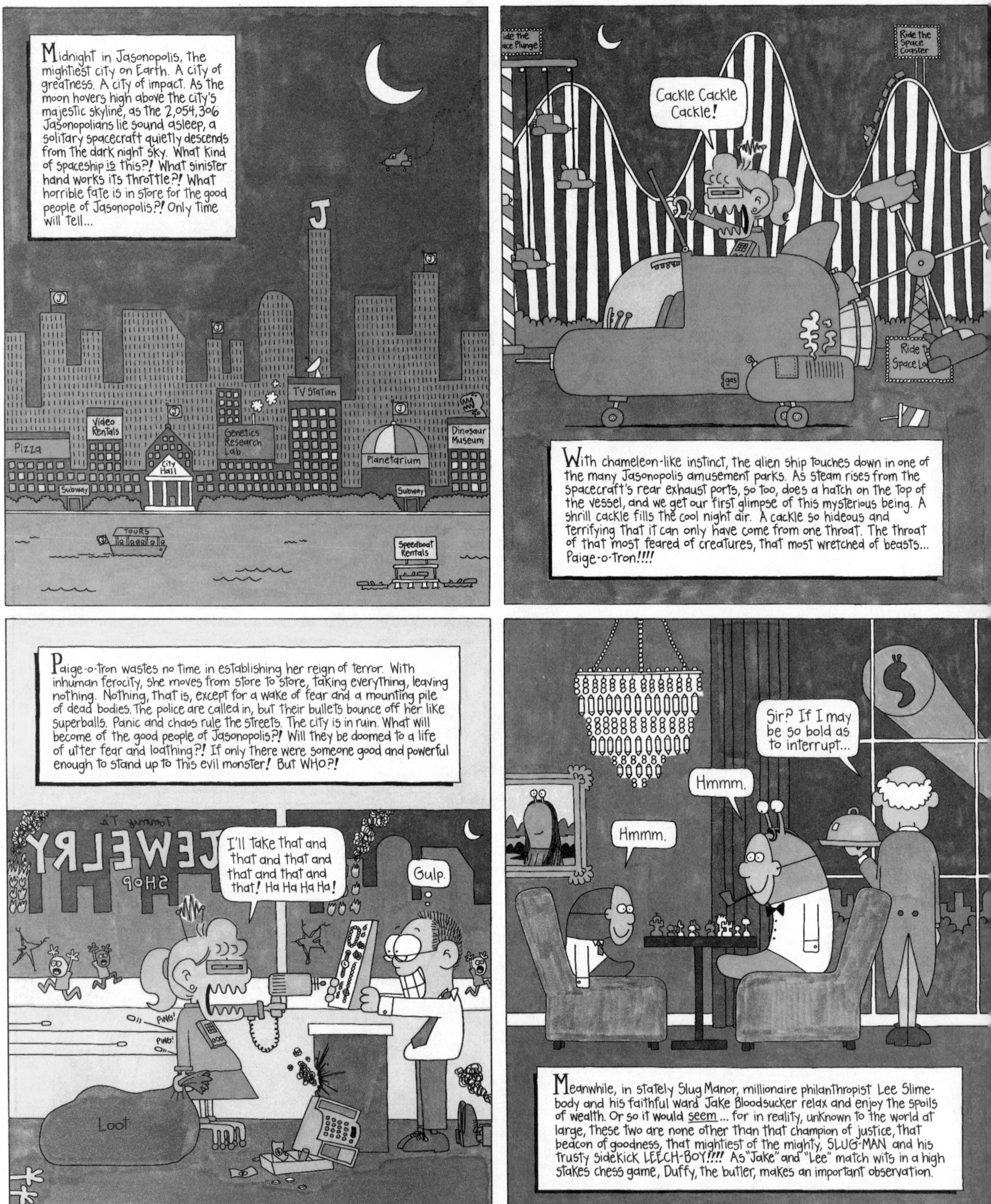
Midnight in Jasonopolis, the mightiest city on Earth. A city of greatness. A city of impact. As the moon hovers high above the city's majestic skyline, as the 2,054,306 Jasonopolians lie sound asleep, a solitary spacecraft quietly descends from the dark night sky. What kind of spaceship is this?! What sinister hand works its throttle?! What horrible fate is in store for the good people of Jasonopolis?! Only time will tell...
J
TV Station
Video Rentals
Genetics Research Lab
Dinosaur Museum
Pizza
City Hall
Planetarium
Subway
Subway
TOURS
Speedboat Rentals
Ride the Space Coaster
Cackle Cackle Cackle!
gas
With chameleon-like instinct, the alien ship touches down in one of the many Jasonopolis amusement parks. As steam rises from the spacecraft's rear exhaust ports, so too, does a hatch on the top of the vessel, and we get our first glimpse of this mysterious being. A shrill cackle fills the cool night air. A cackle so hideous and terrifying that it can only have come from one throat. The throat of that most feared of creatures, that most wretched of beasts... Paige-o-Tron!!!!
Paige-o-Tron wastes no time in establishing her reign of terror. With inhuman ferocity, she moves from store to store, taking everything, leaving nothing. Nothing, that is, except for a wake of fear and a mounting pile of dead bodies. The police are called in, but their bullets bounce off her like superballs. Panic and chaos rule the streets. The city is in ruin. What will become of the good people of Jasonopolis?! Will they be doomed to a life of utter fear and loathing?! If only there were someone good and powerful enough to stand up to this evil monster! But WHO?!
I'll take that and that and that and that and that and that! Ha Ha Ha Ha!
Gulp.
PING!
PING!
Loot
Sir? If I may be so bold as to interrupt...
Hmmm.
Hmmm.
Meanwhile, in stately Slug Manor, millionaire philanthropist Lee Slimebody and his faithful ward Jake Bloodsucker relax and enjoy the spoils of wealth. Or so it would seem ... for in reality, unknown to the world at large, these two are none other than that champion of justice, that beacon of goodness, that mightiest of the mighty, SLUG-MAN and his trusty sidekick LEECH-BOY!!!! As "Jake" and "Lee" match wits in a high stakes chess game, Duffy, the butler, makes an important observation.

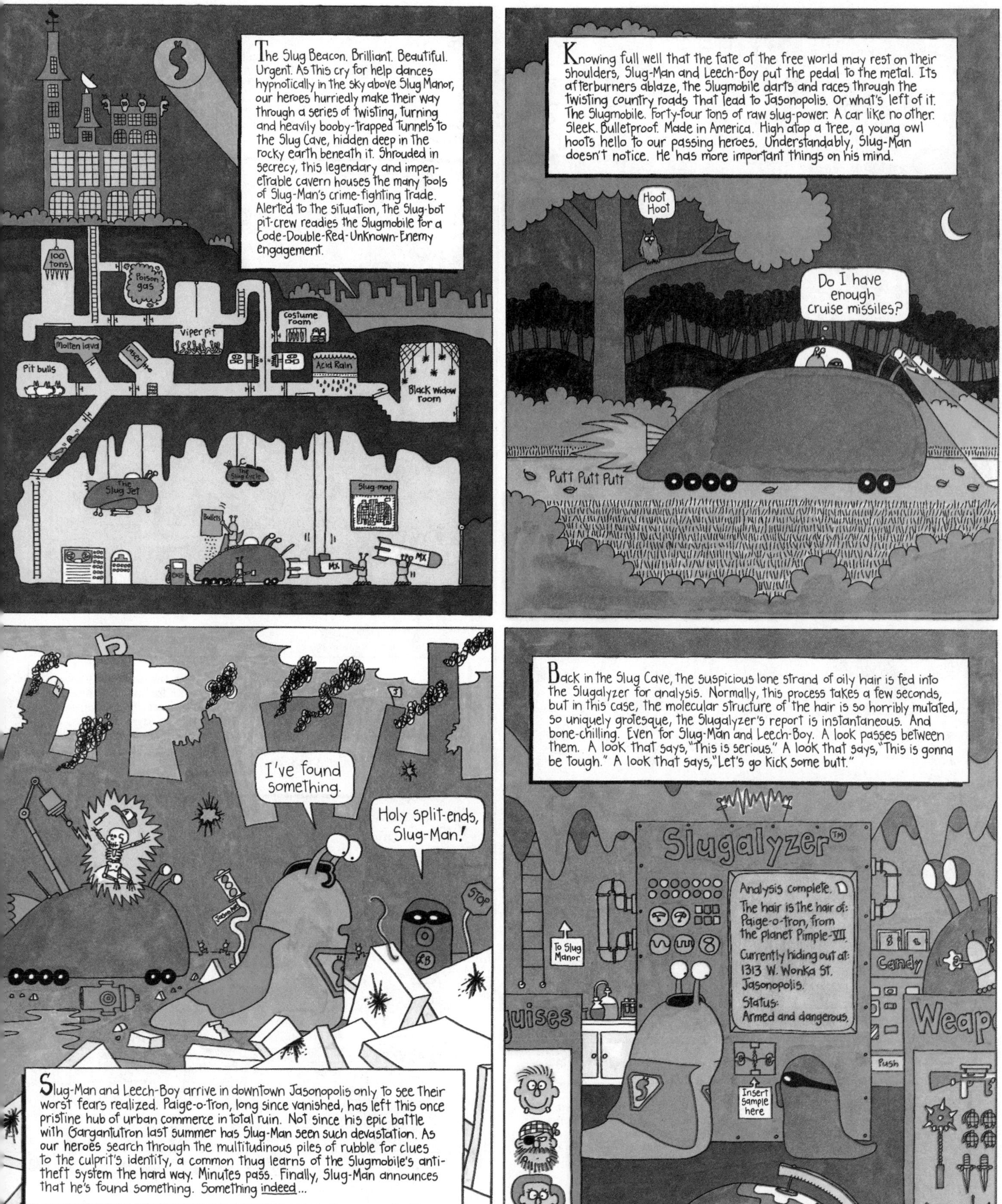
The Slug Beacon. Brilliant. Beautiful. Urgent. As this cry for help dances hypnotically in the sky above Slug Manor, our heroes hurriedly make their way through a series of twisting, turning and heavily booby-trapped tunnels to the Slug Cave, hidden deep in the rocky earth beneath it. Shrouded in secrecy, this legendary and impenetrable cavern houses the many tools of Slug-Man's crime-fighting trade. Alerted to the situation, the Slug-bot pit-crew readies the Slugmobile for a Code-Double-Red-Unknown-Enemy engagement.
100 tons
Poison gas
Costume room
Viper pit
Molten lava
Laser
Acid Rain
Pit bulls
Black widow room
The Slug Jet
The Slug Cycle
Slug-map
Bullets
MX
MX
Knowing full well that the fate of the free world may rest on their shoulders, Slug-Man and Leech-Boy put the pedal to the metal. Its afterburners ablaze, the Slugmobile darts and races through the twisting country roads that lead to Jasonopolis. Or what's left of it. The Slugmobile. Forty-four tons of raw slug-power. A car like no other. Sleek. Bulletproof. Made in America. High atop a tree, a young owl hoots hello to our passing heroes. Understandably, Slug-Man doesn't notice. He has more important things on his mind.
Hoot Hoot
Do I have enough cruise missiles?
Putt Putt Putt
I've found something.
Holy split-ends, Slug-Man!
STOP
Slug-Man and Leech-Boy arrive in downtown Jasonopolis only to see their worst fears realized. Paige-o-tron, long since vanished, has left this once pristine hub of urban commerce in total ruin. Not since his epic battle with Gargantutron last summer has Slug-Man seen such devastation. As our heroes search through the multitudinous piles of rubble for clues to the culprit's identity, a common thug learns of the Slugmobile's anti-theft system the hard way. Minutes pass. Finally, Slug-Man announces that he's found something. Something indeed...
Back in the Slug Cave, the suspicious lone strand of oily hair is fed into the Slugalyzer for analysis. Normally, this process takes a few seconds, but in this case, the molecular structure of the hair is so horribly mutated, so uniquely grotesque, the Slugalyzer's report is instantaneous. And bone-chilling. Even for Slug-Man and Leech-Boy. A look passes between them. A look that says, "This is serious." A look that says, "This is gonna be tough." A look that says, "Let's go kick some butt."
Slugalyzer™
Analysis complete.
The hair is the hair of: Paige-o-tron, from the planet Pimple-VII
Currently hiding out at: 1313 W. Wonka St. Jasonopolis.
Status: Armed and dangerous.
To Slug Manor
Insert sample here
Candy
guises
Weapo
Push

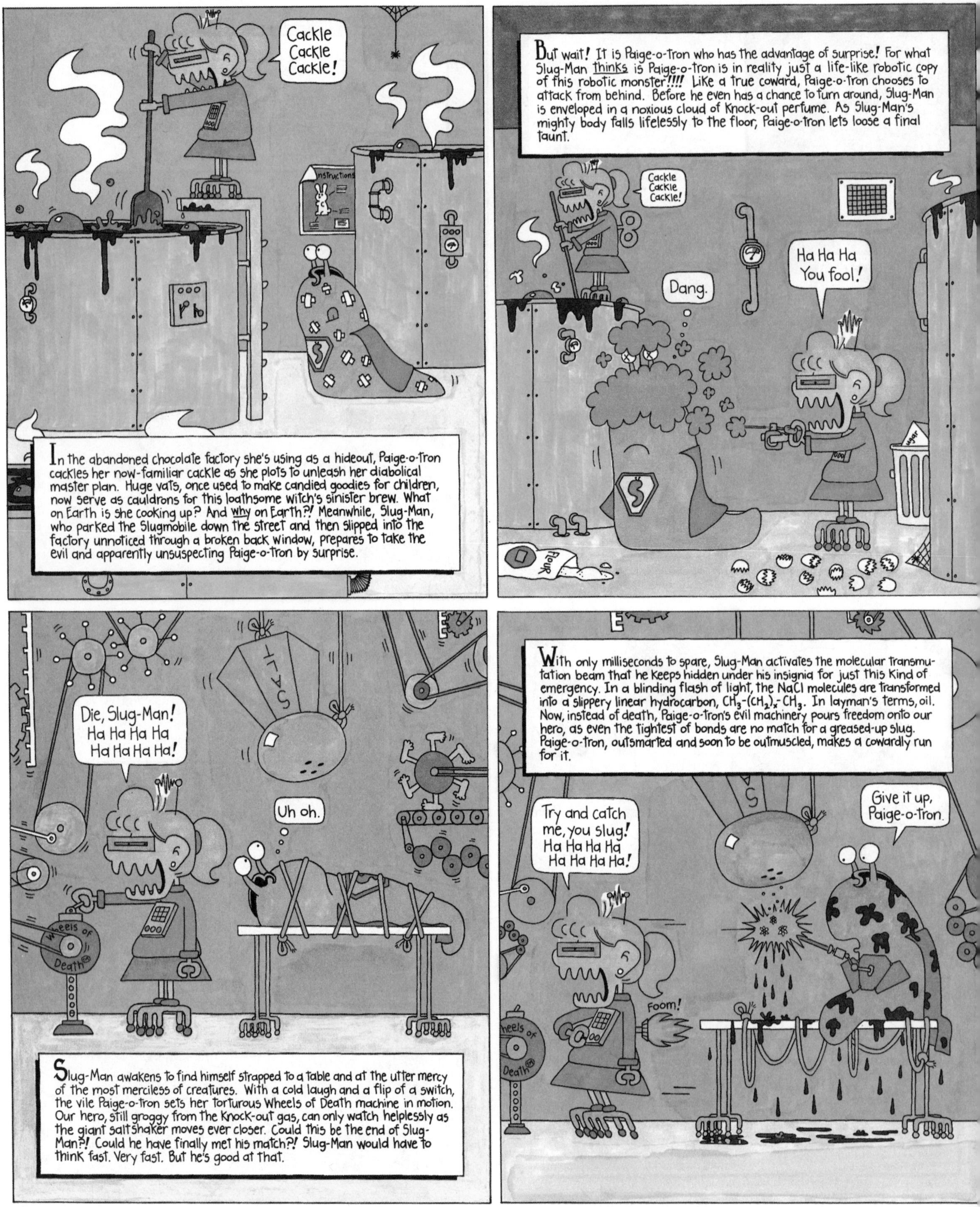
Cackle Cackle Cackle!
Instructions
In the abandoned chocolate factory she's using as a hideout, Paige-o-Tron cackles her now-familiar cackle as she plots to unleash her diabolical master plan. Huge vats, once used to make candied goodies for children, now serve as cauldrons for this loathsome witch's sinister brew. What on Earth is she cooking up? And why on Earth?! Meanwhile, Slug-Man, who parked the Slugmobile down the street and then slipped into the factory unnoticed through a broken back window, prepares to take the evil and apparently unsuspecting Paige-o-Tron by surprise.
But wait! It is Paige-o-Tron who has the advantage of surprise! For what Slug-Man thinks is Paige-o-Tron is in reality just a life-like robotic copy of this robotic monster!!!! Like a true coward, Paige-o-Tron chooses to attack from behind. Before he even has a chance to turn around, Slug-Man is enveloped in a noxious cloud of Knock-out perfume. As Slug-Man's mighty body falls lifelessly to the floor, Paige-o-Tron lets loose a final taunt.
Cackle Cackle Cackle!
Dang.
Ha Ha Ha You fool!
Flour
Sugar
SALT
Die, Slug-Man! Ha Ha Ha Ha Ha Ha Ha Ha!
Uh oh.
Wheels of Death
Slug-Man awakens to find himself strapped to a table and at the utter mercy of the most merciless of creatures. With a cold laugh and a flip of a switch, the vile Paige-o-Tron sets her torturous Wheels of Death machine in motion. Our hero, still groggy from the Knock-out gas, can only watch helplessly as the giant saltshaker moves ever closer. Could this be the end of Slug-Man?! Could he have finally met his match?! Slug-Man would have to think fast. Very fast. But he's good at that.
With only milliseconds to spare, Slug-Man activates the molecular transmutation beam that he keeps hidden under his insignia for just this kind of emergency. In a blinding flash of light, the NaCl molecules are transformed into a slippery linear hydrocarbon, CH_3-$(CH_2)_x$-CH_3. In layman's terms, oil. Now, instead of death, Paige-o-Tron's evil machinery pours freedom onto our hero, as even the tightest of bonds are no match for a greased-up slug. Paige-o-Tron, outsmarted and soon to be outmuscled, makes a cowardly run for it.
Try and catch me, you slug! Ha Ha Ha Ha Ha Ha Ha Ha!
Give it up, Paige-o-Tron.
Foom!
Wheels of Death

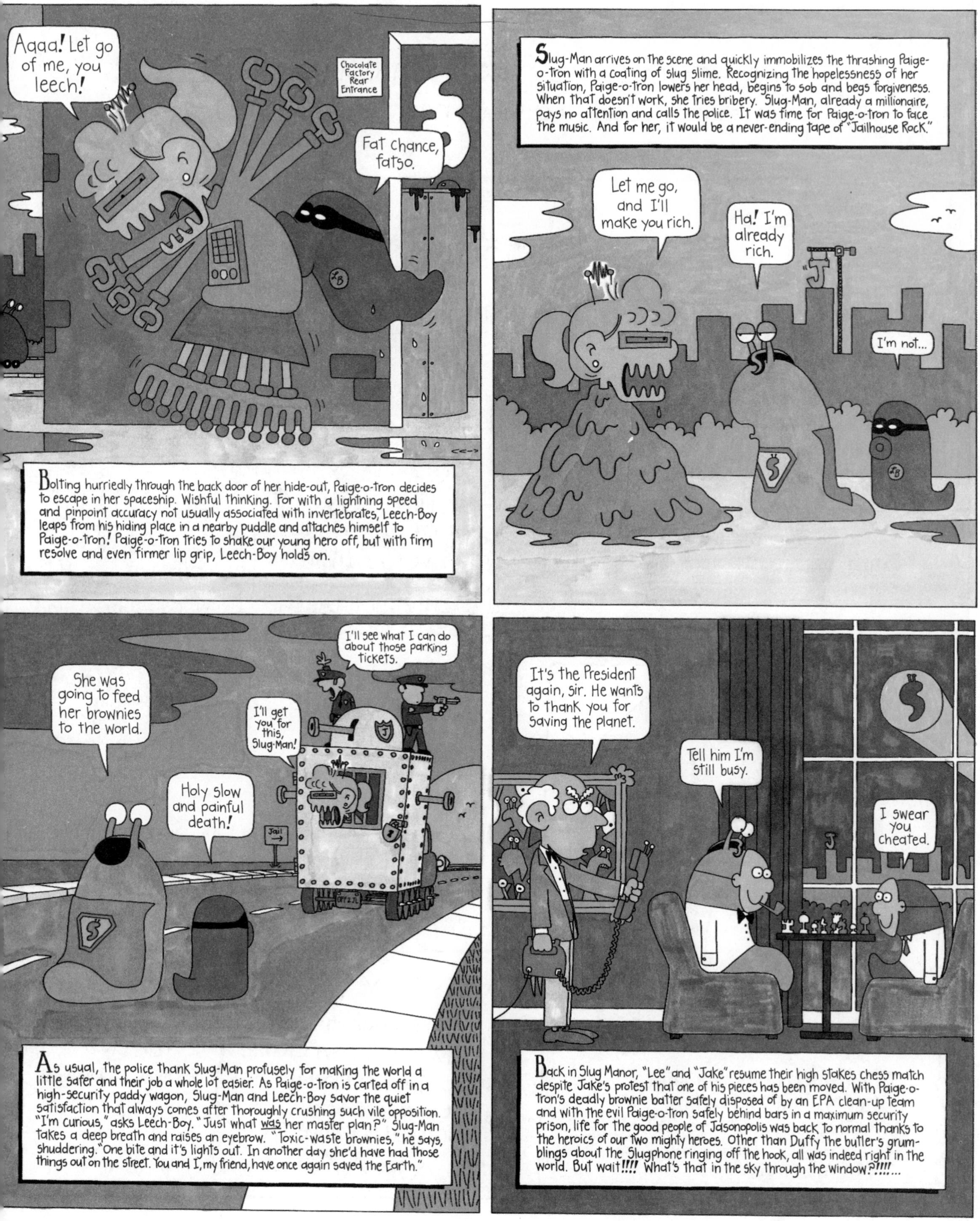
Aaaa! Let go of me, you leech!
Chocolate Factory Rear Entrance
Fat chance, fatso.
Bolting hurriedly through the back door of her hide-out, Paige-o-tron decides to escape in her spaceship. Wishful thinking. For with a lightning speed and pinpoint accuracy not usually associated with invertebrates, Leech-Boy leaps from his hiding place in a nearby puddle and attaches himself to Paige-o-tron! Paige-o-tron tries to shake our young hero off, but with firm resolve and even firmer lip grip, Leech-Boy holds on.
Slug-Man arrives on the scene and quickly immobilizes the thrashing Paige-o-tron with a coating of slug slime. Recognizing the hopelessness of her situation, Paige-o-tron lowers her head, begins to sob and begs forgiveness. When that doesn't work, she tries bribery. Slug-Man, already a millionaire, pays no attention and calls the police. It was time for Paige-o-tron to face the music. And for her, it would be a never-ending tape of "Jailhouse Rock."
Let me go, and I'll make you rich.
Ha! I'm already rich.
I'm not...
She was going to feed her brownies to the world.
I'll see what I can do about those parking tickets.
I'll get you for this, Slug-Man!
Holy slow and painful death!
Jail
As usual, the police thank Slug-Man profusely for making the world a little safer and their job a whole lot easier. As Paige-o-tron is carted off in a high-security paddy wagon, Slug-Man and Leech-Boy savor the quiet satisfaction that always comes after thoroughly crushing such vile opposition. "I'm curious," asks Leech-Boy. "Just what was her master plan?" Slug-Man takes a deep breath and raises an eyebrow. "Toxic-waste brownies," he says, shuddering. "One bite and it's lights out. In another day she'd have had those things out on the street. You and I, my friend, have once again saved the Earth."
It's the President again, sir. He wants to thank you for saving the planet.
Tell him I'm still busy.
I swear you cheated.
Back in Slug Manor, "Lee" and "Jake" resume their high stakes chess match despite Jake's protest that one of his pieces has been moved. With Paige-o-tron's deadly brownie batter safely disposed of by an EPA clean-up team and with the evil Paige-o-tron safely behind bars in a maximum security prison, life for the good people of Jasonopolis was back to normal thanks to the heroics of our two mighty heroes. Other than Duffy the butler's grumblings about the Slugphone ringing off the hook, all was indeed right in the world. But wait!!!! What's that in the sky through the window?!!!!...

Wow!

Presenting the Slug-Man Collection
(coming soon to a store near you!)(maybe)

Super Wow!

Slug-Man T-shirts!!!
Colorful design rendered expertly in permanent marker! (Shirts previously worn, but clean).

Help me! I'm covered with Leeches!

Leech-Boy Suction Toys!!!
Don't let <u>this</u> craze pass you by! Includes booklet "1001 Uses For a Suction-Cup Leech."

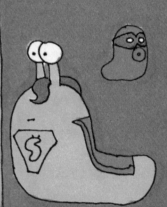

Limited Edition Slug-Man Figurines!!!
Individually hand-crafted from only the finest Play-Doh, each is a signed and numbered tribute to this legendary heroic duo.

NEW For Fall!!!

Slug-Man's Tip For the Day:

Buy Slug-Man Products.

In the works:
- Greeting Cards!!!
- Coffee Mugs!!!
- Lunch Boxes!!!
- Gift Wrap!!!
- Exploding Paige-o-tron dolls!!!
- Plush Toys!!!
- Bed Linens!!!
- And More!!!!!!

Slug-Man/Leech-Boy Halloween Masks!!!
Guaranteed to command attention! Lightweight construction! 100% recyclable! Available in Large, Medium and Lunch sizes.

Announcing the Slug-Man Fan Club!!! To join, send a self-addressed, stamped envelope to: →

Slug-Man Fan Club
c/o Andrews & McMeel
4900 Main St.
Kansas City, MO
64112